DATE DUE

FEB 11 1983			
DEC 02 1983			
MAR 27 1985			
JUN 12 1992			
NOV - 5 1997			

GAYLORD PRINTED IN U.S.A.

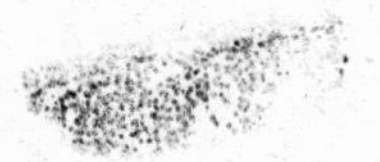

Personnel and Labor Relations

AN EVOLUTIONARY APPROACH

"I am afraid this is not a propitious time for a raise, Adams. Or, as my father would have said, why the devil should I give you a raise? Or, as my grandfather would have said, GET THE HELL OUT OF HERE!" (Reprinted with permission from the *Saturday Review*, August 14, 1971, p. 42.)

Personnel AND *Labor Relations*

An Evolutionary Approach

ALLAN N. NASH
JOHN B. MINER

Both of the Behavioral Science Division,
College of Business and Public Administration,
University of Maryland

THE MACMILLAN COMPANY New York
COLLIER-MACMILLAN Publishers, London

Printed in the United States of America

The Macmillan Company
866 Third Avenue, New York, New York 10022

Collier-Macmillan Canada, Ltd., Toronto, Ontario

Library of Congress catalog card number: 72–77148

Printing: 1 2 3 4 5 6 7 8 Year: 3 4 5 6 7 8 9

To the memory of
Carroll and Esther Nash,
Tracy, Minnesota,
who had to cope with the
problems discussed herein

Preface

As originally conceived this was to be a book of selected papers and articles to be read in conjunction with *Personnel and Industrial Relations: A Managerial Approach,* by the second author, and other texts designed for use in the beginning course in personnel management and labor relations. We think that objective has been effectively achieved, but what has emerged seems to us to have a wider application as well.

Much that is contained here may be new and interesting even to those who have spent many years in the field of personnel management as practitioners, teachers, or researchers. In fact we feel that some background and knowledge in the field may make the reader's experience considerably richer than otherwise would be the case. Certainly those familiar with the field of personnel management as it exists today will come away from the present volume with a greater appreciation of the fact that many of the problems and practices now viewed as new and modern are similar to those of the past. History does appear to repeat itself, which of course enhances its value as a teacher for the present.

The basic purpose of the book is to provide both a reasonably representative firsthand picture of problems and events in the evolution of the integrated fields of personnel management and labor relations and an overall picture of the situation today. The decade of the 1970's represents the end of approximately one lifetime of concerted efforts to improve and change relations between employers and employees in this society. By going back to the beginning of the fields of personnel and labor relations and tracing these relationships, we hope to provide a better basis for viewing the nature of change and the extent to which it might be expected to occur in the future. We have attempted to provide materials showing how this society has reacted to problems in the past. It is interesting to note, for instance, the consistent negative reaction of our society to efforts for revolutionary change made by such groups as the Knights of Labor, the Syndicalists, and the Industrial Workers of the World. This reaction contrasts with the belated but real success of Samuel Gompers and his American Federation of Labor. In this latter case, labor's interests were advanced while working within the system, with a very pragmatic approach to problems. Also, a considerable similarity may be noted between the past struggles of disadvantaged groups in our society and the results they have achieved with various tactics and strategies, and struggles between groups we see today.

The evolutionary approach we have taken in the design of this book has some possible disadvantages. It does sacrifice some current knowledge of personnel and labor practices, which other collections provide, for the portrayal of the past. However, we do not view this as a serious problem, because the latest editions of most good basic texts in the personnel and labor area incorporate material existing in current articles which makes a significant contribution to our present understanding. There is very little value added from a readings book which either includes material that overlaps with the text it is designed to supplement or includes many articles that do not in fact make much of a unique contribution to the understanding of personnel and labor problems.

It could be argued that most current texts do review the historical development of personnel and labor relations, and many do this quite well. However, it is a difficult enough task for most authors to do a good job of reviewing *current* literature in its original sources, to say nothing of being able to review seventy or seventy-five years of literature from such sources. Thus they must rely on unoriginal sources. It has been noted often that the meaning of a statement can be misconstrued after it has been interpreted by many analysts, quoted out of context, or perhaps occasionally selected out of a mass of conflicting statements to *prove* an analyst's point. A case in point would appear to be that of Frederick Taylor, widely recognized as the "father of scientific management," who often has been maligned as antihumanist by those who quote selectively from statements he has made but who ignore many more statements which show him to have been greatly concerned with the welfare of workers. He has also been described as having contributed little which was original, sometimes taking other men's ideas without giving them due credit. A reading of a representative sample of Taylor's original writings, some of which are included as selections in this book, makes it clear that he was willing to give others due credit when he used or referred to their work. In essence, then, we feel that to understand the past fully as a prologue of the future it is necessary to go back beyond condensations and syntheses to original sources. That is what this volume does.

Another possible limitation of the evolutionary approach, as we have used it here, is that only an overview of the evolution of the total fields of personnel management and labor relations is presented, leaving out any detailed portrayal of how the various functional areas within such fields as manpower planning, recruitment, selection, employee training, compensation, appraisal, and the like have developed. Also, the significant contributions that research has made to the solution of relevant problems have not been emphasized in this volume. Evolutionary and research-oriented treatments of these topics are clearly needed. However, space limitations are real, and we have chosen in this particular book to document the rise of personnel management in depth rather than to present a cursory coverage of a broader assortment of topics.

The book itself is divided into four sections. The first attempts to provide an overview of the basic employment-related problems and issues that have confronted workers, management, and society as a whole. The second traces the development of the field of personnel management from its beginnings, considering this field as that concerned with problems which arise between an employer and his employees as individuals. The third does the same for the field of labor relations, concentrating on problems arising between organizations and their members when the latter join formally organized groups such as labor unions. The last section attempts to present a description of some of the pioneering efforts in the fields, depicting both organizations and the people who led them.

We would like to express our appreciation to the scholars and practitioners whose work is presented. They, along with their publishers, are the ones who deserve credit for the contributions they have made to our understanding of the fields within which they have written. Unfortunately, because of our inability to find background material for some of the earliest authors we are unable to provide equivalent biographical sketches for all who have contributed.

A. N. N.
J. B. M.

Contents

Personnel and Labor Relations

AN EVOLUTIONARY APPROACH

SECTION I
A Lifetime of Problems

The material presented in this part of the book is intended to provide a portrayal of the basic human problems that have occurred over the past three quarters of a century between organizations and their employees within the context of the employment relationship. The first selection by Erskine and Cleveland was chosen because it dramatically describes the management philosophy and practices which often existed during the early part of the twentieth century. It suggests that many organizations were inclined to regard their human resources like any other organization resource, in the sense that they were considered virtually interchangeable with other humans and warranted about as much (or less) loyalty as a machine or dollar bill. It also demonstrates the problems many organizations had with the management of their human resources beginning with the recruitment and selection end of the spectrum on through the other personnel functions when they had no staff personnel department to concentrate on such activities.

The selections by Taylor and Gompers present two sides of what is basically the overriding issue around which all personnel and labor activities revolve; that is, getting a good day's work from each employee under conditions that are reasonably acceptable to that employee. The next selection from the Labor Review *(now titled the* Monthly Labor Review*) indicates some of the problems which developed when organizations perhaps overreacted to allegations of inhumanism, on the one hand, and threats of unionism, on the other. It shows what it was like living in a "company town" dominated by a paternalistic, welfare-oriented organization which decided it ought to control and influence virtually every facet of its employees lives both during and after work. Part of the impetus for such a philosophy was the not unsubstantiated belief that many employees did not have the self-discipline to regulate their own lives* *sufficiently to meet their obligations to their families and the organization.*

Two further problems that existed for many years, but that did not attain constructive attention in the form of efforts to alleviate and prevent them until the 1920's and 1930's, are discussed in the next few selections. The first concerns the waste and suffering which accompany fluctuations in the demand for labor resulting from instability in our economic system. Repercussions of such instability have been accentuated by lack of centralized planning and control over the allocation of human resources which is an outgrowth of our "free market" system, the mechanization of jobs which causes at least temporary displacement of labor, and the inequality of economic power between organizations and individual citizens. The remarks of Clare Lewis calling attention to the abrupt drop in job openings for young people in 1927 stir one's curiosity concerning the extent to which such a phenomenon may be a generalizable precursor of economic recessions. Whiting Williams' description of unemployed worker attitudes during the early stages of the Great Depression suggests that personnel practices of the 1920's may have been somewhat effective in building the confidence and image of organizations in the eyes of their employees. Unfortunately, the overwhelming impact of the extended depressed conditions vividly described by Mahon forced organizations to cut back on some such practices, and losses from others, such as employee investment in the employer's stock, actually accentuated their distress and bitterness.

The second problem, which is briefly discussed in the selection by Stuart Chase, raises the issue of how serious the repercussions may be of overspecializing work without paying enough attention to the way the job may be designed best from the standpoint of the worker. Interest in this issue has prevailed to the present time.

The seriousness of these problems and initial attempts to cope with them, which created more problems, are portrayed in the selection from Fortune *magazine published during the late 1930's in which virtual open warfare broke out between industrial and labor organizations. The advent of World War II created a generally observed moratorium on such struggles, but they again broke out shortly thereafter, although not generally over the issue of recognizing union organizations as bargaining representatives of employees, which was the point of contention in the late 1930's.*

 Professor Heneman's remarks forcefully suggest that the basic problems and issues really did not change much during the 1940's and 1950's, although modest progress was made toward their solutions, as will be noted in the following sections. Dunnette's comments represent a shift in attention from the industrial environment to the academic, but they provide a glimpse into some of the problems within academia which have lessened academic contributions to the solution of societal and organizational problems. Finally, the brief article by Murray provides an interesting indication of some of the difficulties that personnel managers presently face, many of which are reminiscent of those in the past.

I

The Way It Was: 1900-1920

New Men for Old

LILLIAN ERSKINE &
TREADWELL CLEVELAND, Jr.

If you would know at first hand the big weak spot in our American manufacturing system, throw away the current newspaper editorials on the Menace of the Unrestrained Labor Strike, and set your alarm-clock at 5.30 a.m.

It is worth an early start; for you are on the track of an economic wastage so colossal as to match its hundred dollars of annual loss to every ten dimes of financial injury wrung as the toll of the industrial deadlock.

In the chill of the gray dawn, dressed in the oldest clothing you can muster, turn your face from your familiar haunts in the office section of the city, and make your way towards the ranks of tall chimneys guarding the outskirts of the town.

Slip quickly by the silent bulk of a dead factory, union-picketed without and police-sentried within, which is featured in the morning's headlines; for your errand is not to the plant bleeding from industrial surgery by means of the strikers' axe, but to one whose line-shafting is seldom idle, and whose doors have been untroubled for twenty years by the shadow of a Walking Delegate.

You are in search of what is ordinarily reckoned the most commonplace and normal of all the daily sights in any manufacturing community—a nondescript group of job-hunters, tailing down the block from a factory employment office's closed door. Nevertheless, as you take your place in line, and stand elbow to elbow with them in the keen air of the March sunrise, you have become a unit in a national menace to the employer, to labor, and to society at large.

The Old-Type Employment Agent

At the sounding of the whistle, and the vibrant coming to life of dead shafting and wheels inside, push your way with the others through the now opened door, and await your turn in the process of sifting the chaff of the old, the physically broken, and the alcoholic, from the residue of wheat that has been winnowed by the threshing-machine of industry. With the enforced patience of the job-hunter, try to realize (as they seem instinctively to do) the futility of appeal from the absolute authority of the little man of the hour who sits behind the rail.

Appreciate, as the other job-hunters can not, however, the heavy odds against him in his efforts successfully to fill those yellow slips upon his desk: requisitions sent to him but a few hours before by foremen whom he knows only by sight; from expanded departments he rarely visits; covering work with which he is technically unfamiliar, and subject to an output-standard of which he has barely heard. Fill out, at last, like the rest

Reprinted from *Everybody's*, Vol. 36, April, 1917, pp. 414-427.

of the candidates, the personal questions on an application blank (such as could be duplicated in forty other factories handling an absolutely different class of labor and production), and eventually find yourself "hired," rather than "employed"—with a ninety per cent chance against your having been assigned to the position or department for which you are physically or mentally fitted.

The Old-Type Foreman

Theoretically you represent an outlay of fifty cents to the firm, whose trade-mark has been stamped for a generation on the pay-roll upon which your name is entered. As a matter of fact (if you consent to see the experiment through), costliness will dog your footsteps from the moment you are sent up to your foreman, whom long experience with the hit-or-miss method of the employment office has prepared for the worst.

You are handicapped by lack of technical training, and by your need for supervision as to the handling of the machine on which you have been placed. But you soon discover that your foreman's only remedy against such incompetence is to follow the traditions in which he has been trained, and to threaten to "fire" you as arbitrarily as he fired the long line of your predecessors.

Antagonism is the key-note of your relations with the "man higher up." And this is fostered by the tacit bond of discontent which springs up between you and your fellow-workers. The noon whistle gives you your choice between the shop gossip over a cold dinner-pail in the workroom and hurrying—unwashed and as you come off your machine—to the more open criticism passed about in the haven of a near-by saloon.

But popular or the reverse, you take no orders save from your foreman; and you find you can look to none other than him for instructions in the rare intervals in which he is not setting piece-rates; planning the work assigned to his machines; setting speeds and feeds; deciding on tools and depths of cuts; supervising repairs to equipment; checking stock; adjusting wages; eliminating congestion; and overseeing the thousand and one details of his department.

One morning, when he has been "jumped" by the man higher up, and needs a safety-valve for his temper and over-tried nerves, you find yourself handing in your dismissal slip at the pay-window, while the firm's balance-sheet unknowingly carries the various costly items of your haphazard instruction, your unproductive labor, your retardation of the department's output, your breakage of tools, and your spoiling of material.

Familiar Game of Battledore and Shuttlecock

No one who has experienced at first-hand the "vicious circle" of our still persistent hiring and firing system; no one who has played even a voluntary part in the game of battledore and shuttlecock between the old-type foreman and the untrained employment agent, can be convinced that his experience is exceptional.

As a matter of fact (making allowance for a low percentage of insubordination, incompetence, and "just quitting"), you will find that you can duplicate your case by the thousand in any manufacturing center of the country. Whether you throw in your lot with the unskilled "Hunkie" in the foundry, or with the trained mechanic in the tool-shop, you will learn that, excepting under the best standards of management, your livelihood and your hopes of advancement may lie absolutely at the mercy of a straw-boss, who neither hires you nor pays you a copper of your wage.

Yet it has been because of the very universality of the unregulated Labor Turnover thus engendered—of the percentage of workers who pass into and out of our factories and mills, and the continual and unnecessary substitution of new men for old, of the untrained for the experienced—that the magnitude of the economic losses involved has so long escaped widespread detection. The ebb and flow is silent.

The very fact that the process lacks the spectacular features of the widely advertised strike, renders it the more dangerous. Nevertheless, *it can be proved that the wastage of the Labor Turnover is a hundredfold more costly than that of the strike.* Unlike the strike, however, it automatically yields no hope of industrial or social gain, in better standards of wage or of living, or of broadened purchasing power. Only by its elimination can its constructive possibilities be realized. It may be likened to the daily strewing of countless grains of sand into the complicated machinery of the national output. And the resulting loss to capital and to society at large has been as final and complete as it was needless.

Who Pays the Cost?

If you imagine that your experiment in a factory workroom concerns you more than the firm that took you on, remember the machine you tried to run, failed "to get the hang of," and finally left out of commission when your foreman discharged you.

"I suppose that's typical of where our big leak has been," the General Manager confesses a few days later to the efficiency expert before whom he lays the output-record of your particular machine. "You see, there's a case where we threw away $2,500 on the original price of equipment; and a forty per cent product is all we've got—besides that bill for repairs—to show for our money."

The visitor runs over the sheaf of yellow slips and emits a low whistle. "But you've had thirty-two men on that machine in ten months," he says. "How do you expect to get an output?"

"What's that got to do with it?"

"I suppose you realize that in addition to that $2,500, you wasted nearly $2,000 of good money on breaking those men in. From my point of view, it's cheaper to throw machinery out of the window than to run a Turnover like that."

"I don't get you."

The visitor rises, and, going to the window, points across the factory yard to a group of men entering a door over which is posted a sign of "Help Wanted." "Supposing, Mr. Lawson, we drop the question of machinery for a while," he suggests, "and discuss instead what your employment office is costing you."

The General Manager looks relieved. "I know that labor's the biggest nuisance we're up against," he answers. "But so far as the actual cost of hiring goes, you needn't worry, Hartley. I understand we've cut that down to fifty cents a head."

"Taking on many?"

"Oh, I hardly know. Of course I don't bother with those minor details. We run a steady force here, but there's bound to be some shifting, of course, out of a payroll of six hundred. Maybe we take on a dozen, more or less, a day. Say, Clancy, how many foremen's requisitions are there on file to-day? Twenty-one? Didn't know it ever ran so heavy as that."

"And you say each new man costs you only half a dollar?"

"That's right, isn't it, Clancy? Yes; fifty cents apiece covers our employment costs."

"Suppose, just for the sake of argument," Mr. Hartley resumes as they again seat themselves, "that I tell you you're wrong, and that fifty cents apiece doesn't begin to cover those costs? Suppose I told you that, instead of fifty cents a head, each one of those unskilled men you took on to-day will cost you from $80 to $100 before he's thoroughly broken in and worth his full day's wage? And that every skilled man signed up this morning will stand you from $250 to $300? And that some of your most highly specialized workers can't be replaced under $1,000 apiece?"

"That's easy. I'd say you were off your head."

"But suppose I've got the facts?"

"You'll have to show me."

"What if I prove to you that you haven't, as you think, a 'steady force'? That I've already informed myself that your foremen are shooting requisitions at your employment office at an average rate of twelve per day? That in twelve months—to keep up the 'steady force' you talk about you've hauled 3,600 men through your gates? That you're running a monthly Labor Turnover of fity per cent., and a yearly one of six hundred per cent.? That during the last year and a half covered by the records I found on file, you've practically thrown $350,000 of legitimate profits out of your employment window?"

"The thing's utterly preposterous. Why, you say yourself that we average only a dozen men a day!"

"But you'll find, Mr. Lawson, that if you averaged only twelve a week, you'd nevertheless turn over your entire force once a year. Don't you realize that if—out of every hundred in your employ—only five a month either move away, or become ill, or disabled, or 'just quit' for any trivial cause, a Turnover of sixty per cent.—or a majority of your pay-roll—will swing your yearly labor-balance over to the negative side?"

"Hold on! I begin to follow you. But when you talk of thowing money out of the window—"

"What if I can prove that I'm putting you next to not only your own worst leak, but next to one of the biggest leaks in industry to-day? Suppose I show you that even a little group of twenty of you manufacturers, in this section alone, employed 69,000 new workers this year to keep up your combined regular forces of 44,000 men? Would that mean nothing to you in dollars and cents? Couldn't you figure out for yourself that even if you should cut my estimate of eighty dollars cost a head in halves—even if you make allowance for a heavy shifting of unskilled labor in the less highly organized departments—the total waste of profits for all of your concerns together was in the neighborhood of $2,000,000 for the year? How long do men like you expect to keep it up? Do you think you can get away with this sort of thing indefinitely?"

The general manager is sitting back now, thinking hard, and watching the smoke-rings as they twist themselves out of shape against the invisible currents of the air. Presently he leans forward.

"Mr. Hartley, if you can prove one-quarter of your statements during the last ten minutes," he says, "you'll be putting me next to a bigger thing than even you suspect. Clancy, will you ask the other members of our staff to come here? We'll dig down to bed-rock together on this stuff. And if you're ready with your figures, we might as well get it doped out right."

The Normal Turnover

While, like the general manager, you may begin to be convinced that the substitution of new men for old is costly policy for industry, you are likely to be a believer in the widespread delusion that the worker (whether skilled or unskilled) is a born drifter. The fact is established, however, that not only is the Turnover involuntary on the part of labor, but that no firm is warranted in seeing it slip over the forty per cent danger-line, without a thoroughgoing effort to cure the weak spots in its organization of which such excess is a trustworthy warning.

If you will bear in mind that but 1 per cent of industrial employees die annually; that from but 4 to 5 per cent are replaced because of absence due to prolonged illness; that under 8 per cent leave for legitimate reasons; that only 5 per cent are liable to discharge for cause; that a 6 per cent allowance, only, is necessary to cover those employed on inevitably temporary work (such as building and construction and improvements); and that a 6 per cent leeway is sufficient to include those who—because of race, religion, or politics—may prove temperamentally unsuited to shop organizations, you will begin to understand the scientific foundations upon which each firm may base its calculations, as to the limits within which it can build up a steady, efficient force.

Where the Blame Rests

"Well, Mr. Hartley," the superintendent begins when the half-dozen men are seated in the general manager's office, "I understand you lay our financial losses to our unsuspected Turnover; and put the responsibility for that Turnover up to the management."

"Squarely. I'm here, Mr. Gray, to be perfectly frank with you all, even if the truth is unpalatable.

"The phrase, 'Unregulated Labor Turnover' is polite efficiency-English for 'Administrative Incompetence.' I've run down the facts of the normal Turnover, and I know that anything beyond it is essentially involuntary. If it weren't for the demoralization of thousands thrown off by the needlessly seasonal trades, only a small minority of the skilled workers—and a steadily dwindling majority of the unskilled—would be drifters."

"But hold on!" exclaims the assistant superintendent. "You say 'the needlessly seasonal trades.' You don't mean to tell us that every plant can run on an even keel twelve months of the year, do you?"

"If they don't learn how to do it, they'll be crowded to the wall. I can show you plants—once seasonal—that by revolutionizing their rush methods of intermittent manufacture, of advertising, of salesmanship, and of order-placing, and by occasionally laying off the entire force one day a week when they are only running on stocking-up on low-cost standard supplies, have cut their Turnover from an even higher figure than yours, to well within a fifty per cent limit."

"And save money?"

"And made money. Don't you believe me when I say that the Turnover is your biggest leak?"

"That's what we want to clear up," the general manager answers, picking up pencil and pad. "How do you figure on the estimates you gave me a while ago as to our labor losses during the last year and a half? We've been sweating blood here trying to pare costs a thousand here and ten thousand there, and yet you talk of our having thrown $350,000 out of our employment-office window, and nothing to show for it."

What's the Real Product of a Factory?

"In the first place," Mr. Hartley begins, as he jots down some figures on the sheet of paper before him, "you've got to learn the latest economic truth that 'the real product of a factory is not materials but men.' It's as dangerous to efficiency—which, after all, is only another name for harmony—to keep on ripping out a trained worker here and there and replacing him at random, as it would be to rip out essential parts of your machinery, and then replace them with any old junk you happened to have handy on the premises.

"There isn't such a record in the country as a fifty-cent maximum cost for a new employee. You may hold the overhead charge for the upkeep of the employment office at that figure—provided you don't follow the best standards for investigating personal character and living conditions, for verifying working references, and for physical examination and efficiency tests. Even if your office charges (including the salary of a trained employment agent) stood you ten dollars apiece for every man taken on, you'd probably find it a big economy in the end. For the whole wastage of the Turnover hinges on not putting the right man on the right job at the right time, and on your not keeping him there by a square deal after you've taken the trouble to get him.

"I've followed this up in about every kind of plant, and you can take it from me that the first thing a man's up against, and the first expense the firm that hires him is up against, is his need for instruction."

"What's the matter with his foreman?" demands the assistant superintendent.

The Problem of Instruction

"There are usually a good many things the matter with his foreman. I'll come to that later. So far as the instruction goes, however, the trouble is that the foreman hasn't the time, or in most cases the faculty, to help him. Just knowing how a thing ought to be done, doesn't necessarily mean that a man is qualified to pass the information on. Particularly when a foreman has to do it so often that he is heartily sick of the job.

"Look here! Let's try to be fair. You put a foreman over a department to get the stuff out; and then you jump all over him because he can't do it with one hand, while he runs a school for new employees with the other. If he trains his men thoroughly, in a plant like this, he's bound to fall down on overseeing his end of the production. If he passes the new man over to some other worker, it's the same story. Either the fellow-worker won't bother with him, or somehow he can't get the information across. Or else, while he is doing it, maybe for several days running, he loafs on his job, and so balls up the balance of production.

"I've seen 100 machines standing idle on one floor, because (in the department next preceding it) two new men had smashed their machines, and blocked the whole flow of output for the factory. No one had warned them when they were put on their machines to 'turn her over easy' before they started up. So they had simply grabbed the belt-shifter, started full speed, and in addition to the damaged machinery, they landed two fellow-workers in the hospital, with broken pieces of steel in them."

"You don't mean to advocate having special men to train new employees, do you?" queries the general manager.

"You hardly get a really one hundred per cent efficient force of men, in a highly organized plant, without trained instructors. Nor can you hold your force steady, after you've got them, without constant supervision to make sure that each individual standard is being maintained at the high-water mark."

"You think, then, that we probably waste several dollars while teaching a new man as we do it now?"

"If you'll run over the figures I've just been jotting down, Mr. Lawson, you'll find why I was more interested in your Turnover than in your cost of recent equipment."

Cost of Instruction

Although the lack of expert supervision of new employees is one of the leading factors in the shifting of labor, it is only lately that students of the question have been able to offer such figures as the expert now offers to the general manager—*a minimum* schedule of *actual instruction costs*, based on the experience of some of the leading employers in this country. These are listed as:

Unskilled laborers	$2.00 to	$3.00
Clerical force	4.00	7.00
Handy men and helpers	5.00	
Skilled mechanics	7.50	10.00
Semi-skilled workers	15.00	18.00

Add to these approximate figures the initial cost of 50 cents to $10.00 for employment costs, and you have the first two items of outlay for the employers involved in the substitution of new men for old.

Cost of Damage to Equipment

In addition to the ten odd dollars wasted on lost time in a majority of cases, it must be remembered that it is primarily the new man who breaks tools and wrecks machinery. The more costly the equipment, the higher must be the estimate of the loss to the employer. Hardly a firm that has worked out this angle of the expense of the Turnover, is willing to list the damage to equipment at less than an average of seven dollars per head.

Handy men and helpers	$7.00 to	$10.00
Skilled mechanics	1.00	10.00
Less skilled mechanics	5.00	10.00

Even with this third estimate added, you have only cleared away the preliminaries of employment, instruction, and breakage costs. You are now ready to deal with the more serious aspects, and the less easily determined financial wastage of the Turnover.

Cost of Lowered Production

No one need go into a factory himself in order to realize that at entry no new man can measure up to even a low standard of production. There are shops that have proved the fact (from their own experience) that it takes the average new mechanic from one to three months to meet the time-limits of his foreman. As a matter of actual record, he falls from three to five hours a day behind the pace of the seasoned piece-worker. But this phase of the question is economically bigger than the individual waste of wage.

In a well-organized plant each division depends for efficiency upon the continuous output of the division next preceding. Sometimes the slowing down of pace due to the breaking in of new employees is startling. It is because every minute so wasted leaves its mark on the balance-sheet of the firm that you will find this the most costly aspect of the "hiring and firing" problem.

For the sake of fairness to a wide range of industry, take the following *minimum* estimate of the costs of reduced production, which is based on the acknowledged losses involved for the less highly specialized type of plant:

Unskilled workers	$5.00 to	$8.00
Semi-skilled mechanics	18.00	30.00
Skilled workers	20.00	34.00
Piece-workers, miscellaneous helpers	25.00	33.00
Clerical force	20.00	

We must realize, however, that these figures do not attempt to cover the more demoralizing factors resulting from such decrease of output. The sense of friction, of uncertainty, and antagonism developed under such conditions, is as destructive to the machinery of shop-efficiency as if oil of vitriol were to be habitually substituted for a lubricant.

The Cost of Spoiled Work

For the same reason, any calculation as to spoiled work must be unsatisfactory, because it is based on incomplete data which will vary in the case of each individual plant. Nevertheless, the following estimate is at least worth quoting, because it is drawn from losses in a wide enough variety of factories to make it a danger-sign on the pathway along which no factory management should persist in traveling:

Handy men and helpers	$5.00 to	$10.00
Highly skilled mechanics	10.00	15.00
Less skilled	15.00	20.00

Something Bigger Than the Employer's Direct Loss

The superintendent passes the penciled memoranda to the general manager with a confirmatory nod. "So that's how you ran up that eighty dollars—including employment costs—you loaded on us, Hartley."

"I'll guarantee that not a new man entered your gates during the last year who cost you a copper less."

"Yet you, yourself, halved that eighty dollars when you were talking about the group of twenty firms having thrown away nearly $2,000,000 of profits during the last twelve months."

"I did that because this stuff is so new I wanted to be conservative. Yours is a highly organized plant, where the costs of shifting labor run higher than in the rough trades employing few skilled workers. Nevertheless, I wanted to strike a fair average for all concerned.

"You men think these figures too startling only because it's a new slant on old problems that you've accepted much as you accept the law of gravitation. Their financial menace lies in the fact that they can be duplicated at random in any manufacturing center of the country. Of course I'm simply talking business now, and giving you what—from my point of view—is the less costly dollars-and-cents end of the Turnover."

"Does that mean you think there's something bigger involved than even the direct loss to the employer?"

"Something so big, Mr. Gray, that the calculations of simple arithmetic can't cover it. Look here. I don't mean to get sentimental over the worker. These days, he's out for something more substantial than sympathy. But I've been in this Turnover game at first-hand, and I know pretty well how it hits the decent chaps who get their walking papers.

"I'm not fool enough to think that all foremen are 'petty tyrants,' or that all of the men they fire are suffering angels. The average foreman is what generations of the man higher up have made him. He's the product of the system he's been trained in, and that gives him a power he hasn't been educated to wield. But there isn't a factor today that contributes more to unemployment, and the so-called 'unrest' of labor, or that spreads more of bitterness, and the belief in the duty of antagonism toward the authority of the employer, than the existence of the unregulated Turnover. And as long as you let it remain unchecked, you'll find the inevitable by-products of your factories are idleness, discouragement, intemperance, and poverty.

"I don't need to ask if any one of you men has ever given a thought to what probably went on in the minds of those two thousand-odd workers you wasted last year; men who, for no legitimate reason, walked out of your factory gates for the last time on the say-so of Tom This, or Mike That. I tell you frankly that it's no wonder men come out of some of these plants ready to go in for any form of organization that will help them to get back at the system they realize no man is strong enough to break down alone.

"I could show you two hundred skilled workers, whom I've talked with—decent men, every one of them—who were thrown out without cause or warning from one plant last year. To-day they're doing more to breed class bitterness, and to foment labor disaffection in this locality, than all the I.W.W.'s the police are ever likely to round up.

"You'll never again convince any one of those two hundred men that there can be such a thing as a square deal between capital and labor. And this instance isn't exceptional. It's what goes on all over the country. It's the logical outcome of a rotten system. But it hits back not only at the industry that fosters it, but eventually at the whole social fabric."

Employment Managers' Association

One of the most hopeful signs of the change in the relations which may some day develop between capital and labor, has been the formation, in a dozen states, of Employment Managers' Associations to discuss those errors in shop-organization that lie back of the unregulated Turnover.

The records of the companies represented (who during the past five years have proved their ability to conquer employment problems by a readjustment of values which placed equipment before men) speak for themselves upon their balance-sheets. Not only have they demonstrated the commonsense basis of wage, hour, and working conditions essential for keeping the Turnover within its normal limits, but they are doing pioneer work in establishing equilibrium in the seasonal trades and in developing that spirit of common fellowship which we are beginning to understand is vital to industrial efficiency.

How Some Companies Have Increased Profits

As a typical example may be quoted the experience of a member of a certain firm (handicapped by a seasonal output) who took over the administration of the employment office, and set himself to investigate the causes that lay back of a costly Turnover of 150 per cent.

As a result he raised the standards of equipment and of tools, and developed a scientific employment and service division, extending the functions of the employment office so as to include the training and hygienic supervision of new employees. *He forbade the discharge of employees except through the authorized channels of the employment and welfare division.* He raised the average weekly wage by thirty-seven per cent and reduced the weekly working hours from fifty-four to forty-eight.

He made provision for special instruction of foreign employees; for periodic physical examination, with special care of teeth and eyes; for sanitary standards in workrooms, dressing-rooms, toilets, lavatories, lunch-rooms, and rest and recreation rooms. He organized a systematic follow-up system for absentees.

He reduced seasonal fluctuations in production by means of better methods of advertising, purchasing, and order-placing; and also by a uniform reduction of fifteen per cent of the weekly working hours throughout the plant, during the weeks when trade conditions did not warrant a full-time schedule.

Nor did he rest there. *He substituted the transfer for the discharge of employees who fell below the standard.* He systematized advancement as a reward for efficiency; eliminated accidents; reduced tardiness to one-third of one per cent of the working force, and he reduced the number of absentees to one and one-quarter per cent (of which only one-half of one per cent were without excuse).

He established a rate of pay for advance notice of quitting, adding a day's pay for each week of notice, not to exceed four weeks.

Finally, he assured daily contact with the employment and service division to at least one-fifth of the force, with the opportunity to all for complaint or suggestions.

That this was an experiment in good business, rather than social philanthropy, is proved by the fact that *he reduced the Turnover from 150 per cent to 33.5 per cent; and that owing to increased efficiency, manufacturing costs were reduced by 10 per cent*, and production was increased by 42 per cent.

2

On the Subject of an Age-Old Problem: "Goldbricking"

Shop Management

FREDERICK W. TAYLOR

On the part of the men the greatest obstacle to the attainment of this standard[1] is the slow pace which they adopt, or the loafing or "soldiering," marking time, as it is called.

This loafing or soldiering proceeds from two causes. First, from the natural instinct and tendency of men to take it easy, which may be called *natural soldiering.* Second, from more intricate second thought and reasoning caused by their relations with other men, which may be called *systematic soldiering.*

There is no question that the tendency of the average man (in all walks of life) is toward working at a slow, easy gait, and that it is only after a good deal of thought and observation on his part or as a result of example, conscience, or external pressure that he takes a more rapid pace.

There are, of course, men of unusual energy, vitality, and ambition who naturally choose the fastest gait, set up their own standards, and who will work hard, even though it may be against their best interests. But these few uncommon men only serve by affording a contrast to emphasize the tendency of the average.

This common tendency to "take it easy" is greatly increased by bringing a number of men together on similar work and at a uniform standard rate of pay by the day.

Under this plan the better men gradually but surely slow down their gait to that of the poorest and least efficient. When a naturally energetic man works for a few days beside a lazy one, the logic of the situation is unanswerable: "Why should I work hard when that lazy fellow gets the same pay that I do and does only half as much work?"

A careful time study of men working under these conditions will disclose facts which are ludicrous as well as pitiable.

To illustrate: The writer has timed a naturally energetic workman who, while going and coming from work, would walk at a speed of from three to four miles per hour, and not infrequently trot home after a day's work. On arriving at his work he would immediately slow down to a speed of about one mile an hour. When, for example, wheeling a loaded wheelbarrow he would go at a good fast pace even up hill in order to be as short a time as possible under load, and immediately on the return walk slow down to a mile an hour, improving every opportunity for delay short of actually sitting down. In order to be sure not to do more than his lazy neighbor he would actually tire himself in his effort to go slow.

[1] Taylor is referring here to a previously discussed high, but attainable, standard of output.—Ed.

Reprinted as an excerpt from *Shop Management*, a paper read before the American Society of Mechanical Engineers, June, 1903.

Frederick Taylor is considered to be the "father of scientific management."

These men were working under a foreman of good reputation and one highly thought of by his employer who, when his attention was called to this state of things, answered: "Well, I can keep them from sitting down, but the devil can't make them get a move on while they are at work."

The natural laziness of men is serious, but by far the greatest evil from which both workmen and employers are suffering is the *systematic soldiering* which is almost universal under all of the ordinary schemes of management and which results from a careful study on the part of the workmen of what they think will promote their best interests.

The writer was much interested recently to hear one small but experienced golf caddy boy of twelve explaining to a green caddy who had shown special energy and interest the necessity of going slow and lagging behind his man when he came up to the ball, showing him that since they were paid by the hour, the faster they went the less money they got, and finally telling him that if he went too fast the other boys would give him a licking.

This represents a type of systematic soldiering which is not, however, very serious, since it is done with the knowledge of the employer, who can quite easily break it up if he wishes.

The greater part of the *systematic soldiering*, however, is done by the men with the deliberate object of keeping their employers ignorant of how fast work can be done.

So universal is soldiering for this purpose, that hardly a competent workman can be found in a large establishment, whether he works by the day or on piece work, contract work or under any of the ordinary systems of compensating labor, who does not devote a considerable part of his time to studying just how slowly he can work and still convince his employer that he is going at a good pace.

The causes for this are, briefly, that practically all employers determine upon a maximum sum which they feel it is right for each of their classes of employés to earn per day, whether their men work by the day or piece.

Each workman soon finds out about what this figure is for his particular case, and he also realizes that when his employer is convinced that a man is capable of doing more work than he has done, he will find sooner or later some way of compelling him to do it with little or no increase of pay.

Employers derive their knowledge of how much of a given class of work can be done in a day from either their own experience, which has frequently grown hazy with age, from casual and unsystematic observation of their men, or at best from records which are kept, showing the quickest time in which each job has been done. In many cases the employer will feel almost certain that a given job can be done faster than it has been, but he rarely cares to take the drastic measures necessary to force men to do it in the quickest time, unless he has an actual record, proving conclusively how fast the work can be done.

It evidently becomes for each man's interest, then, to see that no job is done faster than it has been in the past. The younger and less experienced men are taught this by their elders, and all possible persuasion and social pressure is brought to bear upon the greedy and selfish men to keep them from making new records which result in temporarily increasing their wages, while all those who come after them are made to work harder for the same old pay.

Under the best day work of the ordinary type, when accurate records are kept of the amount of work done by each man and of his efficiency, and when each man's wages are raised as he improves, and those who fail to rise to a certain standard are discharged and a fresh supply of carefully selected men are given work in their places, both the natural loafing and systematic soldiering can be largely broken up. This can be done, however, only when the men are thoroughly convinced that there is no intention of establishing piece work even in the remote future, and it is next to impossible to make men believe this when the work is of such a nature that they believe piece work to be practicable. In most cases their fear of making a record which will be used as a basis for piece work will cause them to soldier as much as they dare.

It is, however, under piece work that the art of systematic soldiering is thoroughly developed. After a workman has had the price per piece of the work he is doing lowered two or three times as a result of his having worked harder and increased his output, he is likely to entirely lose sight of his employer's side of the case and to become imbued with a grim determination to have no more cuts if soldiering can prevent it. Unfortunately for the character of the workman, soldiering involves a deliberate attempt to mislead and deceive his employer, and thus upright and straight-forward workmen are compelled to become more or less hypocritical. The employer is soon looked upon as an antagonist, if not as an enemy, and the mutual confidence which should exist between a leader and his men, the enthusiasm, the feeling that they are all working for the same end and will share in the results, is entirely lacking.

The feeling of antagonism under the ordinary piecework system becomes in many cases so marked on the part of the men that any proposition made by their employers, however reasonable, is looked upon with suspicion. Soldiering becomes such a fixed habit that men will frequently take pains to restrict the product of machines which they are running when even a large increase in output would involve nor more work on their part.

On work which is repeated over and over again and the volume of which is sufficient to permit it, the plan of making a contract with a competent workman to do a certain class of work and allowing him to employ his own men subject to strict limitations, is successful.

As a rule, the fewer the men employed by the contractor and the smaller the variety of the work, the greater will be the success under the contract system, the reason for this being that the contractor, under the spur of financial necessity, makes personally so close a study of the quickest time in which the work can be done that soldiering on the part of his men becomes difficult and the best of them teach laborers or lower-priced helpers to do the work formerly done by mechanics.

The objections to the contract system are that the machine tools used by the contractor are apt to deteriorate rapidly, his chief intrerest being to get a large output, whether the tools are properly cared for or not, and that through the ignorance and inexperience of the contractor in handling men, his employés are frequently unjustly treated.

These disadvantages are, however, more than counterbalanced by the comparative absence of soldiering on the part of the men.

The greatest objection to this sytem is the soldiering which the contractor himself does in many cases, so as to secure a good price for his next contract.

It is not at all unusual for a contractor to restrict the output of his own men and to refuse to adopt improvements in machines, appliances, or methods while in the midst of a contract, knowing that his next contract price will be lowered in direct proportion to the profits which he has made and the improvements introduced.

Under the contract system, however, the relations between employers and men are much more agreeable and normal than under piece work, and it is to be regretted that owing to the nature of the work done in most shops this sytem is not more generally applicable.

The writer quotes as follows from his paper on "A Piece Rate System," read in 1895, before The American Society of Mechanical Engineers:

> Coöperation, or profit sharing, has entered the mind of every student of the subject as one of the possible and most attractive solutions of the problem; and there have been certain instances, both in England and France, of at least a partial success of coöperative experiments.
>
> So far as I know, however, these trials have been made either in small towns, remote from the manufacturing centers, or in industries which in many respects are not subject to ordinary manufacturing conditions.
>
> Coöperative experiments have failed, and, I think, are generally destined to fail, for several reasons, the first and most important of which is, that no form of coöperation has yet been devised in which each individual is allowed free scope for his personal ambition. Personal ambition always has been and will remain a more powerful incentive to exertion than a desire for the general welfare. The few misplaced drones, who do the loafing and share equally in the profits with the rest, under coöperation are sure to drag the better men down toward their level.
>
> The second and almost equally strong reason for failure lies in the remoteness of the reward. The average workman (I don't say all men) cannot look forward to a profit which is six months or a year away. The nice time which they are sure to have to-day, if they take things easily, proves more attractive than hard work, with a possible reward to be shared with others six months later.
>
> Other and formidable difficulties in the path of coöperation are, the equitable division of the profits, and the fact that, while workmen are always ready to share the profits, they are neither able nor willing to share the losses. Further than this, in many cases, it is neither right nor just that they should share either in the profits or the losses, since these may be due in great part to causes entirely beyond their influence or control, and to which they do not contribute.

3

A Different View of Output Restriction

Who Limits Output?

SAMUEL GOMPERS

Cost of living has been rising steadily since the armistice of nearly a year ago. It has risen to a point where relief must be secured. So long as the public was able to pay it paid, though not without complaint. Finally, however, the point of inability to pay has been reached.

The high cost of living situation has not been without its interest for Labor which must find itself involved in everything which has to do with the life of the people. In this case, as in so many other cases, a certain section of the public press has shown its willingness to misrepresent the position of labor, and to report falsely its activities. In the main, there have been two misstatements that tend to give the public a discolored view of the case. These are:

1. That increases in wages are necessarily followed by increases in prices, which in turn are followed by demands for further increases in wages, to be again followed by necessary increases in prices, and so indefinitely around the circle.
2. That there has been an underproduction of goods, due to Labor's determination not to work at full speed. In other words, that there has been a limitation of output by Labor.

In the first place it is not true that increases in wages must be followed by increases in prices to the consuming public. If this were true it would follow that profiteering does not exist. It needs no proof here to establish the fact that profiteering does exist and has existed since the armistice, if not before. So high an authority as the President of the United States has made it perfectly plain that there not only is profiteering, but that this profiteering is of the most flagrant and unjustifiable nature, and that it wants the most drastic action of the nation in the way of curtailment.

Labor has been under the necessity of fighting insistently to maintain the American standard of living. It has been under the necessity of putting forth every possible effort to keep income through wages as near as possible within reach of the rapidly advancing cost of living. It has been the victim of profiteering and in one sense a contributor to that national disgrace.

Labor demands a real relief from profiteering. It understands thoroughly the necessity for production, being engaged constantly in doing the useful and essential work of the world, in shaping and making those things

Reprinted from the *International Molders Journal*, Vol. 58, November, 1919, pp. 878-881.

Samuel Gompers founded the American Federation of Labor in the early 1890's and served as its first president for over thirty years.

by which human life is made possible, and, at times, pleasant. It has a profound understanding of the value of commodities. It looks upon commodities as something to be put to useful purpose. It can have no sympathy with any purpose of any movement which has for its object the attaching of an inflated value to the products of toil.

Labor's effort is and must be an honest effort. There are fundamental reasons why Labor must forever frown upon and fight against all efforts to debase the fruit of Labor in the channels of finance and commerce. With every fibre of its being, for ethical as well as material reasons, it revolts against that which we have come to know and feel as profiteering.

Labor, with ample reason and proof, places the blame for the false situation in which the world finds itself squarely upon those who are masters of the productive machinery of the world. It demands relief of the most fundamental character. In so far as it can contribute thought and good will and helpful effort toward a solution of the world's difficulties, it will so contribute with eagerness and gladness. But there must be relief and remedy at once. To find that relief and that remedy the true situation must be recognized and all false statements and conclusions avoided.

That Labor is a contributory factor to the common distress because of a policy of restriction of output is one of the first and most flagrant examples of falsehood which must be discarded. Only a frank recognition of facts will help toward a final constructive solution and nothing less than that will satisfy a weary and war-worn world.

4

Big Daddyism: 1900-1930

Welfare Work in Company Towns

MONTHLY LABOR REVIEW

The more or less isolated community in which often only one industry is the means of livelihood of the people residing there is found in many localities in the United States. Mining enterprises naturally are frequently located in remote and inaccessible sections, while the location in small towns of one mill only or a group of mills under the same management has been a peculiar development of the textile industry in the South. In other sections, industries are often situated at some distance from manufacturing centers because of available water power, nearness to the source of raw material, or for some other reason which offsets the disadvantages connected with the distance from markets. Whatever the reason for their isolation, such towns have been forced to become more or less self-sufficing units and in order to attract a desirable class of labor or even to maintain an ordinarily self-respecting community the employers in such towns have found it desirable to furnish many of the advantages the

Reprinted from the *Monthly Labor Review*, Vol. 25, August, 1927, pp. 314-321.

provision of which properly comes within the province of the State, the community as distinct from the company, or other business or social agencies.

While hardly anyone will dispute the fact that the provision of churches, schools, a proper milk supply, town sanitation, and other features of communal life does not properly come within the scope of the employer's duties, or even that it is not desirable that he should provide them, the fact remains that many of these towns have been so developed and that frequently an amazing number of activities are assisted or controlled by the company.

While no survey of company towns as such was made by the Bureau of Labor Statistics, the material collected in connection with a recent study of employers' personnel activities included information regarding the life in such towns which, it is thought, may be of some value in contributing to an understanding of the various problems which have been presented in the development of these villages. The present study was not in any sense a critical one but was made for the purpose of showing what has been done along the line of personnel work and, in so far as possible, what has been successful.

Some of the community work has already been touched upon in earlier articles[1] as it was not possible entirely to separate it from the phases of personnel work which dealt more particularly with the employees in their relation to the industry.

Among the most important activities in these towns are the measures taken to safeguard the health of employees and their families through the provision of the services of physicians and visiting nurses and the maintenance of various clinics and classes in home hygiene and the care of the sick as well as by insuring a proper water supply and supervising the other details of the town sanitation. The educational facilities in these towns would often be inadequate without the assistance of the company, as in some of the States the school year is short and school funds are not sufficient to provide a satisfactory teaching force. As a result, the company frequently pays the salaries of the teachers for that portion of the school year that the schools would otherwise be closed. In many instances, also, the companies have built and equipped the school and turned it over to the authorities to run. Part-time schools and night classes for cotton-mill workers are also found, as well as domestic-science classes for girls and women, and instruction where there are many foreign workers in their native handicrafts.

Playground supervision for the children is customary and in the cotton mills where many women are employed it is not uncommon to find a well-equipped nursery where babies and small children are fed and cared for during the day. Houses are quite generally provided at moderate and often cheap rentals and in the South the rent usually includes electric light and water. The houses in many of the towns have running water, bathtubs, and fireplaces. There is a quite general tendency to encourage employees to make their homes attractive, and plants and seeds are often given to them and prizes awarded for the most attractive yards. Nearly always there is space for gardens and sometimes additional ground on the edge of town for those who wish more room for vegetables. In a number of cases free

[1] See *Labor Review*, January, 1927, pp. 7-19. Medical and hospital service for employees; and May, 1927, pp. 1-16: Outdoor recreation for industrial employees.

pasturage is provided for cows, and a few companies maintain a dairy and good milk is sold to the employees at a moderate price. The difficulty of obtaining milk in some sections of the South makes this an important service. Boarding houses for single men are usually maintained in mining communities and several textile mills have attractive houses with such conveniences as laundry tubs, electric irons, etc., for the girls. In the majority of these towns the community affairs are centered in a community clubhouse or in an industrial branch of the Y.M.C.A. or the Y.W.C.A.

The trained staff which supervises and administers the various activities in the community is, in the cotton mills of the South, under the direct control of the company in nearly every case. In other sections, however, the employees participate more largely in their management. A coal-mining company on the Pacific Coast has a thoroughly organized program covering industrial, health, and recreational activities. This company has four mines within a radius of about 50 miles, a town being located at each mine. The affairs of each camp are administered by a mine council composed of workmen elected by popular vote of all the employees. This council handles such questions as wages, welfare, social, and general questions pertaining to the camp, and a central council made up of four elected members from each mine council deals with such problems as relate to all the mines.

This central council has organized a safety association and carried on safety campaigns, developed systematic first-aid and mine-rescue work, and organized social clubs, a mutual-benefit association, thrift campaigns, and systematic savings plans, bands, orchestras, Camp Fire Girls and Boy Scouts, Americanization and citizenship schools, elementary school training of employees, traveling library, and sports. These activities are directed by trained specialists paid by the company. In addition to the mine council composed of employees, a mutual service director acts as conciliator in case of controversy and in an advisory capacity when his services are required.

In other company towns, if the employees have a direct voice in the control of community affairs it is usually through a community club in which membership is open to all.

Medical and Other Health Services

Among the companies providing the services of one or more visiting nurses who either give employees nursing care or visit the homes to see that sick employees are receiving proper attention, a considerable number also extend this service to the families of employees. These nurses are found almost without exception in the mining towns and in many of the textile mill villages. Frequently their entire time is spent in home visiting and, in addition to actual care of the sick, advice and instruction in nursing is given to the women of the village. The nurses give prenatal care and are often of great assistance in helping young mothers to care properly for their babies and young children.

In one town in which a baby clinic is held regularly, charts and accurate records showing the babies' progress are kept and each year a baby show is held and a prize is given to the baby showing the highest score whose mother has attended the clinic. In the baby clinic held by the medical department of another company, children from 6 weeks to 6 years of age are watched by the nurse who weighs them regularly and gives them the attention they need. The school children are also weighed by the nurse every three months and those who are 5 pounds or more underweight are sent to the nutrition class which meets once a week at the dispensary. As soon as these children reach the proper weight they are dropped from the class. A course of 15 lectures on home hygiene and care of the sick is given by the nurse, the mothers and school girls attending in the afternoon and the mill girls in the evening.

Children of school age usually receive free dental treatment and often such surgical attention as the removal of diseased tonsils, adenoids, etc. In addition to these special services, the medical departments in the company towns usually furnish the regular medical and often a considerable part of the surgical care which is needed by the employees and their families.

Although the nurseries conducted by the companies in a number of these villages do not have a health motive as their primary object, their effect from a health standpoint is good, as the children are given expert care. The children are usually taken from 6 to 8 weeks old up through the kindergarten stage and it is undoubtedly a great relief for mothers who are obliged to work to have a place to leave them where they will be properly fed and cared for. In one of the southern mill towns a matron and three helpers are employed in the nursery which the company maintains. The house has all necessary equipment, including bedrooms where the childen may take their naps, and a sun parlor. The children are given three meals a day. There is no charge for this service, although in some of the towns there is a fee for taking care of the children which varies from 5 cents per day per child to $1 a week.

A company in the Middle West has a free nursery for children 5 years of age and under which has a large sunny playroom equipped for kindergarten work and for recreation. The sleeping room has cots and bassinettes and the children take a nap in the afternoon, or, if their parents are on the evening shift, they are put to bed after supper. They are given a light lunch of orange juice and crackers and a regular luncheon of milk, fresh vegetables, cereals, and a simple dessert. The factory physician examines the children, and medical record cards are kept for each child with data as to weight, health, vision, etc. A kindergarten teacher has direct supervision of the children and a trained dietitian prepares the lunches.

In several towns all underweight school children are given milk at recess and a regular balanced meal at noon prepared by the domestic science class.

Education and Clubs

The education work in the company towns includes the provision of kindergartens, assistance to the public schools, classes in cooking, sewing, millinery, fruit canning, etc., for the girls and their mothers, manual training for the boys, and evening classes for the employees in subjects for which there may be a demand.

A paper company in New England holds classes throughout the winter for the girls in the factory and for the wives of employees. Instruction is given in sewing, fine needlework, candy making, and various handicrafts such as dyeing, enameling, parchment shade making, etc., the aim being to provide the same opportunities that can be obtained in larger communities where clubs and needlework guilds help in solving household and clothing problems, gift making, and home decorating. A fee of $5 covers everything taught in these classes. The personnel service director and his wife teach the classes, and in order to keep up to date they go to New York each year to take instruction, the expense of this instruction being borne by the company.

A southern company pays part of the principal's salary and the salary of several special teachers in the public school. The special teachers include a playground teacher, who teaches folk dances and gives the children physical exercises and drills, an art teacher, and a voice teacher who drills the children in chorus singing. This company also has two evening schools giving grammar and high school courses at which some of the men in the mill are enrolled, and there is also a class for illiterates.

In another town in which the company spends a great deal of money in the schools there are two cooking and two sewing teachers hired by the firm. All material is furnished for the cooking classes and there are 160 girls enrolled in this course. Both the cooking and the sewing lessons are very practical and the children gain experience in preparing meals by cooking and serving dinners for the different clubs.

The welfare department maintained by a company which has been very progressive in the matter of developing the capabilities of the members of the community has six workers who give special attention to constructive and educational work. In the two mill towns of this company these workers have a house which is used as a demonstration home and domestic science school. The enrollment during the year in the women's classes is about 700, the subjects given the most attention being cooking, sewing, and basketry. The cooking classes teach menu planning, balanced meals, food values, economical buying, use of left overs, and proper feeding of children; and in the sewing classes women are taught plain sewing, the use and alteration of commercial patterns, making of house dresses and clothing for infants and children, selection of materials, and determination of styles and colors for different types of garments. House furnishing, millinery, and fancywork are also taught. There is a well-equipped cannery in each village for the use of the housekeepers and the women bring their fruits and vegetables and put them up under the supervision of trained experts.

A company which has a separate kindergarten building with a large enrollment of pupils has rooms in the basement for cooking and carpentry classes. These courses are very popular and there is always a waiting list of boys for the carpentry work.

The club work carried on by the companies includes many troops of Boy Scouts, Campfire Girls, and similar organizations and a variety of clubs among factory employees and the older members of their families. The companies generally pay a great deal of attention to the younger children who are enlisted in the different clubs. The social service workers usually supervise these organizations or sometimes one of the mill employees acts as scoutmaster to the boy scouts' troop. Summer outings are arranged for them and the members of these groups are often given a week in a summer camp by the company.

A textile mill located in a large city hires a worker each summer to take the small children to the playgrounds and direct their play. The children are frequently taken into the country for the day in company trucks, a lunch including a pint of milk for each child, being furnished by the plant cafeteria. Each week during the summer a group of children is taken to a camp at some distance from the city which is leased each year by the company.

The community social affairs are of a varied nature, including parties, dances, amateur theatricals, and usually a Christmas entertainment.

Several of the mills promote interest in flower culture by holding annual rose, dahlia, or chrysanthemum shows at which prizes are given and in a number of cases bulbs and plants are furnished to the residents of the town from the company greenhouses.

A great many of the companies maintain bands and orchestras which furnish one of the favorite forms of entertainment, particularly the outdoor concerts in the summer. Customarily the company buys the uniforms and music and the more expensive instruments for the members of the band and often there is a special room provided for rehearsals.

The musical organization in one of the textile mills includes two bands, one made up of mill employees and the other composed of school children. A large band hall, comfortably furnished with wicker furniture and containing cabinets for the instruments and music, a piano and a victrola, is provided by the company. A full-time director is employed by the firm, and instruments, music, and winter and summer uniforms are furnished for the players. The junior band numbers about 30 and credit is given the members on their school work and they are given one-half hour a day from school attendance for practice. They use the same instruments that are used by the adults but with different mouthpieces. Outdoor concerts are given by these bands throughout the summer, and they participate in all community affairs.

Community Centers

The social, educational, and recreational activities of the company towns are usually centered in a clubhouse or in a group of buildings in which the various club and game rooms, the gymnasium, and sometimes the auditorium are located. In many cases, however, the school auditorium is used for the community entertainments. Frequently there is either an indoor or outdoor swimming pool which is almost invariably largely used.

A northern textile manufacturing company provided outdoor bathing for the employees and their families by converting the river near their community house into a bathing beach. A section of the shore was cleared and many truck loads of sand and gravel were drawn in and spread and a float with diving boards at different heights, and chutes, etc., were added to the attractions of the beach. Instruction in swimming is given to operatives and their families by the personnel director. So much enthusiasm was aroused that a water carnival has become an annual event on the Fourth of July. There are various events, and swimmers and divers for miles around compete for the prizes, although competition for the prizes in some of the events is confined to operatives in the mill.

An example of well-organized community life is that of a village in New England where the company for more than a quarter of a century has taken an active interest in providing attractive living and working conditions for its employees. This company has many employees who are foreigners—mainly Portuguese and Italians—and it is of interest to note that an unusually large percentage have had a long term of service in the plant. About 10 per cent of the total number of employees have been with the company more than 25 years, while 30 employees have been with it more than 40 years.

The grounds around the plant and the community buildings are laid out like a park and the different activities are centered in different buildings. There is a separate restaurant building, the dining room on the first floor being used largely by woman employees, by members of the employees' families, and by outsiders; the men use mainly the one on the second floor where they can smoke and play cards. The prices charged employees represent only the cost of the food, but regular prices are charged the general public. The library, which is also housed in a separate building, contains about 20,000 volumes. There are three reading rooms, one of which is specially fitted up for children, with smaller tables and chairs, one is for men and boys and has mainly books of travel, biography, and history, and the other is a general reading room. Books may be taken out by employees and their families, by the teachers, and by outside school children for their work, while the reading rooms are open to any one. A kindergarten building has three classrooms, a large assembly room, and a sand room. All the rooms have special decorations suited to the small children. This is for the exclusive use of employees' children and there is no charge except a small enrollment fee. The auditorium or community building is one of the newer buildings and has reception rooms, cloakrooms, and a lounge, together with parlors for the women and smoking rooms for the men. There is an auditorium (with a fine lighting system) on the second floor, and this has a seating capacity of 600. This building serves as the social center of the town, and here frequent card parties are held and a dance is given each month by the men's club; various lodges and clubs hold their dances and social affairs in this building.

The men's club, membership in which is open to all male employees, their grown sons, and to stockholders of the company, has a clubhouse given by the company, which was a fine old farm house altered to suit the club's needs but in which the colonial finish was preserved as far as possible. There are bowling alleys, billiard and card rooms, a reading room, and a large lounging room. The company furnishes the house rent free, but the running expenses are paid by the members and the management is entirely in their hands.

Sewing, embroidery, dressmaking, etc., are taught at the "art craft" shop. The materials are sold at cost to families of employees and there is an art department where the women may leave their fancy work to be sold if they wish. The provisions for outdoor recreation include baseball and football grounds, a children's playground which also has tennis courts for the use of the children, and bathhouses on the beach with a swimming instructor provided. Houses have been provided since 1899 and all houses now have modern plumbing and hardwood floors. Reasonable rents are charged, the maximum being about $20 a month, and employees who wish to build their own homes are loaned money by the company for this purpose.

While the community work varies in different places and localities according to the different conditions present, its chief value would seem, in viewing it as a whole, to be the attention given to safeguarding the health of the children and the opportunity given them to secure a better education often than their parents have had, as well as the chance to have any special capability recognized and fostered.

5

An Ominous Portent?—1927

News Notes of Member Organizations: Vocational Service for Juniors

CLARE L. LEWIS

We are indebted to Miss Clare L. Lewis, of the Vocational Service for Juniors, for the following statement of an unusual employment condition, and the steps that are being taken to remedy it.

The weeks just past (October, 1927) have presented a situation in the employment office of the Vocational Service for Juniors unknown, at this season of the year, since the period of general industrial depression in 1921. September and October are ordinarily the peak months of the year as far as junior employment in New York is concerned. Business is brisk, openings for boys and girls are numerous and often salaries paid are somewhat higher than at other times of the year. Many children at this time secure jobs, and often desirable ones, through friends or relatives and others obtain work through the newspaper ads or through the numerous "help wanted" signs displayed in front of various business establishments. Applicants at the placement office of our organization can usually be afforded a choice of five to ten different openings. (That is, the boys and girls applying for employment during the fall months are not usually called upon to take just anything as a makeshift. Instead, if they have a definite desire for some sort of work, the chances are good that that desire may be gratified.) This is a state of affairs which many of the children, and the teachers in the Continuation School where our placement office is located as well, have come naturally to expect and to count upon, but this year matters have been radically different. The situation for September was as follows:

The demand for junior workers on the part of New York employers has shown a marked decline this fall, not only as compared with our figures a year ago, but also, as chart 1 shows, as compared with those of any year since 1921.

The contrast between September of this year and September of last year is particularly marked. The figures for these two years are as follows:

Number of Openings Available for Juniors

	Boys	Girls	Total
September, 1926	1,181	666	1,847
September, 1927	550	333	883

 Reprinted from *The Personnel Journal*, Vol. 6, 1927-28, pp. 314-316.

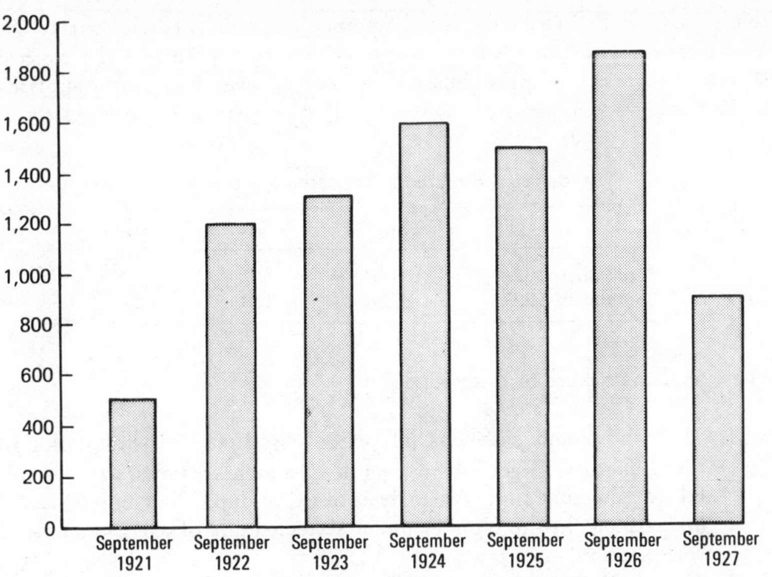

Figure 1. Total number of openings available for juniors each September from September, 1921, to September, 1927.

These figures, as may be seen, show a falling off of exactly 50 per cent in the number of openings for girls and a decrease of slightly more than 50 per cent in the jobs available for boys.

In some lines of work the shortage of openings was more apparent than in others. An analysis of the kinds of jobs available during September, 1927, as compared with September, 1926, reveals the following facts:

1. The total number of trade opportunities for both boys and girls shows a falling off of 68 per cent in September this year as compared with the figures for September a year ago.
2. Factory openings decreased 56 per cent.
3. Office and clerical openings fell off 52 per cent.
4. Mercantile openings fell off 46 per cent.
5. Errand jobs decreased 39 per cent.

The present situation would seem to be due not to any general slump in business but rather to the present period of keen business competition, combined with falling prices, the result of which is to make margins of profit exceedingly narrow, especially for the smaller or less efficiently managed firms. An employer must cut his current expenses to a minimum if he is to make any reasonable profit and one way by which he can do so is to lay off many of his youngest and most unskilled workers, in other words, the boys and girls with whom the Vocational Service for Juniors deals.

There is yet another side to the situation as the employment bureau sees it, that of the applicants themselves. Unable to secure work this fall as usual through friends and relatives or perhaps through newspaper ads, more boys and girls are turning to the placement office than ever before at this season of the year. The total number of applicants applying to the Vocational Service for Juniors for work during September of this year shows an increase of approximately 56 per cent over the number applying in September a year ago. The figures for the two years are as follows:

Number of Individuals Applying for Work

	Boys	Girls	Total
September, 1926	150	162	312
September, 1927	286	200	486

These applicants were of three kinds:

1. Those boys and girls who left school last June and who, owing to their inability to get jobs during the summer, are going to work this fall for the first time. An analysis of this group shows an increase of 38 per cent in the number under sixteen years of age as compared with September of last year.
2. Those who have worked but have been laid off by their employers and told that business is "slack" and who have found it difficult to secure employment again.
3. Those who, studying the chart in the employment office and expecting a great variety of openings to be available in September as usual, quit the jobs they had, hoping to secure something better. Publicity along this line last year brought to the office a number of such cases and the counselors were dismayed at first by their arrival, the situation being what it is. Fortunately, however, although these boys and girls could not always be given jobs which were decidedly better than those they left, they at least could be sent to openings which were as good.

Such being the present situation, the outlook for the coming months, as far as junior workers is concerned, would appear none too encouraging. Hence, as a measure of preparedness, every effort is being made by the members of the placement office staff to make contacts with as many new firms as possible so that more openings may be found. Also the West Side Continuation School, in which the office is located, has been fully apprised of the situation and, with the coöperation of the teachers there, efforts are being made as never before to get the boys and girls to consult the placement counselors before they voluntarily quit any jobs they now may have. By such measures as these it is hoped that some of the threatening unemployment among junior workers may be prevented.

6

Problems of the Work Itself Emerge: 1930

Fatigue, Morale and Output

STUART CHASE

I must come to you this evening as a layman, not with the charts and graphs of a specific piece of research, such as you listened to this morning, but rather with the observations—and with apologies to Dr. Dewey—the observations of a journeyman philosopher as to this question of fatigue in industry. I would like to come to you with a specific research document in my pocket dealing with the fatigue in Wall Street since October 24th, not so much the fatigue of the margineers as of the clerks. I think there is a very interesting study for somebody to make of the way the clerical forces in Wall Street have been working since the crash, and how they have worked.

"Whither Mankind" started me, I suppose, as a sort of a spring-board into these larger problems of what specifically the billion horses, more or less wild in the modern world to-day, are doing to us; and no more had I got started in this inquiry than I was faced with the specific problem, among others, of the robot, the flesh-and-blood automaton. Are we turning as a race into robots, automatons, half-men, dominated and undone, our souls destroyed by these wild horses?

The first thing that I chose to find out in this particular problem was how many robots there were in the United States of America. I took the 1920 census of occupations, and tried to find out how many persons were confronting the machine throughout eight hours of their daily labors; and I discovered that something over ten million, about one-quarter of the gainfully employed, were in actual confrontation.

Then I began to carry the analysis a little deeper. Are those ten million necessarily dominated? Are they slaves to mechanization? Obviously and immediately it appeared that great sections of them were not slaves. Is Lindbergh a slave? Yet he is a machine tender. All of us who drive automobiles know the exhilaration we receive from piloting a powerful engine across country roads. The same way in the factory. There are many jobs where the machine tender is not dominated by the rhythm of his mechanism, but where he uses the mechanism and lets something of its vigor and vitality into his own veins.

There are workers in a jewelry establishment in Newburyport, for instance. They use machines, yes, but they use them only to make their handwork more delicate, because a machine can hammer a plate surface more finely than can a human hand. So I revised my figures, trying to find out the number of robots in the country who were dominated by the machine, and it came down to something over five million, which in 1920 was about 5 per cent of the population.

Reprinted from *The Personnel Journal*, Vol. 8, 1929-30, pp. 333-37.

Taken from a speech by Mr. Chase at an annual meeting of the Personnel Research Federation, November 15, 1929. He was a widely read author and commentator on various aspects of society during the early part of the twentieth century.

Now that is a rather low ratio to form the basis for a conclusion that we are being turned into slaves of the machine. Furthermore, that ratio is dropping. As the automatic and semi-automatic gains ground in industry, and it is gaining ground all the time, machine-tenders give way to skilled planners, inspectors and dial watchers. In the new oil-burning liner, California, three white-garbed firemen, watching dials and throwing switches, have replaced 120 stokers. That sort of thing is going on throughout the industrial structure. I suspect that to-day the ratio of robots is 4 per cent, but still, lest we grow over-optimistic, four or five million men and women in chains, dominated by the machine, dominated by monotonous repetitive jobs, is a ghastly total and presents a tremendous problem.

Let us carry the analysis further. Dr. Myers finds that in monotonous and repetitive work there are three classes of workers. There are, first of all, those with a low intelligence quotient, who apparently do not object to monotony, if the speed is not geared too high, who day-dream as they work. My friend, Fred Colvin, one of the editors of the *American Machinist*, tells the story of being very much perturbed by this question of monotony in industry, and of going out to one of the big automobile establishments and telling the managing staff, "Here, you ought to shift your jobs. You shouldn't keep these people working at this same repetitive work; it should by changed around." Under the belt-line was a gentleman lying on his back on a cradle that moved in and out of the assembly line. He had fixed up a cushion for himself to lie on, and as the frames of the cars came by overhead he reached up and screwed on a bolt or something of the sort. They suggested that this gentleman should be transferred to another job. He crawled out from under the assembly-line very, very mad and said, "Change my job? Well, I guess not. I'll quit if you change my job. I've got the softest job in the shop; nothing to do but lie down all day." He belonged to Class 1, and a great many of our fellow-citizens belong to Class 1.

Secondly, there are those who object to monotonous work but who compensate by outside activities, and, of course, that is where the whole question of play and recreation enters. It becomes cardinal in industry to give a proper balance to jobs that will inevitably remain monotonous, no matter how fast the automatizing process goes.

Thirdly, there are those who are injured by monotonous work and who can find no outlet or compensation; and that, my friends, is the tragic exhibit.

To illustrate: Here is a group of intelligent girls who were put on a monotonous cross-stitching job. They learned their work quickly. In a short time their output exceeded the duller girls' who normally did the work, but in three or four weeks the output curve fell until the intelligent girls were turning out far less than the others? Why? Because they were slowly being bored to death. They could not stand the monotony of it. In other words, we are faced with a problem of selecting workers of the proper type for our industrial processes, and, other things being equal, it is necessary to select them presumably in such a way that industry itself will not be unduly handicapped by the process.

Here I want to make a personal confession. I called myself a journeyman philosopher, and as such I am not a business man. I am not interested in corporate profits except academically. I am interested in men and women and the reactions of the modern world on men and women. I would rather have a poor state with happy people in it than a rich state with millions in misery, psychological or otherwise. But it happens that there may be a compromise between these two points of view on this particular problem. We have been finding compromises lately, strangely enough.

Take the doctrine of the economy of high wages. Enlightened business men in America to-day, particularly in the larger establishments, are announcing at such banquets as this—and I believe also in their own hearts—that wages should be high, in order to promote that flow of purchasing power which will keep mass-production functioning with a minimum overhead cost. Now that is a doctrine to make Adam Smith and the Manchester School turn in their graves. It has always been held that the lower the wages the lower the costs and the bigger the profits; but under this new doctrine apparently it is not true.

Another compromise is found in the Safety First movement. It costs money, lots of money, to introduce the necessary devices needed for adequate safety for industrial employees; but it has been found that that money in the end is well spent. The Engineering Council finds that in those plants where output is at a maximum, accidents tend to be at a minimum. In other words, it pays in dollars and cents to reduce industrial accidents.

Why can we not carry over that same compromise into this question of monotony and fatigue? I think we can. In fact, I think that it is already beginning to be done. The whole movement toward shorter hours and the five-day week is in line with such an assumption. Careful studies have proved that in specific industries and trades, output is as great on an 8-hour day as it used to be on a 12, and sometimes greater.

Now in the specific problem of fatigue and the toxins which it sets up, the Industrial Fatigue Research Board in England—to give a typical example of the sort of studies that are being made—puts counters on the looms in the weaving sheds, and meters on the motors for measuring power-consumption. Undoubtedly you know more about these studies than I do. They have found that on Tuesday morning between 8 and 10 o'clock output is at a maximum, and that on Friday evening at 5 o'clock output is at a minimum, with a variation between the two of 12 per cent. It finds the daily and the weekly output in a fatigue cycle. Then it starts to find out the reasons, and it appears that the reason in this particular case seems to be temperature. That is, as the machines get under way, the weaving sheds warm up. They not only warm up during the day and cool down in the evening, but they warm up cumulatively throughout the week. By adjusting the temperature, output is increased, and the men and women in this particular job are made more comfortable and more healthy. The two points of view have been coördinated, brought together, unified.

As such studies are made the remedies may take account of all sorts of variations. It may be temperature, it may be ventilation, it may be the speed of the machinery, it may be the specific motions of the workers themselves.

Mr. Walter Polokov, the distinguished mechanical engineer, has made fatigue-studies here, using as a quantitive measure, carbon dioxide expelled by the lungs. He has worked on compositors on the night shift and measured the carbon dioxide they give out, and has charted very pretty curves.

Professor Kitson, of Columbia, has worked out a study in the measurement of work-interests, a scale which he proposes to apply and has already applied to certain trades and occupations.

The National Institute of Industrial Psychology in England has served over a hundred clients. It is not a humanitarian organization; it is an organization in business for income for professional workers, and it finds that lessening fatigue pays for its services and pays the organization which has the work done in its shops.

Mr. Ordway Tead, whom I see in the audience to-night, has blocked out a very interesting and significant approach to such studies as I am referring to here, particularly in the field of the psychology of the worker, that is, throughout the industrial world. These studies are being made now and my plea is for more and more of them.

I am not interested, as I said before, primarily because there is profit in it. I think such studies will pay for themselves; but my main interest is that they will serve, when we get a sufficient body of accredited research opinion, to meet this challenge of the machine, the accusation that it is wrecking the bodies and the minds of our industrial workers. If we can point in shop after shop to the careful work that has been carried out, to the actual health statistics, physical and mental, of the employees therein, that challenge and that accusation will break down.

Enter the next ten factories that you pass and ask the manager if he uses fatigue-curves. He will think that you came directly from the nearest speakeasy. Not until you reach the ninth will you see them actually upon the walls; but if they mean lower costs, bigger margins in the competitive struggle, they are bound to come, just as automatic machinery and mass production have come. They open limitless possibilities for keeping the bodily mechanism of the worker at par, the bodily and the mental. And his soul—I wonder how long it is necessary to lie awake worrying about a healthy man's soul!

7

Optimism in the Face of Adversity: 1931

The Worker's Mind Today

WHITING WILLIAMS

"Why should *they* come lookin' fer work" one of my fellow job-seekers answered my query outside the gates of a big Cleveland factory where I had expected to find hundreds instead of a handful of applicants. "All the regulars here know that as soon as work opens up they'll be *sent for*."

3

Reprinted from *The Personnel Journal*, Vol. 9, 1930-31, 401-406.
Whiting Williams was an industrial writer and consultant during this period.

"It's only us floaters," he went on, "that's worried about grabbin' a job, just fer the day."

His explanation was repeated later at many plant gates in Cleveland and also in such other cities as Pittsburgh, Homestead, Detroit, South Bend, Gary and Chicago, in addition to Montreal and Toronto, all of which I visited last July and August in order to learn the unemployed worker's state of mind.

That explanation brought the first of a whole series of agreeable surprises in the field of industrial relations as compared with what I experienced as a worker back in 1919. At that time, for instance—the depression of '21 was just beginning—it was a small plant indeed which did not show, especially on Monday morning, its scores and hundreds waiting to make sure that no stranger took away their place on the payroll.

This summer, as well as then, it is perhaps well here to explain, it proved surprisingly easy to be accepted as one of the waiting crowd—at least in the physical sense. Mentally, it was sometimes hard to remember just who I was at the moment; for instance, to keep from saying, "Hello, Jim," to a good friend and well known member of the Chamber of Commerce who almost brushed my knees as I sat on the low railing in our Public Square trying to learn the response of my companions to the smooth-tongued Communist orator.

Decidedly embarrassing would the result have been if I had failed to "come to" just when I did one early morning in Detroit. There, while the "law" (hobo for policeman), his ugly blackjack in hand, was ordering a couple of near down-and-outs to stop their fighting and move on, I stood close to him smiling my approval, as though to tell him how we minions of respectability ought to stand together against such roughneck trouble-makers. Luckily, an instant later, I was able to move and move fast as he suddenly looked me in the eye and shouted:

"And that goes for ALL you bums! BEAT IT—before I break your G——d—— necks!"

It took several furtive looks behind to give certainty that the blackjack was not following the bunch of us up the alley.

So it was not from the employers or their agents but from the workers themselves that testimony came for making plain these agreeable surprises. High upon the list was this one: as compared with my worker experiences in this country during 1919, I found my workless worker friends of last summer enjoying a greater vested interest—a sense of ownership in a piece of property called their job. Even though this property was not producing greater dividends than the earnings of more than a day or two of work per week, it nevertheless helped hugely to a man's standing with both himself and his grocer, as compared with no place whatever on anybody's payroll.

To a degree unknown in any previous depression, all existing work has been divided up among the workers share and share alike. As never even dreamed of before, also, the largest and most typical employers have refrained from cutting wage rates. In Cleveland, for example, the same group of industrialists whose starting wage rate fell during the depression of 1921 from 48 cents to 36 cents per hour, held their starting rate during this depression to a net change from 44.4 to 44.0 cents per hour.

"They cut down hours," it was explained outside one well known Cleveland establishment, "but they ain't laid off a man—not in a year!"

More than ever before has it been possible for the jobseekers to get such counsel as I received outside a certain great steel plant.

"Ye've got no chance here," explained one of the regulars who lived near the gate where I was loitering, "W'y, in there they've even gone so far as to transfer their regular furnace men on to the odd jobs o' buildin' the new extension, 'stead o' layin' 'em off, see?"

Beyond question, these new practises of job-sharing, transfer and job protection represented closer and more understanding contact between employer and employee than has existed in any similar depression in history. To be sure, none of these improvements increases the total of wages actually paid to the working force as a whole. But, as compared with the older, more hard-boiled methods, they certainly do produce a huge betterment in *feeling*. They serve to make a man's job into something like a piece of property. Even if for a season this property pays little, nevertheless it helps a lot if its owner knows it's there, waiting its chance to come back to normal earning. Infinitely better than no job at all is the feel of a job which gives every week a couple or more days of work.

The repeated assurance from the employment office that no stranger could get their places away from them and that a man was wasting shoe leather even to come to the office pending the arrival of the promised message—this is what kept literally thousands of workers away from those dreary and demoralizing hours of plant-gate loafing and substituted instead those immensely less discouraging days of fishing or perhaps of bathing with one's family at one of the park beaches.

To these cushionings is to be added the fact that the American family enjoys today a wider dollars-and-cents base line than ever before. If Father or John has no job the chance is greater than in any previous depression that either Mother or Mary is bringing home a pay check.

In addition it is certain that partly as a result of all these improvements, the American worker entered into this depression as himself more of a capitalist than before. If he did not own his house or a savings account, or even a few shares of stock in his own or some other company, then at least the chance was good that he enjoyed the self-respect which came from his ability to hold on to the family car.

"Nothin' but a stray day's work or two in weeks," explained one husky young fellow as we sat on the curb outside a great factory. "Not a cent for even the makin's of a little home brew." Followed a moment later by his: "Well, I can't see no job around here so I guess I might as well *run the old flivver down town*!"

Still further any fair observer taking the trouble to get close to the worker must report that an additional cushioning for helping him weather the current joblessness has been given him by the present freedom of our street corners from saloons. As a substitute for that ancient, if not especially honorable, institution, so my experiences this summer taught me, the modern speak-easy is a total flop. In neither money nor alcohol is one of the old saloons equalled by as many as 30 or 40 speak-easies. The chief reason is that these lack almost entirely the saloon's former lure.

It is my belief that, thanks largely to the attention given these past fifteen years to industrial relations, the country's *psychology* last summer was better than the *arithmetic* of its actual unworked man-hours. This impression is made all the surer by my observation that in Canada, where employers and workers remain considerably farther apart, the country's feeling was *worse* than the situation's actual arithmetic of unemployment.

Along with these improvements in the situation of the worker, this depression has also demonstrated a more socialized employer. As never before the country's most typical employers are today feeling a deep and active sense of responsibility for both the maximum security and also the maximum opportunity for their employees. Best of all, also, this feeling has come not as a paternalistic worry about the weak on the part of the strong, but rather a recognition by wise men of the dependence of each upon the other. This feeling is sure to grow as rapidly as modern mass production demonstrates further to the mass producer that he is, sooner or later, simply out of luck unless supported by prosperous mass buyers.

It is nothing less than a huge tribute to all those developments I have mentioned that most of our Communist visitors appear to make slight progress among even such discouraged men and, for the most part, finish their days of exhortation and depart in disgust.

"Here I've handed out to you guys," complained one thin-chested but wiry and agile-minded pleader for the Russian plan, "a lot of books and pamphlets worth every cent of twelve good dollars. The law won't let me pass the hat, but I certainly got a fine idea of the gumption of you Clevelanders. With that hat down at my feet for one good hour, you send me away with—let's see—thirty-five, forty-five, *fifty-five cents*!"

Now with these improvements in our industrial set-up as demonstrated by our present crisis, the country has a greater right than ever, surely, to look to the industrialist for wise leadership in handling both the emergency and the more permanent situation.

The elimination, or at least the strict control of the private employment bureau and the substitution of public exchanges; the training of workers into several different kinds of skills; the adding of factory products calculated to stabilize year-round operations; the announcement to workers of the amount of employment they can now expect; the payment of separation allowances when lay-offs are unavoidable—all these are of the utmost importance, not only to every city's workers, but through them to the entire body of every city's business men and citizens of every type, bar none.

But further, that remarkable ingenuity and initiative of our typical American worker and that equally remarkable spirit of cooperation between him and his leaders and his employers, make it altogether of the utmost importance that, in our effort to handle either the emergency or the permanent problem, we should not by any chance whatever utilize those methods which represent an admission of defeat. Instead of more relief doles, every conceivable effort must be made by the government, by industry and by the domestic householder to give work. If we are to embark upon a program of insurance against unemployment, we should make sure that all its emphasis is upon not mere palliation but prevention. That country is skidding toward demoralization whose public begins to imagine that a man receiving $15.00 a week without work is anything like half as well off as a man earning $30.00 at his lathe or bench. In all the world there is no substitute for a job except another job. Men pray to receive not only the daily bread but the daily job because this job feeds not only the body but also a man's self-respect.

As Americans, we have developed for our entire population the highest standard of living known in the world. We must not consider back-tracking to those lower levels which are sure to follow upon any lessened use of the machine or upon any permanent policy of part time work and a part time paycheck. On the contrary, we must plan better to coordinate our resources of individual initiative, freedom, intelligence, and responsibility in order to find ways to promote such still higher standards of living here and abroad as will consume the products of our workers in charge of increasingly productive machines.

Such coordination will mean immensely more teamwork than we know now—teamwork within a given community, such as Philadelphia, for instance, is now working for. Also more teamwork between the members of entire industries and then of groups representing related industries and, still further, between these related industries and government. If this is all forbidden by the Sherman Act, then we should change the Act.

Something of this type, in combination with our American individual responsibility and freedom, is sure to help every industrialist to do his planning on, say, a three year basis, making sure that with the help of longer planning, his products and his methods keep constant step with the changing needs and demands of his customers. Such longer planning will go far toward supplying the needed jobs by means of the invention of products now undreamed of—products the making of which will employ the men laid off through the improvement of processes and methods. It is all wrong from the viewpoint of our longer future that today hardly five per cent of the scores of millions expended annually in our thousand and more industrial research laboratories, is devoted to the discovery and invention of new products. The chief reason is, according to our best research experts, that we are today too budget-minded—willing to take a chance on the inventor's studies, provided only that he will guarantee to bring in a new product before the end of the current fiscal year!

If we are to look wisely at the present situation we must face the fact that the ability to consume goods is infinite on the part of both America's and the world's workers. It is more helpful to consider the problem as a problem in under-consumption than in over-production, especially when we consider that we here in America earn a national income of around ninety billions yearly, which is roughly equivalent to the yearly income of the earth's remaining billion and a half of people. To these others we shall never be able to sell as much as we should till we grow more internationally minded.

Such increased coordination within and between our industries, combined with such three or five-year budgeting and the resultant product research, and increased international-mindedness, would only represent our growing recognition that all our political, all our social and all our economic institutions are in danger unless we can somehow contrive to give a better answer to that prayer of our fellow citizens—'give us this day our daily job.'

Unlike Italy or Russia, where such coordination and such longer planning have gone farthest, our American emphasis would be to make sure that the increased security of our workers should by no means come to lessen their maximum conceivable opportunity. Only in so far as our workers are helped not simply to stand safely still, but rather to grow and expand in material and social well-being, can we look forward to a continuously successful American; and such courageous efforts here can not fail to be of value to the other peoples of the world.

8

Optimism Gone Sour: 1933

The Panic Picture

W. D. MAHON

For a person to get a real view of the industrial panic now prevailing and its effects upon the people of the country, you have got to be in touch with the industrial situation prevailing. My work in the last seven months has carried me from Boston on the Atlantic seaboard to the Pacific Coast, reaching all of the large cities throughout the East, central states and up and down the Pacific. Everywhere you go you find the parks and public resorts filled with idle men, the beggary hand of want protruding from every side. On the western railroads you see the freight trains loaded with men, and in some cases women, beating their way to the westward. On the highways you see hundreds of men and women hitch-hiking. You will also see whole families—father, mother and four or five children—with all their worldly belongings, packed into an old Ford car, going they don't know where, just hoping against hope.

That is the general picture one gets from traveling through the country and getting in touch with the situation. But when you come down to study the results from a close view by analyzing the facts within the organizations of the workers, you find still a more alarming and serious situation.

In the Amalgamated Association of Street and Electric Railway Employees of America during the last 13 months we have paid 1,047 death claims. Out of that number 15 of these members shot and killed themselves. Thirteen hung themselves. Two killed themselves by taking gas. Two drowned themselves. One crushed his own skull. Then there were three cases of mysterious death that the coroner was in doubt about, but they indicated suicide. There you have some 36 suicides out of one industrial group of about 90,000 members, and remember that in this organization we have been making great sacrifices by assessing our membership, dividing our work and doing everything we can to relieve those that are in depressed conditions.

Now, what must be the condition in the groups of workers that have no organization, and have made no specific efforts to give relief and aid to their fellow workers? This picture, to my mind, gives us an idea of the terrible conditions prevailing, and it brings forth the picture of a situation that calls for every thoughtful man and woman who are interested in the future welfare of humanity to make every effort within their power to bring to an end this terrible condition and establish a new civilization for mankind.

Reprinted from the *American Federationist*, Vol. 40, February, 1933, p. 149. 4

Mr. Mahon was president of the Amalgamated Association of Street and Electric Railway Employees of America when he wrote this article.

9

Armageddon: 1933-1938

The Industrial War

FORTUNE

To progressive sociologists it is axiomatic that the U.S., most advanced of the industrial nations, has had the least developed philosophy of labor. These people contend that until the present Administration took office, labor legislation in the U.S., despite innumerable laws and commissions, had resulted in little essential change in organized labor's standing. They especially emphasize such significant facts as that before the current U.S. union drive, no more than 18 per cent of U.S. nonagricultural labor was organized into trade unions, compared with over 35 per cent in Britain and more than 70 per cent in Sweden. And on the basis of these figures and various supplementary observations that we need not develop here, they hold that U.S. labor has lagged behind U.S. industry in the matter of self-fulfillment.

The U.S. businessman does not admit that his labor philosophy is backward. It is of course impossible to speak for *all* businessmen, and in attempting to speak for even a few one runs into insuperable difficulties in social terminology. . . . Here we can only say that in general, as the businessman sees it, this is a free country, with jobs open to all who can get them and the rights of private property inherent in every economic and political fiber. He has on the whole no "objection" to the organization of labor provided that this will not impede his free action as an owner (or representative of owners) of private property; provided he can hire and fire as he sees fit; provided his individual employees can work when they want to; provided, that is to say, that traditional labor relations are not materially changed. If an "advanced" labor philosophy presumes the existence of national labor unions that curtail this familiar freedom of action, then the average American businessman does not want an advanced philosophy. Confronted with the possibility, or the threat, he takes his position upon the sturdy democratic tradition bequeathed to him by his forefathers, thus placing all those who are opposed to him in the awkward predicament of seeming to oppose that tradition. So that they become what Al Smith calls Communists.

Now whether you believe that this philosophy is backward, or whether you believe that it is the best that any democracy has so far devised, depends roughly upon which side of the private-property line your lot is cast. And as between those two irreconcilable extremes it is not the province of this article to choose. We are not here concerned with theory but with fact: the fact, namely, that for the past four and a half years the U.S. has been in the throes of a major labor upheaval which can fairly be described as one of the greatest mass movements in our history. If one bars the irrepressible conflict of the sixties, the only historical phenomenon

5

Reprinted with permission from *Fortune Magazine*, Vol. 16, November, 1937, pp. 104ff.

comparable to the labor movement is the great trek westward, beginning in the Mississippi Valley and ending on the Pacific Coast. And if that classic American migration looms up to our generation as something far more permanent and vast it is well to remind ourselves that the labor movement likewise has a history. There has been labor unrest ever since there was a factory system, but the movement referred to here can properly be traced back to 1866-87, a period of open warfare characterized for the first time by a series of important strikes on the issue of the right to organize and bargain collectively through nationwide unions. The claim to that right, now widely conceded in Britain and the European democracies but still resisted in the U.S., is the keystone of the American labor movement—is indeed what dignifies it as a movement rather than an intermittent and aimless war. Not that employers by and large are opposed to collective bargaining in principle. If they are involved in conflict, even as deeply involved as Mr. Girdler, it is with national unions as instruments for achieving it. The various local unions and independent unions that many employers prefer are in themselves—since the passage of the Wagner Act—an important aspect of the industrial war; but we are here concerned with labor's longer attempt to achieve collective bargaining through nationwide unions such as are organized into the A.F. of L. and the C.I.O.

The history of that struggle can be had from any textbook and need not detain us here. At present we are considering its most modern phase—a phase that, corresponding roughly with the Roosevelt Administration, is in itself a compound affair illustrating an exceedingly rapid change. In the early days of the NRA there was no C.I.O., there was no Wagner Act, there was no La Follette Committee, and no Mohawk Valley Formula, Big Steel had not yet "sold out" to labor, a sitdown strike had never been heard of in lay circles, and the American automobile was still for the most part innocent of unionized hands. Those things and those events were part of an evolution that was in its turn a part of the long labor movement above referred to. Not to understand this is to miss the point of every major event, every tactical decision, every judgment or error in judgment in the current labor world.

As a medical diagnosis can be reached only by a study of the symptoms, so it is necessary in an analysis of industrial warfare to reach into the heart of the problem by way of the strikes. For the strike is the external manifestation of labor's unrest, the thing that happens when an irresistible force meets an immovable body. The modern evolution we are speaking of has made itself manifest by a series of strikes, reaching a tremendous crescendo in the spring of 1937; and for the purpose of obtaining a better perspective on that evolution *Fortune* has isolated five of them, to be examined in some detail presently. As this article will show, strikes resemble wars in this at least—that they seldom break when or where they are expected. But, as of October 1, when this article went to press, there had been a three-month lull in the storm of big strikes. Whether or not this lull is to continue, it seems a likely moment to take stock of the complex modern phase—to recapitulate, to acquire a broader understanding of forces more subject to misapprehension and misinterpretation than any others to which society is heir.

From May, 1933, to July, 1937, a period of a little more than four years, there were some 10,000 strikes drawing out no less than 5,600,000 workers. This was aside from all the thousands of quickies, sitdowns, and other protests that tied up industry during that period—a "strike," as defined by the Department of Labor and used in this article, being an affair involving at least six workers for at least one day. But that was not all. Although a wave of strikes after any economic dislocation such as a war or a depression is supposed to be a normal phenomenon, the present strike wave did not entirely adhere to this pattern. It began conventionally enough with 1,695 strikes in 1933 (as against only 841 in 1932), and it rose on schedule to 1,856 in 1934, 2,014 in 1935, and 2,172 in 1936. In the latter year it gave signs of relaxing, the number of workers involved having dropped from 1,117,000 in 1935 to 789,000. But instead of following these indications the wave took life again in 1937, such that there were some 2,500 strikes in the first six months of this year, or more than in 1936 alltogether. And these strikes involved some 1,200,000 workers as against 789,000 workers for the full year 1936. During the spring labor observers began to predict an all-time high for 1937, with a total of at least 5,000 strikes, the previous high having been made in 1917 with 4,450.[1]

As already stated, there is now little reason to suppose that the 1917 strike high will be surpassed in 1937. Many an employer feels more secure, and many have fallen back upon the comfortable theory that the 1937 wave, while slightly off pattern, is after all part and parcel of a normal post-depression disturbance. For all anyone knows, these comfortable theorists may be right; but before jumping to that conclusion the wary observer ought to examine the field for himself.

To begin with numbers, the labor movement has been growing prodigiously, displaying an inherent power in the face of numerous emergencies and setbacks. While labor's membership claims are to be taken with some reserve, recent performances make it unwise to discount them too freely. Thus the C.I.O., which had 1,000,000 members in September, 1936, now claims 3,700,000; and the A.F. of L., which then had some 2,600,000, now claims 3,600,000. From these figures, adding in the railway brotherhoods and other independents, one may conservatively estimate the strength of organized labor at over 4,000,000 as of September, 1936, and over 7,500,000 as of September, 1937—a gain of around 90 per cent in twelve months.

The more spectacular record is of course provided by the C.I.O. Today every passenger automobile manufacturer except Ford, Hupp, and Nash has a signed C.I.O. contract. The big committee claims some 400 contracts in the textile industry, covering 275,000 workers. It has signed up many companies, including such giants as U.S. Steel and American Viscose, without going so far as to call a strike. And while considering this angle of the situation it is well to remember that despite the strike in Little Steel, the Steel Workers' Organizing Committee has continued to grow, and now claims 400 contracts and a membership of 510,000. To visualize the progress that the committee has made in steel the reader might profitably turn to *Fortune* for October, 1936, where the membership of the Amalgamated Association of Iron, Steel & Tin Workers was somewhat cautiously guessed to be 50,000.

Next, it is important to note the very marked increase in the number of strikes that labor has won during the past decade. Labor won about 26 per

[1] This was the high for number of strikes, but 1919 constituted the high for the number of workers involved. Nationwide steel and coal strikes, calling out 800,000 workers, helped the total to 4,100,000.

cent of its 707 strikes in 1927 and made partial gains in 25 per cent more; and things remained at about this level through 1932. But in 1933, bolstered by NRA, 37 per cent of labor's strikes resulted in victories, and in 1936 the victories reached what is probably an all-time high of 46 per cent, another 24 per cent of the strikes involving partial gains. If these mounting percentages are applied to the rising number of strikes, the effect is startling. In 1927 labor won or compromised about 360 strikes; in 1936 about 1,500.

Some of the reasons for this will become apparent as we proceed. Here they may be summarized as: (1) new legislation making illegal a number of practices traditionally used by employers (such as subsidizing company unions); (2) new techniques, especially that of the sitdown; and (3) a more highly developed strategy, for which the C.I.O. has been largely responsible and which has changed the nature of labor warfare. The C.I.O. approaches an industry with elaborate and forethoughtful plans; organizes on the basis of peace just as long as possible; acquaints itself with sales problems and seasonal swings; and ferrets out weaknesses in the balance sheet.

Third, during the same decade there has apparently been a marked trend (in this case downward) in the number of days lost per worker as the result of strikes. The 1927 strikes, while few in number, were painfully prolonged, with the result that each striker lost an average of 108 days of work. This was largely the result of the soft-coal miners' strike, which frittered along into the next year. By 1928 the average was down to only eighty-eight days. During the depression it dropped substantially; and then fell further in 1933 to an average of only eighteen days, and in 1934 to fourteen, and in 1935 to thirteen. A slight rise in 1936 does not materially affect this general trend, which is strongly illustrated by the fact that for the six pre-NRA years the average time out was fifty-one days per worker, while for the four succeeding years it was eighteen.

Various factors have been responsible for this, among them the sitdown and the techniques and strategy already referred to. But for the quicker settlement of their strikes the laborites have above all to thank the U.S. Government. Congress has boosted collective bargaining by a series of recent enactments, beginning in 1926 with the Railway Labor Act. In 1932 came the Norris–LaGuardia Anti-Injunction Act; in 1933 the Bankruptcy Act amendment and NRA (including labor's famed Magna Charta); in 1934 an amended Railway Labor Act; and in 1935 the stormy Wagner Act, which was upheld by the Supreme Court shortly before the Little Steel strike in 1937. As between industrial warfare (as presented, for instance, in the illustrations to this article) and the orderly process of collective bargaining, Congress has repeatedly condemned the former and embraced the latter, even at the risk of violating what many industrialists are prone to call the American tradition. The Wagner Act was the most radical step in this direction that Congress has ever made, and whatever problems it involves, the Board that this act set up is perhaps the most effective instrument for the settlement of industrial disputes that the country has ever had. The NLRB is cocky, and . . . many employers accuse it of prejudice and unfair procedures. But between August, 1935, when it was established, and October, 1937, over 7,600 labor disputes involving 2,225,000 workers have been dumped on its doorstep, and it has acted on over 4,500 cases. It claims to have averted 392 strikes involving 95,000 workers and it has adjusted 2,679 cases informally in addition to its highly publicized elections, hearings, and decisions.

Fourth, and perhaps most significant of all, there has been a marked trend in the causes of labor disputes, with the emphasis increasingly on the issue of union recognition. A labor movement fighting merely for better wages might or might not be a "movement" in the profound sense: it might be a kind of guerrilla warfare, indicating unrest but without historical direction. On the other hand, when men strike for union recognition they are striking for collective bargaining, which we have already described as the keystone of the American labor movement. This collective bargaining theme has not always been to the fore by any means. Of the great 1919 strikes, only about 24 per cent were fought chiefly on this issue, while 55 per cent were fought chiefly for wages and hours. (The balance were "miscellaneous.") Up through 1926, indeed, the organization issue never represented 25 per cent of the total. Thereafter there was an abrupt rise, stimulated partly by the general prosperity, and by 1929 about 40 per cent of the strikes were fought for collective bargaining. Then, after declining during the depression, the curve proceeded upward, breaking through 40 per cent in 1934, and reaching 50 per cent in 1936 and 53 per cent for the first half of this year—which so far as the record goes is an all-time high. This can be expressed in another way. In the fourteen-year period beginning with 1919 there were in round numbers 20,000 strikes. Of these 5,000 were primarily for union recognition. But in four years beginning with 1933 there were some 7,000 strikes. Of these, 3,000 were primarily for union recognition.

The fact that half of the 1936 strikes were fought for a principle, with the trend continuing into the stormy spring and summer of 1937, is of such significance that those who follow labor closely are inclined to doubt the comfortable theory already mentioned, to the effect that the current wave of strikes is just a normal post-depression phenomenon. Coupled with the prodigious growth of union membership, the increased percentage of strikes won and compromised, and the apparent trend toward quicker settlements, it would seem to indicate the recrudescence of a major mass movement with its roots far in the American past. One must, to be sure, make allowances for Roosevelt "prosperity," which has made it possible for the worker to afford to fight for principles. And one must make a big allowance for assistance rendered by the government. This latter element, however, is itself symptomatic of a real pressure, for the machinery of Washington, unpredictable as its motion may be, does not operate in a vacuum of pure idealism. Washington has strengthened labor's position, not just for the hell of it, but in response to forces that the depression stimulated and revitalized.

So much, at any rate, the realist must admit. It is useless in a situation such as this to hide one's head in the sand—to suppose, as some employers do, that labor's recent drive has been stopped. It may be that the lull in big strikes will continue for some time. But it is possible that even if it does—and even if the violent manifestations of labor's unrest are somehow avoided—labor is in a position to consolidate and even increase its new gains. It has the machinery, whether for peace or for war. And it is rapidly acquiring the men.

The examples of U.S. Steel and American Viscose, which signed with the C.I.O. without waiting for strikes, enable one to speak of peace in connection with a modern labor drive. But certainly peace has not characterized past drives, and it is with these that we are of necessity concerned. As already stated, the modern phase of the labor movement, the post-NRA phase, represents a distinct evolution, and the progress of the evolution has been fraught with warfare of the most harrowing character. It is of course impossible to choose from the 10,000 strikes included in this phase any several that would give a complete evolutionary picture; but it is possible to choose a few strikes to illustrate the more important points. Eliminating the San Francisco General Strike of 1934 as a special affair and the Minneapolis truck drivers' strike of that year on somewhat the same ground, *Fortune* has arbitrarily compiled a list of five samples, which, presented as case histories from an impartial point of view, may at least open the door to an elementary understanding of what has been going on. They are presented herewith.

Textiles, 1934: Mushroom Unions

If you were a union worker in the southern cotton-textile industry on September 1, 1934, your earnings were around $11 a week—and in general you could expect a wage of little more than half the national average for workers in manufacturing. You probably lived in a town of less than 10,000 people. Unlike the 100,000 weavers, spinners, loom fixers, card grinders, smash hands, slubber tenders, and other cotton-textile workers of the North, you lived in a region where the traditions of organized labor were not strong. You were new to industry, and there was much you disliked about it. Your great complaint was what you called the stretch-out, for if under the NRA cotton-textile code, you worked a basic forty-hour week, you insisted that you produced more than formerly in fifty hours. For instance, you used to make 144 dozen bloomers in ten hours, but now in eight hours you turned out 200 dozen bloomers. You might complain of "docks," of fines, of cases where a week's work brought in $5.88. You were one unit in a vast, disorderly, depressed industry, made up of some 1,200 mills operated by some 850 companies. And, you were probably in a union for the first time in your life.

More immediately, since June your position had grown worse. In that month the cotton-textile code authority had reduced production 25 per cent, which meant a sharp cut in your wages. There was a statewide textile strike in Alabama. The delegates of your local, meeting at the national convention of the United Textile Workers in August, had voted for an industry-wide strike, demanding a thirty-hour week with no wage reduction, more uniform wages in the North and South, establishment of maximum work loads, reinstatement of workers fired for union membership, and—which has most bearing on this article—recognition of the union. Francis Gorman, Fifth Vice President of the Union, had sent the demands to George Arthur Sloan, President of the Cotton-Textile Institute and Chairman of the Cotton Textile Code Authority. He replied that no one could bargain for the entire industry and that the strike was a strike against the code. And the cotton-textile code was no ordinary code. The first of all NRA codes, under which average hourly wages increased 65 per cent in a year, it outlawed child labor, established a labor board to handle disputes, and was generally regarded as one of the most liberal, as Sloan himself was judged a liberal trade-association head. But the union charged that 2,000 cases brought before the board brought no appreciable results. And after six weeks, on September 1, 1934, at 11:30 P.M., you, as a good union man, went on strike.

You were caught up, in fact, in the first surge of the strike wave already described in statistics—and your strike accounted for almost 400,000 of the 1,467,000 workers who were involved that year. Above all, it was a strike of a union that had increased its members enormously under the impetus of the NRA drive, the United Textile Workers having grown from some 15,000 before the NRA to claim 300,000 in cotton textiles alone.

The textile strike was a strike involving primarily workers new to organized labor, pitted against a bitterly depressed industry, which meant that it was violent and brief. Twelve strikers and one deputy were killed in the three weeks that it raged. It was also emotional. "God is with us," cried a southern organizer as the strike began, "He will not desert us in this just struggle for ourselves and our families." It was characterized by what liberal economists politely call "employer resistance to collective bargaining." "Mobs of hoodlums and thugs!" thundered the President of the Alabama Manufacturers' Association, after a clash in the mill town of Boaz, "producing something like civil war in the South!" And the New England trade journal *Fibre and Fabric* asserted: "A few hundred funerals will have a quieting influence." The strike was followed by a period of disillusionment with section 7A and the elaborate mediation apparatus of the New Deal. With consequences that will presently be examined.

Largely because of its mushroom growth, the union could not support a long-drawn-out struggle. Facing enormous expenses, it had less than $1,000,000 in the treasury, and the strike might involve 500,000 cotton-textile workers—to say nothing of about 700,000 other workers in silk, wool, rayon, and other branches of the industry. It had four regional offices covering thirteen states and seventy organizers. When Gorman handed out his orders for simultaneous transmission to 500 locals of the union, he knew that the strike could not last longer than three weeks—or, as time is measured during strikes he had 500 hours in which to win or lose.

The picket lines of fresh recruits tightened around hundreds of the industry's mills, and they stopped production so effectively that textile trade papers reported, along with indignant accounts of violence, that the employers felt they had been outgeneraled by an "audacious and intelligent minority." In the South, during the first week of the strike, fifty flying squadrons of pickets, with from 200 to 650 men in each column of cars, were operating along a 110-mile front from Gastonia to Greenville in the Carolinas. At Trion, Georgia, a deputy sheriff, a picket, and the strike sympathizer were killed and fifteen strikers were wounded in a two-hour pitched battle; at Greenville another strike sympathizer was killed, and during the strike's course there were clashes between pickets, deputies, non-strikers, and Guardsmen as far afield as Woonsocket, Rhode Island, Lancaster, Pennsylvania, and Augusta, Georgia, where three more strikers were shot, one fatally. At the gate of the Chiquola Manufacturing Co.'s plant at Honea Path, South Carolina, a group of armed men opposing the strike charged the picket line, firing, killing six pickets and wounding fifteen. The union said that the armed group were deputies; the employers said they were nonstriking workers. By the second week of the strike more than 15,000 National Guardsmen had been mobilized in seven states, and a concentration camp for pickets had been set up in Georgia.

The strike's violence created so much bitter controversy that its fundamental issues were obscured. The union's introduction of flying squadrons of pickets, a then relatively unfamiliar weapon that it took over from the coal miners, caused a furor in the press. The employers claimed that the use of these groups of strikers in automobiles, descending on towns suddenly and unexpectedly, was proof that the union had the support of only a minority of the employees in each plant.

For this charge the union's rejoinder ran roughly as follows: the employees in company towns, especially in the South, could not form picket lines because of armed guards employed by the companies. Nor could ordinary organizing procedure be followed. At Rockmart, Georgia, the president of the local was kidnapped and driven from town; at Winfield, Alabama, two union officials were caught by thirty-three armed guards of the Alabama Mills Co. and ordered to leave the county. And so forth. Against such odds, the union said, the only way a picket line could be established was by means of a flying squadron. At Fitchburg, Massachusetts, for instance, Organizer Powers Hapgood led fifty pickets to the edge of town, but was turned back by police. Later he returned with a flying squadron of 500 recruits drawn from a number of striking mills and succeeded in establishing a picket line. Whereupon the plant in Fitchburg also came out.

But underlying this was the matter of a union with limited resources and a vastly increased membership, waging a strike over an enormous area and around hundreds of mills, unevenly organized within the industry, with inexperienced strikers to man its picket lines—picket lines, the union asserts, that were attacked with forces strong enough to demoralize the most seasoned of hard-bitten unionists. And when the Winant Board issued a report that was a moral victory for the textile workers (since it recognized their basic grievances as real) but was a practical defeat (since it made no provisions for immediate or specific relief), the union called the strike off. "The union has won an overwhelming victory," said Gorman, the union complaining three weeks later that 25,000 strikers had been blacklisted. By the next year the membership claim of the United Textile Workers declined by about two-thirds.

Thus, if you were an average textile worker who went on strike on September 1, 1934, you probably came out of it three weeks later burdened with considerable doubt as to the effectiveness of section 7A. You had been a part of a mushroom growth of unionism that came into being with the signing of the NRA and fell away soon after.

Remington Rand, 1936: The Back-to-Work Movement Develops

If you were an aligner, say, in Remington Rand's ancient red brick Ilion plant your union experiences were of a far more complex character. As an aligner you were one of the most skilled workers in the complicated field of typewriter and business-machine manufacture, but during the depression you may have earned as little as $350 a year, and girls in the factory got as little as sixteen cents an hour. You probably owned your own home in Ilion, but it was mortgaged. In 1933, soon after the NRA was signed and while the textile workers were being organized, a federal union was chartered in the factory, the old craft unions expanded, and by intricate steps too numerous to be traced here, you presently found yourself in

John Frey's Metal Trades Department of the A.F. of L., organized, along with the employees of the four—later six—Remington Rand plants, into a Joint Protection Board of Office Equipment Workers.

Your union went through some of the typical troubles of the new unions of that period. Mr. Rand would not recognize it as exclusive bargaining agent, and on May 9, 1934, you went on strike. After five weeks, the union was recognized as a bargaining agency for its members (it claimed 90 per cent of the production and maintenance workers).

But the troubles of your union were only beginning. Through the winter of 1936, as a good union man, you were worried at rumors that Remington Rand had bought a huge abandoned automobile factory at Elmira, New York, and planned to move operations there, developing a new typewriter known as the Madame X. The union was worried because of the contract with Rand, covering the employees of six Rand factories. Would the contract apply in the new Elmira plant? And was the plant at Ilion to close? With these questions agitating them, union officials tried to see Rand. They charged, and the Labor Board later upheld them, that Rand's refusal to see them was a violation of their right of collective bargaining. To the company their questions were an unwarranted intrusion into management and an attempt to find out plans that could not be announced without disclosures to competitors. Plant managers conferred with union people discussing other matters of the contract, but could give no satisfactory answer to the crucial question of what was going to happen at Elmira with Madame X. For these and other reasons a strike vote was taken on April 28, and by a vote of 3,200 to 568, union officers were empowered to call a strike if, in their opinion, "all other means have failed to bring about a satisfactory conclusion."

The union contract contained a confidential clause. It read: "It is understood and agreed that any discrimination or intimidation on the part of the employee toward any other employee shall be just cause for discharge." As the union understood it, this only confirmed the public clause of the contract, which pledged both parties to the maintenance of peace and harmony—"We were not to bother or harm the few scabs, and they were to keep their skirts clean," was the union's interpretation. But on May 21, three weeks after the union authorized the strike, this confidential agreement became the mainspring of action. All employees of Remington Rand had received ballots distributed by the management, reading: *Are you dissatisfied with present working conditions? Are you in favor of a strike?* In the Syracuse plant the union leaders stopped work until the balloting was called off. Whereupon the company closed the plant for two weeks. Rand informed the mayor that he would reopen after the sixteen union leaders had been discharged—the point being, he insisted, that they had violated the confidential agreement in preventing the balloting. In Ilion, Syracuse, Tonawanda, Middletown, and Norwood, the union prepared for a strike, sending a last wire asking Rand if he was not letting "anger instead of reason rule." There was no reply. The second Remington Rand strike began.

If you were a good union man in Ilion you probably went to the strike meeting at the Temple Theatre on the night of May 25, listened to the speeches and turned out on the picket line the next morning. You may have eaten a sandwich at strike headquarters nearby. You may have watched the thirty-odd newly hired guards of Foster's Detective Bureau arriving to patrol the plant interior. And then things began to happen—not only to you, but to the mayor, the chief of police, a number of small city businessmen, the employees of Remington Rand in other cities, and a number of professional guards. In Ilion a Citizens' Committee was started by Barney Allen, Ilion's retail dealer in General Electric supplies. He was afraid Remington Rand would move out of Ilion, taking the $12,000-a-day payroll that was the town's main income. An organization called the Ilion Typewriter Employees' Protective Association was started by Reginald Boote, a young aligner who opposed the strike. It opened an office and began signing up employees who wanted to go back to work. A "For Sale" sign appeared on the factory. There was one tense moment the second day, with a threatened riot arising out of a brief encounter between strikers and guards. The Citizens' Committee appealed to Governor Lehman to send state troopers to supplement Ilion's six regular officers. He refused, since there had been no violence. Failing, the Citizens' Committee demanded that the mayor appoint 300 special deputies. In an atmosphere of growing hysteria, the Citizens' Committee held a mass meeting, Barney Allen called upon the mayor to coöperate or resign, the mayor agreed to coöperate (but he refused to ring the fire bell to summon the volunteer firemen to be deputized), and 300 deputies were signed up.

On the morning of June 10 the streets near the plant were roped off. Tear-gas guns were mounted in the factory windows. Across the street members of Reginald Boote's Ilion Typewriter Employees' Association gathered for an open meeting. There were a few skirmishes between strikers and nonstrikers, ending when tear-gas bombs were fired. Then the members and sympathizers of the Ilion Typewriter Employees' Protective Association (500 says the union, 800 say Reginald Boote) entered the factory, the flag rose on the factory flagpole, the "For Sale" sign was taken down, and Rand arrived to address the returning employees. That night a state of emergency was declared in Ilion on the strength of rumors that a flying squadron of strikers from Syracuse was rushing to town to help the Ilion pickets. All roads were blocked. The union headquarters were padlocked. During the "siege of Ilion," as the strikers called it, Union Leader Harold Beer (who had worked for Remington Rand for twenty-five years) entered Ilion by going on foot through the woods that lie behind the town. And the siege ended when the strikers broke, more than 1,200 returning to work two days after the strike began.

If you were a union man in Remington Rand's Ilion plant in 1936 you were one atom in the working out of a new force, which, amid charges and countercharges, accusations of prejudice, partisanship, plotting, and worse, was to be analyzed and defined by the National Labor Relations Board as the Mohawk Valley Formula. The nine steps of the Mohawk Valley Formula it found to include: (1) conducting a forced balloting under the direction of foremen to misrepresent the strength of the union, calling strike leaders "agitators," forming a Citizens' Committee under threat to move the plant; (2) arousing the community by calling for "law and order" because of "wholly imagined violence"; (3) calling mass meetings of citizens; (4) calling for armed deputies; (5) starting a back-to-work movement; (6) setting a date for opening the plant; (7) staging the opening theatrically; (8) turning "the locality into a warlike camp"; (9) keeping up a campaign of publicity to convince the remaining strikers that the plant is in full operation.

Thus the Labor Board pictured Rand as a superstrategist of strikebreaking and the originator of a foolproof strikebreaking technique. It revealed that during the Remington Rand strike the company paid, in all, $25,800 to Pearl L. Bergoff for his services and the services of 200 guards and "missionaries," whose function it was to discourage the strikers, $30,000 more to Captain Foster of Foster's Industrial and Detective Bureau, and an additional $25,000 to Raymond J. Burns of the William J. Burns International Detective Agency, Inc. The latter two, according to the company, for protection because of the recurring violence of the strike, which in some of its six towns lasted longer and was more bitterly fought than at Ilion. The Labor Board found Rand guilty of unfair labor practices and ordered him to offer reinstatement to all strikers unemployed, the case going to the courts, where it still remains. The Joint Committee of Remington Rand Employees' Associations (the Board called the one at Ilion "a puppet association . . . secretly organized by the employer") denounced the Board and said its conclusions were based on the false statements of disgruntled ex-employees. And Remington Rand, which had not called witnesses at the Labor Board hearings, called the Board's charges a slander.

In the history of the Wagner Act, and in the Remington Rand strike itself, these charges and countercharges are of primary significance. But in the wave of 10,000 strikes, of which the Remington Rand strike was only a part, they are of less importance than the trends the strike revealed. For the Remington Rand strike shows quite clearly what other strikes barely suggest—the mechanics of a modern back-to-work movement.

Rubber, 1936: The Sitdown Begins

Some observer poised high above the class struggle about that time might have thought that capital now had all the advantage, with labor's enthusiasm for the NRA ended and the spectacular, coördinated, theatrical Mohawk Valley Formula presently to come into being as an instrument for breaking strikes almost as soon as they got under way. And it might have seemed that with some of the mushroom unions of the NRA period smashed in their attempt to achieve recognition (as in the textile industry) and others broken after they had achieved it (as in the Remington Rand strike), the strike wave was now due to shrink to the proportions of an episode in labor's uneven history.

Instead, out in Akron, Ohio, at three in the morning of February 14, 1936, something happened that sent the strike wave surging to a new high—although its results were not immediately apparent. A major strike began in the rubber industry, growing out of a tangle of accumulated grievances, but taking a form that gave it historical importance. The form it took may have been a natural development in a long chain of brief stay-in and slow-down strikes. But whatever the reason, on that night a group of tire builders in Goodyear Tire & Rubber Co.'s Plant II sat down on the job. Theirs was not the first sitdown. But theirs grew into the Goodyear rubber strike that lasted five weeks, involved 14,000 employees, saw an eleven-mile picket line, and was described by the Department of Labor as "characterized by a lack of violence." It gave the sitdown nationwide publicity, ended with partial recognition of the union, and launched a drive that swept Akron's rubber union membership from less than 2,000 to approximately 37,000, the United Rubber Workers of

America from about 3,000 to an organization of 75,000 with 136 locals and the reputation of never having lost a strike.

But it did not begin impressively. On that stormy St. Valentine's day in Akron, Goodyear's management distributed some unwelcome valentines to sixty-nine tire builders of Plant II—the pink slips that meant a layoff. (February sales had been bad, said the management.) The first three men who got them, according to the story, "swore and sat down." They and many others remained sitting down while production heads hurried to the factory. The later shifts coming to work elected committees to support them, and—most important—the conveyors leading to the department were filled and the hot and steamy curing department immediately beyond had no tires to prepare. At nine in the morning the first sitdowners left the plant. At nine-forty that night Goodyear's outraged management gave notice that anyone not back at work in forty minutes would be dropped from the payroll. At ten-thirty the foremen began handing out notices. One hundred and thirty-seven men were dismissed. Thereafter the progress of the strike became confused—over the issues involved (it grew out of the union's opposition to increased hours and the threat of a wage cut); over union politics (since the union was one of the mushroom unions of the A.F. of L. involved in the split with the C.I.O.); over a back-to-work movement that flourished briefly and died; and over the numerous settlements proposed to end the strike. In the rubber strike itself, in Akron politics, and in the struggle between the A.F. of L. and the C.I.O., these subtleties were of first importance. But in the wave of strikes the sitdowns in Goodyear rubber were consequential because they introduced one of labor's answers to the Mohawk Valley Formula or the less highly organized back-to-work movements of the other side. In the auto strikes that came soon after the sitdown it was to make history on a grand scale. And in the strike in Little Steel, the Mohawk Valley Formula was (perhaps) to be applied on a scale no less sweeping.

Autos, 1936-37: The Sitdown

By November, 1936, the strike wave we have been describing had added up to over 7,000 strikes. It had included at least six general strikes, the great maritime strikes of the East and West Coast, a nationwide miners' strike, and a multitude of small strikes that followed in the wake of the big ones. It had passed through two distinct stages, suggested by our accounts of the textile strike and the strike at Remington Rand. And it looked as if it were going to decline. The number of strikes had increased slightly through 1936 but the number of men involved had gone down—which meant that the strike wave was now reaching smaller plants, and the figures were swollen by the inclusion of later strikes, strikes of grocery clerks, even by a strike of the graveyard workers of Minneapolis.

Then—to set an arbitrary date for the beginning of the next surge—at eight-twenty-five on the sunny morning of November 18, 1936, five men in the trim department of General Motors' Fisher Body plant in Atlanta were laid off because they came to work wearing union buttons. To General Motors that was a violation of company rules. To the union their dismissal was part of a general attempt to smash the United Automobile Workers, and a sitdown strike occurred. If you were a member of the union and had observed it rise and fall, you probably believed that the systematic firing of union men was part of General Motors policy. You may have joined the auto workers union in 1934 when, as a skyrocketing federal union of the A.F. of L., it claimed 200,000, with 60,000 members in Detroit. You may have been with it in 1935 when it plummeted down to the point where William Green could complain: "Today, I am sorry to say, we have 35,000. A year ago there were more, but for different reasons they are not with us now." Among these reasons was one later revealed by the La Follette Committee: that General Motors had spent $839,000 in two and a half years on detective services, that a Lansing local had five members, all officers and all stool pigeons provided by a spy agency hired by the company.

If you were a rank-and-file union man among General Motors' 135,000 employees, your biggest grievance was the "speedup"—the most likely cause for "a conflagration in the automobile industry," the NRA's Research and Planning Division had reported. And as a union man, the subsequent months of that conflagration were the most important of your union experience. There was a strike at the Kansas City Fisher Body plant when a union man was fired for jumping over the assembly line. There were three sitdown strikes in the auto-parts industry: at Bendix in South Bend and at Midland Steel and Kelsey-Hayes in Detroit. In Cleveland and Norwood, Ohio, there were General Motors walkouts; at the General Motors Guide Lamp Plant in Anderson, Indiana, there was a sitdown involving 2,400; and in the long, rectangular, brick factories that house the Fisher Body plants of Flint, the strike was touching the heart of the General Motors empire.

Deep in the interior of Fisher I, about a mile away from the imposing group of factories in the central General Motors plant, a sitdown started on December 30. The union had presented a contract to the company a few days before, and now the strikers saw (or thought they saw, for the company says it never happened) preparations being made for removing the big dies from which turret-top bodies are made. Which, they assumed, must mean that the plant was being abandoned. Or that a scare was being thrown into Flint, 45,000 of whose 150,000 work for General Motors. At Fisher II, across Chevrolet Avenue from Chevrolet II, three inspectors who were union men were demoted to the assembly line. (Because they were union men, said the union; because they were supervisors, said the company, and supervisors could not belong to the union.) Workers sat down in both Fisher plants. During the rubber strike, the sitdowners left the plant, formed their picket lines outside. But at Flint several hundred strikers remained in Fisher I and II. The union listed eight demands, including a thirty-hour week, seniority rights, a national agreement, and joint determination of the speed of the line. The company replied that the plants had to be vacated before there could be any discussion. The stage was set for what motor makers still call Detroit's sociological nightmare.

Seen only in relation to Detroit, or to the state of Michigan (where for a period one person in every thirty-three was on strike), or to the automobile industry, the sitdown certainly assumed nightmarish proportions. And because during the General Motors strike there was dancing twenty-four hours a day in Flint at the strike headquarters at Pengelly Hall, plus ball games in the struck plants, plus food prepared for the strikers by a union chef formerly of Detroit's swank Athletic Club, the sitdowns seemed to take place in a nightmare world where the laws of capitalism, if they operated at all, worked the way the laws of gravity do in a dream. But if viewed in relation to the 1933-37 strike wave, the General Motors strike becomes part of a great pattern. It saw, for example, a back-to-work movement, as well as an injunction against the strikers. The injunction was defied, and the back-to-work movement collapsed, for reasons connected not only with the sitdown but with the change in labor's tactics in general.

During the strike General Motors got an injunction to evict the sitdowners. But the injunction lost some of its authority when the union promptly disclosed that Judge Edward Black, who issued it, owned 1,000 shares of General Motors stock. Whereupon General Motors got another injunction from another judge. But the sheriff who went inside the plant to read it to the strikers was greeted with boos and catcalls. And Governor Murphy refused to order the National Guard to enforce the injunction until all peaceful means of settlement had been exhausted.

As for the back-to-work movement, in this case called the "Flint Alliance for Security of Our Jobs, Our Homes, and Our Community," it came to its own peculiar kind of grief. While it was growing to claim 12,000 and making preparations for a mass meeting, Governor Murphy was holding conferences with General Motors and the union. On January 11 there was an unexpected crisis: the sitdowners remaining in Fisher II thought an attempt was going to be made to evict them. Heat was cut down; the company guards who had previously handed food into the factory now refused to let it enter. But according to General Motors the strikers had for the first time prevented the office force from going to work, which was why the heat was turned off, and although the company guards would no longer hand food into the plant, they would permit it to be handed through the windows. Whatever the reason, the situation suddenly became ominous. By nightfall police had assembled around the plant. In the beginning of a battle that lasted for seven hours, the police broke a window in the plant and fired a tear-gas shell inside; the strikers built a barricade of autos in the street, doused the tear-gas bombs with water from a fire hose and held their ground. On the third rush the police fired, and fourteen strikers were wounded. And the next day militia massed at Flint, the Fleetwood plant went on strike, while from Washington John Lewis announced that the auto strikers would have the full support of the C.I.O. and Homer Martin hurried to Washington to confer with him.

During the forty-eight crowded hours after the riot in Flint, the ascetic Governor Murphy (whose picture, labeled "Our Friend," looked sternly down on several hundred sitdowners) arranged the famous "Lansing Truce." By its terms the union agreed to evacuate the plants, General Motors agreed not to resume operations in the struck plants, and the union temporarily waived its sole bargaining demand. So it came about that on Saturday, January 16, the sitdowners left the Guide Lamp plant in Anderson, Cadillac and Fleetwood in Detroit. But in Flint a hitch occurred. Talkative ex-Mayor George Boysen, once a Buick paymaster, organizer of the Flint Alliance, told a reporter that at four o'clock Sunday afternoon General Motors would announce that it was going to deal with the Alliance. The sitdowners were scheduled to leave the plants at one o'clock. Informed of this, the union refused to evacuate Fisher I and Fisher II in Flint, and the General Motors strike flared up again.

Such happenings gave a good share of Michigan's population its conviction that law and order had collapsed. But seen in perspective against the strike wave, they illustrated how profoundly union tactics, as well as unions themselves, had changed in the period since the textile strike. Unlike the Remington Rand strikers, the auto strikers had successfully countered a back-to-work movement. They had developed a new organizing technique and a new strike strategy. But more profoundly, they had developed a new concept of strike action, which is nowhere better illustrated than in the story of the seizure of Chevvy IV. By the end of the first month of the strike union leaders wanted a bold stroke to bolster union morale. Half a dozen of them went to the bluff overlooking the seven plants on Chevrolet's eighty-acre tract and decided that they had to capture Plant IV, which assembles motors for all Chevrolet automobiles. If the union could get and hold that plant, they could give General Motors all the rest of its establishment and still stop enough production to count.

But a direct attack on Chevvy IV was out of the question. Hardly a hundred feet from this plant was the personnel building, which served as the headquarters and arsenal for the company police. It was too well guarded. Furthermore, the union was not very strong there. They decided to make a false attempt to take Chevrolet IX, a bearing plant on the other end of the tract. Not more than eight strike leaders knew the full details of the plan.

First, thirty-five shop stewards were called to a meeting. It was held after midnight in Fisher I, where the sitdown was in progress, to impress them with its importance and secrecy. Among them, by design, were men known by the organizers to be informers. They were told that an effort would be made to capture Chevrolet IX. This plan met with strong objection because the men knew that the bearing plant would he hard to take—and also that it was relatively unimportant to production because General Motors could get bearings elsewhere. Nevertheless, the program was decided on.

At 3:00 P.M. on February 1, a mass meeting was held in Pengelly Hall. At 3:20 a note was handed up to Bob Travis, chairman of the meeting, who then announced that there was trouble at Chevrolet IX and that everybody should go down there at once. Actually, nothing had yet happened at Chevrolet IX, but promptly at three-thirty at the change of shift the men refused to work, refused to leave the plant, and set up a terrific din. When the strikers from Pengelly Hall arrived at three-thirty-five the "trouble" at Chevrolet IX was in progress.

As had been expected, guards rushed to the plant. Meanwhile, at Chevrolet VI, far from the scene of the trouble, promptly at three-thirty-five a union steward named Ed Cronk sounded a siren, picked up an American flag, and started marching around the factory. He led the march to Chevrolet IV. But in his excitement he forgot to look around, discovering when he got to Chevrolet IV that he had only twenty-five men with him. He rushed back and marched around the factory again, carrying the flag, and this time collected more followers. Once in Chevvy IV the strikers quickly ejected foremen, plant officials, and non-union workers and began to barricade all the doors. Fourteen minutes had elapsed between the time the commotion had started at Chevrolet IX and the time Chevrolet IV was barricaded.

Out of all the sensational news of the auto strike, the seizing of Chevvy IV was the high point. In terms of the auto strike alone it was either the final indignity offered outraged property rights—if you were on the side of the employers—or an illustration of labor's growing initiative—if you were not. But in terms of the 1933-37 strike wave its significance is of a different order. When you compare it with the moves made during the textile strike it serves as a landmark, measuring how far labor had traveled in less than three years and through some 4,000 strikes.

Little Steel, 1937: Back to Work Again

The strike in the twenty-seven plants of Republic, Youngstown Sheet & Tube, and Inland Steel broke under circumstances that will probably make discussion of it one of the classic problems of union shoptalk, like the seizing of Chevvy IV in the auto strike. It broke less than three months after U.S. Steel signed its agreement with the Steel Workers' Organizing Committee of the C.I.O., six weeks after the Supreme Court declared the Wagner Act constitutional, and five days after the union won a consent election, conducted by the NLRB, at the two great plants of Jones & Laughlin. Because of these facts (and because it was lost) the strike in Little Steel posed its questions for the innumerable grandstand quarterbacks of the labor movement: could it have been won if held back a little longer, until the S.W.O.C.'s organizing campaign had advanced more? Or, could it have been won if more care had been paid public opinion and less reliance placed on public officials? And, finally, what does its loss mean to the C.I.O., and the immediate future of American labor?

Before you can consider these posers in detail, it is necessary to look back on the great steel organizing drive of the C.I.O., begun last year and described in *Fortune* of October, 1936. Forearmed with exhaustive economic studies of the steel industry financed with a $500,000 war chest contributed by the ten original unions of the C.I.O., manned with skilled old-line organizers of the United Mine Workers (as well as with young recruits from the mushroom NRA unions and a few from the insurgent company unions), that drive was directed primarily at the traditional anti-union fortress of U.S. Steel. In November, 1936 (when the General Motors strike was beginning in Atlanta), the S.W.O.C. held a convention of organizers and announced that 82,000 of the steel industry's 500,000 employees had been signed up. And on March 2, 1937, the quiet of the S.W.O.C.'s office on the thirty-sixth floor of the Grant Building in Pittsburgh was shattered by the most sensational news in the history of steel labor: John L. Lewis and Myron C. Taylor had come to an agreement by whose terms U.S. Steel recognized the S.W.O.C. as the agency for collective bargaining. Thirty-five thousand members, the union claimed, were signed up in the next two weeks. Before the outbreak of the strike in Little Steel, the S.W.O.C. could boast that it had negotiated 140[2] agreements, established fifty-two administrative offices, and brought 400,000 workers into 797 local lodges.

All of which had brought an answer from the masters of Little Steel. Their argument against unions in general and the S.W.O.C. in particular, distilled from opinions in steel journals, the speeches and writings of steel men, would run about like this: if the proportion of union members to total nonagricultural workers in the U.S. has remained below that of the

[2] Of these, however, the greater number were in smaller fabricating plants. In steel production, the S.W.O.C., with agreements with U.S. Steel, Wheeling, Jones & Laughlin, and some forty others, could claim to have agreements in plants employing about 50 per cent of the workers.

European democracies, it has not been because collective bargaining has been resisted more strenuously by American employers. It has been because American workmen are not greatly interested in national labor unions. From this it follows that national unions are foreign importations, the outgrowth of the rigid class divisions of Europe. From this point of view the issue of collective bargaining is false, since these people maintain that local unions, independent unions, employee-representation plans, and the like provide collective bargaining. Where the Labor Board has decided in a number of cases that such organizations are simply the old-fashioned company unions, revamped to comply with the Wagner Act, the answer is that the Labor Board is prejudiced and unfair. The figures on the increase of union membership are answered by the assertion that the figures are exaggerated, that most members do not pay their dues, and that the labor advance we have described is less a mass movement than the result of a political alliance between the Administration and the leaders of organized labor—who, even if their claims are granted, represent only a small percentage of the total industrial population. This point of view, to be sure, is found in other circles than in steel, but in no other industry has it been so vehemently advanced. "I won't have a contract, verbal or written," said Mr. Girdler, "with an irresponsible, racketeering, violent, communistic body like the C.I.O., and until they pass a law making me do it, I am not going to do it."

The density of union membership in all branches of an industry during a union drive is one of labor's essential secrets. But it was no secret, before the strike in Little Steel, that most of the S.W.O.C.'s organizing effort had gone into the campaign against Big Steel. (In Monroe, Michigan, for example, which was to be a crucial outpost in the strike, the S.W.O.C. office was not opened until late in February.) Nor was it a secret that many of the organizers in the Little Steel area were old-line officials of the United Mine Workers, accustomed to handling strikes in the intensely pro-union mine country; or that the 360 strike functionaries—relief directors, clerical force, organizers—were largely directed by men whose experience had been in other lines than steel. All of which, in the opinion of the hot-stove-league experts of labor, pointed to inadequate preparation in the critical pre-strike months. But to answer that, the S.W.O.C. had been organizing in Youngstown a year before the strike and had two groups, each of 500 picked men, called the organizing committee, in Youngstown Sheet & Tube alone. It had prepared a list of 200 lawyers in spots where trouble was expected, and had investigated 100 of these; an exhaustive study of state laws had been made; and an intricate, foolproof, revolving-fund strike-relief system, making possible cash payment for all supplies, had been laid out. "The S.W.O.C. was ready," said one observer, "but not for what happened."

For what happened began outside the area of Little Steel. It began when the Supreme Court on April 12 upheld the constitutionality of the Wagner Act in five cases dealing with discriminatory discharge for union activity—among them the case of ten employees of Jones & Laughlin Steel Corp., who were ordered reinstated with full back pay. It was carried forward the next month when a strike was voted at the two Jones & Laughlin plants, when S.W.O.C. organizers met in Pittsburgh, and, in anticipation of trouble with Republic Steel and Youngstown Sheet &

Tube, authorized Chairman Philip Murray to call a strike at his discretion. On the day before the Jones & Laughlin strike began, the C.I.O.'s regional director Clinton S. Golden met Republic Steel's director of industrial relations, Mr. J. A. Voss, in Cleveland, there to define, with that mixture of politeness, strain, diplomacy, and plain speaking that distinguishes big-time union negotiations, the position of both sides. To Republic as well as to the other independent steel companies, agreements had previously been submitted identical with those U.S. Steel had signed. The companies refused to sign, giving as reason their unalterable opposition to the closed shop and the checkoff. The union replied simply that it was not asking for the closed shop and the check-off. Wages and hours were not an immediate issue—although the stability of wages was. But the issue became identified in the public mind as solely over a signed contract—which, in the opinion of the S.W.O.C.'s critics, meant that the union was going into battle with two strikes against it.

Meanwhile at Jones & Laughlin the forty-hour strike ended peacefully with a consent election conducted by the Labor Board, the union winning a sensational 70 per cent of the votes cast. There was a premonitory clash between Republic and the S.W.O.C. on the night before the balloting began: the union asked warrants for the arrest of eight Republic employees who appeared in Aliquippa, charging they were there to create a disturbance that would disrupt the voting. Republic asserted they were there only as observers. In this period at least seventy-five cases of discharge for union activity in Republic plants were filed with the Labor Board, as well as more cases of threatened discharge; Republic's tinplate mill at Canton was closed and its Massillon plant, where the union was strong, suspended operations. The Massillon local, without authorization of S.W.O.C.'s headquarters, took a strike vote. After signing an agreement with Jones & Laughlin, which made the S.W.O.C. the sole bargaining agency, Philip Murray rushed to a meeting of 200 delegates in Youngstown. It had been hastily called to forestall runaway strike action. It voted a strike in three of the five companies of Little Steel. "Our membership had to be protected," Philip Murray said, making the question of whether the strike was called prematurely largely an academic one.

From the bridges over the Mahoning at Youngstown you can look down upon the giant by-product coke ovens, the blast furnaces, the open-hearth furnaces, the Bessemer converters, the blooming mills, the billet and bar mills, the skelp mills, and the spike plant of Republic's Youngstown works; on the smaller mills of Youngstown Sheet & Tube, set almost in the center of the city. You can look down too upon a stretch of grim and smoke-darkened streets, on the section given over to its lurid night life, beside the fence surrounding the Youngstown Sheet & Tube Works. You can see the Bessemer converter that stands like a howitzer beside the red-light district, and from which flames periodically shoot skyward with a volcanic roar, blanching the street with a sulphurous light. You can look down upon a section of gray wooden houses where live a good share of Youngstown's 32,938 foreign-born, alongside her 14,552 Negroes. And on the far side you can see the tree-shaded residential streets, equally remote from the mills and the slums, so closely knit that dwellers there insist that Youngstown, for all its 170,000, is essentially a small town.

Up and down the Mahoning, as the strike got under way, the picket lines formed. They were established at mill gates and along the railroad embankments, organized into groups of five doing six-hour turns, with one leader for each group, four division captains (one for each turn), and a head picket. Forty-two cars patrolled the Campbell picket line. In Warren the line stretched over the eight-mile circuit around the Republic plant. In Monroe it crossed the road beside the Raisin River that led to the main gate. In South Chicago, on the first day of the strike, it formed near the plant entrance at 116th Street and Burley Avenue, but was dispersed by the police, and twenty-three pickets were arrested. Within Republic's plants, by the company's count, a large number of men were still at work—2,400 in Warren, 1,400 in South Chicago, "several hundred" at Niles, 2,900 at Buffalo—and food was brought in to them by airplane and sent parcel post. At Youngstown a train, crashing though the picket line at Youngstown Sheet & Tube, led to violence in the first days of the strike. The planes were fired on, the mails were stopped, and after the train at Youngstown crashed through the picket line pickets cut the rails with acetylene torches.

In every strike the men who remain at work—the loyal workers of embattled management, the scabs of strikers—draw on themselves the accumulated resentment of the picket lines. But in the strike in Little Steel, for reasons that will presently become apparent, the status of nonstriking employees decidedly changed, and with it there was an equally momentous change in the attitude of the union toward them. It was to protect these loyal workers, Republic Steel claimed, that it armed its plants. (Ninety-two riot guns, 2,295 long-range projectiles—tear and sickening gas—326 short-range gas cartridges, and 2,029 gas grenades were purchased by Republic and its subsidiaries in May and June—a total expenditure of $43,901.) And the police of Chicago claimed that it was while protecting the 1,400 (company's figure) workers who remained in the South Chicago works of Republic Steel, on Memorial Day, when the strike was four days old, that the pickets were dispersed, with four killed outright, six fatally injured, and ninety wounded, some thirty of them by gunfire.

Read the report of the La Follette Committee on what it calls the Memorial Day incident and you will find a story as savage as any in the dark annals of American labor struggles. You will read of the strike starting on the day of the general strike call, of gas costing $3,300 stored in the plant, of how the first picket line was dispersed, with twenty-three arrested, and how, afterward, Mayor Kelly stated that peaceful picketing would be permitted. You will read of the increased police force around the plant, of a mass meeting called near the factory, followed by a march toward it to establish the picket lines over "a stretch of flat waste sparsely-inhabited prairie land east of and adjacent to the South Chicago plant of the steel corporation—the plant itself is bounded on the west by the Calumet River, on the north by steel scrap piles, the south by low prairie land, and on the east by a barbed-wire-topped fence and the tracks of the Pennsylvania Railroad." You will read also of the marchers approaching the line of 264 police, of a discussion about picketing suddenly interrupted by a stick thrown by the inevitable unknown, a tear-gas bomb tossed at the moment the cameraman was changing his lenses, and, after a graphic report of the subsequent gunfire, the brutal treatment of the injured, and the sixty-seven arrests, the grim conclusion that "the consequences of the Memorial Day encounter were clearly avoidable by the police."[3]

As has been pointed out in the Remington Rand strike, the back-to-work movement of contemporary strikes occupies the center of the stage. Early in the Little Steel strike Philip Murray charged that the Mohawk Valley Formula was being followed step by step, and when the strike spread to Johnstown the New York *Times* correspondent, F. Raymond Daniell, found its pattern repeated in the events that led to the formation of a Citizens' Committee and a demand for the reopening of Bethlehem's Cambria plant. But a strike involving 83,000 and extending over seven states is a vastly different affair from one in a small city dependent upon a single industry, and only at Monroe, Michigan (where the small Republic-owned Newton Steel Co.'s plant was an unimportant unit in Republic's production, but of vital consequence to the community), did events correspond to those in Ilion.

There the mayor polled the employees to determine how many wanted to return to work. Out of a total of 1,350, it was officially claimed 826 voted for, 20 against, and 504 didn't vote. After some 300 men had been deputized, a date was set for opening the plant. It was postponed at Governor Murphy's request. He called a conference in Lansing, to be attended by the mayor, the union organizer, and representatives of the back-to-work movement. While the conference was on, at three in the afternoon of June 10, some 200 deputies marched to the picket line, ahead of the members of the back-to-work movement, organized into an independent union. Given two minutes to open the road, the picket captain gained twenty minutes more in order to telephone Governor Murphy. But while negotiations were going on the ubiquitous tear-gas bomb was thrown toward the pickets while a stone simultaneously sailed toward the deputies, and within ten minutes the pickets were in flight, at least nine automobiles were dumped into the Raisin River by the deputies, and the nonstriking employees returned to work.

At Massillon the back-to-work movement ran into greater difficulties and led to a more tragic ending. There the chief of Massillon's police force of eighteen men refused to permit a poll to be taken because, he said, it would cause trouble unless conducted by the Labor Board. But after a month in which, he testified, he was warned by Republic officials that if the mills closed Massillon would be "just a junction with no need for a mayor or chief of police," and during which he was urged to deputize special policemen and guards, he blew up: "I said all right I would appoint the whole damn outfit. I would give them everything they wanted." The deputies were sworn in and armed. In spite of the unwillingness of the officials to take this course on the grounds that violence would follow, nothing happened until the night of Sunday, July 11, when Police Chief Switter took "a little drive in the country for a glass of beer." When he returned he found that in his absence a riot in front of union headquarters had cost the life of a union member, that thirteen had been injured, and 160 arrested.[4]

[3] The verdict of the coroner's jury was made public the day before the report of the La Follette Committee. The shootings were termed "justifiable homicide."

[4] The full account of the Massillon incident is told in the record of the NLRB hearings, which opened in Washington on July 21, 1937. Republic's witnesses who denied in many particulars the testimony of the city officials of Massillon on the course of the strike there were heard in Canton, Ohio, three weeks later.

But for observing the process by which a full-grown back-to-work movement comes into being (as well as the tension it may create), Youngstown provides a better specimen for study than smaller communities. In the first days of the strike the Independent Association of Republic Employees and the Independent Society of Workers of Youngstown Sheet & Tube opened adjoining offices in the Dollar Savings & Trust Co. ("paying no rent," said the Labor Board's investigator sourly) and began collecting signatures of employees who wanted to return to work. While Governor Davey was calling peace conferences, airplanes were dropping food into the plants and the back-to-work movement spread among the pleasant homes of Norwood Avenue and Poland Manor—an intense drive, made up of employees who did not support the strike, of businessmen who believed that a minority of pickets was preventing the majority of employees from working, of clubwomen who telephoned their resolutions to Boake Carter, wrote letters to the President, and sent a delegation to Governor Davey at three in the morning.

The strike was in its third week when Secretary of Labor Perkins appointed a Steel Mediation Board, President Roosevelt declared that companies willing to make oral agreements should put them into writing, and another night riot left two dead and some thirty to fifty injured in Youngstown. The Steel Mediation Board negotiations soon broke down, not over the question of a signed agreement, but over a proposal that the companies recognize the S.W.O.C. pending Labor Board election, the agreements to be torn up in plants where the union lost. The Senate Post Office inquiry was proceeding. That inquiry resembled a La Follette Committee hearing turned around, for in place of reports of violence against strikers by police or company guards, it was filled with reports of violence by pickets against nonstriking workers—stories of men beaten, stripped, or driven from home. In Youngstown the sheriff deputized a hundred men, and Republic Steel and Youngstown Sheet & Tube had already announced that their plants would be reopened on Tuesday morning, June 22. "In the name of God and the overwhelming majority of steel workers of Youngstown," the union wired the President, ". . . we urge you to immediately intervene in this critical hour and avoid a calamity and disaster that Ohio may remember for decades to come." The United Labor Congress threatened a general strike, the truck drivers struck, union sympathizers streamed into town. Word came at midnight that the mediation conference had broken down, and in the office building of Youngstown Sheet & Tube reporters crowded into two rooms overlooking Shop 14, where the heaviest concentration of pickets was massed before the gates. After midnight word came that by the President's request the mills would not reopen. At Governor Davey's order 5,000 National Guardsmen marched in, and in the morning to the accompaniment of cheers from the picket lines, the tension was broken. And, although it was not apparent until later, so was the strike.

Three days later on June 25 Governor Davey completely reversed his position and, issuing a statement, "the right to work is sacred," ordered National Guardsmen to protect returning workers. The picket lines had been withdrawn, and the Guard now made the reëstablishment of the picket line impossible. Attempts to bring in supplementary pickets from Akron and elsewhere were thwarted and simultaneously arrests of strikers and sympathizers began—225 were arrested in Youngstown alone.

In terms of its immediate importance, the Little Steel strike is consequently involved with politics—with the union's belief that it had Governor Davey's support no less than with the labor policy of the Administration, and with whatever decisions were forming in Franklin D. Roosevelt's mind when he wished a plague on the house of John L. Lewis and on the house of Tom Girdler. But in terms of the wave of 10,000 strikes that swept higher while the Little Steel strike was in progress, it marked the first big strike after the Supreme Court decision upholding the constitutionality of the Wagner Act. In the five strikes described (although it was more complex than any except the auto strike) it most nearly resembled the textile strike of 1934.

But its outcome was less clear. . . . At present the C.I.O.'s partisans insist that, although the union lost the strike, the companies did not win. If the employers believe that the strike turned public opinion against the C.I.O., the union believes just as strongly that public opinion was turned against the companies because of Girdler's refusal to settle. There is a general agreement that in the strike-bound communities themselves only careful publicity could have forestalled the growth of back-to-work movements, and that the union's reliance on Governors Earle and Davey to intervene constituted the main weakness of the strike. But union officials are also careful to point out that the loss of the strike in Little Steel bears no relation to the loss of the steel strike of 1919, which stopped organizing efforts in steel for twelve years.

They further point out that the Labor Board hearings in the steel companies are still proceeding. Eventually, they expect, elections will be ordered in the plants. Which leads to the profound change in contemporary strikes that the steel strike demonstrated. When it became apparent that the strike could not succeed, the union's attitude toward the men remaining at work underwent a transformation. The nonstriking workers, the historic object of resentment in labor disputes, became the voters of the future, to be appealed to as potential supporters rather than denounced as scabs. This development occurred too late in the steel strike to be of great importance. What it means for the future conduct of unions depends on the next stage in the evolution of the National Labor Relations Board.

These are only five of the 10,000 strikes of the 1933-37 wave. They provide a cross section illustrating such features of contemporary labor disputes as the back-to-work movement and the NLRB. But they do not include an illustration of the way the rivalry between the C.I.O. and the A.F. of L. has worked out in the recent past, or suggest how it may work out in the future. Developments in a critical section of interunion struggle—marine labor—were brought up to date in the September issue of *Fortune*. Since that appraisal appeared the complicated struggle of the C.I.O.'s West Coast longshoremen (plus the East Coast seamen) and the A.F. of L.'s West Coast teamsters (plus the East Coast longshoremen) has advanced a stage, and San Francisco has seen A.F. of L. pickets stopping the hauling of C.I.O.-handled freight. Expelled from the Central Labor Council, the C.I.O. unions of San Francisco have set up a rump Labor Council of their own.[5]

[5] In a number of cases, local Central Labor bodies sympathetic to the C.I.O. have refused to act on the expulsion orders of the A.F. of L.'s executive committee. In others, they have technically complied and set up a unity committee representing both C.I.O. and A.F. of L. unions.

In Flint a Fisher Body construction job was tied up over a fine point: if the C.I.O. dug the foundation, would the A.F. of L. erect the building? In Cleveland a strike of the C.I.O.'s International Ladies' Garment Workers' Union plunged into the most up-to-date kind of labor confusion: the four employers involved signed contracts with the A.F. of L.; the I.L.G.W.U. called the strike; a Labor Board election held in three of the plants gave the C.I.O. a majority in two plants and the A.F. of L. in one. In Philadelphia 25,000 teamsters were called on strike when the C.I.O. signed an agreement with the bakery employers; the C.I.O. agreed to give up the agreement if it lost the Labor Board election; the A.F. of L. won. One of the most clear-cut cases of A.F. of L.—C.I.O. rivalry broke when the National Electric Products Corp. of Ambridge, Pennsylvania, recognized an A.F. of L. union, granting the closed shop and the check-off, at the height of a C.I.O. organizing campaign in the plant. The Labor Board declared the contract void. A federal district court ordered the company to carry out its contract with the A.F. of L. The Board ordered an election, which the A.F. of L. won by 105 votes. But the C.I.O. challenged 155 ballots. In general, labor observers claim that such cases are isolated, the bulk of the C.I.O.'s membership (and most of its current organizing drives) being in mass-production industries that the A.F. of L. has hardly touched. But the number of conflicts is increasing, and only in the last few months, despite the long battle of their organizations, have John Lewis and William Green stopped speaking.

Which leads us to a new if not typical pattern that emerges from the wave of recent strikes—a pattern that persists despite local peculiarities, the infinite variations in the conduct of strikes, or the personalities of strike leaders. If you put it in its most up-to-date form, that pattern would include (1) an employer whose moves are considerably circumscribed by the rulings of the National Labor Relations Board, (2) a C.I.O. union involved in a constantly accelerating race with a rival union of the A.F. of L., (3) a Central Labor Union consequently divided by the rivalry of the two organizations, (4) a group of employees organized into an independent union opposing the strike, and (5) a citizens' committee leading a back-to-work movement.

This pattern is subject to challenge at each of its points: you would have a hard time convincing labor people, for example, that the Board had noticeably circumscribed Mr. Girdler's moves during the steel strike or Mr. Rand's moves during the strike at Remington Rand. Moreover, they could tell you that while it is now illegal for an employer to set up a company union, cases have been heard of where independent organizations greatly resembling the company unions of the pre-Wagner Act period have found large donations in their voluntary collection boxes. With these charges and denials, however, we are not at the moment concerned, the point being that in the wave of strikes the pattern of labor disputes has begun to change since the signing of the Wagner Act.

Or, more exactly, since the Supreme Court decision upholding the constitutionality of the act. In the eighteen months of its existence before April 12, 1937, some 2,425 complaints were filed with the Board. In the seventy-five days after the decision there were 3,137. Even that increase does not suggest how large the Board now looms over every threatening strike situation and every organizing drive, how greatly it figures in the plans of organizers and the literature of trade associations. In the Little

Steel strike, when witnesses at its hearings testified that the steel companies had brought pressure to bear on public officials, or in the National Electric Products situation, where it declared void a contract upheld by the district court, the Board has taken steps whose significance cannot be measured by statistics. But statistics will show how deeply a part of the strike pattern the Board now is: during the past year (October 1936-37) the A.F. of L. and the C.I.O. have each filed more than 2,000 complaints, the Board settling slightly more than 700 for the A.F. of L. and slightly less than 700 for the C.I.O. The A.F. of L. has lost as many plant elections as it has won; the C.I.O. has won three times as many elections as it has lost.

The Labor Board is the most recent figure added to the pattern of labor disputes, and with its appearance the positions of the other figures in that pattern have changed. Before the Supreme Court decision, for example, there was a bombardment of injunction suits against the Board (eighty-three up to the time of the Remington Rand strike), and twenty of them resulted in temporary injunctions granted by federal district courts. "The process was like a rolling snowball," the Board complained. "Employers were never complying with our orders. . . . They always challenged us to take them into court." Since the decision the Board, no less than the Federal Trade Commission or the Interstate Commerce Commission in their early days, faces the period that every regulatory body goes through, of innumerable court fights on its intricate issues, fought through until a series of Supreme Court rulings defines its powers.

It is no secret that one reason why the close advisers of the President were vitally concerned that his Supreme Court proposal should be vigorously pressed was that they anticipated—and on good precedent—the Court's rejection of the Wagner Act, and the consequent impotence of the Labor Board. It is also no secret that Mr. Justice Roberts reads the newspapers; and it was his vote that validated the act. Without that validation, said many a Washington observer partisan to the President, the labor situation in the U.S. might swiftly have become blood and chaos. Now that the act exists and has been pronounced to conform to the Constitution, Washington breathes more easily. But industry's breathing is still labored—and whether it will become softer or harsher because of the act in 1938, is anybody's guess. The doctors disagree.

10

Not Very Much Change in the Basic Issues: 1940-1960.

Manpower Management: New Wrapping on Old Merchandise

HERBERT G. HENEMAN, Jr.

No self-respecting conference on industrial relations is considered complete without a "stocktaking and forecasting" wind-up session. This conference has always aimed at respectability and hence this paper. I have often puzzled over the value of such sessions, and have concluded that perhaps the wailing, gnashing of teeth and breast smiting provide some measure of catharsis. At the same time, I'm fearful that they have little, if any, effect upon the lives of the practitioners who make penitent and contrite confessions in all sincerity, and then go on their merry ways as before. Indeed, a job description of manpower managers might well include the phrase: "Consider the lilies of the field—they toil not, neither do they spin—they shuffle papers." Today's crying need in manpower management should not be for "the thinking man's filter," but rather a plea for the thinking man.

Most of the stocktaking and forecasting sessions with which I am familiar (and there is a plethora of these) involve long-term population and labor force projections and their expected consequences, coupled with pleas for (undeserved) professional recognition, and statements that we live in an era of unparalleled change and innovation. Older men point out that manpower management began in World War I, and younger men trace its lineage to World War II. Men still living are described as the father of personnel management or in some cases the father of *modern* personnel management, although of a certainty many of today's personnel techniques are obviously fathered outside the bonds of holy matrimony.

I cannot condone the viewpoints that the manpower management problems we face are new, or that we have made conspicuous progress toward their solution. I was struck forcibly with this proposition recently while reading about early oriental civilizations. As some of you know, at the University of Minnesota Industrial Relations Center we are concerned greatly with today's hot-shot research problem, the problem of criteria. We are studying ways and means of gathering absence data as a step in obtaining better criteria. Only a small proportion of firms keep absence records and these are kept on the most haphazard basis. So we are taking a plunge into unchartered waters. Or are we?

Returning to my reading about oriental civilizations, I find that several thousand years before Christ, even before the invention of coinage, the

Reprinted with permission from *Special Release # 2*, July, 1960, Industrial Relations Center, University of Minnesota, Minneapolis, pp. 3-15.

Dr. Heneman is Professor and Director of the Industrial Relations Center.

ancient Egyptians were working on this problem. Frankly, their classification of reasons for absence may be better than ours in many respects. It was quite simple. There were three categories of absences: (1) sick; (2) placating the gods; and (3) lazy. And these Egyptian absence studies, by the way, were probably old stuff then. Just one other example: the ancient Egyptians were concerned with strikes. So were other early civilizations. In 300 B.C., the Chinese were concerned with public intervention in labor disputes much as we are today.

I don't know who originated the phrase "history repeats itself," but I do know that manpower management problems repeat themselves, and that both manpower managers and manpower management professors can lose perspective anew during each succeeding generation. It still is a widely held proposition that a 1960 textbook is superior to a 1959 text.

Now lest we become too discouraged need I remind you that progress comes slowly in all fields. Let's take mathematics as an example. The early Egyptians valued Pi (the ratio of the circumference of a circle to its diameter) at 3.16. It took *four thousand years* to refine this to 3.1416—and we have since added numerous decimal points. Unfortunately, however, few of us have bosses who will let us wait 4,000 years to answer the employment problems in our firms. But in a more pragmatic vein, may I suggest that if you read the proceedings of these very conferences over the past 18 years you will find that we work largely with "hand-me-downs." Some of you may recall that your first suit was reconstructed after an older brother had worn it and outgrown it, and that it had been altered somewhat for him when "pa" got his new suit. The present state of the arts in manpower management may be described as a "hand-me-down" era of concepts and cutting old cloth to different, if not new, patterns. Again, I raise the basic question, "Oh Lord, how long . . . ?"

Today manpower management stands at a new peak of dubious respectability. We have many more practitioners than ever before, they are higher paid, have more acceptance from top management, and more public interest in their activities. We've sold such a bill of goods that we should worry about our ability to deliver. The demand for our graduate students at IRC is at an all time high. We are so short of graduate students in proportion to demand that we feel queasy about answering phone calls when you call us in your recruiting efforts for your own departments.

More and more manpower managers now have that coveted stamp of approval, a vice presidency, and more are becoming top line managers. Our professional literature is bursting at the seams with a quantity that puts the ancient Egyptian pyramids to shame, and a quality that gladdens the hearts of paper re-processors. We don't have any really professional associations yet, but our crude facsimiles coupled with generous expense accounts and management development junkets provide a soothing unction. Yea, we have the Balm of Gilead for the downtrodden practitioner, bruised by his ever-pressing responsibilities in the taxing realms of "dealing with people," unethical practices of depth interviewing, and prescribing untested human relations "love and happiness potions" to satisfy the needs, and cure the ills, of our numerous trusting patients, employees, bosses, unions and all. So, where do we stand today in manpower management? Why we've got it made—we have it good—the only problem left is how I get my share of the glory. Indeed, if we pursue our present trends, I predict the next startling development will be a major breakthrough in the design of suitably dignified epaulets for personnel officers.

Fortunately, in this epidemic of personnel paresis, there are a few stout unbelievers. Many of those present at this conference may be classed as heretics. In the conviction that we can have a hand in shaping our destinies, and in the belief that unbelievers in the present state of the arts in manpower management are the persons to lead the way, I offer several personal prejudices for your consideration as directions in which we should move if we are not content with putting new wrappings on old packages.

Basically, we must place revised and new emphasis upon objectives, goals and criteria—and these are synonymous in my way of thinking. Our goals are too shallow, too negative, too simple and too static.

The Shallow View

More often than not we dodge the goal problem by "copy-cat-itis," borrowing from somebody else, thereby effectively pooling ignorance. We add to the confusion with what we believe is a down-to-earth bread and butter approach and get extremely interested in programs per se, in terms of their twin obstacles to thinking—content and techniques. Even bread and butter satisfy more basic goals, physiological, social and psychological. We need to develop *basic* employment goals, not superficial ones.

Our concepts of employment goals are far too shallow. Take just two examples, motivation and identification in work and in work teams. Why do people work? What do they want from work? Why do employers offer jobs? What do they want from work? In what ways do these reasons agree? How do they conflict? These are difficult but basic questions. They require a vast expansion of research activity if we are to get answers. If there is economic motivation, how will this be affected by rising standards of living? At the end of this decade 40% of all families will have annual incomes of $7500 or more *after taxes*. How do taxes affect motivation to work? Such problems are not just for economists or fiscal students, but should directly concern us in manpower management.

Research into manpower management requires inter-disciplinary research efforts, as has been suggested for many years. But it requires more than efforts of many disciplines working separately, or side-by-side, like a chemical mixture. It requires a cohesive approach more like a chemical compound. It requires vastly more support from people in industry; this can't be accomplished by university people alone. I'll concede that we must worry in the present about such pressing short-run topics as why middle-management fails to be motivated by our present ineffectual organization structures, wage and salary programs, and management development programs. But we must put some of our resources aside, and with blood, sweat, tears and *cash* dig into the basic problems of understanding, as well as pursuing the task of attempting to put out fires armed with an arsenal of ignorance. If instead of sending 500,000 people to management development programs each year, we sent only 250,000 and spent the rest on basic research, we would have a chance to get some place. If instead of spending $1,000 per year per employee on fringe benefit placebos, we spent half of this on basic research—we might get something for our money. If we raised our sights from the non-thinking level—for example, the plethora of surveys of personnel practices and policies—we might begin to see what we are missing.

From these basic studies we could progress toward other simple but exceedingly difficult questions instead of shallow, specious pap. Has our present industrial society buried the individual? Is the shift to "groupism" a cause or an effect? What about ethical foundations? Or will we prefer to wallow around with the latest panacea—brainstorming, sensitivity training, creative listening or the mad rush to put businessmen in politics? We are moving very rapidly in manpower management, kicking up a lot of very shallow water, but we can't swim because we don't know how. The shallow view leads nowhere. So let's quit fooling ourselves.

Negative Goals and Criteria

Manpower management was born in part because of the shallow views of line managers about employment. Unions came much closer to understanding basic employee needs. They may have arrived at this intuitively, but regardless of how they did it, they forced management to consider employment problems with more respect. At first, management's reactions were negative and defensive. They resisted unions and union demands. They created bigger manpower management staffs and programs at least in part to keep unions out. This negative approach has permeated the very fibre of manpower management. The unions called attention to problems, and management's response was to deal with problems—not to prevent them.

Look at our criteria of effectiveness—turnover, absences, grievances, tardiness, strikes and lockouts—all negative. What of productivity, as an example of a positive approach? The theoretical scholar in the ivory tower has a naive belief that this is important. But not so the hard-hitting, practical, down-to-earth businessman. In Bernstein's[1] study of more than 1,000 wage arbitrations, unions offered productivity considerations in 4% of the cases, employers in 1%, and arbitrators used productivity considerations as basic in 0% of their awards. Productivity claims figure loud and long in recent basic industrial labor disputes. Only one catch. The data are worthless and a national disgrace. I'm not criticizing the Bureau of Labor Statistics—we won't give them the money or the data to do the job. In most cases we can't give them the data because in our obsession with negative criteria we don't measure positive accomplishment. And please don't try to tell me that we get reasonable estimates of productivity or efficiency from employee merit ratings. These are typically so shabby that they defy description in a mixed audience. Fortunately, in many cases unions won't buy them even though many managers will insist upon their prerogative to use them regardless of their quality, and the damage they can (and actually) do to the efficiency of the work team, especially at leadership levels.

If we don't want productivity as a positive goal what do we want? Job satisfaction? Continuity of employment? Let me give you just two other illustrations of our lack of positive goals. Our personnel departments work furiously on retirement plans, but not on providing selective employment

[1] Bernstein, Irving. *Arbitration of Wages*. Berkeley: University of California, 1954. 125 pp.

opportunities for oldsters. We set up employee benefit divisions in personnel departments as a standard operating practice. But I don't know of a single personnel department that has a division called "productivity" or "output." Does that sound like we are really interested in productivity or have positive objectives?

Simple Objectives and Criteria

Employment is a complex process. Employment goals are complex also. However, we treat many of our goals as simple or as clear-cut single purpose goals. We frequently take a simple general method, e.g., a general wage increase, and try it as a means of cutting turnover. This it may or may not do, but the important lesson here is that we generally ignore side effects of our prescriptions and we are surprised to find these exist. Or in a similar vein we fail to appreciate that goals may have inter-correlations. We are giving people more leisure today in the form of premature retirement at age 65. Many of these people don't like their new leisure. Why not? Because they want leisure *and*—leisure and a certain minimal retirement income above that which they are getting. In many cases the problem is concerned with balancing goals, e.g., job satisfaction and efficiency, leisure and income, and conflict and cooperation.

It is important that we identify and measure goals properly. This is seen best perhaps in research where we can often get failure in prediction and too often blame it on the independent variable or tool and not often enough upon the dependent variable or criterion. Shabby criteria can defeat prediction and control just as easily as can shabby prediction instruments. In this connection it seems appropriate to point out that far too many manpower managers with factory floor and clerical outlooks seem to regard manpower research as a luxury and not a necessity—as something apart from the realities of life, when in reality research is the indispensable handmaiden of practical decision making.

Static Objectives and Criteria

Goals and criteria should always be sharply defined, unambiguous, and relevant. All too frequently we use static or horizontal rather than dynamic or longitudinal objectives and criteria. England and Paterson[2] in their IRRA article on selection and placement point out that most testing devices seem to have reached a plateau of predictive validities. They urge the development of more realistic longitudinal criteria to improve this situation. This is not to say that present predictive instruments are perfect—indeed they recommend a moratorium on our present bankrupt employment interview techniques and articles on "how to interview," until they can show demonstrated effectiveness.

Employment behavior in the last analysis is human behavior, and human behavior is dynamic, not static. The acid test criteria in our field must be in terms of human behavior and changes in human behavior. Research and understanding must be predicated upon a solid formation of biological, behavioral and social sciences and not the thin veneer of dollars and cents costs.

[2] England, George W., and Donald G. Paterson, "Selection and Placement—The Past Ten Years," in *Employment Relations Research*, H. G. Heneman, Jr., et al., editors, Industrial Relations Research Association Publication No. 23. New York: Harper and Brothers, 1960. Pp. 43-72.

Before I leave the subject of criteria may I voice a danger in our present personnel research. Weary and frustrated by lack of decent direct criteria our researchers are turning feverishly to criteria substitutes. This doctrine of despair can drain off much of our best research talents from the direct approach main road into the pleasant but profitless by-ways of intellectual diddling. Faint heart ne'er won fair lady!

Substance and Form

Our most pressing conceptual needs, I feel, are those I've outlined above. They are intended to emphasize substantive rather than procedural problems. I have tried to indicate that we are not attacking substantive problems sufficiently. Instead, we prefer to attack each other—labor attacks management and vice versa on trifling and subsidiary issues of status, prerogatives and rituals. We prefer to wallow in expediency and smite each other with platitudes, prejudice and opinion. Research in the field of labor relations is almost non-existent or so amateurish as to defy belief. Conferences on labor relations produce results reminiscent of 18th Century cures for warts, and generous doses of leeches and bloodletting thrown in for good measure. Employers have policies that accept and reject unions simultaneously. Legalistic approaches and past practice are *the* hallmarks. Enlightened groups such as the NAM refuse to sit down with labor groups to discuss anything, general or specific. Many, if not most, employer associations faithfully mirror this weird paranoia.

Frankly, the time has come to ask rather sharply whether all of this conflict is necessary. Don't we have enough substantive employment problems to solve without adding unnecessary procedural ones? Do other professional practitioners such as doctors and lawyers have to get angry, sore and pigheaded before they can help their patients and clients? Is our profession unique in its requirement that emotion be substituted for objectivity? This attitude of hostility and distrust is one we as practitioners can ill afford.

We argue about symbols and semantics. The public is interested in *results*. As a nation we are committed to a policy of full employment. When labor and management fail to provide this, the government steps in. Our recent experiences in disputes settlement in basic industries provide classic examples of flagrant irresponsibility and immaturity. Only a few more demonstrations of such incompetence, and betrayal of professional responsibility, are needed to take collective bargaining and disputes settlement into the hands of governmental control, with a short step remaining to wage and price controls, priorities, rationing and allocation. This problem of incompetency and bankruptcy in manpower management, I submit, is not primarily a political or ethical issue. It is an economic or efficiency issue. Apparently our industrial relations practitioners are just plain incompetent and have been found out.

Nor is this just a matter of injured feelings on the part of practitioners and the public alike. This is a deadly urgent matter of national survival as well. Few manpower managers act as if they are aware of our current mortal economic warfare—the perils involved in the clash of the U.S. and communist worlds. In generous measure this is a conflict in efficiency of different systems of industrial relations. Our economic troops apparently prefer to maul each other and ignore the enemy. Obviously no war has ever been won using this approach. In this conflict of industrial relations systems, little interest has been displayed in the question, "who is right?" Instead we should devote much interest and attention to the contingency that the Russian or Chinese system may be better. We should study their manpower management systems lest the manpower management gap be greater than the missile gap—such an occurrence could be far more deadly.

A Constructive Approach

For all of these reasons let us turn our course as sharply as possible away from petty conflict to constructive mutual attacks on major problem areas. Permit me to suggest several. Employees want job security. Employers want flexibility in worker assignment to jobs. Employers say we can't give GAW because we can't stabilize employment. But many of these same firms already have stabilized employment for the majority of their work force. Unions say our members need to protect jurisdictional job rights to provide job security. Employers damn seniority systems. Here I would ask two questions, "what have employers got to offer that is better?"; and second, "why shouldn't *both* labor and management seek out *better* job rights systems instead of quarreling over a remedy suitable for 1930 conditions?" Isn't this a case where the multiple goal idea would work—a coupling of employment stabilization with flexibility in work and assignment? This could serve the added goal of facilitating and accommodating job changes to changes in consumer buying preferences, especially for new products. It is silly to gear employment policies to the past, and marketing and production policies to the future.

Let's take several other examples of where we need cooperation rather than conflict. As some sage observed, "the Russians claim to invent a new product one week and the Japanese produce it cheaper than we can in the following week." International labor costs comparisons can and will have an increasingly sharp impact upon American industry and industrial relations. Here the famous wage-price inflationary spiral provides a closely related problem area. Instead of management trying to prove that the unions are the culprits, and vice versa, let's get going on the problem, not on each other.

Still another, but closely related, problem area is represented by our crazy patchwork quilt of economic security plans, private and public. In our frenzy to tack on more little pieces we lose sight of goals and consequences, ranging all the way from employee motivation to control of industry. "If 20% of the pay check in fringes doesn't dull motivation, will 30% do the job?" seems to be our approach. Twenty per cent of total personal income in the U.S. now goes out in government checks for veterans' payments, social security, agricultural adjustment payments and the like. And from the standpoint of control of industry, when will welfare and trust funds have invested enough in industrial stocks to run the show? What will be the consequences? Are there better alternatives? Several other areas such as automation, mental health in industry, problems of older workers, leisure, and productivity of service and governmental jobs, readily suggest themselves as fruitful areas for highly intensified mutual cooperative effort.

There is, however, another area less popular in terms of verbiage devoted to the subject, but potentially of gravest consequences. Almost all of our forecasting includes a statement, "assuming no war. . . ." This is not only a most dangerous but a needless assumption. Realistically, the manpower management profession should develop mobilization plans. There will be survivors of atomic holocaust; their mobilization can be greatly facilitated and expedited by manpower experts. The time element will place a premium on speedy action with heavy, if not fatal, penalties for delay—even delay for planning. It is neither fair nor realistic to meet this potential problem situation with flip remarks such as, "who would want to survive if they dropped the bomb?" Such remarks are totally irresponsible from any group or person claiming to be professional. Can you conceive of surviving doctors refusing to meet their responsibilities? They devote time and energy to mobilization planning. Can we do less?

Management, Labor and Small Business

In the few moments that remain let me catalogue briefly several other problem areas that require exploration. The whole concept of management needs re-definition. Converging trends must be accommodated or amalgamated in recognition of three types of competence. These are scientific competence as personalized by the "R and D" man, the mathematical decision maker with his operations research—linear programming, computers and matrices, and finally the "leader of work teams" type who is a combination captain, coach and teacher. Will the new manager be one of these types, a combination, or something still different? Do the older Tayloristic concepts of line and staff have meaning any longer? Or even more bluntly, have we overloaded our organizations with excess baggage of staff positions? This is a subject that should be of particular concern to manpower managers.

And while we're speaking of managers, when will we begin to provide respectable personnel programs for managerial people and positions? Will we continue to ignore this area like we did for rank-and-file, and thus ask for unions of managers? When will we get around to study of management needs, opinions and their correlates? Or do we prefer to keep managers frustrated, packed with tension and restricted in output by fear of authority? Our ignorance in this area is dangerous and poses a threat to the continued existence of the American free enterprise system.

Paralleling studies on the management side we need similar studies of unions and union leaders. Definitions of union goals and objectives, membership needs and participation, and union leadership development are examples. We need a vast expansion of labor education for rank-and-file union members to help equip them to meet the responsibilities they are assigned when they are given corollary rights and privileges in collective bargaining. The entire union structure and the relationships of its component parts, e.g., relationship of central bodies to international, and internationals to locals, need re-examination and study.

One of the most compelling areas crying for attention is the problem of translating effective manpower management to smaller organizations. Is it true that small firms must continue to be bread and butter oriented while the larger firms can have the advantages of specialized manpower management practitioners? Is it not possible to develop better tools to put in the hands of these small general practitioners? Certainly the general practitioner in medicine located in a small town has less disparity in available techniques and tools as compared with the big city medical specialist, than the wide disparity we find between large and small firms in terms of manpower management practice. The small town doctor doesn't have to do tailor-made research and experimentation in his every diagnosis and treatment. Can't we develop something akin to standard practice for smaller employing units? Part of the problem here, in my opinion, stems from a certain intellectual smugness on the part of many universities and professors who prefer to deal exclusively in theory and principle and other lofty concepts, with statements or implications that interest in techniques is anti-intellectual, degrading, and that practice can be learned only in the firm. One is tempted to ask why do university medical schools bother with techniques?

If the long-haired boys in the schools want something respectable to think about, let them worry about the integration of findings from the various disciplines underlying manpower management. Bio-mechanics, blending characteristics of individuals with physical environment is a step in this direction. But to these must be fused social environment as well. This is only illustrative of the kind of problem ahead as industrial relations moves out of its cocoon as a "problem area" into a separate and distinct discipline. This transition can be facilitated if it is recognized. But the tendency toward segmentalism is a counter-force that must be dealt with.

Conclusion

In conclusion, there are two facets of the word "discipline." One refers to a systematic body of specialized knowledge. We don't have that today in manpower management. And we don't stand much chance of getting it unless we apply the other facet of discipline which involves "severe and systematic training, especially with a view to right conduct or prompt and effective action." Out of this formal definition I would draw two concepts for special comment—"action," and "guts."

We can continue to take manpower management as it is handed to us or we can decide to do something about it. We badly need fewer do-gooders and more good-doers! This may require giving up our specialized competence as viewers of TV westerns. And a program of action requires guts—guts to get started, guts to stick with it, and guts to stand up for knowledge and research. Take one simple example. Learning is facilitated by reward and punishment. We know that. But we lack the guts to practice it. How many salary cuts has your firm made? In 1958 when a few firms tried to cut executive salaries the hue and cry went the length and breadth of the land. We lacked the guts to stick to our guns. All too often this is true.

It's nice to be nice to people, but per se it doesn't make for professional competence. We need a rebirth of intellectual vigor and toughness of mind coupled with a dedicated purpose. In large measure this is an attitude. We need to say we're tired of wrapping up old shoddy merchandise in bright new wrappings. And then we need to translate purpose into action. Here are a few examples of what we can do:

1. Spend some money on manpower research—dollars, not pennies.
2. Develop vigorous cooperation between business, unions and universities. Do more joint long run basic studies like those carried on in the IRC's Management Development Laboratory.
3. Develop graduate fellowships in industrial relations. At the University of Minnesota we have a grand audited total of zero for this purpose.
4. Expand internship arrangements in two directions—let us send

student interns and professors to you; and you send mature executives as students to us—not for two days but for three months or longer.

5. Develop programs to exchange research and other information. We need problem clinics and dissemination of research and experience results. Better than 90% of such information currently is lost in the sense of not being shared. We must recognize and accept a professional responsibility to do this.
6. Then let's quit selling "small potato" manpower management concepts to the leaders of our organizations. Instead, let's speak with vision, courage, and foresight. We must not only raise our sights, but we must help management raise its manpower sights as well. Let's quit blaming top management for lack of manpower vision, when all too often we ourselves don't have enough vision to sell.

None of these illustrative "next steps" is new or original. Most of you probably agree with them. But we continue to procrastinate and bury ourselves and our sights in the shifting sands of clerical detail, expediency and fear of authority as exemplified by our top management. Strangely, however, while we fear to act like true professionals because we think the boss won't go for it, surveys show the bosses are more desirous of having their manpower managers take a professional approach than are the manpower managers themselves.

We are fortunate that ours is one of the newest professions. We can still make our future what it should be if we really so desire. So let's quit putting more tinsel on the old packages. Let's *deliver the goods*—of truly professional quality.

II

Some Academic Problems: 1960-1970

Fads, Fashions and Folderol in Psychology

MARVIN D. DUNNETTE

This seemed to be a great idea when the 1965 Division 14 program was being arranged. When I chose the title, it seemed *very* clever, and I looked forward to venting my spleen a bit and to saying sage things about what is wrong with psychology and how its ills might be cured.

Marvin D. Dunnette, "Fads, Fashions, and Folderol in Psychology," *American Psychologist*, Vol. 21, No. 4, April, 1966, pp. 343-352. Dr. Dunnette is Professor of Psychology and Industrial Relations, University of Minnesota.

It was not long, however, before I felt misgivings about the whole enterprise and doubted whether I could meet the challenge to put up or to shut up that my own foolhardiness had cast upon me. At first I thought I knew the things in psychology that bothered *me*, but would there be consensus about this? Suddenly, I had the sobering thought that I might be the only one out of step and that, really, all was well with psychology.

So–seizing upon one of my own pet types of methodological folderol–I decided to run a survey! I contacted older or wiser heads,[1] to inquire what, if anything, was currently bothering them. Their responses might conservatively be described as a vast outpouring. The volume and intensity of their replies caused me to give up my speculations about joining the French Foreign Legion and show up here today after all.

With their suggestions, however, I was faced suddenly with a plethora of fads, fashions, and folderol and the need to make some systematic sense of them. Let me give you the flavor of my survey results by simply mentioning some of the things listed by me and by my respondents.

Fads–those practices and concepts characterized by capriciousness and intense, but short-lived interest–included such things as brainstorming, Q technique, level of aspiration, forced choice, critical incidents, semantic differential, role playing, need theory, grids of various types, adjective checklists, two-factor theory, Theory X and Theory Y, social desirability, response sets and response styles, need hierarchies, and so on and so on.

Fashions–those manners or modes of action taking on the character of habits and enforced by social or scientific norms defining what constitutes the "thing to do"–included theorizing and theory building, criterion fixation, model building, null hypothesis testing, sensitivity training, being productive at work, developing authentic relationships, devising "cute" experiments, simulation, using "elegant" statistics, and so on.

Finally, folderol–those practices characterized by excessive ornamentation, nonsensical and unnecessary actions, trifles and essentially useless and wasteful fiddle-faddle–included tendencies to be fixated on theories, methods, and points of view, conducting "little" studies with great precision, attaching dramatic but unnecessary trappings to experiments, asking unimportant or irrelevant questions, grantsmanship, coining new names for old concepts, fixation on methods and apparatus, seeking to "prove" rather than "test" theories, and myriad other methodological ceremonies conducted in the name of rigorous research.

But, even armed with my list, about all I could say is that there are many things going on in psychology that reasonably responsible people were willing to label faddish folderol. It accomplished the aim of identifying some of the less honorable things we are all doing, but it seemed rather sterile as a source of prescriptive implications. What was needed was a better taxonomy for listing psychology's ills than the rather artificial trichotomy established by my title.

One approach might be through some form of cluster analysis–but my data did not prove amenable to any of the widely used methods such as

[1] I should like to thank the following persons for their readiness to come to my aid, but please understand that I do so only because of a strong sense of gratitude and with no thought of having them join me out at the end of the limb. They are: David P. Campbell, John P. Campbell, Alphonse Chapanis, Edwin E. Ghiselli, Mason Haire, James Jenkins, Quinn McNemar, Paul Meehl, William A. Owens, Jr., Bernard Rimland, Auke Tellegen, Rains Wallace, and Karl Weick.

Pattern Analysis, Elementary Linkage Analysis, Hierarchical Linkage Analysis, Hierarchical Syndrome Analysis, Typal Analysis, Rank Order Typal Analysis, Comprehensive Hierarchical Analysis, or even Multiple Hierarchical Classification.

Just when I was facing this impasse, I received the best-selling book by Eric Berne (1964) titled *Games People Play.* I was stimulated by this magnificent book to give thought to the games psychologists play. Somewhat to my surprise, I experienced no difficulty slipping into the robes of a medical clinician—intent on describing fully and completely the behavioral symptomatology of psychology's distress in terms of the games we all play—many of which may reflect underlying pathologies leading us down the primrose path to nonscience.

The games can be discussed under six broad headings—The Pets We Keep; The Fun We Have; The Names We Love; The Delusions We Suffer; The Secrets We Keep; and The Questions We Ask.

The Pets We Keep

Subtitled "What Was Good Enough for Daddy Is Good Enough for Me," this game is characterized by an early and premature commitment to some Great Theory or Great Method. One major effect is to distort research problems so that they fit the theory or the method. The theory, method, or both can be viewed as pets inherited by fledgling psychologists and kept and nurtured by them, in loving kindness, protecting them from all possible harm due to the slings and arrows and attacks from other psychologists who, in turn, are keeping their own menageries.

At a general level, the premature commitment to a theory is usually accompanied by the set to *prove* rather than to modify the theory. The problem and its potentially bad outcome was outlined years ago by T. C. Chamberlin (1965), a well known geologist. He stated:

> The moment one has offered an original explanation for a phenomenon which seems satisfactory, that moment affection for his intellectual child springs into existence; . . . there is an unconscious selection and magnifying of the phenomena that fall into harmony with the theory and support it, and an unconscious neglect of those that fail of coincidence. . . . When these biasing tendencies set in, the mind rapidly degenerates into the partiality of paternalism. . . . From an unduly favored child, it [the theory] readily becomes master, and leads its author whithersoever it will [p. 755].

It is not difficult in psychology to recognize the sequence of events described by Chamberlin. A pessimist might, in fact, find it difficult to identify any psychological theories which do *not* currently enjoy this form of affectionate nurturing. On the other hand, a more optimistic view might accord to theories the important function of ordering and systematizing the conduct of research studies. What is to be avoided, of course, is the kind of paternal affection and closed mind described by Chamberlin.

The problem in psychology is made more severe, however, by the inexplicitness (Fiegel, 1962) and, as Ritchie[2] has called it, the "incurable vagueness" with which most theories are stated—but then, it should be

[2] B. F. Ritchie, unpublished work.

clear that vagueness in theory construction may simply be part of the game, insuring higher likelihood of a pet theory's long life.

Methodologically, our favored *pets* include factor analysis, complex analysis of variance designs, the concept of statistical significance, and multiple-regression analyses. It is common for psychologists to apply so-called sophisticated methods of analysis to data hardly warranting such careful attention. I shall not try to enumerate the nature of the painstaking activities included in the game of statistical pet keeping. I refer those of you who are interested to excellent papers by McNemar (1951) and by Guilford (1960). The net effect, however, is that attention to relevant and important scientific questions is diminished in favor of working through the subtle nuances of methodological manipulation. As my colleague, David Campbell remarked,[3] "We seem to believe that TRUTH will be discovered somehow through using more and more esoteric techniques of data manipulation rather than by looking for it in the real world." Or, as Platt (1964) has said, "Beware of the man of one method or one instrument, either experimental or theoretical. He tends to become method-oriented rather than problem oriented; the method oriented man is shackled [p. 351].

The Names We Love

An alternate title for this game is "What's New Under the Sun?" Unfortunately, an undue amount of energy is devoted to the Great Word Game—the coining of new words and labels either to fit old concepts or to cast new facts outside the ken of a theory in need of protection.

Just one from among many possible examples is the great emphasis in recent years on Social Desirability—a new label for a phenomenon in test-taking behavior dealt with extensively by Meehl and Hathaway (1946), Jurgensen, and others many years previously, but which did not create much interest because they failed at the time to coin a label sufficiently attractive to "grab" other psychologists.

As Maier (1960) has so aptly pointed out, one major effect of the Name Game is to sustain theories even if the facts seem to refute them. If facts appear that cannot be ignored, relabeling them or renaming them gives them their own special compartment so that they cease to infringe upon the privacy of the theory.

Perhaps the most serious effect of this game is the tendency to apply new names in psychological research widely and uncritically before sufficient work has been done to specify the degree of generality or specificity of the "trait" being dealt with. Examples of this are numerous—anxiety, test-taking anxiety, rigidity, social desirability, creativity, acquiescence, social intelligence, and so on—*ad infinitum.*

The Fun We Have

A suitable title for this game would be—quite simply—"Tennis Anyone?" But the game has many variants, including My Model Is Nicer Than Your Model!, Computers I Have Slept With!, or the best game of all—A Difference Doesn't Need to Make a Difference if It's a Real Difference.

As should be clear, the underlying theme of the game—Tennis Anyone?—is the compulsion to forget the problem—in essence to forget what

[3] Personal communication, 1965.

we are really doing—because of the fun we may be enjoying with our apparatus, our computers, our models or the simple acts of testing statistical null hypotheses. Often, in our zest for this particular game, we forget not only the problem, but we may even literally forget to look at the data!

The most serious yet most common symptom of this game is the "glow" that so many of us get from saying that a result is "statistically significant." The song and dance of null hypothesis testing goes on and on—apparently endlessly. In my opinion, this one practice is as much responsible as anything for what Sommer (1959) has called the "little studies" and the "little papers" of psychology.

As so many others have pointed out (Binder, 1963; Grant, 1962; Hays, 1964; Nunnally, 1960; Rozeboom, 1960), the major difficulty with psychology's use of the statistical null hypothesis is that the structure of scientific conclusions derived thereby is based on a foundation of triviality. When even moderately small numbers of subjects are used nearly all comparisons between means will yield so-called "significant" differences. I believe most psychologists will agree, in their more sober and less fun-loving moments, that small differences and inconsequential correlations do not provide a sufficient yield either for accurately predicting other persons' behavior or for understanding theoretically the functional relations between behavior and other variables. Yet, most of us still remain content to build our theoretical castles on the quicksand of merely rejecting the null hypothesis.

It may seem that my criticism of this particular game is unduly severe. Perhaps the differences reported in our journals are not really all that small. In order to examine this question, I asked one of my research assistants, Milton Hakel, to sample recent issues of four APA Journals—the *Journal of Applied Psychology, Journal of Abnormal and Social Psychology, Journal of Personality and Social Psychology,* and *Journal of Experimental Psychology.* He selected randomly from among studies employing either t tests or complex analysis of variance designs, and converted the t or F values to correlation ratios (eta) in order to estimate the strength of association between independent and dependent variables.

The distribution of the 112 correlation ratios ranged from .05 to .92 with a median value of .42. Five percent of the studies showed values below .20; over one-sixth were below .25; and nearly one-third failed to reach .30. The only encouragement I derive from these data stems from my identification with industrial psychology. At a time when many in industrial psychology are worried because predictive validities rarely exceed .50, it is at least reassuring—though still disconcerting—to note that our brethren in social and experimental psychology are doing little better.

It is particularly informative to note the conclusions made by the authors of the articles sampled by Hakel. Authors of the study yielding the eta of .05 concluded "that rating-scale format is a determiner of the judgment of raters in this sample [Madden & Bourden, 1964]." In an investigation yielding an eta of .14, the authors concluded "that highly creative subjects give the greatest number of associations and maintain a relatively higher speed of association throughout a 2 minute period [Mednick, Mednick, & Jung, 1964]."

Surprisingly, these rather definite conclusions differ little in tone from those based on studies yielding much stronger relationships. For example, a study yielding an eta of .77 is summarized with "Highly anxious subjects tended to give sets of word associates higher in intersubject variability than nonanxious subjects [Brody, 1964]." In like manner, the conclusion stated for a study yielding an eta of .63 was simply "It was found that reinforcement affected subjects' verbalizations [Ganzer & Sarason, 1964]."

It seems abundantly clear that our little survey provides convincing and frightening evidence that playing the game of null hypothesis testing has led a sizeable number of psychologists to lose sight of the importance of the strength of relationships underlying their conclusions. I could not agree more fully with Nunnally (1960), who has said:

> it would be a pity to see it (psychology) settle for meager efforts . . . encouraged by the use of the hypothesis testing models. . . . We should not feel proud when we see the psychologist smile and say "the correlation is significant beyond the .01 level." Perhaps that is the most that he can say, but he has no reason to smile [p. 650].

The Delusions We Suffer

This is probably the most dangerous game of all. At the core, it consists of maintaining delusional systems to support our claims that the things we are doing *really* constitute good science. The game develops out of a pattern of self-deceit which becomes more ingrained and less tractable with each new delusion. Thus, an appropriate subtitle is "This Above All, to Thine Ownself Be *False*!"

The forms of these delusions are so numerous and so widespread in psychology that time permits only brief mention of a few.

One common variant of the game can be called, "Boy, Did I Ever Make Them Sit Up and Take Notice!" The argument is often made and seemingly almost always accepted that if a new theory or method stimulates others to do research, it *must* be good. Although I greatly dislike analogic arguments, I am compelled to suggest that such reasoning is very similar to stating that accidental fire must be good simply because it keeps so many firemen busy. Unfortunately, an inestimable amount of psychological research energy has been dissipated in fighting brush fires spawned by faddish theories—which careful research might better have refuted at their inception

It is probably far too much to hope that we have seen the last of the studies "stimulated" by Sheldon's notions about physique and temperament, or by the overly simplified but widely popular two-factor theory of job motivation (Herzberg, Mausner, & Snyderman, 1959).

A second common delusion seems to arise out of the early recognition that gathering data from real people emitting real behaviors in the day-to-day world proves often to be difficult, unwieldy, and just plain unrewarding. Thus many retreat into the relative security of experimental or psychometric laboratories where new laboratory or test behaviors may be concocted to be observed, measured, and subjected to an endless array of internal analyses. These usually lead to elaborate theories or behavioral taxonomies, entirely consistent within themselves but lacking the acid test of contact with reality. Last year, McNemar (1964) summarized once more for us the evidence showing the pathetic record of factor analytically derived tests for predicting day-to-day behavior. A former professor at

Minnesota used to say—when describing a lost soul—"He disappeared into the Jungle of Factor Analysis—never to be heard from again." Psychologists who choose to partake of the advantages of the more rigorous controls possible in the psychometric or experimental laboratories must also accept responsibility for assuring the day-to-day behavioral relevance of the behavioral observations they undertake.

A third unfortunate delusion rationalizes certain practices on the grounds that they are intrinsically good for humanity and that they need not, therefore, meet the usual standards demanded by scientific verification. In this regard, Astin (1961) has done an effective job of analyzing the functional autonomy of psychotherapy and offers a number of reasons why it continues to survive in spite of a lack of evidence about its effectiveness. In industrial psychology, a most widespread current fashion is the extensive use by firms of group-process or sensitivity-training programs; the effectiveness of such programs is still proclaimed solely on the basis of testimonials, and a primary rationale for their inadequate evaluation is that they are a form of therapy and must, therefore, be good and worthwhile.

Finally, yet another pair of delusions, representing polar opposites of one another, were discussed by Cronbach (1957) in his American Psychological Association Presidential Address. One extreme, shown chiefly by the experimentalists, treats individual differences as merely bothersome variation—to be reduced by adequate controls or treated as error variance in the search for General Laws. Such assumptions cannot help but lead to an oversimplified image of man, for the simplification is introduced at the very beginning. We cannot expect a science of human behavior to advance far until the moderating effects of individual variation on the functional relationships being studied are taken fully into account. People do, after all, differ greatly from one another and they differ even more from monkeys, white rats, or pigeons. It should not *really* be too heretical to suggest that many of the lawful relations governing the behavior of lower organisms may be inapplicable to the human species and, moreover, that laws describing the behavior of certain selected human subjects—such as psychology sophomores—may upon examination prove only weakly applicable to many other individuals. It should be incumbent upon the experimentalist or the theorist either to incorporate a consideration of individual differences into his research and theorizing or to define explicitly the individual parameters or population characteristics within which he expects his laws to be applicable.

The other extreme, actually extending considerably beyond the correlational psychology discussed by Cronbach, is just as delusory and even more detrimental to the eventual development of psychology than the one just discussed. Differences between individuals are regarded as so pervasive that it is assumed *no* laws can be stated. The likely outcome of a strong commitment to this point of view must ultimately be an admission that the methods of science cannot be applied to the study of human behavior. Yet, this outcome is not often openly recognized or honestly accepted by those believing in the ultimate uniqueness of each individual. Instead, they speak of "new approaches," less "mechanistic emphases," and a more "humanistic endeavor."

Cronbach, nearly a decade ago, sounded an urgent call for his fellow psychologists to cast aside the delusions represented by these two extremes. Unfortunately, today we seem no closer to achieving this end than we were then.

The Secrets We Keep

We might better label this game "Dear God, Please Don't Tell Anyone." As the name implies, it incorporates all the things we do to accomplish the aim of looking better in public than we really are.

The most common variant is, of course, the tendency to bury negative results. I only recently became aware of the massive size of this great graveyard for dead studies when a colleague expressed gratification that only a third of his studies "turned out"—as he put it.

Recently, a second variant of this secrecy game was discovered, quite inadvertently, by Wolins (1962) when he wrote to 37 authors to ask for the raw data on which they had based recent journal articles. Wolins found that of 32 who replied, 21 reported their data to be either misplaced, lost, or inadvertently destroyed. Finally, after some negotiation, Wolins was able to complete seven re-analyses on the data supplied from 5 authors. Of the seven, he found gross errors in three—errors so great as to clearly change the outcome of the results already reported. Thus, if we are to accept these results from Wolins' sampling, we might expect that as many as one-third of the studies in our journals contain gross miscalculations. In fact, this variant of the secrecy game might well be labeled "I Wonder Where the Yellow (data) Went." In commenting on Wolins' finding, Friedlander (1964), impressed by the strong commitments psychologists hold for their theories, tests and methods, suggests that "Hope springs eternal—and is evidently expressed through subjective arithmetic"—a possibility which is probably too close to the truth to be taken lightly.

Another extremely vexing and entirely unnecessary type of secrecy is clearly apparent to anyone who takes but a moment to page through one of our current data-oriented psychological journals. I chose a recent issue of the *Journal of Personality and Social Psychology*. It was very difficult to find such mundane statistics as means or standard deviations. Instead, the pages abounded with analysis of variance tables, charts, *F* ratios, and even *t* tests in the absence of their corresponding means and *SD*s. The net effect of this is to make very difficult and often impossible any further analyses that a reader might want to undertake. The implication of this, it seems to me, is that many authors have actually failed to bother computing such statistics as means or *SD*s and that, further, they probably have not examined their data with sufficient care to appreciate in any degree what they may really portray.

Other examples of the secrecy game abound. They include such practices as dropping subjects from the analyses—a practice discussed at some length in the critical review of a sampling of dissonance studies by Chapanis and Chapanis (1964), experimenter-biasing factors, incomplete descriptions of methodology, failure to carry out or to report cross-validation studies, and the more general problem of failure to carry out or to report replication studies.

I believe you will agree that these tactics of secrecy can be nothing but severely damaging to any hopes of advancing psychology as a science. It seems likely that such practices are rather widely applied in psychology by psychologists. I suggest that we vow here and now to keep these secrecy games secret from our colleagues in the other sciences!

The Questions We Ask

There are many titles that might be appropriate for this last game that I shall discuss. One might be, "Who's on First?"—or better yet, "What Game Are We In?"—or a rather common version in these days of large Federal support for research, "While You're Up, Get Me a Grant." My major point here is quite simply that the other games we play, the pets we keep, our delusions, our secrets, and the Great Name Game interact to cause us to lose sight of the essence of the problems that need to be solved and the questions that need answers. The questions that get asked are dictated—all too often—by investigators' pet theories or methods, or by the need to gain "visibility" among one's colleagues. One of my respondents—a younger but undoubtedly wiser head than I—summed it up nicely.[4] He said:

> Psychologists seem to be afraid to ask really important questions. The whole Zeitgeist seems to encourage research efforts that earn big grants, crank out publications frequently and regularly, self-perpetuate themselves, don't entail much difficulty in getting subjects, don't require the researchers to move from behind their desks or out of their laboratories except to accept speaking engagements, and serve to protect the scientist from all the forces that can knock him out of the secure "visible circle."

Another of my respondents, a verbal behavior researcher, illustrated the dilemma by mentioning a fellow researcher who phrased his research question as: "How do the principles of classical and instrumental conditioning explain the learning of language?" This sort of question is clearly illustrative of the tendency to defer too readily to existing popular points of view and to allow them to distort the direction of research activities. It would be better simply to ask "What is learned?" rather than making the premature assumptions that (a) language is learned in the sense that the term *learning* is usually used or (b) *all* learning is of only two types.

An even more serious and, unfortunately, probably more common form of the question-asking game is the game of "Ha! Sure Slipped That One Past You, Didn't I?" Here, the investigator shrewdly fails to state the question he is trying to answer, gathers data to provide answers to simpler questions, and then behaves as if his research has been relevant to other unstated but more important and more interesting problems. The vast majority of studies devoted to measuring employee attitudes have committed this error. It is no trick to develop questionnaires to gather systematically the opinions of workers about their jobs. It is quite something else, however, suddenly to begin talking about measures of employee *motivation* and to suggest that the employee responses have direct relevance to what they may actually do on the job. The literature on response set and response style is another clear case of new questions being designed to fit existing answers. Showing high correlations between scores on empirically developed scoring keys and the numbers of items keyed *True* or some other item index should not be taken as having any bearing on the empirical validities of these keys. Yet for over a decade, our literature has been burdened with all sorts of set and style studies characterized by

[4] J. P. Campbell, personal communication, 1965.

seemingly endless factor analyses and silly arguments between persons committed to acquiescence and those committed to social desirability.

Thus, we all are far too eager to ask such questions as: "What problems can be *easily* answered?" "What else can I do with my test?" "What problems or questions does my theory lead to?" "What aspects of behavior can I study with my computer or with my apparatus?" or "What problems can I find that I can fit this method to?"

Certainly, as psychologists—as scientists presumably interested in the subject matter of human behavior—we should be able to do better than this!

The Causes

You may have inferred by now that I feel some sense of pessimism about the current state of psychology. Based on what you have heard so far, such an inference is probably appropriate. I *do* believe that the games I have described offer little that can be beneficial for psychology in the long run. The behaviors underlying the games represent enormous and essentially wasteful expenditures of our own research energy.

Even so, my mood is not basically pessimistic. In fact, we should be able to emerge from this soul searching with a constructive sense of discontent rather than one of destructive despair. The description of our condition carries with it a number of implications for corrective action. Moreover, we may infer from the condition some possible causes, and listing them should also suggest possible correctives.

To this end, let me consider briefly what I believe to be the major causes of psychology's fads, fashions, and folderol.

The most important, I believe, is related quite directly to the relative insecurity of being a scientist, a problem that is particularly acute in psychology where we must cope with such complex phenomena as those involved in the study of human behavior. The scientist's stance includes the constant need to doubt his own work. Moreover, the long-range significance of his work cannot often be forecast, and rarely can the scientist—least of all, perhaps, the psychologist—preplan his inspirations and his ideas. It is little wonder, then, that many seek, through their theories, methodologies, or other of the games we have discussed, to organize, systematize, and regularize their creative output. When viewed against the backdrop of publication pressures prevailing in academia, the lure of large-scale support from Federal agencies, and the presumed necessity to become "visible" among one's colleagues, the insecurities of undertaking research on important questions in possibly untapped and unfamiliar areas become even more apparent. Stern (1964) has recently very effectively stated the case for the desirability of moving from research into equally fulfilling careers of teaching and administration. But we cannot forget that the value system of science places research and publication at the peak, and it should, therefore, be no surprise that the less able researchers in psychology—learning early that no great breakthrough is in the offing—simply seek to eat their cake and have it too, by playing the games and the song and dance of scientific research, usually convincing even themselves that the games are "for real" and that their activities really "make a difference."

The perpetuation of this state of affairs is related to our present system of graduate education. Many psychology graduate students today find themselves under the tutelage of a faculty member who has bought the system wholeheartedly. Such students live for a period of from 3 to 8 years in an environment that enforces and reinforces the learning of a particular approach, a narrow point of view or a set of pet methodologies which come to define for them the things they will pursue as psychologists.

The Remedy

But here I am—sounding pessimistic and noxious again, and getting farther out on the limb than I really want to be.

In order to convince you of my good intentions and my hope for the future, I had better get on with some constructive suggestions. My suggested remedy—if it can be called that, for indeed it may be more painful than the disease—can be summarized in five imperative statements:

1. Give up constraining commitments to theories, methods, and apparatus!
2. Adopt methods of multiple working hypotheses!
3. Put more eclecticism into graduate education!
4. Press for new values and less *pretense* in the academic environments of our universities!
5. Get to the editors of our psychological journals!

Let me elaborate briefly on each of these recommendations.

First, I advocate a more careful and studied choice of research questions. As should be apparent, I believe research energy should be directed toward questions that contain as few as possible of any prior unproven assumptions about the nature of man. We must be constantly alert to the narrowing of research perspectives due to prior theoretical or methodological commitments. I am calling for less premature theorizing—particularly that which leads to vaguely stated "wide-band" theories that are often essentially incapable of disproof.

I am not advocating the abandonment of deduction in psychology; in fact, psychology needs stronger and more specific deducations rather than the weak and fuzzy ones so typical of so many current theories. What I am advocating is the more systematic study of lawful relationships *before* interpretations are attempted. When explanation *is* attempted, the data should be sufficient to allow hypotheses to be stated with the clarity and precision to render them directly capable of disproof. As the philosopher Karl Popper has said, there is no such thing as proof in science; science advances only by disproofs.

This leads directly to my second recommendation which is to state and systematically test multiple hypotheses. Platt recently advocated this approach which he calls *Strong Inference* (Platt, 1965). The approach entails devising multiple hypotheses to explain observed phenomena, devising crucial experiments each of which may exclude or disprove one or more of the hypotheses, and continuing with the retained hypotheses to develop further subtests or sequential hypotheses to refine the possibilities that remain. This process does not seem new; in fact it is not. It simply entails developing ideas or leads, stating alternative possibilities, testing their plausibility, and proceeding to develop predictive and explanatory evidence concerning the phenomena under investigation. One might say that the research emphasis is one of "studying hypotheses" as opposed to "substantiating theories." The difference seems slight, but it is really quite important. However, in psychology, the approach is little used, for, as we have said, the commitments are more often to *a* theory than to the process of *finding out*.

The method of multiple hypotheses takes on greatly added power when combined with greater care in the analysis and reporting of research results. Instead of serving as the sole statistical test of hypotheses, the statistical null hypothesis should always be supplemented by estimates of strength of association. The psychologist owes it to himself to determine not only whether an association exists between two variables—an association which may often be so small as to be trivial—but also to determine the probable magnitude of the association. As Hays (1964) has suggested, if psychologists are content to adopt conventions (such as .05 or .01) for deciding on statistical significance, they should also adopt conventions concerning the strength of association which may be sufficiently large to regard as worthy of further investigation. Obviously, such conventions cannot be the same for all areas and for all research questions, but it should be clear that an emphasis on magnitude estimation will demand that researchers give much more careful thought than they now do to defining ahead of time the actual magnitudes that will be regarded as possessing either theoretical or practical consequence.

By now, it is apparent why my fifth recommendation has to do with our journals. It will require a new kind of surveillance from both the editors and their consultants if we are to implement the greater care in research conception and in data analysis and reporting that I am advocating. When and if null-hypothesis testing is accorded a lower position in the status hierarchy and comes to be supplemented by emphases on Strong Inference and magnitude estimation, I would predict that the bulk of published material will, for a time, greatly diminish. That which does appear, however, will be guaranteed to be of considerably greater consequence for furthering our understanding of behavior.

One of the possible loopholes in the method of Strong Inference, it should be clear, is the great difficulty of designing and carrying out crucial experiments. Recently Hafner and Presswood (1965) described how faulty experiments had led physicists astray for several decades as they sought to explain the phenomenon of beta decay. We must broaden our conception of multiple hypotheses to include as one quite plausible hypothesis the possibility of poorly conceived or poorly conducted experiments. This, of course, simply speaks to the need for more replication in psychology of crucial experiments, a practice which undoubtedly would become more widespread if psychologists possessed fewer of their own theoretical pets and stronger motivation to examine systematically whole sets of contending hypotheses and alternative explanations.

My third and fourth recommendations need not be elaborated extensively. Both are intended to foster less pretense in the conduct of psychological research by enabling those scholars who may be ill fitted for the research enterprise to gain rewards in other endeavors. The change in the academic atmosphere would need to take the form of according more status to good teaching and to good administration. Perhaps this change would be most rapidly fostered if the scientific games I have described would be more readily recognized for what they are and appropriately devalued in the scheme of things within academia.

Obviously, greater eclecticism in graduate education is crucial to the successful outcome of my other suggestions. It is difficult to know how this can be implemented. But, at least, the goals seem clear. We desire to teach the core of psychology's knowledge and methods, its subject matter and its questions, the statistical methods and their appropriate applications—but most of all, through selection or training or both, we should seek to turn out persons with intense curiosity about the vast array of psychological questions and problems occurring everywhere in the world around us, with a willingness to ask *open* questions unhampered by the prior constraints of a particular point of view or method. Let us hope that graduate education, in the years ahead, will become more eclectic and that even the Great Men in our field may adopt a sense of humility when transmitting knowledge to the fledglings of our science.

The Outcome: Utopia

How do I envision the eventual outcome if all these recommendations were to come to pass? What would the psychologizing of the future look like and what would psychologists be up to?

Chief among the outcomes, I expect, would be a marked lessening of tensions and disputes among the Great Men of our field. I would hope that we might once again witness the emergence of an honest community of scholars all engaged in the zestful enterprise of trying to describe, understand, predict, and control human behavior.

Certainly our journals would be more meaty and less burdensome. There would be more honesty in publishing the fruits of one's labors. Negative results—the disproof of theoretical formulations and the casting aside of working hypotheses—would be a more important part of the journals' contents. In consequence, the journals would contribute more meaningfully to the broad effort to achieve understanding, and we should expect to witness a sharp decline in the number of disconnected little studies bearing little or no relation to each other.

Moreover, I expect that many present schisms in psychology would be welded. The academic-professional bipolarity described by Tryon (1963) would be lessened, for the advantages to both of close association between basic researchers and those practicing the art of psychology should become more apparent. The researchers would thereby establish and maintain contact with the real world and real problems of human behavior, and the professional practitioners would be more fully alert to the need for assessing their methods by generating and testing alternate deductions and hypotheses growing out of them.

Thus, in the long run we might hope for fewer disputes, a spirit of more open cooperation, greater innovation in the generation and testing of working hypotheses, greater care and precision in the development of theoretical formulations, and increased rigor in specifying the magnitude of outcomes such that they have both practical and theoretical importance.

Does this sound like Utopia? Indeed it does. But is it too much to expect of a science now well into its second 100 years? I think not. Let us get on then with the process of change and of reconsolidation.

R E F E R E N C E S

Astin, A. W. The functional autonomy of psychotherapy. *American Psychologist*, 1961, 16, 75-78.

Berne, E. *Games people play*. New York: Grove Press, 1964.

Binder, A. Further considerations on testing the null hypothesis and the strategy and tactics of investigating theoretical models. *Psychological Review*, 1963, 70, 107-115.

Brody, N. Anxiety and the variability of word associates. *Journal of Abnormal and Social Psychology*, 1964, 68, 331-334.

Chamberlin, T. C. The method of multiple working hypotheses. *Science*, 1965, 148, 754-759.

Chapanis, N., & Chapanis, A. Cognitive dissonance: Five years later. *Psychological Bulletin*, 1964, 61, 1-22.

Cronbach, L. J. The two disciplines of scientific psychology. *American Psychologist,* 1957, 12, 671-684.

Feigel, H. Philosophical embarrassments of psychology. *Psychologische Beitrage*, 1962, 6, 340-364.

Friedlander, F. Type I and Type II bias. *American Psychologist,* 1964, 19, 198-199.

Ganzer, V. J., & Sarason, I. G. Interrelationships among hostility, experimental conditions, and verbal behavior. *Journal of Abnormal and Social Psychology*, 1964, 68, 79-84.

Grant, D. A. Testing the null hypothesis and the strategy and tactics of investigating theoretical models. *Psychological Review*, 1962, 69, 54-61.

Guilford, J. P. Psychological measurement a hundred and twenty-five years later. Invited address presented at American Psychological Association, Chicago, September 1960.

Hafner, E. M., & Presswood, S. Strong inference and weak interactions. *Science*, 1965, 149, 503-510.

Hays, W. L. *Statistics for psychologists*. New York: Holt, Rinehart & Winston, 1964.

Herzberg, F., Mausner, B., & Snyderman, B. *The motivation to work*. New York: Wiley, 1959.

Madden, J. M., & Bourdon, R. D. Effects of variations in rating scale format on judgment. *Journal of Applied Psychology*, 1964, 48, 147-151.

Maier, N. R. F. Maier's law. *American Psychologist*, 1960, 15, 208-212.

McNemar, Q. Lost our intelligence? Why? *American Psychologist,* 1964, 19, 871-882.

Mednick, M., Mednick, S. A., & Jung, C. C. Continual association as a function of level of creativity and type of verbal stimulus. *Journal of Abnormal and Social Psychology*, 1964, 69, 511-515.

Meehl, P. E., & Hathaway, S. R. The K factor as a suppressor variable in the MMPI. *Journal of Applied Psychology*, 1946, 30, 525-564.

Nunnally, J. The place of statistics in psychology. *Educational and Psychological Measurement*, 1960, 20, 641-650.

Platt, J. R. Strong inference. *Science*, 1964, 146, 347-352.

Rozeboom, W. W. The fallacy of the null-hypothesis significance test. *Psychological Bulletin*, 1960, 57, 416-428.

Sommer, R. On writing little papers. *American Psychologist*, 1959, 14, 235-237.

Stern, C. Thoughts on research. *Science*, 1964, 148, 772-773.
Tryon, R. C. Psychology in flux: The academic-professional bipolarity. *American Psychologist*, 1963, 18, 134-143.
Wolins, L. Responsibility for raw data. *American Psychologist*, 1962, 17, 657-658.

12

Shades of Yesteryear: 1971

It's Hell in Personnel

THOMAS J. MURRAY

One day every month, a group of long-haired, hippie-looking young people stand at the street corners along Market Street in downtown San Francisco peddling what is probably the only underground newspaper to come out of a major U.S. corporation. Called *The Stranded Oiler*, the paper is published by employees of the Standard Oil Co. of California. The policy of the *Oiler*'s editors is clear enough: to criticize the policies of the company that pays their wages. In any one issue can be found articles censuring individual members of SoCal top management, berating the company for its personnel and labor policies, objecting to its political views and attacking its alleged pollution of the waters.

SoCal top management, at least publicly, laughs off *The Stranded Oiler* as being of no importance and claims it has done nothing to stop its publication. But while perhaps relatively insignificant in itself, the existence of an underground company newspaper is symptomatic of something much bigger: the revolutionary new forces—both internal and external—that are challenging the traditional values of the corporation and causing turmoil. Political militants are infiltrating employee ranks, bomb threats are becoming almost a daily occurrence, minority and women's groups are demanding better jobs, employees are restless and rebellious, and drug abuse is a lot more serious than most companies are willing to admit.

As these massive social pressures intrude on corporate life, the job of coping with them is increasingly falling on the shoulders of one man: the company personnel manager. But he is hardly the personnel manager of old. In most companies not so long ago, he was low man on the management totem pole. Relatively untrained, his job was a simple one: hiring and firing, keeping records, handling routine grievances. The personnel function was often, as clinical psychologist Harry Levinson, a professor at the Harvard Business School, puts it, "an unfortunate dumping ground" for people the company had no place else to put.

Reprinted by special permission from *Dun's*, March, 1971, pp. 40-43.
 Mr. Murray is an editor of *Dun's*.

A Lifetime of Problems

Now, as the "people" problem erupts in a dozen different guises, the "people" man suddenly finds himself with one of the most confusing and complicated jobs in the company. "The whole world," sighs Willard W. Peck, personnel vice president of Metropolitan Life Insurance Co., "has changed more in the past five years than in the previous 25. For us, it has brought changes we never had to deal with before—from drugs to demonstrations.

To be sure, as the personnel man's responsibilities have grown, so has his prestige within the company. The question is: Is the prestige worth the tremendous burden of the job? Few personnel managers express any longing for "the good old days"—and most, indeed, seem to relish their new eminence. But more than a few would agree with one personnel man, who prefers to remain anonymous as he says bluntly: "It's hell in personnel."

Take the problem of the militants. Most companies don't even like to talk about it. But there is no doubt that, wearing a dozen different disguises, militant groups such as the Students for a Democratic Society and the Black Panthers are infiltrating employee ranks, particularly in California, where much of the radical activity is centered.

Two years ago, for example, wood products company Menasha Corp. received well-publicized threats by the SDS to infiltrate their members into summertime jobs at the company's Anaheim plant and then radicalize the work force. Shortly after, Menasha discovered that two young SDS members had successfully penetrated the company.

The potential damage to the corporation of this kind of militant action is pointed out by James C. Hanifin, Menasha personnel director. "I figure I have a lot of power over people as the personnel director," says Hanifin, "but I don't have the power to shut down the company. One hourly worker with the power of persuasion can do just that. Out of 350 workers, such as there are at this plant, there are bound to be some who are susceptible to the kind of thinking espoused by the SDS."

Henifin, who believes that a personnel man these days cannot do his job without reading Jerry Rubin's *Do It* and other literature emanating from the radical ranks, attacked the SDS problem in a unique way. He secured a copy of the SDS manual blueprinting its infiltration program, duplicated it and distributed a copy to every worker in the plant. The point, he explains, was to inform every employee of the specific kinds of action they could expect from the SDS. "We cut them off at the pass," Hanifin adds, "but as far as I'm concerned any personnel manager who isn't spending a major part of his day finding out what his people are thinking, knowing who the militants are and their strengths, and helping to shape attitudes, is simply not doing his job."

Another infiltration was uncovered by Ameron, Inc., the former American Pipe & Construction Co., which discovered that it had four Black Panthers, trained in the use of automatic weapons, working at one plant. And Broadway-Hale, the big West Coast retail chain, found that it had one young summer worker from the ranks of SDS.

Broadway-Hale has had more than its share of trouble around the politically volatile San Francisco-Bay area. There have been seven fire bombings in its stores, and bomb threats, says Howard Carver, vice president of personnel, come in at the rate of one a day. Although he prefers not to be specific about the circumstances, Carver also admits:

"Over the past year some militants have managed to churn up a terrific amount of tension between our black and Puerto Rican employees in the area."

Radicals, though, cannot operate in a vacuum. What they largely feed upon is the malaise and job dissatisfaction that is becoming more and more prevalent among corporate employees. From the blue-collar ranks manning Detroit's assembly lines to the clerks filing checks for the banking industry to the young executives on the first rung of the management ladder, millions of bored, frustrated employees are fed up with repetitive, undemanding jobs and are showing their disenchantment in growing absenteeism, tardiness and sloppy job performance. "There are a lot of people in management," says Harvard's Harry Levinson, "who think they're running an army by control and command and try to operate that way in an authoritarian system. But life isn't like that anymore, and people have all kinds of ways of kicking back. Unless management learns to understand what is going on and work with it more constructively, we'll just get outselves into an impossible bind."

It is, of course, the outspoken, anti-Establishment young employees who are "kicking back" hardest. They are, for one thing, demanding more meaningful work and a greater participation in the company. At California's Security Pacific National Bank, young employees have become highly vocal in insisting on more purposeful work and in questioning the bank's traditional ways of doing business. "They want to know exactly how they influence the company," says George Moody, vice president of personnel. "We never had to put up with these kinds of demands before."

Scores of other personnel men, trying to help satisfy the same kinds of demands, are knee-deep in sensitivity training, job-enrichment programs and a host of other behavioral-science techniques. At Metropolitan Life, for example, an experimental job-enrichment program got under way in one division late last summer and caught on so fast that other divisions jumped ahead with their own programs before any results were in. "Recognizing the change in attitude of our employees," explains Willard Peck, "we have had to change ours. It's not just combining six simple jobs—that's job expansion. It is giving them the responsibility for an entire job, rather than just a small part of it, so they can see what they've accomplished.

The young are also bringing their heightened social consciousness into the company. Ecology, in particular, has become a sensitive issue that personnel men must learn how to deal with. On college recruitment trips, says Robert Bales, personnel manager of Precision Castparts Co., he knows he must be prepared with the right answers when the company's role in pollution comes up. Quips Howard Carver: "These days our personnel people are walking around talking to themselves about the things young employees are asking for—like time off to go to an ecology demonstration. We're surrounded by demonstrations," adds Willard Peck.

Even the "mod" clothing and odd grooming habits of the young can drive a personnel manager crazy. Whether to allow long hair or beards for men or mini-skirts or pants for women are not exactly problems of earth-shattering importance; having to make those kind of niggling day-to-day decisions, though, can be a big pain in the neck. When mini-skirts first became popular, Metropolitan's Willard Peck got dozens of calls from different departments of the company asking how short a skirt personnel would allow. Finally Peck, a normally calm, mild-mannered man, burst out in exasperation, "I just can't go around with a tape measuring everyone's skirts!"

The dissension in the ranks is evident on every level. As reported in *Dun's* ("Revolt of the Middle Managers," September 1969 and "Executives in Ferment," January 1971), discontent and rebelliousness are spreading through middle-management ranks. Equally disturbing to personnel men is the militancy of young union members who are quick to reject management-labor settlements. To James E. Carr, vice president for industrial relations at Ameron, the era of rational labor negotiations is over. "The trend now," he asserts, "is for them to demand all they can get—or else. A thirty-day strike doesn't even ruffle their feathers."

The personnel men expect to see more of this rank-and-file intransigence as union leaders lose control over their young members. William L. Mobraaten, personnel vice president for Pacific Telephone & Telegraph Co., in fact, views this rising group of union rebels as a coming "third force." Says Mobraaten: "With their anti-Establishment point of view, they are sympathetic neither to the unions nor management. They intend to stand apart."

All the while, external problems crowd in to cause more dissension and make the personnel man's life a nightmare. Since the new law was passed, personnel managers find the issue of equal-opportunity employment one of the most complex and time-consuming of all, as they spend more and more time consulting with legal counsel and studying law journals and government directives. Pacific Telephone's William Mobraaten figures he spends half of his time on equal-employment matters. Agrees James Watson, vice president of industrial relations for Hunt Wesson, "It has had one hell of an impact on Personnel. The problems it has raised—from answering charges to having to deal with more than a half-dozen regulatory agencies—are making it difficult for a company to operate."

To complicate the personnel man's life even more, Women's Lib groups are also demanding their equal-opportunity rights. At Libby-Owens-Ford last year, female employees successfully sued the company, so that now it must allow women to displace men with less seniority. The displaced men, in turn, can bump women with less time in service. How is it working? "It hasn't made the men very happy," sels Melvin Burwell, vice president for employee relations. "But then, some of the women aren't too happy either. Now they can be replaced by men."

A related problem is the hiring and training of the so-called hard-core unemployed. According to James Carr, vice president of industrial relations at Ameron, the biggest difficulty is not the time and effort it takes to train such personnel, but having to cope with the emotional reactions of old-time employees and supervisors who work directly with the trainees. Some employees complain that work standards are lowered to accommodate the hard-core employees. And supervisors do not like the idea of getting involved in the personal life and problems of the newcomers. "They claim they don't want to have to get the guy out of bed and to the job on time," says Precision Castparts' Bales.

As a result, personnel men have had to take a hand in developing programs to prepare first-level supervisors and other employees for the experience. "It means educating them in patience, understanding and acceptance," says the personnel director of a Midwest insurance company.

Finally there is perhaps the most potentially explosive issue of all: the worrisome and growing drug problem. While many companies claim to have little or no problem with narcotics use by employees, statistical evidence says otherwise. Last January, the California Chamber of Commerce released the findings of a state survey that concluded: "The large California company that doesn't have a drug-abuse problem is the exception rather than the rule." In a survey of eighty companies, Research Institute of America found that 80 percent of the medium-sized and large firms had incidences of drug abuse. And the Chicago Industrial Relations Council believes that three out of every four plants with fifty or more employees have serious narcotics problems.

What drug abuse is costing business in days lost through absenteeism or in poor production through sloppy work can only be guessed at. But Menasha's Jim Hanifin, who has spent a good deal of time on the problem, believes it is considerable. "Personnel people have been pretty naive about what's going on," says Hanifin. "They don't want to admit they have a real problem. But since I make speeches in public on the problem, my name has gotten around, and many personnel men from other companies contact me privately to ask how we're handling it."

By and large, though, most personnel directors seem to be at about the same stage their predecessors were years ago when alcoholism was first recognized as a major corporate problem. They just do not know what to do about it. "It's a very tricky business," says Ameron's Carr. "In the first place, we know very little about the problem. Then there's the difficulty of having to prove the use of drugs. And on top of that, unions can be very sticky about any harsh action we might take."

For the most part, companies are taking a hard line on drug use. Western Electric in Los Angeles says it uses undercover security agents to detect users in its ranks, then follows a policy of "dismissal only." Security Pacific National Bank, among others, trains its supervisors to identify users. Background checks are being intensified, and a growing number of personnel chiefs are quietly circulating blacklists of known users through their industries.

In addition to dealing with all the new critical problems that have come to haunt them, the personnel men, of course, are still responsible for their traditional chores of hiring and firing, wages and hours, and so forth, in short, the job has become almost incredibly complex.

But the more farsighted of today's personnel men expect it to become even more so as all the newly emerging problems begin to accelerate and cause even deeper havoc in the corporate ranks. "In the decade ahead," says Howard Carver, who though close to retirement is youthfully alive to all the forces around him, "the personnel manager is going to have to shift gears and move faster than he ever dreamed. He will have to listen more than he ever did, for that has been our biggest failure. And if he doesn't," concludes Carver, "he is going to have more trouble and change than we are having now."

SECTION II
The Development of Personnel Management as a Distinct and Important Organization Function

The problems discussed in Section I represent a challenging array. The objective of Section II is to describe how the field of personnel management has grown over a lifetime and to indicate the direction of efforts made to cope with some of these problems. As was suggested previously, one of the difficulties in coping with them arose out of the lack of an organizational unit specifically charged with their attention and solution. The first selection by Frederick Taylor is presented because it portrays an interesting early approach that he took in trying to deal with the dilemma at the first-line management level. His idea of splitting up the supervisor's job into several functional subunits and of having foremen specialize in each was novel. Unfortunately, it never gained widespread adoption because essentially it ignored the principle of unity of command, which emphasizes the need to issue orders from only one source.

The article by Carpenter is the earliest published discussion suggesting that the management of human resources deserves the same specialized attention accorded to other organization resources. He recommends the creation of a "labor department." Fitch's article does a good job of describing the fledgling years of the field and some of the early enthusiasm which accompanied them. Unfortunately, the enthusiasm was more enduring among the people in the field than it was among their line management superiors, as is suggested in the brief discussions from Personnel *and* Iron Age *published during the recession of the early 1920's.*

The discussions by the Donalds and Mathewson provide an interesting overview of progress made during the mid- and late 1920's. One of the clearest conclusions about such progress is that the vesting of line authority in personnel departments of the previous decade over such decisions as hiring and firing of workers still did not cope adequately with the issues of unity of command and parity of accountability and authority. It was during the 1920's that the idea of a "staff" relationship emerged as a better role for such departments.

Leiserson, Balderston, and Brown present a varied picture of some of the changes in personnel practice and thought which occurred during the 1930's. Although it is tempting to sympathize with Leiserson's view that the progress of fifteen years pretty much went down the drain during the 1930's, the comments by Balderston and Brown do not support this view fully. It should be recognized that Leiserson was a very active leader in the field during its early years and felt that personnel practitioners should properly play the role of impartial mediators in working out problems which arose between management and operative employees. His disappointment in seeing this role scuttled during the Depression is understandable. It became apparent from the experiences of personnel people during this decade that evangelism was not going to maintain their jobs in organizations struggling to survive the economic catastrophe facing them. Only by demonstrating to management that they were doing something with impressive economic ramifications for the organization were they likely to attain an enduring role within it.

As the country came out of the Depression and World War II arrived, a new opportunity for progress in personnel management emerged. The problems discussed in Owen's article reflect the growth of the number of practitioners in the field and it recommends decentralization as a way of facilitating the performance of the several facets of their role. James Worthy, a leading practitioner with Sears, Roebuck & Company, presents a provocative discussion which vividly describes some of the dilemmas that the personnel manager of the 1940's faced in defining his role and performing his job. Frustrations resulting from experiences of the 1930's apparently created a tendency to overreact. The personnel manager felt a need to demonstrate his contribution to the goal attainment of the organization but was unable to do so in economic language as easily and convincingly as some of his detractors in other departments.

William Foote Whyte's discussion draws attention to an

additional disrupting influence that resulted from the forceful entry, beginning in the late 1940's, of people trained in the behavioral sciences, such as psychology and sociology, into personnel domains. Although people from these "pure" disciplines have much to contribute, the coordination of their relatively specialized areas of expertise with problems of the traditional personnel manager, who needs to be a "jack of all trades" has not been a smooth process, nor is it yet complete. The interchange between Dunnette and Bass, representing behavioral scientists, and Patten, who presents the practitioner's view, suggests some of the difficulties.

Henning and French provide an interesting picture of what they believe is the real situation regarding authority-influence relationships between personnel managers and other segments of the organization. Subsequent research work by them has substantially verified their view that apparently contrasting pressures to behave in either a line or staff capacity have resulted in considerable variability in the role personnel managers assume among the various activities involved. Gross's intriguing discussion provides insight into why such a mixed picture has developed for the personnel practitioner. He recommends that the most feasible role for the personnel manager is that of monitoring human resource activities within the organization.

The current picture remains somewhat muddled, as reflected in data presented by Ash which show that personnel activities in large organizations, which tend to be centralized at a headquarters or corporate level, are different from those which are customarily decentralized toward operating level units. As he points out, there seems to be a perceptible tendency to centralize broad policy making, those activities requiring uniformity of action, and information relevant for decision making in many areas not normally available in local organization units. Sokolik suggests there is a need to reorganize personnel activities in order to better cope with a current emphasis in personnel work on integrating the particular needs of special groups into the mainstream of organization life.

Finally, Frank Fischer provides a glimpse into the future, in which he foresees personnel practioners becoming more important, creative, and assertive in fostering the accomplishment of both organization maintenance and productivity goals. Dunnette's remarks suggest some rather startling changes may be on the horizon in the not too distant future for personnel management and related disciplines.

13

The Problems of Straight-Line Organization and an Abortive Attempt to Remedy Them–The Functional Management Approach: 1890-1900.

Shop Management

FREDERICK W. TAYLOR

It is, of course, evident that the nature of the organizations required to manage different types of business must vary to an enormous extent, from the simple tonnage works (with its uniform product, which is best managed by a single strong man who carries all of the details in his head and who, with a few comparatively cheap assistants, pushes the enterprise through to success) to the large machine works, doing a miscellaneous business, with its intricate organization, in which the work of any one man necessarily counts for but little.

It is this great difference in the type of the organization required that so frequently renders managers who have been eminently successful in one line utter failures when they undertake the direction of works of a different kind. This is particularly true of men successful in tonnage work who are placed in charge of shops involving much greater detail.

In selecting an organization for illustration, it would seem best to choose one of the most elaborate. The manner in which this can be simplified to suit a less intricate case will readily suggest itself to any one interested in the subject. One of the most difficult works to organize is that of a large engineering establishment building miscellaneous machinery, and the writer has therefore chosen this for description.

Practically all of the shops of this class are organized upon what may be called the military plan. The orders from the general are transmitted through the colonels, majors, captains, lieutenants and noncommissioned officers to the men. In the same way the orders in industrial establishments go from the manager through superintendents, foremen of shops, assistant foremen and gang bosses to the men. In an establishment of this kind the duties of the foremen, gang bosses, etc., are so varied, and call for an amount of special information coupled with such a variety of natural ability, that only men of unusual qualities to start with, and who have had years of special training, can perform them in a satisfactory manner. It is because of the difficulty—almost the impossibility—of getting suitable foremen and gang bosses, more than for any other reason, that we so seldom hear of a miscellaneous machine works starting in on a large scale and meeting with much, if any, success for the first few years. This difficulty is not fully realized by the managers of the old well established companies, since their superintendents and assistants have grown up with the business, and have been gradually worked into and fitted for their especial duties through years of training and the process of natural selec-

Reprinted as an excerpt from Taylor's paper on *Shop Management*, American Society of Mechanical Engineers, Saratoga, New York, 1903.

tion. Even in these establishments, however, this difficulty has impressed itself upon the managers so forcibly that most of them have of late years spent thousands of dollars in re-grouping their machine tools for the purpose of making their foremanship more effective. The planers have been placed in one group, slotters in another, lathes in another, etc., so as to demand a smaller range of experience and less diversity of knowledge from their respective foremen.

For an establishment, then, of this kind, starting up on a large scale, it may be said to be an impossibility to get suitable superintendents and foremen. The writer found this difficulty at first to be an almost insurmountable obstacle to his work in organizing manufacturing establishments; and after years of experience, overcoming the opposition of the heads of departments and the foremen and gang bosses, and training them to their new duties, still remains the greatest problem in organization. The writer has had comparatively little trouble in inducing workmen to change their ways and to increase their speed, providing the proper object lessons are presented to them, and time enough is allowed for these to produce their effect. It is rarely the case, however, that superintendents and foremen can find any reasons for changing their methods, which, as far as they can see, have been successful. And having, as a rule, obtained their positions owing to their unusual force of character, and being accustomed daily to rule other men, their opposition is generally effective.

In the writer's experience, almost all shops are under-officered. Invariably the number of leading men employed is not sufficient to do the work economically. Under the military type of organization, the foreman is held responsible for the successful running of the entire shop, and when we measure his duties by the standard of the four leading principles of management above referred to, it becomes apparent that in his case these conditions are as far as possible from being fulfilled. His duties may be briefly enumerated in the following way. He must lay out the work for the whole shop, see that each piece of work goes in the proper order to the right machine, and that the man at the machine knows just what is to be done and how he is to do it. He must see that the work is not slighted, and that it is done fast, and all the while he must look ahead a month or so, either to provide more men to do the work or more work for the men to do. He must constantly discipline the men and readjust their wages, and in addition to this must fix piece work prices and supervise the timekeeping.

The first of the four leading principles in management calls for a clearly defined and circumscribed task. Evidently the foreman's duties are in no way clearly circumscribed. It is left each day entirely to his judgment what small part of the mass of duties before him it is most important for him to attend to, and he staggers along under this fraction of the work for which he is responsible, leaving the balance to be done in many cases as the gang bosses and workmen see fit. The second principle calls for such conditions that the daily task can always be accomplished. The conditions in his case are always such that it is impossible for him to do it all, and he never even makes a pretence of fulfilling his entire task. The third and fourth principles call for high pay in case the task is successfully done, and low pay in case of failure. The failure to realize the first two conditions, however, renders the application of the last two out of the question.

The foreman usually endeavors to lighten his burdens by delegating his duties to the various assistant foremen or gang bosses in charge of lathes, planers, milling machines, vise work, etc. Each of these men is then called upon to perform duties of almost as great variety as those of the foreman himself. The difficulty in obtaining in one man the variety of special information and the different mental and moral qualities necessary to perform all of the duties demanded of those men has been clearly summarized in the following list of the nine qualities which go to make up a well rounded man:

Brains.
Education.
Special or technical knowledge; manual dexterity or strength.
Tact.
Energy.
Grit.
Honesty.
Judgment or common sense and
Good health.

Plenty of men who possess only three of the above qualities can be hired at any time for laborers' wages. Add four of these qualities together and you get a higher priced man. The man combining five of these qualities begins to be hard to find, and those with six, seven, and eight are almost impossible to get. Having this fact in mind, let us go over the duties which a gang boss in charge, say, of lathes or planers, is called upon to perform, and note the knowledge and qualities which they call for.

First. He must be a good machinist—and this alone calls for years of special training, and limits the choice to a comparatively small class of men.

Second. He must be able to read drawings readily, and have sufficient imagination to see the work in its finished state clearly before him. This calls for at least a certain amount of brains and education.

Third. He must plan ahead and see that the right jigs, clamps, and appliances, as well as proper cutting tools, are on hand, and are used to set the work correctly in the machine and cut the metal at the right speed and feed. This calls for the ability to concentrate the mind upon a multitude of small details, and takes pains with little, uninteresting things.

Fourth. He must see that each man keeps his machine clean and in good order. This calls for the example of a man who is naturally neat and orderly himself.

Fifth. He must see that each man turns out work of the proper quality. This calls for the conservative judgment and the honesty which are the qualities of a good inspector.

Sixth. He must see that the men under him work steadily and fast. To accomplish this he should himself be a hustler, a man of energy, ready to pitch in and infuse life into his men by working faster than they do, and this quality is rarely combined with the painstaking care, the neatness and the conservative judgment demanded as the third, fourth, and fifth requirements of a gang boss.

Seventh. He must constantly look ahead over the whole field of work and see that the parts go to the machines in their proper sequence, and that the right job gets to each machine.

Eighth. He must, at least in a general way, supervise the timekeeping and fix piece work rates. Both the seventh and eighth duties call for a certain amount of clerical work and ability, and this class of work is almost always repugnant to the man suited to active executive work, and difficult for him to do; and the rate-fixing alone requires the whole time and careful study of a man especially suited to its minute detail.

Ninth. He must discipline the men under him, and readjust their wages; and these duties call for judgment, tact, and judicial fairness.

It is evident, then, that the duties which the ordinary gang boss is called upon to perform would demand of him a large proportion of the nine attributes mentioned above; and if such a man could be found he should be made manager or superintendent of a works instead of gang boss. However, bearing in mind the fact that plenty of men can be had who combine four or five of these attributes, it becomes evident that the work of management should be so subdivided that the various positions can be filled by men of this caliber, and a great part of the art of management undoubtedly lies in planning the work in this way. This can, in the judgment of the writer, be best accomplished by *abandoning the military type of organization* and introducing two broad and sweeping changes in the art of management:

(a) As far as possible the workmen, as well as the gang bosses and foremen, should be entirely relieved of the work of planning, and of all work which is more or less clerical in its nature. All possible brain work should be removed from the shop and centered in the planning or laying-out department, leaving for the foremen and gang bosses work strictly executive in its nature. Their duties should be to see that the operations planned and directed from the planning room are promptly carried out in the shop. Their time should be spent with the men, teaching them to think ahead, and leading and instructing them in their work.

(b) Throughout the whole field of management the military type of organization should be abandoned, and what may be called the "functional type" substituted in its place. "Functional management" consists in so dividing the work of management that each man from the assistant superintendent down shall have as few functions as possible to perform. If practicable the work of each man in the management should be confined to the performance of a single leading function.

Under the ordinary or military type the workmen are divided into groups. The men in each group receive their orders from one man only, the foreman or gang boss of that group. This man is the single agent through which the various functions of the management are brought into contact with the men. Certainly the most marked outward characteristic of functional management lies in the fact that each workman, instead of coming in direct contact with the management at one point only, namely, through his gang boss, receives his daily orders and help directly from eight different bosses, each of whom performs his own particular function. Four of these bosses are in the planning room and of these three send their orders to and receive their returns from the men, usually in writing. Four others are in the shop and personally help the men in their work, each boss helping in his own particular line or function only. Some of these bosses come in contact with each man only once or twice a day and then for a few minutes perhaps, while others are with the men all the time, and help each man frequently. The functions of one or two of these bosses require them to come in contact with each workman for so short a time each day that they can perform their particular duties perhaps for all of the men in the shop, and in their line they manage the entire shop. Other bosses are called upon to help their men so much and so often that each boss can perform his function for but a few men, and in this particular line a number of bosses are required, all performing the same function but each having his particular group of men to help. Thus the grouping of the men in the shop is entirely changed, each workman belonging to eight different groups according to the particular functional boss whom he happens to be working under at the moment.

The following is a brief description of the duties of the four types of executive functional bosses which the writer has found it profitable to use in the active work of the shop: (1) gang bosses, (2) speed bosses, (3) inspectors, and (4) repair bosses.

The gang boss has charge of the preparation of all work up to the time that the piece is set in the machine. It is his duty to see that every man under him has at all times at least one piece of work ahead at his machine, with all the jigs, templets, drawings, driving mechanism, sling chains, etc., ready to go into his machine as soon as the piece he is actually working on is done. The gang boss must show his men how to set their work in their machines in the quickest time, and see that they do it. He is responsible for the work being accurately and quickly set, and should be not only able but willing to pitch in himself and show the men how to set the work in record time.

The speed boss must see that the proper cutting tools are used for each piece of work, that the work is properly driven, that the cuts are started in the right part of the piece, and that the best speeds and feeds and depth of cut are used. His work begins only after the piece is in the lathe or planer, and ends when the actual machining ends. The speed boss must not only advise his men how best to do this work, but he must see that they do it in the quickest time, and that they use the speeds and feeds and depth of cut as directed on the instruction card. In many cases he is called upon to demonstrate that the work can be done in the specified time by doing it himself in the presence of his men.

The inspector is responsible for the quality of the work, and both the workmen and speed bosses must see that the work is all finished to suit him. This man can, of course, do his work best if he is a master of the art of finishing work both well and quickly.

The repair boss sees that each workman keeps his machine clean, free from rust and scratches, and that he oils and treats it properly, and that all of the standards established for the care and maintenance of the machines and their accessories are rigidly maintained, such as care of belts and shifters, cleanliness of floor around machines, and orderly piling and disposition of work.

The following is an outline of the duties of the four functional bosses who are located in the planning room, and who in their various functions represent the department in its connection with the men. The first three of these send their directions to and receive their returns from the men, mainly in writing. These four representatives of the planning department are, the (1) order of work and route clerk, (2) instruction card clerk, (3) time and cost clerk, and (4) shop disciplinarian.

Order of Work and Route Clerk. After the route clerk in the planning department has laid out the exact route which each piece of work is to travel through the shop from machine to machine in order that it may be finished at the time it is needed for assembling, and the work done in the most economical way, the order of work clerk daily writes lists instructing the workmen and also all of the executive shop bosses as to the exact order in which the work is to be done by each class of machines or men, and these lists constitute the chief means for directing the workmen in this particular function.

Instruction Card Clerks. The "instruction card," as its name indicates, is the chief means employed by the planning department for instructing both the executive bosses and the men in all of the details of their work. It tells them briefly the general and detail drawing to refer to, the piece number and the cost order number to charge the work to, the special jigs, fixtures, or tools to use, where to start each cut, the exact depth of each cut, and how many cuts to take, the speed and feed to be used for each cut, and the time within which each operation must be finished. It also informs them as to the piece rate, the differential rate, or the premium to be paid for completing the task within the specified time (according to the system employed); and further, when necessary, refers them by name to the man who will give them especial directions. This instruction card is filled in by one or more members of the planning department, according to the nature and complication of the instructions, and bears the same relation to the planning room that the drawing does to the drafting room. The man who sends it into the shop and who, in case difficulties are met with in carrying out the instructions, sees that the proper man sweeps these difficulties away, is called the instruction card foreman.

Time and Cost Clerk. This man sends to the men through the "time ticket" all the information they need for recording their time and the cost of the work, and secures proper returns from them. He refers these for entry to the cost and time record clerks in the planning room.

Shop Disciplinarian. In case of insubordination or impudence, repeated failure to do their duty, lateness or unexcused absence, the shop disciplinarian takes the workman or bosses in hand and applies the proper remedy. He sees that a complete record of each man's virtues and defects is kept. This man should also have much to do with readjusting the wages of the workmen. At the very least, he should invariably be consulted before any change is made. One of his important functions should be that of peacemaker.

Thus, under functional foremanship, we see that the work which, under the military type of organization, was done by the single gang boss, is subdivided among eight men: (1) route clerks, (2) instruction card clerks, (3) cost and time clerks, who plan and give directions from the planning room; (4) gang bosses, (5) speed bosses, (6) inspectors, (7) repair bosses, who show the men how to carry out their instructions, and see that the work is done at the proper speed; and (8) the shop disciplinarian, who performs this function for the entire establishment.

The greatest good resulting from this change is that it becomes possible in a comparatively short time to train bosses who can really and fully perform the functions demanded of them, while under the old system it took years to train men who were after all able to thoroughly perform only a portion of their duties. A glance at the nine qualities needed for a well rounded man and then at the duties of these functional foremen will show that each of these men requires but a limited number of the nine qualities in order to successfully fill his position; and that the special knowledge which he must acquire forms only a small part of that needed by the old style gang boss. The writer has seen men taken (some of them from the ranks of the workmen, others from the old style bosses and others from among the graduates of industrial schools, technical schools and colleges) and trained to become efficient functional foremen in from six to eighteen months. Thus it becomes possible with functional foremanship to thoroughly and completely equip even a new company starting on a large scale with competent officers in a reasonable time, which is entirely out of the question under the old system. Another great advantage resulting from functional or divided foremanship is that it becomes entirely practicable to apply the four leading principles of management to the bosses as well as to the workmen. Each foreman can have a task assigned him which is so accurately measured that he will be kept fully occupied and still will daily be able to perform his entire function. This renders it possible to pay him high wages when he is successful by giving him a premium similar to that offered the men and leave him with low pay when he fails.

14

The First Published Advocacy of a Department for Managing People: 1903

The Working of a Labor Department in Industrial Establishments

C. U. CARPENTER

The "Labor Problem" now confronting us cannot be solved until the same principles of organization that have been such great factors in commercial success are brought to bear upon it. Manufacturers generally, though they have recognized the seriousness of the situation for some time, are just beginning to realize the necessity for a general and comprehensive plan of organization. Practical experience has already proven the great value of strongly organized bodies of employers to meet and bargain with the existing organizations of labor. Experience also shows that these organizations of labor will themselves be benefitted ultimately by the existence of such bodies of employers.

It is my purpose not to dwell upon the value of such organizations, but to bring out the great benefits to be derived by applying the general ideas of organization and specialization to this subject in the case of the individual manufacturer.

 Reprinted from *The Engineering Magazine*, Vol. 25, No. 1, April, 1903, pp. 1-9.

The Working of a Labor Department

Whether employer and employee be organized in mutual bodies or not, one of the greatest needs of the present day is the development of some plan that will bring about a closer personal relation between them. To the loss of this "personal relation" and feeling of mutuality of interest can be attributed most of the trouble of the present day. In this day of huge corporations the employers are entirely out of touch with their workmen. That this works untold harm cannot be doubted. Most employers are fair-minded and would be willing to grant to their employees justice in regard to any complaints that they may have. The majority of them are willing that their workmen shall earn as large a wage as the conditions surrounding their business justify them in paying. The tendency amongst most of them is toward the providing of better working conditions for their employees. These facts are, however, seldom recognized by the workmen. Nor does it seem possible to cultivate any better feeling on the part of the employee toward his employer unless some attempt is made to restore the old-time "personal touch" between the two that to this day exists in the small shop. Trouble seldom comes upon the small shop, owing to the fact that difficulties are usually met and settled by the employer himself before they can grow into an unwarranted importance. Why not adopt a plan in the case of the large corporation that will ensure that all difficulties shall be met in the same manner?

"The Time to Stop Trouble Is Before It Begins." Some plan of organization must be adopted to make this possible. Some method should exist whereby employer and men could get together and discuss their mutual difficulties before trouble begins. For when once trouble does arise, and it has become so acute as to require the attention of the employer, he may be certain that by that time the feelings and prejudices of all who have attempted to handle the proposition have been aroused to a high pitch. There is certain to be a large degree of bad feeling and doubt of good intention on the part of both parties to the controversy.

Many times the workmen's proposal is too absurd for the employer to entertain for a moment. The workmen, on the other hand, often embittered by delays and lack of consideration on the part of their immediate superiors, at times insist upon its acceptance. Or, on the other hand, the employer upon considering the case, will often see in the proposal a large element of justice which he would have admitted without hesitation if the proposition had come to him "first-handed." He however often feels obliged to refuse such proposals for the sake of discipline and his desire to stand by his subordinates. Many bitter strikes have occurred under such conditions—strikes which could have been easily avoided had the questions been met *fairly, firmly*, and *promptly*. Whether or not the proposals are fair, in either case most desirable results can be accomplished by giving them prompt attention together with just and firm consideration at the time when they are first presented.

Consider the actual questions that give rise to strikes, lockouts and, following these, arbitration and conciliation committees. Consider the gist of the questions that these important bodies must investigate after the trouble has reached the point where, for the sake of the manufacturer, the workman, or the public, they must be called upon. Are not they the practical and fundamental questions of wages, hours, conditions under which men work, discharges, unreasonable demands, unjustifiable and unreasonable rules and practices, restrictions upon employment, limitation of output, etc.? Should we not begin at the lower end of the problem and provide some adequate means whereby the manufacturer and his men can come face to face and consider these questions and problems, fairly and squarely, before the matters get to such a serious issue as to render it necessary to call in outsiders to make a settlement? And settlements so made are rarely wholly acceptable to either party to the dispute, and when finally accepted, leave behind a bitter feeling of resentment.

Both logic and practical experience show the necessity for developing some plan of organization to meet such conditions.

No better introduction to the discussion of the work of the labor department in large industrial organizations can be given than a quotation from Mr. Hermann Justi's address on "Arbitration" delivered at Minneapolis some months ago:

> *Organization of the Employer Class.* All talk of arbitration or anything akin to it is well-nigh idle unless we take account of organization—not only as applied to employees, but organization as applied to employers. Whether we oppose it or favor it, organized labor has come to stay, and it must therefore be considered because we must deal with it. The employer class must organize to a point of excellence and efficiency where organized labor will respect it.
>
> I am convinced that only by organization can common labor get the maximum wages for its hire. I am equally well convinced that only through organization of the employer class will capital obtain from organized labor the most and the best service in return for the wages paid.
>
> *It is my belief that all great departments of industry must have their departments of labor, if serious friction is to be avoided and wisely adjusted. When we pause to reflect, is it not remarkable that all the departments of great business enterprises have their especially appointed heads to direct and to manage them, with the exception of the department of labor?* This is allowed to get along as best it can, and yet what department of any great business enterprise is of equal importance? This seems the more inexplicable and indefensible in view of the fact that when we reduce the whole problem of business competition to the concrete form, there are only two propositions after all with which the business man has to deal—the price of labor, and the rate of interest.

And are not these the absolute facts? What work requires more specialization, more continuous and tactful attention, than the handling of the labor question? And yet upon whom does this delicate and difficult problem actually fall? Is it handled by a department composed of men specially fitted for this question by their education, broad study of labor, and knowledge of labor conditions all over the country? Men selected for their fair-mindedness and practical experience in handling large bodies of men, and of such character as to gain the confidence of the workmen? Men of experience in making labor contracts, who know where the rights of labor end and the transgressions of the rights of capital begin even according to the union constitution?

No! this is seldom the case. The active, actual, everyday working policy of handling labor, the part that is vital to the working man and the manufacturer, is dictated *not by him but by his foreman.*

The superintendent is usually so loaded down with duties and responsibilities that it is almost impossible for him to give this subject the close attention it deserves. Again, he is often in the same condition as the higher officials. He is seldom in close touch with the workers. The foremen who are superintending the departments are exercising the direct and consequently the real potential influence over the men for good or bad. No matter what the manufacturer may desire to do for his men, no matter what his actual policy may be, their feeling toward the firm is governed more by their feeling toward the man who has them in daily control than by any other factors. If this man is weak, the workmen will impose upon him and the company. If harsh, unjust, or inclined to "play favorites," they will be discontented. The foreman will either augment or annul the effect of any good action or purpose of the employer.

The Working of a Labor Department

These considerations but still further emphasize the necessity for special departments, whose work may be developed along lines similar to those given herewith, and whose functions may be such as actual experience proves necessary.

Work of a Labor Department. This department should be in control of the labor question with full authority to settle all questions that the men and foremen cannot settle. There should always exist the right of appeal to this department on the part of either workmen or foremen. It should be its constant aim to settle all questions before they reach an acute stage and assume an unwarranted importance. The questions should be considered directly with the employees affected, no outside influence being permitted to enter. The department should also investigate those practices on the part of the workmen which are unjust to the firm and endeavor to have them corrected. In actual experience great good has been accomplished by investigating and taking up with the workmen such matters as restriction of output, opposition to improved machinery, unjust wage demands, unreasonably high wage rates, unreasonable opposition to justifiable discharges, etc. Many important matters bearing directly upon economy of production, efficiency of workmen, and discipline of the shop have been amicably settled, that would probably have ultimately resulted in serious trouble had they been handled through the usual course in the customary manner.

Such is the nature of the work that a standing advisory committee should be formed, composed of men who are highest in authority in the company, before whom shall be brought all important matters of labor policy and any very serious affairs that cannot be satisfactorily settled. This advisory board should be called together by the labor department on emergencies, and also for monthly reports, these reports to indicate clearly the nature of the troubles settled and progress made.

This work should not be undertaken in a spirit of hostility to the workman. It should be carried out along the lines of justice to all concerned, coupled with firmness in demanding and insisting that that which is right should be granted, and that which is wrong should not be tolerated.

Thorough investigation, prompt action, just decisions, and a firm stand for that which is right should mark the work of such a department.

Wage Question. The importance of a just and scientific wage system, both from the standpoint of satisfying the workmen and of producing work with the greatest economy, can hardly be over-estimated. The lack of attention to this matter causes much of the trouble between employees and employer. Where it is possible, the supervision of the wage system, together with the power to advise the adjustment of inequalities in wages, should be committed to the care of this department.

This department can with great profit watch for undue shrinkage in output or any tendency toward its limitation. A study of the reason for such conditions, and the changing of the conditions themselves, are often vital to the success of the business.

Increasing the Efficiency of the Factory Force. The important questions of "employment" and "improving the personnel of the factory force" have a most important connection with efficient production. That the efficiency of the factory force can be largely increased by scientific methods is a fact not generally recognized. In this connection, systematic steps to separate the poor workmen from the efficient for their education and improvement, or, in case they prove totally inefficient, their discharge, are important factors in improving a factory's efficiency. In a properly systematized factory it is not difficult to obtain very accurate information concerning the character, ability, and earning capacity of the different workmen, even though they number thousands. Such data are also valuable in checking up on the discharges of the workmen, as any discharge for an unjust cause can be noted at once. The data for all of this work are usually found necessary for the proper use of a wage system. A full consideration of this part of the subject would require an entire article, hence it is not possible to elaborate upon it at this time.

Improvements in Working Conditions. This department should investigate and have installed such improvements in sanitary and working conditions as experience has shown to be practical. The importance of such work when carried out along practical lines is becoming more and more apparent. It is thoroughly justified on the grounds both of humanity and of economy of production.

Study of Legal Decisions. An acquaintance with legal decisions bearing upon the rights of capital as well as of labor is often very important. The study of associations of labor and capital and a knowledge of the conditions of both throughout the world are necessary.

Foremen's Meetings. The work of such a department will be largely ineffective unless it has the support and co-operation of the foremen or men who are in direct charge of departments. These men should be brought into sympathy with its aims and purposes. Generally the responsibility for this labor question is something that they will gladly relinquish, but the seeming interference with their preconceived ideas of the boundaries of their own authority, which its work must involve, will be at first resented. Nothing, however, need or should be done to interfere with the necessary authority of a foreman.

These men must be instructed and trained in the best methods of handling men; most effective ways of increasing their working efficiency, in a manner not detrimental to their health; of increasing their interest in their work, and, especially in union shops, the most effective methods of securing the best results for the company and the men under union conditions.

Certain it is that this department must be so conducted as to deserve and win the confidence of the workmen and foremen in its fairness and firmness. Its decisions must be along the lines of honesty and justice for both company and men, and unless the foremen will give their support to this policy much of the effect of its good work will be lost.

In order to gain the desired results, weekly meetings should be held of all the foremen and assistants for the purpose of discussing the problems and difficulties that they meet every day and of finding some solution.

Where union conditions exist unionism should be discussed, frankly and fairly, in all its phases. The difficulties experienced in regard to it and methods of overcoming their troubles; the best methods of handling men and getting good work from them; methods of encouraging workmen to take more interest in their work; *methods of encouraging all workmen to attend their union meetings and to take an active part in the proceedings; encouraging good workmen to act as officers and members of union committees.* In many cases in my experience when unions were recognized by a company, foremen were found making it so unpleasant for union shop committeemen that only the worst and most radical men would serve; the better men not only would not serve on committees but would not even attend meetings, not caring to be identified with the movement, especially in view of the foremen's attitude. As a direct consequence of this policy the union leaders were invariably of the type that would continually stir up strife and trouble, and would insist, even to the point of strikes, upon the granting of the most unreasonable demands. The conservative men, bound by their obligations and by the company's acceptance of unionism, would be compelled to follow the lead of these men whenever trouble arose. In such cases a policy of encouraging the men to attend their meetings and serving on their committees will result in great good. It should always be kept in mind that these committees are not only the representatives of the men before the company, but also practically the representatives of the company before the unions.

The aims of such a method of education should be:

> *First.* The instilling into the minds of the foremen the general policy of the firm upon labor matters. A foreman should not be permitted to adopt his own policy and enforce his own rules in regard to such matters, but should be forced to follow the lines laid down by the company and compelled to work in harmony with its general policy and so aid in the development of one harmonious plan.
>
> *Second.* The foremen should, through their discussions, get better ideas as regards the proper methods of handling men.
>
> *Third.* They should, if wisely guided, learn many things that would result in direct economies in their departments.
>
> *Fourth.* Such meetings should develop a most desirable *esprit de corps* amongst the foremen themselves.

Personnel of Labor Department. It is evident that the men responsible for such work must be chosen with great care. Though representing the employers' interests, they must be careful to carry out the work in such a manner as to deserve and gain the confidence of at least the more conservative elements in the body of workmen. In this plan the introduction of any of the employees as members of the department is not contemplated or even suggested.

More will depend upon the ability, character and experience of the man at the head of such work, than upon any other factors.

He should have had a wide experience in the handling of large bodies of men, both union and non-union. He should have an acquaintance with the heads of existing manufacturer's associations and prominent labor leaders, as well as a thorough knowledge of union methods. He should be thoroughly informed on modern factory systems and methods, especially as applied to wage systems. Mechanical experience is very desirable. Inasmuch as many of the disputes that will arise will concern the question of wages and output, he should be able to devise methods of ascertaining the output that could be fairly expected from any job. He should be capable of introducing methods of increasing the interest of the workmen in their tasks. Such work requires a combination of tact, good judgment, experience in handling men, and executive ability and fairness. In short the man guiding such a department, formed to undertake such work as a safeguard to the company's interest, should possess no small degree of ability. No work is more worthy of the close attention of those high in authority in the company. It is indissolubly linked with the highest and most important interests of the employer. The commercial success of any business depends upon the securing and developing of markets, the development of the economic possibilities of the factory, and the existence and continuance of satisfactory relations between employer and employee.

As can be seen, the work of a labor department, properly developed and carried out, is vitally concerned with the last two factors mentioned.

Such methods have been carried out by the labor department in a large corporation for over a year. It was originally organized by Mr. John H. Patterson, president of the National Cash Register Company, and has been developed along the lines laid down in this article.

This particular company employs almost four thousand men. It is thoroughly unionized, there being represented in the factory eleven international union organizations, twenty-four local unions, and thirty-six shop committees. The policy outlined has had its vindication through the change in the attitude of the workmen. The men now limit their complaints to those which are fair. They deal directly with the company through its labor department, many questions being settled before they are brought up in union meetings.

Representative workmen are chosen for the officers and committees. Very little outside influence is brought to bear upon matters that pertain to the shop. Most of their former illiberal practices are done away with. The tendency is constantly toward a more conservative policy. The practical results attained in this case have more than justified the assertion made of the needs and value of such systematic work directed by a well organized department.

Whether or not a factory is unionized, it is certainly advisable to make a careful and unbiased investigation of actual conditions and ascertain what causes for dissatisfaction exist between the workmen and the management. See that opportunity is given the men to earn a wage such as the business can afford to pay under such a system of pay as is both economical and just. Provide them with sanitary conditions which modern industrial science has demonstrated it pays the employer to give them, and which humanitarian principles dictate as just and fair. Try to establish relations of confidence between yourselves and your employees and provide some means whereby you and they can meet on common ground, so that each can learn of those things that are unfair in the attitude or conduct of the other, and consider these in the spirit of justice. Hear their complaints, correct promptly all evils, insist that they do their share, and that they too correct the evils that they are responsible for, and the desired result will in time be attained. This does not by any means imply a weak policy of handling the question. It is the policy of strength.

15

The Field Gets Off the Ground: 1910-1920

Making the Boss Efficient

JOHN A. FITCH

Several hundred men from all over the country met a few weeks ago in Philadelphia to consider the problems involved in the relationship between employers and employees. They spent two days in frank discussion of industrial methods, they pointed out where managers and foremen were at fault and they talked about justice to the worker. There was earnest consideration of the question of legitimate grievances.

It was not a convention of an international trade union. Quite the contrary. The men present were the employment managers of some of the largest corporations in America. But they were meeting to exchange experiences and get new ideas in order that they might handle their jobs better, lessen the strain on industrial relations, and create more general satisfaction among employees.

These men were representatives of a new idea—an idea so hopeful and full of promise that there is just a possibility of its being the forerunner of policies and methods that will revolutionize industry. Whether it is as big an idea as that remains to be seen, but unquestionably it means new things.

When Saint Peter on the Day of Judgment begins to balance his books and tabulate his statistics he will find that until about midway of the second decade of the twentieth century employers of labor in general and critics of labor policies in general had one sin in common. They both believed that it didn't cost anything to replace one man in a factory with another.

There were exceptions, but in general the critics have expressed the idea almost exultantly. It makes a fine climax to a ringing denunciation of the employers' disregard of human welfare. "Aha," they have said, "he takes good care of his machines, new ones cost money. But his men? If he squeezes them dry and throws them on the scrap heap, what's the difference? A new man doesn't cost anything."

With certain honorable exceptions, the employers have believed the same thing. They have hired and fired with careless abandon. As a

Reprinted from *Survey*, Vol. 38, June 2, 1917, pp. 211-215.

competent critic observes, "they have wasted human efficiency like water." The only thing many of them have cared to know has been whether men were standing at the gate, seeking employment. So long as men were in reserve they have been indifferent to discharges and resignations.

With the employers holding to a theory like that, and their most active critics—even the unions—silent or acquiescent in the fallacy that a new man costs nothing, what could you expect? The Ford Motor Company in 1913 hired 54,000 new men to keep 13,000 jobs filled—more than four times as many men as there were jobs. To put it in terms of modern business problems, the "labor turnover" of the Ford company was over 400 per cent.

That was four years ago. Things have changed since the men began to get five dollars for an eight-hour day. But even now in other industries the Ford experience of 1913 can be duplicated. At the Philadelphia meeting a representative of the Goodrich Rubber Company said that in recent years it had been necessary to hire in a twelve-month nearly twice as many men as were on the payroll at one time in order to keep the plant fully manned. And he declared that, at the time of speaking, the labor turnover of that company was higher still.

Hiring and Firing

That there is a shocking social waste about such a condition has of course long been evident to everyone. That it is exceedingly discreditable to a society that permits it has been pointed out again and again. Even though we haven't known and do not know now just how fast the work of hiring and firing has gone on, we have seen it and been appalled by it in the seasonal industries.

We have blamed society for it, and rightly, where it has been due to the lack of training and guidance of the men and women who must be engaged in industry. We have deplored the blind alley jobs where a boy learned no trade and is turned out at maturity, too old for the job that spoiled his best learning years and incompetent for a better job, to drift from one unskilled task to another, never satisfactory and never satisfied. We have scored the employer for ruthlessly turning off his "help" whenever it suited his purpose.

We have seen that the whole proceeding is tremendously costly for society. The carrying of a dead weight of incompetents who might have been trained to skilful service and the maintenance of an industrial reserve to await the pleasure of the employer has been a heavy burden on the public. We have seen, too, how, above all, it has been costly for the employee. Every member of this shifting army of labor feels in his own body the effects of unemployment and stamped on his mind is the discomfort and misery of constant economic uncertainty.

The High Cost of New Men

But we have continued to believe that it costs the employer nothing. How wrong we have been, the employer himself is now beginning to point out. There have been employers here and there who knew it all the time, but there was no talk about it. There was no general understanding. Most of the employers were wholly in the dark, and many of them continue in it.

The study made in 1913 by Magnus W. Alexander was the first attempt to grapple with costs. There were few guide posts pointing the way, but Mr. Alexander found no fewer than five distinct elements of cost in hiring and training new employees. These were:

1. Clerical work in connection with the hiring process.
2. Instruction of new employees by foremen and assistants.
3. Increased wear and tear of machinery and tools by new employees.
4. Reduced rate of production during early period of employment.
5. Increased amount of spoiled work by new employees.

He admitted that these were not the only costs and named two others: "Reduced profits due to reduced production," and "investment cost of increased equipment on account of the decreased productivity of the machines on which new employees are being broken in." He made no attempt, however, to estimate these costs.

He found next that these elements of cost varied with different classes of employees. After making due allowance for each of the five items of cost, and for each of the five classes of employees, Mr. Alexander estimated that the cost of hiring a new man was between $35 and $40.

It was stated above that over 42,500 new employees were hired by twelve factories in a year that began with over 37,000 employees on the payroll and ended with about 44,000. After making deductions for changes due to unavoidable causes, Mr. Alexander came to the conclusion that 22,000 employees were unnecessarily hired, at an expense to the twelve factories involved of $831,000.

Mr. Grieves, who made a study of twenty factories in 1914, where 69,000 new employees were hired to maintain a force of 44,000 found the same elements of cost as those considered by Mr. Alexander. He estimated the average cost of hiring to be $40 per man and figured the extra cost of hiring unnecessary employees for the twenty factories was $1,760,000. John M. Williams, secretary of Fayette R. Plumb, Inc., of Philadelphia, in an address delivered in April, declared that $40 is an extremely low estimate of the cost of hiring a new man. His investigations led him to place the figure nearer $100.

Now that men are not so easy to get, employers are in a frame of mind to consider the new idea in employment, which has spread so rapidly within the last two years. That idea is simply this: That the employment problem should be studied as carefully and scientifically as any other business problem. To make this possible the function of hiring and discharging is taken away from the foremen and placed in the hands of a centralized employment department. Foremen are hired, not for their ability to select good workmen, but for their technical knowledge and their ability to get out the work. It is a loss of energy and a detriment to the plant for the foremen to do the work of hiring new men—and in addition they are, as likely as not, incompetent for that particular task.

An executive of a manufacturing company that adopted the new method of employment last year said recently:

> One of the first benefits we derived was in freeing the foremen from the daily necessity of looking over men they needed at the factory door. Under the old system the first hour of each morning and the

most critical hour from a departmental standpoint, was signalized by the absence of the foremen from their departments. The new system automatically changed this, and foremen were free to supervise work in their own departments, rather than lose hours daily in interviewing applicants for work.

By placing the function of hiring in a specialized department with a responsible executive in charge, it is possible to acquire a knowledge of the sources of labor supply that never could be had under the old system. At the same time a capacity for judging men and making wise selections is developed.

The first great function of an employment department, as I get it from the prophets and leaders of this movement, is the selection of the employee from an organized labor market—not at the gate. The fact that the old methods did not result in wise selections is one of the strongest reasons for the development of the new methods. Any analysis of labor turnover under the unregulated, hit-or-miss methods of a few years ago will show a constant shifting because the men hired were not fit for the jobs. A very large part of the work of eliminating this waste consists in hiring the right men the first time—in getting men who are fitted to the jobs. Trained, intelligent, experienced employment men can do that far better than men whose training is exclusively in another field and whose experience is in operation rather than in hiring.

Round Pins for Round Holes

Not even men of experience and training can select men with 100 per cent success, however. They may be mistaken altogether, or they may have sent men to wrong departments or placed them in the wrong jobs. The second chief function of an employment department, therefore, the leaders and wise men in this field tell me, is the training of men and the constant endeavor to place them in positions for which they are fitted or to which they are adapted.

When the hiring and firing is done by the foremen a man seldom gets a second chance to make good. He may be eminently fitted for some other job in the plant, but the foreman hasn't time to inquire into that. He simply discharges the man and tries another. Under the newer system the foreman has no power of discharge. He merely refers an unsatisfactory employee back to the employment department with a statement of his reasons for considering him unsuited to the work of his department. The employment manager does not then discharge the man except for the gravest of reasons. He studies his case, tries him out somewhere else and continues to try him until it becomes perfectly clear that he is hopelessly incompetent.

Most important of all from many points of view is the third function of an employment department conducted according to the new idea. Here is where new ground is being broken. The importance of hiring men who are fitted for the jobs has long been recognized. It is a new thing, however, for an employment department to consider whether the jobs are fit for the men. But that is what employment managers are now doing, seriously and in dead earnest. This is where, most of all, there enters what Meyer Bloomfield of Boston, calls "the new profession of handling men."

Loss from Trained Men Who Quit

Studies of employment problems have revealed that a high labor turnover is not due exclusively to hiring the wrong men. There are two elements in turnover—the discharge of undesirable workers and the voluntary leaving of desirable ones. The first element can be attacked effectively by careful selection. Discharges for incompetency may be reduced to a reasonable minimum. When this is done, however, the terrible drain due to the second element in the situation, the voluntary quitting of good men, is only emphasized.

Accordingly, the new employment department makes a careful study of the reasons for quitting. Many of them have a rule that a man cannot leave without passing through the office of the employment manager. A requirement that the signature of the employment manager must be secured before the last pay can be drawn enables the manager to have a face-to-face interview with every man as he leaves the company's employ. Of course it is not always possible to induce men to give their real reasons for leaving, but a tactful official can get pretty close to the facts in a majority of cases.

What this procedure means is that the management is getting the most accurate and valuable check it could possibly have on its own competency from the standpoint of dealing with labor. It is thus enabled to test the capability of foremen and gang bosses, and it receives illuminating reports on the physical condition of the plant and the acceptability of working conditions and of the scale of wages.

Nothing would illustrate the point better than the experience of a Philadelphia company that reorganized its employment methods only a little over a year ago. Speaking before a conference of employment managers in Philadelphia recently, John M. Williams, secretary of Fayette R. Plumb, Inc., explained that their employment manager has a chance to interview every man who is leaving the company's employ. He said:

> Some of the results are illuminating. When men quit or are discharged they have no reason for withholding information. Complaints are heard of nagging foremen, lost time in waiting for work and other complaints bearing on shop efficiency. These are investigated and if the fault is with us it is remedied.
>
> These complaints brought to light the weakness of one of our best foremen. He always had a "chip on his shoulder," approached his men with that attitude and caused a great deal of friction before this fault was discovered. A talk by our superintendent convinced him that while that sort of attitude may have been all right ten years ago, it can't be done—not now.
>
> Another case: a man quit, and on being asked for reasons stated that he had to lose too much time waiting for one indispensable tool, and for material for his work. Likewise was advised that his work was O.K. by one inspector, only to finish it up and have half a day's work thrown back by another inspector. An investigation proved that the man was justified; the case was settled and the man is still with us. As this man was an experienced hand in the department in which I stated it cost us $100 to break in a new man, it looks as though this was a fair day's work.

Other accomplishments of the new employment department in this plant, as related by Mr. Williams, are most impressive.

One of our departments demanded personal investigation, as we found it impossible to keep men or to maintain production. An analysis by the employment department showed poor shop conditions in many phases.

(A) Inadequate artificial lighting at dusk, so bad that no one but the individual workman bent over his work could tell what he was doing. This part of room dark and cheerless.

(B) Bad drainage in the rear of the machines, which were fed with water. The water collected in spots. This section of the department had a dank unwholesome smell.

(C) The foreman was inefficient, had no control over his men, and therefore none over his department. He wasted most of his time doing clerical work that he dragged out almost over the entire day. The men who worked under him were as a class heavy drinkers and independent, worked when they wanted to and quit when they wanted to. The following remedies were suggested and adopted:

(a) Improved lighting. One hundred watt Mazda lamps were installed every twenty feet.

(b) Drain was put in which took care of all excess water, relieving both the discomfort and odor.

(c) The foreman was discharged and a capable man from another department put in his place. This move stiffened up discipline and improved personnel of department.

(d) The entire layout was inspected, safety guards put on all machines where there was any chance of a workman getting injured. Everything possible was done to make the operation of the machine safe and convenient for the men.

(e) Two instructors were installed to teach new men.

(f) All piece rates were carefully analyzed and prices adjusted so that there were no "good jobs" and "bad jobs." They were all made "fair and square jobs." Rates were equalized and set so that men could make an average sum per hour on any kind of work done in the department. Since then there have been several adjustments and still a few to make, but we keep in close touch with the work, and "raise before we are compelled to." This is the department that increased production 18.4 per cent. with five hours per week less running time, and last month had the largest production in the last three years. . . .

Transfers in the factory had never been attempted. If a man did not suit his foreman, he was fired and no questions asked. Now we look into unsatisfactory cases, try to find the cause, remedy it if we can, and if we can't, try to locate the unsatisfactory man in another department.

Just a few cases of what we have done:

We have one young man, of undoubted ability, good personality, pleasant and obliging. He became a regular Monday absentee, took all that was told to him as a reprimand with a lackadaisical air, and had evidently lost his "pep." We found upon investigation that he was fast becoming disgusted with his outlook, and felt that he was up against a blank wall. We transferred him to a semi-executive position in another department, gave him larger responsibilities and a larger salary, and he has more than made good.

Another man was a boss trucker, who made a flat failure of the job. He was then made head inspector of one of our hardest departments, and has done wonders in bringing up the general efficiency of the department. He was temporarily unfitted for one job, and fitted for the other. . . .

To show you how far we have gone I will cite the way disputes were handled before and have been since the creation of this department. Formerly men would stop work in a bunch, demanding something, and refuse to return to work until it was granted. In one case they gave us one hour to consider a question involving fifty men in one department, and before we had time to even digest the demand the hour was up and they walked out. Since April 1, 1915, we have had no strikes nor no threats. We have had two requests, and the men have stayed at work until a decision was reached. I wish to say that if our employment department had done nothing but produce this feeling of personal responsibility to each other on the part of the men and on the part of the firm, it would have justified its existence and its cost.

In conclusion I feel that in the study of employment problems we are trying to solve issues ages old, and while the reward is great from the standpoint of efficient factory management, the reward is still greater if we can but help to solve the principle of humanity involved, and so insure that cooperation without which we can make no progress, and with which the watch-word will be "prosperity for all" and not "prosperity for one."

Four years ago the Vocation Bureau of Boston awoke to a realization that something was wrong with employment methods. Their best efforts in placing young people in the right positions were nullified by a lack of effective cooperation toward the same ends on the part of most employers. There seemed to be little effort to fit the man to the job or the job to the man. A boy would be placed in a position only to lose it or leave it in a short time. In order to get a chance at least to talk things over the Vocation Bureau invited into conference a group of men connected with the various industries in Boston who dealt with the problem of hiring. From that initial conference grew a desire for regular and frequent conferences for the interchange of opinion and experience, and the first association of employing executives in the country.

Managers Organizing in Many Cities

Accordingly the Boston Employment Managers' Association was organized. Not all of the members were "managers" at the outset. The employment problems that were given an airing at these meetings, soon led to the conviction, however, on the part of most of the members, that the man in charge of employment should be a manager in a real sense—an executive with recognized responsibility and authority.

Almost simultaneously, in other parts of the country, notably in Detroit, similar organizations with similar convictions and aims have come into being. From these pioneer organizations the idea has grown until there are now in a dozen cities, from Boston to San Francisco, organizations known as executives' clubs, employment managers' associations and the like which meet regularly to discuss employment problems. Three national conferences have now been held, the first in Minneapolis and the second in Boston—both of these were held last year, the third in Philadelphia in April.

It is difficult to say what this movement may mean to industry. The fact that it is a "movement" is what gives it significance. The individual conceptions in this new idea of employment are not themselves new. Some of them have been practiced for many years by individual employers. The important thing is their rediscovery and their restatement in a form that has taken hold of the imagination of employers the country over and so is gathering adherents like a new crusade.

The movement must give a great impetus to education and to the conservation of human skill. So much it must accomplish merely from the standpoint of getting the right kind of workers into industry. When industrial managers analyze industry itself to see whether it offers a fit career to the kind of men whom they would like to employ, the possibilities in the way of social betterment are very great.

The aims, the full intent of the new type of employment manager, cannot be described except in his own language. Robert C. Clothier, of the Curtis Publishing Company, has said, "The raising of the standard of efficiency of the working force, individually and as a whole, in order that the purchasing power of the wage-dollar may be increased—this as we interpret it is the broad function of the employment department." And he names among the essential principles to be observed, intelligent selection, instruction work, the creation of a "satisfied spirit," the stimulation of hope of advancement by filling positions from within the organization, and the avoidance of arbitrary or unjust dismissals.

President Hopkins, of Dartmouth, who reached his present position through the unique route of employment manager in several large corporations, speaks of the efficiency of a high wage and reasonable hours. "The truth is," he says, "that seemingly there is not yet any general understanding among employers that a high gross payroll does not necessarily result from a high individual wage, or expressed in slightly different terms, that cost per unit of production may be larger the lower the rate of pay to the individual worker."

The same idea is expressed by Boyd Fisher, secretary of the Detroit Executives Club when he says: "One of the most basic remedies for turnover is the payment of an adequate wage. . . . By adequate wage I don't mean merely a minimum wage. I mean a good fat wage. . . . Start your men right, promote physical efficiency, foster good habit, make your work an unfolding career and a sufficient future, and all the time encourage self-expression, not only of complaints but of suggestions and of cooperative interest and activity."

Mr. Fisher, who is one of the most irrepressible optimists in this movement, even goes so far as to recommend that when men must be fired—for he believes that "there is a legitimate place yet for the tin can"—"every discharge should be certified by a committee on which workmen are represented." This sounds like a radical proposition, yet at the Filene store in Boston no employee has been discharged for years without right of appeal to a board on which not only are employees "represented," but which is composed exclusively of employees. This board has reinstated some employees who have been discharged by the store, and others they have refused to reinstate. No one can come in contact with its work without being deeply impressed by the uncompromising standard of justice that has been set up toward the store management as well as toward the employees.

The Promise for Both Masters and Men

It would be too much to expect that industry in general will soon be conducted in accordance with these ideas. The labor policies of some of the largest corporations in the country are based on theories that are vastly different. But the fact that these new ideas in employment are finding such wide acceptance among employers and industrial managers does justify the hope that great changes are on their way—changes that will mean vastly improved conditions of living and of work, more amicable industrial relations and better industrial practice in every way, affording benefits to the employee and to the employer as well.

The new idea in employment methods must have the effect of changing altogether the attitude of mind of the employer as he approaches any question involving the satisfaction of his employees. The old, narrow-minded attitude that refuses to meet a committee must give way to a more tolerant, a more scientific spirit. An employer doesn't refuse to give any consideration to a machine that has broken down, he tries to get at the cause; he doesn't curse a piece of material that fails to meet the required test, he sends it to the chemist for analysis.

It doesn't pay to have a different formula for treating human reactions. Dissatisfied men are expensive men to employ. The new attitude towards these matters is going to lead the employer sooner or later to consider coolly and on its merits every conceivable need and desire of the workers in his plant. It will lead him out into the community to discover whether there exists an opportunity for comfortable living at the wage he pays. And finally it must lead him to consider the question of the participation of the employees in problems of management. One of the biggest shoe companies in the country has 20 per cent of its employees in training all the time for executive positions. That number of men alternate between work on their machines and on executive work. Another has found it worth while to spend time explaining to the men its production problems. It turns over to the men all the knowledge in its possession, leads them to see the job not as a mechanical process but as a problem to be solved and thus it enlists their cooperation and at the same time gives them something worth working for.

"The Voice with the Smile Wins"

The way you meet and greet a fellow worker can make a friend or enemy of him. You know that. But do you know that if he is a foreigner it can do more? It can make him more friendly to America, or it can make him more hostile to America. Why? Because the foreigner must judge America mainly by the Americans he meets and the way they greet him. Put a smile in your voice. Don't make "good morning" sound like "bad cess to you."

Reprinted from *Personnel*, Vol. 1, No. 2, 1919, p. 3.

It isn't industrial democracy—whatever that is—not yet. But the men in this new movement have said goodby to tradition. They have turned their backs on prejudice and the closed mind. They are ready to give a hearing to new methods in dealing with employees and even to give them a trial. When a big idea gets into the minds of men like that they are worth watching and the whole world is before them.

16

Storm Clouds on the Horizon: 1920

Looking Forward

PERSONNEL

The pessimistic tone prevailing for the past few months seems to be gradually disappearing and in its place there is an undertone of optimism that increases in volume daily. Here and there the silver lining of the dark clouds that have been obscuring the industrial skies begins to show and it is fast becoming the general opinion that the lowest point has been reached and that the next few weeks will see the beginning of a gradual return to normal.

Wages are coming down, it is true, but so are prices. With the Christmas trade out of the way, there is every likelihood that retail prices will drop to within a short distance of where they were in pre-war days. It is extremely probable that they will never again get down to the point reached during 1912-13. In-as-much as wages are unlikely to drop to the point where they were in those years, this fact is immaterial. As long as the purchasing power of the dollar gets somewhere near normal, all that the worker needs is the work.

At this point it would seem to be the providence of the industrial heads to make and develop their plans for the good times coming. In many cases the changed conditions necessitate new or greatly changed organizations. Careful study of production methods is necessary in order that when work is resumed the highest efficiency at the lowest cost may be secured. War time methods must be changed to peace time—and probably severe competition—methods. In this period of slackening would seem to be the time to build the foundation for the future.

In some quarters there has been the fear expressed that Employment and Personnel work would die out now that reconstruction was being effected. There need not be this fear. This fear is ungrounded. Instead, there will be a greater field for the work. Based on common sense and shorn of the frills of theorists, it will be a more integral part of industry than ever before. On the proper relationship between men and management rests the success of the industry. The bringing about of this relationship will require the services of men and women with good, hard common

 Reprinted from *Personnel*, Vol. 3, No. 1, January, 1921, p. 6.

sense; who know the human equation and who will be able to accomplish real results, so that instead of being the non-productive branch it has heretofore been held, the Employment and Personnel Departments will be able to show real dollars and cents earnings to the company.

17

Rain: 1922

Industrial Conditions Cause Postponement of St. Louis Convention

PERSONNEL

Existing industrial conditions caused the Board of Directors of the Industrial Relations Association of America, on March 10, to vote to postpone the annual convention scheduled for St. Louis, May 3, 4 and 5, until an improvement is noted. The action, taken after a lengthy and serious discussion, should commend itself to industrial heads throughout the country as one of the chief considerations causing the postponement, was the saving of money and the time of the employment and personnel director. The curtailment of expense in all branches of industry has been absolutely necessary during the period of readjustment and it was the general opinion that the action of the Board in keeping down the outlay of money at this time, would be heartily welcomed by the higher executives. It is estimated that the cost to industry, based on an attendance of less than 1,000, would have been over $200,000 had the Convention been held at this time.

The action taken, however, does not mean that a convention will not be held during 1921. Should conditions improve in the manner now indicated, during the Spring and Summer months, plans already under way will be perfected for the holding of the annual session during the early Fall months, either September or October.

Encouragement

Just a word of encouragement and hopefulness for the future to those who are passing through periods of Industrial inactivity. There may be some discouraged because there is little call at this time to use their talent to employ. May we not profit by grasping this opportunity

Reprinted from *Personnel*, Vol. 3, No. 3, March, 1921, pp. 1, 4, 6.

This was the last issue of *Personnel* until 1927, when the American Management Association revived it.

to take account of stock and set our departments in order for the busier times ahead, to simplify and perfect any of the practices which have been followed under great pressure.

Though our energies in the past have been centered with great intensity on employing it may be that we have come to think of this work as the chief aim of the Employment Manager. We should now work intensively to cultivate the human touch—the working-point of contact—to be better able to meet the demands that will be made on us in the future.

Efficient employment practices have found such justification in the results experienced by both employers and employees alike, that we may expect the basic principles to be retained and the work to forge ahead following the present temporary lull in business. Notwithstanding the fact that the immediate outlook justifies the conservation of resources, particularly along the lines of large money expenditures for certain projects in Industrial Relations, nevertheless, the far-seeing employers are retaining, and if anything, strengthening their interest in Employment Relations. They will unquestionably look in the future to the Employment Managers Industrial Relations Heads for much assistance when business is actively resumed.

J. M. LARKIN
President, I. R. A. A.

Testing Out "Industrial Relations"

Some cynicism is developing out of the readjustment in industry as it affects employment and wages and in general the relations of employers and employees. A good many employers are quick to say that the events of the past three or four months have put a quietus on the "employee representation" movement that for a while had so much attention. The so-called experts on co-operation between workmen and managers, who were so much in demand two or three years ago, to a large extent have lost their occupation. Some of the employers who turned to these men for help, when their production problems had become their despair, are now rather disposed to say that it was not so much of a shower as they took it to be. Labor union leaders who held up national trade organization as labor's only ark of safety and frowned on local or shop solidarity as a delusion and a snare, are now saying that events have proved that they were right. Workers who accepted shop councils or any other plan of employee representation are reminded by these leaders that they had fair warning.

Sometimes the whole argument is put into a question, like that an organizer asked last week of a group of unemployed men: "What good did 'industrial democracy' or the Bridgeport plan do you at Ams when they decided they hadn't anything for you to do?" Of course, the deciding referred to was not done by the management, but by the usual buyers of the product of these works, who for the time being were getting along without it. But the agitator chose to put it the more sinister way.

A New York paper prints a long article from an "industrial expert" who starts out by saying that "the mushroom growth of industrial relations departments that sprang up during the war has been washed out to a large extent by the reversal of trade and labor conditions." He cites various cases, and what he says of an Illinois automobile parts company and of an electric company will serve for the rest. In the spring of 1920 the former company employed an industrial relations superintendent to develop many phases of this work with employees.

A promising beginning had been made when cancellations of orders trickled in. Presently these cancellations were pouring in so fast that it was deemed expedient to weed out the less desirable employees. This was done gradually, until the plant was running at 50 per cent capacity. The company found that the employees retained were so eager to hold their places at reduced wages that the industrial relations department seemed unnecessary. The staff of this department was released, but two of the features installed were saved and their supervision was taken over by a member of the firm. . . .

One of our largest electric companies, which was said to have more than half a hundred persons on its industrial relations staff under an expert labor man who has been building up the department for over four years, has dispensed with all of this personnel force, and is said to have reverted to the plan of using a few record clerks for foremen's hiring and "firing."

It is doubtless the fact that very much of the industrial relations work of 1919 and 1920 was an expedient. Many employers turned to it as a solution of their well-nigh impossible production problems. They spent a certain amount of money—a good deal of money, many of them—to get their production up, chiefly by getting employees into a better state of mind regarding their work. Now that that part of the old force which is employed is doing more work, the laying aside or the scrapping of the special machinery for increasing output is one of various measures of economy. It is true, as said in the article quoted from above, that "the best of the industrial relations departments have made progress in interpreting the management and the operatives to each other" and the author is probably right in adding that "when the cycle is complete and trade and labor conditions are again swinging across the upper half of the circle, we may expect another crop of these departments."

Obviously, however, this opportunist treatment of the great questions involved in industrial relations comes out nowhere. If there is need of a better understanding by employees of the economic principles underlying modern business, it would be well to have educational work in that direction go on continuously. If contact between management and workmen was desirable when the plant was full of work, it is desirable now when labor union leaders are sending the word out to employees that their employers are trying to take an unjust advantage of them. There are companies, not a few, which set out some years ago to establish a better understanding with their men and have kept on in that endeavor, with no thought of making the relation merely a fair weather one. The plants of these companies are affected by the depression just as others are, but if there has been sincerity in the effort carried on heretofore, there will be more give and take in these months of slack work and less of the spirit of "let him take who can." The fact that pessimism will be fashionable for some time in respect to industrial relations work should not mean the loss of all that has been built up patiently in good times and bad. The autocratic unionism that fastened so many uneconomic restrictions upon industry during the war and since, and that thrives on division between employers and employees, would be well pleased to see every plan for local co-operation in industry go on the scrap heap. That fact should give the pessimists food for thought.

18

Modest Progress: 1922-1929

Trends in Personnel Administration

W. J. DONALD AND E. K. DONALD

There are so many different industrial sections of the United States of America, each of them influenced more or less by the dominance of different types of industry and affected by different stages of industrial development, that any attempt dogmatically to indicate the personnel trends in America is likely to be subject to so many lines of dispute as to make the effort almost reckless.

This paper will, therefore, attempt simply to survey the most outstanding new developments and to indicate trends which are likely to become most marked in the next few years.

Organization of Personnel Administration

The time was when personnel work was largely regarded as the job of the personnel man and there were many persons who argued that the personnel department should have entire control of personnel administration. This was true particularly of the period from approximately 1914 to 1920, when personnel administration was being rapidly developed and when personnel men were struggling for a degree of recognition, influence, and even authority which previously they had not had. The natural result was that with notable exceptions there was an over-emphasis of the authority of the personnel man and an under-emphasis of the personnel functions of the line organization from foreman to president. This resulted in many conflicts of jurisdiction and authority which were very disturbing to the effective execution of a personnel program.

Since the great depression in 1920 and 1921, including among many other things some deflation of the personnel movement, a rather different point of view has grown up.

In the first place, it has become a generally accepted principle that personnel administration is a function of every person who supervises others in the organization. One hears speakers and finds writers discussing the qualities of foremen in terms of whether or not the foreman is a good personnel man, and there are even references to presidents and general managers as good personnel men. There are not a few presidents of companies who openly make the statement that they are the chief personnel directors of their companies.

 Reprinted from the *Harvard Business Review*, Vol. 7, 1928-29, pp. 143-155.

As a result, personnel men, instead of claiming that they have absolute power in selection, placement, and dismissal of workers, regardless of any preference or conviction on the part of the foreman, are now claiming that it is the function of the personnel department to facilitate the work of the supervisor in dealing with the personnel problems involved in management. "Facilitation," the admirably expressive term used by Mr. Oliver Sheldon in his excellent book, *The Philosophy of Management*, is a term which is beginning to make its influence felt in the United States and a term which gradually is being used more and more generally. The personnel department is thus being recognized as a facilitating department, its functions being to assist the organization in the preparation and execution of personnel policy through research, advice, and cooperation.

Organization for Selection

An employment manager, for instance, does the initial job of weeding out the applicants for employment, selecting those who would have a fair chance of fitting well into the organization, and referring them to the supervisor who is in need of additional help. In making this selection, the employment manager, of course, weeds out persons whom the supervisor might be disposed to employ but who would not fit well into the organization. It is still true, and probably will continue to be true in the majority of companies, that no supervisor will be permitted to employ men who have not had the approval of the employment department. But the power of employment managers to prevent a foreman from dismissing an employee from his department has practically disappeared. Every foreman has, or should have, the power to dismiss from his department, referring the employee to the employment department either for a final separation from the company or for transfer to some other department. On the other hand, most personnel departments have the responsibility of transferring men from one department to another within the company even against the wishes of department heads who may wish to keep men in their respective departments. In common practice department heads have learned the value of cooperation in this matter, and transfers are made without friction.

In the light of this newer point of view, responsibility for results is clearly indicated and there is no confusion as to authority in regard to the administration of any department of a company. In cases where supervisors have an unusual turnover or seem unwilling to cooperate with the employment department, either by releasing men for transfer or by accepting a reasonable proportion of men selected by the employment department for employment, the solution of such difficulties lies in the possibility of the employment department's recommending to executives, higher up than the offending supervisor, the possibility of the removal of the foreman or the correction of the abuses for which he has been responsible.

In the development of the principle that personnel administration is an integral part of management, there have been several other evidences of progress. For instance, it is customary for supervisors to participate in the preparation of such documents as a manual of employment procedure or a syllabus of instructional outlines for the training of employees. Members of the line organization, including the foreman, are much more likely to cooperate in carrying out the personnel program when they have had a part in the preparation of the policy and program and of the tools which are to be used in making them effective.

One very logical corollary of the newer point of view is an effort to train the supervisor in the process of carrying out the company's personnel program. In some companies this has been done informally for years and is simply instinctive good management. Indeed, there often is no thought-out philosophy with regard to such an interpretation of policy. It is merely an expression of the good sense or natural inclination of the leaders of the business. But in very large organizations, even though the upper executives have this spirit and vision, it becomes extremely diluted before reaching the lowest ranks of supervisors. Therefore, it is highly desirable that some more or less formal steps should be taken to convey this policy effectively down throughout the organization.

In the last two or three years a few companies have begun to train the supervisor in the carrying out of the company's personnel program. Without such steps, the personnel work of a large organization is likely to fall down at its weakest point, and all the energetic, intelligent and well-informed efforts of the director of personnel will scarcely get past first base unless steps are taken to strengthen all the positions on the team by which the personnel program of the company must be carried out.

Organization for Training

This need for training all along the line finds expression most clearly in a company's program for the training of employees. The training of rank-and-file employees has been conspicuous in American industry for nearly 30 years. At first the emphasis was primarily on what might be called education as distinguished from training. In a good many cases such an educational movement was initiated by an executive officer of the company who himself had had comparatively few educational advantages and who was inspired to give to his employees advantages which he had not enjoyed himself. The motive was essentially philanthropic rather than economic, and the driving power was emotional rather than intellectual. A contributing factor was the need for training in English and citizenship for the large number of non-English-speaking immigrant workers. A good deal of the instructional material had little bearing on training for the job and might be regarded as a substitute for the work of the public schools.

During the war and its attendant industrial boom, industry was forced to lay emphasis on training for the immediate job, the consequence being a rapid growth of vestibule schools which provided quick instruction in the elements of performing the job. Consequently, there was a shift from an emphasis on what may be fairly called industrial education to job training.

Meanwhile, industrial training began to feel the influence of different pedagogical ideas. Whereas the earlier instruction offered by companies was conducted by what was called "corporation schools" with formal class rooms, instructors, et cetera, the newer tendency was for training the worker in actual production under an instructor foreman, and this change in method brought such quick and effective results that it was a very large factor in making possible the increase in wage levels which took place during the long boom period from 1914 to 1920.

The Project Method of Teaching

Into American business has come of recent years a group of advanced pedagogical thinkers from the university schools of education. They have brought with them the project method of teaching, involving what we now commonly call training on the job, and the preliminary steps that were taken during the war have in some quarters been carried much further to the extent that the supervisor, regarded as the real teacher of the worker, is being trained in the process of teaching so that he may perform his functions better than ever before, better than the training function was performed by corporation schools and better than it was performed by the foreman or the journeyman before the era of corporation schools began.[1]

The president of one of our most progressive companies has frankly said that management is in large measure an education and training job. He illustrates this by telling how on one occasion a number of executives of his company analyzed management in terms of specific operations and that after classifying all the typical operations, nine out of ten of them were listed under education and training. The reasonable inference from this analysis is that a great proportion of the training falls upon the shoulders of the supervisor and, in order to get that training done effectively, he himself must be taught to train. This naturally raises the question as to what is the function of an educational or training department. The answer may be given under four main headings.

1. To provide that enthusiasm and promotive quality which spreads interest in training throughout the organization and creates desire and willingness on the part of every supervisor to take part in the training process.
2. To help to prepare the instructional outlines to be used by supervisors in the training of their workers. One says "help" advisedly because it may easily be recognized that when the supervisors themselves have prepared the instructional outlines with the help of an educational department, they are much more likely to take an interest in the training program and to feel a definite responsibility for making it actually effective.
3. To prepare, improve, and constantly revise the procedure for carrying out the training program, thus facilitating the work of the supervisor.
4. To take a very active part in training the supervisor to train.

On this point it might be argued that the higher executives ought to have the responsibility of training the supervisor to train, and doubtless as time goes on they will participate more generally in this phase of the training program. There are instances where a general manager has actually

[1] One of the largest electric manufacturing companies has practically done away with all formal classroom instruction of employees and is concentrating its efforts on training the foremen to train others. A syllabus for supervisors in an electrical public-utility company consists almost wholly of material which deals with teacher training for foremen. The assumption is that in order to make the training program really effective, steps must be taken to have the training of the worker continuous from the time of entering the plant until he leaves it, and the principle is followed that the best training is that which is given in connection with actual work under normal circumstances of supervision, incentive, and responsibility.

taken this position, and, having done so, has expected his associates next in line to take the same attitude with those further down in the organization.

Labor Supply

When the personnel movement first began in America, the chief emphasis was placed on those problems which have to do largely with the manual working force. This was intensified during the war period by the comparative dearth of labor. There is, of course, no less attention to these problems today than ever before, thanks partly to immigration restrictions and the fact that were it not for increased output per man-hour due to "labor saving machinery," "labor saving management," and better morale, the United States would be faced with a serious dearth of labor today. The labor-supply problem in America is likely to continue to be an important one. Indeed, there are those who believe that the present situation, in which there are comparatively few strikes and a small surplus of labor for employment, may not continue for many years.

During the last three or four years the output per man has been greatly increased through vast installations of effort-saving machinery and the introduction of incentives for factory workers and other similar measures, but it is a serious question whether the rate of increase of output per man-hour can be kept up and whether, with the growth of American industry and continued immigration restriction, a dearth of labor will not reappear in serious form in the course of the next decade.

Research

Reference has been made to the advisory relationship of a personnel department to the line organization. It will be recognized, of course, that the effects of sound advice must be based not only on the personality and promotive qualities of the director of personnel activities, but also on scientific research in the field of personnel management. Incident to this changing conception by reason of which the personnel job has been placed squarely on the shoulders of the supervisor, the personnel department has been relieved to a considerable extent of what may be called operating personnel responsibilities, and is thus left time for more intensive research into the personnel problems of the company. Consequently, personnel departments are less disturbed than formerly by interruptions and are better able to concentrate on more fundamental investigations of personnel problems. These have taken many directions, such as research on hours of work, bonus plans, pensions, profit-sharing systems, group insurance, suggestion systems, employee investments in company securities, savings plans, mutual-benefit plans, discovery of methods of labor stabilization, and have even led to the developing of wholly new lines of products intended to fill in seasonal gaps in employment.

Sales and Office Personnel Problems

The end of the war marked the beginning of more severe competition due in part to excessive plant capacity. But the competitive struggle became intensified through increasing competition between lines of industry producing substitute commodities—the radio has begun to take the place of the talking machine, cement is making inroads in the construction industry, giving brick and steel construction a new line of competition more severe than they ever experienced within their own industry. Improved transportation facilities bring sources of supply in competition with each other which formerly were serving non-competing territories.

The result has been a severe demand upon the manufacturing end of business to bring costs of production down to even lower levels. The factory executives have begun to protest and to urge that similar economies and reductions of unit costs be made in the marketing and administration expenses. As a consequence, personnel problems, which at one time seemed to be confined largely to the manufacturing side of business concerns, now are beginning to be recognized more and more clearly in the distributing and adminstrative departments. Office-personnel departments and sales-personnel departments have been established in many American companies during the last few years. Banks and insurance companies are giving attention to office personnel problems in much the same manner that was formerly given to manual workers by manufacturing companies. The careful selection and training of salesmen has become recognized as important as the training and selection of labor.

Organization of Personnel Departments

Another result has been that not infrequently a company may have several personnel departments existing side by side. An office manager who is also a manager of the office personnel department, a factory personnel department, and a sales-personnel department may be found in the same concern. In a company with several plants there are usually managers of personnel departments at each of the factories, with a central personnel department which has no authority over the personnel men in the various factories or other units, but which cooperates by providing information and advice for the personnel men in the various units as well as for the major executives of those units. There are instances of marketing organizations which have managers of personnel departments in their branch offices.

Some years ago it was not unusual for companies to have several men each in charge of a phase of the personnel work. A company might possess an employment manager, a manager of the educational department, a secretary of the pension committee, a secretary of the mutual-benefit association, a safety engineer, et cetera, et cetera. In recent years there has been a tendency to coordinate these activities into one personnel department in charge of a chief assisted by specialists in the various problems of personnel.

One typical personnel department is headed by a supervisor of industrial relations who has as his associates a safety engineer, a manager of the employment department for headquarters, a personnel statistician, an educational director, a manager of the company store, and a medical director. Most of these have an advisory relation to the executives of branch offices and branch factories as well as to personnel men in those respective units.

The position of the personnel man in the general organization differs in various firms as is often indicated by his title. There are a number of instances of personnel men who are staff vice-presidents of their companies. "Employment Manager" was a title very generally found a few years ago, but at present it has been superseded in many concerns by titles containing the word, "personnel." For a time the title, "Personnel

Manager," was spreading rapidly, but recently such titles as "Director of Personnel Activities" and "Supervisor of Industrial Relations" have become more common. The fact that the title, "Personnel Manager," is gradually disappearing reflects the point of view that the personnel man does not manage or direct the personnel, but rather manages or directs the work of the personnel department. The management of the personnel has become increasingly the province of the line supervisor. There is, however, very little uniformity in titles: "Manager of Personnel Activities," "Service Manager," "Manager of Training Activities," and many others are found at present in common use.

Certain definite trends may be recognized in the various phases of the activities of personnel management.

Wages and Salaries

There has been a very marked tendency toward the growth of extra incentives in the compensation of employees. There are, as is well known, a great variety of formulae for setting up a compensation plan, about 25 of them being known by the names of the men who invented them. There are, in addition, a great many others which are adaptations of these.

One of the most significant developments is a comparatively rapid growth of group bonus plans for manual workers, intended to give additional compensation to the group on the basis of the output of the group. Sometimes these groups consist of men engaged in work of the same kind but in which several men must cooperate. In other cases, the group consists of men who carry on a series of operations through their several steps. In some cases the foreman is included in the group or at least receives extra compensation based on the output of the group.

One of the distinct advantages of the group bonus plan is that it puts a premium on cooperation, encourages workers to insist upon their fellow-workers doing a fair share of the work, and being on the job promptly each day. In some cases, it encourages the worker to help train his fellow-worker.

In dealing with the sales force extra incentives through commission plans or bonus plans are becoming very general. Until recently, however, there have been comparatively few instances of compensating office employees on the basis of a measured output. This has been due, in large measure, to the difficulty in measuring the output of various classes of office employees. In the last few years, however, some very substantial work has been done in developing methods of measuring office-employee output. The number of companies which are applying these methods is rapidly increasing, and new techniques have been evolved for measuring certain classes of office work which previously had defied measurement.

This development is making it possible to compensate office employees on the basis of their output, and the next few years will probably see a very substantial development in this direction.

An intermediate stage in the compensation of office workers has been the development of what is usually referred to as job classification and salary standardization, in which jobs are rated and classified and minimum and maximum limits set for classes of jobs.

Profit-Sharing

In general, it may be said that the growth of profit-sharing as applied to rank-and-file workers has practically been abandoned in America. The conviction has grown that, while profit-sharing may be an excellent arrangement as applied to persons of some responsibility, it has comparatively little effect on the rank and file, and is always in danger of creating ill will when a period of low profits or of no profits arrives.

Incentives, which are based on the actual output of the individual and an extra compensation paid very shortly after the production period has been completed, have in large measure taken the place of profit-sharing as applied to rank-and-file employees.

Compensation of Executives

In the days when ownership and management were almost inseparable, the compensation of the manager was equivalent to the profits of the business, but with the practical divorce of management from ownership which came with large-scale industry and the development of the corporation, the first tendency was to put the manager on a salary, his dividends from stocks comprising a comparatively small part of his total income. There were, of course, many private "deals" in which the manager was paid a salary and received as additional compensation either a bonus based on profits for the year or the dividends on stocks which were assigned to him and which by good management he might make extremely valuable. These cases applied, however, chiefly to the president or general manager of a company.

In recent years there has been a distinct tendency toward applying the principle of extra incentive to other executives—factory managers, district sales managers, the foreman and other supervisors, and even to staff men—the result of whose efforts it is usually comparatively hard to measure.

Some of these plans take the form of the more or less old-fashioned profit-sharing plan. In general, the tendency, however, has been to base the extra compensation, so far as possible, on a measurement of the results of the efforts of the particular individual. The net result of this departure is to reintroduce into large-scale business in America some of the elements of incentive which were general when business was small and when the manager was also usually owner and thus had a direct interest in the business.

Hours of Work

The work time per day and per week has been decreasing in America over a long period of years. One of the greatest issues of public importance was the steel industry's twelve-hour day, which three years ago became a thing of the past. The elimination of the twelve-hour day in the steel industry does not seem to have in any way justified the alarming predictions which some persons were disposed to make. In fact, there were many people in the steel industry who believed that it could have been done long before.

During the last two years the most significant occurrence was the adoption of the five-day week by the Ford Motor Company and the growth of a good deal of propaganda in favor of the general spread of the five-day week. There has been comparatively little evidence that the movement is spreading widely, but there are those who predict that five or ten years from now the five-day week will be as general then as the five-and-a-half-day week is today.

Vacations for Manual Workers

Vacations with pay for executives and office workers have long been general, only a comparatively small number of companies holding out against vacations with pay for office workers.

More recently vacations for manual workers have become more general. In some quarters the opinion is held that this vacation with pay increases the loyalty and efficiency of the worker and that it pays profits to the company even though it does somewhat upset the production schedule. A great deal depends upon the character of the industry and the custom of the community.

It may fairly be said that, while there is no well-thought-out attitude on the practice of vacations with pay and that the practice is more or less a matter of expediency, nevertheless it is probably gradually becoming an unwritten part of the contract of employment.

No American state has made vacations with pay a legal requirement. Even in Canada, where this step has been agitated by labor organizations, no such action has been taken, nor is there any likelihood that such legislation will be passed in view of the rapid spread of vacations with pay.

Pensions

Pensions have been rapidly becoming a part of the industrial fabric of America, at first slyly in the form of informal pension plans in the nature of special treatment of individual cases, and later more openly through the adoption of formal pension plans. The topic is subject to a great deal of dispute, and some companies, which established pension plans some years ago on a rather liberal basis, are beginning to find that the accumulating pension cost is much higher than they had anticipated. The tendency now is, partly in order to keep down the pension cost of companies, to put pension plans on a contributory rather than the non-contributory basis on which most of the earlier pension plans were based.

Stock-Purchase and Savings Plans

A good many companies have provided for the purchase of the securities of the company by the employees. At first such plans were established largely in the expectation that they would increase the loyalty and the efficiency of the employees by giving them an interest in the company. Some of these plans were very generous, the company in many cases making a partial contribution.

More recently, the emphasis has been placed on the thrift and savings aspect of the purchase of company securities by the employees, and the contemporary stock-purchase plans have therefore taken on a somewhat more conservative aspect.

One large company has established what is practically an investment trust, an affiliated securities corporation, the shares of which employees buy. The securities corporation in turn purchases a variety of securities, including the bonds, preferred and common stocks of the manufacturing company, as well as the securities of other companies.

Insurance and Benefit Plans

Group life insurance has been one of the substantial developments of the last ten years. Altogether there was approximately six and one-half billion dollars of group life insurance in effect at the beginning of 1928. At first, a large proportion of group life-insurance plans were non-contributory—that is, the company paid the whole cost—but more recently there has been a very strong tendency toward having the employee share in the cost.

Similarly, there has been a decided growth of benefit plans, a movement which began earlier than did group life insurance. These benefit plans provide a scale of benefits for certain disabilities including accidents, sickness, and death. In many cases they exist side by side with group life insurance. In other cases they are more or less a substitute for group life insurance. As in the case of group life insurance, there has been a movement toward requiring contributions from the company and also toward the administration of the mutual-benefit fund by an employees' committee with the advice and cooperation of executives of the company.

Vocational Adjustment

The importance of the preparation of job descriptions and job specifications has been much discussed, but until recently the discussions had not led to much definite action, the logical step following job analysis. Such specifications are essential for any plan of job classification and salary standardization. One distinct tendency in job analysis is the setting-up of a statement accentuating the "job difficulties."

The introduction of new employees to their jobs, especially to the foreman and to the fellow-workers, and to their environment is being performed more effectively than ever before with distinct advantage not only to the company but also to the employee. Increased output and increased earnings during the initial period of employment and reduced turnover among new employees are the results to be gained.

Gradually the idea of transfers and promotions from within the organization is spreading, without, however, taking the form of a rigid rule which prevents the recruiting of necessary specialists from outside the organization.

The rating of rank-and-file employees, which was much practiced some years ago, has largely been eclipsed by the growing attention to the rating of persons of possible eligibility for promotion to executive positions of greater responsibility.

Promotion within the company is a policy adopted by a few companies with good effects on the morale of the organization.

Health and Sanitation

Promotion of health and sanitation has probably been the least effective of all movements in personnel administration, but this is a subject which is beginning to attract a great deal more attention. The costs to the company and to the employees of ill health, consequent absence from work or inefficiency on the job, are regarded by many as vastly more important than the accident problem to which a great deal of attention has been given in the past.

In nearly all large companies medical examination prior to employment is the rule, but compulsory periodic medical examination for those already on the payroll has not yet been generally adopted. There are some companies following this policy and they are emphatic in their praise of it, claiming that it has been attended by no serious complications or objections on the part of the employees.

In most companies, however, emphasis has been placed on health education rather than upon compulsory examination, and the general practice has been to concentrate not so much on the rank-and-file employees as upon the supervisors, who in turn carry the message of the health program to the employees. This is another good illustration of the advantages of a decentralized responsibility in personnel administration.

Safety

Because of the spectacular losses resulting from industrial accidents, a great deal of effort has been expended on reducing the number and seriousness of such accidents. Workmen's compensation legislation has been passed in all but three of the states, and safety work is vigorously promoted in many companies both large and small.

Results from this phase of industrial-relations work can be isolated more easily than from any other, and this very quality of tangibility has undoubtedly had a great deal to do with the interest shown in accident prevention. Certainly the record of accomplishment is so remarkable, in companies where sustained and intelligent effort has been made, that it should serve to convince any set of officials of its value.

Figures issued yearly by one large corporation indicate what can be done. From 1906 to 1926 serious and fatal accidents decreased 60.22 per cent, and from 1912 to 1926 disabling accidents (including all accidents with loss of time greater than the working turn) were reduced 83.81 per cent. This decrease has been concurrent with a marked expansion in properties and in numbers of employees. The results have been accomplished by careful engineering, which has removed physical hazards in the plant or on machines; by keeping complete records of accidents subdivided by cause, which indicate where added precautions are necessary; and by a ceaseless campaign of education. Each is necessary, but perhaps the educational campaign has yielded the greatest returns.

About $20,000,000 has been spent on accident prevention since January 1, 1912. Had accidents continued at the 1906 rate, however, far more would have been paid out under the various state compensation laws to the injured and their families. If, as a large insurance company recently stated, it is true that to every dollar of compensation cost resulting from an accident must be added four dollars to pay for lost time, labor turnover, waste of materials, interference in production, and other conditions arising out of the accident, the saving from accident prevention is many times greater.

While for some years safety education was directed largely toward rank-and-file employees, it has been found by another very large company that still greater improvement can be made by concentrating the safety educational personnel activities and of carrying out the personnel program through and by the line organization.

Service to Employees

In the early stages of the personnel movement in America, a relatively large proportion of attention was devoted to what was called welfare work, comprising such activities as social clubs, recreational activities, camps, athletic activities, employee publications, company stores, sales and discounts for company products, legal aid, housing, and restaurants.

Probably as much is done by companies today as formerly along these lines, but this general group of personnel activities is much less conspicuous because it is being overshadowed by many newer and relatively more important activities.

There has also been a tendency to eliminate certain classes of personnel service and to continue only those which have a direct bearing on the efficiency of the employee, his earning capacity and, by implication, his value to the company.

Other activities which have a much less direct bearing on the company's interests are being turned over more and more to actual administration by the interested employees themselves, and many of these are financed almost entirely by the employees. This gives employees an increased measure of autonomy and a more self-respecting status. This tendency is a good illustration of the trend away from a paternalistic attitude toward employees.

Joint Relationships

The term "joint relationships" is used in the United States to designate the dealings between management and employees on matters of mutual interest, particularly as affecting such vital subjects as wages, hours, and working conditions; discipline and grievances; and efficiency and economy of operation. In industries in which employers recognize trade unions, joint relationships usually are handled between the management and the union organizations. Union contracts customarily cover wages, hours of work, and general conditions in the shop, and occasionally they include agreements for the mediation or arbitration of disagreements, for unemployment insurance, or for other subjects outside the routine of ordinary union negotiations. There has also grown up in some industries a system of union-management cooperation, having for its purpose joint endeavors toward the promotion of operating efficiency, the reduction of costs, and the building-up of morale. The union labor movement is treated in another paper in this series.

Employee Representation

Perhaps the most impressive development of recent years in connection with joint relationships in American industry is employee representation. Under this classification are included all formal agreements for direct dealing between management and representatives elected by and from the employees in an individual company or plant.

The representation movement as a conspicuous part of industrial management dates from about 1915 and the period of its greatest growth did not begin until after the United States entered the World War. In the period of business depression beginning in 1921, a considerable number of plans were abandoned, but in the last five years representation has shown a steady growth.

Under the typical plan of employee representation the workmen of a single company elect representatives from among their own number, usually by voting districts arranged in such a way that each representative has for his constituents fellow-workers with whose conditions and jobs he is intimately familiar. These employee representatives deal with representatives of the management through joint conferences and joint committees and in other ways. The authority of the shop committees or works councils and the scope of subjects which they are authorized to consider vary in the procedure of different companies. While in a few cases, employees are prohibited from joining unions or from joining a particular union that has been in active opposition to the employing company, it is usual for a representation plan to provide explicitly or tacitly for the undiscriminating employment of union and non-union men.

In addition to the organized practices in joint relationships that have been discussed, there are many less formal methods of dealing with subjects of mutual interest. In some companies the approach of the employees to the management is limited to line officials, with whom the individual workman is required to take up grievances or suggestions. In others the personnel department functions as the point of contact between management and employees. There are infrequent cases in which members of the company's boards of directors are elected by rank-and-file employees.

An important function of any procedure in joint relationships is the exchange of information and opinions between management and work-people. Sometimes this is effected through a representation plan or an agreement for union-management cooperation, sometimes through employees' newspapers or other plant publications, and sometimes through more or less formal suggestion systems under which workmen are encouraged to submit to the management their ideas as to improving conditions or methods of operation. Usually these suggestion plans include the payment of awards for valuable ideas that are adopted.

Interest in Personnel Administration Growing

In the last few years there have been times when, on the surface, it might seem as though the personnel movement in America had received a set-back. This impression was caused largely by the fact that at various times there seemed to be an unusual number of personnel men looking for positions. It may be stated that there is vastly more interest in personnel administration in America than ever before and that this interest is on a sounder basis. For some years it was difficult to get the factory manager or the president or other line officials to take an interest in personnel problems, the inclination being to refer all such matters to the personnel man. With the growing recognition that personnel administration on a sound basis has a definite relation to the business success of the organization, a good deal of this former indifference has disappeared.

Furthermore, it is being recognized that sound management has a very definite relation to the interests of the employees, and that the introduction of effort-saving machinery and labor-saving management and the development of better morale almost inevitably result in greater output as a result of which the employees receive increased earnings.

An interest in personnel administration has become an eminently respectable subject for discussion in business meetings, especially as the subject-matter is approached in terms of management. Indeed, it would be practically impossible to keep the subject of personnel out of any meeting of executives discussing almost any management problem, whether it be a meeting of treasurers or comptrollers at a conference on financial management; of factory executives at a conference on production; of sales executives at a conference on marketing; of office managers discussing office management; or at a round-table of presidents discussing problems of general management.

What appeared to be a period of declining interest in personnel administration from approximately 1920 to 1924 may now be interpreted as a period of transition which has led to a sounder concept of the function of personnel activity in the management of the concern and of its relation to the welfare of the community at large.

19

Survey of Practices: ca. 1930

A Survey of Personnel Management in 195 Concerns

STANLEY B. MATHEWSON

The purpose of this article is to present some facts as to actual use of various principles, practices and instruments in personnel management. To do this it was necessary to obtain accurate information concerning the development of personnel management in some of the most important industrial organizations throughout the United States. It is difficult to obtain such information. No matter how carefully a random sampling is sought, the end-product is likely to be a selected list of concerns. The selection, however, is a natural one; natural for the reason that a concern having little or no development in personnel management might likewise have small interest in answering a long list of questions about their personnel methods. Therefore the conclusions which follow concern those organizations which were sufficiently interested to furnish a mass of detail for the purpose of this summary.

We do not imply, of course, that all concerns who failed to answer communications have also failed to develop personnel management to a high degree. It should be equally evident that the list to which questions were directed did not include every concern giving this subject major attention.

In preparing the original list for the survey, we selected 500 national advertisers, picked at random from various publications. To these 500 was sent a detailed questionnaire covering the principles, practices, and instruments of personnel management. One hundred and ninety-five answers were received in sufficiently complete form to make them statistically useful. These answers came from 41 kinds of businesses in 21 states and

Reprinted with permission from *The Personnel Journal*, Vol. 10, No. 4, 1931-32, pp. 225-31.

Although this was not published until 1931-1932, the data were undoubtedly collected before the Depression had had much effect.

the District of Columbia. These 195 enterprises employ 2,391,000 workers; the numbers in the organizations ranged from 100 to 240,000.

Comparisons

A study of the returned questionnaires discloses many interesting comparisons. For example, no concern was found to use strength tests, while psychological tests, which were hailed so enthusiastically, appear to have lagged behind trade tests as an employment device, and clerical-stenographic tests have come into much more general use than either trade or psychological tests. Job analyses are not nearly as prevalent among the reporting concerns as man analyses, indicated by the more general use of the Master Personnel Record or Qualification Card.

For purposes of comparison here, we somewhat arbitrarily grouped Personnel Management into:

Employment.
Maintenance.
Payment.
Insurance.
Development.
Research Control.

Under each of these is given a number of items, and the percentages of those answering the question who use the item are shown in figures 1 and 2.

From these graphs it becomes apparent that interviews for the selection of applicants are the most generally used employment device, since 93 per cent of the concerns answering stated that it was their practice to interview applicants. Also it appears that 92 per cent of the concerns give new employees some form of training on their jobs. Application Blanks, the next most commonly used device, are reported by 89 per cent. First-aid Stations have come into very general use as they are operated by 87 per cent of the group. Records of Labor Turnover are kept by 82 per cent, many of whom not only keep turnover records for the whole organization, but keep them by departments as well.

At the opposite end of the scale we find the use of psychological tests is reported by only 17 per cent, the repeating of initial employment tests to check up on progress is used on only 7 per cent of the cases. It is surprising to note that Group Life Insurance is reported by 55 per cent and Suggestion Systems by 54 per cent.

Two practices which have been widely discussed are Foremanship Training and Employee Representation. It is significant that in only 34 per cent of the cases is there any claim of the former, and in only 19 per cent is there any form of Employee Representation. Plans for the acquistion of common stock by the employees and Company Housing Plans have reached almost identical development, as they are offered by 25 and 27 per cent, respectively.

Without access to the facts it might logically be assumed that certain practices might go hand in hand. It would not appear illogical to assume that a concern using Trade Tests to find out what an applicant knew about a job would also use Job Analyses, also that the introduction of an employee representation plan might be accompanied by a stock acquisition program. These devices, however, were found to accompany each

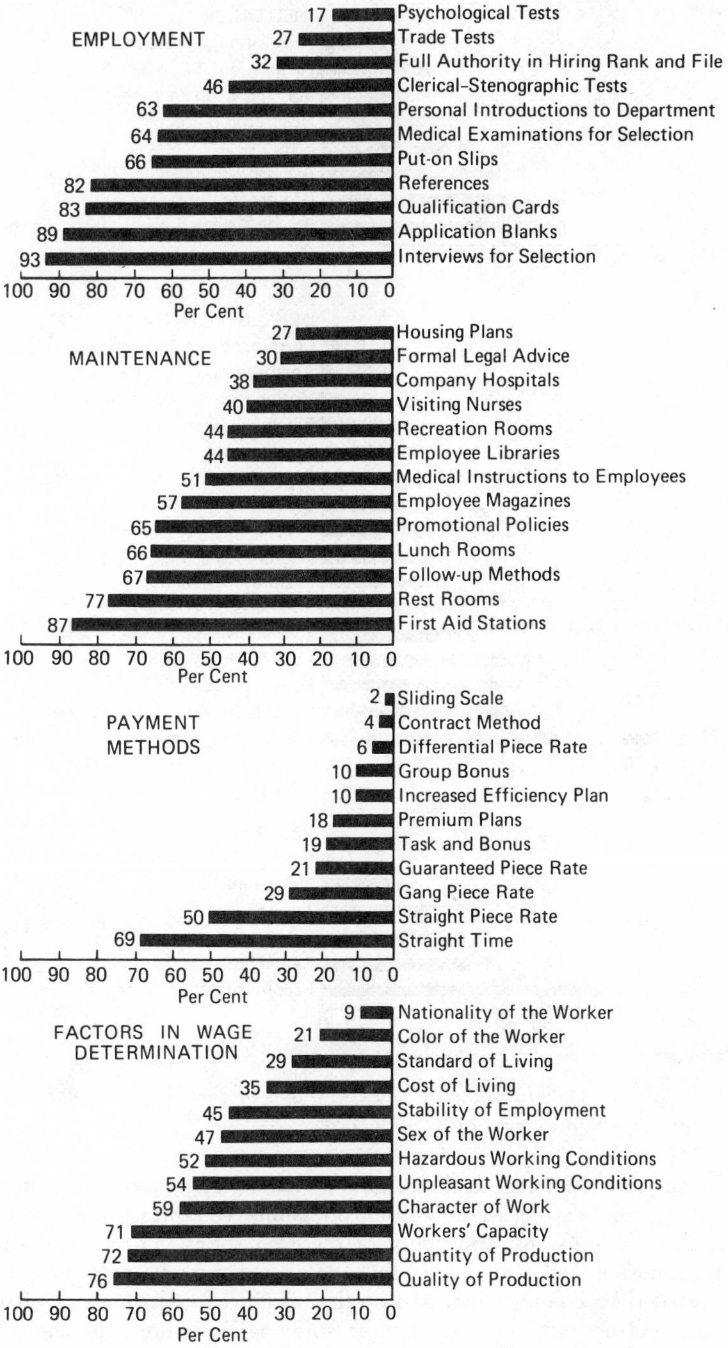

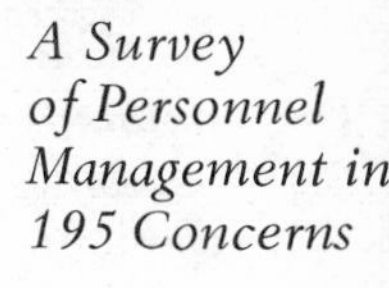

EMPLOYMENT
17 Psychological Tests
27 Trade Tests
32 Full Authority in Hiring Rank and File
46 Clerical-Stenographic Tests
63 Personal Introductions to Department
64 Medical Examinations for Selection
66 Put-on Slips
82 References
83 Qualification Cards
89 Application Blanks
93 Interviews for Selection
100 90 80 70 60 50 40 30 20 10 0
Per Cent
MAINTENANCE
27 Housing Plans
30 Formal Legal Advice
38 Company Hospitals
40 Visiting Nurses
44 Recreation Rooms
44 Employee Libraries
51 Medical Instructions to Employees
57 Employee Magazines
65 Promotional Policies
66 Lunch Rooms
67 Follow-up Methods
77 Rest Rooms
87 First Aid Stations
100 90 80 70 60 50 40 30 20 10 0
Per Cent
PAYMENT METHODS
2 Sliding Scale
4 Contract Method
6 Differential Piece Rate
10 Group Bonus
10 Increased Efficiency Plan
18 Premium Plans
19 Task and Bonus
21 Guaranteed Piece Rate
29 Gang Piece Rate
50 Straight Piece Rate
69 Straight Time
100 90 80 70 60 50 40 30 20 10 0
Per Cent
FACTORS IN WAGE DETERMINATION
9 Nationality of the Worker
21 Color of the Worker
29 Standard of Living
35 Cost of Living
45 Stability of Employment
47 Sex of the Worker
52 Hazardous Working Conditions
54 Unpleasant Working Conditions
59 Character of Work
71 Workers' Capacity
72 Quantity of Production
76 Quality of Production
100 90 80 70 60 50 40 30 20 10 0
Per Cent

Figure 1. Graphs showing the use made of various personnel management devices in 195 concerns.

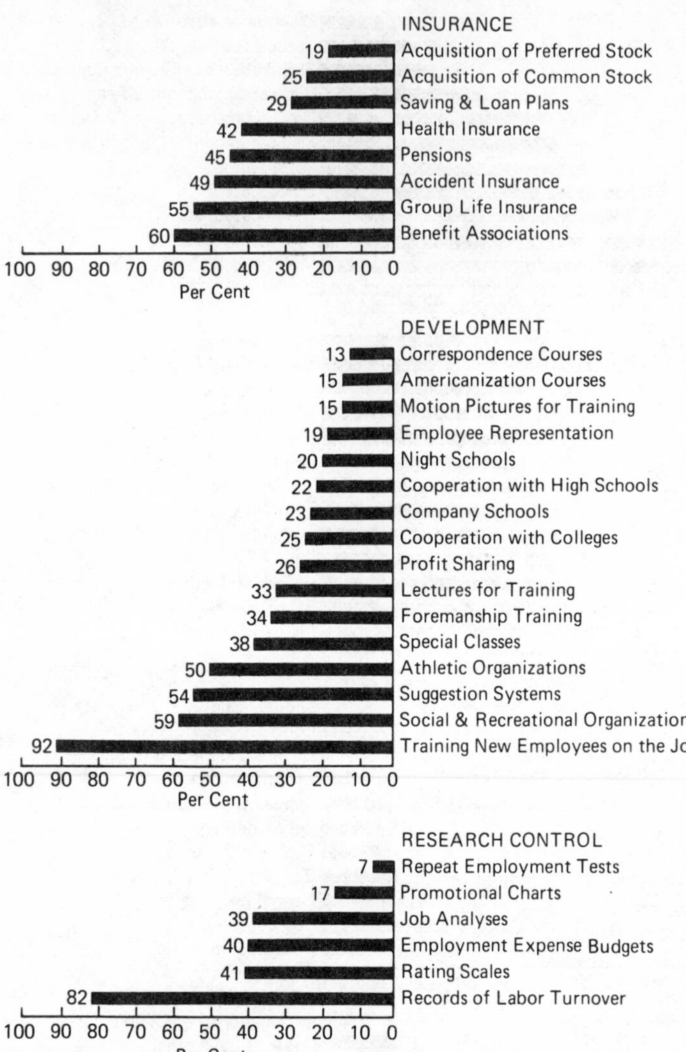

Figure 2. Graphs showing the use made of various personnel management devices in 195 concerns.

other in only 9 per cent of the cases. A still more logical assumption might be that profit sharing would accompany employee representation, yet of the 177 concerns answering both of these questions, 35 used employee representation and 49 had profit sharing, yet only 9, or 5 per cent, reported their common use. Many other significant relationships of this nature will occur to the reader upon studying the more complete comparison of pairs in figure 3.

Conclusion

Twelve years after the World War is too short a period in which to reach any final conclusions concerning the socioindustrial forces set in motion by that conflict. Just why some industrial practices have been

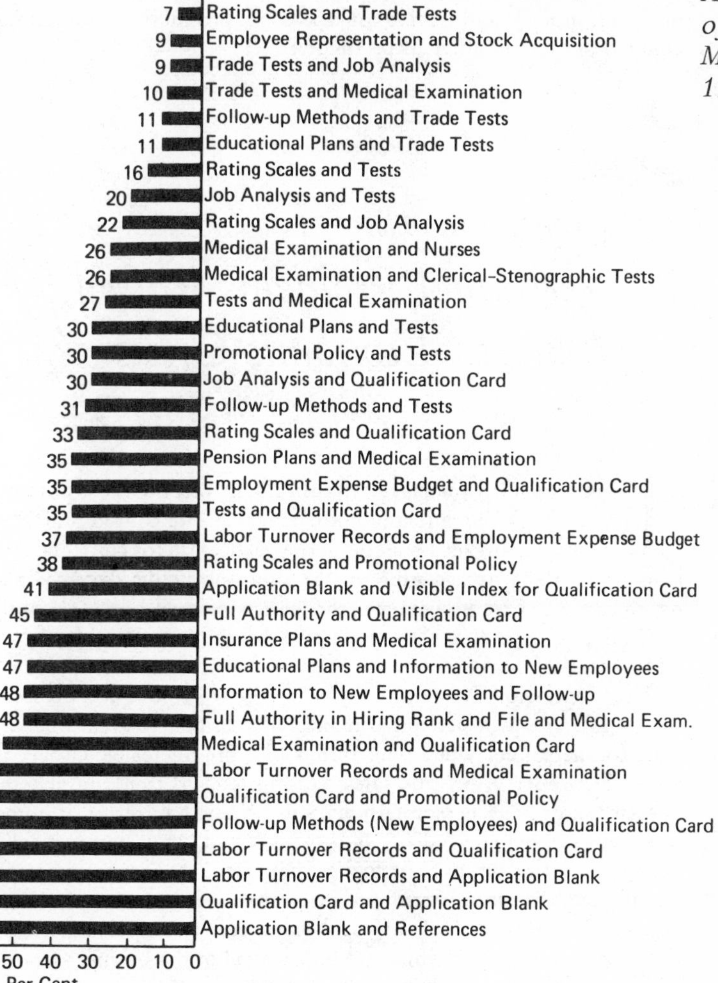

Figure 3. Graph showing paired comparisons of various personnel management devices in 195 concerns.

more generally adopted than others is impossible to determine with accuracy. This article suggests a number of anomalies. One can only guess at why the appeal of Pensions (45 per cent) had led to a development two and one half times that of Employee Representation (19 per cent). Pensions not only appeal to executives, but are also rapidly coming into the foreground in the minds of lawmakers. We are in a fair way for the early passage of Federal laws making them obligatory.

As to the mechanics of Personnel Management, the simpler devices, such as Interviews (93 per cent), Application Blanks (89 per cent), Qualification Cards (83 per cent), and the like, from our survey appear to have far outstripped the more complicated procedures, such as Job Analyses (39 per cent), Motion Pictures for Training (15 per cent), and Promotional Charts (17 per cent). While the introduction and use of the latter group might be more expensive and troublesome, the probable dividends in bettered morale and saving of waste in production should more than compensate for the difficulties involved.

20

A Cloudburst: 1930-1937

Personnel Problems Raised by the Current Economic Crisis

WILLIAM M. LEISERSON

The personnel management movement was the most potent factor in stopping the trade union movement in the United States. Personnel management set up a competing leadership for labor and stopped the labor movement by cleaning up the shop, providing decent air and light, by the safety first movement, through personnel contacts, and through conceding the principle of collective bargaining through the employee representation movement.

This depression has undone fifteen years or so of good personnel work. The whole trend in personnel management since 1931 has been to hire a man for personnel work who thinks like the higher executive, that is, in terms of property, profits, sales, etc., instead of thinking in terms of the human factor. The personnel man who thought in terms of human beings was gradually being weeded out as being "wild" and "impractical." Personnel men, in the opinion of higher management, became saner and saner. They thought more in terms of business than in terms of human beings. A personnel man, to be of any real value to the employer, must think in terms of human values which are impractical in the business world.

From the point of view of the individual business, at the present time business is solvent, but from the point of view of the community, business is now bankrupt. A great number of people who are not now making a living through business enterprise are living at the expense of the community. The community must, therefore, be taxed to support them. From the point of view of the community, business ought to be supporting them because that is the reason for which business exists.

Labor is going to look to legislation and not to personnel management for a solution of the unemployment problem. Unemployment insurance is coming with reserves and maintenance for human investment in industry. We need a three-fold scheme: 1. Public agencies; 2. Unemployment insurance for the great body of workers; 3. Crisis relief on top of unemployment insurance because no unemployment insurance system will take care of the depression that extends over a period of five or six years.

Reprinted from *The Management Review*, April, 1933, Vol. 22, No. 4, pp. 114-115.

Dr. Leiserson was an active leader during the early stages of the development of personnel and labor relations.

21

Status of Personnel Work During the Depth of the Depression: 1933

Recent Trends in Personnel Management

C. C. BALDERSTON

Ten years ago, personnel managers placed special emphasis on the supplying of effective workers. Their problem during the past few years has been to maintain an efficient staff with a high morale in the face of the changes incident to the business landslide. The emphasis shifted from the building up of a force to the paradoxical problem of keeping it efficient while it was being decimated.

Chief executives are once more devoting more of their own attention to industrial relations. It is now clear, as it should have been before, that personnel management is not something separate from general management, which can be turned over to an obscure department while the responsible heads attend to more pressing matters. Personnel policies are effective only when actually carried out by line executives in their supervision of those reporting to them.

We shall first discuss what general management has done with questions affecting people. Take, for example, the adjustment of the executive pyramid to a reduced income and volume of sales—i.e., the reduction of the administrative force in order to decrease expense. A few years ago, we would have thought that the demotion of men either in salary or in job would reduce their morale so greatly that their retention on the payroll would be inexpedient. Yet companies have reduced men from one rank to another, with apparent success. That high officials have been able to induce their associates to take positions lower down the ladder has meant that fewer old and middle-aged executives are walking the streets than would otherwise have been the case. Many concerns have worked on the problem of making their executive pyramid and their administrative expense more flexible so that it can either be reduced or expanded according to the volume of business at a given time. This is a logical development not only to meet depression emergency but to safeguard the future permanence of the concern if we continue to do business in the midst of rapid change.

Over 150 of our large manufacturing plants, railroads and utilities are paying a dismissal wage in some form to those laid off. One of the trends is that increasing emphasis is placed upon age in the determination of the amount of dismissal compensation. Another tendency is to pay it even to those dropped for incompetency, although the amount may be smaller, and to make eligible for it men of relatively short service.

Reprinted from *The Management Review*, Vol. 22, No. 9, September, 1933, pp. 259-269. Dr. Balderston was Professor of Industry, Wharton School of Finance and Commerce, University of Pennsylvania.

Wage rates were, of course, reduced, but two very significant differences are evident: 1. In concerns sensitive to the problem of maintaining *esprit de corps*, the sequence of dividend, salary and wage cuts has been the reverse of 1921. 2. One of the wage cuts has frequently been used to realign salaries and to bring the rates into tune with the difficulty and responsibility of the job. The realignment of salaries and wages to wipe out inequalities is difficult unless the general level is either rising or falling. Consequently, many progressive managements have taken this opportunity to iron out the injustices and ill-feeling caused by salaries that are out of line. In a period of good business, such as we had between 1923 and 1929, it seems inevitable that salaries in some departments should be advanced faster than in others, either because of more aggressive department heads, or because of nepotism. At the end of such a period men working side by side may feel that they are not being paid fairly, that the rates of pay have little connection with the contribution to the company. The fact that employees are mute when other jobs are unavailable does not lessen the injustice.

In addition to these questions that have been encountered by general management, it may also be worthwhile to consider the recent tendencies in the activities of the personnel departments proper. They may be divided into two groups, those that are clear, and those that are uncertain.

Among the obvious depression trends are the following:

1. Increased emphasis upon relief activities.
2. Many departments busier because of company and community relief work together with the time-consuming investigation of individual cases prior to the dismissal.
3. The expenses of personnel departments have been reduced by the decrease or elimination of company contributions to employee activities.
4. The less essential routine records have been eliminated, as well as many company magazines and training courses.
5. Turnover for reasons other than layoff has shrunk to negligible proportions, often less than 10 per cent.
6. In connection with financial provisions for employee security, the sentiment for credit unions has increased, but except in unusual circumstances, plans for the employee purchase of stock have come to be considered dangerous.

Among the trends that are confused and indefinite might be included:

1. The tendency to decentralize the responsibility for training, the emphasis upon training for the job rather than for cultural background, and the significant growth of retraining employees to increase their versatility.
2. The increased centralization of the guidance of the personnel activities.
3. The unification of financial plans for employee security.

Relief work has been emphasized especially in companies located in small or medium-sized communities where they are expected to take the lead and to provide both money and guidance. There is considerable variation in the methods of handling relief work. If it is over-centralized so that the employees do not participate in its administration, or if the employees are given loans that must be cashed at the company store, ill feeling is engendered. In contrast, an employee of one large corporation told me that the active participation of his associates in the relief program and the evident sincerity with which the company was backing it might in the future prove to be the strongest asset on the personnel balance sheet.

The expense of the personnel and employment departments has been generally reduced. Because the hiring activity atrophied, the employing staff were either transferred or dismissed. Many personnel records are no longer kept current and reliance is placed upon special studies to provide such information when needed. Company contributions to the athletic games and social activities have been curtailed and often eliminated.

Financial Provisions for Employee Security

We have had a real disillusionment in industry concerning employee ownership. Our most authorative source of information on employee stock ownership, the Industrial Relations Section of Princeton University, finds that of 50 plans surveyed, 60 per cent had become inoperative before the end of 1932.[1] The general sentiment seems to be that there are great dangers involved in sponsoring the sale of common stock to rank and file employees. The costly nature of our recent experiences, in money and in the loss of morale, has probably taught us a lesson. Yet we still find some advocates of the sale of common stock who believe in the principle with various protective features. These would either limit the purchase to a selected group, make offerings only in selected years, or guarantee the payments until the expiration of the plan. Others advocate offering only preferred stock, and, if possible, stock which would have priority in case of failure.

I feel that the provision of a systematic channel for employee saving is altogether desirable, but that with the exception of special cases, employee stock purchase is not a financially sound investment plan for employees, and is a questionable management policy. The difficulty is that many companies have copied their plans from others and have omitted the safeguards. Consequently there are three reasons for not using it unless the company is very stable and can offer its employees safeguards that will protect them in case of a debacle like the one we have been experiencing.

1. It is poor advice to ask any workman to invest his savings in the same company from which he draws his pay check. If that company meets financial adversity, he not only loses his source of current income, but the savings on which he relied to carry him through the valley as well.

2. It is unsound financial advice to suggest to a workman, let alone to urge him, to invest in the common stock of any one company unless he has first accumulated a "rainy day" fund the principal of which can be realized at any time. Yet, that is exactly what many companies have done frequently in the past.

3. The argument is advanced that employee stock ownership builds morale and loyalty. And yet, curiously enough, in companies which have urged their employees to purchase stock, the cart seems to have gotten

[1] See "Employee Stock Ownership and the Depression," prepared by Eleanor Davis. Industrial Relations Section, Princeton University, 1933. 41 pages.

before the horse. The more loyal the employees, the more loath they are to sell out. They feel there is something disloyal to the company in running to cover, even though they suspect the stock may fall further than it has. Instead of building morale, this procedure destroys it. If an employee stock purchase plan cannot be relied upon to increase the *esprit de corps* in a company, why have it?

The original objective of systematic saving and the development of an interest in the company is admirable but I believe that the safeguards which surround a few unusual arrangements such as the guarantee of principal or sale below market price, have been forgotten by the majority of stock purchase plans. It is my confident hope that the mechanisms used in the future will represent sounder methods because the price of failure has been high.

In contrast to the fall of employee stock purchase, we have the rise of credit unions. There are now approximately 1,600 credit unions in the United States, and they seem to have survived the depression rather well. One thing in their favor is that the lending of the fund is handled by the man's own buddies. Since they are familiar with his situation at home, they put a brake on loans that are excessive or speculative. Another is that a man is less willing to have his associates lose than he is for the company to lose. Consequently, the loans are probably a better risk if the man knows that the money is lent him by his fellow employees than from a reserve fund of the company.

There are advocates of the unification of all the financial provisions for employee security. The Eastman Kodak Company has such a unified arrangement. But however logical it may seem to have a homogeneous plan linking death and disability insurance, a plan for regular savings, and provision for retirement, there are practical difficulties involved. In the first place, when the matter is under consideration, a company usually discovers that its scattered plans covering some of these contingencies have developed traditions, and that their fusion into a new comprehensive scheme would be confusing and disturbing. Moreover, it is to be questioned whether a comprehensive scheme can be explained in sufficiently simple terms to be understood and accepted. Finally, there is always the danger that unless the administrative heads face each of the financial risks of the employees frankly and separately, they will not all be provided for.

Employee training, of course, may emphasize the improvement of a man's ability to do his job, or it may emphasize his general development and cultural background. Some companies, like the American Rolling Mill, have recently drifted toward the former, yet still others feel they need a properly balanced ration of both types of instruction. In fact, a given company seems likely to swing from one position to the other in a cyclical fashion. The most significant development in the whole field of training has been the retraining of employees in this emergency. As a part of work spreading, it was often essential, but where it actually opened up new jobs for men who would otherwise have been laid off, the efforts of companies like Kohler have been very constructive. To the extent that specialized work and training have narrowed the usefulness of workers, the latter's security has been lessened. It is not only a social obligation, but probably good business for companies to broaden their executives and other workers.

A number of pioneer companies have increased the centralization of control over the personnel activities during the last two or three years. There are undoubtedly gains to be made from such centralization in administering salaries uniformly, insuring that work will be spread fairly, and that layoffs will be so made that the best qualified and most deserving employees are retained. On the other hand, boards of directors occasionally feel that highly centralized departments of any kind make for administrative expenses, and that economy dictates the distribution of the personnel staff among the operating departments.

Lessons of the Depression

In times like these, it would be natural, in any survey of industrial relations, to see the wreckage of abandoned hopes and promises. On the other hand, one must not ignore the constructive developments, many of which are encouraging. Most fundamental of all is the development of a personnel philosophy or attitude among the operating management and owners. Without the growth of such a philosophy, the conduct of affairs during this depression would have been far different. Moreover, there are signs that plans are being tailor-made to fit the needs of individual companies. At least, one can find more evidence now of real analysis prior to the adoption of a new scheme.

Evidences of improvement that are more tangible are to be found in the decreasing accident rates, explained partly by the laying off of the less experienced workers, but also by the constant emphasis upon safety. There has probably been a similar trend in the sickness rate. In the provision of security against the risks of death, disability, accident and sickness, old age and unemployment, there have been some definite gains. At least, group life insurance with some total disability protection has grown apace. There are likewise, according to Industrial Relations Counselors, Inc., some 420 pension plans, under which 3,750,000 employees have been protected. Of a large group of plans, roughly one-half were both funded and on an actuarial basis.[2]

In addition to these tangible evidences, discussion of the problems of old age and unemployment has grown tremendously. An analysis of the personnel literature of the past decade reveals a great increase in the number of articles upon worker security and wage policy. Out of all this discussion and thinking, there will undoubtedly come more experiments and more action.

Needless to say, depression has revealed mistakes in policy and procedure. The mistakes made in connection with employee stock ownership and pensions are typical. It is now clear that if employees contribute to a pension fund, their money should be invested only in the most conservative manner. Employee funds and company funds that support contractual arrangements must be treated as trust funds if corporations are to keep faith with their employees. Moreover, it would appear that certain corporations have fallen in the esteem of their employees and the public because of the injudicious manner in which pre-retirement cases have been treated. To lay a man off within a few years of his retirement age may be necessary, but unless fair provision is made for him the action is interpreted as an attempt to reduce the number of pensioners. The answer is to make the provision as to the age of retirement flexible.

[2] See "Industrial Pension Systems" by Murray W. Latimer. New York: Industrial Relations Counselors, Inc., 1933. 2 volumes.

Other lessons of the depression add to our humility. The inability of operating and personnel managers to continue their personnel policies in the face of adverse economic forces, for instance. Although the recent trend of business has by no means minimized the need for effective personnel programs, it is painfully apparent that the program within a given company can operate only within limits that are set by economic forces.

Perhaps the solution of the personnel problems just ahead is to strive for flexibility on the one hand, and for more adequate insurances on the other. Many of the constructive steps toward flexibility must necessarily be taken by the general management, for they involve expansion policies, the financial structure and reserves, and the choice of products to be sold. The impact of economic forces has demonstrated that general management decisions have more to do with the welfare of employees and their families than do many so-called personnel policies.

With regard to the complicated problem of financial provisions for employee security, might we not be on safer ground if we attempted to determine the minimum a company can afford to provide for the various personnel risks, and then begin the re-education of employees in the virtues of individual thrift? No one can expect employee contributions to be made to a pension plan in many industries at present; but we did not save enough, as individuals, in the balmy days of 1923-1929. What we did save, we invested unwisely. Now workers are disillusioned by the loss of their savings, especially when they were advised or urged by their companies to enter an unsound investment or pension arrangement.

During the happier years of the next decade, the extra earnings of employees over and above what they will be earning during a moderate work week, say of 35 or 40 hours, and part of the extra profits of our companies, could be devoted to building up greater economic security for employees. Annuity plans could be so arranged that in prosperous years employees would be encouraged to buy their annuities for two or three years ahead. Companies could likewise use their extra profits of those years to build up reserves, or to buy annuities for their employees. If workers are to have more than the minimum of financial security, it will have to be provided when both they and their companies can afford to set aside the money.

We are scarcely learning our lessons fast enough. For instance, have we learned not to put our faith in mere phrases, like "high wages and prosperity," nor to copy blindly what other companies are doing? Perhaps the latter habit is to be blamed for personnel programs that are poorly integrated and without clearly defined aims. Not only do concerns need to re-define their objectives, and to look where each part of the program is leading them, but to recognize that, year by year, their personnel administration is in danger of depending too greatly on general rules and decisions.

It is obvious that on matters like salary administration, generalizations and policies are needed to give uniformity. Whatever science there may be in personnel management therefore demands them, but their application is another matter. Perhaps in the past too many executives have thought in terms of classes, and too few in terms of the individual people who comprise them. Those who have emphasized programs to the exclusion of the individual need to refocus their attention upon him. Such emphasis is the essence of good personnel administration; unless department heads and personnel managers have a real interest in, and a liking for people, paper policies will be ineffective. Unless the individual who carries out the so-called policies is an experienced person, one who has passed through some of the vicissitudes of life, he can scarcely talk to his fellows on a basis of confidence.

Will we continue to be content with organization arrangements that separate personnel and general management so that the operating departments think of the personnel department as a step-brother? Personnel management, considered apart from general company management, is merely window-dressing and a delusion. One hopes to see more company programs reach the adult stage typified by a high degree of integration, with less emphasis on hobbies, and with the program in actual operation as well as on paper.

22

Weeding Out, but Not Total Abandonment of Personnel and Labor Activities: 1935

Industrial Relations Activities Survive a Critical Test

H. F. BROWN

There have been two leading theories of the place of industrial relations activities in the scheme of management. According to one of the theories, these activities represent a parasitic growth on the system of labor relations, and owe their existence either to a misplaced paternalistic idea of philanthropy, or to a studied policy of trying to hood-wink employees and wean them away from ideas of class consciousness and class struggle, or to both. With such a basis, these activities would obviously be a product of prosperous and high profit periods, and would pass out of the picture when hard times removed the temptation to be unnecessarily generous at the company's expense, or to maintain unessential techniques for hiring, training, and adjusting employees to jobs.

Believers in the other theory contended that industrial relations policy, as developed during the last decade, was far more than a sop thrown to labor; that the various activities introduced for the purpose of developing cooperation between management and working force served the interests of both parties and so were sound and equitable, and that activities providing individual financial benefits represented well merited rewards for accomplishment and service. If this theory were correct, those activities

Reprinted with permission from *The Personnel Journal*, Vol. 13, 1934-35, pp. 258-262. Mr. Brown was employed by the National Industrial Conference Board when this was written.

must be a definite and integral part of management policy, and should be affected by a business depression only to the extent that other features of operating policy were affected.

A more searching test of industrial relations activities than the business depression which began in 1929 could hardly be contrived. A prolonged recession in business activity, covering not months but years, and the necessity to curtail drastically all operating expenses, provided ample justification for discarding any features of industrial policy that had not fully proved themselves. If industrial relations activities succumbed at such a time, they would not be discredited, but they might be criticized as prosperity extravagancies. If they survived such a protracted period of deflation, even though curtailed in some respects, the claim that they were an important and established part of operating policy would be well substantiated.

Opinions are likely to differ with regard to what stage in the depression we have now reached, but there can hardly be any question that we have been through sufficiently trying times to permit an appraisal of the staying qualities of industrial relations activities. Accordingly, with the horizon somewhat brighter and industry hopeful that the worst was over, the National Industrial Conference Board set out to survey the results of the storm, to find what was to be learned from the experience of the last several years.

Such an investigation might be approached from either of two angles. The attempt might be made to select as a sample a thoroughly representative cross-section of American industry with proper regard for size of establishments, their location, and their distribution between industries, but without regard to their previous experience in administering industrial relations activities. Or it might be felt that the only true test of these activities could occur in companies that had seriously developed a program of such activities before the depression and had had an opportunity to judge their value before financial retrenchment challenged them to justify their worth. The Conference Board believed that the latter group of companies could contribute the more valuable information, and that their experience would offer a truer line on what past experience revealed with regard to future probabilities in this field than could companies selected at random. From its records, therefore, it selected a list of companies which before the depression had well developed industrial relations programs and asked their cooperation in answering the question what the effect of the depression had been on industrial relations activities. Through the courtesy of 233 companies, significant information was obtained.

How Personnel Activities Fared in the Depression

One of the most informative features of the inquiry was a listing of over a hundred activities which involved employer-employee relations, with the request that companies indicate in appropriate columns those activities which are now maintained, those which had been discontinued as a result of the depression, those dropped on account of the N.R.A., those adopted since the National Industrial Recovery Act, and those that they were considering adopting. Such information would indicate not only what activities were most widely maintained by industrial companies, but also how the various activities had stood up under the impact of the depression.

Industrial Relations Activities

The picture presented by the results of the survey is one of remarkable vitality on the part of industrial relations activities.[1] Particularly noteworthy is the strength displayed by those which involve no inconsiderable expense. For example, 41 companies had formal pension plans and only 3 had been dropped during the depression, while one such plan had been adopted since the N.I.R.A., and 8 companies were considering adoption of pension plans. Informal pension plans were in force in 77 companies, and only 4 such plans had been dropped during the depression. Group life insurance was carried on by 162 companies, 2 had dropped it during the depression, 5 had taken out such policies since the N.I.R.A., and 3 others were considering such action. Only one of 134 mutual benefit associations had been discontinued during the depression.

Some activities, on the other hand, had suffered rather heavily. Employee stock purchase plans were in effect in 24 companies, as compared with 25 in which they had been discontinued. Suggestion systems were still operative in 102 companies but had been discontinued in 22 concerns. Twenty-five companies had dropped their plant restaurants or cafeterias and 124 companies had retained them. Vacations with pay were still provided for wage earners by 37 companies but had been discontinued by 28.

Medical and accident prevention work had been well maintained. Educational and training activities had suffered surprisingly little when the large labor surplus and ready availability of most types of labor is considered. Recreational activities had quite naturally been somewhat curtailed. Employment procedure, tests, job analysis, time study, and other features of modern employment technique had been interfered with very little considering that they are still generally regarded more as refinements than as essentials of plant policy.

Particular interest at this time attaches to the record of agencies for employer-employee negotiation. Individual dealings with employees were maintained by 101 companies. In 126 companies there were plans of employee representation, and 17 companies operated under agreements with organized labor unions. Of the employee representation plans, 43 were of the employee committee type, and nearly twice as many, 83, were joint committees, including representatives of employees and also of the management. Forty-two of the employee representation plans had been started since the N.I.R.A., and 9 of the union agreements. In 12 companies employee representation plans were under consideration, but no companies reported the expectation of entering into an agreement with a labor union.

Cost of Personnel Programs

A subject on which information is frequently sought is the cost of maintaining industrial relations programs. Such information is difficult to secure because segregation of the exact amount of cost assignable to different activities is almost impossible, and many companies lump much of the cost of maintaining these activities under some general heading of administrative cost. However, a number of companies covered in the survey contributed more or less complete figures with regard to these costs

[1] For full results of survey see National Industrial Conference Board, "Effect of the Depression on Industrial Relations Programs," 1934.

during 1933. Because of the wide variation in the figures reported by different companies, the median rather than the arithmetic mean was used to denote the average. Figures were reduced to a basis of cost per employee in order to make data from the various companies generally comparable, and companies were classifed in three size groups: those with 1 to 750 employees, those with 751 to 2,000, and those with more than 2,000 employees.

The median total cost per employee of maintaining industrial relations programs during 1933 in 63 companies which provided such information was $14.06. This median cost varied from $26.66 in companies employing not over 750 persons to $11.25 in companies with 751 to 2,000 employees, and was $11.87 in the large companies. The lower cost per employee in the larger concerns is probably attributable to the greater number of employees among whom the more or less fixed factors in cost may be distributed.

These figures can not, of course, be regarded as comparable except in one sense. They represent the median cost of maintaining the personnel activities which were in force in the various companies and therefore constitute the cost per employee of whatever program was maintained. But the activities included in the various company programs may have varied considerably, and therefore these figures do not show the differing costs of maintaining similar activities.

A closer approach to comparative costs of identical activities is found in figures provided by some companies. The median cost per employee of maintaining medical service in 73 companies, for example, was $2.70; for pensions in 51 companies was $10.33; for group insurance in 69 companies, $6.25; for profit sharing in 5 companies, $34.50. The spread between costs of these activities in the three size groups was relatively considerably less than in the case of total costs.

Another angle of the cost of personnel programs is its proportion of total payroll. In the 49 companies that furnished information of this character, the median per cent of payroll spent on industrial relations activities was 1.85 per cent. Corresponding figures for the three size groups of companies were 2.1 per cent in concerns employing 1 to 750 persons, 2.3 per cent in companies with 751 to 2,000 employees, and 1.4 per cent in those with more than 2,000 employees.

The Place of Industrial Relations

Conditions affecting the relationship of employee and employer have undergone considerable change during the past year and a half. Regulation of the employment relationship in private industry has been assumed by the federal government, and what was formerly a matter for decision by employer and employees is now subject to approval of government boards and other agencies. Unless voided by court decisions, legislation of 1933 and 1934 has created a new and fundamentally different situation in industrial relations. How will this affect the status and importance of personnel programs?

Executives in 56 per cent of the companies which cooperated in the survey believe that the National Industrial Recovery Act has had no effect on industrial relations; that they are neither more important nor less important than before the Act became effective. In 43 per cent of the companies it is believed that industrial relations have become of greater importance since the Act, while one executive thinks that they have become less important. If this is representative of industrial opinion generally, it is widely recognized that industrial relations policy in the future calls for the best thought that can be applied to it.

The function of an industrial relations policy might be said to be to provide a medium for translating a management's philosophy of the rights and obligations of employer and employee into terms of actual plant relationships. Many plans have been worked out during the last few years to assure the employee easy access to a responsible representative of management, to assure healthful and sanitary working surroundings, to adjust wages and working hours in an equitable manner, to prevent favoritism and provide equal opportunity for all, and to provide such financial benefits as particular companies believe that they can afford. These plans will undoubtedly be reexamined by many companies with a view to their applicability to present conditions when so much depends on establishing beyond question the management's desire and intention to be absolutely fair with its employees.

However long and wordily the controversy may rage over the question whether the interests of employer and employee are basically identical or antithetical, the fact remains that the two must work together in a common enterprise in the success of which the fortunes of both are linked together. To make this joint association as free from friction and as mutually productive as possible in an economic world where change and unsettlement seem to be the rule, is the task which industrial relations policy must assume. The quality of its contribution is likely to be an important factor in industrial accomplishment during the next few years.

23

Personnel Work Becomes Established and Has Some Growing Pains: 1940-1950

Decentralize Personnel Work

WILLIAM V. OWEN

Personnel managers of twenty years ago were selected from the shop on a basis of "understanding men." When top management felt the need for establishing contact with employees, industrial relations departments were set up and the task of managing such a department was assigned to a person who became known as the personnel manager. Foremen who had no problems of discipline provided suitable raw material for good personnel men. A promoted ex-foreman did not pass through a course of training; he merely put on his "Sunday Suit" on Monday morning and took his post in an improvised office as personnel manager.

Reprinted from *The Personnel Journal*, Vol. 19, 1940-1941, pp. 65-68

Dr. Owen was Professor of Industrial Management at Purdue University when this was written.

A Man Not an Office

He was a pioneer, which meant that he was forced to develop his own methods. He was on trial; his old colleagues, the foremen, were sometimes unwilling to allow interference with their prerogatives of hiring and firing. His job depended on "getting along with people." Soon, everyone in the shop (if the shop was not too big) knew the personnel manager by his first name, and referred to him as "Charlie" or "Bill." Workers with grievances were told to see "Charlie," rather than told to report to the personnel office.

There were few trade agreements to which the personnel manager could refer for guidance in settling disputes. He was forced to use his ingenuity in solving his problems. The fact that he "knew" the men with whom he was dealing was a great boon in the promotion of industrial peace. "Cases" were in the form of human beings, and not records. He was a one-man board of arbitration who could be trusted with incriminating evidence. His advice was sought concerning all manner of problems which were outside the scope of employment. In short, he was unscientific.

Loses Direct Contact

The first World War, and the subsequent brief period of prosperity provided ideal soil for the growth of this new organism; so, as business institutions expanded, the duties of the personnel manager became more complex. It was no longer possible to "know" the men and the foremen. The knowledge, which had been the personal property of the personnel manager, was now obtained by his interviewers, who made a record of each "case," which was placed on file.

The manager of men was becoming a manager of records. Reports of labor turnover had to be drawn up, as well as reports of the meetings of the shop council. Welfare programs were organized and administered; the company paper had to be edited. Thus, the old personnel man gradually became an executive who worked with curves, charts, figures and words, rather than with human emotions.

This process of management based on system and science had only begun in the middle twenties. Scientists had been working behind academic walls constructing whole batteries of scientific tools which are now in the hands of personnel managers. Tests of skills, intelligence and attitudes, as well as rating scales were being produced by industrial psychologists. Furthermore, the employment of thousands of persons under one management provided a fertile field for the statistician. Books on personnel management now contain a chapter on statistical methods, and these statistical methods have become a definite part of the equipment of the personnel expert of today.

Now Deals with Legislation and Unions

The Social Security Act, the National Labor Relations Act and the Fair Labor Standards Act have added more duties to the personnel specialist. He functions, both as an agent of the government in making out the required reports, and also as an agent of top management in interpreting government legislation, as it applies to a particular firm. Owners of firms may look to personnel officers for advice as to coverage, and here any wrong advice as to coverage may prove costly. Violations of the N.L.R.B.

which may invite annoying investigations have created a quasi-legal responsibility which must be discharged by the busy personnel executive.

Decentralize Personnel Work

So, it would seem that the old "dressed up" foreman who "understood men" is supplanted by a person who has been trained in economics, political science, psychology, statistics and law. He has become an executive in charge of a variety of "relationships," with his firm on one end, while on the other are to be found labor (organized and unorganized), State administrators armed with State laws, and Federal administrators with their Federal laws.

Almost without warning the field of labor management finds itself engaged in research, collective bargaining, the selling of the State's social reform to employers and the firm's policies to the State in addition to all the ordinary duties of hiring, promotion, safety, etc. That one person can be proficient in discharging all the functions of a present-day personnel office is improbable.

Now a Coordinator

Because of the complexities of modern labor relations, a personnel man with the necessary capacity becomes of necessity a coordinator. By division of labor he delegates authority to his subordinates. Thus, he becomes further removed from the workers and may very probably take on the coloring of management rather than of men. Another possibility is that labor management may become involved in research.

Research in industrial relations may have one of many motives, such as discovering means of reducing labor costs, the truth for the sake of truth, or the promotion of the welfare of the workers. Research may result in the conclusion that management is paying a wage less than the value of labor's product. Will the scholar in industrial relations, who discovers exploitation on the part of his employer, be able to convince his employer that wages should be raised? Is industry interested in discovering its social responsibilities, and is industry willing to pay a scholar for showing industry how to discharge its social responsibilities?

Personnel officers may be forced to think of their own security as well as that of employees. The gravest possibility is that personnel management may degenerate into mere office routine of reporting and record keeping. Record keeping may offer the utmost in job security to the personnel worker, but the least in the development of labor management.

Despite the fact that the old industrial relations specialist was unscientific, he did perform a very necessary function. He provided "ears" which would listen and *not record* the woes of the workers. It is doubtful that trade unions furnish the "ears" which modern personnel management has lost.

How to Restore Personal Touch

The listening function could, however, be restored by reorganizing the personnel department. Such reorganization would consist of setting up several "branch personnel offices" within a plant. Each sub-division would serve no more than a few hundred employees. In this way the old "personal touch" could be restored. Centralized record keeping need not be disturbed.

It would not only be possible to restore the lost personal element, but considerable simplification of the tasks of each "branch office" could be realized by assigning each branch to a group of shops. One office would have jurisdiction over foundry workers, another, over the machine shop, etc. Quite obviously, there wouldn't be the same number of workers in each division, and adjustments would have to be made.

The division of functions as between the central office and the "branch offices" would be determined by experience. Perhaps record keeping should be confined to the central office, while skeleton cards containing but little detailed information would be filed in the branches. It might be desirable to have the central office select workers, which would obviate the objection of having applicants walk through the plant to the regional offices. In general, the chief functions of the outlying offices would be: to carry out the policies formulated in the central office, to provide "ears" for complaints, and to advise the central office.

Cannot Do It with Foremen

It has been suggested that the personal touch lost by the complexities of system and science and the increase in the number of employees can be restored by the foremen. This doesn't seem feasible for at least two reasons. In the first place, it would be unwise to add to the burden of foremen, whose tasks are already very difficult. In the second place, a foreman is the immediate "boss" and it is very doubtful that a worker would feel free to confide in his "Boss."

Furthermore, the task of informing workmen as to their rights under the Social Security Act, the Labor Relations Act and the Fair Labor Standards Act requires the services of a specialist. It would be unreasonable to expect a foreman to have the knowledge necessary to inform a worker concerning his unemployment insurance benefits, old age benefits, etc.

If it is possible, and apparently it is, for a large business corporation with widely separated production units, to have a central personnel office which functions through the plant offices, why isn't it reasonable to apply the same plan to a large producing unit, which has outgrown its centralized industrial relations office?

24

Finding a Niche in a Quagmire of Ambivalency: 1948

Changing Concepts of the Personnel Function

JAMES C. WORTHY

Personnel administration is a relatively new specialized function of management. Because it is new, there are wide areas of disagreement as to its proper role. Actually, there is no common understanding as to the responsibilities of the personnel administrator and no generally accepted system of techniques and methods for carrying out his responsibilities. In this respect, personnel administration is far behind such other specialized management functions as accounting, finance, engineering, and the like. In a real sense, personnel may be said to be in its adolescent stage—well past its infancy but not yet grown to man's estate. As is characteristic of adolescents, it is not too sure of itself and not yet quite certain what it wants to be when it grows up.

At the present time, the role of the personnel administrator varies widely from company to company and can be understood only in terms of a particular management's reasons for establishing a personnel department and in terms of the type of individual selected for personnel work. It is possible, however, to distinguish a number of rather well-defined roles which are fairly characteristic of the personnel function in industry today.

Some Concepts of the Personnel Function

At one end of the scale is the concept of personnel as primarily a record-keeping function, necessary because of the requirements imposed by legislation and the need for centralizing certain fairly routine activities. While many personnel offices continue to function today at this rudimentary level, it is probable that most of us in management have begun to think of personnel in higher terms.

There is also the personnel department which was established because it was "the thing to do"—because of a feeling on management's part that "no well-run business should be without one." Where personnel departments and personnel activities are established as a means of "keeping up with the Joneses," the resulting program can be little more than a façade to the organization. Its orientation is not primarily toward the organization it is set up to serve but toward what others are doing, and it is therefore likely to employ techniques and methods poorly adapted to the real problems of the firm.

Reprinted by permission of the publisher from *Personnel*, Vol. 25, No. 3, November, 1948, pp. 166-175.

James Worthy was with the personnel department at Sears, Roebuck, & Company when he presented this paper, and is currently Professor of Management at Sangamon State University, Springfield, Illinois.

Another important reason for the increased use of personnel departments is the growth of unionism and management's need for adequate facilities to administer collective agreements. One difficulty with personnel departments which originated primarily to serve this need is that they are likely to become so occupied with the intricacies of collective bargaining that they lose sight of the real problems of human relations in the organization. Thus they may also lose sight of the constructive, rather than the merely defensive, contribution they can make to their managements.

A closely related type of origin is management concern at evidences of increasing friction with its employees and recognition of need for improving employee morale. While this is a constructive attitude as far as it goes, management may be too anxious for quick results from the new department. In such cases, the personnel administrator is in an exposed position. If management does not soon see evidences of improved morale, the administrator is likely to be replaced by someone who will attack the problem more vigorously. He is in a position where he must try to find a panacea which will solve all his problems in one swoop. He has little opportunity to develop the activities and the day-by-day contacts with the organization which are the slow but only sure way of building high employee morale and sound employee relations.

The Scientific Approach

A much more realistic and promising approach to the problems of personnel administration is represented by developments of the past ten years or so which may be loosely described as "scientific personnel administration." Considerable strides have been made toward the introduction of rational methods and techniques in personnel, and, as a result, personnel work is gradually taking on some of the characteristics of a profession. There can be no question that many products of this approach—merit rating, job evaluation, psychological testing, and the like—represent great improvements over former methods.

Valuable as this progress has been, however, the so-called scientific approach has shown some serious shortcomings which have undermined the contribution it could be making—and in many cases has made—to management success. Too often the goal of the "scientific" personnel adminsistrator is to install a variety of highly systematic procedures. From textbooks or elsewhere he may have picked up the idea that a well-run personnel program should consist of certain standard parts, each represented by some type of system, and he may not feel that he has his job under control until he has established corresponding systems in his own organization, whether it really needs them or not.

What Is "Good Personnel Practice"?

Many people who have reputations as topnotch personnel administrators today think of their jobs primarily in terms of "good personnel practice," which is often only a euphonious way of saying "bigger and better systems." There is, of course, a rationale for this attitude because in any organization large enough to require a specialized personnel department it is necessary to establish systematic procedures.

The assumption is that if employees are properly selected, well trained, adequately paid, and fairly supervised, job satisfaction will automatically result, production and efficiency will be high, and all will be right with the world. The personnel administrator guided by this philosophy therefore has a relatively simple task in planning his program. All he has to do is catalogue the necessary elements of sound employee relations—which he can find spelled out in detail in any good book on personnel—and then set up the necessary systems, the good personnel practices, to see that each element is properly provided for.

Undue Emphasis on Systems

There can be no quarrel with systems as such. In a company of any size there must be an organized means for reaching certain basic objectives, and activities related to personnel—no less than those related to sales, production, or finance—must be systematically ordered if results are to be achieved. But the strong tendency to overelaborate the systems used and to place undue reliance on such systems for building and maintaining sound employee relations is certainly open to question. Let us take an example—job evaluation. The primary objective of a job-evaluation program is to provide an orderly set of wage differentials between various jobs in the organization which will be recognized as just and fair by the employees and which will serve as guides in wage administration. So far, so good. Too often, however, a highly complex system results, and the essential objective becomes clouded in a maze of abstruse statistical and rating procedures.

Personnel literature is cluttered with endless arguments on behalf of different sets of such procedures, and considerable ingenuity has been exercised in the development of more and more complex job-evaluation systems. This welter of activity often results in a system too complex for employees to understand. Far from being convinced of management's fairness in handling the highly important matter of wage differentials, the employees become deeply suspicious of the whole thing.

The same tendency toward overelaboration is apparent in many other personnel activities—training, periodic interviewing, testing, employee benefits, house organs, morale-building programs, and so on. Personnel administrators as a group, in fact, display a remarkable bent toward systemization, a bent so strong that speculation as to its origin and significance may be profitable.

The Struggle for Status

One reason for this tendency, I think lies in the fact that personnel administration is among the newer specialized functions of management. Personnel administrators as a group are engaged in a struggle for status and recognition in the management hierarchy. Much of the energy of personnel executives goes toward trying to establish personnel as a legitimate function of management, to "sell" themselves to management and the line organization. In this struggle for status, they are under a heavy handicap in the fact that management often has only a nebulous idea of what it expects from personnel, and the further fact that there are no commonly accepted standards by which the personnel job may be judged.

Production, sales, finance, and other specialized management functions have the great advantage of being able to offer relatively objective measures of their effectiveness. Personnel, on the contrary, has nothing to compare with balance sheets or sales and production statistics. After all, what basis does management have for evaluating the importance of its personnel department or the worth of its personnel administrator? As a personnel man myself, I would hate to be judged largely in terms of whether or not I was successful in avoiding labor trouble or in reducing personnel turnover. Such matters are only partially within our control and, in any event, represent only limited aspects of the personnel job.

To win the confidence and recognition of management, the personnel administrator must find some means of convincing management that he is operating vigorously and effectively within the areas of his responsibility. In this situation, a "good system" is often highly effective. Management may be concerned with what it feels is a jumbled wage situation. If the personnel administrator can come up with a precise plan backed up by attractive charts and an impressive set of statistical tabulations, management is likely to react favorably because it has the comforting feeling that a thorough and logical job has been done and that this problem, at least, is settled for the time being.

The point is not that thorough, logical work is not important. It is that in too many cases the real purpose of the charts, the statistics, and the show of reasoned logic is not so much to accomplish a job as to convince management that it has a very bright and capable personnel administrator. Because management is accustomed to a high degree of systemization in the more technical phases of its work, it may be unduly impressed with evidences of similar methods in the field of personnel. And personnel administrators, being human, are likely to be led to overelaboration of their systems and to the introduction of highly mechanical procedures in areas of their work where more informal methods would produce more effective results for the organization.

Competition for Line Authority

Another aspect of the struggle for status is the attempt, implicit in many personnel systems, to gain a degree of control over the line organization. Staff departments—personnel included—are often painfully conscious of the more solid position of the line, a position whose strength lies largely in its direct responsibility for producing the goods and services which are the lifeblood of the organization. It is a fairly common tendency of staff departments to attempt to inject themselves into the line by establishing control over certain line activities such as hiring, placement, training, promotion, wage administration, and so on.

These attempts are easily understandable, of course, because in any line organization there are bound to be problems which require correction. However, instead of trying to strengthen the line organization so that it is better able to deal effectively with its own problems, the temptation is to set up some sort of system of control which may have the incidental effect of strengthening the staff department at the expense of the line. It often has the further effect of requiring some sort of policing action which, while it may remedy the immediate problem, very often creates other problems which are as bad or worse. The result is more bureaucracy, more pieces of paper, more "controls to make the controls work." There is a gradual aggrandizement of power and authority by the staff and a weakening of the line.

As a personnel man, I will not deprecate the importance of the personnel job or attempt to relegate it to a lower status in the organization than it should enjoy. But I am very much concerned at misguided and misdirected efforts to achieve that status which I firmly believe a well-conceived and well-executed personnel program would merit. I submit that any effort to secure undue control over line activities, whatever its initial advantages, is a blind alley, essentially unsound and inevitably self-defeating.

Don't Invite Resistance

One evidence of this fact is the sense of frustration exhibited by many personnel executives. The line will tolerate a great deal, but it can be pushed just so far. Beyond that point, the personnel staff meets increasing resistance, which it is likely to interpret as bullheaded stubbornness. A common topic of conversation when personnel men meet is the obstructive attitudes of the line organization, the need for more power and authority to compel the line to follow "good personnel practices," and the lack of enlightenment on the part of management in not providing personnel with the necessary authority to get things done.

While management is inclined to be system-minded and is likely to be impressed with charts, statistics, and precise, well-ordered procedures, it is also likely to have a fairly sure instinct about what is really workable in terms of the organization as a whole. And management most probably would back up the line organization in any direct contest for authority and control.

Too often, I fear, the status angle may play a larger part in the personnel administrator's thinking than he may care to admit. In such cases the real needs of the organization may be sacrificed to the ambitions of an individual or group. Such a situation is not only bad in itself but, in the long run, can only result in undermining the status and prestige the administrator is working so hard to achieve.

The Human Function of Personnel Management

What, then, should the aims of the personnel administrator be, and how should he go about accomplishing them? To answer these questions we must look at the goals of management and explore the possible contributions personnel administration can make to achieving those goals.

In broad terms we may define management's task as that of putting together and maintaining an effective organization which can accomplish the economic aims of the enterprise. This task has both a technical side and a human side. On the technical side, management must provide an efficient plant with necessary machines and processes, in the provision of which it is aided by its engineering and related staffs who constantly feed in ideas for technical improvements and who assume responsibility for working out various technical problems which require solution. On the human side, management's task is that of building a cooperative organization, an organization of people with drive and enthusiasm, who work together and who are responsive to management's leadership in the common effort to achieve the economic aims of the enterprise.

The function of the engineering staff is to aid management in the performance of its technical tasks. The function of the personnel staff should be to aid management in the performance of its human tasks—to assist in the development and maintenance of an effective human organization.

Mechanistic Approach to Human Problems

To perform his function adequately, the personnel administrator must develop a considerably broader point of view and an entirely different set of skills from those ordinarily represented by so-called scientific management. There has been too great a tendency for personnel people to adopt, more or less uncritically, the methods and points of view of the engineer and to attempt to apply these to the solution of the human problems in organization.

One of the serious stumbling blocks to effective human organization is a deep-seated attitude characteristic of our times. The physical scientist and the engineer have exercised a profound influence not only on the outward aspects of modern life but on our inner thought processes as well. Among other things, they have strongly influenced our thinking about problems of organization and human relations. The transference of their mode of thought to a field for which it was never designed has distorted our apprehension of our human problems and has seriously misdirected our efforts to deal with them.

If we consider closely our generally accepted theories of organization, we cannot help but note a curious parallel to the machine. Actually, our ideal of an effective organization is a "smoothly running machine," an organization in which all parts function smoothly with minimum friction and maximum economy of effort. Each component is carefully designed for its particular task, and the whole responds automatically to the touch of the operator's hand.

Our very phraseology employs mechanical images. Organization charts are frequently referred to as blueprints. A common argument for the use of psychological tests cites the care with which machines are selected to insure their suitability for the task at hand and urges that people be selected and placed with at least equal attention to their abilities and capacities. "Management engineering" and "human engineering" have become important and respected professions. Our thinking about organization displays a strongly mechanical turn of mind.

Human Aspects of Organization

The nature of human organization cannot be properly understood in terms of mechanistic concepts. The machine and its component parts have only one purpose—that for which the engineer designed them. The purpose of a human organization, whether business or otherwise, can be defined only in terms of the purposes of the people in it. Unlike the component parts of a machine, the people who comprise a human organization are something more than just parts of that organization. They are flesh-and-blood men and women, with sentiments, ambitions, and needs of their own ranging far beyond the confines of the organization. The extent to which these people serve the needs of the organization willingly and enthusiastically depends upon the extent to which the organization serves their needs as sentient, aspiring human beings.

In these circumstances, the effort to apply primarily technical rather than social skills to the solution of social problems is likely to have grave consequences, since the two kinds of skills are not synonymous and not mutually interchangeable. Elton Mayo, in his book, *The Social Problems of an Industrial Civilization*, draws the following distinctions between the two skills: "Technical skill manifests itself as a capacity to manipulate things in the service of human purposes. Social skill shows itself as a capacity to receive communications from others, and to respond to the attitudes and ideas of others in such fashion as to promote congenial participation in the common task."

The attempt to apply to human problems methods and concepts originally developed for the manipulation of things almost inevitably inhibits effective communication and undermines that "congenial participation in a common task" referred to by Mr. Mayo.

Need for Improved Social Skills

Unfortunately, the social skills required for effective cooperation have not been developed to anything like the degree that technical skills have been developed. The task of the personnel administrator comes down to this: If he is to function as effectively in aiding management on its human problems as the engineer aids it on technical problems, he must develop as high an order of conscious skill in his field as the engineer has already developed in his.

This is a sizable task. one which cannot be accomplished overnight. For one thing, social skills are poorly understood and many personnel administrators and men in management who have developed intuitive social skills have great difficulty in talking about them or defining them. Until these skills are more precisely identified and until they can be more adequately classified and described, they are communicable only to a limited degree and cannot gain the wide application required.

A great deal of creative work along these lines is being done in some of our universities, which are working closely with business and industry in their areas. Personnel administrators and management cannot wait, however, for the work of the social scientists to come to full fruition. Faced with problems here and now, we must deal with them to the best of our ability. But we can at least make a start, and I think it is important that it be a conscious start—a purposive effort to develop a higher order of skill which we can place at the service of management.

Pattern for Industrial Democracy

Actually, we have ready at hand, as a deeply ingrained part of our thinking, the ideas which can serve as the basis for our badly needed social skills. This basis is simply the ideals of the democratic society, ideals which are fundamental elements of our culture universally accepted by management and workers alike. These ideals are usually expressed in terms of "rights"—the very word "rights" implying their essentially moral and ethical nature. For our present purposes, we may summarize some of the more significant of these rights as follows:

1. The right of every man to be treated as an individual and respected as a person.
2. The right of every man to a voice in his own affairs, which includes his right to contribute to the best of his ability to the solution of common problems.
3. The right of every man to recognition for his contribution to the common good.

4. The right of every man to develop and make use of his highest capacities.
5. The right of every man to fairness and justice in all his relationships with superiors.

These democratic ideals are not platitudes but actual working principles of effective human organization. Their validity has been proved over and over again, both by our historical experience and by modern research in the social sciences. In my own company, we have cooperated with the University of Chicago on extensive research into the nature of effective organization and the factors which make for cooperation in human relations. Throughout this research we have been impressed with the extent to which the fundamental notions of our democratic society have been validated.

For example, we have been impressed with the number of times the fundamental notions of participation, human dignity, freedom to speak one's piece, and the right to advance on one's own merits have proved crucial factors in the maintenance of a high level of cooperation and teamwork. These are not merely ideals; they are practical principles of how to live and work in a free society.

Control or Cooperation?

Another thing we have learned is that an organization with an extensively developed supervisory hierarchy is more rigid, less adaptive, and less satisfying to the employees than a "flat" organization, which places considerable responsibility on the individual and keeps supervision and formal controls at a minimum. In an organization where there are many layers of supervision, employees feel restricted, controlled, and policed. There is little opportunity for creative effort and the development of ideas. In organizations with fewer layers of supervision and fewer controls, there tend to be higher morale, better feeling, and more creative effort, infinitely greater adaptability and flexibility, and a higher development of cooperation between employees and management. I hardly need point out that this latter type of organization more closely approximates the democratic ideal than the former.

What are the implications of these democratic ideals in terms of the practical problems of business and industrial organization? In politics we are all familiar with the ideas represented by the democratic and the authoritarian states. Despite our unshakeable faith in the superiority of democracy as a form of civic government, a great many managements apply strict authoritarian principles in the administration of their business affairs in the belief, apparently, that business and politics are two different orders of things.

Actually, the two institutions—business and government—are closely similar in their most essential aspect: Both are organizations of human beings, and both depend in the long run on the creative intelligence and effort, on the voluntary support and acceptance, of the people who comprise them. One of the great paradoxes of our society is that we have failed to apply to the internal affairs of our businesses the principles we all recognize when applied to political organization as largely responsible for the tremendous growth in national wealth and the superb social progress we have enjoyed.

Authoritarianism in Industry

Many business organizations closely resemble the authoritarian state in the sense that all direction, all thinking, all authority tends to flow from the top down. While the top administrator may delegate certain parts of his responsibility and authority, the delegation is largely in terms of implementing and effectuating at lower levels of the organization the policies and directives which have already been set up at the top. While a directive may be broken down into a series of parts and parceled out to different people, and while these people may be expected to show initiative and drive in executing their work, their activity is essentially that of carrying out an order.

To make such an organization work, management is forced to set up a rigorous system of controls to see that things get done and that people do not make too many mistakes in carrying out orders. In other words, a minimum of reliance is placed on the people in the organization, and the system depends primarily on the initiative and judgment of those at the top.

A corollary of this tendency is the elaboration of staff organizations, because where the exercise of judgment and skill is largely reserved to top administrators, they must be assisted by specialized advisory staffs. The result is a further extension of the system of controls through the initiative of the staff departments, as well as a considerable complication of the organizational structure, leading in turn to the necessity for other controls to hold the organization together and make it work. At the same time, because of the necessity for operating these controls and because employees at each successive level must be closely directed in their work, the supervisory hierarchy becomes more and more extended.

Effects on Supervision

Let us consider the manner in which the personnel administrator frequently acts in this type of organization. For one thing, he is likely to develop a feeling that supervisors can't be trusted to use good judgment ("good judgment" usually means what *he* would do in a particular situation). He feels impelled, therefore, to establish precise rules to govern every contingency. Or he must appropriate broad areas of responsibility from line supervision and vest them in the personnel department—all for the purpose, naturally, of guarding against the possibility that line supervisors or executives will make mistakes.

Certainly some broad framework of policy is necessary within which the supervisor should be required to work, but this should not lead to the substitution of an elaborate system of bureaucratic controls for the good judgment which should arise from the supervisor's own intimate knowledge of the immediate situation. The effect of such minute controls is to undermine the initiative and judgment of supervisors, so that ultimately their judgment really cannot be trusted because they have never had an opportunity to use it.

What Happens to the Rank and File?

What is the effect of this elaborate system of supervision and control on the rank and file? I refer the reader to the bitter complaints of management itself over the apathy of employees, their lack of initiative, their lack of interest in the affairs and problems of the enterprise, their antagonism to management, and so on. Instead of blaming this state of affairs on agitators, on faults in the educational system, or on errors in family methods of raising children, many managements need only look within their own organizations.

In effect, all that some organizations demand of lower-level employees is their animal energies, their muscle power. Some managements have done everything possible to take all judgment away from the operator, to relieve him of all initiative, to reduce his work to the lowest possible repetitive, mechanical level. This is usually justified in terms of supposedly greater efficiency, shorter training time, ability to use less skilled workers, and the greater proficiency of the operator which can come from repetition of simple movements.

Granted all this, but how much does industry lose in depriving the worker of all creative relation to this job? I hazard the opinion that industry has lost far more than it has gained. A very serious consequence of this process has been to destroy all meaning of the job for the worker—all meaning, that is, except in terms of the pay envelope. It has had the equally important effect of seriously undermining the confidence of workers in management. Furthermore, because they are restless and discontented, employees are easily influenced by strong leadership which may arise in opposition to management. Their jobs have made so few demands on their higher faculties, they have had so little opportunity to think, to take initiative, or to make their own contribution to the improvement of their jobs, that when aggressive antimanagement leadership arises, promising workers an opportunity for self-expression that management has not provided, they readily respond. Without question, one of the great appeals of unions is their promise of giving the workers a more effective voice in matters that affect their jobs—their assurance that employees no longer have to do just what they are told but can stand up and be men.

Toward Increased Participation

If management is to restore more cooperative working relations and more efficient production, it must give serious thought to ways and means by which it may restore the highest possible level of individual and group participation in solving problems. This does not imply the necessity for management-worker councils, shop committees, or any other formal devices, although under given circumstances these may have a certain utility. When problems arise at the workplace, however, rather than have someone in supervision or management do all the thinking and tell the workers what he has decided, it is only necessary to call the workers together and say: "Here is the problem; let's figure out the answer." Give them a chance to express their own ideas, and let them know that their thinking is needed and valued.

This is a simple device, but it can be tremendously effective, whether a personnel man is trying to get the cooperation of the line, an engineer is trying to introduce a technical change, or a foreman is trying to increase output. Employees, instead of waiting around to be told, will have the opportunity to express their own ideas with all the satisfaction such expression offers. If people are simply told what to do, they have no responsibility for what happens. But if they have a voice in working out a problem, part of the responsibility is theirs and they'll do everything they can to make it work.

Similar devices can be improvised to deal with a wide variety of situations. They can be of great value not only in dealing more effectively with the practical problems involved but, more important, in building better teamwork and cooperation. Moreover, these devices can be readily applied. They need not wait on changes in the character of the organization structure or in the system of administration.

The fundamental issue, however, must be dealt with in terms of organization structure and managerial attitudes and skill. So long as a company's management is authoritarian, its organization unduly complex, its staff and supervisory hierarchy unduly extended—and so long as controls are overprecise and overelaborate—the people in the organization will be stifled, their capacities and creative energies smothered by the sheer weight of the bureaucracy bearing down upon them.

In our efforts to extend the democratic process in industrial organizations I am not suggesting that we take over intact the apparatus of the democratic state. Business cannot be run by the ballot box, or by a parliament or congress. These were devised to solve the problem of effective participation by the citizenry in the affairs of its government. We must develop other inventions, adapted to the special circumstances of business, which will give employees at all levels of our organizations a greater sense of personal participation and "belonging," a greater sense of dignity and recognition of their worth both as individuals and as respected members of the industrial community.

25

An Interdisciplinary Focus Emerges: 1950-1960

Social Science and Industrial Relations: How Management Can Use the Human Relations Specialist

WILLIAM F. WHYTE

From all sides, social scientists are bearing down upon the field of industrial relations. In an area where just a few years ago only economists were active, today we find social anthropologists, sociologists, psychologists, and psychiatrists. Economists have long been active within business in analyzing economic conditions, but these new activities are bringing social science into industrial relations.

Reprinted by permission of the publisher from *Personnel*, Vol. 27, No. 4, January, 1951, pp. 258-266.

Dr. Whyte is Professor of Industrial Relations, New York State School of Industrial and Labor Relations at Cornell University.

Industrial managers are coming increasingly to believe that social science offers them aid on their industrial relations problems, but the field is in such a state of rapid development and resulting confusion that it is difficult for them to know where to turn.

How Did We Get Here?

Perhaps more than any other group, the social anthropologists have contributed to the ferment and growth in social science today. They began many years ago with studies of primitive tribes. There they developed both the methods of intensive research upon human relations and the point of view that characterizes their studies of modern civilized society. For decades, social science had been so wrapped up with ethics that real scientific development was impossible. Social scientists were more concerned with determining what was right and what was wrong than in discovering what *was* and how it got to be that way. The social anthropologists, studying societies completely different from our own, could approach them with a new perspective and were forced to recognize that their own middle-class civilized values did not apply to the behavior they saw before them. They had first to describe systematically what they observed and then seek to discover what put the behavior in this observed pattern. With the methods and point of view thus developed, it remained for W. Lloyd Warner to take the step of studying the modern American community of Yankee City. Since factories were a prominent part of Yankee City life, the path led naturally from the community to the factory itself, and to the related study of unions.

Sociologists have arrived at very much the same methods and point of view, coming along an entirely different route. A few decades ago, sociology consisted of the study of delinquency, crime, various forms of abnormal group behavior, and the family. The only thing they studied that did not naturally fall under the heading of a social problem was the family, and even here sociologists tended to devote much of their time to studying what they called family disorganization. They seemed to be concerned either with the things that were abnormal about society or with the phenomena that were left over from other disciplines—the family, for example. It was this view of the field that Louis Wirth once referred to as "the garbage can conception of sociology."

The day of the garbage can has passed. Most sociologists now look upon their field as the study of group behavior, and group behavior runs from the small informal clique to the large institution or organization. Sociologists have come at last to recognize that the factory is not only a technological and process organization; it is also a human organization which can be studied by methods and theories that can be used upon groups and organizations of all sorts. It was in this way that the field now called industrial sociology arose.

The psychologists were in the industrial relations field early, but at first it was only those psychologists who were developing methods of testing the characteristics of individuals. Some of this psychological testing effort has borne fruit and is useful today, but in the early stages the effort did not pay off as richly as it promised to do. It was found in the Western Electric research program, for example, that the men who tested highest in aptitude for the job were not necessarily the highest producers, nor were the ones who tested low necessarily the lowest producers. In fact, it was discovered that the individual's productivity was strongly influenced by his relations with other members of the group: His behavior could be explained only through examining his relations with other individuals. With this insight, growing numbers of social psychologists are developing methods for studying group process in industry. The work of Kurt Lewin and his followers, in what they called "group dynamics," has led to some ingenious social experiments.

The psychiatrists are the most recent arrivals in industrial relations. While a few of them have served in departments of industrial medicine, there is as yet little to report of a distinctly psychiatric nature in their industrial relations work. This development is being fostered particulary at Cornell's New York State School of Industrial and Labor Relations, where a grant of funds from the Carnegie Corporation has enabled us to set up a program to provide psychiatrists with the training they need in human relations in industry and other industrial relations fields.

While economists were the first in the general field, they were until recently concerned primarily with studying the national economy, trends in collective bargaining on a total industry basis, and other subjects of so large a scope that the student could not make any first-hand observation of behavior. However, the trend is now reversed and we find more and more economists working on case studies in industrial relations.

Standards for the Social Scientist?

To describe in detail the contributions of various branches of social science to the understanding of industrial relations is not my present task. I should like to make the assumption that social scientists have made a contribution to this field of knowledge and that they will be increasingly called upon to contribute. Nevertheless, the present use of social science in industrial relations is rather limited compared to the possibilities the field has to offer. This, then, is addressed to the man who is convinced that the social scientists can make a contribution but is confused about tying in social science with his own practical problems.

The problem is a difficult one for management. If the executive wishes to hire a medical doctor, he will not consider anyone who doesn't have a degree in medicine, and he is relatively safe in assuming that the training provided by high-ranking medical schools and hospitals will equip the man for his job. The case is quite different in the field of industrial relations. The men active in research in that field represent an extraordinary variety of educational background and training. Who can say what training qualifies a man to analyze the human problems that arise in industrial relations? The whole field is in such an early state of development that to standardize would impose a strait jacket upon future developments. For some time to come, we will have to cope with a field populated by men with the most diverse training and qualifications.

Furthermore, since the field involves dealing with people, the man of action (who deals with people all the time) is inclined to consider himself an expert. So he may have confidence in his ability to select men who know about people, regardless of their background and training. As a result, the personnel field has been prey to all sorts of fads. People have successfully peddled everything from vitamin pills to courses in phrenology as a cure for human relations problems.

Fortunately, this patent-medicine approach is rapidly losing ground as executives become more sophisticated in industrial relations; but too often, experience with alleged cure-alls has resulted in a skepticism and even a distrust of experts of all sorts.

Expert or Quack?

If social science is to be used more effectively in industrial relations, the executive needs some reliable method of distinguishing between the expert and the quack. Since the social sciences are in such a state of ferment, the executive cannot accept the Ph.D. degree as providing the assurance of competence that the M.D. does in medicine. There are, nevertheless, certain fairly reliable questions that the executive can ask himself as he attempts to distinguish between the quack and the expert in social science.

• *Has the man done research, or is he just a good talker?* The answers to new questions in industrial relations depend upon research, just as they do in the natural sciences, and the only man who can be trusted to do that research is the man who has already had some research training.

We can make this even more explicit by distinguishing among various types of research. Is the research man a field man or a library man? Social science research used to be primarily a matter of studying books, articles, and other documents. But the field of industrial relations is so undeveloped that the research man can find only a small portion of what he needs to learn in the library. He needs to get out into the field, to learn his way around the industrial organization, to observe people at work and in their leisure moments, to interview them about their problems, to sit in on discussions with them, and so on. There is no substitute for this first-hand experience. The valuable ideas that may be gained from reading the literature cannot be applied effectively unless the research man has had some first-hand experience with the raw data of human behavior. Many of the important ideas in industrial relations have been expressed in general terms, and the job of relating them to a specific situation can be done only when that specific situation has been studied.

• *Does the man make a diagnosis before he examines the patient?* Suppose you went to a doctor and told him, "I've been having the most terrible headaches." Suppose that without further ado he handed you a package of pills, saying, "Take this remedy. I have been prescribing it for all my patients with headaches, and they say it does wonders for them." How would you size him up? Obviously, you would decide he was a quack.

The same principle holds for industrial relations. Suppose you tell a consultant, "We have a bad problem of absenteeism and labor turnover in Department X." Suppose he immediately proposes a course of action. What conclusion do you reach about him? Well, that man is a quack too. He has a patent medicine to sell and he tries to sell it without investigating the needs of the patient.

The point is that investigation should come before prescription. On some highly complicated problems, we may have to do research for months to arrive at useful conclusions. When a problem is sufficiently similar to those we have worked over in detail in other cases, we can recognize the common elements after a brief preliminary investigation; then we can move rather rapidly from research into an action program. But whether the research time required is long or short, a reliable diagnosis of industrial relations problems is impossible without some sort of investigation. Therefore, beware of the man who has a patent medicine to sell.

• *Is the man interested in follow-up studies of the changes he recommends?* All too often, a consultant prescribes a course of action that is adopted only after he has left the situation. He may learn later that the executives were enthusiastic about the results, or he may learn that they were disappointed. But he has not learned anything of scientific value if he leaves before the program has been followed to a considerable extent. Even if the executives report that the program was highly successful, he cannot safely assume that he knows the reasons for that success. Often a given action program may be effective for reasons quite different from those that were used to justify it. If the consultant does not learn why the program succeeded by observing it in action, he may recommend the same program in a situation so different that the reasons for success in one case will not be present in the other. If he has followed up on the first case, he is in a better position to prescribe treatment in a similar case.

Of course, there are times when management does not permit follow-up studies. And there may be problems on which extensive follow-up studies can legitimately be dispensed with. But the essential point remains: The real scientist is not satisfied with giving good advice. He wants to expand his own knowledge through testing the results of any program he recommends. He wants to follow up whenever the appropriate opportunity arises.

• *Does the man promise that he will reform* other *people in the organization?* In recent years much attention has been given to training foremen in the skills of supervision. Since the foreman is the management man in most frequent contact with the employees, it may seem that frictions in the plant are due to a lack of skill on the part of the foreman. This is a comfortable point of view for the executive to accept—if only the foreman had the skill that he and his higher executives have in handling human problems, everything would be all right; therefore, improvements must be effected through working on the foremen. This point of view tends to make foremen the scapegoats for many difficulties that are not really their own responsibility. Our studies have shown again and again that members of higher managemt tend to set the pattern of human relations in the organization. The foreman who clashes with workers and union steward is in many cases simply responding to pressures from above. Higher management does not want him to handle his human relations the way he does; but higher management, nevertheless, unwittingly creates the pressures that drive the foreman into a conflict situation. Therefore, anyone who proposes to solve some of the basic human problems of the organization solely through foreman training should be recognized as a quack.

In the field of engineering, the vice president in charge of production may authorize the expenditures necessary to have a new machine or process introduced into the organization. This new machine or process may necessitate considerable adjustment on the part of people down the line, but it will not require adjustment from the vice president except as dissatisfaction at lower levels comes to his attention.

In human relations, the problem is different. The top management man who wishes to effect improvement in this field must first be willing to examine his own behavior. To do an effective human relations job, the executive needs to have skill and understanding as well as goodwill. If he is not willing to consider the possibility that he may have to change his behavior in order to achieve the results he wishes, then he had better not call upon a social scientist to help his organization.

An industrial organization is a social system made up of interdependent parts; the parts are the relations of people at all levels of the organization to each other. Top executives are in such a strategic position to affect behavior that the effects they have upon the organization must certainly be studied.

It is flattering to the executive to make the assumption that his behavior cannot possibly cause any problems and that existing problems have arisen solely at lower levels. However, the sophisticated executive will be wary of this approach. If he is not willing to have himself studied, he cannot expect much from a research program.

• *Does the man promise to set you on a definite course of action?* Time and again studies have come out with recommendations for action based upon adequate research—and nothing has happened. The gap between formal recommendations and an action program is large indeed. People do not change their behavior simply because they are told to do so, even when the recommendations are based upon the most cogent and logical analyses of the problem. Changing behavior is a slow and difficult task. Changes cannot be imposed from the outside; they can take hold only if the people who are to change become actively involved in the process of working out solutions to their problems. This does not mean that the executives themselves must do the research—research is a specialized job that requires special skills and training. It does mean that executives must be involved step by step in the discussion of findings and in the planning of action. Only in that way can we bridge the gap between research and action. Therefore, beware of the man who has too pat advice to offer.

What Kind of Expert Do You Need?

If he uses these measuring rods, the executive may have better success in distinguishing between experts and quacks in the field of industrial relations. However, there still remains the question of distinguishing among various types of experts. The social sciences are certainly interrelated, yet they cover such a broad territory that no individual can be expected to be competent in all of them. However, the specialist should know something about the possibilities and limitations of work with other techniques and bodies of theory. We will naturally expect him to think his own specialty is the most important approach to industrial relations problems, but we ought to demand of him that he recognize work in related fields and be able to distinguish problems that his own techniques and theories are not adequate to deal with. In talking with the social scientist, the executive can present a variety and range of problems to see whether the social scientist considers himself able to prescribe competently in all these areas, or whether he can talk instructively about work that is going on in related fields, at least in general terms. But beware of the social scientist who professes to be able to tackle all industrial relations problems.

While this approach may be helpful to executives in choosing social scientists, it can be no final answer. In the last analysis, the research man is himself the best judge of other research that is currently going on. Despite any personal biases he may have, he nevertheless has standards of judgment based upon training and experience that are not available to the layman. Though an organization which decides to move into work with social scientists will need to have more than one, the first choice is necessarily the crucial one. In this field, as in any other, a bum tends to select other bums to work with him, while a good man tends to select good people. There seems no alternative in this rapidly developing but confused field but to bank on one man carefully selected to build such social science research staff as the size of the business and its needs will justify. We can only hope that the first will be a man of broad enough interests so as not to be tied down to any narrow doctrinaire approach.

Ideally, of course, the industrial relations director, while not a research man himself, will have some familiarity with research problems and methods. Such a background is invaluable in selecting the director of research and can be exceedingly helpful in working with the research director to select and develop his staff.

Fitting Research In

Management can work with social scientists on industrial relations problems in either of two arrangements, singly or in combination. The research can be handled by contract with a university or with a commercial consulting organization; by developing within management an industrial relations research unit; or by having an industrial relations research unit and calling upon outside groups for specialized work that the management unit is not equipped to handle.

The need for industrial relations research in management is increasingly realized, but let us be clear about what we mean by research. A short time ago a man with a nationwide reputation in the personnel field discussed the functions that every good personnel department should have and mentioned research as one of the important functions. But to him, the research department or unit should function to study what other companies have been doing in the personnel field. With this background, they should be able to inform their own management about the latest developments in personnel. All too often, this activity degenerates into a game of "follow the leader." The personnel man discovers that a new practice has been developed by the XYZ Company. He talks with some of the personnel men and executives of the company. They are enthusiastic about the effectiveness of this new practice. Now, he already knows that the XYZ Company is one of the largest in its field and is reputed to be highly profitable and well managed. When he reports about this new practice to his own management, they are inclined to think that the XYZ people are really shrewd operators and if this practice works for XYZ, it must also be a good thing for them.

One of the first things we learn in human relations research is that the executive's concept of the effectiveness of any practice or policy must be taken with a good deal of salt. Whether the practice of the XYZ Company is as effective as its executives would have us believe can be determined only through research into its human relations: We would have to determine factors that make it effective with XYZ before we could predict confidently that it would be effective in another corporation.

This practice of finding out what a prestige organization is doing and then trying to do likewise is still too common in personnel work today. If we are going to play follow the leader in that way, we ought not kid ourselves that we are carrying out research.

Your Own Laboratory

The management that wishes to sponsor research in industrial relations would do well to consider its own organization as the laboratory for study and experimentation. This is not completely unknown in industry today. About a generation ago, the Western Electric Company developed a research program with the Harvard School of Business Administration, and it still has a human relations research unit as a regularly functioning part of the management organization. More recently, Sears, Roebuck and Co. developed a personnel research unit in its personnel department. The first work was done in collaboration with Burleigh Gardner of the University of Chicago's Committee on Human Relations in Industry, but as the program developed from 1944 on, more and more of the research came to be done by a staff employed directly by the company. The organizational studies being done today in Sears seem to compare very well indeed with the best that is being done in universities.

There is today ample experience to provide the principles for sound development of human relations research in industrial organizations. However, it would seem unwise for management to rely for its research entirely upon outside organizations. If it does, how is it to develop its own understanding of the possibilities and limitations of research, and how can the executive know what kind of research is appropriate for what type of problem? The management that has its own research organization should be best able to determine what is needed in research and what resources should be called upon if they are not available within the organization.

The small company will certainly not be able to afford a human relations research unit, but it would do well to consider having at least one man with human relations research training. Even if he does not have time for intensive research, he has a research way of thinking about human problems. The social scientist may be most useful in helping executives to think more effectively about their human problems.

26

A Coalescing and Reassessment of Ideas and Practice: The 1960's

The Mythical Personnel Manager

DALE HENNING AND WENDELL FRENCH

The personnel man as described in textbooks and journals is like the Abominable Snowman—much talked about but seldom seen. Traditional usage would lead us to believe that the personnel man is a "staff" man—that is, an official with advisory and consultative rights, but advisory and consultative only, who performs certain "service" activities.

In our opinion, this is far from the actual case. The word "staff" simply does not fit what the personnel manager is and does. As Hayakawa would say, "The map does not fit the territory."[1] Use of the word "staff" is symptomatic of a general misconception of the personnel manager's role.

The Myth

In this article the activities and position of the personnel manager are examined in terms of the kinds of influence and authority exercised by him. The position discussed is that of the chief personnel officer of a company, whether he be called a vice-president, personnel director, director of industrial relations, or any of a number of other titles. Various personnel functions are examined in order to portray his role more accurately.

Before looking at the "real" personnel manager, however, let us review some typical definitions of the word "staff" when this word is used in describing personnel and industrial relations, for much of the myth of the personnel manager revolves around this concept.[2] McFarland, for example, defines staff as being "devoid of the right to command or to veto." And he goes on to refer to the personnel function as a staff function.[3] Myers and Turnbull describe staff as "advice-giving" and repeatedly use the word in describing industrial relations in contrast with "line" departments.[4]

Both authors are professors in the Graduate School of Business Administration at the University of Washington, Seattle.

[1] S. I. Hayakawa, *Language in Thought and Action* (New York, Harcourt, Brace and Co., 1949), pp. 31-33.

[2] We are taking these quotations without some qualifying comments which may appear earlier or later in the manuscripts because these statements point up vividly the problem to which we are addressing ourselves.

[3] Dalton E. MacFarland, "The Scope of the Industrial Relations Function," *Personnel*, January-February, 1959, pp. 42-51.

[4] Charles A. Myers and John Turnbull, "Line and Staff in Industrial Relations," *Harvard Business Review*, July-August, 1956, pp. 113-124. (Without saying so, Myers and Turnbull point up the inadequacy of the word "staff" as we shall see later.)

Sayles and Strauss define staff as designating "a group in the organization that is not charged with the responsibility of getting the work done—as distinct from the line departments."[5]

Mee and Williams say "As the personnel department is conceived as a staff unit, there is seldom any operating or line authority for final decisions delegated to its people other than for internal personnel department affairs."[6] It is clear that McGregor has a "staff" concept of personnel administration, although he takes note of an occasional delegating of personnel administration responsibility to the "staff," a practice which he deplores.[7]

And so it goes. Personnel departments tend to be referred to as staff, and staff traditionally is defined as advice-giving. To say that the personnel department performs an auxiliary function cannot be denied, but to refer to it in terms meaning advice-giving, and to ignore other aspects, we think, departs substantially from reality.

Is He Strictly Staff?

Some authors who define staff as advice-giving, and who refer to the personnel department as being "staff," ignore their own definitions by describing personnel administration in practice as being something quite different. For example, Myers and Turnbull use the term "staff" in talking about personnel functions, yet carefully document that a great deal of effective decision-making often rests with the personnel officer.

In referring to interviews conducted with personnel executives, they note, "One of the most striking results of the interviews was the contradiction between belief and practice . . . the typical response was that he operated in the staff capacity or, at most, in some combination of staff and line capacity. But when he went on to describe how he handled particular personnel or labor relations functions, it was clear that in a number of situations *he made the effective decisions*."[8]

Saltonstall[9] also contradicts himself. He starts out by saying that the personnel director exerts implied authority and functional controls as well as performing advisory activities. He concludes, however, by classifying the division of responsibility between "staff" and "line" in such a way as to imply that the personnel director has little or no authority. He uses words like "develop," "consult," "plan," "interpret," "evaluate," "diagnose," "research," "investigate," and "recommend," with reference to personnel people; and such words as "direct," "control," "decide," "enforce," "apply," "perform," and "instruct," in referring to the responsibilities of supervisors in departments other than personnel.

Although Saltonstall has made a contribution in shedding some light on

[5] Leonard Sayles and George Strauss, *Personnel, The Human Problems of Management* (Englewood Cliffs, N.J., Prentice-Hall, 1960), pp. 395-396.

[6] John F. Mee and Edward G. Williams, "Managing a Successful Personnel Relations Program," *Indiana Press Information Bulletin No. 33*, Bureau of Business Research, Indiana University, 1958, p. 24.

[7] Douglas McGregor, "Line Management Responsibility for Human Relations" in Building up the Supervisor's Job. (*Manufacturing Series*. No. 213, American Management Association, 1953), pp. 27-35.

[8] Myers and Turnbull, see note 4, p. 114.

[9] Robert Saltonstall, "Who's Who in Personnel Administration," *Harvard Business Review*, Vol. 33, No. 4, July-August, 1955, pp. 75-83.

the role of the personnel executive, we do not believe that he goes far enough in documenting the authority typically found in that position.

It Isn't Necessarily So

There are, however, a few organization theorists whose theories, we believe, can readily be applied to personnel management. For example, Stahl asks . . . "would it not make sense to divest ourselves of the abracadabra that divides 'line' and 'staff' into incongruous kinds of activity and to recognize that *all* such activities are simply specialized subdivisions of that organization's work?"[10]

He goes on to say: "I find it convenient to think of the work of an enterprise as a network, a grid, or a checkerboard in which vertical program subdivisions are interlaced with horizontal sustaining activities. The chief executive sits in a position at a top corner from which he holds both the vertical lines and the horizontal lines."[11]

Applying his conceptual scheme to personnel administration, we find the personnel director involved in the development and control of the framework or the boundaries within which program operators must perform—particularly the framework and boundaries pertaining to the quality of the treatment of the people and the procedures used to assure equity and control.

Urwick[12] lends support to this view: "This staff relationship is at present very imperfectly understood and applied in civil life. It has been suggested . . . that a 'staff' officer's position should be 'purely advisory.' This suggestion is an escape. The phrase 'purely advisory' is usually an attempt to avoid personal misunderstandings and clashes of authority due to inability on both sides to form a clear picture of a correct position. But it is equally obvious that a subordinate who merely adds to the numbers of advisors cannot do much to relieve a chief or an increasing burden and complexity of command and particularly in the work of coordination."

Network of Authority

Anderson's[13] functional executive is similar to the military "staff" officer concept of Urwick and is also consistent with Stahl's concept of the "network of authority." Anderson says in effect, that the line officer rarely has full authority and that functional officers (of which the personnel officer would be an example) typically exercise controls over certain aspects common to the various line units.

This is the way he puts it: ". . . As soon as the first step is taken toward dividing up the work of the enterprise into operating units, there must be initiated some method of getting the divided parts or units back together again into an integral whole . . . .

". . . The managers or supervisors of such units find accordingly their spheres of activity diminished and their independence curtailed, and since the chief executive, due to limitation of his span of attention and control,

[10] A. G. Stahl, "The Network of Authority," *Public Administration Review*, Vol. 18, No. 1, Winter, 1958.

[11] *Ibid.*

[12] L. Urwick, "Personnel Management in Relation to Factory Organization," Institute of Labor Management, Aldwych, London, W.C.2, England, 1943, p. 17.

[13] E. H. Anderson, "The Functional Concept in Organization," *Advanced Management*, October, 1960, Vol. 25, no. 10, pp. 17, 18.

cannot personally supervise all the activities necessary for coordination and control, his only recourse is to appoint special assistants for the task. . . ."

Stahl, Urwick and Anderson, then, provide a useful framework for thinking about the role of the personnel director. All three talk about controls and authority exercised by what are often labeled "staff" people. We think the personnel director is a case in point.

Basic Thesis

Here, then, is our central thesis: In addition to advice-giving and directing the work of his own subordinates, the job of the corporate personnel director involves a type of functional authority which is exercised horizontally and down throughout the entire organization, and that this authority can only be understood by examining the subcomponents of major personnel functions. The word "staff" with its connotation of advice-giving glosses over the personnel director's role and either ignores or denies major parts of it. We will first cite what we think are appropriate tests of authority, and then try to show how the personnel manager meets these tests.

Influence or Authority?

In reality, is the personnel manager influential or is he authoritative?"[14] We submit that there are two tests of authority which will help us answer this question. The foremost of these is that there must exist the institutionalized right to limit choice. A secondary test and one which by itself does not suffice is that the recipient of an authoritative communication "holds in abeyance his own critical faculties for choosing between alternatives."

In order to understand and to utilize these tests of authority in our analysis, it is first necessary to examine the nature of authority and power as contrasted with influence. Figure 1 gives this comparison in a summarized fashion.

FIGURE 1

Power	Influence
Is the ability to limit choices for social action.	Is the ability to cause others voluntarily to choose alternatives favored by the influencer.
Coercive.	
Based on inequality.	Persuasive.
May or may not be formalized or institutionalized.	Always informal.
If institutionalized, is referred to as "authority."	May exist either within or outside a formal organization.
When in the form of authority attaches to a position.	Based on free choice and perceived superiority of the alternative chosen.
When in the form of authority, involves rights—the right to command, to limit choice.	Attached to ideas, doctrines, persons.

[14] It goes without saying that he exercises authority within his own department. We are not here concerned with this, but rather with his exercise of authority in other organizational units.

Authority is institutionalized power. The existence of authority in an organization results from conscious efforts to structure power relationships between people. We artificially assign extra power in the form of authority, to certain positions whose occupants will hopefully use this extra power to further the goals of the enterprise. Thus, we create what is in a sense an artificial power inequality.

Authority usually involves the ability to broaden as well as to limit choices. Thus, we speak of someone having authority to grant a subordinate a pay increase. This ability to broaden choices results in applications of authority that are sometimes more subtle than mere restrictions of choice which are negative in character.

To illustrate, it is quite obvious that a foreman is limiting choice when he says "Do this job, or draw your pay." It is much less obvious that choices are being restricted when he merely refrains from giving a promotion or a transfer.

"That's an Order"

There is another aspect of authority that helps us to recognize it. Where authority is manifest, the recipient of a communication "holds in abeyance his own critical faculties for choosing between alternatives."[15] A person who receives an order does what he is told, suspending his judgment about other courses of action (provided, of course, he chooses not to challenge the authority of the communicator as we shall point out).

We have now suggested two conditions which indicate the presence of authority. The most critical of these is the institutionalized right to limit choice. The second is that the communicatee holds in abeyance his own critical faculties for choosing between alternatives.

Where both conditions prevail, authority undoubtedly exists. Where the former condition exists alone we submit that authority exists even if the recipient of a communication questions the directive or refuses to obey.

Chester Barnard and other theorists argue that this makes the authority nonexistent, a point of view with which we take issue.[16] However, using Barnard's acceptance theory of authority one still comes to the conclusions set forth below.

Limitation of Choices

Where only the suspension of judgment about alternatives exists, authority is absent. Many people in an organization are technically expert and their suggestions are often accepted and acted upon uncritically. But if the technically expert persons lack the right to limit choices of the communicatee, the situation is either one of influence (where the communicatee *could* choose freely if he wished) or one of power (where the communicatee is coerced but the communicator lacks the *right* to limit choice).

[15] Herbert Simon, *Administrative Behavior* (New York, John Wiley and Sons, 1958), p. 126.

[16] The superior retains his authority through time. In the *particular* instance where compliance is not forthcoming, this authority is ineffective and hence can be argued to be nonexistent. For a discussion of this point of view see Chester Barnard, *Functions of the Executive* (Cambridge, Harvard University Press, 1938).

Influence vs. Authority

How does the personnel manager fit into this authority-influence picture? Is he authoritative? Is he influential? Is he both? We are convinced that he is both.

He is influential, of course, because he accomplishes much through persuasion, but we submit that typically, he also has authority. Let's look at the personnel manager's activities, using the two criteria mentioned above—limitation of choice and communicatee's suspension of judgment about alternatives.

Does the personnel manager have the right to limit choice? Here we think the answer is an unqualified "yes." Typically, the personnel manager is given functional authority—the right to determine and enforce many personnel methods, procedures and policies. (Like all other executives, sales, finance and production included, there are some policies he will determine unilaterally, some after consultation with peers, and others will be submitted to the president for approval.)

The personnel manager's functional authority is a broad authority in the sense that it covers all, or almost all, departments of the enterprise, and it is a narrow authority in the sense that it is restricted to personnel policies, procedures and methods. Where the personnel manager is given functional authority (that is, the right to determine and/or enforce personnel procedures, methods, and policies), he has the right to limit choice.

The production manager, the foreman, the sales manager, and the purchasing agent may no longer determine individually what personnel practices will be within their respective departments—there has occurred a "reduction or limitation . . . of alternatives to the social action of one person or group by another person or group." This has come about by virtue of the rights granted to the personnel manager.

"But," it is often said, "the personnel manager really is just acting for the president or general manager, and he has no authority in his own right." We consider this a spurious disqualification—cannot the same be said of the sales manager and of the production manager? Yet their "authority" is unquestioned.

He Limits Action

The personnel manager limits choice in every instance when he exercises the functional authority granted to him by his superior. He does this when he directs that no person shall receive a pay rate in excess of the rate range allowed for his job. He does it when he directs that employees are not allowed to smoke on the job, are not allowed in restricted areas, or will not have access to confidential files. He limits choice when he directs that all new employees must undergo indoctrination procedures, and executives must follow procedures established by him in the discharge of personnel.

The second test of authority we have posed is the uncritical reception of a communication without reference to alternative courses of action. How does the personnel manager meet this test? We submit that typically his communications are accepted without overt challenge; that his order is not treated merely as one of the evidential bases for making a choice; and that the recipient of the order does indeed "hold in abeyance his own critical faculties for choosing between alternatives."

He Gets Compliance

The foreman who receives a notice that merit ratings for his department are due in the personnel office on July 1 does not say to himself, "Well, that is a pretty good suggestion, but there are alternatives to doing it this way, and I'll just mull this over and make up my mind about its feasibility later on." More likely the foreman says, in effect, "This is what I've been told to do so I'll do it."

Can't Fire Dissenters

But what happens if he *doesn't* do it—when he refuses to carry out the directives of the personnel manager? If a subordinate challenges the authority of, say, the sales manager, he may be dismissed or otherwise punished. Are there similar sanctions open to the personnel manager? He may not discharge the person challenging his authority, for his functional authority covers only the establishment of policies, procedures and methods and does not include the right to fire (except, of course, in his own department).

But, He Can Block Raises

However, there are other ways in which he may limit choices of those who refuse to conform to his directives. He might, for example, just refuse to approve pay raises for those persons whose merit ratings were not received at the time and in the form indicated, to use the example cited above. Or, he might decline to place on the payroll the names of those employees who were hired in violation of procedures he had laid down.[17] Choice limitations such as these are likely to bring about conformance.

Punitive choice limitations such as those just mentioned, however, may be temporary. Sooner or later the personnel manager's right to take such punitive action will be challenged. When conflicts of this sort arise they must be resolved either between the disagreeing parties or by a superior executive, usually the president.

At this point the president has to make a decision about preserving his organizational integrity. How much value does he place on functional organization as a way of doing business? How valuable is it to him to have the specialist actually give the orders, actually determine the methods, procedures and policies, rather than merely giving advice?

There are many other factors involved, of course, but ultimately this is the decision the president must make. Much can be done to minimize these potential conflicts, not properly the subject of this writing, but the potential will always exist as long as functional units such as the personnel department are used.

He Writes "Directives"

Even in the absence of punitive measures such as those mentioned above, the personnel manager has authority. He has the right to limit choice, and his communications are generally accepted uncritically. True, his authority is subject to challenge. But so is all authority in a democratic society. The sales manager's authority can be questioned. Even his right to

[17] Note that if the personnel manager goes to his superior and asks that the superior force his subordinate to comply, influence rather than authority is being manifested, i.e., the personnel manager *influences* his superior to use his *authority*.

FIGURE 2

Examples of Areas of Authority and Persuasion for the Personnel Manager

	Area of Authority → Area of Persuasion		
Function	Maximum Use of Authority	Combined Use of Authority and Persuasion	Maximum Use of Persuasion
Salary Administration	Direction of payroll calculations Establishing and administering job evaluation system Establishing and administering wage and salary plan Exemption ruling	Inter-departmental data gathering	Salary changes under rules of Applying job evaluation factors to a specific job
Performance Review	Establishing and administering performance standard systems and plan, and merit rating		Changing recommendations about a specific individual under plans
Training, Orientation, Management, Development	Orientation procedure	Determination of number of participants in a training program	Determining who will attend advanced management seminar
Hiring and Recruitment	Recruitment program Rejecting candidates Establishing beginning salaries and pay grades		Employment of individuals recommended by personnel department
Safety and Health Program	Making area "off limits" until hazardous material is removed	General housekeeping, removal of dangerous objects from work areas	Which foremen attend off-hours safety conference at University
Discipline	Administration of discipline procedure	Establishment of discipline procedure Whether disciplinary layoff will become discharge	Initiating discipline
Transfer	Transfer rules		Transfer of individuals under rules of system

take punitive measures can be questioned—it can always be appealed to higher levels in the organization. The personnel manager's authority's being subject to challenge does not make it nonexistent.

We think it can be shown conclusively that the personnel manager (1) limits choice, (2) has a right to do so, (3) has his communications received, interpreted, and implemented while the recipient's "own critical faculties for choosing between alternatives" are held in abeyance.

In Figure 2 the personnel director's role is analyzed in terms of the authority he uses as compared with the influence he exerts. The reader will note that it does not suffice to look only at broad functions of personnel administration, such as salary administration, or hiring or recruitment.

He Administers Pay Plans

Rather, these broad activities must be subdivided in order to determine more accurately the role of the personnel executive. For example, we find the personnel director having a great deal of authority in establishing and administering wage and salary plans, but that in making actual salary changes for specific individuals, the department head involved has considerable latitude—as long as he stays within the limits established in the plan. Within these latter limits, therefore, the personnel director can only use persuasion in accomplishing his ends.

Figure 3 is essentially a continuation of the first two columns of Figure 2, and lists various broad functions and typical command statements (stripped of pleasantries) which the personnel director might make. Such command statements are often couched in persuasive terms, but this does not change their authoritative nature.

FIGURE 3

Typical Authority and Command Statements

Function	Typical Command Statements
Wage Policy	"Time off with pay because of tornado warning will count as time worked for computing overtime."
Wage and Salary Administration	"Salary recommendations under the salary plan are due _______. You are not permitted to exceed the limits of the ranges of the plan under any circumstances."
Exemption Rulings	"Mr. Jones is now exempt under the Wage-Hour Laws and will no longer fill out a time sheet. He will draw straight time for any scheduled overtime. Incidental overtime will not be paid."
Merit Rating and Performance Standard Procedures	"No more than 25% of your employees may be placed in the 'superior' category." "Performance standards must be worked out between subordinate and superior with concurrence of higher authority." "The following format is to be used."

FIGURE 3 (*continued*)

Function	Typical Command Statements
Recruitment and Screening	"This man will not be invited to the plant." "We are going to visit ______ College this year and try to recruit some of their graduating physicists."
Orientation Procedure	"All newly hired employees will attend an orientation meeting at 10:00 in the cafeteria the Monday following the day they report to work."
Establishment of Beginning Salaries	"If we hire this girl, in view of her experience, skill, and the pay plan, her beginning salary will be $350.00 per month."
Safety and Health Program	"All employees entering room 30B must wear respirators until repairs can be made."
Administration of Benefit Plans	"Issue a check for $40.00 to Mr. Olson to cover cost of X-rays at XYZ clinic."
Discipline Procedure	"You may put a man on immediate disciplinary lay-off pending a review of his case, but you may not unilaterally discharge him without personnel review."
Termination Procedures	"All terminating employees must pick up their checks at the personnel department and be interviewed."
Transfer Procedure	"Except in unusual cases senior employees are not to be made available for transfer because of technological change. The least senior employees are to be made available for transfer. You cannot transfer Mr. Smith."
Confidential Records	"I am sorry. We do not disclose that information."
Testing Procedures	"No one, including department heads, may see the results of the testing validation sample just completed."
Compliance with Federal and State Laws	"That would be a violation of state wage-hour laws, and as a matter of policy, this company is not going to violate these laws."

His Reach Is Company-wide

An observation of these two charts will show that the personnel manager exercises functional authority as we have previously defined it—namely, the right to determine methods and procedures and policies for personnel activities throughout the firm. (To be sure, he may seek the support of the president and a few major executives, as may any executive when making changes of major consequence.)

This functional authority is characterized by being specialized—it is limited to *personnel* activities—and by being comprehensive—it covers all or almost all of the units in the organization. As is seen in the preceding charts, his authority is so closely intertwined with the authorities of other department heads that they have, in effect, shared authority; for example, the determination of specific pay rates within the various pay ranges as previously mentioned. But this in no way refutes the contention that he does indeed have authority.

His Relations with the President

We can tell something more about how much authority the personnel manager has by looking at his relationship to the president. The president may delegate important policy-making and planning authorities to him, or he may delegate only relatively minor authorities dealing with procedural matters. The most important kinds of decisions usually have something to do with planning—with setting down future courses of action.

If the personnel manager makes important planning decisions it can be shown that he is more authoritative than if the president makes all the planning decisions and the personnel manager is left only to carry out the plans.

Figure 4 lists various alternative hypothetical situations. The left side of the figure indicates a situation in which the personnel manager makes a few important decisions. His only real function here is to prepare the plan for his superior's approval and then to make routine decisions about its implementation.

In the center category we find him performing all of the steps in planning and implementing with the exception of the critical decision on approving the final plan. At the far right of the figure the personnel manager has nearly complete freedom to plan, approve the plans, and implement them without reference to his superior.

A Continuum

Obviously, where one operates on this continuum will depend not only upon the importance of the decisions involved, but also upon forces in both the president (e.g., his desire to develop his subordinates) and the personnel manager (e.g., his imagination, initiative, and willingness to take on responsibility).

Most authors would have us believe that the personnel manager falls to the left side of the figure. We submit, however, that personnel managers find the subcomponents of their functions distributed over the entire continuum.

The Velvet Glove Plus

As we have indicated, in his daily actions the personnel manager may sound more like an advisor than a functional executive. He may depend upon persuasion and expertness much more than on his ability to "order" that any action be taken. Indeed, in the long run his success depends very much upon his expertness and persuasiveness. But the production manager and the sales manager also are much more dependent upon persuasion than upon the exercise of bald discipline. This is true of all executives.

In conclusion, we find the use of the word "staff" in referring to the personnel director to be symptomatic of popular misconceptions about his

FIGURE 4.

Exercise of Authority in Planning, Directing, and Controlling of Personnel Activities

AREA OF AUTHORITY USE BY SUPERIOR

Superior sees problem and need for plan, directs personnel manager to draw up plan, personnel manager performs data gathering and other intermediate planning steps, superior approves final plan; personnel manager implements plan, makes routine decisions, makes nonroutine decisions after consulting superior.	Superior sees problem and need for plan, approves undertaking of planning. Personnel manager performs intermediate steps in planning, superior approves final plans. Personnel manager implements plans, making routine and nonroutine implementation decisions without reference to superior.	Personnel manager perceives problem and need for plan, undertakes planning on his own without superior approval, performs intermediate steps in planning. Superior approves final plan. Personnel manager implements plan, making decisions without reference to superior.	Personnel manager perceives problem, sees need for plan, undertakes planning, performs intermediate steps in planning, approves final plan, informs superior, implements plan. Superior controls through frequent and continuing post-action review.	Personnel manager perceives problem, need for plan, undertakes planning, performs intermediate steps, approves final plan, implements plan, informs superior. Superior controls through infrequent periodic review. Disapproval, nonsupport, or veto of personnel manager's decisions very unusual and infrequent.

AREA OF AUTHORITY USE BY PERSONNEL MANAGER

role. This word implies that the personnel director is solely advisory—that he accomplishes all his work by virtue of persuasion and expertness. This does not square with reality, with real personnel directors and real business organizations as we have observed them.

Conclusions

We find it useful to analyze the personnel director's role in terms of the authority he exercises, in contrast to the influence he exerts; to compare his authority in planning with the authority he exercises in the implementation of plans, and in the kind of authority he possesses in contrast to that possessed by executives in nonfunctional organizational units.

Also, we find it useful to break down the major components of the personnel manager's job for purposes of analysis. A study of these subcomponents indicates that the authority he exercises varies considerably between and within the various components of a given personnel activity. To focus solely on the major components without subdividing them obscures the real nature of the role.

In summary, we think that the authoritative aspects of the personnel manager's position are as much in evidence as are the influential aspects of that position. We think it would be highly useful to relegate the mythical personnel manager to the realm of folklore and to focus greater attention on the real authorities vested in real-life personnel managers in the modern corporation.

27

Attack from Academia

Behavioral Scientists and Personnel Management

MARVIN D. DUNNETTE AND BERNARD M. BASS

The search for the philosopher's stone which would transmute base metals into gold occupied alchemists for hundreds of years. Although they were concentrating on the wrong problem, many of the alchemists' techniques and much of their lore served eventually as the basis for the budding science of chemistry.

Like alchemists, personnel managers have concentrated on the wrong problem, trying one technique after the other in a long search for a psychological touchstone to solve all the human problems of industry.

Reprinted with permission from *Industrial Relations*, Vol. 2, May, 1963, pp. 115-130.

Marvin Dunnette is Professor of Psychology and Industrial Relations, University of Minnesota, and Bernard Bass is Professor of Psychology and Director, Management Research Center, University of Rochester.

Meanwhile, particularly during the last decade, the behavioral sciences have developed principles and techniques which have proved immediately applicable and useful to the art of management. These developments are long overdue; they are occurring after more than a century of philosophizing and experimenting with various concepts of work, employment, management, and manpower marketing.

Prescientific management, in the Smith-Ricardo-Marx tradition, regarded work as a commodity to be bought at the lowest price and sold at the highest, with the worker an interchangeable part to be maintained at minimum cost in the production process. Taylorism, which followed, focused on rationalizing work, the workplace, and incentives in order to maximize output and induce workers to exert maximum effort in return for material gain. Paternalism, the precursor of the human relations school, sought to win employee loyalty either through crude bribery or more subtle and sophisticated manipulation. Faulty logic, coupled with false assumptions about the nature of man, resulted in generations of unnecessary conflict, rule-making and rule-breaking, dissatisfaction, and curtailed production.

Modern personnel management includes vestiges of each of these approaches in the programs it seeks to promote as its raison d'être. The tendency to regard labor as a commodity is reflected in the continuing practice of paying wage earners by the hour rather than on a salaried basis. Taylorism is reflected in job simplification, specification, and specialization, when job enlargement might be more appropriate. Paternalism has resulted in hidden labor costs and in fringe benefits as high as 40 per cent of the total payroll, creating what Bendix has called the new industrial feudalism.

Toward a Science of Industrial Behavior

During the past decade, efforts to promote the scientific and objective study of human behavior in industry have successfully penetrated management practice. Paralleling this movement, many of the leading schools of business and industrial administration have shifted from the descriptive study of current personnel practices to the application of principles of the social sciences to the analysis of organization problems. Emphasis is placed on creativity, disciplined thinking, and the appropriate use of analytical tools for effective decision-making. The behavioral sciences are making rapid strides and are moving to a central position in the study of industrial behavior. Yet personnel management seems intent on pursuing a pattern of increasing stagnation and lack of significant innovation. As a result, behavioral scientists are being employed by businessmen not only to undertake research but also to apply their findings to the actual operation of the enterprise. Psychology, sociology, and related disciplines are responding to the call of a new and enlightened management. Personnel management, with its traditional practices, appears to be ill-equipped to face the business and industrial needs of the future.

If this indictment of personnel management is valid, it raises some disturbing questions and has some interesting implications for the future role of the behavioral sciences in industry. This article will be concerned, therefore, with the following important questions:

1. In what respects has personnel management defaulted in meeting

businessmen's needs for innovation in handling the problems of human behavior in industry? Why has this occurred? Is it too late to do anything about it?

2. What has been the role of the behavioral sciences in relation to the human problems of industry? How have the behavioral sciences responded to the changing needs and emphases of modern business?
3. What will be the role of the behavioral scientist in the business organization of the future? What problems of human behavior may he be asked to help solve, and what will be his mode of attack?
4. What are the "development needs" of personnel management? What kind of manager will the personnel manager of the future be? What contributions will he be expected to make to the business enterprise? To what extent will he depend on behavioral science? What will he contribute to the development of the behavioral sciences?
5. Finally, how will human behavior problems of the business firm of the future be handled? How will personnel management and behavioral science interact and supplement one another?

The Failure of Personnel Management

Evidence of the failure of personnel management to adapt to the changing climate of business is widespread and well-documented. Drucker was one of the first to call attention to the shaky future of the profession. In 1954, he assigned to the personnel function such chores as housekeeping, filing, and firefighting and suggested that it was destined to become a cluster of unrelated functions such as accounting, office management, and the handling of administrative arrangements—in other words, a sort of staff office boy to the rest of the organization.[1] Odiorne also finds little reason for optimism.[2] He suggests that too many personnel officers still reflect the naiveté of the early twenties and that many still practice the rites of the profession as if nothing had changed since 1925. The personnel program in most companies is not central to the enterprise and, indeed, is rapidly coming to be regarded as a function entirely ancillary to the major purposes of the firm. Herbert Heneman has provided a most discerning and thorough analysis of the present problems and uncertain future of personnel procedures.[3] Personnel management, in his opinion, has been marked by shallowness, negativism, static concepts, and oversimplified approaches to complex problems. Instances of these limitations are not hard to find.:

1. The personnel interview continues to be the most widely used method for selecting employees, despite the fact that it is a costly, inefficient, and usually invalid procedure.[4] It is often used to the exclusion of far more thoroughly researched and validated procedures. Even

[1] P. F. Drucker, *The Practice of Management* (New York: Harper, 1954).

[2] G. S. Odiorne, "Company Growth and Personnel Administration," *Personnel,* XXVII (January-February, 1960), 32-41.

[3] H. G. Heneman, Jr., *Manpower Management: New Wrapping on Old Merchandise* (Minneapolis, Minn.: Industrial Relations Center, University of Minnesota, 1960).

[4] See, for example, R. Wagner, "The Employment Interview: A Critical Summary," *Personnel Psychology*, II (1949), 17-46; G. W. England and D. G. Paterson, "Selection and Placement—the Past Ten Years," in H. G. Heneman, editor, *Employment Relations Research* (New York: Harper, 1960), pp. 43-72; M. D. Dunnette, "Personnel Management," *Annual Review of Psychology*, XIII (1962), 285-314.

when the interview is used in conjunction with other procedures, it is almost always treated as the final hurdle in the selection process. In fact, other selection methods (e.g., psychological tests) are often regarded simply as supplements to the interview.

The continued uncritical use of the personal interview offers a clear illustration of what is perhaps personnel management's prime problem—that is, the great resistance to carrying out fundamental research on its practices and techniques. Careful programs of research have been conducted to assess the validity of other selection techniques, and progress has been made toward specifying their validity under a variety of conditions. Until similar research has specified the conditions under which the interview does have predictive value, its continued use must be rationalized as a public relations device rather than as a personnel procedure. Even so, there are still many outspoken and ardent supporters of the personal interview, many of whom are wedded to the device as their raison d'être.

2. Typical management development programs clearly illustrate the shallow and oversimplified approaches denounced by Heneman. Again, in connection with such programs, personnel management displays overenchantment with gadgetry and techniques, ignoring the need for research on the enormously complex problems of human behavior in industry. As Taylor has pointed out, these gimmicks in management development programs range from role-playing and brainstorming to management by committee and so-called "new" techniques of conference leadership.[5] Many personnel men have been only too ready to pose as experts in the difficult science of human development and behavior change. They have used gimmicks to promote an *art* of management development, without first undertaking the solid scientific research required to develop the principles on which a sound program might be based. No wonder the programs, so widely promoted by personnel staff departments, have gone from "fad" to "old hat" in less than a decade. Widespread disillusionment with management development programs has contributed substantially to the demise of personnel management.

3. Negativism, shallowness and static concepts are particularly evident in wage and salary administration. On the basis of an exhaustive review of the literature of the last ten years on employee and executive compensation, Belcher concludes that wage and salary administrators have developed an array of programs but have given practically no attention to evaluation of their relative merit.[6] Salary administration functions in far too many firms constitute either holding actions or, at best, practices of keeping up with (but not ahead of) the Joneses. The old-fashioned idea of using money as an incentive to effort has very nearly disappeared. Even at the level of executive compensation, personnel men are concerned with gimmicks, procedures, and techniques to the near exclusion of principles of human motivation. An accounting philosophy and idle speculation about "programs" pervades their thinking.

It is extremely unfortunate that many early personnel men were "burned" when they tried to institute compensation schemes which conflicted

[5] E. K. Taylor, "Management Development at the Crossroads," *Personnel*, XXXVI (March-April, 1959), 8-23.

[6] D. W. Belcher, "Employee and Executive Compensation," in Heneman, editor, *op. cit.*, pp. 73-131.

with nonmonetary drives (e.g., social motives).[7] The salary and wage administration functions of many firms have, as a result, become shrouded in a veil of secrecy, and the possibility of innovation in the use of money as an incentive to effort, in conjunction with fundamental knowledge concerning employee motivation, seems remote. Thus, even though it has been abundantly shown that money is an effective incentive when used in combination with other motivating principles, most personnel managers lack the spirit of innovation and research mindedness necessary to work out effective combinations of money and other types of motivation.

4. Most personnel training programs, according to Bowles, are merely acts of wishful thinking on the part of the training directors responsible for them.[8] The principles of human learning spelled out so well by McGhee and Thayer are rarely given heed in industrial training efforts.[9] Indeed, if our public school systems carried out their educational functions in the manner of the typical industrial training program, the wailing and anguish of critics could probably be heard from here to the moon. In contrast to the situation in education, the lack of carefully designed training evaluation studies in industry is startling.[10] Personnel men apparently are unwilling to test the usefulness of training procedures by conducting periodic, experimentally designed audits of their programs.

Other writers have commented on the problems of personnel management in this country, Canada, and Western Europe.[11] There seems to be substantial agreement that classic personnel procedures have everywhere been found wanting. As a group, personnel managers have been too easily content with their "servicing" jobs. Early successes based on systematic applications of certain techniques and skills (e.g., recruitment practices, accounting systems for wage and salary payments, counseling, and "human relations" programs) apparently promoted a premature freezing of procedures. Generally, personnel men are content to follow the dictates of a technique-bound profession and have resisted opportunities to study problems involving human behavior in industry from a scientific point of view.

We believe that personnel management, as presently constituted, must yield its position to broader and more innovative behavioral sciences, which are proving capable of fulfilling management's needs for research as

[7] See, for example, Frances Torbert, "Making Incentives Work," *Harvard Business Review*, XXXVII (September-October, 1959), 81-92; William F. Whyte and others, *Money and Motivation* (New York: Harper, 1955); H. R. Northrup, "The Other Side of Incentives," *Personnel*, XXXVI (January-February, 1959), 32-41.

[8] W. J. Bowles, "The Mismanagement of Supervisory Training," *Personnel*, XXXVIII (March-April, 1961), 50-57.

[9] William McGehee and Paul W. Thayer, *Training in Business and Industry* (New York: Wiley, 1961).

[10] For excellent outlines of methods for evaluating training programs in industry, see D. L. Kirkpatrick, "Techniques for Evaluating Training Programs," *Journal of American Society of Training Directors* (1959-1960), pp. 13-14; L. K. Randall, "Evaluation: A Training Dilemma," *Journal of American Society of Training Directors*, XIV (1960), 29-35; T. A. Mahoney, *Building the Executive Team: A Guide to Management Development* (Englewood Cliffs, N.J.: Prentice-Hall, 1961).

[11] D. B. Strother, "Personnel Management in Theory and Practice," *Personnel*, XXXVI (May-June, 1959), 63-71; J. D. Kyle, "Personnel Administration Must Embark on a Program of Rigorous Self Development," *Personnel and Industrial Relations Journal*, VIII (1961), 9-17; F. T. Malm, "The Development of Personnel Administration in Western Europe," *California Management Review*, III (Fall, 1960), 69-83.

well as for the application of research results to the solution of problems of human behavior in industry.

Crisis in the Behavioral Sciences?

Clearly the behavioral sciences have not yet entirely come of age. In fact, they too nearly fell by the wayside as a result of premature crystallizing of techniques and procedures. For example, during the early and middle fifties, industrial psychologists were frequently criticized, usually justifiably, for a tendency to distort business problems to fit their pet measurement and testing procedures rather than to study actual human problems in business in order to develop novel approaches to their solution. As late as the fall of 1958, in his presidential address before the Division of Industrial Psychology of the American Psychological Association, Lawshe called attention to such practices and criticized industrial psychologists for them.[12] In a sense, the fifties constituted years of crisis for industrial psychology. In its applications to industry and business was it slated to become merely an occasionally useful adjunct characterized by sets of mechanistic tests, global case studies, and *a posteriori* reasoning? Or could it respond imaginatively to the growth of industry and the enlightenment of a new type of management seeking novel solutions to old problems?

The seeds of crisis were felt by many industrial psychologists early in the postwar years. Some of the more imaginative ones began to alter their ways and to develop more diversified approaches to business problems. However, the majority simply let the business world move by, as Leavitt has suggested:

> . . . classical industrial psychology is maybe a little bit under the weather. Its practitioners are apt to be . . . conflicted. If they have stuck to the pure and true—to test construction and job evaluation—they are finding themselves relegated to peripheral technicians' roles; at once outside the mainstream of the organization and also outside the mainstream of psychology. They have had a piece of bad luck too; the bad luck of allying themselves with the once promising young profession of personnel management. If not . . . moribund, that profession turned out to be at least disappointingly stodgy and unimaginative.[13]

In other words, industrial psychology, like its sister profession, personnel management, became technique-bound. The simple-minded paradigm of the classic selection model persisted for over half a century.[14] Psychologists played a large part in developing and promoting various wage and salary "plans," employee rating procedures, attitude scales, and an impressive array of other mechanically oriented devices. These pet techniques and psychological "instruments" became the stock in trade of the industrial psychologist. It is little wonder, then, that he fell into the habit of

[12] C. H. Lawshe, "Of Management and Measurement," *American Psychologist,* XIV (1959), 290-294.

[13] H. J. Leavitt, *Toward Organizational Psychology* (Pittsburgh, Pa.: Carnegie Institute of Technology, Graduate School of Business Administration, March, 1961).

[14] That is, the classic test validation technique of dividing employees into "good" and "poor" groups and comparing their performance on a series of psychological tests. Although this is still a common technique of industrial psychologists, many more sophisticated approaches have been developed, these are discussed in a later section.

seeking or inventing problems to fit his methods, rather than devoting his time to the solution of actual business problems.

Moreover, the classical model of industrial engineering, designed to rationalize work and the workplace, has undoubtedly created more human problems in industry than it has solved. Here, too, the difficulty has been a too ready acceptance of simple procedures for the solution of complex problems. Indeed, industrial engineering appears to have been seized by a panacea complex and to have been incapable of coping effectively with the industrial employee as a human being.

While industrial psychology was often rendered sterile by a simple-minded reliance on shotgun data collected without any underlying rationale, its sister social sciences, such as industrial sociology and anthropology, suffered from a muddleheaded desire to explain the whole situation. Case studies, sometimes with samples consisting of a single subject, were often used as the basis for sweeping generalizations which, as Homans would put it, were interesting but not necessarily true.[15] The dependence on participant-observers or on limited data from interviews seriously biased conclusions. The reliability of observations was considered less important than whether the observations were consistent with a pronouncement by Durkheim or Pareto.

Even so, the insights and speculations of sociologists and anthropologists have changed our conceptions of worker motivation, of the significance of the work group, and of the discrepancy between prescription and description in the large organization.[16] The trend toward greater objectivity and reliability in sociology has been influenced by the work of Bales on small groups, Lazarsfeld and his coworkers, Guttman on attitude measurement, and many others.[17] Indeed, successful attempts have been made to reproduce in the laboratory certain societal phenomena, such as cycles of innovation and ritualization, which were previously merely a matter of speculation and crosscultural observation.[18] Moreover, reliable generalizations have been based on respectable numbers of observations, for example, in the examination of as many as 150 primitive cultures, using anthropological data.[19] Indeed, industrial sociology and anthropology have been transformed into a more general behavioral science of business. Weber's classic work on bureaucracy, formerly accepted as the sine qua non for understanding the large, formal business organization, now serves merely as an introduction to the subject.[20]

[15] G. C. Homans, *The Human Group* (New York: Harcourt, Brace, 1959).

[16] See F. J. Roethlesberger and W. J. Dickson, *Management and the Worker* (Cambridge, Mass.: Harvard University Press, 1943). See also, P. M. Blau and W. R. Scott, *Formal Organizations* (San Francisco: Chandler, 1962), for the best available summary of the literature on the sociology of organizations.

[17] R. F. Bales, *Interaction Process Analyses* (Cambridge: Addison-Wesley Press, 1950); P. F. Lazarsfeld, *Latent Structure Analysis* (New York: Bureau of Applied Social Research, Columbia University, 1957); L. Guttman, "A Basis for Scaling Qualitative Data," *American Sociological Review*, IX (1944), 139-150.

[18] R. L. Hamblin and J. A. Wiggins, *Ambiguity and the Rate of Social Adaptation*, Technical Report 1, ONR Contract N 811 (St. Louis, Mo.: Social Science Institute, Washington University, 1959).

[19] S. H. Udy, Jr., *Organization of Work: A Comparative Analysis of Production Among Non-Industrial Peoples* (New Haven, Conn.: Human Relations Area File Press, 1959).

[20] Max Weber, *The Theory of Social and Economic Organization*, translated by A. M. Henderson and T. Parsons (Glencoe, Ill.: Free Press, 1947).

New Directions

These years of crisis for the behavioral sciences, painful though they were, did stimulate rapid growth and significant change. In addition to a small handful of industrial psychologists, other social scientists accepted the challenge of addressing themselves to the human problems of business.[21] By the mid-fifties, at least three new kinds of industrial behavioral science had emerged:

1. A science devoted to the purpose of assuring adequate recognition of human capabilities in the design of equipment and systems (predominantly military and weapons systems) came into being. Engineering psychologists, specializing in such work, are concerned with developing rules for designing equipment which can be operated efficiently by the *typical* human being. More broadly, they are concerned with identifying the sources of variation or error in any man-machine system. Thus, they use the knowledge and methods of experimental psychology, physiology, statistical methodology, and industrial engineering in attempting to solve complex equipment and systems-design problems.

2. As an unhappy alternative to the rather rigid and mechanistic approach of the classical industrial psychologist, there has been continuing widespread use of subjective and clinical procedures in connection with the human problems of business. Thus, executive counseling (with no discernible emphasis on research or evaluation) is enjoying a heyday, while projective techniques and depth interviewing are being widely used in personnel assessment programs. Since these methods are essentially unscientific, they cannot be subjected to objective tests. Even so, the therapeutic relationships established between executives and their counselors have often resulted in greater frankness among company managers, better adjustment to the pressures of modern-day business, and a more effective handling of interpersonal relationships in business. Although it is unlikely that clinical methods will persist in personnel assessment, there does appear to be sufficient evidence of improved human relationships to warrant the continued utilization of the clinician in industry.

3. The most promising development in the behavioral sciences takes the form of a merging of individual, experimental, and social psychology and the sociology of formal organizations, buttressed by computer technology, game theory, and related techniques. A vigorous new group of behavioral scientists is at the forefront with recent studies designed to gain an understanding of organizations and the human interactions which comprise them. This new discipline has been characterized by Leavitt as organizational psychology. Its nature, diversity, and high potential for successfully attacking the human problems of business are apparent from Leavitt's thumbnail description:

> Organizational psychology occupies itself with the study of organizations and organizational processes. It is as much descriptive as normative; as much or more basic as applied; as much interested in developing theories of organizational behavior as ways of improving organizational practice. It is close on one of its boundaries to human relations

[21] See, for example, Leavitt, *op. cit.*; M. Haire, "Business Is Too Important to Be Studied Only by Economists," *American Psychologist*, XV (April, 1960), 271-273; M. Haire, "Problems Relevant to Business and Industry," *Psychological Bulletin*, LVI (May 1959), 169-194.

> psychology, especially the social-experimental part of that field. It is also touched with experimental psychology and the rapidly growing field of empirical sociology. Its other boundaries are quite different: predominantly economics and mathematics—the game theorists, the operations researchers, the computer people.[22]

Thus, it is clear that organizational psychology is a fortunate blending of the science of psychology, with its emphasis on the formulation and testing of general rules and principles, with more immediate day-by-day applications to the art of business management. Each branch serves and is served by the other in a fortunate symbiotic combination. The behavioral scientist of today is much less prone to display the inflexibility which has been characteristic of personnel management or of the technique-bound social sciences in the past. Instead he is alert to problems and research opportunities which can aid in the development of behavioral science while also improving the over-all effectiveness of business management.

Theories and Their Applications

The adaptations stimulated by the years of crisis in the behavioral sciences have resulted in a new industrial science—one well equipped to play a central role in the business management of the future. Already this new school of broadened and more comprehensive psychology has produced insights (both theoretical and empirical) which are having widespread impact on the business community. For example:

1. A revolution may well be under way in industrial training. At long last, experimental work in learning has been adapted to educational methods in the form of programmed instruction,[23] characterized by an effort to break instructional content down into highly organized, logical stages which demand a continuing active response from the trainee. After each response, the trainee receives "feedback" or knowledge on how he did. Thus he receives immediate reinforcement or reward for learning. In a pioneering study, Hughes compared the effectiveness of programmed instruction with that of conventional classroom instruction in training IBM customer engineers to learn the nomenclature of the IBM 7070 computer.[24] The group receiving programmed instruction required 27 per cent less classroom time and showed a learning gain of 10 per cent over that shown by the group in the conventional classroom situation. With such results as these, behavioral scientists are moving rapidly into the field of industrial training. The emphasis on motivation in programmed instruction and its use of important principles of learning, such as reinforcement, immediate knowledge of results, and attention to individual differences help to explain its role in providing a critical breakthrough for behavioral science in industry.

2. Business executives are being taught to become better decision-makers and to make more effective use of the abilities of other persons in

[22] Leavitt, *op. cit.*

[23] See, for example, McGehee and Thayer, *op. cit.*; A. A. Lunsdaine and R. Gleser, editors, *Teaching Machines and Programmed Learning: A Source Book* (Washington, D.C.: National Education Association, 1961); E. Galanter, editor, *Automatic Teaching: The State of the Art* (New York: Wiley, 1959); B. F. Skinner, "Teaching Machines," *Science*, CXXVIII (1958), 909-977.

[24] J. L. Hughes, *The Effectiveness of Programmed Instruction: Experimental Findings for 7070 Training* (New York: International Business Machines, 1961).

solving complex business problems.[25] The methods were developed from the theoretical and methodological contributions made in group dynamics by Kurt Lewin. Beginning in the late forties, under the leadership of Leland Brandford, training sessions in "human relations" were held in Bethel, Maine, under a grant from the Carnegie Corporation. Lewin's theories and group dynamics concepts received rigid testing for a number of years and were modified accordingly—a clear example of the testing of psychology's scientific insights in the rugged arena of actual application. The early programs tended to be somewhat "soft headed" and overly emphasized a namby-pamby kind of adjustment to other persons. Today, however, the most successful industrial programs provide simulated or contrived group-conflict situations, in which the participants become deeply involved and, with the help of instructors, gain insight into their own and others' problem-solving behavior. The goal, of course, is to train participants to be applied human scientists, who will approach problem situations according to systematic principles, carefully gathering and sifting all available information rather than relying on haphazard, rule-of-thumb, or simple habitual techniques, as has been the typical pattern in the past. Although the evidence is not yet in, the results so far seem far superior to those accruing from any previous effort to teach human-relations and/or problem-solving methods applicable to complex business problems.[26]

3. New approaches to problems of industrial selection have been suggested and tried out. Foremost among these has been the utility model elaborated by Cronbach and Gleser.[27] This approach emphasizes the desirability of computing the utility and/or cost associated with various kinds of selection outcomes.[28] Moreover, these authors suggest the use of a sequential program in the selection process. In other words, selection is based on a series of decisions related to the varying validities of different procedures for distinguishing among the applicants for various jobs. Personnel selection in the firm of the future is likely to be based on evidence supplied by careful behavioral research, rather than on a single

[25] See H. A. Shephard, "An Action Research Approach to Organizational Development." *Management Record*, XXII (June, 1960), 26-30; R. R. Blake and J. S. Mouton, "Group Dynamics in Decision Making: A Series," *Petroleum Refiner*, Vol. XXXIX (May-December, 1960); *Sensitivity Training: Curse or Cure* (New York: Industrial Relations Newsletter Special Report, March, 1962); C. H. Kepner and B. B. Tregoe, "Developing Decision Makers," *Harvard Business Review*, XXXVIII (September-October, 1960), 115-124.

[26] See B. M. Bass, "The Management Training Laboratory—A Way to Improve Organizational Effectiveness," *Advertising Management*, XXV (1960), 11-15. For examples of evaluation studies of this approach to training, see R. S. Soar and N. C. Bowers, *Evaluation of Laboratory Human Relations Training for Classroom Teachers*, U.S. Office of Education Cooperative Research, Project No. 469, Vanderbilt University, 1962; and M. B. Miles, "Human Relations Training: Processes and Outcomes," *Journal of Counseling Psychology*, VII (1960), 301-306.

[27] L. J. Cronbach and G. Gleser, *Psychological Tests and Personnel Decisions* (Urbana, Ill.: University of Illinois Press, 1957). See also S. R. Wallace, *What Price Selection* (Hartford, Conn.: Life Insurance Agency Management Association (1960).

[28] For example, what is the cost to a firm of making a poor decision in selecting a salesman? Does the cost of a poor decision exceed the cost (recruiting, screening, etc.) of insuring a good decision? If it does not, it may well be argued that careful selection procedures are not warranted. This line of reasoning does not seem "new," but it is startling to observe the lack of attention given to utility and cost factors by the classic industrial psychologists.

technique (such as the interview), as it is in most firms today. As Dunnette has pointed out, the selection expert of the future

> will not be blindly attempting to utilize identical methods for all his selection problems. Instead, he will be a sort of statistical clinician. He will have developed, through research, a wealth of evidence showing the patterns of validities for different techniques, candidates, jobs, and criteria. He will be a flexible operator, attentive always to the accumulating information on any given candidate, and ready to apply, at each stage, the tests and procedures shown to be optimal and most valid.[29]

4. Perhaps the most impressive and far-reaching contributions lie in the area of organizational theorizing and its implications for managerial and employee behavior in the firm of the future. A large and growing literature provides impressive evidence of the increasing interest in this approach.[30] Although the rash of activity in organizational psychology has as yet resulted in few applications to the actual art of managing,[31] it is precisely in this field that the interaction between management and the new industrial psychology are likely to be most evident and most productive.

Only a sampling has been provided of the contributions already made, and it is merely suggestive of the innovations to be expected from this rapidly expanding field in the years ahead. The years of crisis are essentially over; the shakeout has been accomplished. The evolution from technician, or academic observer, to educator-trainer and research specialist on human behavior in the industrial organization is well under way. Let us, therefore, speculate a bit concerning the developing role of the behavioral sciences in industry and the possible nature of their contributions to effective management in the future.

Optimizing the System

Current thinking in the behavioral sciences and in microeconomics suggests that any attempt to maximize some aspect of organizational output or to minimize some aspect of organizational input or waste is bound to end in less than the desired result somewhere else in the system. One can't have one's cake and eat it too—and the staff specialist in

[29] Dunnette, *op. cit.*

[30] A partial listing of significant contributions in the area of organizational psychology includes the following: James G. March and Herbert A. Simons, *Organizations* (New York: Wiley, 1959); Mason Haire, editor, *Modern Organization Theory* (New York: Wiley, 1959); G. B. Strother, editor, *Social Science Approaches to the Study of Business Behavior* (Homewood, Ill.: Dorsey Press, 1962); D. McGregor, *The Human Side of Enterprise* (New York: McGraw-Hill, 1960); B. M. Bass, *Leadership, Psychology and Organizational Behavior* (New York: Harper, 1960); Chris Argyris, *Understanding Organizational Behavior* (Homewood, Ill.: Dorsey Press, 1960); R. M. Stogdill, *Individual Behavior and Group Achievement* (New York: McGraw-Hill, Press, 1959); Rensis Likert, *New Patterns of Management* (New York: McGraw-Hill, 1960).

[31] One outstanding example, however, has been reported to us by Dr. Arthur Kuriloff, Vice President, Manager of Performance and Development, Non-Linear Systems, Del Mar, California. Twenty-four months ago, the firm undertook a complete organizational change in accordance with the principles of McGregor's Theory Y and according to the functional alignments suggested by Drucker. It is noteworthy that the firm is still in business and over-all productivity per employee has increased by a factor of 31 per cent, the highest ever achieved in the 10-year history of the firm—and the ceiling has not yet been reached.

personnel must not only stop searching for the magic incantation or philosopher's stone but also cease to act as if he has already found it. Rather, he must become an applied behavioral scientist, using the principles and methods of modern psychology, sociology, and economics to help management and workers optimize the total system that is the business organization.[32]

Experts in human affairs in industry must be trained in psychology, sociology, economics, and organization theory (note we do not say personnel management, as such) to know the relevant principles and methods that must be applied in seeking answers to certain types of managerial problems. These problems concern the interaction of inputs, outputs, and waste of (a) men and money or (b) men and materials.

For example, a typical question on which research might be conducted follows:

If we increase our management trainee budget, will we increase individual management growth and satisfaction, or increase waste of money and our inventory of unused talent? In his search for valid answers, the behavioral scientist must consider as interacting components: output (men) and input (money) with input (men) with waste (money) and waste (men).

Many important questions of this sort, for which solid research answers can be found, might be enumerated. For example, we suggest a sample of questions on which any respectable behavioral scientist of the future should be prepared to conduct appropriate research, applying appropriate methods and drawing on his knowledge of the literature:

1. What can we do to get people in an organization to say what they think, instead of merely saying what they think their bosses want to hear? How can the full range of ideas available in a group be brought to the surface? How do interpersonal relationships either facilitate or inhibit problem-solving effectiveness in business? How may group and personal interactions be capitalized upon to maximize organizational problem-solving effectiveness?
2. We have just discovered that our salesmen can't figure simple percentages. If they can't compute percentages, is it because they don't know how to divide, or what? Can we use some simple diagnostic tests to find out how widespread and serious the problem is? What kinds of self-training techniques are available for those needing them? If remedial action is inadequate, should salesmen use simple slide rules in front of their customers or do the figuring with them? Or, should all calculations be made at the office?
3. How do we use our computer facilities to increase feedback to employees? What kinds of information will contribute positively to the motivation of employees? What measures of results may be developed to enhance the learning and/or continued productive efforts of all employees—managerial as well as rank and file? May the measures be "computerized"? In what form may information be presented most effectively to employees?
4. What are the implications of the current and future racial composition of our employees on our over-all operations? Can we or should

[32] We are indebted to Jack Dunlap for this idea.

we maintain different policies in different regions? Are our current selection tests as valid for our Negro as for our white applicants? What are the reactions of white jobholders in an occupational category in which Negroes begin to find employment? What about Negro supervisors and white subordinates?

5. Should our diversification of organization be along product, process, or geographical lines? What are the significant human factors to be considered here, as they interact with purely economic and engineering issues? What is likely to be the effect of the type of diversification on management development and organizational flexibility?
6. What effects may be expected from flattening the structure of our organizational hierarchy? What new managerial skills may be required? How will they be developed? What new controls may be necessary that are not required in a more vertically organized company? How will these be developed and implemented?

Currently, it is the Ph.D. in psychology or associated behavioral disciplines (not necessarily industrial psychology) who receives the education necessary for the "tough-minded" research demanded by an enlightened management. What other companies have done will not provide adequate answers to the really important questions—and too often the past education of the personnel manager has provided him with nothing more than the ability to follow where industrial engineers, industrial psychologists, or, much worse, industrial faddists have led.

In addition to an ability to search out answers, and to rephrase questions so that they are answerable, the behavioral scientist (formerly known as a personnel manager) will be able and eager to initiate new programs of research and training without waiting for the issues to arise. Thus, he may press for organizational gaming—developing specific games to meet particular needs in management and employee training and research through the stimulation of the system or subsystems. Or, he may, with top management, plan his own long-range educational program for such personnel needs as an executive training and replacement schedule.

Other important trends may be discerned. Like the Ph.D. in chemistry, who is beginning to be found in all types of positions in the chemical industry, the behavioral scientist of the future may more frequently become a member of line management.[33] This would be the opposite of the current tendency to rotate into personnel management from the line and would resemble the tendency for men who have advanced degrees in engineering to become executives.

The future research specialist in human factors may receive his education in behavioral science in schools of business administration as well as in departments of psychology, sociology, or related fields. He is also likely to have more training in associated areas, such as operations research, mathematics, and statistics. At the same time, he will tend to make more contributions to basic psychology and sociology, particularly in such areas as: human interaction, communications in organization, decision-making, emotional factors in learning, design of experiments, and bureaucracy.

[33] There are, of course, already well-known examples of behavioral scientists serving as corporation presidents and members of top management in a variety of businesses and industries. But, we guess that the number is likely to increase.

Indeed, the time may come when (as now occurs in certain branches of chemistry) a Ph.D. in psychology, sociology, or one of the other behavioral sciences commonly elects to join an industrial firm rather than remain at a university, so that he may have adequate facilities and opportunities to pursue his research interests.[34]

We believe, then, that the personnel man of the future will be an expert in the difficult and complex science of human behavior. What his formal label will be is not important, but his function will be that of a professional scientist and adviser, to whom problems of human behavior in business will be referred. The central role we anticipate for the behavioral sciences in the firm of the future is a far cry from the technique-bound services of present-day personnel management or from the myopic empiricism or global muddleheadedness of early social scientists. During the past decade, this new behavioral science of business practice began to develop. An enlightened management is calling for more industrial behavioral scientists such as we have described; our educational institutions should respond by training an increasing number of these personnel specialists of the future. It may be that they will be called neither personnel managers nor industrial psychologists. However, they will be uniquely equipped to handle the human problems arising out of our continuing efforts to optimize the organizational systems of the future.

[34] Both G.E. and the Bell Laboratories now support experimental laboratories to conduct basic behavioral science research within their organization.

Criticism and Comment

THOMAS H. PATTEN

EDITOR:

The article by Marvin D. Dunnette and Bernard M. Bass, "Behavioral Scientists and Personnel Management" (May 1963), should be commented on by a personnel man who has a professional background as a social scientist. Although I agree with the article's basic thesis, namely that individuals involved in personnel work in industry should have some understanding of the scientific study of human behavior, a number of the assertions made in the article appear to be based on undocumented scholarship. I should like to take issue with some of these unsupported observations and state some personal opinions which I feel may be of interest to other readers.

Specifically, I believe the authors either overstate their case or fail to provide a balanced perspective in regard to: (1) the conservative character

Reprinted with permission from *Industrial Relations*, Vol. 3, February, 1964, pp. 109-118.

Thomas Patten, Jr. was Supervisor, Program Planning Section, Training Department, Industrial Relations Staff, Ford Motor Company when this was written and is now Associate Director, School of Labor and Industrial Relations, Michigan State University.

of personnel management, (2) interviewing and selection, (3) the confidence personnel specialists have in their ability to bring about personnel development and behavior change, (4) the status of industrial training, and (5) the extent to which the behavioral sciences are unappreciated by personnel managers.

Conservative Character of Personnel Management

The authors state, "The behavioral sciences are making rapid strides and are moving to a central position in the study of industrial behavior," and then they indicate that "personnel management [not further identified, but presumably people working in industry in such positions] seems intent on pursuing a pattern of increasing stagnation and lack of significant innovation." It is probably true that the number of articles concerning personnel management being published by behavioral scientists is rapidly increasing, but it is also likely that, at least in large companies, qualified individuals working in various fields of personnel management are aware of and are attempting to use published information as a means of establishing more sophisticated personnel policies and programs.

Since 1950, an increasing number of companies have established personnel research functions or have employed people with qualifications in the social sciences to do evaluative or analytical work. Although this work frequently does not result in uncovering new knowledge, it is used as a basis for improving in-house policies and programs. Using the accepted techniques of the social sciences, studies are designed to measure the predicted and the actual effects of programs and to determine any action implications within the value system of the particular organization. This new analytical work would not suggest "stagnation" of the personnel function and is a distinct change from the past, although probably not innovative in the scholarly sense.

Without supplying any convincing documentation the authors accuse personnel managers of being too easily content with their "service" jobs. Essentially, personnel administration is a service function in the sense that expert advice is provided to the line organization and certain control systems are established to introduce some degree of rationality and justice into the supervision of people in organizations. Personnel management cannot be an end unto itself (or at least it should not be). Increasingly, personnel managers have become concerned with personnel planning as, for example, in projecting long- and short-range manpower needs by employee classification, identifying and rotating above-average performers, determining the total pattern of replacements in an organization, etc. Personnel planning as defined above is of a service nature to the organization, but involves a degree of social science knowledge which would elevate the personnel function above that of "staff office boy" (to use the phrase by Drucker, which the authors apparently agree is an accurate characterization of the personnel function).

Interviewing and Selection

Dunnette and Bass cite some sources to support their assertion that the personnel interview is the most widely used selection method and "that it is costly, inefficient, and usually invalid." They then go on to state that until research specifies conditions under which the interview has predictive value, its continued use must be regarded as primarily a public relations device. However, until psychological selection tests become available for various jobs and positions and can be properly validated on industrial populations employed by a specific firm, there is hardly any alternative to interviewing. This is particularly true in selecting personnel for supervisory or managerial positions, where the state of the art or science of testing is generally agreed to be very primitive. In these circumstances, the interview is the best tool available and probably could be shown to have predictive value, based on the ability of managers to pick candidates who prove later to be adequate or better for the job. At least there is no reason to assume interviewing is usually invalid. Also, the public relations value of interviews should not be unduly minimized, for frequently the same people who apply for employment are also consumers of an organization's products. Courteous attention to their inquiries regarding employment possiblities can hardly be regarded as unjustified, costly, or inefficient.

Personnel Development and Behavior Change

Personnel men are accused of being "too ready to pose as experts in the difficult science of human development and behavior change." It has been my experience that most personnel men are very reluctant to pose as experts in these areas and are simply trying to perform their jobs. Personnel development cannot be shunned in industry. Learning inevitably takes place once a person starts work; the problem is, we have insufficient knowledge of how people learn most effectively. To be sure, there exists some knowledge about child or adolescent development, but who really knows much about how people develop as adults?

Many of the larger American companies have conducted extensive research before launching programs of management development. Much of this research has been conducted by company-employed social scientists or outside consultants who are fully competent to do the research required. The bulk of this research unfortunately never finds its way into scholarly publications, but management-employed social scientists who are acquainted with one another meet at professional gatherings (such as the Executive Study meetings of the Educational Testing Service) and periodically exchange insights and reports on research under way.

The authors suggest that executive counselling and projective techniques are widely used for personnel assessment. Several large American companies with which I am familiar have executive counselling arrangments. Each of these firms emphasizes research and evaluation, plus a professional approach directed by seasoned Ph.D.'s who are fully aware of the limits of the contribution they can make. Personnel tests have increased in use since World War II, but there is little evidence that projective tests are "widely used," depending of course upon what is meant by the latter phrase. The authors should supply some evidence for this assertion.

I believe most industrial trainers would agree that, in the final analysis, all development is self-development. However, most would also agree that organizations can use the training activity as a staff function to assist in identifying the circumstances that foster learning and to modify some aspects of the environment so that people who are motivated can learn and later apply their learning in the work situation. Judicious use can be made of the methods and tools of the social sciences in this context.

Status of Industrial Training

Industrial training and the lack of carefully designed training evaluation studies are criticized. The authors state: "Indeed, if our public school systems carried out their educational functions in the manner of the typical industrial training program, the wailing and anguish of critics could probably be heard from here to the moon." I think it behooves the authors to provide evidence that education carried out in the public schools is much different from that provided in-house by firms or that available in universities and community colleges utilized by companies for part of their industrial training program. No evidence is provided that public school education is generally more effective than in-house industrial training; in fact, in this instance are the authors not contrasting unlike systems with unlike objectives?

Industrial training specialists are well aware of their problems in determining training needs, conducting programs, and evaluating the results of training. A careful reading of the literature of personnel and training would indicate that a variety of attempts are being made to remedy existing defects. Program evaluations sometimes involve *follow-up studies* of what happens to trainees after the training; *expert appraisals*, i.e., retaining university professors or consultants to observe and report on the quality of instruction provided in a classroom or conference room; *testimonial questionnaires* given to program participants who complete training; *before-and-after studies*, which measure changes in scrap rates, safety, grievances, and other types of objective items; and *subject matter examinations* (as in a high school or university). We have arrived at no final answers in this complex field, but work is under way; and more importantly, personnel people are attempting to increase their sophistication, as would be evident to persons attending meetings of the American Society of Training Directors or the American Management Association.

The authors attach much significance to current changes in industrial training. I believe it is too soon for us to assess the impact of programmed learning. There is a growing commercialism in this field, but there are also some solid attempts at research and program development. We do not know the extent to which different types of subject matter can be programmed to improve learning or which types of program style, format, or length are best in specific circumstances.

For teaching such subjects as management problem-solving and decision-making the new training programs that simulate industrial situations (not, as the authors suggest, involving destructive group conflict, but rather emphasizing competition) do seem to be worthwhile. In discussing decision-making training, the authors seem to applaud new programs that are concerned with the analytical skills involved in devising the "best" answer to a production or sales problem in terms of costs, delivery possibilities, quality, etc., rather than the human relations problems involved in reaching a decision. In my opinion, both types of programs have value depending upon the needs of the persons undergoing training. These programs simply focus on different aspects of managerial behavior involved in decision-making.

Simulations and laboratory training obviously have their places. However, for training in blueprint reading, shop arithmetic, work standards, fire prevention, or economics, it is likely that the lecture, movie, slidefilm, or directed reading, plus having an instructor available for consultation, may be preferable. To sum up, we should use a variety of methods and approaches, new and old, depending upon the needs in a particular area.

Behavioral Sciences and Personnel Managers

Dunnette and Bass have much to say about industrial psychology and sociology and the virtues of the behavioral sciences. At the risk of being picayune, I should like to comment on their views.

The authors indicate that during the mid-fifties industrial psychologists were frequently criticized (and in their opinion justifiably) for a tendency to distort business problems to fit their pet measurement and testing procedures instead of studying actual human problems in business in order to develop novel approaches to their solution. This criticism is probably quite supportable, inasmuch as social scientists working in industry (not only industrial psychologists) may be prone to adopting myopic points of view regarding company problems. However, this phenomenon may be the price of specialization or "trained incapacity," regardless of one's position.

Industrial psychology takes its lumps, but industrial sociology and anthropology are more severely treated because they have allegedly "suffered from a muddleheaded desire to explain the whole situation." No documentation is provided for this assertion other than a reference to George C. Homan's *The Human Group*, which is a book consisting of an analysis of research almost entirely conducted by others (including a segment of the Western Electric studies) within Homan's small-group interaction frame of reference. The authors state that: "The reliability of observations [presumably made by the industrial sociologist] was considered less important than whether the observations were consistent with a pronouncement by Durkheim or Pareto." The latter hardly is the case and is not supported by documentation. Implicit in the assertion, though, is perhaps a charge of naive academic genuflection. Since 1950, very few industrial sociologists have concerned themselves directly with the theory of Durkheim or Pareto in interpreting their research findings, although it is still useful to apply the concepts of anomie or equilibrium where appropriate since these terms have long since found their way into general sociological thought.

Finally, while the work of Bales, Lazarfeld, and Guttman have been influential in the work of sociology in general, its imprint upon industrial sociology has been minimal. When we think of the latter field, we think of William F. Whyte, Wilbert E. Moore, Robert Dubin, Melville Dalton, Harold Wilensky, Reinhard Bendix, and Seymour M. Lipset. These individuals have used the quantitative or questionnaire techniques associated with the aforementioned, but they have also made use of historical materials and, more especially, interviewing and observation methods. Also, in recent years more and more attention has been given by industrial sociologists to the theory of large-scale organization as outlined by Max Weber. In fact, many erstwhile industrial sociologists today define their field as "complex organization." Weber was the pioneer here, rather than Durkheim or Pareto. In any event, I see no evidence in these developments of "a muddleheaded desire to explain the whole situation."

From the standpoint of their intellectual outlook, the authors see considerable promise in the development in the behavioral sciences of a "merging of individual, experimental, and social psychology and the sociology of formal organizations, buttressed by computer technology, game theory, and related techniques." This merger, they suggest, using Leavitt's term, has resulted in the discipline of "organizational psychology." If there is such a new discipline, the authors fail to indicate how these basic sciences have merged, and this writer doubts that there is any merger on the conceptual level among these disparate disciplines. Also, it is not clear what the authors mean when they say that the behavioral scientist possesses the virtue of being less inflexible than the "technique-bound" social scientist or the personnel manager. If anything, the personnel manager has been probably too flexible over the years and, as the authors suggest earlier, too prone to follow the fads and gimmicks. In addition, there may be some evidence to support the point that a number of mature social scientists have been rather flexible and wide-ranging in their interests, such as Kenneth Boulding, Talcott Parsons, David Riesman, and Robert K. Merton, to name a few. These scholars have not been "technique-bound," but have, on the contrary, displayed broad intellectual interests crosscutting economics, law, philosophy, psychology, history, sociology, etc. Interdisciplinary research and conceptual merging of disciplines are separate considerations which should be carefully treated; the authors' statement that, "Each branch [of the social sciences] serves and is served by the other in a fortunate symbiotic combination," beclouds the matter for me. I believe Dunnette and Bass have not stated their case very clearly or specifically in regard to the distinct virtues of "organizational psychology."

The authors conclude their article with some comments on organization theory and sample suggestions for further research in behavioral science. Admittedly a sample is not a complete assortment or array. However, it is worth noting that these suggestions do not add up to a consistent theoretical statement indicating concepts which may be systematically related and integrated to form a body of knowledge either insightful or useful to the personnel manager. Instead, these suggestions appear to be a potpourri of the interesting. The specific contribution which the social scientist is uniquely able to make regarding these suggestions is not very clear, although I would obviously feel he is not unqualified to do these things.

The authors also suggest that the future personnel manager must become an "applied behavioral scientist, using the principles and methods" of the various social sciences in his work. This is all well and good, but as the late Bernard DeVoto argued in the Foreward to Homans' *The Human Group*, there are no generally agreed upon principles of sociology (i.e., reliable general propositions about human behavior that have been established), and this view would probably find considerable support today as well. What are sometimes considered principles in the typical first or introductory course in the social sciences turn out to be basic concepts that are commonly used in describing and analyzing the range of phenomena of interest to the sociologist, psychologist, economist, etc. Few staff specialists in personnel are looking today for the "philosopher's stone"; let us not, on the other hand, be deceived that there is a body of *principles* in the social sciences which we can turn to and readily apply. Probably greatest utility can be drawn at the present time from applications of the *methods* of social research to the analysis of personnel and industrial relations problems and issues. It would be worthwhile for someone to take it upon himself to spell out in systematic detail what "principles" of the social sciences apply where and how in specific industrial situations.

Reply to Mr. Patten

MARVIN D. DUNNETTE AND BERNARD M. BASS

EDITOR:

We are gratified that our article stimulated the careful soul-searching shown by Mr. Patten's letter. In writing it we had hoped to gain the attention of people in industry who might be in a position to do something about the sad state of personnel management. It would certainly appear that Patten is in just such a position, and we are happy to learn that he views the scene with somewhat greater optimism than we do. Unfortunately, however, his optimism concerning personnel management is even less well documented than was our pessimism, and we can only conclude that his comments are based primarily on his personal opinions, gleaned presumably from experience in the Training Department of the Ford Motor Company.

We should like to comment briefly on each of the five areas discussed by Patten.

Conservative Character of Personnel Management

When we argued that the behavioral sciences were moving to a central position in the study of industrial behavior, we were referring to the recent influx of trained behavioral scientists into industrial settings. We view this movement as necessitated by the demonstrated inability of personnel management to respond creatively to the need in industry for the scientific study of behavior. The personnel research functions mentioned by Patten are being manned by behavioral scientists, not personnel managers. However, even though there is some increase in personnel research, a recent survey by Minnesota's Industrial Relations Center revealed an average of only two people (including clerical and supporting staff, as well as professionals) in personnel research jobs for every 10,000 employees.[1] Thus, there is a good deal of room for improvement. We hope and believe that more and more behavioral scientists will research in industry and that personnel managers will continue to perform their housekeeping functions. As a matter of fact, this was perhaps the major point of our article.

Interviewing and Selection

Patten's statement that, "the interview . . . probably could be shown to have predictive value, based on the ability of managers to pick candidates

[1] Roberta Nelson, George England, and Dale Yoder, "Personnel Ratios, 1960: An Analytical Look," *Personnel*, XXXVII (November-December, 1960), 118-128.

who prove later to be adequate or better for the job," is typical of the unfounded confidence that people seem to have that interviewing is a valid selection tool. There are a few published studies which yield modest evidence in support of interviewing validity, but even in these cases it is strongly probable that *higher validities would have been obtained by more objective procedures.* One extensive study suggests that the inferences made by interviewers show steady decreases in validity with increasing confidence on the part of the interviewers in their abilities to "size up" the candidates.[2] Perhaps the most extensive industrial validation effort to date is the Early Identification of Management Potential Study. Standardized tests yielded a cross-validated correlation of .70 with a carefully developed measure of managerial success. In contrast, inferences made from an extensive interview with each manager failed to add sufficiently to the prediction equation to justify the time and expense of its continued use.[3] Thus, psychological tests do have demonstrated validity for selecting supervisors and managers, as well as for selecting personnel in other jobs; as far as we know, the interview has no such demonstrated validity. However, we certainly did not intend to minimize the public relations benefits of the interview; in fact, it is a very important public relations tool, and we suggest it to be continued *as such.*

Personnel Development and Behavior Change

We want to underscore Patten's statement that we lack sufficient knowledge about effective learning in industry. Because of this, we would prefer to see money being spent for research on human learning in industry, rather than on the numerous so-called "development" programs now being undertaken and supported by industry. We are surprised by Patten's claim that many larger companies have conducted extensive research before launching management development programs. If he knows of such instances, he should have described them. The only such "research" that we are aware of has been characterized by surveys of what other companies are doing and/or traveling around to conferences to get an idea of what is being offered. To us, this seems a far cry from fundamental research.

Status of Industrial Training

We must plead guilty to the charge that in comparing public school education with industrial training we were contrasting unlike systems with unlike objectives. We fell into this trap primarily because we are impressed with the fact that public education has at least made the effort to define the terminal behaviors to be developed in the educational process. In contrast, training in industry has not often coped with the problem of identifying training needs and expressing the desired training outcomes in terms of the behaviors to be developed. Too often, it seems to us, industrial training just simply happens; training design is based on fads, fashions, and haphazard notions of what should be taught, rather than on

[2] E. L. Kelly and D. W. Fiske, *The Prediction of Performance in Clinical Psychology* (Ann Arbor: University of Michigan, 1951).

[3] Harry Laurent, *Summary Report of the Early Identification of Management Potential Research Project*, Employee Relations Department, Standard Oil Company of New Jersey (1961).

knowledge of the learning process or on careful specification of, and fundamental research on, the behaviors to be learned.

We believe that programmed learning will bring about a revolution in industrial training because it tends to force training managers to attend to what is going on in the learning process. Programmed learning formalizes the guidance, feedback, and reinforcement features of learning and must, of course, begin with the specification of terminal behaviors. We do not view programmed learning in the narrow context of a teaching machine or a scrambled text, but rather as a broad statement of important principles in learning. Thus, we agree with Patten that training should be fixed on no single method, but that it should use a variety of approaches, new and old. But all of these should be carefully pretested, programmed, and sequenced to instill the desired job skills, knowledges, and attitudes in the repertoire of the learners. Again, we believe that behavioral scientists rather than personnel managers are the ones who are more likely to innovate in this area.

Behavioral Sciences and Personnel Managers

Replying here, we must join our critic in risking being picayune. We too think of William F. Whyte, et al., as the leaders in contributing to . . . changing "our conceptions of worker motivation, of the significance of the work group, and of the discrepancy between prescription and description in the large organization." Footnote 16 called attention in particular to Blau and Scott's excellent review of the field. We had no intention of devaluing industrial sociology as such, but we see observation (the primary method of industrial social science) as an early stage in the growth of any science. What must follow is the drudgery of measurement and experimentation now being conducted both in industry and laboratory. We could be mistaken, but we think that much of social psychological observation needs to be put to the test. It is important for pioneering observers to pull together into a meaningful whole what they have perceived. The structure they build still must stand the test of verification. For example, Parkinson's gift for putting into interesting, stimulating, and humorous language his observations on administrative growth doesn't make his law correct. And when it is tested by careful, painstaking statistical studies, it not only fails to be verified for banking systems or for 211 Ohio firms, but the facts suggest that the "law" may be stating the reverse of what is true about administrative growth in American and German manufacturing establishments.[4]

The merging of disciplines into a field of organizational psychology will be described in a chapter by Harold J. Leavitt and Bernard Bass in the *Annual Review of Psychology* for 1964. A text on the subject has also been completed by Bass and will be published within the year. Such an approach to the field involves examining both the *rational* as well as the motivational aspects of decision-making, organizational conflict, organizational structure, communications, labor-management collaboration, super-

[4] F. W. Terrien, *The Effect of Changing Size Upon Organizations* (San Francisco: Institute for Social Science Research, San Francisco State College, 1963); A. L. Stinchcombe, "Bureaucratic and Craft Administration of Production," *Administrative Science Quarterly*, IV (1959), 168-187; A. W. Baker and R. C. Davis, *Ratios of Staff to Line Employees and Stages of Differentiation of Staff Functions* (Columbus, Ohio: Bureau of Business Research. Ohio State University, 1954).

vision, and so forth. The interdisciplinary view would be of particular value in instances in which a worker or manager *intends* to be rational, but is limited by the uncertainties and complexity of a problem (the subject matter of certain branches of economics and mathematics) as well as by his own past history and current motivation (the subject matter of psychology) and the situation in which he and the problem are embedded (the subject matter of social psychology, sociology, and anthropology).

We can only reply to the charge that a few examples fail to demonstrate the concepts or issues of organizational psychology by providing another example—that of labor-management conflict. In doing this we shall illustrate the difference in viewpoint between organizational psychology and traditional personnel management. For organizational psychology, the social aspects of labor-management conflict are part of a fundamental phenomenon which arises when groups of any kind compete. Similar problems arise, for example, whether the conflict is between departments over transfer prices, between line and staff, or between engineers and machinists. The conflict can be simulated in the laboratory and mathematically, using game theory. Knowing the elements in the game, one can predict quite well whether collaboration or deadlock will occur. For example, if it is a zero-sum game, a win-lose situation, then each group will unrealistically overvalue its own position and undervalue the opposition, see more differences than really exist, etc.

The typical personnel manager, we submit, has been trained in a tradition that focuses his attention in a labor-management conflict on such things as disagreements over wording and intent of the contract, keeping records of grievances, or advising management about other firms' wage scales. We expect that in his assessment of the conflict he is fairly strongly committed to management's point of view, rather than to a more objective, neutral position.

Relevant to this discussion is Stagner's demonstration of the gullibility of 68 personnel managers, in which 50 per cent ranked the same glittering personal generalities as amazingly descriptive of themselves after they had completed a personality test.[5] The study has relevance, for it suggests that even in housekeeping procedures such as personnel selection, the personnel director may be doing more of a disservice than a service to management by his failure to remain objective and self-corrective, as would be demanded of any scientist.

The moral of all this may be that if personnel directors want to be involved in more than the "conservative character of personnel management," they ought to start by examining the results of psychological experiments on themselves.[6] As Simon would say, personnel directors may be satisfied with the job they are doing, but they are not necessarily doing the job as well as it could be done.

Someone does have to keep the records, make manpower forecasts, provide stability, and monitor personnel services, but these routines are

[5] Ross Stagner, "The Gullibility of Personnel Managers," *Personnel Psychology*, XI (1958), 347–352.

[6] See also, Harry C. Triandis, "Factors Affecting Employee Selection in Two Cultures," *Journal of Applied Psychology*, XLVII (1963), 89-96. In this study, Triandis found that, when making hiring recommendations, personnel directors both in the United States and Greece placed more weight than did college students on irrelevant factors such as race, age, sex, religion, sociability, and wealth and less weight on mere competence to do the job well.

only a minor portion of what management might be offered to assist it in its efforts to optimize the utilization of its human resources to the satisfaction of all concerned: owners, managers, workers, and the public.

28

Concern with Problems of Authority and Influence

Sources of Lateral Authority in Personnel Departments

EDWARD GROSS

Authority in organizations is usually discussed solely in terms of the hierarchy—the issuance by a superior of orders to a subordinate and the probability of obedience to, alteration of, or subversion of the orders. Such a focus ignores a major form of authority which is not hierarchical; namely, lateral authority—the authority of one department over another. This paper is concerned with the forms of lateral authority available to personnel departments.

Most organizations are organized on a departmental basis (although there have been recent proposals that this be altered).[1] As a result the typical employee is isolated from all but other members of his own department and departmental, rather than organization-wide, loyalty is rewarded. When a man has done his job, it is his superiors in his own department who evaluate him and recommend the appropriate reward, the highest of which is an elevation in the hierarchy of the department itself. Since the head of the department is himself judged by how well his department does its job, he cannot help but judge his subordinates primarily by their contribution to the department. As long as departments can in fact be isolated from one another—as, for example, in the Sears retail stores investigated by Worthy[2]—no particular problem is raised. But whenever there is a flow of work from one department to another—whether such flow takes the form of materials, problems, or clients—then clearly one department's ability to do its job is very much affected by how others do theirs. When the candy department at Sears runs out of nuts, sales in the shoe department are not affected. But when the rivet depart-

Reprinted with permission from *Industrial Relations*, Vol. 3, No. 3, May, 1964, pp. 121-133.

Edward Gross is Professor of Sociology, University of Washington, Seattle.

[1] For example, see P. G. Herbst, *Autonomous Group Functioning* (London: Tavistock, 1962); and Robert T. Golembiewski, "A Behavioral Approach to Wage Administration: Work Flow and Structural Design," *Academy of Management Journal*, VI (December, 1963), 267-277.

[2] James C. Worthy, "Organizational Structure and Employee Morale," *American Sociological Review*, XV (April, 1950), 169-179.

ment in a factory slows production because of machine breakdown, then all departments using rivets must also slow their production. Consequently, other departments will seek to stabilize their supplies and this means entering into the affairs of the rivet department. While the problem we describe may not be faced by all line departments, it *is* faced by all staff departments, for they are, by definition, related to the line which they serve or control in some manner. In fact many staff departments are judged by the performance of the line departments they serve.

When the fate of a department is so intimately tied up with the fate of another, it will certainly attempt to influence the other's work. However, the department wishing to have this effect cannot simply depend on being able to use influence or power to protect its interests,[3] for this would mean waiting until some clear crisis occurs and then acting. By then, the damage might be too extensive or costly. In any case, the department might not have enough power when needed. Instead, we may predict that it will attempt to regularize or stabilize its power over the other department. Since the department seeking control is, by definition, an outsider with no "rights," it will seek to justify the regularized power it seeks. And justified, regularized power is legitimate power, or authority. We are using "authority" here in the standard Weberian sense of legitimate power in which the source of legitimacy is a set of values which the subjects of the power-wielder accept. By looking at the different sorts of values to which legitimacy comes to be attached, we secure a picture of the different sources of organizational authority.

A staff department which is especially revealing of sources of authority is the personnel department. It is newer than many others and still in the process of establishing authority; furthermore, its four different functions are based on quite different sources of authority. Three of these functions—services, recordkeeping, and manpower management—have clear, effective sources of authority and are, hence, the occasion for few problems. The fourth function—advising and counseling—is highly ineffective. Our analysis will show that this ineffectiveness is traceable directly to unclear and weak authority. At the same time, a search for new sources of authority will suggest a new function for the department—namely, that of monitoring the manpower variables in the organization. Our over-all goal is to show how an analysis of organizational authority sheds light on structural relationships among departments.

The Service Function

Personnel managers administer services such as recreation programs, lunchrooms, medical aid, company stores, and plant newspapers. As Strauss and Sayles point out, the threat of union organization and the fear of Communism after World War I led to a great flowering of these services.[4] Managers, assuming that employee discontent was the basic problem, tried

[3] Excellent studies of lateral tactics of power and influence are provided in George Strauss, "Tactics of Lateral Relationship: The Purchasing Agent," *Administrative Science Quarterly*, VII (September, 1962), 161-186; Melville Dalton, *Men Who Manage* (New York: Wiley, 1959); and Henry A. Landsberger, "The Horizontal Dimension in a Bureaucracy," *Administrative Science Quarterly*, VI (December, 1961), 299-332.

[4] George Strauss and Leonard R. Sayles, *Personnel* (Englewood Cliffs, N.J.: Prentice-Hall, 1960), pp. 397-398.

to anticipate this discontent by a paternalistic approach. Since it was not always clear just what would alleviate discontent, a great many different services were provided. First, a rest room might be put in. Then, if union organizers made gains in spite of it, a cafeteria would be installed. When that failed to stem organization, attention shifted to soft music or day-care services for children of female employees. Once such services were installed, unions saw to it that they were maintained, with the result that the services became a regular part of the fringe benefits bargained for by the unions.

The source of authority for the service function of the personnel department is, hence, twofold: the provisions of the union contract and the general pattern of expectations of the workers (that is, the values associated with employment at the particular concern). Armed with such authority, the personnel man feels no hesitation in taking a worker off his job to interview him for a story in the plant newspaper, posting bowling league scores on the shop bulletin board, or rearranging work schedules to permit time off to vote in a local municipal election.

Recordkeeping and Collective Bargaining

Recordkeeping, the second function, involves a different source of authority. Recordkeeping is tied in with the service function, since the latter involves keeping current files on insurance and pension programs, health records, and so forth; but it also bears an intimate relationship to collective bargaining, since many records are kept for the purpose of supporting the management's position in collective bargaining.[5] Management desires accurate data and careful measurements to justify what it would have done earlier "by intuition."

The authority, then, for the recordkeeping function, with its attendant mountain of forms, comes partly from the service function, as already discussed, but also from the connection of the department with collective bargaining. In large firms, a portion of the personnel department may be renamed "industrial relations" and spend the whole of its time in negotiations or preparations for them. As such, the authority of the department is the authority of management itself, with the department acting as a supply house of weapons in the power struggle against the union.

Manpower Management

The third function may be called manpower management.[6] As in the case of collective bargaining, the source of authority is management itself. However, unlike the case of collective bargaining, the personnel department here acts not as an agent of management (whom it assists or advises) but *as* management itself in the sense that the department is given the right to make binding decisions on such subjects as recruitment, selection, induction, training, management development, wage and salary administration, personnel rating, promotion, transfer, and separation. It has been mainly these activities which have led to the staff erosion of line authority

[5] William F. Whyte, *Men At Work* (Homewood, Ill.: Dorsey and Irwin, 1961), p. 502.

[6] The term is drawn from Dale Yoder, *Personnel Management and Industrial Relations* (Englewood Cliffs, N.J.: Prentice-Hall, 1962), chap. 1. However, my usage is narrower than his since I specifically exclude labor relations, recordkeeping, and the provision of advice and counsel. See his p. 8.

noted by many.[7] Such erosion has occurred because members of personnel departments are often younger, more aggressive, better educated or trained persons who seek to dominate line officers and because line officers are often happy to yield decision-making power in exchange for escaping responsibility for the effects of a decision. When employees find that the personnel department can reverse a foreman's decision on a disciplinary matter and that more money can be made by getting a loose rate from a time-study man than by "cooperating" with the foreman, then the foreman becomes someone to by-pass on the way to the personnel office.[8] Such a "payoff" serves, as does the "payoff" described by Seymour M. Lipset in *The First New Nation*,[9] to legitimate the power of the personnel department and hence add support to its authority.

Advice and Counsel

In the functions described so far—services, recordkeeping, and manpower management—the sources of authority are clear and their impact is strong. These sources are legal (provisions of the union contract), normative (worker expectations and values), and structural (when personnel officers act as management, agents of management, or use their positions to administer rewards or other satisfactions). The case is altogether different with the fourth function—the provision of advice and counsel to line officers on "human relations" problems, that is, the manipulation and modification of behavior in line with organization wishes or values. In this area, personnel officers find they are least effective and least listened to.

The usefulness of a search for sources of authority is confirmed here, for it is precisely in terms of the lack of a clear source of authority that the above "ineffectiveness" may be understood. At the same time, our analysis will suggest that the need to find a workable source of authority has the paradoxical effect of altering the "advice and counsel" function till it becomes a "control or monitor function."

Knowledge as a Source of Authority

The legitimacy usually claimed for the advice and counsel role is the authority of the professional or expert. Listen to me, says the personnel officer, because I am a psychologist, or I am trained in the techniques of scientific research. Such a legitimation rests, at bottom, on the knowledge this person may be presumed to have by virtue of his having been validated as a professional. Those who see the authority of the personnel officer as

[7] See, for example, George Strauss, "The Changing Role of the Working Supervisor," *Journal of Business*, XXX (July, 1957), 202-211; and Whyte, *op. cit.*, chap. 21.

[8] Further contributing to this trend was the emphasis of the human relations school on supervisory training programs. Since conflict was held to be due to lack of human relations skills, the supervisor, as the person closest to the worker, was blamed. Such supervisory training was usually carried out by members of the personnel department, a fact that dramatized their superior knowledge and competence.

[9] (New York: Basic Books, 1963), pp. 45 ff. In discussing the problem new rulers face in establishing legitimacy, he writes: "All claims to a legitimate title to rule in new states must ultimately win acceptance through demonstrating effectiveness . . . even claims to legitimacy of a supernatural sort, such as 'the gift of grace,' are subjected on the part of the populace to a highly pragmatic test—that is, what is the payoff? For new states today, demonstrating effectiveness means one thing: economic development."

being based on his knowledge will, it may be predicted, attribute any lack of effectiveness to an insufficiency of knowledge either on the part of the particular officer, or on the part of the field the officer represents. The solution to ineffectiveness will be seen, then, in a program of up-grading and research.

The most thorough-going statement of this position is provided in a discussion by Dunnette and Bass who indict personnel management for its "shallowness, negativism, static concepts, and oversimplified approaches to complex problems."[10] This denunciation is illustrated by pointing to the continued reliance on the personal interview in selection (when more reliable and valid methods are available), the use of gimmicks and fads, the lack of evaluation of alternative wage and salary programs, and lack of attention to research in areas such as learning. The solution, they suggest, lies in making the personnel manager into a kind of applied behavioral scientist. Such a person would be trained in what Leavitt[11] has called "organizational psychology"—a sort of amalgam of "individual, experimental, and social psychology and the sociology of formal organizations, buttressed by computer technology, game theory, and related techniques."[12]

Such a claim has a certain plausibility, for, after all, what else does the professional's authority rest on but his knowledge? The problem is that the claim ignores the fact that the professional is in an *organization*. The model that is tacitly being used is that of the isolated scientist in his private laboratory, the consulting engineer in solo practice, or the physician in private practice. I am the expert, thinks the professional in the personnel office, so let the people come to see me (as they would their physicians) and I shall advise and counsel them. Such a picture is not even adequate for the isolated professional, for it is not his knowledge which draws persons in off the streets. Instead, recent research in medical sociology has documented the extent to which an elaborate structure is necessary to *bring* the patient to the physician in a state of *willingness* to follow the physician's advice.[13] It is precisely this willingness which is absent in the case of line personnel who the professional in industry expects will come to him for advice and counsel. The professional will often further delude himself by thinking he has a captive clientele—the line officers have no alternative but to come to him. But they do indeed have an alternative: they can refuse to listen. So the problem comes down to one of creating a structure which will produce a willingness to come and a willingness to follow the advice.

[10] Marvin D. Dunnette and Bernard M. Bass, "Behavioral Scientists and Personnel Management," *Industrial Relations*, II (May 1963), 117. See, also, correspondence on this article in *Industrial Relations*, III (February, 1964), 109-118.

[11] Harold J. Leavitt, *Toward Organizational Psychology* (Pittsburgh, Pa.: Graduate School of Business Administration, Carnegie Institute of Technology, March, 1961).

[12] Dunnette and Bass, *op. cit.*, p. 123.

[13] See Talcott Parsons, *The Social System* (Glencoe, Ill.: Free Press, 1951), chap. X, especially the discussion of the sick role on pp. 436-447; Robert N. Wilson, "Patient-Practitioner Relationships," in Howard E. Freeman, Sol Levine, and Leo G. Reeder, editors, *Handbook of Medical Sociology* (Englewood Cliffs, N.J.: Prentice-Hall, 1963), chap. 11; and Thomas J. Scheff, "The Role of the Mentally Ill and the Dynamics of Mental Disorder: A Research Framework," *Sociometry* XXVI (December, 1963), 436-453.

Professional Knowledge Is Not Enough

We have a good deal of evidence now which casts doubt on the claim that increasing the professional's knowledge will also increase his influence with line personnel. The best such evidence is offered by the reports of the experience in bureaucratic organizations of physical scientists, such as chemists and physicists.[14] When no one listens to a social or behavioral scientist, he can always comfort himself by insisting that people "just don't realize" the tremendous contribution such sciences have to make. When callous industrial managers speak of the "so-called" behavioral sciences, the behavioral scientist conceals his wince and bravely looks forward to the day when he will be properly appreciated. Meanwhile, he plans a campaign to "educate" the benighted. There is clearly no such problem with, say, chemists. No one ever speaks of the "so-called" science of chemistry, and no one could claim that people "just don't realize" their tremendous contribution. So the chemists represent a sort of Nirvana for the social and behavioral scientists.

But physical scientists seem to be among the most dissatisfied of all industrial employees.[15] A major reason for their dissatisfaction is that they are *not* listened to with respect. Their relationships with line personnel are shot through with conflict and their recommendations are often accepted only after great pressure has been brought to bear on line officials. Then, if we look further, we discover that it is not only chemists that have this trouble, but also engineers, accountants, purchasing agents, sales personnel—in fact, all staff departments. We begin to recognize that the problems the personnel department has in dealing with the line and in getting its recommendations accepted are not due to its weakness, not due to the lack of reliable, valid knowledge, not due to the scarcity of behavioral scientists, but are one case of a whole genre—line-staff conflict.

Research reveals that such conflict has structural sources.[16] As stated above, staff men are usually younger, ambitious persons, seeking to prove their usefulness and to advance rapidly. As such they are immediately represented by older line officers who oppose general "knowledge-about" expertise in favor of their own "acquaintance-with" experience. At the same time, staff men discover that promotional opportunities are better in the line and that if they wish to move up very high, they will often have to move over into the line in order to do so. Such a situation leads staff persons to increase pressure in order to demonstrate their ability to "advise" on line problems. Line personnel are resistant to staff ideas because such ideas are often innovations[17] which upset relationships a line officer may have spent years developing, cast aspersions on a line officer's habitual way of doing things, and reveal matters they would rather keep secret. Very early, the effective personnel man learns that, to operate at

[14] See, for example, William Kornhauser, *Scientists in Industry* (Berkeley and Los Angeles: University of California Press, 1962); and Simon Marcson, *The Scientist in American Industry* (New York: Harper, 1960).

[15] David G. Moore and Richard Renck, "The Professional Employee in Industry," *Journal of Business*, XXVIII (January, 1955), 58-66.

[16] See, for example, Melville Dalton, "Conflicts Between Staff and Line Officials," *American Sociological Review*, XV (June, 1950), 342-351.

[17] See Tom Burns and G. M. Stalker, *The Management of Innovation* (London: Tavistock, 1961).

all, he must "appreciate" the line officer's problems and learn to play ball. As professionals the world over have lamented, the result is compromise with all of its "impure" consequences.

No amount of upgrading of the personnel staff will increase its authority, for its problems result from relationships with other parts of the company. Even more striking evidence that this is true is provided by two reports on supervisory training programs. Fleishmann, Harris, and Burtt report that a program at the International Harvester Company did not improve supervisor-worker relationships.[18] A similar study in two divisions of the Detroit Edison Company found a net loss in one division and a net gain in the other.[19] The explanation cannot be sought in the training programs themselves. They appear to have been carefully thought through and based on the best that modern sociology and psychology had to say on learning and the alteration of behavior. The most likely explanation emerges from a comparison of the two divisions in Detroit Edison and provides us with a perfect case of what Haire has called "encapsulated learning."[20] In the successful division, it was found that the supervisors' managers themselves supervised as the supervisory training program directed. In contrast, the managers of the supervisors in the unsuccessful division did just the opposite. The success of the training program was thus shown to depend not merely on whether scientifically sound principles were being taught, but on whether higher management indicated there would be a payoff for following the principles by itself exemplifying them.[21] In short, the personnel department that initiates any program or approach, however sound scientifically, will have to give separate attention to the problem of getting the program accepted. The mere scientific desirability of the program is hardly enough.

Resistance to Advice

Thus the personnel officer should become an expert in those social and behavioral sciences which deal with receptivity to and resistance to change.[22] A common misperception is that all resistance is pigheaded or irrational. But, it is just possible that the personnel manager may be

[18] Edwin A. Fleishmann, Edwin F. Harris, and Harold E. Burtt, *Leadership and Supervision in Industry: An Evaluation of a Supervisory Program*, Monograph 33 (Columbus, Ohio: Bureau of Educational Research, Ohio State University, 1955).

[19] Norman A. Maier, *Principles of Human Relations* (New York: Wiley, 1952), pp. 184-192.

[20] Mason Haire, *Psychology in Management* (New York: McGraw-Hill, 1956), chap. 5.

[21] Another interpretation of these findings is that they represent a special case of a congruence between the values of the trainees and those of the company (as represented by top management). After a study of engineering managers, House and Tosi conclude: ". . . we infer that those people who are most likely to benefit from training are those who have already demonstrated an acceptance of the values of the organization and who feel secure in the position." See Robert J. House and Henry Tosi, "An Experimental Evaluation of a Management Training Program," *Academy of Management Journal*, VI (December, 1963), 303-315 (quotation is on p. 314).

[22] See, for example, Lester Coch and John R. P. French, "Overcoming Resistance to Change," *Human Relations*, I (1948), 512-532; Kurt Lewin, "Studies in Group Decision," in Dorwin Cartwright and Alvin Zander, editors, *Group Dynamics* (Evanston, Ill.: Row, Peterson, 1953), pp. 287-301; William F. Whyte, *Money and Motivation* (New York: Harper, 1955), chap. 10; and Strauss and Sayles, *op. cit.*, chap. 12.

wrong, and one of the functions of social conflict is to determine who is right and who is wholly or partly wrong.[23]

It is of the first importance to note that people troubled by conflict rarely seek out scientists. In marital conflict, for example, a couple may look for a counselor, a church minister, a psychotherapist, or if all else fails, a lawyer—but not a scientist. There seems to be good reason for this choice, for the scientist has a trained incapacity to handle conflict. The scientist seeks the truth and uses the criteria of the scientific method to find it. Confronted with conflicting claims, the good scientist will let the chips fall where they may. But the management of conflict requires much more than a determination of truth by the abstract standards of science. It requires a *resolution* which both parties can live with, with a saving of self-respect and pride. And such a resolution is, as often as not, a matter of compromise, negotiation, appeals, pleadings, tears, and sometimes even lying. The good scientist keeps hold of his emotions and certainly never lies. So he has much to contribute to the understanding of the bases of conflict and may advise on programs to reduce the likelihood of conflict, but I do not look to him to solve particular cases of conflict. Of course, this is not to deny that individual scientists may be very capable in the handling of conflict. But there is little in their training that prepares them for the role. As for what they know about conflict, they can make it available to others.

The first characteristic, then, of the structure which will bring the line "client" to the personnel officer in a state of willingness to listen is an unexpected one. It is not one in which the client arrives, waits to be taken care of, and then meekly does as he is told. Rather, the structure is one of continuous conflict. This is not of course to say that conflict in itself produces a willingness to listen and be guided by advice. Rather, it is to say that conflict implies an engagement of the parties and a possibility of a change in behavior. It means the professional does not always win, but, given the actual limits of his knowledge, this is not always catastrophic for the client. Again, the medical model so frequently used leads us astray. Even in the case of the physician-patient relationship, there is a great deal of conflict, but it is submerged because the patient has been well socialized to his role.[24] (Western physicians in the newer countries often find that their patients, being much less socialized, protest violently, or refuse to cooperate altogether.) In any case, the authority of the physician is usually strengthened by his high status; the personnel man, on the other hand, is usually of lower status than his line "client."

Further clues to the nature of the "willingness structure" may be sought in an examination of the "advice and counsel" role itself. Those who provide such counsel are often naive in their relationships with those they counsel. Having provided counsel, they feel it to be no more than their due that the worth of the counsel (assuming it is a good counsel) will freely be acknowledged by the recipient. Yet it seems to be the fate of those who volunteer unsought advice to be without honor among those they advise. Blau's research among white-collar persons showed that the acceptance of

[23] See Lewis Coser, *The Functions of Social Conflict* (Glencoe, Ill.: Free Press, 1956).

[24] See Parsons, *op. cit.*

advice always implied a debt which had to be repaid.[25] It implied the advice-giver was one's superior and that one should pay him in the coin of deference or gratitude. Such a price was a high one to have to pay, and hence, workers turned from experts (who could really give helpful advice) to their peers (who knew no more than they did) because the latter's advice could be repaid easily by returning the favor. Line officers are similarly reluctant to accept advice from personnel men, for to do so is to admit the latter's superiority and to incur a debt which must be paid sometime.

Blau's workers would often "talk out loud" about their problems, as if simply repeating them to themselves, thereby permitting anyone who wished to offer suggestions or advice. The man who brought up the problem would thus not have placed himself in the situation of coming to others, hat in hand, and asking their help. He could claim any suggestions offered to be ideas he had already thought of, later actually adopting one of them to solve the problem. So too, a line officer might well accept a personnel officer's advice, but he does not want the personnel officer to remind him of the help or to use it as the basis for a claim later on that the line officer owes the personnel officer anything.

As suggested earlier, this sort of dilemma is commonly faced by staff or auxiliary departments. All departments are interdependent and each department's actions have repercussions on others. At the same time, each department will wish to increase its share of credit for accomplishments and reduce its share of blame for difficulties.

In this situation, the personnel department can only render appropriate service if there is a demand for its special skills. In order for there to be that demand, the department will have to make its contribution highly visible. But visibility alone is not enough; if it were, the placards and cartoons that personnel departments are fond of bringing out, together with the customary activity reports (which count the number of inquiries received and telephone calls made), would have long since earned for personnel a top honored position. Besides being visible, the contribution must be highly valued, that is, it must relate to the values of those whom power-holders seek to influence.

A first step is to establish *criteria* by which the presence of problems may be detected. For each department, personnel could gather data on subjects on which it might be able to offer assistance, such as turnover, training, absenteeism, efficiency, merit rating records, and measures of supervisory effectiveness. Chapple and Sayles suggest the use of statistical measures similar to those employed in quality control.[26] Thus, data on absenteeism might be kept for a year and broken down by department, skill group, sex, age group, seniority, and other variables. Variations beyond sampling error might be noted and correlated with other variables, such as seasonality, training programs, policy changes, and recruitment source shifts. Through such means as these, it is possible to present highly convincing evidence that a department is below other departments or below its own average in the past, and to suggest possible explanations.

[25] Peter B. Blau, *The Dynamics of Bureaucracy* (Chicago: University of Chicago Press, 1955), pp. 99-248, especially pp. 108 ff.

[26] Elliot D. Chapple and Leonard R. Sayles, *The Measurement of Management* (New York: Macmillan, 1960).

In addition, the personnel department could play a major role in evaluating the effects of organizational change. This it might do through before-and-after studies of management development programs, shifts in recruitment, and changes in sales approaches. Such evaluations would be valuable, but there should be no illusions about their possible effects. A carefully controlled evaluation will produce results that favor one manager and throw another under a cloud. Consequently, resistance should be expected.

The Personnel Department as Monitor

Thus, I should like to suggest that the personnel function should increasingly be that of evaluating how well the organization functions. For this purpose it should develop a set of statistical controls which provide a running record of work in departments or other structurally significant divisions. While the devising of these controls would require intensive training in the social and behavioral sciences and in statistics, the resulting information could be highly meaningful and valuable to supervisors in those departments and to other managerial officials. Just as cost control information provides guidelines to departmental operations, so indices of grievances, transfer requests, turnover, etc., are likely to provide equally useful guidelines, though their interpretation requires the expertise of the personnel department.

It is essential that these and other such indices have a public, objective quality about them. They should make it impossible for anyone to claim that the personnel department is creating a job for itself. At the same time, they must refer to operations which are of obvious importance to line operators and be used as evaluating devices by the operators' superiors. The public, objective character of the indices enables the personnel man to be given credit when he solves the problem. If it was he who discovered that the volume of grievances had gone up in a department after some new piece of machinery was installed, if he instituted a program to reduce those grievances, and if they were in fact reduced, he can claim at least some credit for the change.

The Failure of the Medical Model

I bring up the matter of credit because there is a kind of advice to which my remarks do not apply, for which the personnel officer cannot be given credit, and which, in my judgement, had better be abolished altogether. I refer to the private consultation, where a line officer seeks out a personnel officer, asks his advice on a work problem, and perhaps acts on the advice. Even should the personnel officer be willing to give "free advice" with no thought of future return, he is, in fact, hampered from so doing for two reasons.

First, for a line officer to be able freely to confide in a personnel man, or any other adviser, the officer must trust the personnel man not to reveal his confidences to higher management. Otherwise, he will be reluctant to admit any problem which might reflect on his ability to do his job. It is precisely the "human" problem that most managers feel reluctant to discuss, for they are, as managers, presumed ot be highly skilled in handling men. Yet the personnel officer, as a staff man to management, is expected to keep management informed on special human difficulties that arise. Therefore, the personnel officer may find that his job requires him to violate confidences.

The second objection is suggested by Whyte.[27] In many respects, personnel officers are viewed by management as "inspectors," who conduct "audits" on the company's employee relations policy, salary policy, and other matters. Indeed, the role of monitor *is* an inspector role. But there is obviously a fundamental conflict between being a consultant, on the one hand, and an inspector, on the other. Clearly, if the man whom one consults on a problem is also the man who will evaluate how one solves the problem, then one would be wise to accept his advice, whatever it is.

It is ironical that when an occasion does arise when the medical model might seem to be applicable, the personnel man cannot act. Yet his realization of this fact is, in a sense, but a recognition of the structural imperatives of the organization in which he is employed. It is, of course, possible for a personnel man to manipulate the structure and to carve out his own destiny in his own way. Thus a personnel man might have private consultations and promise to keep the information secret, though this promise violates his responsibility to his superiors. Personnel men do this all the time (and not only personnel men), and they may use secret knowledge to push their careers or to attain other goals by demanding, later, a payoff for services rendered. But such considerations take us into a discussion of power and how it is achieved in organizations, whereas our concern in this paper has been with the sources of authority.

[27] Whyte, *Men at Work* . . . , p. 509.

29

Current Status of Personnel Management

Measurement of Industrial Relations Activities

PHILIP ASH

While each company must shape its industrial relations function to suit its own particular local needs and situation, it is desirable from time to time to evaluate how this function is being discharged, either by comparison with other companies to determine the extent of divergence from the common pattern, or by manipulation of internal data without comparison.

From Philip Ash, "Measurement of Industrial Relations Activities," *Journal of Applied Psychology*, Vol. 51, No. 5, 1967, pp. 387-392.

Philip Ash was with the Inland Steel Company when this was written and is now Professor of Psychology at the University of Illinois, Chicago Circle, Chicago, Illinois.

Where intercompany or interindustry benchmarks are available the evaluation will provide a more realistic appraisal than would be possible in the absence of such benchmarks.

In recognition of the desirability of creating benchmarks for comparative purposes, the Industrial Relations Center of the University of Minnesota, under the direction of Dale Yoder, undertook an annual survey of salaries and staffing ratios in industrial relations. In all, between 1949 and 1962, when the project was abandoned, 13 annual surveys were published (Nelson, England, & Yoder, 1963). The central statistic developed was the personnel ratio (*PR*) : the ratio of the number of employees in industrial relations to the total employment in the company. This ratio has been widely used in industry to assess the industrial relations function (Mee, 1958, p. 112). As Gray (1965) and others have pointed out, however, the *PR* provides less than unambiguous information. The ratio also may be correlated with company size (American Management Association, 1961, Table 12; Nelson, England, & Yoder, 1960; Wortman, 1963), limiting the possibility of applying an average industry figure to evaluate the industrial relations functions in different-sized companies.

Furthermore, the number of employees in a function such as industrial relations is not necessarily a very good indicator of what they do, considering the wide range of possible activities in the function.

A more sophisticated statistic to evaluate the industrial relations function (or any other corporate activity, for that matter) on the basis of comparative work-force data is a regression equation including the predicted number of employees in the function as the dependent variable, and total employment as the independent variable, namely,

$$IR = a + bE$$

where *IR* is the predicted number of employees in industrial relations, *E* is total employment, and *a* and *b* are the constants.

It may be noted that if the linear relationship does exist, it follows that the *PR* systematically varies with total company employment:

$$PR = \frac{IR \text{ employment}}{\text{Total employment}}$$

$$= \frac{a + bE}{E}$$

$$= \frac{a}{E} + b$$

The American Management Association (1961, Table 12) study of 14 industries, cited above, showed that a linear-regression line fits the data very well. The correlations between *IR* employment and total employment ranged from .73 to .99 for the 14 industries, and was .89 for all companies combined without respect to industry. In 7 of the industries, the intercept (a) was positive: the PR *decreased* with increasing company size. In the remaining 7 industries, however, the intercept was negative: the PR increased with increasing company size.

A third approach to evaluating the industrial relations function has involved the construction of an index based upon activity measures such as accession and separation rates, grievances, suggestions submitted, safety data, etc. (French, 1954; Jackson, 1961; Merrihue & Katzell, 1955). Typically, in such an index, six to eight measures of industrial relations activities are combined into a weighted composite to provide a single-number measure of the state of the function. At least in the published studies, one important limitation has been the lack of cross-company comparison and, indeed, the practical impossibility of making such a comparison, since the same functions, measured in the same ways, do not seem to occur across any large number of companies.

Method

The present study was an attempt to develop other measurement concepts and benchmarks which might contribute to understanding the ways in which industrial relations staff may be deployed to accomplish many different objectives, with particular emphasis on the conceptualization and measurement of level of activity and of centralization versus decentralization.

Forty-three[1] major corporations provided, via a lengthy questionnaire, data on organization structure and on general employment and industrial relations employment, and responses to a 38-item scale of industrial relations activities (listed in Table 3). The 43 companies included 13 steel companies ranging in employment size from 9,700 to 244,000 workers; the median was 16,000. The 30 other companies were distributed among 12 manufacturing industries and reported total employment ranging from 11,400 to 38,000 employees; the median employment was 30,000. For the sample as a whole, median employment was 26,950.

A correlation analysis was made of data on 11 variables, and measures of centralization were also compared with qualitative data on centralization policies and practices. The 11 variables included:

First, three measures of employment size:

1. total employment,
2. total industrial relations staff,
3. headquarters or corporate industrial relations staff.

Total headquarters work force was also noted, but not treated as a separate variable.

Second, two traditional personnel ratios:

4. total industrial relations personnel ratio (industrial relations staff to total employment), and
5. corporate industrial relations personnel ratio (corporate staff to total employment).

Third, two measures of centralization of staff based upon employment figures:

6. the ratio of corporate industrial relations staff to total industrial relations staff, and

[1] Not all companies reported complete data. For each variable, the number of responding companies is shown in Table 1.

7. a personnel concentration index based on a comparison of the previous ratio with the ratio of total corporate staff to total work force.

This index measures the extent to which the industrial relations function is more or less concentrated at the corporate level than are all other company functions.

Fourth, two measures of industrial relations activity based on responses to the 38-item scale. For each item, the responding company indicated that (a) the corporate staff conducts and administers the activity (e.g., labor negotiations), (b) the corporate staff reviews and approves, (c) the corporate staff provides advice and counsel only, (d) the activity is not a corporate activity, or (e) there is no active program in the area in the company.

The two measures based on this score are:

8. an activity centralization index, a score based on the first four response categories.

This score can vary from 0 (none of the listed activities is a corporate responsibility) to 3.00 (all activities centrally located, conducted, and administered), and

9. an activity ratio—the number of activities coded to reflect corporate responsibility for at least advice and counsel (Codes a, b, or c checked), divided by 38.

Finally, two measures of the ratio of professional, technical, and managerial (exempt) staff to clerical (nonexempt) staff:

10. the exempt-nonexempt ratio for the total industrial relations function, and
11. the exempt-nonexempt ratio for the corporate industrial relations function.

Results

Tables 1 and 2 summarize, respectively, measures of central tendency and dispersion on the 11 variables and the intercorrelations among the variables.

Employment and the Personnel Ratio. While the three employment-size statistics are highly correlated with one another (as might be expected), they are related to only a limited extent to the rest of the measures. The correlations of total employment with the various ratios and indexes are all insignificantly different from zero. It might be noted that the correlations between total employment and both *PR*s (total *PR* and corporate *PR*) are both negative. At least in this sample, as company employment size increases, the *PR* tends to decrease. The absolute size of the corporate industrial relations staff, however, is *positively* related to the corporate *PR*.

Total PR and Centralization. The total *PR* is negatively correlated (–.40, –.38) with the two measures of centralization (personnel concentration index and activity centralization index). Decentralized companies,

TABLE 1

Medians, Quartiles, Means, and Standard Deviations for All Industrial Relations (IR) Measures

Measure	No. responding companies	*M*	*SD*	Q 1	*Mdn*	Q 3
1. Total employment	43	32826	40647	14801	26950	31548
2. Total IR staff employment	28	284	334	100	176	315
3. Corporate IR staff employment	37	35	37	13	26	41
4. Total IR personnel ratio	28	1.01	0.59	0.63	0.85	1.12
5. Corporate IR personnel ratio	37	0.11	0.10	0.05	0.09	0.16
6. Corporate IR staff to total IR staff	26	16.00	10.61	8.93	15.60	19.90
7. Personnel concentration index	26	5.12	3.66	2.66	4.55	6.97
8. Activity centralization index	42	1.65	0.53	1.26	1.72	1.93
9. Activity ratio	42	70.20	19.30	64.00	74.90	82.90
10. Exempt/Nonexempt ratio: Total IR staff	26	1.08	0.61	0.73	0.87	1.35
11. Exempt/Nonexempt ratio: Corporate IR staff	26	1.66	0.86	1.16	1.62	2.22

TABLE 2

Intercorrelation Matrix

Variable	Variable 2	3	4	5	6	7	8	9	10	11
1. Total employment	89	71	–08	–15	–10	18	12	03	–17	–16
2. Total IR staff employment	–	72	36	–03	–16	–00	–05	–02	–26	–25
3. Corporate IR staff employment			08	51	39	18	31	22	–19	–23
4. Total IR personnel ratio			–	–20	–06	–40	–38	–10	–30	–09
5. Corporate IR personnel ratio				–	71	02	20	25	04	–18
6. Corporate IR staff to total IR staff					–	25	44	50	08	00
7. Personnel concentration index						–	–04	–04	30	–21
8. Activity centralization index							–	53	06	30
9. Activity ratio								–	12	10
10. Exempt/Nonexempt: Total IR staff									–	35
11. Exempt/Nonexempt: Corporate IR staff										–

Note – Decimal Points Omitted

in other words, tend to have larger industrial relations staffs in relation to their total employment than do companies in which the industrial relations function is more centralized at the corporate level.

Centralization and Level of Activity. Centralization of functional responsibility at the corporate level (activity centralization index) tends to be related to a wider range of industrial relations activities (activity ratio; $r = .53$), and both functional centralization (activity centralization index) and a wider range of activities (activity ratio) are associated with larger corporate staffs vis-à-vis industrial relations staffs ($r = .44$ and $.50$, respectively.

Exempt-Nonexempt Ratio. Contrary to original expectations, the ratio of exempt to non-exempt personnel did not seem to be related to any of the other indexes or measures that were computed. Organizations that have fairly well-centralized industrial relations programs are about as likely to have low exempt-nonexempt ratios as high exempt-nonexempt ratios, and decentralized programs reflect similar variety. It had been thought that as industrial relations programs increase in size, extent, and variety of functions, and degree of centralization, the ratio of exempt to nonexempt employees would go down because larger numbers of clerical people would be required to accomplish all the details of administration. This hypothesis is at least partially sustained in the comparison of the ratios for the total industrial relations force with the ratios for the corporate industrial relations force. The latter are consistently higher, reflecting the relatively larger number of clerical personnel involved in processing of forms and records at the plant level. However, there does not appear to be a consistent pattern across the companies surveyed for either of the ratios considered separately.

The Activity Centralization Index and Perception of Centralization. For the sample as a whole, the index ranged from 0.00 to 2.69 with an overall median of 1.72 (the steel industry is characterized by a slightly higher tendency toward industrial relations centralization—median 1.83—than nonsteel companies—median 1.53).

To test the index against management *perceptions* of centralization, respondents were asked for their views concerning the extent to which industrial relations activities are, or should be, centralized at the company-headquarters level. Companies with high activity centralization indexes generally reported that the function *was* centralized, and the leading reason cited was the need for uniformity of action arising out of master labor agreements.

For example, a steel company with a score of 2.69 said

> . . . from our experience there is a great need for a close review and approval of the activities listed through a central staff functioning at Corporate or Company Headquarters. Unless this is done there can be misinterpretation of policies which would ultimately go far afield of the original purpose and intent of such policies. We have found this to be very definitely the case even where operations are closely integrated. It is very easy to create misunderstanding involving such matters as Employee Benefit Programs (insurance and pensions), through wrong interpretations at plant levels. Such matters can be corrected quickly where general clearance is established through centralized headquarters staff. . . . In certain areas such as those related to safety, the actual operations must be carried out at the plant and departmental levels. However, the great majority of the other activities depend primarily on strict interpretation of policies established by top management and therefore should be administered from headquarters to be most effective.

A nonsteel company with a score of 2.32 said

> In the Industrial Relations or any other field, decentralized *administration* is highly desirable. The central group can provide three important

things: *Company policy manuals* to give guidance to local administrators; *staff assistance* (especially to small plants) in the development of employee safety manuals, training material, and the like which are beyond local plant staff capacity; *periodic audits* or inspections to provide assurance to top management that decentralized administration has not resulted in failure of a location to carry out important Company policies.

We find that a high degree of central control is necessary in the negotiation and interpretation of contracts (to prevent the unions from playing one plant off against another) but that most other phases are best handled by local administration and responsibility within broad policy limits.

However, companies with somewhat similar problems, but with low activity centralization indexes, tend to deemphasize administrative consistency and to emphasize reporting, auditing, and counsel.

For example, a nonsteel company with a score of 0.94 said

> We believe the industrial relations activity should be decentralized into the individual plants to the greatest degree possible. Operations and employee relations are so inter-related that the effective administration should be exercised at the local level and essentially by the same management. The limit on the degree of decentralization depends on the effect of local actions on the other plants and divisions of the company, and the responsibilities retained by corporate management governing broad policy application and expenditures. In this area corporate industrial relations staffs function best—clearing and advising both local and corporate management.

And another with a score of 1.12 said

> A good rule of thumb: Centralize information—decentralize action.
>
> This does not mean that the Corporate Industrial Relations Department does not get into the actions which are normally decentralized. They do. But only when needed. For example, collective bargaining is decentralized, but with detailed, continuous reporting of local bargaining, the Corporate Department can and does step in (1) when the trend of the local bargaining may substantially affect more than one local unit; or (2) when unorganized units are organized for the first time; or (3) when management changes bring new, inexperienced management to the local bargaining table.
>
> This "rule of thumb" also means centralized records—but decentralized wage and salary administration—with the Corporate staff stepping in when special problems arise or major revisions of the local wage-salary program are contemplated.

In almost all the comments, the underlying theme seems to be, "Centralize policy, decentralize practice." But in working out this slogan, there seems to be a wide divergence concerning what policy embraces, which practices may be delegated, and how far.

Activity Centralization Across Companies. An analysis was also undertaken for each of the 38 activities, based on the responsibility classifica-

TABLE 3

Activity Centralization Index and Activity Ratio, by Activities (for 42 Responding Companies)

Activity	Activity Centralization Index	Activity Ratio
Union contract negotiations	2.45	97.7
Contract interpretation	2.14	97.7
Supervisory training	1.76	92.9
Employee benefit administration	2.20	92.9
Grievance procedure administration	1.74	90.5
College recruiting	2.34	85.8
Management development	2.08	85.8
Induction and orientation training	1.51	85.8
Skills and apprentice training	1.46	85.8
Personnel records	1.95	83.4
Industrial relations research	2.63	81.0
Executive health programs	2.35	78.6
Safety training	1.55	81.0
Selection testing	1.77	78.6
Other safety activities	1.40	76.2
Occupational hygiene	1.57	73.9
University management programs	2.13	71.5
Salaried job evaluation	1.76	71.5
Employee attitude survey	2.23	69.1
Tuition aid programs	2.22	69.1
Hourly job evaluation	1.40	69.1
House organs	1.73	66.7
First aid and medical programs	2.59	64.3
Community relations	1.05	64.3
Employee communications	2.48	62.0
Recreation programs	1.09	62.0
Test validation	1.59	59.6
Merit rating	1.39	59.6
Eating facilities	1.02	59.6
Employee counseling	1.23	57.2
Plant security	0.95	54.8
Testifying before governmental bodies	1.31	52.4
Speeches	1.29	52.4
Participation in industry associations	1.13	52.4
Public relations	1.03	47.7
Credit union	0.86	45.3
Time and motion study	0.74	31.0
Lobbying	1.24	12.0

tions assigned by the 42 companies that completed the scale, to identify the most frequently occurring activities and the relative degree of centralization of each activity, over these 42 companies.

For the combined sample, the five most frequently occurring corporate industrial relations functions (as indicated by the activity ratio) were: union contract negotiations, contract interpretation, supervisory training, employee benefits administration, and grievance procedure administration. Supervisory training and grievance procedure administration tend to involve advisory responsibilities primarily but the other three involve administrative or review responsibilities.

At the other end of the scale, the functions (among the 38 listed) that occur least frequently among corporate industrial relations staff responsibilities are: lobbying, time and motion study, credit union, and public relations. Generally, industrial relations responsibility for public relations is advisory only. This reflects the fact that the public relations function is part of the industrial relations function in only a minority of the companies surveyed. Where the two are in one department, however, the corporate staff generally exercises administrative responsibility.

From the point of view of centralization–decentralization (as measured by the activity centralization index), the five most centralized activities were: industrial relations research, first aid and medical care, employee communications, union contract negotiating, and executive health programs. The five least centralized activities were: time and motion study, credit unions, plant security, eating facilities, and community relations. For these latter activities, if the corporate industrial relations staff had a role at all, it was primarily advisory and consultative in nature.

Conclusion

The actual distribution of statistics of the small sample of companies surveyed is not intended to provide benchmarks, particularly for companies that are substantially smaller or substantially larger than those surveyed. It is suggested, however, that the methods and measures outlined do offer a way of reducing to common scales some very complex concepts, and collection of data over samples of companies comparable in size and structure would provide useful comparisons for a company engaged in evaluating its own industrial relations organization.

REFERENCES

American Management Association. *Statistical analysis of the 1961 Red Book data. Group 10 research report.* Saranac Lake, N.Y.: American Management Association Academy, November 1, 1961. Unpaginated.

French, S. H., Jr. Measuring progress toward industrial relations objectives. *Personnel*, 1954, 30(5), 338-347).

Gray, R. D. Evaluating the personnel department. *Personnel*, 1965, 42(2), 43-56.

Jackson, W. C. The Personnel Activity Index: A new budgeting tool. *Personnel*, 1961, 38(1), 47-52.

Mee, J. F. (Ed.) *Personnel handbook*. New York: Ronald Press, 1958.

Merrihue, W. V., & Katzell, R. A. ERI-yardstick of employee relations. *Harvard Business Review*, 1955, 33(6), 91-99.

Nelson, R. J., England, G. W., & Yoder, D. Personnel ratios, 1960: An analytical tool. *Personnel*, 1960, 37(6), 18-28.

Nelson, R. J., England, G. W., & Yoder, D. Personnel ratios and costs, 1962. *Personnel*, 1963, 40(1), 19-26.

Wortman, M. S. Personnel ratios and personnel departments. *Personnel Administration*, 1963, 26(6), 46-51.

30

New Structures for New Challenges

Reorganize the Personnel Department?

STANLEY L. SOKOLIK

Personnel-staff departments of larger firms are usually organized on a function- or task-oriented basis. This pattern seems to have developed as a natural concomitant of the increasing personnel expertise which has come about in the last twenty-five years. Growth in staff specialization has become possible only to make assignments on the basis of more specifically prescribed technical areas (e.g., compensation planning, benefits analysis, technical training, employee publications, college recruitment).

Of course, some of this division of labor also results from the personnel specialists' own efforts to preserve and add to appurtenances of their status. Though an oversimplification, it is not too far wrong to say that personnel specialists have generally equated task specialization with gaining and reinforcing acceptance of their role as the authority in management of their firms' human resources.

However, all has not gone well with personnel departments which have developed on this basis. Their growth and, even more importantly, their particular contribution to the profitable growth of their firms have not kept pace. Symptoms persist to indicate that personnel-staff management is increasingly left at the starting gate in important corporate efforts, if considered at all as anything more than interested onlookers. Surely, in all too many cases, personnel-staff management has failed to earn the direct commitment of top-management resources—the convincing arguments of some of their most persuasive practitioners notwithstanding. This situation seems appropriately described as a malaise. Four strongly foreboding symptoms stand out:

- Work productivity and worker satisfaction continue to languish, and few personnel departments are able to show material gains in either area.
- Tasks are being splintered off from the personnel departments' responsibilities and established not only as separate divisions, but often in competition with those who sired them.
- The personnel field continues to have difficulties in attracting outstanding men, both from among college students and within management ranks, no matter how exposed some of the potential candidates' "helping" interest is.

Dr. Sokolik is Professor of Administration, Sangamon State University, Springfield, Illinois.

• Personnel departments are all too seldom in the midst of the creative leadership generated by corporate responsibilities in a changing urban America.

Cries of the bankruptcy of personnel management have been heard for some time. Criticism of the personnel staff's ability to generate effective responses to new and growing problems from within and without the firm is never far from the formal and informal discussions of managers of every stripe (at times, even those who hold management positions within the personnel department). Although not the first to do so, Peter F. Drucker met the question head-on in his book, *The Practice of Management*, concluding that the field (while not bankrupt) was "certainly insolvent, certainly unable to honor, with the ready cash of performance, the promises of managing worker and work it so liberally makes. . . . [Its] assets are frozen."[1]

Thirteen years later, the claims of the creditors do not appear to have been satisfied. Personnel departments have not achieved long-run improvement in work productivity or worker satisfaction, presumably the key reasons for their existence.

To the extent that a malaise exists, corrective action is needed to enable personnel departments to make the unique contribution which can be theirs. A first step—surely a major one—would be giving them a more viable organization structure. Structure must be clearly attuned to purpose. Unless it is, it cannot be expected that personnel specialists will reach out for more creative programs, let alone respond in such a way as to surmount the increasing pressures which beset them today. The consequence of an orderly change now could well be such extreme dysfunctioning that answers will be sought elsewhere—from others who deal with human resources from outside the personnel-staff ranks or from those who would have the enterprise depend far less upon people.

I will present two organizational models which may provide the basis for effectively redesigning personnel departments. The first was recently suggested by Frederick Herzberg, and the second is an outgrowth of my search for a renewal of personnel-staff capacity. Neither is simply achieved, and each requires major realignment and reorientation in how personnel-staff specialists work together. On the other hand, both are within the grasp of those now in the field.

In the last of his trilogy about job attitudes, Herzberg offers a challenge to even the hardiest and most successful personnel practitioners as he observes, "Present personnel programs, which in effect serve to minimize the natural symptoms of an amputated individual, can lead only to temporary, opiate relief and further the basic psychic pathology."[2]

Herzberg's thrust is direct and piercing as it focuses upon the direction of the historical growth of personnel-staff departments. He finds and questions the almost exclusive concern with the "maintenance" needs of workers (Fig. 1). So directed, the personnel specialists end up working at odds with their own best interests. Though they proceed to launch more and more programs as well as intensify or update the old ones, their efforts

[1] Peter F. Drucker, *The Practice of Management* (New York: Harper and Brothers, 1954), p. 287.

[2] Frederick Herzberg, *Work and the Nature of Man* (Cleveland and New York: World Publishing Company, 1968), p. 170.

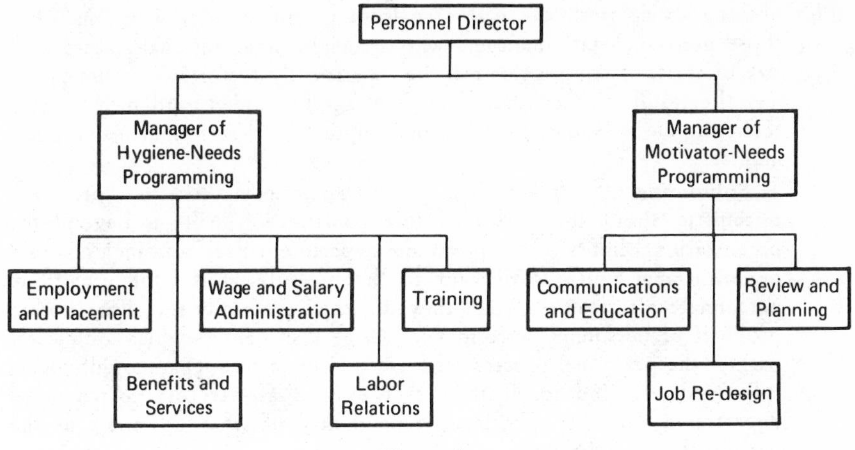

Figure 1.

are largely self-defeating. Little of lasting worth results for the workers and almost nothing for work productivity (as studies by Herzberg and others have verified).

Herzberg, moreover, recognizes a structural causality for some of the present state of affairs. He refers to an increasing regard for professionalism among personnel specialists (certainly something not restricted to them) as ironically becoming a "synonym for gathering [for themselves] the harvest of the hygiene factors of status and money."[3] Winning professional status for themselves has thus been seen by many personnel-staff workers as reassurance that their focus upon task specialization in personnel management is proper. Whatever the fears they have about their preoccupation with the hygienic environment of the employee, they are encouraged by the "professional legitimacy" of immersing themselves in the pursuit of refinements of technique, no matter how abstruse or unmotivating these ends become.

To be sure, such concerns with the growth of personnel-staff professionalism are not shared by all. The opinion of many is, to the contrary, most optimistic. They point to the growth in numbers and variety of staff and programming of personnel departments. Such evidence is, of course, undebatable. There are sizable and still-growing personnel staffs in almost every business organization worthy of mention. From the way things look, indeed, the creditors have been staved off. But does such growth signify success?

Some of this growth, it should be remembered, comes directly from growth in the size of many business firms. There is the increased personnel-staff workload brought on by greater payroll-tax complexities and a myriad of government regulations of employment and labor relations practices, not to mention the growing number of mergers with the planning and consequences which they create for personnel-staff specialists. Then, too, there's the persistence of what Dalton McFarland has termed the "trash-can" pattern which has led personnel departments to become a dumping ground for a broad array of functions which have little or

[3] *Ibid.*, p. 184.

nothing to do with the major goals of personnel administration.[4] For those personnel-staff managers who associate organizational stature with size of staff, of course, this may be a personally fortuitous circumstance. Yet the result is often that they then face the added burden of keeping their emphasis (and their superiors') upon their personnel accomplishments.

Splintering Off of Personnel Tasks. Sometimes those who are more optimistic about the personnel-staff contribution will go beyond the organizational limits of the personnel department itself and include other organizational units as relevant to the measure of the full growth in personnel-staff services. When they do, they are really revealing another problem of personnel performance. Three task centers which are clearly part of the personnel process (at least, as I conceived it) are rapidly being splintered off (indeed, if they ever existed as part of the personnel department) and are growing independently of what is known as the personnel-staff function.

I refer here to the growth of staff departments in labor relations, organization planning, and management development. All three of these staff activities—though perhaps reporting to the same senior executive—are more and more being regarded as separate organizational entities. Ironically, too, these are often the "personnel" activities which receive the greatest attention and the most direct involvement of top management. Of course, when this happens, the personnel department loses out. If nothing else, it is blocked in trying to generate a coordinated program of human-resource management. It also finds itself sterile in achieving a strategic position in corporate planning which would enable it to mount and sustain innovative efforts.

A Helping Posture Without Appeal. The malaise also reveals itself in the lack of appeal which personnel departments hold out for college graduates. Though one would think that a personnel-staff career opportunity would offer a meaningful alternative to the young people who have been turning to the generally recognized "helping professions," the Peace Corps, VISTA, and similar ventures, it does not seem to have worked out that way.

Surely, young people will always have trouble identifying business with a liberal outlook or public service so long as its specialized human-oriented departments are themselves so uninviting. At a time when business in general may be making some headway in attracting more able and creative students, personnel careers are often not among the best, and many who select a "personnel" major in a business school do so for no more deep a consideration than their "liking for people." If the feelings of the college student and graduate offer valid insight into the broader job situation, personnel departments do not appear as the "in" group, offer the greatest challenge, or stand the best chance of rewarding an individual's efforts.

Ineffective Response to Forces from Without. Finally, no matter how much personnel departments are contributing to organizational productivity and development, it's the *exception* to find them playing a viable and

[4] Dalton E. McFarland, *Cooperation and Conflict in Personnel Administration* (New York: American Foundation for Management Research, 1962), p. 49. In contrast to my concern here with internal organization, McFarland's survey focused upon the relationships between the personnel-staff department and those outside of it.

central role in marshalling the organization's capacity to respond creatively to the increased responsibilities thrust upon business firms from without. Indeed, in all too many instances in the past, the answers have been imposed upon—not anticipated by—the personnel department. Civil rights legislation and the summer riots of 1966 and 1967 have truly contributed far more to the renewal of personnel-staff performance than any effort its practitioners have wrought on their own.

Only recently, Alfonso J. Cervantes, Mayor of St. Louis, wrote:

> Either business men *will* learn new techniques of job simplification, personnel management, and skill development, and take over the leadership of the thrust against chronic unemployment, or it will be necessary to withdraw from the central city and to seal it off as the leprous Pandora's box of American society.[5]

In a recent review of the status of race relations in the business community, Arthur Shostak expresses the fear that the social responsibilities which he sets out for future personnel specialists will not be realized since the challenge which "goes to the very heart of the personnel function" has been left unheeded in the past.[6]

Herzberg's Duality Structure. Only recently has there been a creative suggestion for revamping the internal structure of personnel-staff departments into two major divisions. Though I personally do not know of any business firm which has proceeded to institute the change, it stands a good chance of arresting the existing problems, even of making serious inroads in obliterating many of the causative factors. The suggestion comes from Herzberg as he seeks to provide a more operational base for the celebrated research he and his associates have conducted into worker attitudes.[7] Herzberg advocates that two divisions of personnel-staff activity should be formed to deal separately with the dual needs he has identified as significant to worker attitudes and behavior. One would continue to concentrate on the hygiene or maintenance needs, and the other would be charged with sustaining a creative effort to satisfy the motivator needs of workers. (See Fig. 1.)

Herzberg's plan is an offshoot of his own research. As the practical import of his investigations, he even adocates paralleling his delineated duality of worker needs with a dual structuring of personnel-staff performance. In short, he says that the best way to meet man's needs is to reflect the dual structure of man's nature (i.e., his maintenance and motivation needs) in the very organization structure of those departments which are responsible for dealing with man's concerns, problems, development, and utilization on behalf of the enterprise. Such an organization structure could be charted as in Figure 1.

Herzberg would have the first of the formal personnel divisions continue to pursue programs concerned with the worker's hygiene-need system. As he sees it, most of the existing personnel-staff activity of business firms today would fall into this division.

[5] Alfonso J. Cervantes, "To Prevent a Chain of Super-Watts," *Harvard Business Review*, XLV:5 (Sept.-Oct. 1967), 60.

[6] Arthur Shostak, "Race Relations: Questions and Answers for Personnel Men," *Personnel Administration*, XXVII:4 (July-August 1964), 18.

[7] Herzberg, pp. 171-180. Herzberg provides here a very convincing defense for the kind of reorganization he suggests.

The second division would have as its sphere the tasks that have been given far less attention but (as Herzberg's findings evidence) can be far more effective in changing workers' behavior. It would search out and deal creatively with the problems that interfere with workers' psychological growth. Three tasks would predominate in this second division:

- The education or, preferably, the re-education of workers and management as to the realism of worker motivation and efforts to this end.
- Meaningful job enlargement and other structural changes which provide for greater job autonomy.
- "Remedial and therapeutic actions" growing out of periodic reviews of company policies, assumptions, rules and regulations—reviews specifically aimed at uncovering factors which interfere with or do not go far enough in motivating workers.

Some examples of specific objectives for each of these latter subunits will help to appreciate the contrast with the operation of existing personnel departments. Communications and education with the workers as well as those who manage them would treat directly the effect of work upon them, the realistic prospects of gaining greater satisfaction from work performance, the natural changes in workers' levels of needs as they mature organizationally and personally, and the extreme importance of personal communications. Herzberg holds out much for job enrichment as the major means of realizing worker motivation by providing additional opportunities for recognition of achievement, more challenging job complexity and open-endedness and more built-in job fluidity.

It is clear that Herzberg has thought out his proposal well. He acknowledges the practical value of manifesting a clear organizational separation of these tasks and takes pains to project realistically possible results. For example in the wake of changes introduced by the motivator division, he foresees a sharp and dramatic increase in productivity at the creativity level, but an increased number of errors at the operational level. Though he feels that over the long run the creativity output is likely to more than offset the greater errors engendered by the freedom given the individual, he expresses concern that the fear of increased errors at the outset may well block the proposed organizational change. He fears that an agreement to "permit mistakes" might be impossible to achieve.

At the same time, Herzberg stresses the full potential of job environmental factors. Should a firm consequently agree to give the responsibility for the reduction of these errors to lower-level workers, he feels that the way would be opened for additional benefits. It would be giving these workers a motivator factor, errors would be reduced as they learned to fulfill their new responsibility, and higher management would be released for more challenging endeavors.

Though following Herzberg's suggestion would surely bring about a far greater consideration of motivator-need factors, two questions arise as to how successful his model can be in providing an over-all organizational strategy for a creative, growing personnel-staff role. The first has to do with the persisting differences which exist among workers employed at any one time within a firm, whether they are a matter of fundamental characteristics which pre-exist a worker's employment in a particular job (e.g., sex, age, physical or mental handicap) or are organizationally derived (e.g., status as an operative worker, union-represented worker, scientific worker, manager).

Here, from an internal viewpoint, doubt arises as to whether or not significant individual differences can be productively dealt with to the extent that Herzberg would insist is possible with his broad restructuring. Can motivator answers for such differing workers really be found and implemented when corporate personnel departments need to justify new, far higher-risk undertakings in terms of their global economics?

The second question (and perhaps one more verifiable in practice should a business firm adopt Herzberg's model) lies in this plan's wholly internal orientation. In itself, it seems to offer little likelihood of enhancing the personnel department's capacity to reach out and provide personnel answers to the increasing external pressures *vis-à-vis* a firm's human resources. It really can offer little in the way of providing the organizational impetus necessary to fill the present gaps in the capacity of business firms to deal constructively with the needs imposed by the intense external pressures facing them, both as employers and citizens within a changing, complex urban society.

This is a matter of no small significance. Can such dual structuring of the personnel-staff serve more than to help in making possible maximum treatment of individual differences of the currently employed? Or can it also provide the kinds of creative approaches necessary to attract and deal with the culturally disadvantaged, women, the physically and mentally handicapped, the increasingly mobile management and scientific workers, and other distinguishable groups on their terms? As time goes on, it may well be found that the kind of personnel performance really needed today can come about only through a carefully designed set of specialized treatments of such significant differences as these, particularly when done in terms which also stand to give effect to a greater and more specialized concern with their motivator needs.

Take, for example, the spread and growing militancy of collective bargaining. Much of the recent development has been all too little connected with problems growing out of the specific employing organization's immediate employee relationships. Concerned only with an internal orientation, personnel activity (no matter how much it has been able to successfully deal with motivator needs) probably would not be of much help here.

In some instances, it has largely been a matter of the broader labor movement's thrust to regain its economic and liberal dominance or of the competitive maneuvering of various labor leaders. In others, the increasingly troublesome confrontations have stemmed from broader social and economic pressures which have left the unorganized far behind. Teachers, social workers, policemen, firemen, and others are thus turning to power bargaining as their most effective immediate alternative, even though it hasn't been too long ago that these very workers felt that union affiliation would be belittling. This is not to say that a more vigorous personnel effort dealing with motivator needs would not help in meeting the problems of these workers as well. Rather, it raises the question of how much more successful these attempts could be if directed to the motivator needs of these workers seen as union members.

Personnel Segmentation as the Organizational Strategy. My view of the scene has led to a different design for the internal structure of the personnel-staff department. In essence, it borrows from the concept of "market segmentation,"[8] leading to the establishment of various subunits within the personnel department—each concentrating somewhat independently upon different segments of the work force on a temporary or continuing basis. The personnel segmentation approach is intended to afford an opportunity for personnel specialists to program their staff assistance (and so to act) in terms of a definable, more homogeneous group of workers.

Decisions to use differentiated practices, tools, and standards for these formally identified subgroups of workers would be steeped in a careful examination of the particular impact of these groups upon overall productivity and worker satisfaction as well as in terms of how they are best dealt with within the specific job culture.

Through what would be tantamount to a continuing reorganization, these structural patterns and specialized staff would evolve to provide and assist in personnel activity specifically directed to segmented groups of workers distinguishable by:

1. The kind of work they do.
2. Their inclusion in a particular employee representational unit.
3. Their job requirements.
4. Social/hereditary factors of the individual worker.
5. A combination of these characteristics.

The expertise of the resulting staff specialists would become more and more a derivative of their own preparation and experience in dealing with all aspects of personnel performance for one or more of the limited segments of workers assigned as their particular responsibility. The traditional functional specialization would no longer exist, except perhaps at the top corporate units of large-scale firms. One form which this organizational change might take is seen in Figure 2.

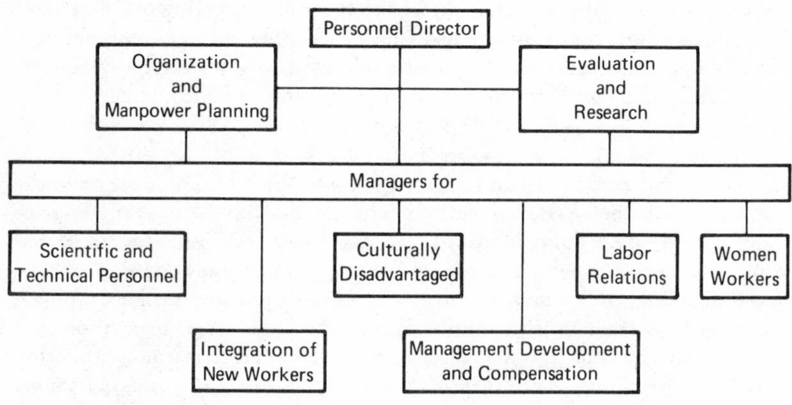

Figure 2.

[8] An early, penetrating analysis of this view of marketing strategy can be found in Wendell R. Smith, "Product Differentiation and Market Segmentation as Alternative Marketing Strategies," *Journal of Marketing*, XXI:1 (July 1956), 3-8.

With such a structural model, both hygiene and motivator needs would be effectively met, since the specific elements in the personnel staff's performance would be carefully focused upon dealing with the dynamic nature of more "manageable" segments. There would be greater certainty, too, of a balanced staff effort, purposefully compensating for the all-too-common one-sided view (i.e., hygiene) of present-day personnel management. Similarly, there would be an improvement of other dimensions of its responsibilities, such as meeting temporary personnel dislocations resulting from operating changes and reaching out to help resolve social and individual problems for which creative employment practices can be of meaningful help.

All this would become possible because the activity and results of each subunit would then be more precisely measureable, the need to deal with an amorphous group of workers being a thing of the past. This would be no small gain. Many personnel-staff efforts in the past have had to deal broadly and therefore in a compromising fashion with far more unimportant differences existing within the specific work culture to which they were directed.

One thing should be made clear. Some aspects of this segmentation approach already exist in the organization structure of many personnel departments. The most general, of course, is the separation of the labor-relations functions (as previously indicated, sometimes in the form of a staff department outside the personnel one) which recognizes the desirability of dealing specially with union-represented operative workers. Here, however, the organizational pattern appears to have come about more as a result of the pressures of having to deal separately with an outside group (i.e., the union) rather than from any planned approach on the part of personnel-staff management to deal specifically with this segment.

I am espousing this alternative: a carefully designed structural arrangement for the entire personnel effort which recognizes the existence of a number of distinct segments which merit and can profit from specialized programming and support, no matter how transitory the need. There would then evolve a continuing interest in reviewing the efficacy of its current design, since the need for and significance of special consideration of particular worker segments would be seen as flowing and ebbing. And, when the particulars changed, there would be a reorganization to suit the new priorities.

Thus, far more organizational changes or at least reassignments of staff would take place, even greater than those made by firms which have vacillated in their resolution of the functional-staff and centralized-decentralized dimensions of their personnel departments. Moreover, the changes would be sought out and expected. A premium, in fact, would be placed upon more effective ways of segmenting the work force so as to serve in a specialized way those segments which appear to benefit the most from specialization.

It should also be recognized that personnel segmentation could lead to some overlapping in personnel-staff activity with more than one subunit dealing with a particular worker. For example, if the worker is a woman returning to active employment in a management position after raising a family, she could be the concern of those specializing in the development and utilization of women and of managers, as well as those concerned solely with new employees. However, this is really nothing new. Today, a worker is often confronted by a number of personnel-staff persons (e.g., employment, training, and benefit specialists). With personnel segmentation, however, the various specialists focusing upon a worker's progress would each be viewing him as a particular kind of worker—as older worker, as technician, as physically handicapped. The fragmentation of service which grows out of functionalism would cease to exist.

Here, then, we propose personnel segmentation as an organizational answer to the fact that pre-existing (as well as organizationally derived) differences do exist among workers and do introduce significantly different obstacles and opportunities in achieving effective personnel-staff performance. Personnel segmentation can really succeed only when it recognizes these differences and makes it realistic to deal with them in ways more certain of meeting the internal and external pressures besetting the management of human resources in larger business firms. The traditional organizational pattern of task orientation cannot so succeed, if only because it implies that workers can be managed similarly, no matter what their intrinsic qualities or their organizational roles.

Just as a seller is urged to recognize that his total market is really quite heterogeneous—made up of several or many smaller homogeneous groups of consumers—the major personnel-staff manager would recognize a number of definable subgroups among his firm's employees. He would do so by aligning his staff to specialize in learning about and serving the needs of each of the subgroups. In this way, the different sets of needs (and opportunities for inducing productivity and satisfaction) which each segment represents become more certain of being identified and met.

The personnel manager himself would thereby gain, having the ability to mount effective differentiation of programming and treatment and to reject the "total market" approach which is unsound, no matter how much of an intense interest he sustains in worker differences. With personnel segmentation, moreover, he would find the kinds of profitable opportunities for expansion of specialized personnel programming not only more readily discernible, but with a greater probability of success. Certainly he would be better able to calculate just how well specific tools and programs would meet the needs of the smaller, more homogeneous groups.

Instead of engaging in wage and salary administration in a way roughly calculated to serve the needs of all workers, personnel segmentation would lead to specialists for particular subgroups of workers, each of whom would perform wage (or salary) administration as one of a range of concerns on behalf of a segment of workers. The risk entailed in "bending" the internal logic of a broad wage and salary administration system to the service of the needs of what are really diverse groups of workers could then be minimized, if not avoided altogether.

Differences between the worker on an assembly line and one who works a drill press, between the salesman and the scientist, between the first-level supervisor and the middle manager—all would be recognized for what they are: differences between formally distinguishable segments of workers, each of which is deserving of a different set of logic when it comes to deciding how and what to pay them. Whatever would be lost from a lack of functional specialization on the part of staff specialists performing wage and salary administration as only one of their varied concerns would be more than offset by the value of their deeper insights and relationships with the particular segment of workers assigned them.

Functional specialists could also be consulted, either from the ranks of professional consultants or from the corporate personnel unit.

Personnel segmentation could thus achieve selective adaptation in personnel-staff performance with accommodations attuned to effectively deal with the pre-existing and organizationally derived differences between workers. The need to justify particular reorganizations and staff reassignments on the basis of keeping personnel performance in tune with current priorities would force out into the open just what the differences are that are being accorded special consideration and how a firm might best deal with them. There would then be far more likelihood that certain differences which are best met head-on and helped to "melt in" in the broader organizational backdrop would not be left to fester below the surface.

Assigned to deal with Negro workers, for example, a personnel-staff subgroup would be permitted to gain depth of understanding in working through the problems besetting the integration and natural utilization and development of these workers. Assigned to establish and sustain a specialized personnel-staff program with older workers, another subgroup might well design an innovative program of retraining, job reassignment, counseling, and special recognition, which would stand a better chance of achieving the maximum utilization of this segment. Permitted such opportunity to specialize with older workers, this personnel unit would develop a more thorough understanding of such factors as the learning inadequacies, personal and family anxieties, and socializing patterns of these workers, as well as gain the base for sustaining a meaningful, unthreatening relationship with them.

Benefits of Segmentation

A critical look at personnel segmentation suggests that it offers much promise. Aside from those benefits discussed so far, two others deserve mention. First, effective use of personnel segmentation—just as with market segmentation—would introduce a beneficial dynamism into personnel-staff performance. It would destroy the myth of organizational stability and encourage personnel staff specialists to think periodically about the modification of their structural arrangements so as to facilitate their dealing with those worker segments of greatest import to the current targets of the firm.

If successful, a movement toward new ways of segmenting the work force would result—somewhat as a result of changing pressures and conceptions of what can be done, but also because previously segmented groups will have been successfully dealt with and their differentiating characteristic will no longer be significant (e.g., true integration of the Negro worker or the woman worker). The personnel-staff organization would thus move more and more in the direction of the greatest need. The specialized programming and treatment of segments of the work force would be dynamically changing, each time moving on to deal with those workers felt to offer the greatest severity of consequences in terms of their problematic situation and those where the potential for achieving a "breakthrough" in personnel-staff performance is predictably the greatest.

At all times, personnel segmentation would hold out the promise of a changing organization structure aimed at the most economic use of staff resources. Too, it would afford greater control over the segments a business purposefully determines to be of greatest consequence to it, as well as to the manner in which these groups are to be managed.

Second, a personnel segmentation approach would tend to place a beneficial stress upon line management, requiring that they act to fill in the gaps and integrate the segmented activity of the personnel specialists. When it becomes a matter of the line manager having to deal with a number of personnel-staff units who seek to view his subordinates in different but integral terms (rather than concentrate upon fulfilling a separate personnel task with them), he is less likely to feel a personal threat that the personnel-staff is doing his job for him. If nothing else, he will be less able to defer to their way of performing the personnel process, since it will be more apparent that the total personnel job cannot possibly be done by a staff which concentrates upon only some of the segmented characteristics existing among his workers. Each line manager will find that all the personnel staff can do is provide him with more certain insights and staff "assists" in managing his workers *qua* worker, no matter how many organizationally segmented differences they individually reflect.

It is as if the salesman finds himself with a customer—needing to uncover which of the various segments represented by him can be most profitably cultivated, calling upon the specific product-service offerings developed for that segment, and then being sure to integrate all that he does with the total marketing effort and (most important of all) with the customer as a profitable customer. If personnel segmentation can be successful in these terms, it is possible to predict that the persisting line-staff conflict in personnel performance may become a thing of the past.

Some Difficulties

There will, of course, be difficulties in the way of achieving personnel segmentation as the organization model for personnel-staff departments. As Herzberg emphasizes, much re-education of both line and staff practitioners will be needed. Too, the personnel manager will initially be hard-pressed to stay on top of the new pressures generated by having to deal in a unifying way with the various divisional heads reporting to him. For him, it will be a constant search for the budgetary wherewithal to plan for all the currently recognized segments of the workforce and still look ahead to improved ways of segmentation that do away with existing arrangements in a way which achieves a more dynamic balance of the total personnel-staff effort.

He must also guard against various divisions losing sight of the over-all development of the organization. On one hand, the result could be a wholly selective development and utilization of a particular segment, with little or no positive influence upon the firm's total human resource values (i.e., the marketer's "primary demand"). On the other hand, it could be that one division would so program its activity that it becomes too differentiated and is looked upon as discriminating in favor of one segment of workers to the detriment of others.

Finally, there would exist a need to guard against the kind of myopia which could lead some staff specialists to become so engrossed in working more and more intensively with the segment to which they are currently assigned that they would be led to preserve, rather than eliminate, irrelevant and inappropriate differences. This is what has happened in a good many situations where a subunit has been set up in the personnel department to deal with women workers. These efforts have led to further and further differentiation of treatment, becoming in "reality" an authentication of stereotyped beliefs about women workers rather than purposeful segmentation. The problems here remain, I might add, even after civil rights and equal-pay legislation specifically aimed at improving the employment conditions of women.

Conclusions. Historically, personnel-staff departments have been dominated by a task orientation derived from their structural arrangements and the pursuit of functional expertise on the part of their specialists. To arrest what is described as a malaise in personnel management and gain a truly decisive corporate role for this staff department, a fundamental reorganization of its operations is in order. The malaise is pinpointed by four general symptoms:

- The objectives of personnel management are not being realized in a way which lives up to their promise.
- Erstwhile personnel-staff tasks are being assigned outside the personnel department.
- The personnel-staff field is continuing to have difficulty in attracting outstanding recruits.
- Personnel departments are often being bypassed in the growing efforts of business firms to respond to the challenges of urban America.

Conclusions

Two broad-base, substantially different models are suggested for reorganizing personnel departments.

First considered was Herzberg's dual structuring to revamp these departments into two major divisions, one for dealing with the hygiene or maintenance factors and the other for the worker's motivator needs.

My model for segmentation entails grouping personnel-staff activities in accord with their relevancy to selected classes of workers. Various subunits would be formed on a temporary or continuing basis to concentrate upon providing and administering personnel-staff services and support in terms of roughly homogeneous workers, e.g., new workers, culturally disadvantaged workers, managers, and clerical operative workers. Each case of organization and staffing for a particular segment of workers would require justification on the basis of the potential benefit to the over-all effort (e.g., resolution of a persisting problem, comparative advantage from specialized attention and programming). Often, the segmentation of personnel-staff performance would find the specialists working themselves out of one job and going on to restructure their work to serve another group.

As in the case of any innovative organizational change, there is a need to put these models to the test of actual application. Without a serious attempt to see if they can work in practice, I can only conjecture about their prospects and limitations. Surely, the need for personnel departments to gain the organizational vitality required to meet the challenges which are facing them today is great enough to assume the risk entailed in a radical change. The alternative is almost certain to be further atrophy of personnel departments and more and more difficulty in harnessing a consistent and coordinated long-range effort in the management of a firm's human resources. The risk may be minimized by first adapting the selected model to the particulars of the existing management climate and existing competence of the staff specialists and, for the large-scale firms, experimentally introducing it in only a single divisional personnel department.

31

A Look to the Future

The Personnel Function in Tomorrow's Company

FRANK E. FISCHER

In the past 30 years technological changes have helped to double the gross national product, and in the next 30 they will more than double it again. In the field of human knowledge, we are told that four times as much is known today as was known 30 years ago and that scientists will learn as much more in the next 15 years as in all of previous history. As for population, we can expect to grow from a country of 200 million people to 226 million by 1975 and 245 million by 1980.

To those engaged in business management generally and in the personnel function particularly these prognostications have a special significance, because all these goods, all this knowledge, all these people will be the concern of a shrinking proportion of the population. The group from which our executives and decision-makers are drawn—the age group from 35 to 55—will have dropped from 47 per cent of the total productive age group to 38 per cent by 1980. Roughly, this means that three managers will be doing the work that four are doing today.

Tomorrow's Manager

To understand what this means for the personnel function, we have to consider first what tomorrow's manager will be like and what kind of work he will be doing. We can be reasonably sure that he will have to know more and learn more than his counterpart today, and that he will be supervising more sophisticated people than he does today. Professor Harold Leavitt of Carnegie Tech predicts that tomorrow's manager will be more of an intellectual, that he will make more of his decisions on the basis of systematic analysis and less by off-the-cuff methods. There is evidence that this is already happening. Not long ago, the American Telephone & Telegraph Co. studied the records of 17,000 college graduates

Reprinted by permission of the publisher from *Personnel*, Vol. 45, No. 1, January-February, 1968, pp. 64-71.

Dr. Fischer is a Vice President of Cresap, McCormick and Paget, Inc. where he serves as Director of Personnel Services.

in the Bell companies and learned that the single most reliable indicator of their success was class standing on graduating from college, and more recently the Prudential Insurance Co. of America came to the same conclusion.

Tomorrow's manager will also be supervising a different kind of workforce. Between 1950 and 1960, the number of professional and technical people employed in business increased 47 per cent, and for the first time white-collar workers in industry exceeded the number of blue-collar workers. This trend is expected to continue. The supervision of primarily professional, technical, and other white-collar employees will require a kind of manager different from the one who is now typical in factory management.

At the same time, despite the best possible preparation for his present job, tomorrow's executive may find himself threatened with obsolescence in mid-career. With "knowledge" compounding at such a rapid rate, no manager can be sure that his skills will continue to be needed or even that his job will exist tomorrow. As MIT's Professor Charles Myers has observed, "It is becoming impossible to learn a skill that will continue for a lifetime." In some companies there is even talk about preparing executives for a second career.

Shifts in Personnel Emphasis

Can personnel specialists meet the needs of tomorrow's manager? Their record in responding to new requirements in the past encourages the belief that they can. The personnel function began as an employment and record-keeping function; later, as workers began to organize, it took on the administration of labor agreements. Increasingly, too, it was charged with carrying out programs largely developed by management.

The personnel department then moved in one or more directions: (1) It became the keeper of the corporate conscience, and concerned itself with the morale of the employees; (2) it became "scientific" and introduced systematic techniques for employee selection, salary administration, and other activities connected with personnel; or (3) it began to concoct programs that proved to be more fashionable than useful.

A number of management fads and gimmicks have originated in the personnel department, particularly in the training function. Not long ago, the magic words were "economic education" and "human relations;" later came "brainstorming" and "group dynamics;" and more recently we have been hearing about teaching machines and "human systems development."

The Recent Record

Aside from busying itself with fads or status-symbol programs, however, the personnel function has shown signs of maturing.

- Appraisals are more goal-oriented, and tied in with management development as well as compensation. They are regarded less as a personnel "program" and more as a management tool.
- Compensation plans and techniques are becoming less complex, top management involvement is more evident, and the plans are better integrated than before. In the past it was not unusual to find responsibility for a company's compensation program fragmented among three or more departments, but now it is recognized that compensation is not a matter of discrete programs, and that companies still following that line are probably

paying total compensation far beyond what they thought they were paying or need to pay. As a result, it is becoming more common for all elements of the compensation program to report to a single executive.

- So-called discretionary bonus plans are giving way to incentive plans based on formulas and distributing funds according to individual performance weighed against planned objectives.
- Personnel records and reports are being centralized and put on computers.
- Greater attention is being paid to personnel research as an assist in making management decisions.
- In divisionalized companies, there is more policy direction by corporate personnel departments but at the same time greater local autonomy in personnel administration.
- There is more effort to collaborate with government in personnel matters, such as equal employment opportunity, collective bargaining, wage guidelines, pricing, retraining, and Medicare. For instance, companies are finding that merely pledging to eliminate discrimination or joining the voluntary Equal Employment Opportunity Councils is not enough. Compliance must be positive, and companies are expected to prove good faith by publicizing the fact that appointments are open to minority groups, by recruiting actively from among such groups, and by establishing programs for training them.
- The personnel department is beginning to operate internationally, particularly in the areas of compensation and employee benefits.
- More attention is being given to the identification of potential managers and to the nurture of talent. As shortages of skills become more acute, recruiting becomes more competitive and companies worry more about how to retain their college trainees and other "elite" groups.
- Training is leaving the classroom and returning to the workplace or a simulation of it. A recent reorientation of the training activity at American Airlines illustrates this trend: Aware of the constant changes in the business environment, the training heads at American Airlines believe that it is not enough to pass on managerial wisdom from one generation to another, that managers have to learn how to relate that experience to tomorrow's requirements. Thus, they act on the principles that the organization should be less a traditional schoolmaster and more a provider of resources and experiences; that training is concerned with improvement in both functional skills (such as budgeting or selling) and social skills (such as communications or counseling); that training should both increase individual competence and improve collaboration within and between groups; and that the best way to teach people management processes like planning, organizing, and controlling is to have them plan, organize, and control.

To implement these principles, the company is making use of problem-solving and simulation techniques, such as business games, in-basket exercises, role playing, and team-task methods.

What's Ahead?

In addition to these developments, there are signs of other changes, some of which may have a profound effect on the purpose, staffing, status, and organization of the personnel department in the future. Four related changes of particular significance are: (1) the growing profit orientation of the personnel function; (2) the shift in personnel work from a mechanistic concept to a creative, innovative one; (3) the interest in furthering an organization, rather than just maintaining or servicing it; and (4) the more direct involvement of top management in the development of the human resources of the business. Just what are the implications of these trends?

1. The personnel function will assume a more important role in the management of the business. It will do more planning and policy-making in the areas of manpower, organization structure, and compensation, among others. It will have more functional authority, especially in large, complex, and growing organizations. In becoming increasingly oriented toward growth and profits, instead of merely administering personnel activities, it will search out profit-improvement opportunities.

This new awareness will mean that personnel people will view their role in a different light. For example: In selecting people, more weight will be placed on what a candidate has accomplished than on the jobs he has held. In management development, more stress will be placed on identifying company and departmental needs and objectives and training people to help attain them. In compensation, it will be important to relate pay to performance and to its motivational impact, as well as to make sure that rates are competitive. In the area of employee benefits, there will be more consideration of the fact that a large part of expenditures are going to people who are not working in the form of retirement benefits, life insurance payments, medical plans and the like.

In appraising performance, there will be more emphasis on accomplishments against expectations, and appraisal results will be more closely tied to a man's compensation. In organization planning, there will have to be major emphasis on aligning responsibilities and relationships in the individual company to obtain maximum results with the least manpower, instead of seeking symmetrical or conventional organization patterns or uncritically following principles of organization laid down by others.

In summary, the personnel function will no longer be able to justify itself to top management by citing numbers or listing activities—the number of people interviewed or trained or counseled, the number of reports prepared or of records maintained, the number of job descriptions written, or the rate of employee turnover. Rather, personnel will demonstrate its effectiveness by raising the qualification levels of the employees hired; reducing the turnover among key managerial and professional people; recommending or drafting plans, policies, and programs that are adopted by operating management; and initiating organizational and staffing changes.

2. The personnel function will become more creative, less mechanistic. In the future, the disparity between the paper programs and actuality will have to be eliminated. The deficiencies of rigid, packaged "personnel programs" will become increasingly apparent.

Most of us are familiar with companies where "management development programs" have been conducted for years, yet half of their top managers are over 55 years old and there are few successors in sight, and the companies go outside to find people for many higher-level jobs, where management positions are invariably staffed without consulting the head of the personnel department; and where although the companies have performance appraisal programs, half the executives don't even bother to complete the required forms.

In such corporations, most of the top management group have had experience in only one function of the business; there are no inventories of management resources, no plans for management succession, and only a dim notion of future management requirements or how to meet them; participation by top executives in outside management development programs is almost nonexistent; a high proportion of the more promising men recruited on college campuses leave the company within two years; and numerous corporate departments are involved with compensation and employee benefit plans, but no department is responsible for over-all policy or coordination in these areas and, for that matter, the compensation plan does not apply to a sizable group of executives in the top levels.

There will be less me-tooism, less concern with imitating industry practice or matching industry averages, and more attention to what's actually required to help the company meet its goals. There will be more concern with ends rather than means, with substance rather than forms, with accomplishments rather than activities. There will be increasing emphasis on what the operating people find workable instead of what is theoretically best or easiest for the personnel department to administer. We already see this trend in the adoption of less complicated job-evaluation plans and in the movement away from automatic merit increases and appraisals based on an employee's activities or traits and toward appraisals based on performance measured against company goals or standards.

3. The personnel function will be responsible for furthering the organization, not just maintaining it. Personnel people will devote more time to proposing and promoting changes than to protecting the status quo. Instead of a miscellany of diverse specialties or activities, the personnel department will be regarded as an integrated general management function, responsible for the effective deployment of the firm's human resources, and, as it becomes more oriented to the requirements of the organization, it will view the needs of individuals in the light of their compatibility with those of the organization.

The personnel managers will recognize and encourage sound management practices, fostering concepts like management-by-objectives and team problem-solving approaches. They will seek new ways to awaken the talents that lie dormant in every organization by searching out opportunities and providing training experiences that are challenging and meaningful, rejecting a commitment to human relations as an end in itself.

In planning and developing his company's human resources, the personnel man will have to raise his sights to plan the form of the future organization and of the firm's manpower requirements; to structure and integrate the work; to identify and select management talent; to appraise and reward performance; to provide learning experiences to ensure growth of both the individual and the organization; and to rotate, transfer, and promote people into appropriate positions.

To handle this responsibility, the personnel man will have to be an individual of singular breadth and influence, sensitive equally to the needs and capabilities of people and to the requirements of the business. How many personnel departments or personnel people today perform this role or qualify for it? Apparently, not many. Some companies establish a separate unit within the personnel department to carry out this creative policy-making and program-planning function. In others, a small, high-level staff, responsible for organization planning and development, is created to work directly with the chief executive officer and his key subordinates, while personnel services for supervisory and employee groups are provided by the regular personnel department.

If this trend continues, there is a real possibility that the personnel department will become, in effect, an employee services organization, catering to the needs of lower-level groups and administering the traditional, routine personnel functions. This threat will be averted only if professional personnel people turn their energies to making the organization more effective instead of making it more comfortable or safe; if they start thinking more about making work productive and meaningful than about making it easy.

4. *Top management will become more directly involved in the deployment and development of human resources.* The chief executives of a growing number of companies are spending a good deal of time thinking about the people in the organizations, reviewing management, manpower needs and resources, assessing the performance and potential of their executives, and planning their future experiences. Michael Haider, Chairman of Standard Oil of New Jersey, recently wrote:

> In the life of a corporation, today's success is largely a product of three types of executive actions taken yesterday: selecting the right people; placing them in the right jobs; and seeing to it that they were able to grow to meet both their own needs and those of the organization. This activity is not a program in the usual sense, any more than selling or making profits are programs. It has no fixed dimensions, no timetable, no cutoff point.

How seriously he regards this activity, Mr. Haider points out, is indicated by the fact that he assumes the executive development function as his personal responsibility. He, the president and four executive vice-presidents of the company, acting as a committee, met 37 times in 1964 to review the company's human resources. This committee is "involved in a continuing examination of management throughout the Jersey organization. . . . Once a year the chief executive officer of each of the larger affiliates meets with the committee and reviews in depth his company's development activities and its replacement situation, and appraises the performance and potential of all his key management personnel. He goes over his replacement tables, his plans for job rotation assignments, and the specific steps being taken to increase the effectiveness of his organization."

A company in which the chief executive regards the development of its human resources as one of his chief concerns will probably provide the kind of climate in which people are encouraged to grow and to innovate. Those engaged in personnel work are in an excellent position to influence—and to benefit from—that climate.

To exert the proper influence, however, the personnel executive will have to adapt to management's changing expectations of his role. Thus, to sum up, the personnel executive in the future will:

- Assume a larger role in profit management.
- Concern himself more with ends than with means, with accomplishments rather than activities.

- Devote his efforts to building the organization instead of just maintaining it.
- Assist top management in the effective deployment and development of the company's human resources.

If the personnel function is going to survive as more than management's maid-of-all-work (to use Professor Paul Pigors' phrase), and if it is to satisfy management's greater demands upon it, there will have to be fundamental changes in its role.

32

Some Mind-Boggling Predictions

Research Needs of the Future in Industrial and Organizational Psychology

MARVIN D. DUNNETTE

Strategies of Prediction

A view of the future ideally should link with both present and past. The past suggests trends. The present induces first despair followed, for some, by hope. Rational Man extrapolates to the future from trends of the past and is usually wrong. Feeling man sees the future through eyes clouded by hope, envisioning a time when despair is gone. He's often wrong too. But at least his hope causes him usually to seek to be an active agent of change while the rational being is more apt merely to sit about, observing and recording the passing scene.

I shall try today to adopt both strategies. First, I shall trace briefly industrial psychology's recent past in order to evaluate its effect on the study of people in organizations. Second, I shall look feelingly, and perhaps somewhat rationally, at current patterns of organizational life in order to formulate my hopes for what those patterns may become within my lifetime. Finally, my hope-based description of what future organizations will be like will be the basis for my own rationally-based dicta about the kinds of research necessary for us to do if we are to move toward this organizational utopia of the future.

Industrial Psychology: Past

Let us look first at the recent past of Industrial Psychology. In order to gain a long range perspective, I define "recent" as the period from about

Reprinted with permission from Dr. Dunnette, who presented this paper as part of a symposium at the 1971 annual American Psychological Association meetings in Washington, D.C.

1930 on. By viewing what's happened over the last forty years, we may sense the trend of events and gain a better appreciation of their meaning for interpreting both present and future. For the sake of brevity today and because of my relative ignorance of history, I shall use the political cartoonist's technique of caricature. By so doing, I seek to distill the essence of our past in order to draw a picture which highlights, admittedly through distortion, its most salient features. I acknowledge its incompleteness and its haziness as to detail. Hopefully, the broad *Gestalt* will be recognizable to most of you.

It's helpful, I believe, to divide industrial psychology's development over the last forty years into three periods: 1930 to 1941; 1942 to 1955; and, 1956 to 1969.

1930-1941: The Era of Instrumentation

Emphasis during the thirties was mostly on trait psychology, recognizing differences between people and developing measures of them. It was the time of the Strong Vocational Interest Blank, the Kuder, the Otis, the Wonderlic, the Bernreuter, and early versions of the Minnesota Multiphasic Personality Inventory. Aptitude testing was becoming big business and early ideas leading to multiple aptitude batteries such as the GATB, DAT, and FACT were first enunciated. Methodologically, it was the time of item analysis, factor analysis, scaling methodology, reliability, and correction for attenuation. In industry, it was the time of the Protestant Ethic, grudging recognition of the importance of the human element, the birth and demise of industrial counseling, and embryonic use of selection testing. Substantively, industrial psychology was oriented mostly toward measuring individuals and then, in theory, guiding them into vocations, occupations and jobs best suited to them. Professionally, industrial psychologists had almost no separate identity. They worked mostly in academic settings or in government or with test publishing firms—with but a few notable exceptions such as Procter & Gamble and Western Electric. Throughout this era, industrial psychology was devoted almost exclusively to the study of white, middle class males.

1942-1955: The Era of Service to Management

Emphasis during the middle years of our development was mostly on developing techniques to aid management in making institutional decisions about people. It was the time of performance ratings, forced choice, critical incidents, *the* criterion, large scale test administration and selection programs, development and widespread use of employee attitude scales, the growth of training technology—flannel boards, filmstrips, charts and diagrams, TWI, human relations, and role playing. Methodologically, it was the time of criterion analysis, validity, multiple correlation and regression, suppressor variables, attitude scaling, tests of statistical significance, and of factoring just about everything in sight. In industry, we saw the dawning of the Social Ethic, of organization man, and an emphasis on the necessity of either finding the right shaped human pegs or of reshaping the available pegs so as to fit into the pigeonhole jobs available in military, government and industrial settings. Substantively, industrial psychology was "thinking" mostly about the statistics of validation, taxonomizing, scaling and, to a lesser degree, about better methods of job study and job analysis. Counseling could perhaps be included as a substantive concern, for its practice in industry—mostly with poor, lonely executives—became big business during this era. Professionally, industrial psychologists began to move into industry, gaining their identity after learning during World War II that applied psychology could, afterall, be fun and profitable. Consulting firms blossomed. Business schools established Industrial Relations Centers, but with a few notable exceptions, they leaned mostly on economists to man them. Industrial psychology became viable as an area of study in psychology departments. Throughout this era too, industrial psychology was devoted almost exclusively to the study of white, middle class males.

1959-1969: The Era of Humanizing and Social Conscience

Emphasis over the last decade or so has seen remarkable changes in industrial psychology's locus, methods and orientation. I view these changes optimistically as indicating a kind of maturing a coming of age, an emerging eagerness to lead and to educate society's institutions rather than merely responding to their cries for help. Because the changes have been great and because we are still so much in the middle of them, this era is quite difficult to characterize. Nonetheless, it is clear that these years have seen the beginning of efforts to *understand* as well as merely predicting what employees do in jobs and job settings. Industrial psychologists, at long last, began trying to assess more fully and to understand the consequences of the impact between the natures of men and women and of organizations. We have seen a sudden renewed awareness by industrial psychologists of what was implicit in the work of the thirties—the importance of human diversity and individuality. And, to that, we have added a recognition of the importance of *organizational* diversity and individuality. Thus, our science has become vastly more complicated in response to the need to understand processes and behavioral mechanisms rather than merely describing, measuring and trying to predict their consequences. Thus, it has been a time of emphasizing job behavior and job enrichment, differential prediction, moderator variables, behavioral processes in problem solving, decision making, communicating, resolving conflict, and humanizing; a time for trying to individualize instruction and training, and a time devoted to the melding of measurement technology, differential psychology, social psychology, and experimental psychology into the beginnings of a unified methodology. Substantively, we suddenly are of a theoretical bent, particularly in the area of work motivation, but also in areas related to taxonomies of work behavior, behavior change, and job commitment. Our locus now is virtually everywhere—psychology departments, business schools, organizations, and institutions of all types—industry, government, consulting firms, unions and schools. Best of all, we finally have recognized large segments of our population which we previously had ignored—the lower class, the disadvantaged, the blacks, and the female sex.

In my opinion, industrial psychology has done well. We have grown greatly. We have matured into a reasonably sophisticated scientific discipline. Best of all, we have penetrated into the nooks and crannies of our society, where presumably, we are now standing ready—on the firing line so to speak—to address ourselves to the needs of the future.

Future Shock

What, then, are the needs of the future? I mentioned earlier what my strategy was to be, namely to describe briefly what the present look is in organization–human interactions, to extrapolate from that to enunciate the areas of concern or despair, if you will, and to move from there to a statement of the organizational Utopia of the future, and the research needed in industrial psychology in order to reach that state.

In spite of my optimism about the maturing of and readiness of industrial psychology to attack and hopefully to solve problems, a glance about us shows that we presently are in rather bad shape as we proceed hazardously through one of the most trying periods in our history. In his recent book, *Future Shock*, Alvin Toffler describes brilliantly the condition of *transience*, the single feature he sees as the most prominent and by far the most dangerous and challenging aspect of present society. Industrial psychology during the seventies and beyond will be the *Era of Coping with Transience.* If we succeed, the chances of a better world are good. If we fail, humanity will be rocketed into a crisis of adaptation from which it will not survive, and we will witness (as we may, indeed, be witnessing in microcosm now) the total breakdown of adaptation that Toffler refers to as *Future Shock.*

The Present Despair

What is the transient society? Primarily, it is change, accelerated beyond the wildest notions, coupled with impermanence throughout society and a loss of any sense of stability. In the words of C. P. Snow, "the rate of change has increased so much that our imagination can't keep up." And, according to our colleague, Warren Bennis, "No exaggeration, no hyperbole, no outrage can realistically describe the extent and pace of change . . . In fact, only the exaggerations appear to be true."

Transience is the temporariness of modern life. It is the impermanence of objects, the nomadic wanderings of people, the fleeting quality of human interactions, the cracking at the seams of organizational bureaucracies, and the kinetic blizzard of information and ideas.

What are the effects of this emerging era of transience in things, places, people, organizations, and ideas? What problems have been wrought? What is the nature of and how deep is the despair with which as applied psychologists, we must begin to cope?

Here are the problems:

People increasingly are alienated, "turned off," deadened, apathetic in response to change and often unwilling to cope with newness. The atmosphere is laden with words, images, noise, poisons, and dirt. Sensory systems are turning inward, seeking renewal of feeling through drugs or its explosive and unrestrained expression in groups characterized by warmth and support, transient though they may be.

Revered institutions are shattering and breaking down. Religion—as the interaction between man and his personal God—is dwindling. For many, God is indeed dead. The nature of marriage as well as the basic structures of all sorts of personal and organizational commitments are changing wildly. Symptoms include the increasing rates of divorce, liberalized laws governing marital dyads and communes, a breakdown of nationalism, and the rampant turnover and shifting about among companies of college graduates during the first several years of employment.

People suddenly are becoming aware not only of the discontinuities of consumption but also of the contaminating effects of our consumption-oriented and still burgeoning population. This, coupled with what amounts to widespread consumer loss of faith in not only products but also ideas, information and ultimately, technology, has laid the groundwork for a "people's revolt."

And finally, our society is witnessing conflict on a massive scale. Our recent history in learning partially to cope with management–labor conflict offers only modest clues for coping with Black versus white, old versus young, the power elite versus power weak, man versus woman, and straight verus hip.

These, then, are the problems that lead us to hope for a better world–alienation and sensory deadening, the crumbling of the institutional rocks of stability, the latent potential of consumer revolt, and intense and widespread inter-group conflict. These are problems we must get our teeth into during this, our fourth stage of development. Let us hope that we are able to cope effectively with transience, and, thereby, avoid the breakdown concomitant with Future Shock.

Adaptation and Renewal

Given these problems, what must we overcome in order to advance toward a better world? Obviously, our present circumstances can suggest a myriad of utopian models as the consequences of successful adaptation–perhaps as many such models as there are people who choose to ponder the future. I shall offer one, flowing from my own speculations and hopes. But, many of you will note, I am sure, that its elements differ little from similar speculations by Warren Bennis in his recent paper titled "A Funny Thing Happened on the Way to the Future."

As we near the year 2000, it is my vision that we will no longer witness individual alienation and apathy, that stability may be derived directly from the quality of life rather than from the sense of needing to belong to or to identify with particular institutions or belief systems, and that humans will have learned to accomplish a unity of purpose which builds constructively on the fact of group differences instead of allowing intergroup conflict to limit or to delay the advance of civilized interaction systems.

Persons in that world of the future will have returned to a sense of the crucial role of individualism, and they will have learned to distrust institutional and organizational, as well as geographic, nationalism. Their values will stress autonomy; yet they will be ready to be helpful and of direct service to others. Their motives will be more diverse, and they will respect and value the fact of this diversity. They will place less emphasis on achievement, and a central aim will be a planned and quite rational structuring of the world toward the simple goal of pursuing pleasure. The worlds of work and nonwork will have merged. Man's capacity for job fulfillment and orientation toward self-actualization will find easy and open expression in all of life.

These people of the future will find themselves in a world where the speed and accuracy of communications technology will demand interpersonal competence from everyone. All decisions will be shared decisions; almost always they will be aided substantially by computer processing of information and knowledge in order to assure the weighing of *all* relevant knowledge and to reduce ambiguity to an absolute minimum.

Organizations will consist of an almost endless set of loosely coordinated groups or task forces of constantly changing membership. Bennis notes that persons will serve a variety of roles within such entities. Their roles in some may be *pivotal* and relatively permanent, *relevant*, but relatively impermanent in others and merely *peripheral* in still others. Organizations will function primarily to accomplish specific task objectives. Their major goals will be to utilize wisely and to conserve mankind's resources—human as well as material and financial—to promote and to be adaptable to individualism and to serve the welfare of society at large. Profits will be earned toward the end of serving these higher objectives. The separate identities of institutions now known as *education, government, union,* and *private business* will no longer be discernible. Staff-line distinctions will be gone and each organization will function much more according to what we see today in staff groups. The only stability within organizations will be a stability of purpose, the effort to maximize returns to individuals, to assure them of fully actualizing their essential humanness. The structure of organizations will be essentially flat or horizontal, and growth—to the extent that it is a viable concept under circumstances such as these—will occur through cell division rather than by adding hierarchical levels or by establishing titles, positions or bureaucratic lines of authority.

Research Needs for Industrial Psychology's Era of Coping with Transience

What are the areas of research that we should pursue in order to implement the move toward the patterns of life I have described? In Bennis' view, we must give attention to nine broad areas: (1) organization adaptation, (2) maintenance of individual identity, (3) study of the psychology of dissent, (4) promoting more broadly attitudes of social responsibility, (5) making the transition from a technology in the service of technocracy to a technology in the service of scientific humanism, (6) promoting better harmony between man and his physical environment, (7) teaching managers to be more flexible in their planning for the future, (8) learning improved means of bringing about social and political justice, and (9) developing a world order to maintain peace and between nations, groups, and persons.

All these suggestions are highly relevant for accomplishing the goal state I have described. But let me recast them in somewhat more substantive terms according to needed research in four areas: Individual Dynamics, Interpersonal Dynamics, Organizational Objectives, and Organizational Structure.

Individual Dynamics

Here, if we are to educate our youngsters to be ready for the future, we need to study the formation of motive systems and of basic value orientations and their behavioral correlates. We need to learn more about the early development, stability and modifiability, and eventual diversity among humans in the values they espouse and the motives which drive them.

Interpersonal Dynamics

It is crucial that we learn much more about the technology of group process training and its impact on people. We need desperately to learn about the parameters of effective training leading to enhanced interpersonal competence. We must become so expert and knowledgeable about the strategies of training and development that we will be able to construct training batteries to accomplish specific learning objectives in much the same way as we have constructed test batteries to assess specific individual attributes. We need research related to rationalizing and defining the nature of learning under different training approaches, on how to assure transfer of learning under different training approaches, on how to assure transfer of learning and its behavior correlates to the "back home" getting. Training gimmickry should fall by the wayside in favor of a proven and known technology. Training needs study as a means of *maximizing* each person's potential as opposed to burying it in the service of accomplishing group goals. In schools, it is necessary to learn how to teach our children to accept the fact of transience and to learn adaptive techniques of constructive coping with constant ambiguity and change.

Organizational Objectives

Here our most critical research need involves the study of how best to change what is perhaps a very fundamental aspect of human nature—the tendency to form groups, commitments and nationalistic loyalties. We must learn how to teach people to adopt the broadest loyalty of all—a deep appreciation for the value of all individuals regardless of superficial memberships, beliefs or back grounds. We must, indeed, learn how to dislodge the nationalism of professional, organizational, and institutional identities. We need an empirically based theory of the sociology of organizational identity and commitment.

Organization Structure

We need, of course, to learn how to implement, with minimal loss, the loosely structured set of constantly changing entities I have envisioned as comprising the organizations of the future. We shall need to learn much more than we now know about the sociology of coordination and of the political and economic strategies for structuring our organizations according to the rather bizarre combination of anarchy and democracy I have suggested. Toffler calls the organizational structure of the future Ad-Hocracy to suggest the fact of its fluid and organic responsiveness to the ad hoc needs of a society confronted with transience. The proper balance between anarchy and democracy is crucial. Bennis states the problem well. In commenting on educational needs of the future, he states: "In short, we need an educational system that can help make a virtue out of contingency rather than one which induces hesitancy or its reckless companion, expedience."

These, then, are the research needs facing industrial and organizational psychology in the years immediately ahead. We must learn much more about individual motives and values, their development, modifiability and behavioral correlates. We must develop an empirically based technology of training processes and training outcomes. We must learn processes which can speed the constructive destruction of attitudes of organizational nationalism. In other words, we must, in the process of helping persons to lose their commitments to sub-entities, show them the utility of forming the broader most socially relevant loyalty to humanity *and* to individualism. And, finally, we must study the consequences, but more importantly, the strategies for bringing about in a workable way the flat, diffuse, organically dynamic organizational entities of the future.

It appears to me that we're in for a bit of fun and excitement in the years ahead.

SECTION III

The Evolution of Relations Between Organizations and Their Members

The possibility of an organization's employees banding together into an independent "union" has been a crucial factor influencing the efforts of those who have struggled to develop viable relationships between organizations and their employees over the years. Although Leiserson's view as reported in the previous section that fifteen years of good personnel work (in keeping unions out) had gone down the drain during the 1930's with the hiring of "management-oriented" personnel men may have been an overstatement, there can be no doubt that much of what has gone on in employee relations has been spurred in one way or another by the threat that employees might opt for their own independent organization.

In this section of the book, an attempt is made to trace this development of the struggle of employees to organize and bargain collectively with management over conditions of employment. The views of Frederick Taylor were again chosen as a starting point in the analysis. It is apparent that he felt his scientific management methods and results were so successful that they largely eliminated the impetus for employees to form unions. He believed that shared increased profits coupled with respectful supervisory practices and scientifically determined performance standards were enough to dissuade such inclinations. However, those employers who did not follow scientific management principles deservedly could expect labor problems.

Frederick Hay suggests that setting up a labor department would not be a panacea for solving labor problems from the workingman's point of view and he goes on to enumerate some of the complaints which labor had around 1900. John R.

Commons, perhaps our most famous early labor economist, describes in detail the circumstances and events surrounding the great stockyards strike of 1903, which was one of the first large-scale confrontations that did not result in serious violence. It is apparent that either the management of these yards had never heard of Frederick Taylor or it preferred to ignore many of his principles of management. Weinstock, Ballard, and Aishton present the employer's side of the story, indicating that many of them felt irresponsible unions would ruin their businesses if they allowed their employees to join them.

During World War I organized labor found itself in a relatively strong position because of a scarcity of manpower for war-related production and a desire to prevent crippling stoppages in that production caused by labor disputes. Thus, thought was directed at ways of reaching an accommodation that was fair to all the "parties to industry," as John D. Rockefeller, Jr., refers to them. He describes an approach he subscribed to and one that was practiced in many of the corporations he controlled. Willis Wisler presents a provocative analysis of pronouncements by management that the interests of labor and management were really the same, and of pleas by labor spokesmen for solidarity among the ranks and a possible political strategy in coping with industrial adversaries.

William M. Leiserson, one of the outstanding leaders during the formative stages of personnel management and labor relations, provides a thorough analysis of the various approaches to employee representation around 1920. He points out that there were basic differences between the approaches and that the likelihood of attaining enduring success was not the same for each.

Another strategy that was used widely to counteract the threats of organized labor and general industrial unrest was the welfare movement which extended from before 1900 to about 1930. We again turn to comments by Frederick Taylor as a launching point for the discussion of this approach. It is apparent that he felt such activities should have a definite subservient position to the basic issues of wage determination and prescription and procurement of a fair day's work from each employee. Samuel Gompers, the founder and long-term first president of the American Federation of Labor, makes some satirical and humorous comments about welfare work in his brief essay. Whitney's article describes how this approach developed and estimates its costs near the end of World War I.

Epstein buries it with his cynical and caustic assessment of its demise.

During the decade of the 1920's, welfarism, paternalism, and employee representation trends established during the war and shortly thereafter were given the test of extended trial and experience. Leiserson's 1928 article, which was written about ten years after his initial presentation, indicates some of the changes in his views after having had ten years to observe the employee representation movement in action. Sumner Slichter's presentation provides a detailed and accurate description of labor policies existing in American industry just before the Great Depression arrived in late 1929. Cowdrick describes the situation five years later in the depth of the Depression, when social legislation coupled with employee dissatisfaction resulted in a preference for formal collective bargaining between independent unions and industrial organizations as the mechanism to establish conditions of employment. The destruction of the labor movement in Germany as described by Abram Plotkin represents somewhat of a digression from the American scene, but rather vividly portrays an alternative fate that organized labor experienced in another system at about the same time it was establishing an enduring position in our system.

The articles by Lescohier and Cross identify some of the early repercussions of the surge in unionism during the 1930's. It is apparent that the foreman or first-line supervisor was probably the most severely affected because much of his authority and decision-making discretion was constrained by provisions in labor contracts negotiated during the period and by the personnel departments. An outgrowth of this development which must have been the last straw for management is described by Cross, who enumerates some of the circumstances and events surrounding the efforts by some foremen to get on the union bandwagon and join up themselves. Things gradually began to settle down and thought was directed during World War II (as it had been during World War I) to the issue of developing a reasonably stable relationship between labor and management organizations. Knickerbocker and McGregor present their views of this process of accommodation from a psychological viewpoint.

Finally, Robert Macdonald provides an overview of events on the labor-management relations scene since 1945. He points out that the main changes since that year have been in the direction of refining the ground rules and methods of achieving a viable relationship, with the public interest attaining an ever-increasing amount of attention. Growth in unionism since that period has been limited, neither making significant gains nor suffering substantial losses, although significant shifts in the composition of union membership have occurred.

It is apparent from the papers included in this section that the evolution of labor-management relations has been closely tied to the problems noted in Section I and to the evolution of the personnel management function as portrayed in Section II. Although it took a major catastrophe to do it, it should also be noted that our social system did change markedly in the direction of accommodating the interests of organized labor during the Depression.

33

The Philosophy of Scientific Management on Labor Relations: 1900

Shop Management

FREDERICK W. TAYLOR

Regarding the personal relations which should be maintained between employers and their men, the writer quotes the following paragraphs from a paper written in 1895. Additional experience has only served to confirm and strengthen these views; and although the greater part of this time, in his work of shop organization, has been devoted to the difficult and delicate task of inducing workmen to change their ways of doing things he has never been opposed by a strike.

> There has never been a strike by men working under this system, although it has been applied at the Midvale Steel Works for the past ten years; and the steel business has proved during this period the most fruitful field for labor organizations and strikes. And this notwithstanding the fact that the Midvale Company has never prevented its men from joining any labor organization. All of the best men in the company saw clearly that the success of a labor organization meant the lowering of their wages in order that the inferior men might earn more, and, of course, could not be persuaded to join.
>
> I attribute a great part of this success in avoiding strikes to the high wages which the best men were able to earn with the differential rates, and to the pleasant feeling fostered by this system; but this is by no means the whole cause. It has for years been the policy of that company to stimulate the personal ambition of every man in their employ by promoting them either in wages or position whenever they deserved it and the opportunity came.
>
> A careful record has been kept of each man's good points as well as his shortcomings, and one of the principal duties of each foreman was to make this careful study of his men so that substantial justice could be done to each. When men throughout an establishment are paid varying rates of day-work wages according to their individual worth, some being above and some below the average, it cannot be for the interest of those receiving high pay to join a union with the cheap men.
>
> No system of management, however good, should be applied in a wooden way. The proper personal relations should always be maintained between the employers and men; even the prejudices of the workmen should be considered in dealing with them.
>
> The employer who goes through his works with kid gloves on, and is never known to dirty his hands or clothes, and who either talks to his men in a condescending or patronizing way, or else not at all, has no chance whatever of ascertaining their real thoughts or feelings.

Reprinted as an excerpt from Taylor's paper on *Shop Management*, American Society of Mechanical Engineers, Saratoga, New York, 1903.

Relations Between Organizations and Their Members

Above all it is desirable that men should be talked to on their own level by those who are over them. Each man should be encouraged to discuss any trouble which he may have, either in the works or outside, with those over him. Men would far rather even be blamed by their bosses, especially if the "tearing out" has a touch of human nature and feeling in it, than to be passed by day after day without a word, and with no more notice than if they were part of the machinery.

The opportunity which each man should have of airing his mind freely, and having it out with his employers, is a safety-valve; and if the superintendents are reasonable men, and listen to and treat with respect what their men have to say, there is absolutely no reason for labor unions and strikes.

It is not the large charities (however generous they may be) that are needed or appreciated by workmen so much as small acts of personal kindness and sympathy, which establish a bond of friendly feeling between them and their employers.

The moral effect of this system on the men is marked. The feeling that substantial justice is being done them renders them on the whole much more manly, straightforward, and truthful. They work more cheerfully, and are more obliging to one another and their employers. They are not soured, as under the old system, by brooding over the injustice done them; and their spare minutes are not spent to the same extent in criticising their employers.

The writer has a profound respect for the working men of this country. He is proud to say that he has as many friends among them as among his other friends who were born in a different class, and he believes that quite as many men of fine character and ability are to be found among the former as in the latter. Being himself a college educated man, and having filled the various positions of foreman, master mechanic, chief draftsman, chief engineer, general superintendent, general manager, auditor, and head of the sales' department, on the one hand, and on the other hand having been for several years a workman, as apprentice, laborer, machinist, and gang boss, his sympathies are equally divided between the two classes.

He is firmly convinced that the best interests of workmen and their employers are the same; so that in his criticism of labor unions he feels that he is advocating the interests of both sides. The following paragraphs on this subject are quoted from the paper written in 1895 and above referred to:

The author is far from taking the view held by many manufacturers that labor unions are an almost unmitigated detriment to those who join them, as well as to employers and the general public.

The labor unions—particularly the trades unions of England—have rendered a great service, not only to their members, but to the world, in shortening the hours of labor and in modifying the hardships and improving the conditions of wage workers.

In the writer's judgment the system of treating with labor unions would seem to occupy a middle position among the various methods of adjusting the relations between employers and men.

When employers herd their men together in classes, pay all of each class the same wages, and offer none of them any inducements to work harder or do better than the average, the only remedy for the men lies in combination; and frequently the only possible answer to encroachments on the part of their employers is a strike.

This state of affairs is far from satisfactory to either employers or men, and the writer believes the system of regulating the wages and conditions of employment of whole classes of men by conference and agreement between the leaders of unions and manufacturers to be vastly inferior, both in its moral effect on the men and on the material interests of both parties, to the plan of stimulating each workman's ambition by paying him according to his individual worth, and without limiting him to the rate of work or pay of the average of his class.

The amount of work which a man should do in a day, what constitutes proper pay for this work, and the maximum number of hours per day which a man should work, together form the most important elements which are discussed between workmen and their employers. The writer has attempted to show that these matters can be much better determined by the expert time student than by either the union or a board of directors, and he firmly believes that in the future scientific time study will establish standards which will be accepted as fair by both sides.

There is no reason why labor unions should not be so constituted as to be a great help both to employers and men. Unfortunately, as they now exist they are in many, if not most, cases a hinderance to the prosperity of both.

The chief reason for this would seem to be a failure on the part of the workmen to understand the broad principles which affect their best interests as well as those of their employers. It is undoubtedly true, however, that employers as a whole are not much better informed nor more interested in this matter than their workmen.

One of the unfortunate features of labor unions as they now exist is that the members look upon the dues which they pay to the union, and the time that they devote to it, as an investment which should bring them an annual return, and they feel that unless they succeed in getting either an increase in wages or shorter hours every year or so, the money which they pay into the union is wasted. The leaders of the unions realize this and, particularly if they are paid for their services, are apt to spend considerable of their time scaring up grievances whether they exist or not. This naturally fosters antagonism instead of friendship between the two sides. There are, of course, marked exceptions to this rule; that of the Brotherhood of Locomotive Engineers being perhaps the most prominent.

The most serious of the delusions and fallacies under which workmen, and particularly those in many of the unions, are suffering is that it is for their interest to limit the amount of work which a man should do in a day.

There is no question that the greater the daily output of the average individual in a trade the greater will be the average wages earned in the trade, and that in the long run turning out a large amount of work each day will give them higher wages, steadier and more work, instead of throwing them out of work. The worst thing that a labor union can do for its members in the long run is to limit the amount of work which they allow each workman to do in a day. If their employers are in a competitive business, sooner or later those competitors whose workmen do not limit the output will take the trade away from them, and they will be thrown out of work. And in the meantime the small day's work which they have accustomed themselves to do demoralizes them, and instead of developing as men do when they use their strength and faculties to the utmost, and as men should do from year to year, they grow lazy, spend much of their time pitying themselves, and are less able to compete with other men. Forbidding their members to do more than a given amount of work in a day has been the greatest mistake made by the English trades unions. The whole of that country is suffering more or less from this error now. Their workmen are for this reason receiving lower wages than they might get, and in many cases the men, under the influence of this idea, have grown so slow that they would find it difficult to do a good day's work even if public opinion encouraged them in it.

In forcing their members to work slowly they use certain cant phrases which sound most plausible until their real meaning is analyzed. They continually use the expression, "Workmen should not be asked to do more than a fair day's work," which sounds right and just until we come to see how it is applied. The absurdity of its usual application would be apparent if we were to apply it to animals. Suppose a contractor had in his stable a miscellaneous collection of draft animals, including small donkeys, ponies, light horses, carriage horses and fine dray horses, and a law were to be made that no animal should be allowed to do more than "a fair day's work" for a donkey. The injustice of such a law would be apparent to every one. The trades unions, almost without exception, admit all of those in the trade to membership—providing they pay their dues. And the difference between the first-class men and the poor ones is quite as great as that between fine dray horses and donkeys. In the case of horses this difference is well known to every one; with men, however, it is not at all generally recognized. When a labor union, under the cloak of the expression "a fair day's work," refuses to allow a first class man to do any more work than a slow or inferior workman can do, its action is quite as absurd as limiting the work of a fine dray horse to that of a donkey would be.

Promotion, high wages, and, in some cases, shorter hours of work are the legitimate ambitions of a workman, but any scheme which curtails the output should be recognized as a device for lowering wages in the long run.

Any limit to the *maximum* wages which men are allowed to earn in a trade is equally injurious to their best interests. The "minimum wage" is the least harmful of the rules which are generally adopted by trades unions, though it frequently works an injustice to the better workmen. For example, the writer has been used to having his machinists earn all the way from $1.50 to seven and eight dollars per day, according to the individual worth of the men. Supposing a rule were made that no machinist should be paid less than $2.50 per day. It is evident that if an employer were forced to pay $2.50 per day to men who were only worth $1.50 or $1.75, in order to compete he would be obliged to lower the wages of those who in the past were getting more than $2.50, thus pulling down the better workers in order to raise up the poorer men. Men are not born equal, and any attempt to make them so is contrary to nature's laws and will fail.

Some of the labor unions have succeeded in persuading the people in parts of this country that there is something sacred in the cause of union labor and that, in the interest of this cause, the union should receive moral support whether it is right in any particular case or not.

Union labor is sacred just so long as its acts are fair and good, and it is damnable just as soon as its acts are bad. Its rights are precisely those of non-union labor, neither greater nor less. The boycott, the use of force or intimidation, and the oppression of non-union workmen by labor unions are damnable; these acts of tyranny are thoroughly un-American and will not be tolerated by the American people.

One of the most interesting and difficult problems connected with the art of management is how to persuade union men to do a full day's work if the union does not wish them to do it. I am glad of the opportunity of saying what I think on the matter, and of explaining somewhat in detail just how I should expect, in fact, how I have time after time induced union men to do a large day's work, quite as large as other men do.

In dealing with union men certain general principles should never be lost sight of. These principles are the proper ones to apply to all men, but in dealing with union men their application becomes all the more imperative.

First. One should be sure, beyond the smallest doubt, that what is demanded of the men is entirely just and can surely be accomplished. This certainty can only be reached by a minute and thorough time study.

Second. Exact and detailed directions should be given to the workman telling him, not in a general way but specifying in every small particular, just what he is to do and how he is to do it.

Third. It is of the utmost importance in starting to make a change that the energies of the management should be centered upon one single workman, and that no further attempt at improvement should be made until entire success has been secured in this case. Judgment should be used in selecting for a start work of such a character that the most clear cut and definite directions can be given regarding it, so that failure to carry out these directions will constitute direct disobedience of a single, straightforward order.

Fourth. In case the workman fails to carry out the order the management should be prepared to demonstrate that the work called for can be done by having some one connected with the management actually do it in the time called for.

The mistake which is usually made in dealing with union men, lies in giving an order which affects a number of workmen at the same time and in laying stress upon the increase in the output which is demanded instead of emphasizing one by one the details which the workman is to carry out in order to attain the desired result. In the first case a clear issue is raised: say that the man must turn out fifty per cent. more pieces than he has in the past, and therefore it will be assumed by most people that he must work fifty per cent. harder. In this issue the union is more than likely to have the sympathy of the general public, and they can logically take it up and fight upon it. If, however, the workman is given a series of plain, simple, and reasonable orders, and is offered a premium for carrying them out, the union will have a much more difficult task in defending the man who disobeys them. To illustrate: If we take the case of a complicated piece of machine work which is being done on a lathe or other machine tool, and the workman is called upon (under the old type of management) to increase his output by twenty-five or fifty per cent. there is opened a field of argument in which the assertion of the man, backed by the union, that the task is impossible or too hard, will have quite as much weight as that of the management. If, however, the management begins by analyzing in detail just how each section of the work should be done and then writes out complete instructions specifying the tools to be used in succession, the cone step on which the driving belt is to run, the depth of cut and the feed to be used, the exact manner in which the work is to be set in the machine, etc., and if before starting to make any change they have trained as functional foremen several men who are particularly expert and well informed in their specialities, as, for instance, a speed boss, gang boss, and inspector; if you then place for example a speed boss alongside of that workman, with an instruction card clearly written out, stating what both the speed boss and the man who he is instructing are to do, and that card says you are to use such and such a tool, put your driving belt on this cone, and use this feed on your machine, and if you do so you will get out the work in such and such a time, I can hardly conceive of a case in which a union could prevent the boss from ordering the man to put his driving belt just where he said and using just the feed that he said, and in doing that the workman can hardly fail to get the work out on time. No union would dare to say to the management of a works, you shall not run the machine with the belt on this or that cone step. They do not come down specifically in that way; they say, "You shall not work so fast," but they do not say, "You shall not use such and such a tool, or run with such a feed or at such a speed." However much they might like to do it, they do not dare to interfere specifically in this way. Now, when your single man under the supervision of a speed boss, gang boss, etc., runs day after day at the given speed and feed, and gets work out in the time that the instruction card calls for, and when a premium is kept for him in the office for having done the work in the required time, you begin to have a moral suasion on that workman which is very powerful. At first he won't take the premium if it is contrary to the laws of his union, but as time goes on and it piles up and amounts to a big item, he will be apt to step into the office and ask for his premium, and before long your man will be a thorough convert to the new system. Now, after one man has been persuaded, by means of the four functional foremen, etc., that he will earn more money under the new system than under the laws of the union, you can then take the next man, and so convert one after another right through your shop, and as time goes on public opinion will swing around more and more rapidly your way.

I have a profound respect for the workmen of the United States; they are in the main sensible men—not all of them, of course, but they are just as sensible as are those on the side of the management. There are some fools among them; so there are among the men who manage industrial plants. They are in many respects misguided men, and they require a great deal of information that they have not got. So do most managers.

All that most workmen need to make them do what is right is a series of proper object lessons. When they are convinced that a system is offered them which will yield them larger returns than the union provides for, they will promptly acquiesce. The necessary object lessons can best be given by centering the efforts of the management upon one spot. The mistake that ninety-nine men out of a hundred make is that they have attempted to influence a large body of men at once instead of taking one man at a time.

Another important factor is the question of time. If any one expects large results in six months or a year in a very large works he is looking for the impossible. If any one expects to convert union men to a higher rate of production, coupled with high wages, in six months or a year, he is expecting next to an impossibility. But if he is patient enough to wait for two or three years, he can go among almost any set of workmen in the country and get results.

34

Conditions for Conflict–1903

Labor's Complaint Against Capital

FREDERIC HAY

The frequent manifestations of discontent and unrest in the ranks of the many branches of labor, voiced through the medium of their organizations, should, it appears to me, indicate to the intelligent mind that there must be deep-seated causes for the trouble that will not down.

In the article by Mr. Carpenter in the April number of *The Engineering Magazine*, on "The Working of a Labor Department in Factory Management," the subject is dwelt on at great length, and the cardinal point is made, perhaps more forcibly than logically, "that the time to stop trouble is before it begins." That I think may be accepted as an axiom. But the question arises *how to prevent it*?

From the standpoint of the employee (to which class I belong) I feel that while, theoretically, Mr. Carpenter's propositions may seem all that is required to "stop the trouble before it begins," yet they do not practically represent the actual conditions that would be satisfactory to the wage-earner. Workmen are averse to the referring of questions to departments, with the delays consequent upon investigation; nor does Mr. Carpenter indicate the *materiel* of which the Labor Department should be composed, which would be a matter of consequence in the event of his suggestion meeting with approval.

Workingmen, as a rule, are not broad-minded or far-seeing; their minds do not in general range beyond their particular trade, and their party politics. They are suspicious of their employer, believing that any new method introduced is to beat them in some way to the employer's advantage. Labor-saving devices generally do not meet their approval; the time-clock especially is looked on with contempt as an invention designed to make further profit out of them; and many men think it creditable to use the means in their power to get even with it–and they do, too.

Reprinted from *Engineering Magazine*, May, 1903, Vol. 25, No. 2, pp 253-255.

Relations Between Organizations and Their Members

The existence of labor unions in the present day is in itself great evidence of the unwillingness of employers to concede to their workmen what they believe to be a fair share of the earnings acquired by their industry and skill. The unions were not at their inception designed as a menace to the employers but, as descendents of the Guilds of the Middle Ages, associations of trained and competent workmen for the conservation of their rights, and to secure a uniform wage in their various trades—so that to be a member of a labor union is to imply a competent workman.

Labor is more necessary to capital than the latter to the former (though this may not generally be conceded)—without labor capital could not be employed to advantage. Men need not become mechanics.

No special system can be devised to meet all cases, because all men are not alike—there are the zealous and the careless; the industrious and the idle, i.e., the worker and the fakir. The most successful system in the long run will be that which appeals to the men's honor—and to that alone. The men should by a careful and quiet process of weeding be brought, as nearly as possible, to an equal standard.

One reason for the indifference of the workman to the interests of his employer is the drifting apart that has for years been going on. In former times (not so many years ago) the employer was interested in his men. He had been one of the craft himself. His face was seen in the workshop or factory. He knew the men by their first names. He knew something of their condition and their needs. The men could address him personally if they would.

All that is changed now. These are days of large combinations of capital. The capitalist does not require a practical knowledge of the business. He is not in sympathy with the "hands," with whom he holds no communication, should he ever see them, and so the superintendent takes the place which the employer formerly held.

As the object of business is to obtain the largest return on the capital invested, the duty of the superintendent is primarily to produce that return to his employer by restricting the working expenses to the lowest point. On all questions that may arise he is practically the court of appeal. The employer does not desire to be troubled with the affairs of the "shop."

The foreman comes between the workmen and the "super," as he is known in the shop, and controls the working department. He should be a first-class workman, knowing to a hair what is possible for the men to do—a man of firm but equable temper, just to employer and men alike, easy of approach—and should strive to preserve order and content. The average foreman does not in my experience represent these conditions. He requires an homage paid to him akin to that of a sovereign; he resents appeals from his decisions, just or unjust; and if a man displease him, no matter how good a workman, he may expect discharge.

One open cause of discontent on the part of labor is the undisguised hostility on the part of capital. The employer objects to deal with labor's only representative—the union. But objectionable as many features of the union are (and the ranks of labor are aware of them), it is their only protection; through its means have been obtained advances of wages and reduction of hours of labor; it is their bundle of sticks, and for their mutual interests forbearance should be shown by each. After a bitter contention sometimes a slight advance in wages may smooth over the surface for a while; but the discontent remains. That for which labor is contending and without which it will not rest and be satisfied is:

Labor's Complaint Against Capital

Recognition by capital as a factor in the production of profit. The workman sees his employer grow rich, while his income does not advance; his dollar has not the purchasing power of a few years ago, for the things he needs, and if he have family, his mind is exercised how to maintain them properly. He asks himself questions; Why should he toil so many hours a day and be expected to do so much; why when the business is prospering he enjoys no benefit, though if it be dull he may be expected to take three-quarter time; why, when there are legal holidays should he be "docked" his pay and the foreman be paid; and lastly, for the three months' Saturday half-holidays he should lose half a day each week, when he knows that by pressure he has been made to earn his full week's pay? The holidays, instead of being cause for rejoicing, are the reverse.

If the workmen were treated more as helpers to their employers' prosperity and made to feel that their efforts would be recognized—that when the accounts for the year's business are made up a bonus or percentage of profit would be awarded them, discontent would give place to satisfaction and honest pride in their work.

The views expressed in this paper may not be acquiesced in, but they are not theories; they are the results of experience, and in my opinion it is for their mutual welfare that capital and labor should approach each other with recognition of their mutual interest.

35

Labor Relations at the Plant level: 1900-1910

Labor Conditions in Meat Packing and the Recent Strike

JOHN R. COMMONS

On September 9 the Executive Board of the Amalgamated Meat Cutters and Butcher Workmen of North America "called off" the strike of their 50,000 members against the five packing companies. In the Chicago stock yards, where 22,000 came out, followed by 8,000 allied trades, this was the third general strike. For fifteen years after the Knights of Labor strike in 1886 every man or woman who ventured to start an organization was discharged; and after 1890, when the "combine" of packers became effective, many of them were blacklisted. The strike of 1894 was sympathetic and unorganized. The strike of 1904 was a mistake on the part of the union; for the employers had offered arbitration sixteen

Reprinted from *The Quarterly Journal of Economics*, Vol. 19, No. 1, November, 1904, pp. 1-32.

John R. Commons was Professor of Economics at the University of Wisconsin when this was written.

hours before the men went out, and arbitration was what the leaders had asked for. They were out eight days, and went back on an agreement to arbitrate, but were again called out after an hour's work on the ground of discrimination. This was in violation of the agreement just made, which bound them and their employers to submit discriminations and all other grievances to arbitration. The mistake was natural. It followed a history of grievances on both sides, and a conviction on the part of the workmen that the packers were determined to destroy their union.

The national union dates from July, 1897, and is designed to include all wage-earners in slaughtering and packing establishments and all meat-cutters employed in stores. The country was fairly organized before Chicago was attacked in 1900. For a year or more the organizations were secret,[1] but eventually they felt strong enough to throw off their cloak; and in August, 1901, they united in the Packing Trades Council. This eventually comprised twenty-two locals, under the jurisdiction of one national organization. Each local is organized on the line of a department. The cattle butchers form one local. Others are the sheep butchers, pork butchers, beef carriers, beef-casing workers, sausage makers, wool workers, hide cellar men, canning-room employees, oleo and butterine workers, and twelve more. At first only the skilled men in each department were organized; but these gradually extended their numbers to take in the unskilled, and finally departments altogether unskilled were organized. Each local made its own demands and agreements at different times under the approval of the national organization; but in May 1904, a combined scale for all departments and classes of labor was submitted to the employers. It was this scale that precipitated the strike; and the point of division was the demand for a minium wage of 20 cents an hour, afterwards reduced to 18½ cents, for all unskilled labor. Demands of this kind had been made and granted in departments where skilled workmen, like cattle butchers and sheep butchers, prevailed, but had been rejected in other departments.

In analyzing the labor situation in the industry, we may begin with the leading group of workmen, the cattle butchers.

The cattle butchers' local unions number 5,500 of the 50,000 members, and of these about 2,000 are the most highly skilled of all the workmen in the slaughtering and packing industry. Their importance has brought to them the title of "butcher aristocracy." Their strategic position is explained by the character and expensiveness of the material they work upon. The cattle butcher can do more damage than any other workman; for a cut in the hide depreciates its value 70 cents, and a spotted or rough carcass will be the last to sell, with the risk of the rapid depreciation of a perishable product. The sheep butcher merely "pulls off" three-quarters of the hide, but the cattle butcher can pull off only 2 per cent. The entire hide must be neatly cut off, leaving the "fell," or mucous covering, intact on the carcass, to give it a good appearance. The "splitter," too, must make a neat and smooth cut straight down the middle of the ivory-like "fins" of the backbone, or the wholesaler cannot quickly dispose of the piece. Yet, notwithstanding the high skill required, the proportion of skilled workmen in the butchers' gang is very small, owing to a minute

[1] Conditions described in this article are mainly those of Chicago, the centre of the industry.

division of labor. It would be difficult to find another industry where division of labor has been so ingeniously and microscopically worked out. The animal has been surveyed and laid off like a map; and the men have been classified in over thirty specialities and twenty rates of pay, from 16 cents to 50 cents an hour. The 50-cent man is restricted to using the knife on the most delicate parts of the hide (floorman) or to using the axe in splitting the backbone (splitter); and, wherever a less skilled man can be slipped in at 18 cents, 18½ cents, 20 cents, 21 cents, 22½ cents, 24 cents, 25 cents, and so on, a place is made for him, and an occupation mapped out. In working on the hide alone there are nine positions, at eight different rates of pay. A 20-cent man pulls off the tail, a 22½-cent man pounds off another part where the hide separates readily, and the knife of the 40-cent man cuts a different texture and has a different "feel" from that of the 50-cent man. Skill has become specialized to fit the anatomy.

In this way, in a gang of 230 men, killing 105 cattle an hour, there are but 11 men paid 50 cents an hour, 3 men paid 45 cents, while the number getting 20 cents and over is 86, and the number getting under 20 cents is 144, as follows

Typical Crew of Cattle Butchers and Helpers

Rate of Pay per Hour		Number of Men at Rate
50 cents		11
45 cents		3
40 cents		5
32½ cents		6
31½ cents		2
30 cents		2
27½ cents		4
26½ cents		6
25 cents		6
24 cents		1
22½ cents		16
21 cents		4
20 cents		20
18½ cents		5
15 to 18 cents		139
Average 21	Total	230

The following table shows the list of occupations as provided for in the agreement of 1903-04, with the number of men in each occupation for a gang of 230, their rates of pay, and their schedule of output. The agreement went only as far as knife men, who received 20 cents an hour. Those receiving less than that rate were the shifting population of laborers who had never been included in the scale, and who would have been raised to a minimum of 18½ cents, had the demands of 1904 been granted.

The division of labor grew with the industry, following the introduction of the refrigerator car and the marketing of dressed beef, in the decade of the seventies. Before the market was widened by these revolutionizing inventions, the killing gangs were small, since only the local demands were supplied. But, when the number of cattle to be killed each day increased to a thousand or more, an increasing gang or crew of men was put together; and the best men were kept at the most exacting work. At what

Cattle Butchers, Gang of 230 Men

Number of Men	Position	Scale of Wages (per Hour)	Scale of Work (per Hour), 1903-1904
3	Penner	$0.18½	Left to House Committee
1	Knocker, when raising gates and dumping out	.24	60
	Knocking only	.24	80
2	Schackler	.18½	Left to House Committee
2	Hoister	.20	Left to House Committee
	Sticking	32½	Left to House Committee
4	Heading and sticking	.32½	25
	Heading only	.32½	30
1	Dropper	.20	Left to House Committee
2	Pritcher up	.20	Left to House Committee
1	Gullet-raiser	.20	Left to House Committee
3	Foot-skinner	.22½	35
3	Leg-breaker	.25	25 sets
1½	Ripper-open	.25	80
7	Floorman	.50	15
1½	Breast-sawyer	.25	75
1½	Caul-puller	.26½	50
	Pulling cauls and opening eich	.20	40
1	Eich-opener	.20	75
1	Tail-ripper	.20	20
3	Fell-cutter	.27½	25
	Cord-cutter	—	Left to House Committee
2½	Rumper	.40	40
3	Fell-beater	.22½	
	Fell-puller	—	60
2	Gutter	.26½	40
2½	Backer	.45	40
3	Tail-sawyer	.26½	30
4	Splitter	.50	25
2	Hanging off	.22½	60
2½	Clearing out	.30	40
2½	Hide-dropper	.32½	40
	Clear out and drop together	.32½	20
1½	Neck-splitter	.31½	60
2½	Skirt-trimmer	.21	60
3	Ladder-men	.22½	Left to House Committee
4	Bruise-trimmer	.22½	Left to House Committee
1	Scribe-sawyer	.20	Left to House Committee
1	Cutting out tongues	—	100
6	Boning heads	$1.05 per 100	32½
	All other knife men	.20	
	Laborers not covered by agreement	16½ to 19½	

point the greatest economy is reached was discovered by experiment and by comparison of one house with another. Each firm has accurate knowledge of the labor force and the output of every other house, and in this way each improvement becomes general and each superintendent is keyed up. Taking a crew of 230 butchers, helpers, and laborers, handling 1,050 cattle a day under the union regulations of output, the time required for each bullock is equivalent to 131 minutes for one man, from the pen to the cooler, the hide cellar, and all the other departments to which the animal is distributed. But this is made up of 6.4 minutes for the 50-cent man, 1¼ minutes for the 45-cent man, and so on; and the average wage per hour for the gang would not exceed 21 cents, making the entire labor cost about 46 cents per bullock.

Three objects were gained by this division of labor. *First*, cheaper men—unskilled and immigrant labor—could be utilized in large numbers. *Second*, skilled men became more highly expert in the quality of their work. While, on the one hand, this greatly increased the proportion of low-wage men, it also pushed up the wages of the very few skilled men on the delicate and particular parts of the work. An all-round butcher might expect to earn 35 cents an hour, but the highly specialized floorman or splitter earns 50 cents an hour. Some of these expert floormen work a week at a time without cutting a single hide, so deft and delicate becomes their handling of the knife. If the company makes a few of these particular jobs desirable to the men and attaches them to its service, it can become independent of the hundreds who work at the jobs where they can do but little damage; and their low wage brings down the average to 21 cents, where, if all were all-round butchers, the average would be 35 cents. Consequently, in the course of time the companies put a few of the strongest men, and those with a particular knack for their work, on "steady time," paying them a salary of $24 to $27 a week, regardless of the time actually worked; but the other nine-tenths of the gang were hired by the hour, and paid only for the time at work. These steady-time men not only stood by the company, but acted as pace-setters; and in this way a *third* object of division of labor was brought about,—namely, speed. Take the occupation of splitting, for example. In the year 1884 five splitters in a certain gang would get out 800 cattle in 10 hours, or 16 per hour for each man, the wages being 45 cents. In 1894 the speed had been increased so that 4 splitters got out 1,200 in 10 hours, or 30 per hour for each man—an increase of nearly 100 per cent in 10 years. The wages, except for the steady-time men, were reduced to 40 cents per hour. Other occupations had been speeded up, and other rates of pay had been reduced in similar proportions. This was undoubtedly the grievance above all others which led to the organization of 1901; for the first act of the union was not directed towards wages or hours, but towards a reduction of the output. This the union did by adopting a "scale of work," and putting it into force without consulting the foremen, superintendents, or proprietors. In the case of the splitters the output was reduced from an average as high as 30 cattle an hour in some establishments to a uniform 25 an hour, and thereafter, in order that the gang might get out 120 an hour, the number of splitters had to be increased to 5. Similar changes were made in other occupations, the floormen being reduced from an average of 20 to a limit of 15, and so on. An exception is the "head boners" or trimmers, who are the only class of workmen in the cattle gang paid by the piece. In this occupation the rate formerly was 7 cents per head, but it had been reduced to 9 mills per head; and the union, without placing a limit on the amount of work, secured two advances in the rate, bringing it to 1¼ cents per head. At this rate the leader of the boners can make 40 cents an hour.

The packers admit that some of them had gone too far in rushing the men, but they hold that the union has gone too far in restraining them. The union contends that their scale of work is the same as that which already existed in the Hammond plant and in one of the Swift houses. At any rate, the inelastic restriction of output is set forth by the packers as the most objectionable and arbitrary of all the features of the union. They cite the fact that it applies equally and without distinction to "canners" that weigh 800 or 900 pounds and to corn-fed steers that weigh 1,800 pounds. The justice of this criticism is acknowledged by some of the men, though they hold that the quantity of work does not vary in proportion to the weight of the animal, and that, if the limit is low for canners, it is high for steers, so that the average is fair. The packers cite cases where a floorman is compelled to "kill time" sharpening his knife or strolling along in order to hold himself down to the union limit of work. There are undoubtedly exceptional men, and nothing is more surprising to the outsider than these wide differences. One man, whose knife slips down the hide as though he were playing, is turning out twice as much as his comrade, who seems to be a hard worker. Individual splitters have been known to reach as high as 60 cattle an hour, working on canners, at the time when the average was 30; and, of course, when the union sets the limit for each man at 25 an hour, these swift men find spare time on their hands. Taking them as a standard, some of the packers say that the union reduced the output 50 per cent., whereas the reduction below the average might have been 16 to 25 per cent, according to the plant.

After the limit was set, the companies discontinued the "steady-time" men, and placed them all on the hour basis, since their services as pace-makers were no longer useful. This reduction in expense must be considered as a compensation partly offsetting the reduction in work. The steady-time men have opposed the action of the union because their earnings were reduced; but the majority of the skilled men consider the restriction as the main blessing which the union has brought them. For they say that formerly they were speeded up until they were "in a sweat" all day, exhausted at night, and useless after forty years of age; "but now it is a pleasure to work."

In the first written agreement, dated September, 1903, it was agreed that, "in the absence of any skilled man, those doing the same kind of work will attempt to make up the loss in the amount of work caused by such absentee." This was a valuable concession; for otherwise the absence of a floorman would reduce the output of the gang 150 cattle a day, or the absence of a splitter 250 a day, and so on. An offer on the part of one of the companies to pay the time of the absentee to those who made up the loss was declined by resolution of the union, because they feared it would increase absenteeism, and that the greed of the men would thus urge them on permanently to the former speed.

The artificial limit on output works against the employer in another way, for it prevents economical adjustment of the gang. Two floormen handle 30 cattle, but one splitter handles 25. Hence the foreman must hire two splitters, and set them at other work which could be done by cheaper men; with a loss of time, moreover, in changing work. In the earlier days of the industry the number of men to be assigned to one position was determined by speeding up a man, if possible, to the gait of the gang; but, if he could not keep up, another full man was set to help him. Later the idea was adopted of putting a half-man or a quarter-man to help him; and the rate of pay for the half-time or quarter-time was the rate for that occupation. The significance of this device appears in the contention between the union and the employers over "laying off" men in dull seasons. The custom has always prevailed in all departments of laying off a part of the force for three or four months when work is slack, in order to give nearly full time to the others. In a killing gang the foreman would lay off the lowest ranks of unskilled labor, and set higher paid men to doing a part of the work in the lower paid jobs. This dropping down would be carried through to the highest grades of labor, and in this way half-men, one-third men, and one-quarter men were invented. This led to a crisis at one time, when the union insisted that a 50-cent man, who was put quarter time on a 40-cent job, should receive the higher rate of pay for all his time. The union finally receded; but at a later time by threat of a strike, they stopped the practice itself of laying off men, and succeeded in keeping the gang at full number through the year. This episode illustrates the diametrically opposite points of view of the employers and the men. The men preferred to have all of their number employed short time during the dull part of the year, and thus to share equally the disadvantages of slack work. The employer considered it better to attach two-thirds of the men to his work by giving them full time through the year; and he pointed out that it was exactly the complaint of short time that gave force to their demands for higher wages. For it was admitted on all sides that the hourly rates of pay, if they could be earned sixty hours a week, would place the butcher workmen in a better position than that of similar grades of labor in other industries. But, in order to do this, they must lay off a large part of the force; and, consequently, when the packer speaks of steady work, he does not take into account those laid off: it is steady for the others. The union, however, includes all the workmen; and, from their standpoint, steady time cannot be secured except by a different distribution of the work through the year—a thing apparently impossible in a seasonal industry like slaughtering.

Notwithstanding this policy of laying off men, the companies have never been able to furnish full time, even for those who are not laid off. In the killing gangs, for instance, the man who makes full time in December makes only two-fifths to three-fifths time from February to July. Taking it altogether, such a man, regularly employed through the year, has averaged in years past 35 to 46 hours of work per week. This is shown by the following table of hours and wages of the highest-paid labor in the cattle-killing gangs, showing the earnings of a splitter or floorman who "made killing time"; i.e., worked practically all the time when a certain gang was working. All of the time lost by sickness, accident, or other ground of absence, has been added, so that the table shows the full time of the gang, not the full time of any one man in the gang. The table represents the 25 or 30 men, in an establishment of 5,000, who could have earned the highest possible wages for men paid by the hour.

The table shows that the rate of wages per hour, beginning at 40 cents, was raised to 45 cents during the years 1891, 1892, 1893, then reduced to 40 cents until 1899, then again raised to 45 cents, and that two advances, to 47½ cents in 1902 and 50 cents in 1903, were secured by the union. Similar changes were made in the rates for other skilled positions.

It will be seen that the average weekly earnings of this highest skilled workman who had a "steady job," though not "steady time," since he was paid by the hour, have varied from $14.11 in 1897 to $21.70 in 1902, and that the average number of hours per week varied from 35 to 46, so that the time actually worked and the wages actually earned varied from 58.3 per cent. to 76.6 per cent. of possible time and earnings on the basis of 60 hours per week.

Wages of Splitter or Floorman (1888-1904)

Year	Rates of Wages per Hour	Average Number of Hours per Week	Average Earnings per Week	Per Cent of Possible Time and Earnings
1888	$0.40	41	$16.24	68.0
1889	.40	39	15.86	65.0
1890	.40	46	18.46	76.6
1891	.45	39	17.69	65.0
1892	.45	43	19.48	71.6
1893	.45 (7 mo.) .40 (5 mo.)	40	16.66	66.6
1894	.40	37	14.72	61.6
1895	.40	37	14.99	61.6
1896	.40	35	14.20	58.3
1897	.40	35	14.11	58.3
1898	.40	36	14.33	60.0
1899	.40 (9 mo.) .45 (3 mo.)	42	16.60	70.
1900	.45	38	16.15	63.3
1901	.45	46	21.00	76.6
1902	.45 (8 mo.) .47½ (4 mo.)	46	21.70	76.6
1903	.47½ (9 mo.) .50 (3 mo.)	42	20.02	70.0
1904*	.50	34	17.16	56.6

*Six months, slack season.

Taking this position as a standard, it will be seen that the average weekly earnings of the men in the same gang getting 20 cents an hour have ranged from $5.64 in 1897 to $8.68 in 1902, while the men getting 16½ cents an hour have ranged from $4.65 to $7.16. These earnings are for men who have been kept on the force throughout the year, and not laid off by slack work, sickness, or other cause. Evidently, the average earnings of the men who were laid off for three or four months have been still lower, unless they have found work in other industries.

After the strike of 1886 the packers introduced what was known as "the contract system;" i.e., a contract to work, signed by each workman, authorizing the company to keep back ten days' pay and requiring the workman to give two weeks' notice of withdrawal. This practice continued until 1901, when the cattle butchers, irritated by the hardships of a man who was refused his deposit when his child was sick, made a demand; and the system was abolished throughout the industry, and all of the deposits were returned.

Perhaps the most remarkable gain secured by the cattle butchers' union, and one that was shared by all the others, was the adoption of regular hours of work. Cattle reach the stock yards during the night, and are purchased by the packers early in the morning. Seldom, however, can they be driven over the chutes and delivered on the killing floors before nine o'clock, and often not until ten or eleven o'clock. Furthermore, it was always held that they could not be kept over night, and must be killed on the day of arrival, since the charges of the stock-yard company for holding over night are 50 cents a head. Consequently, the men would report in the morning between seven and nine o'clock, as notified the night before. If the cattle were on hand, they began work. If the cattle were not yet ready, after waiting awhile, a notice would be posted to begin work at ten, eleven, or twelve o'clock, as the case might be. The men received no pay for the time spent in waiting; and then they would be required to work often until late at night, in order to dispose of the day's arrivals. It was nearly two years after the union was organized before it felt strong enough to take up this matter. A strike was threatened, but finally a conference was secured with a leading packer. The union spokesman told him of these hardships, compared their position with his own, in that they never knew beforehand when their work would begin or be done, while he could finish up his day's work and go home. The packer only replied that he had never known that such conditions existed. From the date of that interview, although no promises were made, overtime has been abolished for the cattle butchers in all the establishments. The men begin regularly at seven o'clock, and work until the day's killing is done, and go home not later than 5.30 p.m. If, after ten hours' work, there are cattle left over, they are held until the next morning. That a union had to be organized and threaten a strike in order that the owner of the business might learn of conditions of which his own conscience promptly disapproved is a fact full of meaning for all who are disturbed by the modern unrest of labor.

The union also secured four of the legal holidays which they had never enjoyed before, and these were shared by the other departments.

The cattle butchers devoted much time to perfecting a line of promotion, which they say shall be "according to superiority and oldest men to receive promotions." By "superiority" is evidently meant "seniority." This is designed to prevent favoritism on the part of the foremen, to prevent the introduction of outsiders in the lower positions and then "jumping them over the heads" of the older men, to diminish jealousy, and to maintain the feeling of equity and comradeship necessary among the members of a union. These rules of promotion do not find favor with the superintendents, who contend that forced promotion often takes a man away from work that he does well and gives him a position which he may not be able to hold. Neatness and superior quality of workmanship are natural to some men, and never acquired by others; and, if the foreman is required by reason of seniority to promote an awkward man to a position where he may damage the hide 70 cents or retard the sale of the carcass, then the gang as a whole suffers. The antagonism at this point shows clearly the nature of the conflict between capital and labor—a conflict irrepressible, as proved by the strike.

We may proceed now to other groups of laborers.

In a gang of sheep butchers the pace is set by the "pelter," who loosens the hide so that it can be pulled off without tearing the "fell," or mucous covering, and by the "setter," who starts the carcass on the trolley. One pelter and one setter in a gang were formerly steady-time men, and the pelter's speed had been pushed up to 60 and even 75 an hour. The union, which was organized a year after that of the cattle butchers, set the limit at 40 per hour, and later by an agreement with the firms raised it to 46½; and the companies placed all the steady-time men on the hourly basis. The speed of other positions was reduced proportionately; that is, a reduction of 30 or 50 per cent., according as it is measured by the average speed or by the speed of the swiftest men.

Irregular time was a grievance even more serious with the sheep butchers than with the cattle butchers. There are some 12 styles of dressing mutton, according to the locality of the market—"Alleghenys," "Bostons," "New Yorks," and so on. The packer must wait each morning for orders from different parts of the country before he can decide the styles and quantities of work for the day. This compelled the men to wait sometimes until two o'clock in the afternoon, and to go home late at night. They finally refused to work after 5.30 p.m. under any conditions, the reason being that they could have got out the work if they had begun at seven o'clock. When the union was first organized, one of the packers discharged several of the members; but, after a threat to strike by the international union, they were reinstated.

In the hog-killing and pork-cutting departments the local union was organized at the same time as that of the sheep butchers; but in these departments a limit has not been placed on the amount of work. A larger number of mechanical contrivances are used than is the case on the other killing floors, such as a huge wheel for hoisting the shackled hog, a scraping machine to take off the hair, and a trolley on which the carcass is hooked and passed from one worker to the next. The pace-setters are the sticker, the scalder, the hooker-on, the splitter, and the chopper, the latter being in the pork-cutting room; and, since the union has not set a limit on the amount of work, these positions have continued on "steady time." The proposed scale, as submitted in 1904, for the first time set a limit in this department; and, had this scale been adopted, the scalder, for example, would have been restricted to 500 hogs an hour, and his wages placed at 40 cents an hour instead of "steady time."

In this department the seasonal character of the work is more marked than in sheep and cattle killing; but there is, of course, a great improvement over the period preceding refrigeration, when hogs were killed and packed only in the winter months. On account of the very irregular supply of animals the union has not attempted to keep the gang at full force, but it has tried to establish the rule that "the last man hired is the first laid off; and, when the gang is increased, the oldest man with the house shall be hired first."

The sausage department has the credit of furnishing steadier work than other departments. The union of sausage makers, composed mainly of Germans, had a checkered and disastrous career. They imitated the cattle and sheep butchers in demanding a minimum pay for their gang; but they went further, and applied the minimum of 18½ cents to all common labor. This they supported in 1903 by a strike in violation of their agreement. Their union had reached a membership of 1,300; but they found that the unskilled laborers receiving less than 18½ cents an hour could not appreciate the advantages of the union, and would not pay their dues. Since the strike was "illegal," the Amalgamated refused to support them, and the packers filled their places. When the agreements expired in 1904, it was this demand of the sausage makers, applied to all departments, that the Amalgamated took up, and lost in the strike.

In the sausage department piece-work prevails more than elsewhere, except in the canning department. The rates are based on the thousand pounds of sausage. The piece-work system was introduced in 1891 in stuffing sausages by machinery, and up to the time of the union organization in 1902 the rates and practices were such that the best man in the best year could earn a yearly average of $12 a week, ranging from $8 to $16 in different parts of the year. In other years he earned less. In some cases, piece-rates had been reduced; and in 1899, without an organization, a strike forced an increase of 10 per cent in certain bologna prices that had been reduced 20 per cent. After the union was organized in 1902, other rates were increased.

A peculiar feature of the piece-work system in pork sausages, as distinguished from bologna sausages, is the limitation of earnings per hour through the substitution of inferior casings when the men's earnings exceed a certain amount. In first-class casings, without "leaks," 20 feet can be filled at one expulsion of the steam stuffer; but on second and third class casings, the workman must tie the casings wherever a leak appears, and this reduces the number of pounds of sausage to his credit. Since the superintendent is charged with the cost of material and labor, and is credited with the value of the product, sometimes getting a bonus on the margin, it is to his interest to get not only a low labor cost, but also a low cost of the expensive casings, a considerable part of which is purchased in the open market. He, therefore, watches his opportunity to substitute second and third class casings for first class. At what point it is safe to do this depends on the point of hourly earnings below which the workmen will resist, which was found to be the rate of about 27 cents an hour. He refrained from cutting the piece-rates, as he had done in the case of bolognas; and, since the rates are the same for all classes of casings, he contented himself with putting slower work on the men by substituting inferior casings. This might require the men to work overtime in busy seasons to get out the product. Consequently, when in 1902 the union enforced its demand for a one and a half piece-rate on all work done after a ten-hour day, the superintendent in the next busy season furnished first-class casings, and permitted the men to earn 35 to 36 cents an hour.

Women and girls have been taking the places of men in this department during the past five or six years, a peculiar instance being that of trimming meat from the bones and tying casings, where formerly older men, who were kept as a sort of pensioners, have given way to girls, who work much faster. The strike of 1903 opened a place for Slav women to take the places of German men.

The beef "luggers" are one of the most interesting specialities of this most highly specialized industry. They are the powerful men who load the sides of beef into the cars. There are but 60 of them in the yards; but they have taken into their organization the cooler hands and truckers who work with them. Prior to 1891 the luggers were paid 28 cents an hour, and earned $8 to $10 a week. They work irregular hours, beginning at two to four o'clock in the morning, and working only when the cars are switched in place. In 1891, on account of irregular hours, they asked for weekly wages, and in place of 28 cents an hour secured $12.50 a week, without an organization. In 1892 they again asked for an advance, and received $15 for a week of 54 hours. In 1902, after they had formed the Beef Carriers' and Helpers' Local, they got $17, and their demands for 1904 were for $18.50. At $17, "steady time," their yearly earnings were nearly as high as those of the splitter or floorman, who is paid 50 cents an hour "killing time." The luggers also reduced the amount of their work, so that where 5 or 6 men loaded 60 to 70 cars a day, which, in their own words, "certainly was slavery, as any one who understands the work will admit," it thereafter required 8 men to load 60 cars. However, in the fall of 1903, after four men in a house had been making up work for a fifth member of the gang who was sick a month, the firm reduced the number permanently to four. The luggers went out on strike; but, not being supported by the Amalgamated organization, they lost.

The number of women employed in the industry in 1890 was 990, or 2.2 per cent. of the total number of employees. This was increased by 1900 to 2,954, or 4.3 per cent. In Illinois the number is put at 1,473, or 5.3 per cent. This proportion has undoubtedly been increased since the last census year; and it is generally stated that the number of women employees in Chicago alone is 2,000, or about 9 per cent of all employees. This increase has come about partly through the introduction of foreign-born women in the sausage department and meat-trimming rooms at times when the men went on strike. Prior to that time, women were not employed in the large establishments at work where the knife is used, their work being principally painting and labelling cans, soldering and stuffing cans, sewing up ends of bags, packing chipped beef, packing and wrapping butterine.

The majority of the women and girls are paid by the piece; and the Illinois Bureau of Statistics in 1892 showed that piece workers earned from $3.58 to $11.57 per week of 60 hours, the average being $6.78. At that time, girls paid by the week of 60 hours earned $4 to $8.25, the bulk of employment per year ranging from 35 to 40 weeks. Weekly rates were gradually equalized until in 1902 the prevailing rates of pay were $4.50 to $5.50. Much the larger number of women work at piece rates, and these were gradually reduced as the girls acquired greater speed, until in 1900, prior to the organization of the men and without any organization on their own part, the girls in one of the largest canning establishments went on strike against a further cut in rates. At that time the swiftest girl, who one year later died of consumption and overwork, was said to be able to earn $20. This girl, whose high earnings had tempted the company to cut the rates, joined with others of Irish-American stock, and led the strike; and, when they were defeated by the introduction of foreign-born women, they found themselves blacklisted by the other large companies. Nine of them brought suit against the four leading companies for $50,000 damages; but the suits were decided in May and June, 1901, on demurrer in favor of the packers. The court declared[2] that "the defendants agreed not to re-employ those who went out upon a strike. This they had a right to do. According to the allegations of the girls' declarations, the purpose for making this agreement was bad, because by such agreement the plaintiff cannot get employment at her trade, and is thus injured. This gives her no right of action, for a bad motive does not make a lawful deed actionable." The court also intimated that a union was judged by the same standard. "The right of union laborers to quit work or to refuse to work where non-union men are employed is established beyond controversy, and that without reference to how pitiful the consequences may be to him who is thus deprived of an opportunity to earn bread for himself and family."

This decision had undoubtedly an effect upon the men and women in the stock yards in determining them during the next two years quietly and thoroughly to organize the whole industry. The men began to organize in June, 1900, four months after the girls' strike, and several departments were organized by the men before, in March, 1902, a women's local was

[2] Chicago papers, June 11, 1901. The court was not a court of record.

chartered with 14 members. The initiative was taken by the Head Worker of the University of Chicago Settlement, who had noted the exclusion of the women from the men's locals. It was decided to organize the women of all departments in one local, although the men were organized by departments. In this way the women secure representation in the Packing Trades Council and in the conventions, whereas they would be outvoted, were they to be distributed among the department organizations. Since the scales of wages and work are agreed upon by these superior bodies before they can be submitted to the packers, the girls have a voice through their own delegates in formulating them, which they would not have, were they organized by departments.

An interesting illustration of this influence is seen in the compromise agreed upon at the Cincinnati Convention in 1904, respecting the employment and wages of women in the sausage departments. It was in this department that Slav women had been employed in place of Germans out on strike, as described above; and the men afterwards insisted that in the new agreement the women should be discharged. But the girl delegates opposed this demand, even though the women were not members of the union; and, finally, it was agreed that the union should demand that women be paid the same wages as men. This concession to the girl delegates was not faithfully carried out; and the scale, as actually submitted in May, provided for "abolition of women labor in the sausage departments." But the original compromise is significant as showing the standards which the union women were willing to have applied to women's work. These standards were also adopted for all other girls working in those occupations which had been recognized as "women's work," where they were not paid by the piece; and the demands there were the same as for the men—namely, a minimum of 20 cents an hour. This would have amounted to an increase of 100 per cent, since girls paid by the week receive 9 cents and 10 cents an hour, whereas the increase for the lowest-paid men, bringing them up to the same minimum, would have been only 10 to 15 per cent. Even the compromise offer of 18½ cents an hour would have raised the girls 85 per cent. These standards were agreed to by the girls in full view of the fact that, at the same rates of pay (except in piece-work), the women would probably be displaced by men.

Immediately following the organization of the women's local, all the charter members, to the number of 14, were discharged; but in the course of the year, with the assistance of the men's locals, they reached a membership of 1,200. It has never been possible for them to being into their union the non-English speaking women, many of whom are married. But they secured practically all the Irish-American, German-American, and Polish-American girls; and this gave them entire control of some departments where only such happened to be employed. They elected their own business agent, secured reinstatement of several members who had been discharged for union activity (though not their president and secretary), gained advances in some of the piece-rates, and advances of 50 cents to $2 in weekly rates. The normal rate paid now to these American girls is $5 for beginners, rising to $6 with experience. In one department, for example, employing 62 American-born girls, there are only 8 who get as high as $6 a week. Here the girls begin at $5 at sixteen or seventeen years of age. Very few work more than three years, the majority leaving within that period, usually for marriage. Numbers of Slav women return to work after marriage, but this is not the case with the American-born. Bohemian women and girls are increasing in number more rapidly than other nationalities, with the Poles and Lithuanians next; and they are doing heavy and disagreeable work, such as stuffing cans and trimming meat, where in many cases they have displaced men.

A significant fact in the history of the women's local is that, though they are the only class of labor generally employed at piece-work, and though such a method of payment had led them to serious over-exertion, they have yet made no efforts to limit the amount of work, some of which, especially in the can-making departments, depends on the speed of the machine. It seems that for the few years during which most of the girls expect to work in the industry they choose to overlook the strain of excessive speed, which to the men, as they grow older, becomes the greatest of all their grievances. The girls feel like working to their utmost for a period, in order to save up a sum of money, and quit the work for a home of their own.

The number of children under sixteen years of age employed in the industry was 700 in 1890. This had been increased in 1900 to 1,651, or 2½ per cent of all employees. The number in Illinois was 596, or 2.28 per cent. The intermittent work of the packing houses fosters in the children unsteady habits, and even the most industrious workmen trained in this school dislike more than four days' work in the week. The probation officer of the juvenile court strongly urges the boys and girls under suspended sentence not to work in the stock yards, and endeavors to find other jobs for them. The parochial schools of the neighborhood have been defective after the third or fourth grades; and in the Slovak school none of the teachers speak English, while the Polish school has but recently introduced English. The capacity of the public schools has been inadequate, though lately it has been increased. Since the census year (1900) the compulsory school law has been strengthened by amendments to the child labor law, largely through the efforts of the butcher workmen's organizations, which sent a delegation to Springfield in behalf of the proposed law. Many of the men and women now working in the yards began at eleven or twelve years of age; but by the new law the work of children under fourteen years is prohibited, and the work of those under sixteen is limited to eight hours per day. An age and school certificate, showing ability to read and write, is required from the health and school authorities for those under sixteen; and each establishment is required to keep posted in a conspicuous place a list of all children employed and the hours of beginning and quitting work. The enforcement of this law is intrusted to the State factory inspector and his deputies; and, after sixty convictions secured against some of the packers, certain firms have gone so far as to issue orders to their foremen not to employ children under sixteen, though permitted to do so by law. The short-time clause makes the services of children undesirable, except in the offices as messenger boys, where the entire force works but eight hours. The companies usually require an affidavit from children above sixteen as a measure of protection, although an affidavit is not required by law. The union does not admit persons under sixteen years of age. Viewed as a piece of legislation to exclude children under fourteen years of age, the law is effective.

The foregoing are departments of peculiar interest in the industry. The others are composed mainly of unskilled labor, as will be seen from the large proportion of those whose wages are less than 20 cents an hour, such as the oleo workers and glue workers, 95 per cent, wool workers, 70 per cent, and so on. Taking the industry as a whole, it is maintained by the union statisticians that one-quarter of the employees eligible to membership received less than 18½ cents per hour. The packers assert that the proportion was only 6 per cent. It was on behalf of this 25 per cent that the skilled workmen lost eight weeks work and jeopardized their jobs, and on behalf of this 6 per cent that the packers lost several million dollars.

The motives on the part of the strikers were partly sentimental, partly for self-preservation. The sentimental side appealed to the public, and was strongly emphasized. But there was also a profound self-interest involved, in that, through the minute division of labor, promotion from the lower ranks can be made without much training. The packers contended that in the case of the unskilled the law of supply and demand, with its market rate of wages, could not be overruled; and they pointed to the 3,000 to 5,000 transient laborers who gathered every morning at seven o'clock at the several time-keeping stations, asking for work, when not one-tenth of their number could be employed. It was not a question of ability to pay the minimum asked; for the five packing companies controlled the bulk of the business, and through favorable freight rates, their own car lines, utilization of by-products, and minute division of labor, their position was more favorable than that of the "independents," who did not have these advantages, and yet were paying the wages asked for. The packers proposed to reduce the minimum pay of men in the killing, cutting, casing and beef-loading departments to 17½ cents an hour, a reduction of 1 cent. All other classes of unskilled labor were to be left "open" without a wage scale, by which transient labor might be paid as low as 16½ cents. A minimum wage of 18½ cents was more than such inexperienced labor was worth. It was necessary to have this floating supply only in order to fill the places of absentees, so that the gangs might not suffer. But the union contended that, when once employed at 16½ cents an hour, those who were getting 18½ cents would be discharged; and there were known enough cases of men at 18½ cents being discharged and rehired at 16½ cents to convince them that such would happen all along the line. After the strike the packers reduced large classes of their regular unskilled labor 1 and 2 cents an hour.

The demand for a minimum wage above the market rate was also necessary to the permanency of the union, since it had been found that those who received only market wages refused to pay dues. It is true that nearly all of them came out on strike with the others; but it was the union theory that, if a minimum of 18½ cents could be established, the companies could not then afford to employ transient labor, which was worth only 16½ cents, and therefore better men would seek these positions, and union men would be preferred by the employers to non-union men. This was in lieu of a demand for the the "closed shop," for which none of the unions had asked, but which the skilled men had secured in practice, as is shown by the agreement of the cattle butchers that, in the absence of any skilled man, those doing the same kind of work would attempt to make up the loss. A minimum wage would have lessened the number of transient laborers employed, and would have made the position of union laborers steadier through the year. The importance of this factor is seen by consulting the census[3] of 1900, which shows that, in the industry as a whole, the greatest number employed at any one time during the year was 81,416, and the least number employed at any one time 57,119. In other words, 30 per cent of the employees are unemployed in the slack season. This proportion agrees with that of one of the largest houses in Chicago, whose employees number about 4,000 in the slack season, and 6,000 in the busy season. If practically one-third of the employees are laid off, then, of course, there is a wide opening for new men, unless blocked by the "closed shop" or obstructed by the minimum wage. The employers, as compensation for reduction in hourly rates of pay, have promised to make work steadier, so that the yearly earnings will be larger. They began during the strike by enlisting the aid of the commission men, and by sending thousands of circulars to cattle raisers and shippers, urging a better distribution of their shipments throughout the week. The custom has long existed of shipping live stock on Saturday and Sunday, so that the arrivals of cattle during a typical week would be 30,000 on Monday, 8,000 on Tuesday, 30,000 on Wednesday, dwindling to 200 on Saturday. If the shippers were organized, this appeal might be effective; but there is at present no certainty of its results. And, even if shipments were equalized through the week, this would not remedy the more serious inequality in distribution through the year, since live stock is a seasonal product following grass and corn.

Perhaps the fact of greatest social significance is that the strike of 1904 was not merely a strike of skilled labor for the unskilled, but was a strike of Americanized Irish, Germans, and Bohemians in behalf of Slovaks, Poles, Lithuanians, and negroes. The strike was defeated by bringing in men from the companies' own branch houses for the skilled occupations and negroes and Greeks for the unskilled occupations.

This substitution of races has been a continuing process for twenty years. At the time of the strike of 1886 the men were American, Irish, and German; and the strike was defeated by splitting their forces rather than by introducing new nationalities. After that date the Bohemians entered in large numbers, although a few of them had begun work as early as 1882. Bohemians have worked their way forward until, of the 24 men getting 50 cents an hour in two of the cattle-killing gangs, 12 are Bohemians, and the others are German, Irish, and American. The Bohemian is considered to be the coming man in the business. The Americans as wage-earners have practically been driven out of the stock yards, and are being followed by the Irish and Germans. Those who have accumulated money leave for something more certain. The Germans are held mainly by the large number of homes they have purchased in the neighborhood; and this has seemed to be the future of the Bohemians and Poles, who have been purchasing homes for several years, and of the Slovaks and Lithuanians, who have begun during the past two years. The feeling of security since the union was established three years ago has stimulated the tendency to home ownership among all these nationalities, although as yet there are many Slovaks and Lithuanians who return with their savings to their native land. The Irish show wide diversities of character, noticeable in contrast with the uniformity of other races. In general there is a rising class and a degenerating class. Neither class shows any inclination towards home

[3] Vol. ix, p. 398.

ownership. But the Irish of the rising class have a much stronger desire than the Germans or Bohemians to educate their children rather than put them to work. This class of Irish has been leaving the industry, except as held back by a foremanship or skilled trade or by a salaried position in the union, of which they have been the aggressive organizers and leaders. With the defeat of the union, doubtless many more of them will leave. The other class—the degenerating Irish—displaced by the Slav, have become casual laborers, without definite place in any industry.

The older nationalities have already disappeared from the unskilled occupations, most of which now are entirely manned by Slovaks, Poles, and Lithuanians. The Poles began to appear at about the same time as the Bohemians, though not in as large numbers; and they have not advanced in the same proportion. The Slovaks and Lithuanians were first seen in 1899. One Slovak who has been in the yards ten years has worked himself up to a 50-cent job; but he is exceptional, and these two races have as yet only shared with the negroes the unskilled positions. The negroes first came during the strike of 1894, when many were imported from the South and large cities. An intense race hatred sprang up among the Americans and Europeans, who thought the negroes were favored by the employers; and this seemed to be leading to a race war. The conflict was averted by the union, which admitted the negroes on equal terms with the whites. This hatred has been renewed during the recent strike, when several thousand negroes were again imported. Notwithstanding the alleged favoritism towards the negroes, they have not advanced to the skilled positions, mainly because they dislike the long apprenticeship and steady work at low pay which lead to such positions. As strike breakers, they were attracted by the easy work, free board and lodgings, and wages of $2.25 a day instead of the $1.85 asked by the union; but in times of peace they are not steady workers at the low wages of the Slav.

Italians have never found a place in the trade; and the experience of the Greeks, who first appeared in 1904, has been curious. Several hundred Greeks in Chicago have established themselves as fruit dealers. When 300 of their countrymen, recently landed from Macedonia, entered the yards, these storekeepers were boycotted, and several of them bankrupted. Through the Greek consul and the Greek priest the merchants endeavored to persuade the Greeks to withdraw from the yards; but they did not leave until the strike was settled, and then they went in a body to another part of the country.

It will be seen that the mingling of races in the stock yards is similar to that in other large American industries, and the problem is a trying one both for the civic neighborhood and for the union organizers. Unlike the union in 1886 under the Knights of Labor, the present organization sprang from the butcher workmen themselves: the former had been officered from without. In the union meetings the speeches are translated often into three or four languages, and much trouble has been occasioned by dishonest or prejudiced interpreters, though with experience these are weeded out. The races are brought together; and, where four years ago scarcely a Polish, Slovak, or Lithuanian family had a member who could speak or understand English, now nearly all have each at least one such member. Race conflicts were infrequent because the races were kept apart by language, distrust, and the influence of the priests; but there were frequent factional fights between religious societies of the same race, especially among the Poles, each society having its own patron saint. There were also many arrests for drunkenness, wife-beating, and neighborhood quarrels. Curiously enough, these disorderly acts dropped off entirely from the date when the strike took effect, and the arrests fell off 90 per cent. The strike continued eight weeks, and the police inspector in charge of the district is reported as saying: "The leaders are to be congratulated for conducting the most peaceful strike Chicago has ever had. Compared with other big strikes, such as the railroad strike of 1894, the teamsters' strike of 1902, or the stock-yards of 1886, there was no violence."

The substitution of races has evidently run along the line of lower standards of living. The latest arrivals, the Lithuanians and Slovaks, are probably the most oppressed of the peasants of Europe; and 18 cents for a day of 12 or 14 hours in the Carpathian foot-hills becomes 18 cents an hour in the stock yards. Even with only four days work a week the Slovak's position is greatly improved; for in Uhrosko he had no work in winter. Yet his improved position shows itself, not in more expensive living, but in fabulous savings gained by packing sometimes as many as 12 persons in 3 rooms, taking in boarders, and sending his children to work. The new arrivals of this class of labor swell the ranks of the thousands waiting at the packing-house gates every morning, and to them there is little difference between 18 cents and 16 cents an hour. Yet it is most remarkable that those already on the ground came out with the union, and did not go back until the strike was declared off.

It is not surprising that, with wage conditions, racial elements, and former grievances such as they were, the union, when it acquired power, should have carried a high hand. Besides the restrictions themselves, the manner in which they were enforced was irritating. Every department or division had its "house committee" of 3 stewards, who often acted as if they had more authority than the foreman or superintendent; and frequently, when a union rule was violated, they stopped the work "in the middle of the game." When it is stated that the superintendent of one of the largest firms had to deal with 120 of these committees, it need create no surprise to learn that he felt relieved when the strike came. The principal grievance was the violation of their own constitution and agreements, which forbade locals or house committees to stop work and required all matters to be referred to higher officers for settlement with the company. The rank and file and the lower officers were insubordinate. Yet the superintendents observed that the unions, as they gained experience, were electing more conservative leaders and that petty troubles were being more easily handled. This encouraging prospect for the union was blighted by the blunder and disaster of the strike.

36

Management's Bill of Particulars: 1915

The Employer's Viewpoint

HARRIS WEINSTOCK,
S. THURSTON BALLARD,
AND RICHARD H. AISHTON

Representing as we do on this Commission, the employers' side, we are at one with the other members of our Federal Commission who represent the general public, and also with those representing organized labor, in believing that under modern industrial conditions, collective bargaining, when fairly and properly conducted, is conducive to the best good of the employer, the worker, and society. We find that there are many enlightened employers who concur in this view, who in the past recognized and dealt with organized labor, but who now refuse to do so, and who, under proper conditions, would willingly continue to engage in collective bargaining. With good cause, in our opinion, however, they place the responsibility for their refusing to do so at the door of organized labor. There is an abundance of available testimony in our records to show that many employers are frightened off from recognizing or dealing with organized labor for fear that to do so means to put their heads in the noose and to invite the probability of seriously injuring, if not ruining, their business.

The prime objection that such employers have to recognizing and dealing with organized labor is the fear of—

(*a*) Sympathetic strikes.
(*b*) Jurisdictional disputes.
(*c*) Labor union politics.
(*d*) Contract breaking.
(*e*) Restriction of output.
(*f*) Prohibition of the use of nonunion-made tools and materials.
(*g*) Closed shop.
(*h*) Contests for supremacy between rival unions.
(*i*) Acts of violence against nonunion workers and the properties of employers.
(*j*) Apprenticeship rules.

While we have found many sinners among the ranks of the employers, the result of our investigation and inquiries forces upon us the fact that unionists also can not come into court with clean hands; that this is not a case where the saints are all on one side and the sinners all on the other. We find saints and sinners, many of them, on both sides.

The hope of future industrial peace must lie in both sides using their best endeavors to minimize the causes that lead to the growth of sins and sinners on each side of the question.

Reprinted from a report by the *U.S. Commission on Industrial Relations*, 1915.

Sympathetic Strikes

Taking up *seriatim* the objections offered by many employers to recognizing and dealing with organized labor, we come first to that of the sympathetic strike. The employer contends, and we find ourselves in sympathy with his contention, that it is a rank injustice to subject him to a strike of his employees who have absolutely no grievances, to stop work because some other group of workers, possibly at a remote point, have a real or fancied grievance against their own employer, especially when such stoppage of work may not only inflict very serious loss, but may mean ruin to the enterprise of the innocent employer, thus making it, in violation of all the equities, a clear case of punishing the many innocent for the one or the few who may be guilty, who were party to the original dispute.

Jurisdictional Disputes

The employer further points out that not only is his business liable to be ruined by the sympathetic strike, but, more especially in the building trades, he is likely to become an innocent victim of jurisdictional disputes for which he is in no wise responsible and over which he has absolutely no control.

Sidney and Beatrice Webb point out that—

> It is no exaggeration to say that to the competition between overlapping unions is to be attributed about nine-tenths of the ineffectiveness of the trade union world.[4]
>
> Innumerable instances have occurred where jurisdictional strikes have lasted for months and sometimes for years.[5]

In 1910 the secretary of the bricklayers said:

> Our disputes with the operative plasterers' union during the past year have taken thousands of dollars out of our international treasury for the purpose of protecting our interest. The loss in wages to our members has amounted to at least $300,000. The loss to our employers has been up in the thousands, also.[6]

Sidney and Beatrice Webb again point out that in the industries of Tyneside, within a space of 35 months, there were 35 weeks in which one or the other of the four most important sections of workmen in the staple industry of the district, absolutely refused to work. This meant compulsory idleness of tens of thousands of men, the selling out of households, and the semistarvation of whole families totally unconcerned with the disputes, while it left the unions in a state of weakness from which it will take years to recover.

That wise and far-seeing labor leaders keenly appreciate the great wrongs inflicted not only upon the employers, but upon the workers themselves, by virtue of cessation of work in jurisdictional disputes, is emphasized by the following extracts from the report of Mr. Samuel

[4] Industrial Democracy, vol. 1, p. 121.
[5] *The Bricklayer and Mason*, Feb., 1911, p. 127.
[6] *Ibid.*

Gompers, President of the American Federation of Labor, at its convention in 1902:

> Beyond doubt, the greatest problem, the danger which above all others is threatening not only the success but the very existence of the American Federation of Labor, is the question of jurisdiction. Unless our affiliated national and international unions radically and soon change their course, we shall, at no distant date, be in the midst of an internecine contest unparalleled in any era of the industrial world, aye, not even when workmen of different trades were arrayed against each other behind barricades over the question of trade against trade. They naturally regard each other with hatred, and treat each other as mortal enemies.
>
> There is scarcely an affiliated organization which is not engaged in a dispute with another organization (and in some cases, with several organizations) upon the question of jurisdiction. It is not an uncommon occurrence for an organization, and several have done so quite recently, to so change their laws and claims to jurisdiction as to cover trades never contemplated by the organizers, officers, or members; never comprehended by their titles, trades of which there is already in existence a national union. And this without a word of advice, counsel, or warning.
>
> I submit that it is untenable and intolerable for an organization to attempt to ride rough-shod over and trample under foot rights and jurisdiction of a trade, the jurisdiction of which is already covered by an existing organization. This contention for jurisdiction has grown into such proportions, and is fought with such an intensity as to arouse many bitter feuds and trade wars. In many instances employers fairly inclined for organized labor are made innocently to suffer from causes entirely beyond their control.

Labor Union Politics

The third objection of employers to recognizing and dealing with organized labor is the risk they run, especially in the building trade, where power to declare a strike is concentrated in the hands of a business agent, of finding themselves at the mercy of either a corrupt business agent or one who, for the sake of union politics, is endeavoring, in order to perpetuate himself in office, to make capital at the expense of the innocent employer by making unwarranted and unreasonable demands against the employer.

Contract Breaking

The fourth reason offered by the employers for refusing to recognize or to deal with organized labor, is its increasing unreliablity in keeping trade agreements. To give one case in point, our record gives the story, in undisputed statement published in the *United Mine Workers' Journal*, which is the official organ of the United Mine Workers of America, written by Mr. W. O. Smith, ex-Chairman of the Executive Committee of the Kentucky District of United Mine Workers of America, in which Mr. Smith, among other things, says:

> Because of the indifference of the conservative members of our unions, and the activity of the radical element which is responsible for

the greatest menace which has ever threatened the United Mine Workers of America, the local strike, during the past two or three years the international, as well as the district and subdistrict officials, have been confronted with many perplexing problems, some of which seem to threaten the very life of the organization. But I believe I am safe in saying that no problem has given them so much concern as the problem of local strikes in violation of agreements.

Thousands of dollars are expended every year in an effort to organize the 250,000 nonunion miners in the United States, while hundreds of our members go on strike almost every day in absolute, unexcusable violation of existing agreements.[7]

This criticism comes not from an employer, but from an ardent, earnest unionist, in high standing in his organization.

Corroborating the statement of Mr. Smith, comes a statement published in *Coal Age* of December 20, 1913, issued by the Association of Bituminous Coal Operators of Central Pennsylvania, addressed to Mr. Patrick Gilday, President of District No. 2, U.M.W. of A., Morrisville mines, Pa., dated Philadelphia, December 12, 1913, in which, among other things, the following appears:

Whereas, Rules 12 and 13 of said agreement provide, "that should differences arise between the operators and mine workers as to the meaning of the provisions of this agreement or about matters not specifically mentioned in this agreement, there shall be no suspension of work on account of such difference, but an earnest effort be made to settle such differences immediately." Whereas, notwithstanding the fact that Rule 15 provides the right to hire and discharge, the management of the mine and the direction of the working forces are vested exclusively in the operator, the United Mine Workers of America have absolutely disregarded this rule, in that they have at numerous times served notices on substantially every operator belonging to our Association, that unless all the employees working for such operators should become members of the union on or before certain dates mentioned in said notices, that they, the Mine Workers, would close or shut down the operators' respective mines, and in many instances did close the mines for this reason, and refused to return to work unless such nonunion employees were discharged. This conduct is in direct violation of the contract, and specifically interferes with and abridges the right of the operator to hire and discharge; of the management of the mine, and of the direction of the working forces; this conduct in violation of contract on the part of the Mine Workers, as well as that mentioned in the preceding paragraph, has resulted in more than one hundred strikes during the life of our scale agreement.[8]

Numerous other illustrations could be given from the records of the Commission, showing that there are other instances where unions did not observe their contracts, tending to make, in the minds of many employers, a character for all unionism, and thus increasing their hesitancy in recognizing and dealing with unions.

[7] New York Hearings, U.S. Commission on Industrial Relations, pp. 2750-51.
[8] New York Hearings, U.S. Commission on Industrial Relations. pp. 2061-2.

Restriction of Output

Not least among the reasons given by fair-minded employers for refusing to recognize or deal with labor unions, is the fact that many unions stand for a limited output, thus making among their workers for the dead level, and thereby making it impossible for the union employer successfully to compete with the nonunion employer, who is not faced with such handicap.

British industrial conditions are cursed with the practice of limited output, as compared with the absence of this practice in industrial Germany. As a consequence, Germany, in time of peace has industrially outrun Great Britain by leaps and bounds.

The British unionist, by practicing limited output, has thus played directly into the hands of his keenest industrial competitor, the German.

The records of the Commission also show that organized labor, almost as a unit, is very strongly opposed to the introduction in industry of what has become known as Scientific Management, or Efficiency Methods. In relation to this phase of the problem, we find ourselves at one with the statement made and the opinions expressed by Mr. Louis D. Brandeis before the Commission at Washington, in April, 1914, who, when invited to express his opinion on the question of efficiency standards, scientific management, and labor, among other things, said

> My special interest in this subject arises from the conviction that, in the first place, working men, and in the second place, members of the community generally, can attain the ideals of our American democracy only through an immediate increase and perhaps a constant increase, in the productivity of man. . . . Our ideals could not be attained unless we succeed in greatly increasing the productivity of man. . . . The progress that we have made in improving the conditions of the working man during the last century, and particularly during the last fifty years, has been largely due to the fact that intervention or the introduction of machinery has gone so far in increasing the producivity of the individual man. With the advent of the new science of management has come the next great opportunity of increasing labor's share in the production, and it seems to me, therefore, of the utmost importance, not only that the science should be developed and should be applied as far as possible, but that it should be applied in cooperation with the representatives of organized labor, in order that labor may now, in this new movement, get its proper share.
>
> I take it that the whole of this science of management is nothing more than organized effort, pursued intensively, to eliminate waste. . . . It is in the process of eliminating waste and increasing the productivity of man, to adopt those methods which will insure the social and industrial essentials, fairness in development, fairness in the distribution of the profits, and the encouragement to the working man which can not come without fairness.
>
> I take it that in order to accomplish this result, it is absolutely essential that the unions should be represented in the process. . . . When labor is given such a representation, I am unable to find anything in Scientific Management which is not strictly in accord with the interests of labor, because it is nothing more than fair, through the application of these methods, which have been pursued in other branches of

science, to find out the best and the most effective way of accomplishing the result. It is not making men work harder—the very effort of it is to make them work less hard, to accomplish more by what they do, and to eliminate all unnecessary motion, to give special effort and special assistance to those who, at the time of the commencement of their work, are mostly in need of the assistance because they are less competent.

. . . As I view the problem, it is only one of making the employer recognize the necessity of the participation of representatives of labor in the introduction and carrying forward of the work, and on the other hand, bringing to the working man and the representatives of organized labor, the recognition of the fact that there is nothing in Scientific Management itself which is inimical to the interests of the working man, but merely perhaps the practices of certain individuals, of certain employers or concerns who have engaged in it.

I feel that this presents a very good opportunity for organized labor. It seems to be absolutely clear, as Scientific Management rests upon the fundamental principles of advance in man's productivity, of determining what the best way was of doing a thing, instead of the poor way, of a complete coordination and organization of the various departments of business, that the introduction of Scientific Management in our businesses was certain to come; that those who oppose the introduction altogether are undertaking a perfectly impossible task; and that if organized labor took the position of absolute opposition, instead of taking the position of insisting upon their proper part in the introduction of this system, and the conduct of the business under it, organized labor would lose its greatest opportunity, and would be defeating the very purpose for which it exists.

On being asked the question what, in his opinion, would be the status of unionism in the event of Scientific Management becoming a common industrial condition, Mr. Brandeis said:

I think there would be a great deal left for unionism to do, and do not think the time will come when there will not be, as long as there is a wage system in existence. . . . I do not feel that we have reached the limit of the shorter day, certainly not in some employments, nor do I think we have reached the limit of the higher wage; certainly we have not reached the limit of the best conditions of employment in many industries.

All of these subjects are subjects which must be taken up, and should be taken up by the representatives of the men and women who are particularly interested. There will be work for unions to do as long as there is a wage system.

Prohibition of Use of Nonunion-Made Tools and Material

The sixth reason offered by employers for refusing to recognize or to deal with organized labor, is that when they do so they are often not permitted to use nonunion-made tools or materials, thus placing upon themselves a burden and a hardship from which nonunion employers are free, and thus also laying themselves liable to get into all sorts of controversies with the union, which are vexatious, annoying, time-losing, and, frequently, most costly, as they sometimes lead to grave and serious strikes.

Closed Shop

The seventh reason why many employers refuse to recognize or to deal with organized labor (and among these may be mentioned the employers of large bodies of workers who have previously had trade agreements with organized labor) is the matter of the closed shop.

Many such employers are quite willing to recognize and to deal with unions upon a tacit or written open shop agreement, but they have no confidence, based on their previous experience, that an open shop agreement will be respected by the unions. Such employers labor under the fear that, despite an open shop agreement or understanding, the union, at its first opportunity, will force them to compel the nonunion worker to join the union. Employers such as these are unwilling to place themselves in the position where the union can control them despite an open shop agreement or understanding, and, so to speak, put a pistol to their heads and command them in turn to command a nonunion worker, on pain of dismissal, to join the union. Such employers feel that, having an open shop agreement or understanding, if, for any reason, a worker does not choose to join the union, they, as employers, should no more compel him to do so than they would compel him to join any particular fraternal society or religious body. They feel that if they are working under an open shop agreement or understanding, and such nonunion worker is capable, efficient, and has rendered long and faithful service, that they are doing him and themselves a great injustice either to force him into a union or to discharge him because he will not join a union.

Where an employer enters into an agreement with a union which does not stipulate that only union men shall be employed, but leaves the employer free to employ exclusively union men, or some union and some nonunion men as he may prefer, so long as he maintains for all men union conditions, in such an event the union has no right to demand that the nonunionist should be compelled by the employer to join the union or a strike will follow. For the union, under such conditions, to strike, as it has done notably in the Pennsylvania coal fields, and as pointed out also by W. O. Smith, ex-Chairman of the Executive Committee of the Kentucky District of the United Mine Workers of America, whose statements have been quoted herein, is a violation, on the part of the union, of its contract.

It may be held that unionists working under an open shop agreement or understanding always reserve to themselves the right, for any reason or for no reason, to cease to work alongside of nonunion men, and that they further reserve the right to determine the psychological moment at which it is in their interest to cease work or to go on a strike because they will not work alongside of nonunion men. It is the fear of the likelihood of their doing this that frightens off many employers from recognizing or dealing with organized labor. They feel that even when they are operating under an open shop agreement or understanding, which does not deny them the right to employ nonunion men so long as they work under union conditions, they are working with a sword suspended over their heads by a slender thread, which may break at any moment, and are liable to have a strike on their hands at the most critical time, which may spell ruin for their business. Employers, as a rule, do not deem it a good business policy to invite such risks.

An impressive example of this policy on the part of organized labor was brought out in the testimony taken by the Commission at Lead, S.D. Superintendent Grier of the Homestake Mining Company, Lead, S.D., at the hearing held by the Commission at that point in August, 1914, stated that he had recognized and dealt with the Lead City Miners' Union from 1877 to 1909, with the understanding that they were at liberty to employ union or nonunion men as they preferred. Late in October, 1909, a resolution was published in the daily papers that on and after the 25th of November, 1909, members of the Federation would not work with those working for the Homestake Mining Company who failed and neglected to become members of the union in good standing; and in consequence, on the 25th of November, the mine was closed down, and from that day on the company has not recognized nor dealt with organized labor.

We are, however, of the opinion that where an employer enters into an agreement with a union which stipulates that only union men shall be employed, a thing which he has both a moral and a legal right to do, the nonunion worker, in that event, can have no more reason to find fault with the employer in declining to employ him, than a certain manufacturer would have if the employer, for reasons satisfactory to himself, should confine his purchases to the product of some other manufacturer.

Contests for Supremacy Between Rival Unions

Testimony has been given before this Commission indicating in more than one instance, that contests between rival unions, or factions of the same union, have led to strikes causing industrial unrest from which the worker as well as the employer has suffered harm and loss.

Acts of Violence Against Nonunion Workers and the Properties of Employers

The ninth objection raised on the part of the employers against unionism, which has been substantiated abundantly by investigation and by testimony taken by the Commission, is the resort on the part of unionists to violence in labor troubles, and to the fact that unionists condone such violence when committed in the alleged interest of labor.

The most notable case, of course, in modern industrial history, is that of the Structural Iron Workers, which resulted in the plea of guilty on the part of the McNamara brothers, for the blowing-up of the Los Angeles Time Building, killing over twenty innocent people, and which further resulted in Frank Ryan, the President of the Structural Iron Workers' National Union, and a group of other labor union officials, being convicted and sentenced to prison.

As a matter of fact, the bringing into life of this United States Commission on Industrial Relations was due primarily to the long series of crimes committed at the instance of the Structural Iron Workers' Union, which culminated in the blowing-up of the Los Angeles Times Building, with its attendant loss of life of innocent citizens, and which aroused a state of public sentiment demanding that an investigation be made by an impartial Federal body, to inquire into the underlying causes of industrial unrest, the existence of which seemed to be evidenced by the violent activities on the part of labor in various parts of the country.

Vincent St. John, Secretary of the Industrial Workers of the World, in his testimony before the Commission on Industrial Relations at a public hearing in New York, said that he believed in violence when it was necessary to win. He said that if the destruction of property seemed necessary to bring results, then he believed in the destruction of property.

A. Johannsen of California, State Organizer for the Building Trades of California, and General Organizer for the United Brotherhood of Carpenters, in his testimony before the United States Commission on Industrial Relations at Washington in May, 1915, in speaking of the reelection of Frank Ryan, President of the National Structural Iron Workers' Union, among other things thanked the Lord that the union had the courage to reelect him President after he had been convicted as a participant in the dynamiting crimes of the Structural Iron Workers. He further expressed the hope that it was true that the convicted dynamiters, after being re-elected to office by the Iron Workers, were met by a procession of applause at Fort Leavenworth while on their way to prison, and that President Ryan performed his official duties while there, and rendered his official reports as President of a union of 10,000 members and a part of the American Federation of Labor.

In contradistinction to the opinion of Mr. Johannsen, to the effect that he thanked the Lord that the union had the courage to reelect Frank Ryan President after he had been convicted as a participant in the dynamiting crimes of the Structural Iron Workers, we have the opinion of Dr. Charles W. Eliot, President Emeritus of Harvard University, who, in his testimony before the United States Commission on Industrial Relations at New York, January 29th, 1915, in referring to this very instance, said, in answer to the question as to how he regarded the action of the Structural Iron Workers' Union in reelecting Frank Ryan President after his conviction of crime, "As a serious moral offense against the community as a whole."

Speaking about respecting court labor injunctions, Witness Johannsen said:

> I don't think the power of an injunction goes much beyond the courage of those who are enjoined. I think that if a person is convinced in his own mind and his own feelings that his case is just, that his demands for an increase of wages, or whatever the fight may be—if you think and feel you are right, why then go ahead. Never mind about those pieces of paper.

On being asked whether he (Johannsen) believed that Frank Ryan, President of the Structural Iron Workers' National Union, and his associates, were innocent men railroaded to prison, he said that he did, and that he was satisfied they never committed any crime against labor or a better society, and were therefore unjustly convicted. This was his attitude, despite his attention having been called to the opinion and decision rendered by the Circuit Court of Appeals, including Judges Baker, Seaman, and Kohlsaat, against whose integrity and fairness no whisper had ever been heard, and who seemingly went into the evidence in the dynamiting cases most exhaustively and carefully, and who, among other things, in their decision, said—

> The facts thus recited, as proven by the Government on the trial, may be mentioned in part as follows: Almost 100 explosions thus

occurred, damaging and destroying buildings and bridges in process of erection where the work was being done by open shop concerns, and no explosions took place in connection with work of a similar character, where the work was done by closed shop concerns. . . . In connection with this work of destruction, dynamite and nitro-glycerine was purchased and stolen, and various storage places arranged to conveniently store such explosives which were to be used in the destruction of property in the various States referred to. . . . Large quantities of dynamite and nitro-glycerine were at various times stored in the vaults of the Association at Indianapolis, and also in the basement of the building. . . . Four explosions occurred in one night at the same hour in Indianapolis, and explosions were planned to take place on the same night, two hours apart, at Omaha, Neb., and Columbus, Ind., and the explosions so planned did occur on the same night, at about the same time, instead of two hours apart, owing to the fact that one clock was defective. . . . All the dynamite and nitro-glycerine . . . including the expenses incident to the stealing of the dynamite, were paid out of the funds of the International Association, and these funds were drawn from the Association upon checks signed by the Secretary-Treasurer, John J. McNamara, and the President, Frank M. Ryan, plaintiff in error.

The written correspondence on the part of many of the plaintiffs in error . . . furnish manifold evidence not only of understanding between the correspondents of the purposes of the primary conspiracy, but many thereof convey information or direction for the use of the explosives, while others advise of the destruction which has occurred, and each points unerringly not only to the understanding that the agency therein was that of the conspirators, but as well to the necessary steps in its performance of transporting the explosives held for such use. This line of evidence clearly tends to prove, and may well be deemed convincing of the fact on the part of many, if not all, of the correspondents.

Plaintiff Frank M. Ryan was President of the Association and of its Executive Board, and was active manager and leader of the contest, and policies carried on throughout the years of the strike and destructive explosions in evidence. Letters written and received by him at various stages of the contest clearly tend to prove his familiarity with and management of the long course of destroying open shop structures, however guarded in expression. He was at the headquarters of the Association for the supervision of operations periodically, usually two or three days each month, uniformly attended the meetings there of the Executive Board, and made frequent visits to the field of activities. . . . He signed all of the checks in evidence for payments for expenditures for purchase, storage, and conveyance of explosives. . . . Many other letters in evidence, both from and to him, however disguised in terms, may well authorize an inference of his complete understanding of, and complicity for, the explosions, both in plans and execution.[9]

Masses of testimony were filed with the Commissions to prove that organized labor at times resorted to a policy of lawlessness. Among other

[9] Washington Hearings, May 1915, U.S. Commission on Industrial Relations, p. 1004-13.

documents may be cited a magazine under the title of *A Policy of Lawlessness*, a partial record of riot, assault, murder, and intimidation, occurring in strikes of the Iron Moulders' Union, during 1904-5-6-7, published by the National Founders' Association, in which are given, as a partial list taken from court records, a great number of instances of violence on the part of labor unionists in labor disputes; and also a document published as a report, submitted by the Committee on Labor Disputes of the Cleveland Chamber of Commerce, entitled *Violence in Labor Disputes*, giving hundreds of instances where unionists had resorted to violence in labor troubles in that community alone.

Mr. Luke Grant, special investigator for the United States Commission on Industrial Relations, in his report to the Commission on the National Erectors' Association and the International Association of Bridge and Structural Iron Workers, says:

> Do they [the unions] believe in violence? They did not destroy property and they don't know who did. They probably adopted resolutions denouncing the unknown perpetrators, and offering a reward for their arrest and conviction. The Western Federation of Miners, in convention, offered a reward for the arrest of the men who blew up the Independence depot in June, 1904, killing 14 men. Harry Orchard afterward confessed that he and Steve Adams did it, acting as agents for the officers of the union.
>
> In this way do union men collectively approve of violence, that few if any of them would individually permit.

Referring to the industrial war between the National Erectors' Association and the Structural Iron Workers' Union, Mr. Grant continues to say:

> When the hopelessness of the situation became apparent to the union officials, resort was made to the destruction of property. Diplomacy was out of the question, so dynamite was tried.

The report of Luke Grant brings out the fact that the Structural Iron Workers had no grievances against their employers in the matter of wages, hours, or working conditions. The only question at issue was that of the closed shop. To enforce the closed shop, the Structural Iron Workers seemed to feel themselves justified in dynamiting over one hundred properties and destroying many innocent lives.

Police Commissioner Arthur Woods, of the City of New York, in his testimony before the United States Commission on Industrial Relations, in May, 1915, at Washington, D. C., speaking of violence by labor unions, among other things said:

> The result of our investigation shows a course of procedure like this: There would be a strike and the strikers would retain some gunmen to do whatever forcible or violent work they needed. The employer, to meet this violence, would in a comparatively small percentage of cases, and not as many cases as the gunmen were employed on the other side, hire a private detective agency. The function that the gunmen were to perform was to intimidate the workers that were hired to take the place of the strikers. . . . There were three indictments for murder in the first degree.

The question was asked Police Commissioner Woods in how far his investigations had warranted the statement that appeared in the New York Herald of May 14, 1915, reading as follows:

> Several of the indictments mentioned assault upon members of the union, and in this connection District Attorney Perkins said last night that the reign of lawlessness was caused by union leaders who wished to perpetuate themselves in power, who hired assailants to assault contenders in their own unions for their places, and who used their union offices to extort blackmail under threats from employers. Seven men are indicted for assault in a riot for control of the union. Four men are indicted for hiring Dopey Benny's men to go to a nonunion factory and rough-house the employees as they left, and wreck the plant. A dozen workers were wounded in that fight.
>
> Six union men are accused of extortion and assault in using violence to collect a fine of $100 upon an employer. Four others are accused of hiring the Dopey Benny band to shoot up a nonunion factory. Many shops were fired. The factory suffered a damage of $1,000 and several persons were injured. Other indictments mentioned cases where the band was employed by union leaders to attack nonunion workers, to wreck factories, and even to assault nonunion men who opposed the leaders. (pp. 964-5.)

To all of the foregoing, Police Commissioner Woods replied, "That is the general line of things that we found."

> One of the ablest and clear-headed exponents of the cause of labor that testified before this Commission was Morris Hillquit of New York. In speaking of violence in labor troubles, he is quoted as saying,[10] that the resort to violence and lawbreaking was "ethically unjustifiable and tactically suicidal." Mr. Hillquit pointed out that wherever any group or section of the labor movement "has embarked upon a policy of 'breaking the law' or using 'any weapon which will win a fight,' whether such policy was styled 'terrorism,' 'propaganda' of the deed, 'direct action,' 'sabotage,' or 'anarchism,' it has invariably served to destroy the movement, by attracting to it professional criminals, infesting it with spics, leading the workers to needless and senseless slaughter, and ultimately engendering a spirit of disgust and reaction."

Robert Hunter, commenting on the foregoing statement made by Morris Hillquit, says (p. viii):

> It will, I think, be clear to the reader that the history of the labor movement during the last half century fully sustains Mr. Hillquit's position.

Apprenticeship Rules

The question of apprenticeships has led to much industrial strife and consequent industrial unrest, where unions have arbitrarily determined the number of apprentices that the employer may take on.

[10] Robert Hunter, Violence and the Labor Movement, p. viii.

Where this practice has prevailed the union employer has, in competition with the nonunion employer, been seriously handicapped. The remedy for this evil lies obviously in a joint agreement under the direction of the proposed State Industrial Commissions, in which each side has an equal voice in determining the proper quota of apprentices to be employed.

In conclusion, it is our desire to point out that organized labor is chargeable with its fullest share of creating causes of industrial unrest, because of its sympathetic strikes, its jurisdictional disputes, its labor union politics, its contract breaking, its resort to violence in time of trouble, its policy of limited output, and its closed shop policy. There is an abundance of evidence in the records of the Commission to show that organized labor is also guilty of intimidating courts, more especially the lower criminal courts, to deal lightly with labor offenders charged with criminal assaults in labor troubles; and that some judges, more especially in the lower courts, toady to organized labor for vote-getting purposes, and dismiss union labor men guilty of law breaking, or impose on them nominal penalties out of all proportion to the crimes committed.

These various policies have brought about their fullest share among the workers, to say nothing of the injury inflicted on employers and on society, of poverty, suffering, wretchedness, misery, discontent, and crime. Organized labor will never come into its own, and will indefinitely postpone the day when its many commendable objects will be achieved in the broadest sense, until it will cut out of its program sympathetic strikes, until it can prevent cessation of work in jurisdictional disputes, until it can more successfully prevent labor union politics, until it can teach many in its rank and file to regard more sacredly their trade agreements, until it can penalize its members for resorting to violence in labor disputes, and until it can make it a labor union offense to limit output.

Organized labor may ask, "If we cut out the evil policies complained of from our program, what offensive and defensive weapons will be left us with which to protect ourselves against the unfair employer?"

The answer is that when labor is effectively organized, it has two most powerful weapons at its command that the employer, as a rule, dreads, and fears because of the great damage these weapons can inflict on him, namely, the strike and the primary boycott, both of which are within the moral and legal rights of the worker to use.

Generally speaking, the evils complained of have been eliminated from the program of the railway brotherhoods. As a consequence, railway managers do not hesitate to recognize and to deal with the railway unions, to their mutual advantage and satisfaction, with the result that collective bargaining has become the common condition in the railway world. Railway strikes and lockouts have now become most infrequent, and industrial unrest due to these causes in this sphere of activity has become greatly minimized.

If these evils are eliminated by organized labor from its program, much will have been done to stimulate collective bargaining and to minimize the existing causes of industrial unrest. The remedies for all these evils do not lie with the employer; they rest wholly and solely with unionists. The responsibility for the growth of these evils, in our opinion, rests primarily with unionists who neglect their union duties, and who are as unmindful of their duties as union men as are many voters of their civic duty who remain at home on election day.

Relations Between Organizations and Their Members

We have faith in the honesty of purpose, in the fairness of spirit, and in the law-abiding character of the American worker, and we do not believe that the rank and file of American wage earners are in favor of many of the practices of some unions which have subjected unionism to so much severe, but just, criticism. We believe it is the duty of each unionist regularly to attend the meetings of his union, in order that democracy shall prevail in trade unions instead of an autocracy or despotism, which inevitably follows where the best membership fails to attend union meetings, and thus permits the affairs of the organization to get into the hands of incompetent, ill-judging, or dishonest officials, who, for their selfish ends, abuse the power and authority vested in them.

Wherever there are found honest, high-minded, clear-headed, labor leaders—and in the course of our investigations and hearings we have come into close personal touch with many such as these, who have commanded our esteem and respect—it will be found that, as a rule, they represent unions where the better membership takes a lively and active interest in the welfare of the association, and regards it as a sacred duty to regularly attend its meetings.

We say frankly that if we were wage earners we would be unionists, and as unionists we should feel the keen responsibility of giving the same attention to our trade union duties as to our civic duties.

The ideal day in the industrial world will be reached when all labor disputes will be settled as a result of reason, and not as a result of force. This ideal day can be hastened if the employers, on the one hand, will earnestly strive to place themselves in the position of the worker, and look at the conditions not only through the eye of the employer but through the eye of the worker; and if the worker will strive to place himself in the position of the employer, and look at the conditions not only through the eye of the worker but through the eye of the employer.

This, of course, means the strongest kind of organization on both sides. It means that employers must drive out of the ranks of their associations the law breaker, the labor contract breaker, and the exploiters of labor. It also means that, in the interests of fairness, every Board of Directors of an industrial enterprise should have within its organization a committee for the special purpose of keeping the Board of Directors advised as to the condition of their workers. And it finally means that trade unions must, in order to minimize the causes of industrial unrest, among other things remove the weak spots in unionism set forth herein, thereby hastening the day when employers will no longer fear to recognize and deal with unions, and when collective bargaining shall thus become the common condition.

Finally, we feel that employers, individually and through their associations, in common with thoughtful representatives of labor, should give their fullest share of thought and lend their heartiest cooperation in aiding to solve, through constructive legislation and other ways, the great problems of vocational education, continuation schools, woman and child labor apprenticeship, hours of labor, housing, sickness insurance, workmen's compensation, safety measures, old age pensions, and unemployment. The hope is therefore expressed that employers will strive to work *with* rather than *against* intelligent labor representatives in aiding, through these various movements, to lessen industrial unrest and to still further improve the condition of wage earners and their dependents.

37

Appeal to Superordinate Goals

A New Industrial Creed

JOHN D. ROCKEFELLER, JR.

The basic facts as to the fundamental relations between the parties in industry are as right, as just and as vital for the common success of the industry of today as in the earlier times. The question which confronts the student of industrial problems is how to re-establish personal relations and co-operation in spite of the changed conditions. The answer is not doubtful or questionable, but absolutely clear and unmistakable: Through adequate representation of the four parties thereto in the councils of industry (Capital, Management, Labor, and Community).

Various methods of representation have been adopted, of which perhaps the most conspicuous is the labor union. As regards the organization of labor, it is just as proper and advantageous for labor to associate itself into organized groups for the advancement of its legitimate interests as for capital to combine for the same objects. Such associations of labor manifest themselves in collective bargaining, in an effort to secure better working and living conditions, in providing machinery whereby grievances may easily and without prejudice to the individual be taken up with the management.

But organization has its danger. Organized capital sometimes conducts itself in an unworthy manner, contrary to law and in disregard of the interest both of labor and the public. Such organizations cannot be too strongly condemned or too vigorously dealt with. Although they are the exception, such publicity is generally given to their unsocial acts that all organizations of capital, however rightly managed or broadly beneficent, are thereby brought under suspicion.

Likewise it sometimes happens that organizations of labor are conducted without just regard for the rights of the employer or the public and methods and practices adopted which, because unworthy or unlawful, are deserving of public censure. Such organizations of labor bring discredit and suspicion upon other organizations which are legitimate and useful, just as is the case with improper organizations of capital, and they should be similarly dealt with.

Fundamentally Sound

We should not, however, allow the occasional failure in the working of the principle of the organization of labor to prejudice us against the principle itself, for the principle is fundamentally sound. In the further development of the organization of labor and of large business, the public interest as well as the interest of labor and capital alike will be best advanced by whatever stimulates every man to do the best work of which he is capable; by a fuller recognition of the common interest of employers

Reprinted from *Current Affairs*, December 16, 1918, pp. 7, 42-3, 46.

Relations Between Organizations and Their Members

and employed, and by an earnest effort to dispel distrust and hatred and to promote good will.

While labor unions have secured for labor in general many advantages in hours, wages and standards of working conditions, a large proportion of the workers of the country are outside of these organizations and are to that extent not in a position to bargain collectively.

War Labor Board

Since the United States went into the war the representation of both labor and capital in common councils has been brought about through the War Labor Board, composed equally of men from the ranks of labor and the ranks of capital. Whenever questions of dispute have arisen in various industries in which there was no internal machinery which could deal with them to the mutual satisfaction of the parties in interest, the War Labor Board has stepped in and made its findings and recommendations, which have been accepted and adopted by both labor and capital in practically every instance. In this way more continuous operation has been made possible and the resort to the strike and lockout has been less frequent.

In England there have been made during the past year three important government investigations and reports looking toward a more complete program of representation and co-operation on the part of labor and capital. The first is commonly known as the Whitley Report, made by the Reconstruction Committee, now the Ministry of Reconstruction, through a Sub-Committee on Relations Between Employers and Employed, of which the Right Hon. J. H. Whitley, M.P., was chairman.

Whitley Plan

The Whitley plan seeks to unite the organizations of labor and capital by a bond of common interest in a common venture; it changes at a single stroke the attitude of these powerful aggregations of class interest from one of militancy to one of social service; it establishes a new relation in industry. Problems old and new, says the report, will find their solution in a frank partnership of knowledge, experience and good will.

Another investigation and report was made by a Commission on Industrial Unrest appointed by the Prime Minister, which made the following interesting recommendations:

1. That the principle of the Whitley report as regards industrial councils be adopted.
2. That each trade should have a constitution.
3. That labor should take part in the affairs of industry as partners rather than as employes in the narrow sense of the term.
4. That closer contact should be set up between the employers and employed.

The third report, prepared by the Ministry of Labor, on the question of the constitution and working of the works committee in a number of industries, is a valuable treatise on the objects, functions and methods of procedure which have been tried in actual practice.

These reports, together with a report on reconstruction, made by a sub-committee of the British Labor party, outlining its reconstruction program, a most comprehensive and thoughtful document, indicates the extent and variety of the study which has been given to the great problem of industrial reconstruction in England. All point toward the need of more adequate representation of labor in the conduct of industry and the importance of closer relations between labor and capital.

A simpler plan than those to which reference has been made, less comprehensive and complete, building from the bottom up, has been in operation for varying periods of time in a number of industries in this country, notably the Standard Oil Company of New Jersey, the Colorado Fuel and Iron Company, the Consolidation Coal Company, several of the works of the General Electric Company, and others, and is worthy of serious consideration in this connection.

Beginning with the election of representatives in a single plant, it is capable of indefinite development to meet the complex needs of any industry and a wide extension to include all industries. Equally applicable in industries where union or non-union labor, or both, are employed, it seeks to provide full and fair representation of labor, capital and management, taking cognizance also of the community, to which representation could easily be accorded, and has thus far developed a spirit of co-operation and good will which commends it to both employer and employee. The outstanding features of the plan are briefly as follows:

Chosen Representatives

Representatives chosen by the employes in proportion to their number from their fellow workers in each plant form a basis of the plan. Joint committees, composed of an equal number of employees or their representatives and an equal number of officers of the company, are found in each plant or district.

These committees deal with questions of co-operation and conciliation, safety and accident, sanitation, health and housing, recreation and education. Joint conferences of representatives and officers of the company are held in the various districts several times each year, and there is also an annual joint conference, at which reports from all districts are received and considered.

Another important feature of the plan is an officer known as the President's Industrial Representative, whose duty it is to visit currently all the plants and confer with the representatives, as well as to be available always for conference at the request of the representatives.

Thus it will be seen that the employes, through their representatives chosen from among themselves, are in constant touch and conference with the owners through their representatives and the officers in regard to matters pertaining to their common interest.

The employes' right of appeal is the third outstanding feature of the plan. Any employe with a grievance, real or imaginary, may go with it at once to his representatives, who frequently find there is no real ground for grievance and are able to so convince the employe. But if a real grievance exists or dissatisfaction on the part of the employe continues, the matter is carried to the local boss, foreman or superintendent, where, in the majority of cases, questions are amicably and satisfactorily settled.

Further Appeal

Further appeal is open to the aggrieved employe to the higher officers and to the president, and if satisfaction is not had here, the court of last appeal may be the Industrial Commission of the State, where such a commission exists; the State Labor Board, or a committee of arbitration. Experience proves that the vast majority of difficulties which occur in an industry arise between the workmen and subordinate officers with whom they are in daily contact.

These petty officials are sometimes arbitrary, and it is by their attitude and action that the higher officials and the stockholders are judged. Obviously, the right sort of appeal from their decision is important, and, even if seldom availed of, tends of itself to modify their attitude.

A further feature of the plan is the employes' bill of rights. This covers such matters as the right to caution and suspension before discharge, except for such serious offenses as are posted at the works, the right to hold meetings at appropriate places outside of working hours, the right without discrimination to membership or non-membership in any society, fraternity or union, and the right of appeal to which reference has just been made.

Where some such plan as this has been in operation for a considerable space of time, some of the results obtained are:

First–Uninterrupted operation of the plants and increased output.
Second–Improved working and living conditions.
Third–Frequent and close contact between employes and officers.
Fourth–The elimination of grievances as disturbing factors.
Fifth–Good will developed to a high degree.
Sixth–The creation of a community spirit.

Based as it is upon principles of justice to all those interested in its operation, its success can be counted on so long as it is carried out in a spirit of sincerity and fair play. Furthermore, it is a vital factor in re-establishing personal relations between the parties in interest and developing a genuine spirit of brotherhood among them.

Here, then, would seem to be a method of providing representation which is just, which is effective, which is applicable to all employes whether organized or unorganized, to all employers whether in associations or not, which does not compete or interfere with organizations or associations in existence, and which, while developed in a single industrial plant as a unit, may be expanded to include all plants of the same industry, as well as all industries.

If the foregoing points which I have endeavored to make are sound, might not the four parties to industry subscribe to an industrial creed somewhat as follows:

1. I believe that labor and capital are partners, not enemies; that their interests are common interests, not opposed, and that neither can attain the fullest measure of prosperity at the expense of the other, but only in association with the other.
2. I believe that the community is an essential party to industry, and that it should have adequate representation with the other parties.
3. I believe that the purpose of industry is quite as much to advance social well-being as material well-being and that in the pursuit of that purpose the interests of the community should be carefully considered, the well-being of the employes as respects living and

working conditions should be fully guarded, management should be adequately recognized and capital should be justly compensated, and that failure in any of these particulars means loss to all four.

4. I believe that every man is entitled to an opportunity to earn a living, to fair wages, to reasonable hours of work and proper working conditions, to a decent home, to the opportunity to play, to learn, to worship and to love, as well as to toil, and that the responsibility rests as heavily upon industry as upon government or society, to see that these conditions and opportunities prevail.
5. I believe that industry, efficiency and initiative, wherever found, should be encouraged and adequately rewarded and that indolence, indifference and restriction of production should be discountenanced.
6. I believe that the provision of adequate means for uncovering grievances and promptly adjusting them, is of fundamental importance to the successful conduct of industry.
7. I believe that the most potent measure in bringing about industrial harmony and prosperity is adequate representation of the parties in interest; that existing forms of representation should be carefully studied and availed of in so far as they may be found to have merit and are adaptable to the peculiar conditions in the various industries.
8. I believe that the most effective structure of representation is, that which is built from the bottom up, which includes all employees, and, starting with the election of representatives in each industrial plant, the formation of joint works committees, of joint district councils and annual joint conferences of all the parties in interest in a single industrial corporation, can be extended to include all plants in the same industry, all industries in a community, in a nation and in the various nations.
9. I believe that the application of right principles never fails to effect right relations; that the letter killeth and the spirit maketh alive; that forms are wholly secondary while attitude and spirit are all important, and that only as the parties in industry are animated by the spirit of fair play, justice to all and brotherhood, will any plans which they may mutually work out succeed.
10. I believe that that man renders the greatest social service who so co-operates in the organization of industry as to afford to the largest number of men the greatest opportunity for self-development and the enjoyment by every man of those benefits which his own work adds to the wealth of civilization.

The Social Ideal

In the days when kings and queens reigned over their subjects, the gratification of the desires of those in high places was regarded as of supreme moment, but in these days the selfish pursuit of personal ends at the expense of the group can and will no longer be tolerated. Men are rapidly coming to see that human life is of infinitely greater value than material wealth, that the health, happiness and well-being of the individual, however humble, is not to be sacrificed to the selfish aggrandizement of the more fortunate or more powerful.

Modern thought is placing less emphasis on material considerations. It is recognizing that the basis of national progress, whether industrial or social, is the health, efficiency and spiritual development of the people. Never has there been a more profound belief in human life than today. Whether men work with brain or brawn, they are human beings, with the same cravings, the same aspirations, the same hatreds, the same capacity for suffering and for enjoyment.

Standpatters Face Failure

As the leaders of industry face this period of reconstruction, what will their attitude be? Will it be that of the standpatters, who take no account of the extraordinary changes which have come over the face of the civilized world and have taken place in the minds of men, who say: "What has been and is must continue to be—with our backs to the wall we will fight it out along the old lines or go down with the ship," who attempt stubbornly to resist the inevitable, and arming themselves to the teeth, invite open warfare with the other parties in industry, the certain outcome of which will be financial loss, inconvenience and suffering to all, the development of bitterness and hatred, and in the end the bringing about through legislation if not by force of conditions far more drastic and radical than could now be amicably arrived at through mutual concession in friendly conference?

The New Spirit

Or will it be an attitude, in which I myself profoundly believe, which takes cognizance of the inherent right and justice of the principle underlying the new order, which recognizes that mighty changes are inevitable, many of them desirable, which, not waiting until forced to adopt new methods, takes the lead in calling together the parties in interest for a round-table conference to be held in a spirit of justice, fair play and brotherhood, with a view to working out some plan for co-operation which will insure to all those concerned adequate representation, an opportunity to earn a fair wage under proper working and living conditions, with such restrictions as to hours as shall leave time not alone for food and sleep, but also for recreation and the development of the higher things of life.

Never was there such an opportunity as exists today for the industrial leader with clear vision and broad sympathy permanently to bridge the chasm that is daily gaping wider between the parties in interest and to establish a solid foundation for industrial prosperity, social improvement and national solidarity.

Future generations will rise up and call those men blessed who have the courage of their convictions, a proper appreciation of the value of human life as contrasted with material gain, and who, embued with the spirit of brotherhood, will lay hold of the great opportunity for leadership which is open to them today.

In conclusion let it be said that upon the heads of these leaders—it matters not to which of the four parties they belong—who refuse to reorganize their industrial households in the light of the modern spirit, will rest the responsibility for such radical and drastic measures as may later be forced upon industry if the highest interests of all are not shortly considered and dealt with in a spirit of fairness. Who, I say, dares to block the wheels of progress, and to fail to recognize and seize the present opportunity of helping to usher in a new era of industrial peace and prosperity?

38

Competing Rather than Mutual Goals: Pragmatism of American Labor

Wages and Some Industrial Fallacies

WILLIS WISLER

Our present critical condition in industry is due almost wholly to labor's new self-assertion. It is hardly necessary to enter into the many reasons for this new self-assertion of labor. We know its sudden growth has been fostered by the war. Great emergencies have a levelling effect; artificial barriers can not stand up at such times. It is not so much what labor has done that disturbs employers as what it is emboldened to suspect.

Under autocracy this new mood of challenge must lead to some form of protest. The caste that strives to impose its control upon labor must either justify itself by leadership, it must stand aside, or it must establish itself by violence.

The musket made the medieval peasant more deadly than his lanced and plumed overlord, and by this fact it marked the passing of a social order. Trained intelligence may be now about to repeat the event.

If rule by caste, high or low, shall ever come upon the United States it can only be by the creation of some caste lines imposed by an ill-advised industrial Bourbonism. The degree of fear an employer of men expresses concerning the menace of "radicalism" in this country is a fair index of his real autocratic intent and ideals.

Men, however, who are familiar with the spectacle of their fellows rising from the ranks of wage-earners to places of the highest affluence and esteem, can have no intention to tear down the golden ladder of opportunity. The most passing comparison must show the very real differences between our conditions and those of Europe. The very elements making for success of radicalism abroad are until now happily lacking here.

There is, however, a condition—though not a fact—of caste that threatens. It grows out of a shrewd though perhaps mistaken conviction on both sides that solidarity is the best protection.

While the American is a wage-earner he senses the advantages he has in collective bargaining. In solidarity he sees his defense against the monopoly of jobs in the hands of the employers.

The employer, too, compels solidarity so far as he can by keeping labor in the "laboring class." He must look with scant favor on his employe climbing out of the wage and vocational limitations he has tried to fix at the hiring moment.

Yet both violate solidarity when opportunity offers. The wage-earner becomes an employer if he can do so. The employer recruits his executives

Reprinted from the *American Federationist*, Vol. 26, November, 1919, pp. 1036-1040.

necessarily, for the most part, "from the ranks." Thus with us "solidarity" in the old world sense is a technique of industrial strategy rather than a social fact that can be physically perpetuated.

Behind this technique of industrial strategy is functioning a bread and butter philosophy. Perhaps it were better to say a "bread and butter opportunism." Organized labor in America is essentially pragmatic; it gets all it can whenever it can. I am speaking now as a layman. I shall surely not attempt to speak for organized labor. But there has certainly been no stampede to any philosopho-political program such as we are fond of attributing to English labor.

Here in America we are transients in labor—at least we so love to assume. We require no political upheaval to break our way through economic barriers. We ask only to be decently comfortable and self-respecting while we tarry at the bench or at the machine. Only men reconciled to no escape by industrial effort grow urgent and evolve philosophies.

It is our good fortune to represent in the eyes of the world of labor that best standard. When American wages and standards of working and of living conditions shall have become—through international knowledge—world standards, the day of American exploitation of foreign labor and the American use of foreign labor as American labor's competitor will have passed. The fortunes of American industry must rest on some other basis than the misfortune of any group of workers.

For the accomplishment of this great project, the world enfranchisement of labor, the machinery is now in the making. An international labor congress can concentrate, by centralization, the energies and intelligence of labor. Universality of knowledge will level up the workers of all nations. And for this project America is well fitted to furnish the sanest leadership —a leadership which it will he hoped will not attempt to create a fictitious dignity of labor by the perpetuation of a caste, but which will insist on decent living and unobstructed opportunity for wage-earners on the sole basis of their being human beings.

All that sincere persons, who differ in opinion, need do to come to agreement is to argue their differences sufficiently. The reason most controversies end in protracted antagonism is that they have not been carried to the essential limits of definition—the coincidence of meaning in the fact has not been reached.

One of the commonest faults is classification by coincident phenomena. A good illustration of this is the resentment of organized labor against the physical examinations of new employes. Physical examinations of applicants has been sometimes used by employers or their agents to exclude so-called "troublemakers." Therefore, physical examination of new employes needs to be abolished? Surely we are capable of better reasoning than that. It is not the physical examination that is bad, but the misuse of this sound precaution for discriminatory purposes.

This kind of loose reasoning has done much harm. It seems as though this kind of reasoning has placed organized labor at a disadvantage with regard also to industrial representation. The condemnation by organized labor should have been not against industrial representation, because much of it is specious, but it should have been against the obstruction of absolute freedom of suffrage and against the sinister emasculation of its legislative function.

The real ground for objection by American organized labor to industrial representation is better indicated in its reference to these industrial representation plans as "Company or Employer Unions." It is fairly evident that organized labor has all along felt sure of an essential insincerity on the part of American employers.

The American Federation of Labor, it seems, fears that once American organized labor has been disorganized and rendered pliant by the quasi-liberality of industrial representation plans outside of unions, then—so say the leaders of organized labor—the wage-earner will again find himself alone and stripped of his defenses in the perpetual wage war.

This may be so, but it might well work the other way. Company unions, subjected to oppression, might well make common cause with other company unions in their industry and so again coalesce into a national organization with its hands well trained and gripping the very vitals of their industries.

Organized labor might well give this possibility its closest thought. By capturing all genuine works committees and destroying the rest it would have gained access to the essentials of wages, hours, working conditions, and to economic policies through a door which the employer himself has opened to labor. Thus, organized labor might recoup the poor strategy which let employers strip its crafts of their monopoly of that trade skill which employers, by experts and research and vestibule schools, have shrewdly made their property. In the resultant spectacular rise of the semi-skilled—the great menace to craft unionism—should have been read the ominous handwriting on the wall.

Organized labor may be distrustful of the employer's disposition to respect the rights of his employe, but they seem to be no less distrustful of the employe's ability to safeguard his rights. The employer, they say, has access to experts—trained men to advise him. Why, then, shall the employe be denied a like opportunity to avail himself of the organized skill the unions can supply to him? Merely to enfranchise a worker does not automatically endow him with political competency. To elevate him to the office of works representative does not assure to his associates, *ipso facto*, adequate representation. But let us bear in mind that this initial inexperience will pass with time and use and that employers may find themselves in time matched eye to eye with men who can effectively demand from them genuine leadership or retirement.

The facile assumption of the equality of labor and capital, of employe and employer, is *prima facie* untenable. If this were true there would hardly be employes. Nor are their interests at all so mutual as our popular platitude would assume. There is, to be sure, a common interest in the creation of wealth, but in its distribution there can be little of mutuality. Until some equitable distribution, accepted on both sides, by a common compromise agreement or because of an inescapable accuracy of apportionment, this distribution must be governed by the relative strength and the effective force applied on each side.

Managerial skill at the point where planning meets production is the supreme strategic point in future industry. The forces which shall control the production, executives who directly supervising labor, translate plan into product, are the forces that can control industry. Employers already have sensed this and they are hastening to bind to them these minor executives by developing foremen's training courses.

It is about this participation in management and in the division of the wealth produced in the industry that the impending industrial contest must revolve. Profit sharing can not satisfy this contest. The fallacy of profit sharing lies deeper than its mistaken psychology, deeper than its inconsistency in not sharing deficits, deeper than its assessing on the worker in reduced dividends losses usually beyond the effect of his individual enterprise and industry; it lies in an intrinsic dishonesty. Many employers, moved by the most honest intention, have been perplexed at the general and apparently increasing distaste among their employes for profit-sharing systems.

In large measure this disfavor rests in an instinctive resentment against the assumption by the employer in such plans of priority to claim on all surplus over the cost of production. The employer by granting profit sharing takes credit for a special virtue. To the laborer this must often smack of that benevolence of the robber who graciously makes to his victim a gift from part of the spoils.

There are arguments for deferred wages, but for profit sharing—except under a real partnership—none that are economically sound. The conviction of the worker that wages have been curtailed to effect the dividend is, so far as the economic fact is concerned, a correct view. That such is the intention of the employer—either to cover poor management or to keep down the current wage scale—may sometimes be true. But even if it were not true the fact would remain that any attempt to solve the wage problem by a "profit-sharing system" is clear proof of a complete misconception of the meaning of wages.

Adam Smith, back in the eighteenth century, established the cost of living as the controlling factor in the law of supply and demand in labor. There are modifying factors, such as working conditions and sales prices, but in the main, in actual shop practice, little improvement on Adam Smith has yet been made.

When the mechanistic theory of labor came in with Taylor, Emerson, and the "efficiency school," the employers of labor who became adherents of the school of management proceeded confidently upon the scientific concept that labor is a commodity.

So far as labor is a factor to be applied to production like power, and materials, and overhead, they were consistent. The real error lay in not distinguishing between labor as a complex of applied force to be released by a human self-determining being, and value released by an inert and non-sentient mechanism. Even so, labor owes much to this scientific management movement. It replaced the old concept of labor as a chattel, with wages a grudging concession, by the idea of labor as a commodity to be purchased at market rates. Production replaced time, and wages —of necessity under their system—became an incentive rather than a concession.

This, while improving the status of the worker, still fell as far short as ever of the real meaning of wages. For all their bold pretension to science, nothing could be more crudely unscientific than scientific management's interpretation of the meaning of wages. The direct ratio between the worker's actual contribution to the value of the product and his wage they failed to recognize.

To point out that time and motion study assumed such a ratio does not answer this criticism because it is not in any analysis of work into its elements that such a ratio is established, but in the true evaluation of the work performed. In competitive products, where profits are slight, some such ratio may occur but hardly by any consciously deliberate purpose.

The efficiency engineer, persisting in his misconception of wages, tried by the introduction of welfare work to build up the necessary good-will which the mere stimuli of bonuses and premiums could not evoke. Against this there rose inevitably the same unreasoning but proper resentment workers feel against profit sharing. Something that was their own was being withheld to be presented to them in the guise of special reward or benevolence. Wage earners felt deceived and injured even when they knew their employers were well intentioned.

What the wage earner of today wants is that which is his own. If he seems to be asking for a great deal more it is in part because he is human, and in part because he is ill informed; not necessarily ill informed by agitators and extremists, but ill informed in the past by employers and capitalists. So assiduously have these "Captains of Industry" paraded their parlor magic of finance and administration that the groundlings, too well befooled, now clamor for the materialization into their own hands and pockets of the mysteriously conjured coin and rabbits! These impressive gentlemen may have to do more than merely brandish their empty silk hats and turn back their cuffs—they may have to submit, with such good grace as they can muster, to a rather horny-handed and thorough searching.

It will be no easy matter for management to live down the indiscretions of its capitalistic associations. Management, to our thinking, must be divorced from capital. Management must stand on its own merits—a type of labor.

The great problem of the future must be the adequate measurement of the contribution of the three factors—labor, management and capital—to the product so that each may receive its commensurate share.

Capital will continue to scrutinize management before it invests; labor should do the same before it invests. For until labor shall be regarded as an investment and not as an expenditure, no real progress beyond an armed truce can exist.

And if labor shall be regarded as an investment, wages must take some account of depreciation. The worker who invests himself in industry at a wage which aims to meet only current living costs, must expect to find himself in old age a dependent on private or public charity. This is an arrangement neither humane or intelligent. Industry owes a worker, in return for his productive years, a fair and dignified assurance of his being taken care of through his non-productive years. In short his depreciation needs to be written off, whether in the form of a pension by the specific industry he has served, or by the operation of compulsory savings out of an adequate wage, or by the application of state insurance assessed on all industry, it is not necessary at this time to say. The essential principle to keep in mind is that wages that pretend to be a complete return for labor given without making provision for depreciation, disability or superannuation, are economically unsound and can never satisfy labor's unrest.

The time may never come when the refinements of accounting can effect, for the purpose of adequate wages, accurate measurement. In the meantime approximation must do, but approximation by an agency all parties can and will trust.

39

Trying Democracy Out in Industry: 1919

Employment Management, Employee Representation, and Industrial Democracy

WILLIAM M. LEISERSON

Industrial Democracy Means Representation of Organized Interests

Whether we call it "organized labor" or "an organized working force," the subject we are to discuss is democracy in industry; and, as Professor Commons says in his recently published book on Industrial Good-will:

> Representative democracy in industry is representation of organized interests. Individuals who are not organized cannot choose representatives. They must be content with their tacit proxies given to the organized. When once organized they can be consulted in advance of action. The procedure of autocracy is to act first and consult afterwards. . . .
>
> But democracy cannot quickly consult all individuals whose interests are affected. It comes as near as possible to doing this when it consults those who have been freely chosen for the purpose without interference from other classes, so that they really represent the interests of the class affected.

All Employees' Organizations Not Examples of Democracy

The mistake we are likely to make in dealing with this problem is to assume that because industrial democracy necessarily involves an organized labor force capable of acting as a unit through its representatives, therefore every organization of working people in industrial plants is an example of industrial democracy. Committees and employee-representation plans are spreading rapidly throughout the industries of this country and employment managers as well as employers are assuming that all these organizations, no matter what their form or purpose, are providing industrial democracy for their employees.

As a matter of fact, however, a study of the employees' organizations now in existence will show that they classify themselves into three general groups, and the element of democracy is not present in one of them, nor is it present in each of the other two to the same extent.

Reprinted from an address before the *National Association of Employment Managers*, Cleveland, Ohio, May 23, 1919.

Welfare or Shop Committees

The first group of employees' organization plans may be called welfare committees or shop committees proper. These are merely advisory organizations of the working force selected by either the management or the employees for the purpose of conferring with the foreman, with safety directors or personnel and service managers regarding problems related to working conditions in the plants. The matters with which these committees are concerned are primarily safety and welfare work with a small number trying to extend their activities to include grievances. Although these committees are constantly hailed as examples of industrial democracy, they involve no element of collective bargaining or joint control over terms and conditions of employment. Complete authority is centered in the management; the committees merely giving advice and suggestions which may or may not be accepted by the management. The powers, functions, and methods of operation of these committees identify them with the service work of the plants rather than with problems of bargaining, of wages, hours, and shop discipline, which, as I shall show presently, are the subjects that must be handled, and to an extent controlled, by any organization that pretends to provide democratic control of industry.

Employers' Unions

The second group of organizations may be called "employers' unions." In this group are included all those plans which either explicitly say, as does the Midvale Steel & Ordnance Co. plan, "We recognize the right of wage earners to bargain collectively with their employers . . .," or which by implication recognize the principle of collective bargaining between the employees and their employers, as do the plans of the Bethlehem Steel Co., the International Harvester Co., and the Colorado Fuel & Iron Co. The employers' organizations in this group represent a long step in the direction of industrial democracy, for they involve getting the consent of the employees who are the governed in industry, in the making of industrial laws. Our Declaration of Independence says that government derives its just powers from the consent of the governed. As political democracy provides for the consent of the governed in the state, so industrial democracy will provide for the consent of the governed in industry. The difference between these "employers' unions" and the ordinary unions known as "organized labor" is that the former are initiated by the employers; they are confined to one company rather than connected with a national organization of employees, and the management is not excluded from the meetings.

Trade Unions

The third group of organized workers are the ordinary labor unions, and they usually involve written or understood agreements between national unions of the employees and individual firms or associations of employers. The agreements invariably cover wages and hours and usually working conditions as well.

Danger of Misconceptions of Employees' Representation

However much the employer whose workers are included in the third group may object to the principle of collective bargaining, he understands thoroughly that his agreement with the union involves that principle. In the second group, however, in the plans we have called "employers' unions," there is not always this clear understanding on the part of the employer of what his employees' organization involves. Where the principle of collective bargaining is present only by implication, as is true in practically all the plans except that of the Midvale Steel Co., it quite often happens that the employer does not realize that his plan involves this principle. The employees, however, usually assume it does not mean anything unless it gives them the opportunity to bargain collectively with their employers. It is hardly necessary for me to point out to a group of employment managers that any misunderstanding like this of the purposes of a plan of employee representation is likely to cause trouble between employer and employee, making the employees feel that they have been deluded, while the employers are likely to think that the workers are ungrateful for all the things the management has been trying to do for them.

Collective Bargaining Basis of Industrial Democracy

In spite of the danger in misunderstandings of this kind a deluge of shop committees and employee-representation plans is flooding the country. Employers, feeling unrest and distrust among their employees, are seizing on these plans as a sort of panacea for all their labor troubles without clearly analyzing their troubles and the nature of the remedies. A great many of our labor difficulties are caused by poor labor management. Democratic organizations of employees will not remove these. Only good management will help in such cases. Employees' organizations are needed to deal with labor troubles that arise under the best management, that grow out of the democratic movement in industry.

Diagnosing the Labor Problem

Before attempting to deal with organization of his employees the employer ought to have a thorough understanding of the labor question. He must analyze the relations between his own management and his working force, and he must have complete knowledge of the labor administration machinery already existing in his plant, which labor relations this machinery is designed to handle and which it is not equipped to handle. This is the diagnosis part of the job and, unfortunately, diagnosing the industrial ills in a plant is usually neglected by both employers and labor experts. Remedies are applied because of their supposed general healing powers, and just now shop committees seem to be the most popular of these patent medicines. You may have heard of the country doctor who, when he did not know how to diagnose a case, gave his patients a concoction to throw them into fits. And he had a good remedy for fits. We must avoid thinking that all labor troubles are just fits that can be cured by one remedy like committees.

Two Kinds of Labor Relations

Let us, therefore, try to analyze the relations between employers and employees, and see if we can find out the nature of various kinds of industrial ills and which of these can be removed by organizing the working force. In any plan or policy of labor management for industrial enterprises two sets of labor relations must be clearly distinguished. First, the personal relations which present the personnel management problems;

and, secondly, the economic collective relations which cover the problems of bargaining and democracy. The names I have given to these are not very apt, but the different kinds of relations exist and must be dealt with in different ways. Perhaps we can get the distinction more clearly if we describe in more detail the two sets of labor relations.

Personal Relations

What I have called the personal relations presents the problem of managing human beings in industry. It means handling the human element that goes into production with the same understanding of the feelings, instincts, prejudices, and characteristics of the workers as the management has of the materials and mechanical forces which it uses. The personal relations in industry cover such questions as hiring, selection, placement, training, promotion, treatment by foremen, health, safety, recreation, lunches, rest periods, etc. These questions, as we shall see presently, are not essentially controversial in nature; they do not involve conflicting interests and they have to be settled by good management and scientific experts rather than by democratic decisions of majorities.

Economic Relations

The second set of labor relations, those which I have called the economic or collective relations, presents quite a different problem. It has to do with the division of the product of industry, with the government or control of industry, with bargaining, wages, hours, unionism, and shop discipline. The return that workers should get for their labor, the number of hours they shall work for what they get, the authority they shall have in fixing terms and conditions of employment, the voice they shall have in making disciplinary rules and punishing infractions of such rules—these are questions that present controversial issues which cannot be settled by any technical expert. They are matters which require democratic decisions and about which a wide diversity of opinion will be permitted in any democratic system of industry.

Employment Problems One Phase of Personal Relations

The personal relations in industry divide themselves further into two sets of problems. First, the employment problems; second, the service problems. The employment problems require an administrative organization—commonly called a centralized employment department—for properly recruiting the work force, selecting and placing the workers, intelligently training them and educating them in their work, and providing an adequate system of promotion and transfer to give advancement to the ambitious and the capable, to make readjustments for those unsuited to certain work or to certain foreman, and to provide steady employment when the amount of work in different departments of the plant fluctuates.

Service Problems Another Phase of Personal Relations

The service problems are somewhat different from these. They arise from the mere fact that a large number of human beings are congregated under one roof and the management must provide a service organization to meet the human needs that develop under such circumstances. Health problems arise, sanitation and medical care are needed. Safety must be looked after and compensation for accidents provided. Then there is the education and protection of the foreigner, the illiterate, and the juvenile employees; providing eating, rest, and recreation facilities, insurance and pensions, maintaining and building up morale. While the service and employment problems differ somewhat in nature, they are alike in that they do not present essentially controversial questions. They are two phases of the personal relations in industry; both are personnel management problems rather than economic problems of democracy or government.

Personnel Management Required Under Any System of Industry

Whether we have a system of privately owned industry or government ownership, or socialism or bolshevism, these problems remain the same. How to manage the working force with due regard to the fact that it is made up of human beings and not some abstract thing called "labor," how to provide for their human needs and how to use their characteristics, feelings, instincts, ideals, and ambitions to get the greatest amount of production—these are problems that confront not only the private industrial manager—Mr. Burleson is up against them too, and so is Lenin, the bolshevist, and Tchaikowsky, the moderate socialist. Democracy is not the problem here—the problem is scientific, efficient management. In these matters of purely personal relations final authority may be safely lodged in the hands of experts and scientists.

Safety and Sanitation Technical Problems

We have made some progress in this direction in the matters of safety and sanitation. Employers and workers are generally agreed that every place of employment should be as safe and sanitary as it is possible to make it. What constitutes a safe and healthful place of employment is a subject for the safety expert, the sanitary engineer, and the medical man to decide after research and investigation rather than for a decision by a democratic majority. It is easy to see that safety and health problems are technical and not essentially controversial, and that the same holds for the other welfare or purely service problems will also be admitted. But it is not so obvious that the other phase of the personal relations, the employment problems, are also technical and need to be handled by experts and scientific men.

Personnel Management Also a Technical Problem

We have a notion that everything in the world is natural except human beings. The materials and the mechanical forces used in industry work according to their natural characteristics and the laws of their being, but humans, we think, act any old way, and if they are employees they ought to do anything the employer expects of them. A manager would never expect wood or concrete to stand strains and do work that only steel can do. He will employ a trained man who understands these materials to decide the different uses to which they are put. But while the manager will say there are lots of workmen with wooden heads, he seldom thinks of employing a trained man who knows the difference between wooden-headed men and other different kinds of men to decide the different uses to which they shall be put. Qualities, characteristics, and capacities of human beings are subjects of scientific study just as are the qualities and characteristics of materials or steam or electrical power. As we expect an engineer to know something about the boilers or turbines he handles, so we ought to expect the men who want to manage the human engines to know something about the emotions, the intellects, the capacities and the resistance power of human beings. Slowly we are beginning to realize this and the movement for expert employment managers is the best evidence of this.

Democracy in Industry Not Technical Problem

But the employment manager or human engineer is a technical man like the safety expert, the medical man, or the sanitary engineer. He is not a statesman or a politician and it is not his function to deal with questions of democratic control or government of industry. Moreover, the better expert he is at his employment work the less qualified he is likely to be at the controversial questions that comprise the second set of labor relations, which we have called the economic collective relations in industry. He is likely to try to decide these by absolute scientific laws when they are very much a matter of opinion and bargaining power.

Welfare Committee Versus Representative Organizations

Committees of employees may be used by the technical men who handle the personal relations in industry, but they are not the same kind of organizations of employees that are needed to deal with the economic or governmental relations. The first can be permitted to offer to the management only advice and suggestions. The second must have a veto power on the acts of the management and will sooner or later demand an equal voice in determining wages and hours and controlling discipline. What we have earlier in this paper called shop committees proper are nothing more than advisory committees on employment and service problems. Welfare committees might be a better name for them. They deal with personal problems only, with personnel management questions; yet either in ignorance or as a subterfuge they are commonly offered to employees as industrial democracy.

Shop Committees Not Necessary for Good Personnel Management

This is playing with fire, or with dynamite, if you prefer that. Any employer who is not ready for collective bargaining, who is not looking toward turning over to his employees 50 per cent of his control over terms and conditions of employment had better beware of shop committees. If he desires merely to improve the personal relations between his management and his men, if he wants only to be brought into closer contact with his employees for the purpose of insuring a square deal to them *as he sees it*, if he wants to see that justice is done to every employee *as he sees justice*, then all he needs is a good employment and service organization. What he wants to accomplish can best be done by expert employment and service managers. Shop committees are not at all necessary and they are likely to confuse the managers with issues of democratic control of industry while the employees may be misled into thinking they are going to have a real voice in the management and become resentful and rebellious when they find out the truth. If these advisory shop committees are used in personnel management work it is very important that most careful explanations be made to the employees so that they will not misunderstand.

Committees Necessary Only When Employer Gives Up Exclusive Control

It is always dangerous for an employer who wishes to maintain personal control of his business to use representative committees, which are a device of industrial democracy. The administrative machinery of such committees is designed primarily for the collective action required in dealing with the economic or governmental relations in industry. Only when he is ready to administer justice to his employees as they understand justice, only when he is ready to give them a veto power on his acts and to insure them a trial by their peers, a jury of fellow employees, should an employer inaugurate an employee-representation plan. For once he begins to deal with governmental relations in industry he must create wage-fixing committees of employees, arbitration boards, and impartial umpires. In a word, he must be prepared to give up his exclusive control over wages, hours, and shop discipline.

Committees and Unionism

Perhaps you still doubt my statement that representative committees are essentially devices of unionism and collective bargaining. Perhaps you think I am not justified in calling the employee-representation plans "Employers' Unions." Let me, therefore, support my statements with citations from the experience of England and America with works committees.

Works Committees Grew Out of Trade Union Practices

The United States Shipping Board's report of an investigation of "Works Committees and Joint Industrial Councils" finds that:

> Works committees have evolved out of certain shop practices and organizations of union labor. . . . It is evident that the institution of shop or works committees will be easiest where both employers and workmen are already accustomed to collective action through trade union organization. This fact explains the comparatively large number of committees in English establishments and the paucity in American industry. . . . In England the movement has developed quite naturally upon the basis of the craft or shop stewards so that the backbone of the committee system there may be said to be an already existent trade organization.

Whitley Committee Supports Unionism

The Whitley Committee, appointed in England to report on industrial reconstruction problems, which has done more to popularize shop committees than any other single cause, insists throughout its reports that works committees should be based wherever possible on union organization. It says:

> Our proposals as a whole assume the existence of organizations of both employer and employed and a frank and full recognition of such organizations. Works committees established otherwise than in accor-

dance with these principles could not be regarded as a part of the scheme we have recommended, and might, indeed, be a hindrance to the development of new relations in industry to which we look forward. We think the aim should be the complete and coherent organization of the trade on both sides, and Works Committees will be of value in so far as they contribute to such a result.[1]

Employers' Unions Versus Organized Labor

Assuming that employers are convinced that organizing representative committees in their plants means collective bargaining and unionism, should they try to keep the employees they organize into works committees away from the regular labor unions? Will employers' unions be perpetuated as substitutes for organized labor or will these employers' unions develop into bona fide labor organizations?

Warning of the Whitley Committee

On this point let me quote the Whitley Committee again:

> We think it important to state that the success of the works committees would be very seriously interfered with if the idea existed that such committees were used, or likely to be used, by employers in opposition to trade-unionism. It is strongly felt that the setting up of works committees without the cooperation of the trade-unions and the employers' associations in the trade or branch of trade concerned would stand in the way of the improved industrial relationships which in these reports we are endeavoring to further.
>
> In an industry where the work people are unorganized, or only very partially organized, there is a danger that works committees may be used, or thought to be used, in opposition to trade-unionism. It is important that such fears should be guarded against in the initiation of any scheme. We look upon successful works committees as the broad base of the industrial structure which we have recommended, and as the means of enlisting the interest of the workers in the success both of the industry to which they are attached and of the workshop or factory where so much of their life is spent. These committees should not, in constitution or methods of working, discourage trade organizations.

Works Committees Not Substitute for Unions

Please note the insistence that the essential purpose of any attempt to organize the working force—namely, the improvement of relations between employer and employee—will be defeated if works committees or representation plans are to be used as a substitute for organized labor or as a means of destroying it. This is the point I wish to emphasize, in conclusion, also. And you will note in all the intelligently prepared employee-representation plans a clause to the effect that these plans shall not abridge or conflict with the right of employee to belong to labor unions.

The labor organizations that make collective agreements with employers

[1] For the important Whitley reports see *Employment Management* by Daniel Bloomfield. H. W. Wilson Company. p. 331-90.

covering wages, hours, and discipline are here to stay. It is their practices that give rise to shop committees and they will grow in power and prestige with the extension of the committee and employee representation plans. There cannot be complete industrial democracy until bargaining power is equalized between the management that owns a thousand jobs and the man who wants to hold one of these. To bargain on equal terms the thousand men must act as one in dealing with the management. And there can be no such unity until the employees are organized independently of the employer.

Summary and Conclusion

Let not this statement, however, mislead you into thinking that I am advocating trade-unionism to you or to any employer. I am advocating only that the employer should know what he is about when he begins to form organizations of his employees. I point out the democratic trend in industry to show you what you are headed for once you get away from the purely personnel management questions and pass over into the domain of collective and democratic relations between employer and employee. It has been my purpose in this paper to point out that personnel management, the handling of the employment and service problems in a plant, however scientifically and efficiently this may be done, cannot meet the demands of democracy in industrial relations. Mere welfare committees attached to such management is not democracy and when an employer thinks or pretends that it is he is preparing trouble for himself. If he is not ready to give up personal control of justice let him beware of any employees' organization. Once he starts with committees he is on the road to unionism, and he can't stop or go back. Welfare committees in England, the Whitley report shows, have prepared the way for works committees and a strengthened unionism. In this country the employer will find that our shop committees tend to become employers' unions, and these will develop into labor organizations, independent of the employer, to complete the trend toward industrial democracy.

40

A Real Believer

Cleveland Concern Adopts Industrial Democracy

PERSONNEL

Industrial Democracy is now effective in the plant of the American Multigraph Company, Cleveland.

Under date of March 1, a comprehensive co-operative management plan became effective under a scheme that practically follows the form of

Reprinted from *Personnel*, Vol. 1, No. 4, April, 1919, p. 9.

Cleveland Concern Adopts Industrial Democracy

government operative in the United States. The agencies making up this arrangement comprise an Employees' Congress and a Senate.

The Congress is composed of twenty-four members, all employes, twelve of whom are elected by the employees and twelve are appointed to office by the President. Every member must be an American citizen over twenty-one and an employe of the company over one year. Six may be women. Four elective and four appointive members change every year, the term of office being three years.

The Senate is composed of the Production Manager, Chief Engineer, Superintendent, Advertising Manager, Sales Director, Treasurer, Chief Inventor, Chief Inspector, Manager Industrial Relations, Purchasing Agent, Auditor, Vice-President and the managers of such departments as may be formed from time to time.

Among the subjects dealt with by the Congress are Employment and Discharge; Education and Publication; Health, Sanitation and Safety; Wages and Rates; Economics and Suggestions; Rules Procedure and Elections; Shop Training; Sales Cooperation; Recreation, Athletics and Entertainment.

The duty of the Senate is to approve or disapprove such measures as the Employees' Congress shall pass and present for approval. In the event of approval the measures are passed through the Secretary of the Company to the President and his cabinet for final action before becoming a company policy. In the event of disapproval, the Senate presents suggestions that will put the measure in acceptable shape. If the Senate and Congress cannot agree on any measure, an arbitration committee is provided for. A Supreme Court also is provided for in the document under which the arrangement is given life. Either the Congress or the Senate may impeach its members, expulsion from office being the penalty. The member impeached also will have to show cause why he should not be dismissed from the concern.

The President's Cabinet consists of the company executives, their authority being derived from the Board of Directors and their action is final in such matters as are assigned to them by the Directors.

The plan may be terminated January 1, 1920, or upon any anniversary thereafter, should the parties to the agreement have reason to believe that the mutual benefits expected have not been realized.

41

A Former President's Views on Labor Relations

Collective Bargaining

WILLIAM HOWARD TAFT

Organization of labor has become a recognized institution in all the civilized countries of the world. It has come to stay; it is full of usefulness and is necessary to the laborer. It shows serious defects at times and in some unions. These are an apparent willingness to accept benefits enforced through a fear of lawlessness, a disposition to use duress to compel laborers to join unions, and efforts to limit output and to create a dead level of wages, and thus wipe out the necessary and useful difference in compensation of those who are industrious and skillful and those who are lazy and do not strive to increase the product of the employer whom they serve.

These are evils that as the unions grow in wise and intelligent leadership we may well hope are being well minimized.

Much can be done by employers in anticipating just demands of employees. Workers have had too many instances of holding back of employers until they are forced to justice. Too many employers seek to justify failure to raise wages by pointing to their welfare work for their employees. This is of a paternal character and impresses the workers with the idea that they are being looked after as wards and not treated as men capable of exercising independent discretions to their welfare. They are apt to give the employers the idea that it is a generous concession they are making out of the goodness of their hearts and that they are not merely yielding a right for a quid pro quo for what they receive.

The most difficult persons to deal with are the extremists on both sides. On the side of labor there seems to be much suspicion by one leader or another, that few are willing to make a just concession, not because they don't recognize its justice, but because if they admit it they are charged with betraying the cause of labor. Thus they furnish to their rivals in leadership among workingmen the opportunity to undermine their standing with their fellows. This often puts the labor side in an indefensible position and offers to its enemies a basis for criticism that might easily be avoided.

On the other hand, there is among employers the bourbon, the man who never learns anything and never forgets anything; the man who says:

> It is my legal right to manage my business as I choose, to pay such wages as I choose, to agree to such terms of employment as I choose, to exclude from my employment union men, because I don't approve of the tenets of the union, and to maintain a family arrangement of my own. I do fairly by my men; I pay them what I think is right, and they will not complain unless some outside union agent interferes. I run a closed non-union shop, and I am happy and propose to continue happy.

 Original source unknown. Ca. 1921.

Collective Bargaining

This man is far behind in the progress of our social civilization. He lacks breadth of vision extending beyond the confines of his shop. He looks to fear of courts and injunctions and police and militia as the ordinary and usual instruments for continuing his business peacefully and maintaining his rights. He is like the man who regards the threat of a divorce court as a proper and usual means of continuing domestic happiness. He does not recognize that we have advanced beyond the state in which employers and employees are mere laws unto themselves.

He does not see that the whole public is interested in industrial peace. He does not see that the employers have certain duties social in their nature that are not defined and are not enforceable in law, but exist just as family duties of care and affection exist. He has not followed the growth of things.

As long as the system that he insists upon continued, individual laborers were at the mercy of their employers. Whatever they got was a concession. They could not maintain themselves in a contest with their employer, dependent as they were on their daily wage, and independent as he was with accumulated capital. That very unjust situation led to the organization of labor that the employee by massing contributions may maintain himself during an industrial struggle without wages.

This has come to collective bargaining, which is bargaining by the group system. A group of laborers knowing their rights and knowing how to maintain them, put themselves on a level with the employers, and the result reached is far nearer a just one than any before attained. That it may often be unjust, goes without saying, but so are all human attempts to reach the right line. Of course those individual laborers who do not see the advantage to them of the group system have a right to stay out and must be protected in doing so. But whether we will or not, the group system is here to stay, and every statesman and every man interested in public affairs must recognize that it has to be dealt with as a condition, to be favored in such a way as to minimize its abuses and to increase its utility.

The workingmen of the country since the war began and the importance of their group action has been emphasized by the requirements of the war, have been given a sense of power in their united action which we must recognize and deal with. Of course, they may abuse this power; and if so, they may find that they are not the entire community; but if under level-headed leadership they do not push it to an excess they will be able to do much for their members and indeed for the community at large.

The junkers and the hunkers on both sides must stand aside and will be set aside if common sense prevails. The danger from bolshevism is far greater than from reaction to the bourbon type of employment. The intelligent and conservative leaders of the labor movement should be encouraged. Their difficulties in dealing with their extreme constituents should be recognized.

42

Welfare Activities as an Alternative to Unionization: 1900-1930

Shop Management

FREDERICK W. TAYLOR

The writer does not at all depreciate the value of the many semi-philanthropic and paternal aids and improvements, such as comfortable lavatories, eating rooms, lecture halls, and free lectures, night schools, kindergartens, baseball and athletic grounds, village improvement societies, and mutual beneficial associations, unless done for advertising purposes. This kind of so-called welfare work all tends to improve and elevate the workmen and make life better worth living. Viewed from the managers' standpoint they are valuable aids in making more intelligent and better workmen, and in promoting a kindly feeling among the men for their employers. They are, however, of distinctly secondary importance, and should never be allowed to engross the attention of the superintendent to the detriment of the more important and fundamental elements of management. They should come in all establishments, but they should come only after the great problem of work and wages has been permanently settled to the satisfaction of both parties. The solution of this problem will take more than the entire time of the management in the average case for several years.

Mr. Patterson, of the National Cash Register Company, of Dayton, Ohio, has presented to the world a grand object lesson of the combination of many philanthropic schemes with, in many respects, a practical and efficient management. He stands out a pioneer in this work and an example of a kind-hearted and truly successful man. Yet I feel that the recent strike in his works demonstrates all the more forcibly my contention that the establishment of the semi-philanthropic schemes should follow instead of preceding the solution of the wages question; unless, as is very rarely the case, there are brains, energy and money enough available in a company to establish both elements at the same time.

 Reprinted as an excerpt from Taylor's paper on *Shop Management*, 1903.

The Good and the Bad of "Welfare Work"

SAMUEL GOMPERS

The bulletin on "Employers' Welfare Work," recently published by the Bureau of Labor Statistics of the Federal Department of Labor contains some very interesting reports. The purpose of the bulletin is to give an account without comment, of the different kinds of so-called welfare work found in fifty establishments well known for their endeavors along that line. Welfare work has always been regarded by the workers either with indifference or suspicion as it was supposed to be concerned with the welfare of the employer only. This opinion has been repeatedly confirmed by declarations of the employers who have engaged in "welfare work" on the largest scale, that it is good business policy and results in a better labor force. This opinion has been strengthened by the conviction that welfare work was to serve only a business interest in binding the workers to the management by ties of obligation and dependence.

On the other hand, some of the most active promoters of welfare work have been philanthropic societies. This relationship has enveloped the movement with an atmosphere of charity and patronage that is most repugnant to virile, self-reliant workers.

An examination of the types of welfare work claimed by the various establishments is most illuminating. There is such a wide range of endeavor and so many surprises cheerfully labeled "welfare work" that one is overwhelmed with the apparent increasing spirit of "brotherly love" in the business world. Whatsoever you shall do in the name of welfare, shall be imputed unto you as virtue or shall put money in your purse, therefore call supplying even the least convenience a "welfare" deed—such seems to be the prevailing conception. For instance, in the enumeration of its welfare activities, the International Harvester Company seriously and complacently affirmed: "The drinking water is everywhere pure." This astounding good deed of the International Harvester Company perhaps merits public commendation and notice. Perhaps it really is a matter of great self-restraint and inhibition of vicious impulses on the part of the management to refrain from furnishing water polluted by disease germs and dirt. Or perhaps there was intended a comparison between this establishment and the cotton mills of Lowell, Mass., where impure river water was sold at five cents a drink. Truly furnishing pure water does indicate a higher stage of moral development. But it must be remembered there is development even in moral standards. What in medieval times was a praiseworthy achievement in morality, today is considered a matter of commonplace duty, necessary of fulfillment if one would live on terms of peace with one's conscience.

An equally encouraging symptom of world betterment is chronicled of the charity of Huyler's—"Lunch rooms are provided for the women employees where they may eat lunches they bring with them." The

Reprinted from the *American Federationist*, Vol. 20, December, 1913, pp. 1041-1043.

character of the industry in which Huyler is engaged demands scrupulous cleanness—a condition incompatible with using the workroom as a lunchroom also.

This is imputed to its welfare work by the Westinghouse Company: "The Electric Journal is a monthly publication issued by the company, to which the technical employes contribute. It has the second largest circulation of any electrical magazine." Assuredly that is work for the employers' welfare—the magazine can hardly be a financial loss and there is a tremendous advantage in controlling the trade informational matter which goes into the hands of employes.

The Walker & Pratt Manufacturing Company, located at Watertown, Mass., commented upon this virtue: "The foundries . . . are built in the midst of a beautiful and spacious lawn, dotted with clumps of shrubs and flowers. The grounds have been laid off by a landscape gardener." This attempt to satisfy aesthetic instincts is not so general as some of the other kinds of good deeds, but in some parts of the world violence to the sense of sight is regarded as just as offensive as violence to the sense of smell. For instance, France has forbidden the use of billboards about railway stations and permits advertisements made of plants and flowers only. However, it is an indication of public spirit and progressive thought to maintain an establishment that is beautiful when one that was an eye-sore would be allowed without legal penalty.

The welfare work recounted for this report is multiform in type but seems to serve a few underlying purposes. Some types facilitate the work by saving time and material, such as good lighting, where the nature of the work makes that desirable; or ensure sanitary conditions, now desirable because of the increasing alertness of the consuming public in its own interest. Others conserve the health, safety, and lives of the workers—this obviates constant changes of workers and instructing new ones, damage suits, and compensation expenditures; a sound, vigorous worker can do better and more work than one physically hampered. Certain devises are intended to develop a spirit of loyalty to the establishment. Others, classified as welfare, are purely mercenary in aim, such as renting houses to employes, and have been so universally abused that they are thoroughly discredited among the workers.

It should be clearly understood that an employer who employs numbers of workers in his establishments places them under an organization where they individually have no control over environment and are unable to furnish for themselves even the most necessary things such as water, toilet provisions, and things of like nature. Any person who is in any degree responsible for the physical well-being of human beings, can not with good conscience disregard the obligation. If he has intelligent imagination and foresight he will refuse to poison the bodies and lungs of his workers, or to permit them to render their product unfit for use or consumption, to ruin their eyesight or mutilate their bodies. He will do these things to satisfy his own sense of decency and justice, anything less would do violence to his conscience and cause him discomfort. Such deeds are not favors but only a decent respect for humanity.

The spurious kind of welfare work, intended only to rob the workers of independence of action and of just compensation, has met with deserved discredit and disrepute. Justice, not charity however disguised, is the right of all the workers. Let welfare work become what it should be—conscience work.

Administration and Costs of Industrial Betterment for Employees

A. L. WHITNEY

The present article treats of the methods of carrying on betterment work, the costs to the employer, and the effect of the work on the efficiency and stability of the force in the different establishments visited.

Cost to the Employers of Betterment Activities

It was found in this study difficult to get very exact information, both on the costs and on the comparison of the present conditions with those prevailing before service work for the employees began. It was rather surprising to find that few firms had definite knowledge of what the work was costing them. In the majority of cases, even with a fairly well organized department, no separate record of the expenditures was kept, and in those establishments which were able to give the amounts expended, there was so much diversity in the forms of welfare work for which the figures were given that it is difficult to make a comparison or arrive at very definite conclusions as to the outlay which might be considered to be a reasonable one. The costs, as given, vary from a fraction of 1 per cent to 5 per cent of the total annual pay roll. In those cases where the allowance is as high as 4 and 5 per cent, the costs of the pension or group insurance plans and the contribution to the benefit associations or the maintenance of an expensive clubhouse form a large part of the expense. It seemed, taking into consideration the scope of the work in relation to the costs, as reported by the different companies, that excluding unusual contributions to these features a fairly comprehensive program could be maintained for about 2 per cent of the annual pay roll. Another element to be taken into consideration in this matter of costs is the degree of participation of the employees. Those examples of welfare which cost the firms the most are not necessarily the most successful, since advantages are appreciated by most people in measure as they give to them, both of money and effort. The company which, while encouraging and aiding such work, still leaves a share in both the management and the expense to the employee is probably nearer to harmonious plant relations than the employer who gives lavishly but administers the work in a more or less paternalistic spirit.

Comparison of Present Conditions with Those Prevailing Before Welfare Work Began

The date of the beginning of welfare work, as reported by many of the firms, is somewhat misleading. Many firms had an employees' benefit association long before any other work of this character was even thought of, and to accept the dates given by these firms would give an entirely erroneous idea of the length of time over which the movement extends. It

Reprinted from the *Monthly Labor Review*, Vol. 6, No. 3, March, 1918, pp. 199-206.

Administration of Welfare Work and Its Effect Upon Time Lost and Stability of the Force by Industries

Industry	Number of Establishments	Number of Employees	Welfare Work Administered by—		Establishments Having—		Establishments Reporting as to Effect of Welfare Work Upon—			
							Time Lost		Stability of Force	
			Employer Alone	Employer and Employees Jointly	Outside Agencies Cooperating	Welfare Secretary Employed	Improvement	No Change	Improvement	No Change
Automobiles	9	95,683	6	3	3	3	5	1	2	2
Boots and shoes	5	23,930	1	4	1	1	3	—	3	—
Chemicals and allied products	7	13,539	2	5	3	3	4	1	3	1
Clothing and furnishings	13	19,498	3	10	8	10	6	—	6	—
Electrical supplies	5	51,040	1	4	2	1	2	1	1	2
Explosives	5	36,030	2	3	4	4	2	—	2	—
Fine machines and instruments	8	25,326	2	6	2	2	3	—	3	—
Food products	15	17,638*	12	3	6	3	8	—	5	1
Foundries and machine shops	49	143,882	28	21	12	16	18	6	18	8
Gas and electric light and power	10	27,102†	1	9	1	2	2	2	2	1

Iron and steel	40	213,143	33	7	12	9	15	2	9	4
Mining, coal	12	34,807	7	5	4	1	6	3	3	6
Mining, other than coal	12	25,448	5	7	5	2	6	—	7	—
Offices	9	13,814	2	7	—	3	2	1	1	1
Paper and paper goods	7	9,174	3	4	3	2	6	—	3	1
Printing and publishing	10	12,769	5	5	3	4	4	—	4	—
Railroads, electric	17	60,642	6	11	3	4	6	2	5	2
Railroads, steam	10	393,583	4	6	8	1	2	1	2	1
Rubber and composition goods	9	42,847	5	4	3	6	4	1	2	—
Stores	47	125,148	17	30	20	30	18	2	10	3
Telegraph and telephone	15	66,447*	14	1	2	8	2	—	3	—
Textiles	60	71,221	41	19	31	16	21	2	22	2
Other industries	57	138,793*	31	26	18	10	15	4	19	3
Total	431	1,661,504§	231	200	154	141	160	29	136	38

* Not including 1 establishment, not reported.
† Not including 2 establishments, not reported.
‡ Individual plants of 1 corporation have been counted as separate establishments.
§ Not including 5 establishments, not reported.

The table above shows, by industries, the number of establishments scheduled and their employees, the administration of the welfare work, and its effect in regard to the time lost and the stability of the labor force.

is safe to say, that with the exception of a comparatively few of these establishments, the major part of the progress along these lines would extend over only the last 10 or 12 years. The emergency hospital work, for example, has been introduced or extended in many of the hazardous industries since the passage of the various State workmen's compensation laws. The work along the lines of safety and sanitation also has been much influenced by these laws and has grown with amazing rapidity in the last few years. The increase in the number of firms providing a pension system for their employees has been very marked in the last seven years, and group insurance has developed entirely since 1911.

In spite of the fact that so much of this work is comparatively recent, it will readily be seen that, owing to the abnormal labor conditions of the past three years, it was very difficult to obtain from the companies a comparison of present conditions with those prevailing before welfare work was undertaken. The extent to which the output is affected by the welfare work is difficult to determine, both because of the present unusual labor conditions and the fact that few companies had made any study of this point. A few firms, however, gave it as their opinion that the output had been increased by it, although several of these stated that this improvement was only in part due to the welfare work. Quite a number stated that their increased output was due to a reduction in the working hours, a form of welfare which has not been given special consideration in this report.

The stability of the force also has been much affected in many plants by present labor conditions. One hundred and thirty-six of the establishments scheduled reported an improvement in this regard, due in whole or in part to the betterment activities. In many cases this was more than a mere expression of opinion, since many employers have, of late, been impressed with the fact that a large turnover is a very important item in the cost of production, and have been seeking to reduce this turnover by more scientific management of the employment departments and by the introduction of welfare features. One firm which had compiled statistics in regard to the reduction in the turnover had an increase of 13.4 per cent of employees of more than two years' service in 1916 over a similar group for 1914, due entirely, so the management stated, to their welfare work.

One hundred and sixty of the establishments reported an improvement in the time lost. There are probably two reasons for this: One is the work of the emergency hospitals, which care for the general health of the employees and do much preventive work, as well as sort out those most undesirable physically through their examinations on entrance; the other is the installation of safety devices and the education through safety lectures and literature, which has resulted in a large reduction in the time lost through industrial accidents.

Even though only a small proportion of the companies reported on this subject, still enough have done so to prove that welfare work does have an appreciable effect upon the work and health of the employees. It would be reasonable to suppose, even without the confirmation of such reports, that all service work which is carried on in such a spirit that it results in a more contented force, as well as a healthier one, must have the effect of making the employees more stable and more efficient. Another proof of this is found also in the attitude toward welfare work, even of these employers who are least in sympathy with it, for there is an apparent realization among them that much of this work is becoming necessary in order to get and retain a desirable class of employees.

Administration of Welfare Work

It will be found that the administration of this work is by employers alone in slightly more than half of the cases. This also probably gives a somewhat wrong impression, since there are necessarily many firms reported which do not do a great deal along these lines. The companies which do the least are those most likely to control entirely such features as they have, partly becuase the kinds of work first introduced are usually those which naturally remain under the immediate direction of the firm, and partly because it usually takes some experience in order to realize the desirability of giving the employees an active part in the conduct of the welfare activities.

It is natural that the employer should direct the work of the emergency hospital, although there are a number of cases where this has been given over to the benefit association; similarly several firms allow their employees to manage the lunch room, either on a cooperative basis or using the profits for either the benefit or the athletic associations. The employees quite frequently have a voice in the management of the club rooms or houses, in several instances being given entire control of the clubhouse. In the matter of athletics and recreation, more often the employer plays a passive part, assisting financially, and also providing rooms for meeting purposes, gymnasiums, and athletic fields. The work among families, except what is done in connection with the benefit association, is entirely under the direction of the companies through the medium of the welfare secretary or visiting nurses. The administration of the benefit associations is in most cases either mutual or in the hands of the employees. Pension and group insurance funds, being in most cases provided by the firms, are therefore administered by them, as is much of the educational work, although frequently members of the force assist in teaching, especially in the classes in English for foreigners.

Mention must be made of one conspicuous and well-known example of cooperative management by the firm and its employees of both the business and the welfare organization. It has been the policy of this company in increasing degree through the past quarter of a century to give the employees a share in the management. An association of the employees is maintained, to which every employee belongs. The affairs of this organization are conducted by a group elected by the employees, and this executive body has the power to make, change, or amend any rule that affects the discipline or working conditions of the employees. This can be carried even over the veto of the management by a two-thirds vote of all the employees. This association is also represented by four members out of eleven on the board of directors of the corporation. All the parts of the welfare organization have been carefully built up and are controlled and managed by the council of the association through committees. The firm contributes club and business rooms, certain salaries, and any other assistance necessary. The fundamental principle followed by the club in the management, however, is that these activities shall be in the main self-supporting and that financial or other assistance rendered by the firm shall receive a direct return from the employees in increased efficiency. There is no doubt that in this particular instance the generous and broad-minded policy of the firm is reflected in the very unusual personal interest in the business which is evidenced by the employees as a whole.

Cooperation with Outside Agencies

Employers cooperate frequently for the betterment of their employees with certain established outside agencies, such as the local school boards, the Y.M.C.A., and the Y.W.C.A. In the North and West the continuation school work is often carried on beyond the requirements of the law, and several companies also cooperate with the public schools in their apprenticeship courses. In the South the public school terms are often extended many months each year through the contributions and assistance of the companies. The Y.M.C.A. and the Y.W.C.A. also serve as the medium through which the employers carry on the club work for employees, as in the case of most railroad companies which use the Y.M.C.A., since it is so well organized and seems particularly to fill their needs. In a few other instances firms have established their own branches of these organizations or pay membership fees for junior employees in the city branch. In many instances either one or both of these organizations, with the sanction of the company, conduct meetings for employees in the plant. In one western city an association of several of the nursing and charitable organizations does much welfare work for employees and their families in the different industries. This association is supported by voluntary contributions, and recently all the principal industries in the city except one agreed to pay five cents per month for each employee in return for which the association cares for any cases to which the employer calls its attention.

Employment of Welfare Secretary

In 141 cases it was found that a welfare secretary was employed. Very often the secretary's sole duties are supervising the various welfare activities. In other cases the employment and welfare departments are merged into one, part of the time of the manager being given to each, and in still other instances the doctor or head nurse assumes these duties in addition to the hospital work. In quite a number of instances the welfare department employs a corps of trained workers. One large department store has, in addition to its medical department and welfare secretary, a number of college women engaged in educational work, physical culture, and dancing, as well as supervising the library and the girls' clubhouse. Another company which does much community work has, in addition to the head worker, seven others, teachers, librarian, and a visiting nurse who have kindergarten, manual training and other classes, many clubs among both young and old, and also have much general supervision of the townspeople, of whom many are foreigners.

The duties of a welfare secretary are many and varied. She frequently must oversee the work of the emergency hospital, see that the food served in the lunch room is kept up to the standard, and that the kitchens are kept in a sanitary condition, and look after many of the details of sanitation; she often has charge of the library unless it is sufficiently large to require one or more special attendants; her office is so placed that she has a view of the rest and recreation rooms, and in some plants, of the cloakrooms. Often, in cases of special need, she visits the homes, and a number of instances were found where the firm had placed a sum of money at her disposal, to be used at her discretion, in special cases of illness or distress among the employees or their families. In the larger cities there is a great deal of cooperation among those serving different firms in this capacity, in the way of exchange of ideas, and the visiting nurses' association also is utilized often to help out in cases of illness in families. The State factory inspectors suggested to certain establishments, in one large city, which had not yet taken up any work of this sort, that they should allow an experienced woman to start the work for them. This woman, feeling that this particular city was well equipped to do the necessary educational and recreational work, did not include such work in her program, but confined herself to the installation of rest rooms, emergency rooms, and lunch rooms. Even when little space was available she utilized it until such time as the firm could provide more. Two or three months were spent in each plant getting the work under way, when it was turned over to a competent woman, and the same thing begun in another establishment. This particular welfare worker was able to interest the employers, since she believed that production is increased and labor turnover decreased by the introduction of this work.

Conclusion

One might conclude that all welfare secretaries are women since they have been cited especially. In the majority of cases this is true, but in a number of instances this department, especially in those industries employing only men, is managed by a man. In either case the opportunity which is presented for a very broad and helpful service to the employees is very great. It is a difficult position to fill, since, if the policy pursued is not a liberal and broadminded one, the employees may feel that the position is being used to their disadvantage, but if, on the other hand, the one who holds it is gifted with sympathy and tact, the possibilities for help and encouragement of all kinds are almost unlimited.

Employees' Welfare: An Autopsy

ABRAHAM EPSTEIN

Now that millions of American workers are jobless, the leading business men and industrial seers of the nation are heading charity drives and soliciting funds for them. The President's Organization on Unemployment Relief is composed largely of such high-hatted gentlemen. Their appealing voices are broadcast nightly over the radio. By a skilfully devised system of "voluntary" deductions from the pay of the workers still employed, they are able to swell their own contributions to the relief funds. Yet no one appears to question the unselfishness with which they are carrying out the responsibility which they assumed aforetime in their industrial welfare programmes.

A few years ago these programmes were acclaimed as constituting a new departure in employer-employé relationship, and were credited with

Reprinted from *The American Mercury*, Vol. 25, No. 99, March, 1932, pp. 335-342.

ushering in a povertyless, strifeless, and Bolshevik-less America. They were ascribed to the far-sightedness of American industrialists and lauded as peculiarly American in origin. They were supposed to explain why social legislation was unnecessary in the United States. American employers, it was asserted, were "increasingly recognizing their responsibilities toward their workers," and on their own volition were taking over the burden of supporting the victims of the industrial system instead of leaving them to the care of governmental agencies. According to the spokesmen of American industry they had adopted their programmes because of their affection and forethought for the welfare of their workers. But why, then, are these programmes, particularly designed for hard times, not performing their functions now? Why the need for charity appeals and increased governmental expenditures?

The truth is that the relatively few and inconsequential company welfare plans which were inaugurated during the days of prosperity were not actually instituted for the welfare of the workers. They were set up chiefly because of hoped for advantages to the corporations which adopted them. The question of the workers' welfare or security, if it was considered at all, was at best only secondary. The fact that all the plans, with a few isolated exceptions, made the benefits contingent upon the worker staying with the company, with all the benefits ceasing as soon as he left, is proof enough that his security had little to do with the matter. An employé can get no aid under these systems once he has quit or been discharged—in other words, when he needs it most.

The welfare plans were really instituted primarily for the purpose of increasing the worker's loyalty, reducing the labor turnover, frustrating unionization and strikes, and making possible the retirement of inefficient executives, who could not otherwise be dislodged so easily. Upon the discovery that these potential boons did not materialize, many corporations promptly and unceremoniously abandoned their elaborate programmes. Wherever they are still maintained it is because the corporation, rightly or wrongly, believes that they pay, or is fearful of the consequences which might result from scrapping policies which have been advertised with so much ballyhoo.

The major welfare programmes prevailing in American industry today are the following: (1) Industrial Pensions; (2) Mutual Benefit Plans; (3) Group Insurance; (4) Employé Stock Ownership; (5) Unemployment Benefits.

I

The oldest welfare programme directly undertaken by employers in the United States is that of promissory pensions to workers upon reaching the age of sixty-five or seventy, provided they have been with the concern for a period generally running from twenty to thirty years. The first such plan was adopted in this country in 1875. Altogether, four companies were in line before the turn of the century. The greatest development in this direction occurred in the fifteen-year period between 1910 and 1925, when nearly 300 concerns inaugurated retirement systems. With few exceptions these schemes were financed entirely by the corporations undertaking them.

A keen student of the problem aptly describes all such industrial pension systems as "if and maybe" propositions. "In effect," he says, "such a system says to the worker:

> If you remain with this company throughout your productive lifetime,
> If you do not die before the retirement age,
> If you are not discharged or laid off for an extended period,
> If you are not refused a benefit as a matter of discipline, [i.e., because of joining a union, asking for a raise, or, in some cases, for "immoral" conduct],
> If the company continues in business, and
> If the company does not decide to abandon this plan, you will receive a pension at the age of ___, subject to the contingency of its discontinuance or reduction, after it has been entered upon."

Altogether, less than 500 American companies have formally adopted such programmes in the past fifty years. Before the depression set in it was estimated that only 4,000,000 of the 31,000,000 workers in industry and commerce in the United States were covered. The number is certainly smaller today, and it is estimated that only about 110,000 or 1⅔% of the 6,600,000 persons in the country over sixty-five years of age, are actually receiving benefits under such plans.

The National Industrial Conference Board, which for years refused to admit the inherent inadequacy of industrial pensions, was finally forced to acknowledge in its 1931 report on "The Support of the Aged" that

> The chief impediment to an increase in the number of employés who might benefit from industrial pensions is the service requirement, usually from twenty to twenty-five years, since only a very small percentage of workers fulfill this requirement. . . . A weighted composite of five surveys in different parts of the United States shows that only 5.3% of factory workers stay with one firm for more than twenty years. Records of railroad companies, which have had pension plans established for longer periods than any other industry in the country, show that the number of pensioners at any one time equals from 3 to 6% of the total number of employés on their payroll twenty-five years before. Calculations made by actuaries for the purpose of determining costs of pension plans, based on turnover figures for five large companies, indicate that for the typical median employé in industry—that is, a man about thirty-six years of age—the probability of remaining employed by the same company to the age of sixty-five is from 1 to 5%.

Years before the depression set in, the Pennsylvania Old Age Pension Commission prophesied that "the large majority of the pension systems now in operation are so constructed as to preclude any hope of their ever becoming effective instruments in solving the great problem of old age dependency to any considerable degree. . . . As pension obligations are now carried, unless our present business prosperity continues without periods of reaction, it is likely in the long run that public or charitable agencies will be forced to assume the maintenance of many thousands of workers whose employers had led them to expect that they would be granted pensions in their old age." A study of 149 industrial pension plans in New York State by the 1930 Old Age Security Commission disclosed that in only 49 of these plans was there some guarantee of payments, once the pension had been granted.

Although the abandonment of a pension plan is obviously a most serious matter to the workers who are dependent upon it for old age security, the Industrial Relations counselors report that eleven companies have completely abandoned their plans since October, 1929. Meanwhile, three railroad companies have reduced their pension rates, and a number of other large concerns have cut pensions and changed their plans by requiring contributions on the part of their employés. How many companies have given up or reduced their pension payments without official announcement can only be guessed. It is significant that the plans that are presumably sound financially, requiring the actual setting aside of money annually, are being dropped at a greater rate than the unguaranteed schemes.

II

Among the oldest welfare agencies are the mutual benefit societies, now in existence in about 800 American plants. These societies go back half a century. Their main aim is the protection of their members against the hazards of accidents, sickness and death. In the early days they were generally initiated by the workers themselves, who often refused suspiciously to accept contributions from their employers. But when bosses began to be admired instead of distrusted many of the societies welcomed company assistance.

However, most of them now offer only small and inadequate benefits. A study of the subject a few years ago by the National Industrial Conference Board disclosed that the predominating benefit rates were from $5 to $6 a week, granted only for a limited number of weeks. It was also found that "many associations which have been in operation over periods ranging from ten to twenty-five years are still paying the same rates of benefits as they did at the time they were organized." The societies are rarely soundly financed, and in many instances the benefits depend upon the accumulated funds in the treasury and cease when they have been spent.

III

At the moment the most popular form of welfare work—which, although hardly known abroad, has spread rapidly in the United States—is group insurance, i.e., the protection of the dependents of deceased employés by insuring the lives of the living. An English newspaper once described this plan as an "American scheme for giving the family of the deceased worker one year's notice of the demise of the pay check." High pressure salesmanship by the insurance companies has made the scheme the most widespread in the United States today.

The reasons for the growing acceptance of it until recently are not far to seek. It offers the cheapest method of securing practically all the results which employers seek through welfare programmes. The company not only obtains greater loyalty on the part of the workers themselves, but also creates "a desirable influence in the worker's home." Insurance agents are instructed to sell these policies to an employer with the following argument:

> Practically half of your workers have no insurance protection whatsoever for their wives and children. Whenever one dies a hat is

passed around the shop in behalf of the widow. A certain amount of costly time is inevitably wasted in such a collection. But this is nothing compared to the depressing spirits caused in the shop when your employés are reminded of their own fate. Then again, you are generally asked to put something into the hat, and you cannot refuse.

You have also probably been in the habit of giving your employés a basket or a turkey for Christmas. But what happens? It is very much appreciated while it lasts, but your wonderful generosity is forgotten as soon as the leftovers are gone.

Now, for the price you spend on a Christmas turkey, you can procure a group policy providing approximately $1,000 on the death in your service of an old-time employé. You may begin with $100 for those who have been with you only one year and raise the policy $100 for each additional year of service, up to say a maximum of $1,000 after ten years. We shall provide each of your insured workers with a beautifully engraved policy which he can take home and hang in the parlor. John's wife will not only be everlastingly grateful to you for your thoughtfulness of her, but you may be sure she will do everything she can to prevent him from quitting when he is disgruntled, or from going on strike, or joining a union when she knows that if he does so her only protection in the case of his death is gone.

Generous employers need no further persuasion. The more rapacious ones are advised that they need not pay the entire premium themselves. Delicate persuasion can readily secure the "coöperation" of their employés in bearing at least half the burden.

For the extreme misers the insurance agent resorts to one final trick in his bag—a gentle hint to the effect that since the premium rates, being based upon the average age of all the employés, are higher the older the workers, the costs will be reduced if the corporation increases the proportion of younger workers. The charge has been repeatedly made, and soundly, that one of the chief reasons for the employment deadline encountered by middle-aged and older men in finding work is that older workers raise the insurance premiums on group policies.

Despite the eloquence of the insurance agents, the peak of the group insurance business was passed in 1929. The companies authorized to do business in New York—they do more than 90% of the national business—had outstanding at the end of the year 16,563 group policies. Not all of these, of course, covered industrial employés. Some covered National Guard and State police units, fraternal organizations, teachers, clerks, professional associations, and labor unions. At the end of 1930 the number outstanding was only 16,177, or about 400 less than in the previous year. Of 607 policies carried by the Morris Plan in 1929, only 7 did not lapse by 1931. The Metropolitan began 1930 with 548 policies in New York State, but after writing 46 new policies, it wound up with only 545 at the end of the year. The Equitable began with 369, wrote 30 new policies during the year, and ended with 363. Thus several thousand companies have abandoned their promises to the prospective widows and orphans of their workers.

In 1931 the National Industrial Conference Board estimated that "more than 6,000,000 employés [out of a total of 31,000,000 industrial workers in the United States] are now covered by group life insurance, and the average coverage is approximately $1,200." This average, it admitted, "is, of course, inadequate for the support of a family, or even of an individual for a considerable period," but it argued that it "gives the family a new start that may be sufficient to lift it to a self-supporting basis." The New York Old Age Security Commission, however, has another point of view. It says:

> Here again the difficulty of money averages comes in, because the higher policies of officers and executives weight the averages greatly, and the amounts of wage-earners only would fall considerably below the general average. A study by the Bureau of Labor Statistics indicated that the usual minimum is about $500, although some firms set their minimum below $300. The maximum amounts start at $500 and range up into the high levels of executive salaries.

As in all other welfare plans, group insurance benefits depend upon the employé's remaining in the service of the company. Should he die shortly after leaving the company—even after many years of service—his widow and orphans are as unprotected as though he had never worked for it. Although workers upon leaving can continue paying the regular premium rates in accordance with their age, the Old Age Security Commission aptly points out that

> This, however, raises a difficulty group insurance was devised to avoid, the prohibitive cost of insurance to many workers. Those men who could not have purchased ordinary policies when employed would be less able to do so when out of work.

IV

The sale to employés of those (formerly) most precious of all things, industrial stocks, was hailed not only as proof of a paternal and fraternal affection on the part of the industrial leaders of the nation for those who worked for them, but also as evidence of an economic revolution which was making track-walkers and bricklayers colleagues of railroad presidents and bankers. It was frequently asserted that the number of stockholders in the country had increased from less than 5,000,000 in 1920 to about 15,000,000 in 1927. Elated, Professor T. N. Carver, the Harvard economist, declared that this meant "a revolution that is to wipe out the distinction between laborers and capitalists by making laborers their own capitalists and by compelling most capitalists to become laborers of one kind or another, because not many of them will be able to live on the returns from capital alone. This is something new in the history of the world."

The baselessness of these Pollyana claims of the New Era economists was known to all sensible people. But the fable of 15,000,000 stockholders was perpetuated even after the late Joseph S. McCoy, actuary of the United States Treasury, stated that only some 3,000,000 individuals in America owned corporation securities, and that only about 1,000,000 were bond buyers. "Only one in every thirty persons in the United States," said Mr. McCoy before the crash, "now belongs to the legion of capitalists. Investigations have shown that some individuals own as many as 500 different stocks."

How many of these investors were wage-earners? On the basis of extensive studies, the National Industrial Conference Board estimated, before the stock market collapse, that about 1,000,000 employés had subscribed for or owned non-voting stock amounting to about $1,000,000,000, or about 1% of the total market value of all the stock then outstanding. In other words, in the heyday of employé-stock-purchase plans only 1 out of every 31 workers had purchased any stock at all. Were these 1,000,000 "employés" really wage-earners, or were they salaried men and executives? Following two surveys of the subject the Conference Board said categorically that the stocks had been largely purchased by the higher paid employés rather than by the wage-earners. It went on:

> In some companies stock is offered for sale only to a restricted group, consisting usually of executive, sales and office staffs, the managerial and supervisory force in the plant, and perhaps certain key men in the rank and file. But even where no restriction, apart from the nominal service requirement, was placed upon subscription for stock, most of it was found to be held by a comparatively small number of employés. This appears to be due partly to the fact that cancellations and resales by other employés are often absorbed by this group.

What is the import of these stock sales in terms of the worker's security, since, according to the Conference Board, thrift has been overwhelmingly "the chief motive actuating the purchase of company stock by employés"? All stocks have depreciated to a small fraction of their former value. Unless the companies repurchase those held by their workers at the prices originally paid, the savings of the latter have been almost completely wiped out. But of 99 companies which stated their policies in reply to the Conference Board's questionnaire in 1930, only 8 said that they had made a mandatory promise to repurchase employé stock at cost!

Thus, in so far as stocks were sold to wage-earners the movement turned out to be a deception. Gambling in stocks is a risky proposition even for the wealthy. To encourage poor workers to invest their scanty savings in company stock is certainly reprehensible. Many employés bought such stock not only for reasons of thrift but because they believed that their purchases gave them certain privileges and brought them greater security in their jobs. Some corporations actually compelled their employés to subscribe for stock at the risk of losing their jobs. During the past two years, however, many of these stockholders have not only had to dispose of their stock at heavy losses, but have also lost their jobs with the companies in which they fondly thought they were acquiring ownership and partnership. The entire movement, far from offering any security to the workers, has only served to divest many of them of the small savings which they had accumulated through thrift and scrimping during a lifetime of work.

V

The latest *fata morgana* is unemployment relief. The first company benefit plan was inaugurated in 1916 by the Dennison Manufacturing Company of Framingham, Mass. In 1928, twelve years afterward, Mr. Bryce M. Stewart found that only eleven companies, employing approximately 11,000 workers, had set up such plans, and that they covered but 8,500 employés. The total expenditures during that year amounted to but $11,871 *for the entire country.* Two other companies which had adopted such plans had been forced to abandon them prior to 1928.

Notwithstanding the interest aroused by and the wide advocacy of unemployment relief during the present depression, the United States Bureau of Labor Statistics, in a follow-up study made in 1931, found that the number of plans outstanding had risen to but fifteen, and that one of these—the plan of the United Diamond Works—was suspended because of the depression. The second largest system—the joint company plan in Rochester—does not come into operation until January, 1933. Shortly after the publication of this study, the largest of the fifteen concerns—the General Electric Company—also announced the abandonment of its original system of unemployment benefits and the substitution of a new plan of work guarantees.

At the time the Bureau of Labor Statistics study was made, the fifteen companies had about 116,000 employés, but only "slightly more than 50,000 were eligible to benefits." Excluding the Rochester joint plan, which, so far as benefits are concerned, is still inoperative, and the completely altered General Electric Company plan, the total number of employés who were eligible for benefits was no greater in 1931 than in 1928. Thus, after fifteen years of agitation, unemployment benefit systems have been adopted by but fifteen of the approximately 300,000 establishments in the United States, and cover at best but 50,000 of the country's 31,000,000 industrial and commercial workers.

They are confined in the main to a few exceptionally situated companies headed by men especially interested in industrial welfare. There is, to begin with, the Dennison Manufacturing Company, which initiated the movement. There is the Columbia Conserve Company, a small concern practically given over to its employés. There is Deering, Milliken & Company, always conspicuous for its enlightened labor policy. There is the Procter & Gamble Soap Company, headed by Col. W. C. Procter. There is Leeds & Northrup, under Quaker influence. And there is the General Electric Company, headed by the two publicists, Messrs. Young and Swope.

Unemployment plans in which employers and trade unions coöperate are confined almost entirely to the trades manned by foreign workers, who, rooted in the older European Socialist philosophy, have forced contributions from their employers. The largest plan, embracing more than two-thirds of all the workers in question, is managed by a union outside the fold of the American Federation of Labor. Of the eight national and international unions which at this writing are coöperating in such schemes, seven are in the needle trades or related industries.

Unemployment payments under joint plans, as under company plans, are never certain, and, agreement or no agreement, depend almost entirely upon current conditions in the industry. American experience *warrants the conclusion that workers are assured of unemployment benefits only so long as business is prosperous and they are employed.*

Most of the larger industrial establishments which undertook welfare programmes in the days of prosperity were induced to do so only because they believed the total cost would not involve more than the price of a turkey at Christmas. A canvass made by the writer a few years ago disclosed that 514 corporations, employing a total of 3,075,034 workers, had expended during the year but $52,408,384.13, or an average of only $17.04 a worker, on all their welfare work, including expenditures on group insurance, old age benefits, mutual benefit societies, death benefits, restaurant losses, swimming pools, baseball clubs, golf courses, and the like. The *per capita* cost of industrial pensions was approximately but $10.75 a year. The cost of group insurance in 292 establishments amounted to but $0.72 a year. A study by the National Metal Trades Association showed an average cost for the contributory plans of $7.36 for the employer and $6.54 for the employé. The *per capita* cost of mutual benefit societies amounted to $4.99 a year. A study of the cost of health service in industry, by the National Industrial Conference Board, showed an average *per capita* outlay of but $1.33.

Even this small cost the paternalistic American industrialists have shifted in part to the shoulders of their employés. Years ago welfare programmes were generally granted free to employés. Today most companies compel their workers to contribute some part of the cost. Even in the prosperous days of 1926 the National Metal Trades Association reported that "it appears that the percentage of group insurance plans being written on the contributory basis is increasing yearly." The tendency now is to put at least one-half of the cost on the employés. Probably not more than 10% of the group insurance policies written fifteen years ago were contributory, but today approximately 75% are contributory.

In the case of pension plans the same tendency has set in. Says the New York Old Age Security Commission:

> There has been a gradual shift, which is still going on, from systems in which the company pays the whole of the pension to ones under which the employés bear a substantial portion of the cost. Before the end of 1903, except for the one attempt by the Baltimore & Ohio, and the plan of the Grand Trunk, there were no schemes in which the employés participated as contributors. In the period 1906-1910 one of the thirteen plans established was one in which part of the cost was assessed on employés (contributory) and three out of forty-seven in the next five-year period were in the same class. . . . In the period 1916-1920, three out of thirty-three plans were of the contributory type. . . . In the period 1921-1925, four of the twenty-three plans were of the contributory type. . . . In the period since 1926 almost half of the plans established, eight of eighteen, were financed partially by the employés. . . .

Not one of the pension plans adopted in 1931 was on a non-contributory basis. Unemployment benefits likewise began with gratuitous payments on the part of the companies, but the latest and largest plan, that of the General Electric Company, requires contributions from the workers.

But even if the current industrial welfare programmes were really adequate, they would offer little security to most of the 31,000,000 industrial workers of the United States. Substantial programmes are, of necessity, confined to the larger and more prosperous or monopolistic industries. Small concerns, struggling against competitors, cannot afford either the time or the money necessary for such luxuries. Moreover, since all welfare benefits are contingent upon length of service, the overwhelming majority of workers, because of their constantly shifting employment, are never able to qualify for them. Cases of employés being discharged just before they become entitled to benefits are not infrequent. The benefits, even in the contributory systems, are rarely guaranteed. At all times the corporation has the right to cancel its promises whenever it may feel so disposed. Indeed, the history of welfare plans is already strewn with the wrecked anticipations and prospects of workers. And the future, I fear, will witness only more shattered hopes.

43

Democracy in Industry Revisited: 1928

The Employee Representation Movement: Its Meaning for Management

WILLIAM M. LEISERSON

Employee representation is a worldwide movement. In every industrial country works committees or shop councils of some kind have appeared as means of adjusting the relations of employers and employees.

In such a worldwide movement many cross currents are bound to appear. In some countries the councils are mere adjuncts of the trade unions, while in others they attempt to take the place of trade unions; and sometimes the councils have developed mainly in the industries where the trade unions were too weak or inefficient to accomplish their purposes. To a certain extent, also, these different relationships of councils to trade unions are to be found within the same country. Many of the plans have failed; many appear to have established themselves permanently. But those that have succeeded in establishing themselves more or less permanently have accomplished results that appear contradictory. Sometimes they have succeeded in strengthening unions; sometimes, in weakening them. Sometimes they have brought management and wage earners into a more unified organization; sometimes they have succeeded in organizing the employees as a distinct class for bargaining with the management.

The movement is too young to disclose what the ultimate trends will be, what goals the representation plans will finally achieve, what ideals will actuate them. However, and in spite of the dearth of scientifically accurate information as to the practical working of the plans, certain tentative

 Reprinted from *Personnel,* February, 1928.

conclusions may be drawn from the broad facts of the movement that are already available.

First, let us be clear as to the meaning of "employee representation." In an all-inclusive sense the term is sometimes used to cover all forms of experimental schemes for improving labor relations, including trade union arrangements with employers, profit sharing, employee stock ownership, membership on boards of directors, as well as works committees and shop councils. In a narrower sense the term includes only such committees, councils, assemblies, or other forms of representation as are established without the assistance of trade unions. It is in this narrower sense that the term employee representation is used here, and we are excluding from consideration also representation on boards of directors and profit-sharing plans. Our discussion is limited to those representation plans that refuse to recognize trade unions as legitimate intermediaries for the employees and are commonly designated as "company unions."

To a disinterested scientific student of labor relations one of the most significant facts about these company unions is that managers and business leaders have organized them as a means of providing democratic control over wages and working conditions, and that these men who are at the forefront of industrial progress urge the adoption of employee representation as a step toward industrial democracy. There are, of course, many employers and managers who merely follow the crowd and adopt representation plans and talk about industrial democracy without knowing what they are doing or saying, simply because it is the latest style in labor relations. The significant thing is that the really intelligent leaders who have carefully studied employee representation, and who are responsible for setting styles in management devices, should acknowledge the need and attempt to devise the administrative machinery for democratic control of industry.

Henry Dennison writes:

> It may be questioned whether there is the difference between the fundamentals of the problem of industrial management and the problem of political management that some of us think there is. Some of the experiments that are being worked out in industry, even if they seem unsuccessful for a time, but nevertheless rank as experiments in the management of men on a nonautocratic basis. . . . The technique of democracy—how to manage ourselves as citizens—is not very different from the problem of how to manage ourselves as parts of a producing or distributing agency.

Edward Filene:

> Labor . . ., having experienced the advantages of democracy in government, now seeks democracy in industry. Is it any stranger that a man should have a voice as to the conditions under which he works than that he should participate in the management of the city and the state and the nation? If a voter on governmental problems, why not a voter on industrial problems?

These statements go further in the direction of democratic control of industrial management than most employers would be willing to go. And they may be discounted as being mere talk or advertising or general buncombe, given out for public consumption and not really intended to be put into practice. The mere fact, however, that employers and organizers of great capitalistic enterprises find it necessary or desirable to talk industrial democracy and to advocate its establishment as an essential principle of sound management is itself a fact of the utmost significance. For something like a hundred years the term industrial democracy has been a familiar one in the propaganda of socialists, trade unionists, and various kinds of social reformers. Now the leaders of business have taken it over. Why have they done that?

In my opinion, it is because they are enlightened industrial monarchs. They have seen that treating laborers as if they were commodities is unsound and wasteful economically. They have tried paternalism or benevolent autocracy, and they have found that this did not work, just as Frederick the Great and his followers found that benevolent political despotism did not work.

We need not argue about the term "democracy." There are many forms. The main thing is that there shall be consent of the governed. In industry it means that the wage earners shall have an effective voice when they differ with management; that they shall be in a position to have their views enforced as well as represented equally with management.

Whatever the motives of management may be, when it inaugurates employee representation it is handing its employees a constitution for the government of the industry. It may not be much of a constitution. It may give the wage earners little power and few rights, and management may think that employee representation is different from unionism because it does not provide for the right to strike. But management has started a movement in the direction of democracy in industry which is bound to grow. Just as the first political constitutions of European countries did not provide much democracy but gradually led to more and more democratic control by the people, so these employee representation plans may not have much democracy in them at first, yet it is inevitable that once a plan is established the workers will get more and more control over it.

The notion, then, that professions of industrial democracy may be insincere, or that those who establish employee representation do not believe in it and do not intend to have any of it, is quite immaterial. The question is rather whether forces of self-government in industry have been let loose which tend to give wage earners more and more power and control over industry, at the same time that they are being made a part of industry. That workers threaten strikes when managers propose to use their undoubted legal right to drop representation plans, and that sometimes they strike to get plans inaugurated, are straws showing the direction in which the wind is blowing.

When an employer establishes a representation plan and the wage earners say, "We dare you to take it out!"—at that moment you have the beginning of democracy. Industry is a living, growing organism, and it may be evolving democratic control in much the same way as democracy in government was evolved. When kings could not get the money they wanted, they called representatives of the people together in a parliament to vote taxes. Those representatives said, "If we are going to vote for taxes, we might as well ask for a lot of other things." Employee representatives do much the same thing. At first they are timid, and they do whatever management asks. But pretty soon they say, "Let us start doing something for ourselves." They want to know and to test how much power and authority and voice they actually have.

If we want to understand the real meaning and significance of employee representation, we must look at the development of the movement scientifically; that is, objectively and disinterestedly. We must not confuse our own notions of what we should like to see employee representation turn out to be with what it actually is and is becoming. For example, the notion has been expressed that employee representation is a device for restoring the close contact and friendly relations that existed between employers and employees when business was small and masters and men knew each other by their first names. Yes, but when they knew each other by their first names and not by numbers, what did they call each other? What kinds of names? Strikes, boycotts, picketing, blacklisting—all the paraphernalia of industrial warfare arose in small plants between employers and workers who were closely associated.

No, employee representation cannot be a scheme to bring back the close touch and bitter fighting between the small master and his few employees. It might be much truer to say that it is a scheme to keep out of the large industrial establishments the antagonisms and bad labor relations which arose and are still arising in small plants and which are responsible for the militant, fighting kind of trade unionism instead of the cooperating kind that you find in large enterprises—as on railroads, on the big newspapers, in the large clothing plants.

Another preconception is the notion that there is only one true method of giving workers a voice in industry and, therefore, if company organizations are sound, then trade unions are unsound. Organized labor has the same notion, only it thinks trade unionism is the only sound method and, therefore, company unions are wrong. Once we drop preconceptions, however, and study the operations of employee representation with scientific objectivity, we see that the plans work exactly like trade unions; even when they start as mere advisory committees, they tend to become more and more like trade unions. Therefore, I am led by the evidence to the conclusion that employee representation is a form of labor organization.

Its accomplishments are the accomplishments of organized labor. Just as some ill-informed people think there is only one form of political democracy, such as American democracy, and overlook the fact that British, Swiss, Danish, Norwegian, and Canadian democracies are equally good and sometimes more effective, so some employers think company unions are the only form of joining workers and managers in cooperative organizations; and most labor leaders think trade unions are the only proper form of labor organization. Yet there *is* no one true form of industrial democracy. The employee representation movement shows that there will be many forms of this, as there are of political democracy.

What have employee representation plans accomplished that probably would not have been achieved in any other way?

My answer to that is—nothing! Most of what they have accomplished has been done before by the trade unions, and the better-managed unions have done more. There are, of course, many poorly managed trade unions and some rotten, dishonest union men; but in proportion there are just as many poorly managed businesses, rotten businessmen, and dishonest company unions. The honest purpose of unionism is not antagonism but cooperation with management to improve labor conditions and relations, just as the honest purpose of employee representation is not opposition to unionism but cooperation with employees. Some unions practice cooperation; others do not. Some employee representation plans practice cooperation; others do not and are merely anti-union.

Look at the matter disinterestedly and you must acknowledge that if the accomplishments of employee representation have been to give wage earners a voice in determining conditions, to treat the laborer as a human spirit rather than as a commodity of trade, to fix wages on a give-and-take basis, to reduce excessive hours of work, and to prevent arbitrary discipline and discharge, then all these things were established years ago and are being maintained today in many industries by what is ordinarily called organized labor. You will even find this acknowledged by many of the leaders in the employee representation movement.

Do employees get as much or more out of employee representation as out of some other form of employer-employee relations?

That is much more difficult to answer. I think, if you take them as a whole, the unskilled and semiskilled working people of this country in the past six years have obtained more of the things trade unions want out of employee representation plans than they have out of the organized labor movement. Not that they could not have gotten them out of labor organizations if the labor organizations were efficient in handling the problems of the craftless workers in the mass-production industries. But the reason the employee representation movement has grown is because the trade unions have not succeeded in doing their job among the specialized workers in the large-scale industries. There is even evidence that these workers sometimes deliberately prefer company unions to the regular trade unions.

The reason for this preference is that they think employee representation is doing what the unions have failed to do. They think employee representation is doing the unions' job. When they are convinced that the unions are doing a better job they prefer the unions.

As I see it, you have your ordinary labor leader who learned his job under the small employer who knew everybody by name. Then you have the modern industrial relations managers who learned their jobs in the colleges of engineering and business administration, who studied labor psychology and industrial relations and scientific management. You have competition for leadership of labor, and these industrial relations managers are winning out. In my judgment, trade unionism is losing in proportion as employee representation and the other devices of modern personnel management are becoming effective. The trade unions will not go out of existence entirely, but at present they are more or less at a standstill. Why? Because they have not the kind of *trained* leadership that modern personnel management is providing for the employers.

Your industrial relations managers ask new questions—that is why they have learned to handle labor relations in a new way. You object to union leaders as "outsiders"; but your consulting experts, your personnel managers, your directors of industrial relations are the same kind of outsiders. When the unions get leaders of that kind, to ask what appear to be foolish questions about traditional union methods and policies, and thus are led to improve them, then unionism may take a spurt again and employee representation may not have as easy sailing as it has had up to the present.

To what facts can I point in support of this conclusion? Let us begin in Philadelphia. The Philadelphia Rapid Transit plan is as successful as any employee representation plan can claim to be, yet its aims and methods and practices are essentially those of trade unionism. In fact, management took two votes on the question whether the employees wanted the street railwaymen's union to represent them or a company union. Both times the employees voted down the proposition to join the regular union. They voluntarily chose the company union when management was willing to deal with organized labor. They now have a collective contract which is exactly the same as a trade union contract. They have a dues-paying organization, joint committees, arbitration, collective bargaining, and all the other forms and devices of trade unionism.

Let me give another example—Sperry Gyroscope. That company worked out a plan, as many have done, and presented it to the employees, who overwhelmingly voted it down. Two years later, however, the same employees came along with a plan of their own. Management considered it, a vote was taken, and finally it was adopted. This company union, then, is the employees' plan. What is the significance of that? To a disinterested observer it means that the managers of the regular unions were asleep. Here were employees who did not want the company's kind of employee representation. Had the union managers been awake and on the job they might have gone to the employees and told them, "We will organize and operate the kind of representation that you do want." But the employees had to work out a plan themselves. The employees, therefore, keep away from the organized labor movement and have a company union. What they are doing is what intelligently managed unions are trying to do.

Some time ago I spent a few days at a large rubber plant in Ohio, which has a congressional form of employee representation. The factory manager arranged for me to see any representatives I wanted to talk to privately. I put the question to these representatives: "Suppose there were a secret ballot to decide whether you shall have union representation or this company arrangement, with merely advisory powers?" Every one of them, including a perennial candidate for the state senate on the Socialist ticket, said that the vast, overwhelming majority would vote to stay by the company's plan and to keep away from the union plan. "Why?" I asked them. Their answer was that they felt they were getting more than joining the regular unions would give them.

Democracy in Industry

This is democracy in industry, but it is not sharing management with the workers. Managers must be free to manage, must have independent power to manage. But management can never be entirely irresponsible. At present it is generally responsible to stockholders alone. Democracy in industry means only that management shall be responsible to labor as well, that it shall be equally responsible to those who invest their strength and skill and minds in industry and to those who invest their capital.

Investors do not manage corporations. They control managers. Managers must have investors of human labor power in industry as well as the saved wealth which we call capital. If the laborers were actually to manage, we would not have democracy; we would have bedlam—but the same would be true if the stockholders managed. Management must be free to lead, to make decisions, to administer. Democracy in industry does not mean the election of managers any more than democracy in government means the election of a lot of officers. The city manager plan of government shows the essence of democracy—a manager selected to lead and make decisions, without interference, but held strictly responsible to all who are a part of the organization.

It seems strange to see this movement toward democracy in industry developing just at a time when the world is seeing a recession of the tide of political democracy, and when dictatorships and autocracies are being set up in Italy, Spain, Russia, Austria, Rumania, Poland, and other countries. Why is that? Perhaps one of those employers who believe employee representation is industrial democracy has the right explanation. This employer has said that employee representation is taking hold and developing fast because of "general recognition of the fact that political democracy or self-government in the state is somewhat hollow." Where self-government counts nowadays is not in politics or the state, not in religion or the church, but in industry on the job.

The wage earner has been a foreigner in industry. Employers complain that he has not been much interested in his work, or in the business. But why should he be interested? You could kick him out at any time.

What redress has the worker? Look at the reports of grievances adjusted under employee representation plans; in most of them, especially at the beginning, you will find two-thirds, or 70 per cent, of the cases are settled in favor of the employees. Just think of what happened before you had the machinery of employee representation, when management had its own way. Who was at fault? Always it was the worker who had to get out. He did not belong to the industry. He was banished the way they used to banish people who disagreed with the king. Management could not be interfered with, just as the king could do no wrong. Modern management, however, when it establishes employee representation, recognizes that wage earners are a part of the industry. Employee representation is a scheme for bringing them in, making citizens in industry out of them, instead of treating them like commodities or machines or mere burden bearers.

The difficulty has been that we have had no common sense of justice, no agreement on what is right and wrong in labor relations. Most people want to do the right thing, but in labor relations there is no one standard of ethics as to what is right and what is wrong.

What are fair wages, for example? Is it fair if wages go up when there is a shortage of labor and down when there is an oversupply? I have seven children. If I am working as a wage earner, shall I have seven bottles of milk on mornings when the labor market is right, and only two or three bottles when the labor market is oversupplied and there are a lot of unemployed who want my job? The wage earners think fair wages mean one thing; the employer thinks fair wages mean another thing; and we have no common agreement as to what is justice in this respect.

A Common Standard of Ethics

How do we achieve a common standard of ethics in ordinary business relations? It is done through a trade association. There are over 11,000 of these now in existence, and the old idea of one businessman getting the better of the other businessman is gradually disappearing. They agree on what is fair dealing by setting up a standard code of ethics for their industry or business.

You may say these codes are insincere, but I think they are to be compared to what a young fellow tells the girl he wants to marry. He lies like the devil as to what a fine fellow he is and what great things he can do; then, pretty soon, he feels so ashamed of himself for lying that he actually goes and does some of those things. Now, these trade associations are in the same position. Their members may vote for the code of ethics with their fingers crossed, but then they start talking about it, setting it up as an ideal, and pretty soon it becomes habit. When a dispute occurs between members and the association, they settle it according to this code; and thus common rules are established as to what is right and fair in their relations.

In labor relations, however, we have had trade associations of employers on the one side and trade unions of labor on the other, each developing different systems of ethics—with no common code except where a joint agreement was maintained between them.

Now, your employee representation plans are developing codes of ethics and common rules of justice and fair dealing which both employers and workers agree on. The decisions made by joint committees and arbitrators under representation plans, as well as under collective contracts with unions, are gradually formulating into law the points of view of both wage earners and employers as to what is right and wrong in labor relations. And through these plans, contracts, and decisions, management and men are being united into one going concern, one guild for the industry, with one standard of ethics.

The significance of employee representation is that it is making a trade association of employers and employees together in one organization, so that they can develop a common code of ethics by which labor relations can be adjusted every day, just as other business relations are adjusted in other trade associations. But the trade unions are doing the same thing. You are competing. If you don't do a good job, it will be done by the unions. If they don't do a good job, you will.

44

A Review of the Situation Just Before Things Fell Apart: 1929

The Current Labor Policies of American Industry

SUMNER H. SLICHTER

I

To the abundance of cheap immigrant labor are primarily attributable the two outstanding features of American labor policy before the war—the tendency to adapt jobs to men rather than men to jobs, and the policy of obtaining output by driving the workers rather than by developing their good will and coöperation.[1] The immigrants, being largely peasants or agricultural laborers, were available only for the least skilled industrial tasks.[2] The extraordinarily wide differential which thus came about between the wages of skilled and of unskilled labor gave managers a strong incentive to develop methods which demanded little skill and experience. This incentive was all the greater because training immigrants was extremely difficult when many supervisors could not speak the language of their men. Consequently managers displayed amazing ingenuity in adapting work to unskilled laborers, but manifested almost no interest in developing the men themselves.

There are several reasons why immigration encouraged the practice of driving workers rather than of developing their coöperation and good will.[3] Differences in language and outlook between immigrants and their supervisors prevented even employers of good intentions from gaining the confidence of most of the workers, and hence their coöperation. On the other hand, the immigrants were easily driven because they came largely from oppressed classes or races among which a tradition of docility was well established, and because their lack of industrial experience and their ignorance of English made many of them reluctant to leave one job and look for another. And employers were able to prevent concerted resistance

Reprinted from *The Quarterly Journal of Economics*, Vol. 43, May, 1929, pp. 393-435.

Dr. Slichter was a Professor of Labor Economics at Cornell University when this was written.

[1] In 1910, 48 per cent of all persons engaged in mining, 31.9 per cent of those engaged in manufacturing and mechanical pursuits, and 26.3 per cent of those engaged in transportation were foreign born. H. Jerome, *Migration and Business Cycles*, p. 46.

[2] During the period of July 1, 1907, to June 30, 1923, 26.4 per cent of the immigrants declared their occupation as "laborers" and 25.1 per cent as "farm laborers." Jerome, p. 48. Nevertheless it is true that immigration played an extremely important role in supplying men for the skilled handicrafts—so much so that the decrease in immigration since 1915 has caused the problem of apprentice training to become acute.

[3] There were, of course, other reasons for the drive system.

to drive methods by mixing workers of different, and often antagonistic, nationalities.

With labor policies so crude and simple, industrial relations were not believed to require the attention of highly paid experts. The handling of men was largely left to the department foremen, who were free to hire, "fire," and promote as they saw fit, who set piece rates, and who often possessed considerable discretion in fixing hourly rates of pay.

The European war caused net immigration to drop from 815,000 in 1913 to 50,000 in 1915 and 19,000 in 1916. It also created an intense demand for labor. The labor shortage was accentuated by the rapid spread of the eight-hour day,[4] and later by the entrance of several million men into military service. Labor turnover roughly doubled,[5] strikes increased from 1,420 in 1915 to 3,517 in 1916,[6] and 4,450 in 1917,[7] and union membership grew from 2,716,900 in 1914 to 3,508,400 in 1918 and 5,110,800 in 1920.[8] Under these conditions the old drive policies no longer worked—they simply drove men to quit or to strike. Consequently employers suddenly became interested in gaining labor's good will. By the end of 1919, 71 enterprises voluntarily established shop committees through which employees could take up grievances with the management.[9] Many firms began to provide their men with life insurance, and in some cases, with disability and sickness insurance. Sales of group insurance increased from $45,474,000 in 1914 to $178,336,000 in 1917, and $425,574,000 in 1919.[10] The number of concerns which offered old-age pensions to their employees increased from 1914 to 1919. Prior to 1914, 145 old-age pension plans had been established in American industry. During the five years ending in 1919, 90 additional plans were instituted.[11] Most important of all, the control over labor in many enterprises was transferred from the foremen to a newly created executive, the director or manager of personnel.

The severe depression of 1920-21 suddenly changed the labor market from a sellers' to a buyers' market. Except for a few months in 1923, the market has remained continuously favorable to employers. The net immigration, it is true, has been less than before the war, but this has been more

[4] From 1914 to 1919, the percentage of employees in manufacturing who regularly worked no more than 48 hours a week increased from 11.8 to 48.7. United States Bureau of Census, *Census of Manufacturers*, 1923.

[5] For the period 1913-14, the United States Bureau of Labor Statistics found a separation rate of 95 per cent and for the year ending June 30, 1918, of 183 per cent. P. F. Brissenden and E. Frankel, *Labor Turnover in Industry*, pp. 88-89.

[6] *Monthly Labor Review* (April, 1916), pp. 13-18.

[7] United States Bureau of Labor Statistics, *Handbook of Labor Statistics* (1924-26), p. 570.

[8] Leo Wolman, *The Growth of American Trades Unions, 1880-1923*, p. 33.

[9] National Industrial Conference Board, *The Growth of Works Councils in the United States*, p. 10. Forty-nine of these committee plans were initiated in either 1918 or 1919. In addition, eighty firms had established shop committees at the order of the government.

[10] New York Trust Company, *The Index* (May, 1927), p. 7. Group insurance is a plan by which a group of employees is insured. A master policy covering the entire group is issued to the employer, and individual policies are issued to the insured employees. The expense may be borne entirely by the employer or jointly by the employer and employees. The most usual type of group insurance is life insurance, but accident or sickness insurance is sometimes provided.

[11] Pennsylvania Old Age Pension Commission, A. Epstein, *The Problem of Old Age Pensions in Industry*, p. 21.

than counteracted by the enlarged flow of labor from farm to city; labor turnover has been low except for a short time in 1923; and, from 1920 to 1926, the total union membership in the United States dropped about 30 per cent. *In short, every aspect of the post-war labor situation might be expected to cause employers to abandon their newly acquired interest in labor's good will and to revert to pre-war labor policies.*

And yet, except in a few cases, this has not happened. On the contrary, the efforts to gain labor's good will have steadily grown. Shop-committee plans increased from 145 in 1919 to 385 in 1922 and 432 in 1926.[12] Most of the group insurance now in effect has been sold since 1921.[13] During the last five years, over 300 companies have instituted some form of stock purchase for their employees. Of the 370 private industrial pension plans now in existence, 72 were established between 1921 and 1925.[14] Two thirds of 1,058 enterprises which give vacations with pay to manual laborers began the policy since the first of 1920.[15] During the last ten years, industrial good will has been rapidly acquiring an importance in American business comparable to that which consumers' good will has long possessed; employers have been developing the same keen interest in the good will of their workers, the same willingness to make large expenditures in order to obtain it, that they have manifested toward the good will of their customers. The outstanding task of one who essays to account for the present labor policies of American industry is to explain why this interest in industrial good will has continued to grow, despite the shift of power in favor of employers; why, in other words, the passing of abnormal war conditions has not produced a reversion to pre-war labor policies.

II

The failure of the change in the labor market to end the interest of business men in labor's good will appears to have been due to three principal reasons: (1) the dread of labor trouble; (2) the inability or the unwillingness of employers to reduce wages in proportion to the drop in wholesale prices; and (3) a better appreciation by managers of the relation between morale and the efficiency of labor.[16]

[12] *An Advance Report of an Investigation of the National Industrial Conference Board on the Growth of Employee Representation in the United States, Law and Labor*, ix (March, 1927), 61.

[13] Prior to the depression of 1920-21, the largest sales of group insurance occurred in 1919, when $425,574,000 was sold. In 1924, however, the sales were $597,765,000; in 1925, $998,784,000; and in 1926, $1,050,605,000. New York Trust Company, *The Index* (May, 1927), p. 7.

[14] A. Epstein, *The Problem of Old Age Pensions*, pp. 115-126.

[15] *Law and Labor*, x (May, 1928), 113.

[16] It is desirable to point out that ever since 1910 a foundation for better industrial relations was slowly being built up by the growing use of time and motion studies in setting piece rates. The intimate connection between time and motion study and labor policies has been inadequately appreciated. It is easy, however, to see why inaccurate methods of timing operations prevented satisfactory industrial relations. When a rate was based on too liberal a time allowance, a cut in the rate was, sooner or later, inevitable. Such cuts, of course, excited intense ill will. But they did more than this—they led workmen to restrict output, and this in turn led the management to use drive methods. Time study has tended to diminish driving by making rate cuts unnecessary.

The employers' dread of labor trouble reached its apex in 1920. During the preceding six years, the labor movement had threatened the power of American employers more seriously than ever before. Trade union membership, as was stated above, nearly doubled between 1914 and 1920. Unionism even established itself temporarily in such open-shop strongholds as the Chicago packing plants, the mills of the United States Steel Corporation, and the shops of the Pennsylvania Railroad. The employers' alarm was accentuated by the belief that American labor was in danger of becoming radical—a fear that was fostered by the general strikes in Seattle and Winnipeg during 1919, the Boston policemen's strike, the great coal strike of 1920, and the support of the Plumb plan by the heretofore staid and conservative railroad brotherhoods. The dread of radicalism was encouraged by interested groups, such as the National Civic Federation and the National Security League, and even by Mr. Gompers and his lieutenants, who skillfully fostered the country's fears in order to present conservative unionism as a bulwark against irresponsible and dangerous groups.

Business men did not suddenly lose their fear of labor troubles when the collapse of prosperity filled the streets with job-seekers late in 1920. Even at the end of 1921, union membership was a million more than in 1914, and strikes, though fewer than in the immediately preceding years, were still numerous. Furthermore, the precipitous drop of prices made wage reductions imperative, and every cut in wages increased the danger of trouble. At this particular time, however, many concerns were peculiarly unable to risk a strike because, during the boom period, they had speculated heavily in raw materials. When prices fell, these enterprises were left with a large floating indebtedness which they were under the necessity of liquidating as soon as possible. Consequently they were in no position to face the loss of production and the heavy expenses which a strike would entail. The double necessity of reducing wages and of avoiding strikes stimulated the interest of many employers in gaining labor's good will.

In some plants, especially those in which the workers were organized, wage reductions led to strikes, and, in many cases, the unions lost and were destroyed. It is extremely interesting to notice the effect of these victories over unions upon the personnel policies of the enterprises. The management was usually determined never again to be troubled by labor organizations. Accordingly, after driving out unions, many concerns immediately embarked upon carefully planned attempts to gain the good will of their employees. Some enterprises followed the destruction of unions with the creation of shop committees to represent the employees. The General Electric Company, the International Paper Company, and many of the railroads are examples. Especially noteworthy is the great interest which many railroads developed in the welfare of their shopmen following the great strike of 1922. Roads which had done little to cultivate the good will of their shopmen as long as the workers were organized suddenly became greatly concerned about good industrial relations when their men returned to work as non-unionists.

Another outstanding determinant of American postwar labor policy has been the inability or the unwillingness of employers to reduce wages in proportion to the fall in non-agricultural wholesale prices. Between 1920 and 1921, non-agricultural wholesale prices decreased about 31 per cent, and between 1920 and 1922 about 30 per cent.[17] Had employers been more willing to risk labor trouble, they undoubtedly could have reduced wages in proportion to wholesale prices.[18] But the fear of strikes, which has already been explained, checked the reduction in wages. The best measure of wage *rates* is hourly earnings. Between 1920 and 1921, the hourly earnings of factory workers decreased about 14 per cent and between 1920 and 1922 about 19 per cent.[19] Wage rates undoubtedly dropped somewhat more—possibly from 20 to 25 per cent between 1920 and 1922.

Having failed to reduce wages in proportion to the fall in prices, employers were compelled to make their men more efficient. This might have been done by reverting to pre-war methods; but the same dread of strikes which prevented more drastic wage reductions made many managements unwilling to try driving. One course remained—to increase efficiency by developing a stable force and by winning the good will and coöperation of the men. This alternative was widely adopted.

Possibly the most important determinant of post-war labor policies, at least during the last four or five years, has been the growing realization by managers of the close relationship between industrial morale and efficiency. When the severe drop in prices and in sales during 1920 and 1921 caused managers to search meticulously for methods of cutting costs and of increasing sales, many ways were found in which the workers could help *if they would.* Spurred by financial necessity, managers sought the aid of their employees to an unprecedented extent in saving material, reducing the wear and tear on equipment, diminishing the amount of spoiled product, improving the quality of workmanship and even in soliciting additional business. Some concerns, such as the Bethlehem Steel Corporation and the International Harvester Company, have used their shop committees to reduce costs. The committees have suggested ways of saving labor and materials, they have made improvements in the location of tool rooms and in the methods of issuing tools, they have helped increase the value of scrap by segregating materials of varying composition, and they have assisted in raising the quality of workmanship.[20] The Bethlehem Steel Corporation has attempted to interest its employees in saving supplies by calling attention through its committees to the expense of certain things which are often wasted.[21] Public utility companies have endeavored to

[17] *Handbook of Labor Statistics* (1924-1926), p. 517. In addition, the physical volume of manufacturing dropped about 23 per cent between 1920 and 1921. (*Federal Reserve Bulletin*, xiii [February, 1927], 100.) By 1922, the physical volume of manufacturing had recovered to the 1920 level.

[18] The willingness of employers to risk labor trouble in order to reduce wages should be carefully distinguished from their willingness to risk it in order to get rid of unions. The very fear of unions and radicalism which made business men over-reluctant to reduce wages made them over-eager to destroy labor organizations. Consequently, some enterprises recklessly courted costly shut-downs in order to drive out unions, and others timidly refrained from making urgently needed wage reductions.

[19] National Industrial Conference Board, *Wages in the United States, 1914-1927*, p. 29.

[20] *Bethlehem Review* (April 22, 1925), p. 3.

[21] For example, the company calls attention to the fact that in 1925 its expenditures for soap were $8,161; paper towels, $14,780; brooms, $17,255; window glass, $25,855; shovels, $30,000; electric light bulbs, $200,000. *Bethlehem Review* (April 24, 1924), p. 4.

Following the success of the union-management coöperative plan on the Balti-

interest their employees in the more accurate reading of meters and computation of monthly bills. The People's Gas Light and Coke Company of Chicago is an example. Although ten operations are necessary to prepare the bill for each reading, the company reports that in 1926 the errors in meter reading and billing were only about .007 per cent.[22] The Chicago Motor Coach Company and the Boston Elevated Railways have conducted fuel-saving campaigns among their employees. Possibly the most notable attempts to gain the help of employees have been made by the railroads. Almost all roads have instituted fuel-saving campaigns among the engineers and firemen. Many have sought to reduce damage to equipment and freight by appealing to the train crews for smoother handling of cars and to the freight-house employees for more careful handling of less-than-carload shipments.[23] A number of companies have sought the aid of the shopmen in increasing the locomotive mileage per engine failure. Some roads now post the mileage per engine failure in the roundhouses, and the Rock Island publishes the figures by divisions in its monthly magazine. Efforts have also been made to interest the shopmen in reducing the number of locomotives found defective by the federal inspectors,[24] and to gain the coöperation of all employees in improving the "on time" performance of both passenger and freight trains. The Erie, the Missouri Pacific, the St. Louis and San Francisco, the Southern, and the Chicago and Great Western now announce in their monthly magazines the percentage of passenger trains arriving "on time"; the Rock Island publishes the "on time" performance of both passenger and freight trains and also a list of the trains which have maintained perfect records; and the New York Central publishes the percentage of less-than-carload shipments which arrive on time.

Of course, the efforts of managements to reduce costs and to increase sales by persuading wage earners to go out of their way to help would not have persisted had the results not been satisfactory. But the workers responded to appeals for their help with almost startling generosity. And naturally this response has profoundly affected the labor policies of employers. The more plainly the workers have demonstrated the value of their coöperation, the greater has become the interest of managers in labor's good will. During the war, and to a great extent during the post-war

---

more and Ohio, the Canadian National, and other railway systems, several roads have sought to develop a coöperative plan in conjunction with their "company unions." The Atchison, Topeka and Santa Fe and the Union Pacific are examples.

[22] People's Gas Light and Coke Company, *Year Book* (1927), p. 15.

[23] Between 1920 and 1927 payments on loss and damage per carload of revenue freight decreased from $2.66 to $0.72. To a small extent this was due to the drop in the price level.

[24] Some indication of the improved morale and increased efficiency in the railroad shops is given by the decreasing proportion of locomotives found defective by the federal inspectors. In the year ending June 30, 1923, when the percentage was affected by the shopmen's strike in the summer of 1922, 65 per cent of the locomotives inspected were found defective and over 10 per cent were ordered out of service. In the next year, the percentage of defective locomotives dropped to 53 per cent; in the year ending June 30, 1925, to 46; in the year ending June 30, 1926, to 40; and finally, in the year ending June 30, 1927, to 31 per cent. The percentage of locomotives ordered out of service dropped from 8.8 in 1923-1924 and 5.0 in 1924-1925 to 3.6 in 1925-1926, and 2.6 in 1926-1927. The Interstate Commerce Commission, *Sixteenth Annual Report of the Chief Inspector, Bureau of Locomotive Inspection* (1927), p. 1.

depression, managers sought labor's good will largely in order to avoid labor trouble. As the fear of strikes has diminished and as labor has demonstrated its willingness to coöperate, the desire for labor's help has become the most important single influence molding the labor policies of American employers.

III

The methods by which industrial enterprises have attempted to make their workers more efficient and more contented fall into six principal groups: (1) helping their employees acquire property; (2) helping them acquire a "stake" in the enterprise by which they are employed; (3) protecting them against arbitrary treatment; (4) rewarding continuity of service; (5) giving them opportunities to advance to more responsible positions; (6) giving them security.

The rise of about 11 per cent in the real hourly earnings of factory workers between 1920 and 1925 led to a great increase in saving among wage earners.[25] It was natural that the growing tendency of employees to save should be encouraged by business men. The disposition of employers to foster saving was stimulated by their fear of radicalism and by a somewhat naïve faith in the power of even small amounts of property to alter the fundamental economic views of its owners.[26] But even though small amounts of property may influence the economic philosophy of wage earners less than most employers believe, the stimulation of saving is undoubtedly good personnel policy, because a man who is setting aside a small part of his earnings each week cannot escape feeling that he is getting ahead, even though slowly. This may not make him satisfied with his compensation, but it is likely to take the edge off his dissatisfaction.[27]

The most usual method of encouraging saving is for the employer to obtain an authorization from the employee to deposit to the employee's credit in a savings bank a stipulated deduction from his pay. The employee escapes the temptation to spend his money before he has made a deposit of part of it, and he even avoids the trouble of going to the bank. This plan

[25] From 1921 to 1926, saving deposits in banks and trust companies in the United States increased from over $16,500,000,000 to nearly $24,700,000,000; and between 1921 and 1925 the assets of building and loan associations increased from $2,890,000,000 to $5,509,000,000. (Statistical Abstract of the United States [1926], pp. 263 and 267.) It is impossible to say what proportion of the increase was in the savings of wage earners, but these savings probably increased as rapidly as deposits in savings banks.

[26] For example, Mr. John F. Tinsley, vice-president of the Crompton and Knowles Loom Works, says: "Through a savings plan the employers make more capitalists among the wage earners and I think all must feel that this is a desirable end. The more the wealth of the country is distributed, the less socialistic will be the tendencies among the masses of our people." (*New Phases of Industrial Management*, p. 194.) Mr. C. J. Hicks, executive assistant to the president of the Standard Oil Company of New Jersey, writes: "The employee who is saving his money becomes a capitalist and is no longer hostile to capitalism." (*Harvard Business Review*, ii [January, 1924], 200.)

[27] It is true also that the desire to save is likely to increase the efficiency of piece- and bonus-workers, who constitute about half of the employees engaged in manufacturing. (See result of an investigation which I made of this point, and which was published in the *American Economic Review*, xv, Supplement [March, 1925], 94-95.) But, strange to say, I have been unable to discover a single case in which it is acknowledged that saving is encouraged because of the expected effect upon the efficiency of piece-workers.

is followed by the Crompton and Knowles Loom Works. After five years, 80 per cent of its 2,500 employees were participating in the arrangement.[28] Some enterprises offer to hold the savings of their employees. In such cases, the company usually pays the same rate of interest that it would pay a commercial bank for a loan—usually one or two per cent more than the rate paid by savings banks on time deposits. This is the practice of the Commonwealth Edison Company of Chicago, which has an "Employees' Saving Fund," to which, at the end of 1926, 5,165 of its 9,900 employees were subscribers.[29] An exceptionally high rate of interest is paid by the General Electric Securities Corporation which sells its bonds to the employees of the General Electric Company. The bonds pay 6 per cent, to which is added 2 per cent as long as the owner is in the employ of the General Electric Company. Thirty-two thousand employees, or nearly half the force, have purchased these bonds.[30]

Many workers wish not merely to save, but to save in order to acquire homes. From the standpoint of the employer, it is more desirable that an employee have a house which is partly paid for than that he have several hundred dollars in the bank. A man who owns a house near his place of work is more or less tied to his job, unless there are other plants nearby at which he could pursue his occupation. And, more important, a worker who is buying a home is careful to avoid discharge, unlikely to resign (unless he is confident of promptly obtaining another job) or to strike, and more eager to increase his earnings and hence his efficiency. Since the payments on a house usually extend over years, the encouragement of home ownership is an effective way of diminishing the independence of the workers.

Home ownership is encouraged by selling houses or land to employees at low prices, by assisting employees to finance the acquisition of property, by giving free legal and architectural help, and by establishing building and loan associations among employees. The Eastman Kodak Company has built houses in small groups and has sold them at prices which gave the workers the benefit of the economical multiple construction.[31] The Commonwealth Steel Company appraises the land and examines the title without charge, and lends money at 5 per cent, repayable in monthly installments.[32] The Oneida Community sells land at a low rate, provides the services of an architect, assists the employee to borrow from a bank on a first mortgage, and itself lends him money on a second mortgage. On completion of the house, the company gives the worker a bonus of $200. To receive assistance, the worker must have saved ten per cent of the cost of the house.[33] The Bethlehem Steel Corporation guarantees or purchases the second mortgage on the property, and gives the employee free architectural, engineering, financial, and legal advice.[34] The Milwaukee Electric Railway and Light Company has established a mutual savings, building,

[28] J. F. Tinsley, *New Phases of Industrial Management*, p. 176.

[29] Commonwealth Edison Company, *Annual Report* (1926).

[30] General Electric Company, *Thirty-Fifth Annual Report*, p. 21.

[31] *Law and Labor*, ix (May, 1927), 133.

[32] *The Commonwealth*, xiii (June, 1927), 3.

[33] Ester Lowenthal, "The Labor Policy of the Oneida Community, Ltd.," *Journal of Political Economy*, xxxv, 122.

[34] Presidential Address of C. M. Schwab before the American Society of Mechanical Engineers, December, 1927, *Law and Labor*, x (January, 1928), 18.

and loan association for its employees. The assets of the association exceed $8,000,000 and more than four-fifths of the married male employees own their own homes.[35]

From encouraging employees to save, it is a short step to encouraging them to invest their savings in stock of the enterprise which employs them. Some business men and personnel experts have acquired amazing faith in the power of a few shares of stock to make workmen interested in efficiency and unwilling to join trade unions or to strike. Mr. Glen A. Bowers of the Industrial Relations Counselors, Inc., has stated that employee stock ownership "makes the worker a capitalist in viewpoint and this renders him a conservative and immune from radical ideas";[36] Mr. F. H. Sisson, vice-president of the Guaranty Trust Company, that diffusion in the ownership of industry "will decrease class-conscious antagonism by bringing about a partial identification of interests as between laborers and capitalists," and "will discourage the propagation of dangerous and violent social theories";[37] and Mr. T. E. Mitten of the Philadelphia Rapid Transit Company, that "if the principle were applied to all industry, America would within a year become a strike-proof nation."[38] During the last seven years nearly all of the largest enterprises in the country have made special efforts to sell stock to their employees.[39]

No recent development of personnel practice has attracted wider attention than employee stock ownership. And yet it is among the least significant of the new labor policies. When a large proportion of employees owns stock, the ground is undoubtedly prepared for the management to insist upon better workmanship or more output, and, in consequence, the task of improving the efficiency of the force may be somewhat

[35] The Milwaukee Electric Railway and Light Company, *Year Book* (1926), p. 41. It seems clear, however, that in some cases the employees who have been assisted to acquire houses have almost exclusively been minor officials of the company or higher paid, skilled employees. For example, by the end of 1926, the General Electric Company had assisted 1,125 of its 75,000 employees to purchase homes. (General Electric Company, *Thirty-Fifth Annual Report*, p. 21.) Furthermore, the average value of the houses which the employees were assisted to purchase was $8,000—distinctly more than most wage earners could afford. So far as the effect on labor turnover is concerned, it is probable that the workers who have purchased houses are those who are most inclined to be stable, and who in many cases would probably purchase homes without aid from their employers.

[36] *New Tactics in Social Conflict*, p. 4.

[37] *General Electric News, Lynn Works*, ix (December 2, 1927), 9.

[38] Philadelphia Rapid Transit Company, *Service Talks*, vii (Sept. 28, 1926), no. 21.

[39] In order to induce the employees to invest, the shares are often offered at substantially less than the market price. The Union Oil Company of California sold stock to its employees at 5 per cent below the market; the Electric Storage Battery Company at about 20 per cent below. The American Telephone and Telegraph offered stock to its employees in 1925 at $125 a share. The range of the market price for that year was from $130 to $145. Early in 1926, the Pullman Company sold stock at $140. The low for the year on the New York Exchange was $145½ and the high was $199½. Several of the Standard Oil Companies gave the employee a share for every two that he purchased. This, of course, amounted to selling the stock at one third below the nominal price. In still other cases, employee stockholders are paid a special bonus, in addition to regular dividends. General Motors Corporation and the International Harvester Company pay a bonus of $2 a share for five years after the employee has paid for his stock; E. I. du Pont de Nemours and Company pays $3; the Bucyrus Company pays a bonus of $5 a share for five years, regardless of whether or not the stock has been paid for.

easier.[40] But unless the management demands greater efficiency, stock ownership alone is not likely to produce it. Nor is there any real evidence that a few shares in a huge corporation affect the fundamental economic views of the worker, cause him to "feel himself a partner rather than a servant," render him a "capitalist in viewpoint" and "immune from radical ideals," or make him less willing to join a trade union or to strike for higher wages.[41] As a matter of fact, it would be surprising if these results occurred. During 1927 the average factory worker in the United States earned $1,299. In order, therefore, to possess an interest as a stockholder which approximates his interest as a wage earner, the typical factory worker would need about $20,000 of stock. The National Industrial Conference Board has found that the average subscription in 315 corporations is only $1,300.[42] It is scarcely conceivable that the ownership of twelve or thirteen shares would materially alter the attitudes of employees toward wages, hours, or working conditions. Suppose that a man earns $1,200 a year and that he has purchased thirteen shares of $100 each. Dividends at the rate of seven per cent yield him $91 a year. Assume that the men seek a 10 per cent advance in wages. The company replies that such an increase would necessitate cutting dividends in half, a loss to the employee-stockholder of $45.50 a year. But a 10 per cent advance in wages would give him $120 a year. Is it likely that the title to thirteen shares of stock would diminish his interest in higher wages or prevent him from joining a union or from striking in order to get them?

The traditional drive system of management naturally gave rise to many methods of handling labor which created ill will and resentment. In order

[40] In a large number of cases, the proportion of employees owning stock is very large: for example, Bethlehem Steel Corporation, over 60 per cent (*Bethlehem Review* [February 1, 1926], p. 3); the Commonwealth Edison Company, 43 per cent; the Standard Oil Company of California, 86 per cent of 14,200 eligible employees; the Standard Oil Company of Indiana, 71 per cent of 22,000 eligible employees. (Foerster and Dietel, *Employee Stock Ownership in the United States*, pp. 115, 138, 160, 161.)

[41] The defeat of a carpenters' strike in Reading, Pennsylvania, is said to have been aided by the refusal of some carpenters to participate because they owned small blocks of stock and considered themselves "members of the firm." (*Labor Age*, xiv [July, 1927], 24.) But it is obvious that the carpenters may have given this reason to justify a refusal which rested upon other grounds—probably upon a conviction that the strike would fail. In any event, the effect of a share in a *small* enterprise sheds little light on the probable effect of a share in a large concern. For example, the fact that the photo-engravers' union has found it desirable to prohibit its members from buying shares in the small shops which are typical of the photo-engraving industry, or that the International Ladies Garment Workers' Union has experienced difficulty in controlling the small shops manned by working partners and known as "social shops," is scarcely indicative of how a worker will be affected by a $1,000 interest in a billion-dollar enterprise such as the United States Steel Corporation or the General Motors Corporation.

[42] The New York Trust Company, *The Index* (October, 1928), p. 8. Many enterprises limit the number of shares which will be sold to an employee under the stock-purchase plans. The Great Atlantic and Pacific Tea Company restricts subscriptions to one-tenth of the employee's annual earnings; E. I. du Pont de Nemours and Company to one-fifth; and the General Motors Company to one-third. The American Telephone and Telegraph Company permits each worker to purchase one share for each $300 of his annual earnings; the Bethlehem Steel Corporation, one for each $400; and the Electric Storage Company and the Pullman Company, one for each $500.

that enterprises should gain the good will of their men, it was necessary for them to effect substantial improvements in the practices of foremen and other minor executives in dealing with labor. Three principal methods have been used: (1) centralization of control over discharges; (2) foreman training; (3) shop committees. These efforts to improve the handling of men are among the most important developments in American personnel practice.

Of the three methods, that used most extensively has been the transfer of authority to discharge from the foreman to the head of the labor department. In some cases the foreman is permitted to dismiss men from his own department but not from the service of the firm; in others, the approval of the labor manager is necessary even to remove a worker from a department. Some companies, including several of the Standard Oil companies and the Boston Rubber Shoe Company, forbid discharge for the first offense except in the case of a few serious acts which are listed in the book of rules. Restricting the freedom of the foreman to discharge has profoundly affected his methods of handling men because it has deprived him of his chief disciplinary device. This has compelled him to rely less upon threats for obtaining results and to make greater efforts to get along amicably with his men. The consequence naturally has been a drop in the number of petty grievances.[43]

The eagerness of managers to improve the handling of men has led hundreds of enterprises during the last seven or eight years to establish classes in foremanship. Swift and Company, for example, have put 4,600 of their foremen through a training course. The United States Chamber of Commerce has a record of 324 foremanship courses (exclusive of correspondence courses) conducted during the year ending in June, 1926, and of 933 in the year ending June, 1927.[44] So rapid has been the spread of foreman training, that concerns have been created to conduct classes on a commercial basis, and some trade associations, such as the National Metal

[43] As a matter of fact, labor managers almost invariably approve the discharges which the foremen recommend. Nevertheless, the centralization of authority over discharges has a profound effect because the foremen interpret it to mean that discharges are not desired.

The restrictions upon the freedom of foremen to discharge might be expected to reduce the number of discharges, and to some extent this result seems to have occurred. For example, during the period 1910 to 1915, the United States Bureau of Labor Statistics found a discharge rate of 17.5 per cent among 153 establishments. (P. F. Brissenden and E. Frankel, *Labor Turnover in Industry*, pp. 80-81.) Among 78 plants, I found a discharge rate of 12.5 per cent during the period 1910 to 1913. (*The Turnover of Factory Labor*, p. 94.) The Metropolitan Life Insurance Company, however, found a discharge rate of only 6.5 per cent among 300 plants for 1926, and of 5.5 per cent for 1927. (*Handbook of Labor Statistics* [1924-1926], p. 585, and *Monthly Labor Review*, xxvii [July, 1928], 27.)

But discharge rates based upon the average number of workers employed are somewhat misleading. Discharges vary with hirings as well as with the size of the force, because it is the newly hired men who are most likely to be discharged. The principal cause for the decrease in the discharge rate has been the decrease in the number of hirings. Compared with the number of hirings, however, discharges are not clearly less numerous now than before the war. For the period 1910 to 1915, the Bureau of Labor Statistics found one discharge for every 5.5 men hired; but, for the period 1910 to 1913, I found one discharge for every 8.3 men hired. For 1926, the Metropolitan Life Insurance Company found one discharge for every 8.4 hirings and, for 1927, one discharge for every 7.3 hirings.

[44] U.S. Chamber of Commerce, *Growth of Foremanship Courses in the United States*, June, 1926, to June, 1927, p. 11.

Trades Association, have prepared courses for their members.[45] Of less importance than classes on foremanship, but significant of the trend of the times, are the special handbooks for foremen, such as the Bethlehem Steel Corporation's Hints to Foremen, the Scoville Manufacturing Company's Foremen's Manual, and, most elaborate of all, the Lehigh Coal and Navigation Company's Mine Management Policies, running, in the revised edition, to 117 pages.

These policies with regard to foremen—depriving them of authority to discharge and training them in better methods of handling men—do not entirely eliminate grievances. The steady increase in the number of shop committees since 1921 indicates that many managers recognize the undesirablity of permitting grievances to smolder unadjusted. The disposition of the cases handled by these committees is significant. Mere statistics, of course, cannot prove that employees are obtaining justice, but the many decisions in favor of the men suggest that managers consider it wise to be fair in at least a substantial proportion of the cases. The Bethlehem Steel Corporation reports that, out of 2,316 cases, 1,682, or over two-thirds, were settled in favor of the employee.[46] Of more than 1,800 matters considered by the plant assemblies of Swift and Company prior to 1925, about 70 per cent were settled in favor of the employee.[47] At the Lynn works of the General Electric Company, 274 cases were settled by the shop committee in the first two years: 76 were decided in favor of the employee, 99 in favor of the management, 7 were compromised, 21 were withdrawn, 14 were not considered, and 52 were submitted to other authorities for decision.[48] Out of the 45,930 cases considered by the employee committees of the Pennsylvania Railroad during the four years ending 1924, 21,904, or 47.7 per cent, were adjusted or compromised in favor of the employee; 13,320, or 29 per cent, were withdrawn or decided against the employee, and 10,693, or 23.3 per cent, were appealed to the next higher officer.[49]

The acute scarcity of labor during the war caused employers to discover the importance and the cost of labor turnover. The post-war drop in prices, which compelled managers to hunt for every possible way of cutting costs, accentuated the interest of managers in reducing labor turnover. One of the outstanding features of recent American personnel policy, therefore, has been the endeavor to increase the efficiency of labor by encouraging continuity of service.

[45] The current methods of training foremen leave much room for improvement. The situation has been well described by Mr. L. A. Hartley: "It is well to observe here that many of the foreman training activities conducted at present throughout the country are open to considerable question as permanent methods. The success of the short, intensive foreman training conferences is due very largely to the fact that the present methods of foremanship have been so generally poor that almost any kind of a discussion of present problems is helpful." (Chamber of Commerce of the United States, *Employee Training*, p. 17.)

[46] John Calder, "Five Years' Representation Under the Bethlehem Plan," *Iron Age*, cxi, 1,694.

[47] Swift and Company, *Year Book* (1925), p. 51.

[48] E. H. Morell, *The Lynn Plan of Representation*, chart no. 3. But the most significant thing about these figures is the small number of cases which arose during a period of two years in a large force. The conclusion appears to be inevitable that the shop committees failed to command the confidence of the employees, or that there were other more satisfactory ways of having grievances adjusted.

[49] Pennsylvania Railroad Company, *Employee Representation*, p. 47.

Many of the recent developments in personnel practice—such as group insurance, old-age pensions, promotion of home ownership, protection of employees against arbitrary treatment, and vacations with pay—have the encouragement of continuous service as *one* of their purposes.[50] Of special importance, however, are specific rewards for continuous service. Many enterprises now advance the wages of workers at given intervals of employment. The Oneida Community, Ltd., adds one per cent to the worker's wage at the end of the month. This rises by gradual increments to 5 per cent in twelve months, 7 per cent in two years, and 10 per cent in five years.[51] The Eastman Kodak Company pays a wage dividend which is affected by the employee's length of service. For every dollar in excess of the first dollar paid in dividends on common stock, the company pays a wage dividend of $5 on every $1,000 earned by the worker in the preceding five-year period. The company is now paying $8 on its common stock. This makes the wage dividend $35 for every $1,000 earned by each employee during the last five years of service.[52] The Studebaker Corporation pays a bonus of 5 per cent of the worker's last year's earnings on each anniversary of his service, and the Crocker-McElwain Company a differential for each year of service up to five, when the worker becomes eligible to apply for a written agreement guaranteeing him full employment.[53]

One of the most effective ways of encouraging continuous service is to transfer men, after a given period of employment, from the hourly to the monthly pay roll, thus giving them the privileges enjoyed by the regular salaried staff. This is done by the Commonwealth Edison Company of Chicago at the end of a year's service. An employee on the hourly pay roll who is absent a day or so for some reason other than sickness is not compensated, but the man on the monthly pay roll receives full pay. A worker on the monthly pay roll who becomes ill or is injured receives *full* pay for seven working days. Thereafter, until he returns to work, he is paid a *portion* of his salary. The hourly man is given half of his normal wages for the first seven days of his incapacitation, but after this receives nothing.[54] Most important of all is the fact that the worker who is on the monthly pay roll feels that he has a permanent job, because reductions in staff are made by first laying off the hourly men. The Standard Oil Company of California also places all employees, regardless of their work, on a monthly salary after a year's service. Every salaried employee, whether common laborer or manager, receives the same privileges—an annual vacation of two weeks with full pay, a pension after a number of years of service, and compensation during sickness and recovery from accident for a certain period depending upon the length of employment, but regardless of whether the sickness or accident was incurred in line of

[50] Except possibly in the case of the encouragement of home ownership, the predominant purpose is not to encourage continuous service. A principal object of insurance and pensions is to provide a regular way of dealing with situations which have often subjected employers and their men to appeals for charity and which have been injurious to morale.

[51] Esther Lowenthal, *Journal of Political Economy*, xxxv, 118.

[52] *Law and Labor*, ix (May, 1927), 132. An official of the company says: "We believe that the payment of these wage dividends has resulted in greatly reduced labor turnover and increased loyalty and efficiency of employees."

[53] "Stabilizing Employment Plans," *Law and Labor*, viii (May, 1926), 140.

[54] Letter from the company to the writer.

duty.[55] Most effective of all rewards for continuous service is a definite guaranty of steady employment to workers who have served a given time. The Crocker-McElwain Company, for example, guarantees full-time work to each man who has been in its employ five years or more.[56]

A highly significant recent development in American personnel policy has been the creation of definite sequences of promotion and the filling of vacancies in accordance with merit. The mere transfer of the control of hiring and firing from the foreman to the labor manager has tended to bring about advancement on the basis of merit. As long as each foreman hired and promoted his own men, many vacancies were filled, not by promotions, but by hiring new men. In fact, many foremen preferred not to promote their best men. The better a man performed an operation, the more anxious the foreman was to keep him at it, because it meant one less job to worry about. Some foremen deliberately gave the best places to friends. This was done partly out of friendship, but partly also because a group of friends sprinkled throughout the force made the department easier to manage.[57]

The labor manager, on the other hand, has no reason to refuse to promote a worker simply because the man is especially good at a certain job, nor is he seriously tempted to promote on the basis of friendship, because, as a rule, he is intimately acquainted with relatively few wage earners in the plant. In addition, the spread of the policy of promotion by merit has been stimulated by two special causes—the desire to keep down labor turnover and the necessity of adjusting labor costs to the post-war level. Studies of labor turnover revealed that many enterprises were losing good men because workers could obtain better jobs more easily by changing employers than by winning advancement. In order to encourage continuity of service, many labor managers have adopted the policy of hiring outsiders only for the least desirable jobs, and of filling the best jobs by promotion. This policy was still further stimulated by the drop of prices in 1920. In order to reduce labor costs in proportion to the fall in prices, it was necessary to provide every possible incentive for workers to be more efficient, and one incentive offered them has been the opportunity to win better jobs by merit.

Not only has advancement in accordance with merit spread rapidly, but many enterprises have established classes in which employees can prepare themselves for promotion. The Boston Elevated Company offers courses in business English, inter-departmental accounts, and automotive maintenance; the General Electric Company has a vast variety of courses of different grades, including machine design, blue-print reading, shop mathematics, armature winding, mechanical drawing, switchboard testing, and courses for clerical employees.[58] The Milwaukee Electric Railway and Light Company has classes in car wiring, boiler room practice, and the company accounting system.[59] Swift and Company report that on

[55] W. J. Held, *Forbes Magazine* (June 1, 1925), pp. 261-262.

[56] *Law and Labor*, viii (May, 1926), 139.

[57] Occasionally the foreman used his control of jobs to create a personal machine which rendered him more or less independent of his superiors. The firm could not discharge him without causing a large part of the department to quit.

[58] General Electric Company, Education Facilities for Employees of the General Electric Company.

[59] The Milwaukee Electric Railway and Light Company, *Year Book* (1926), p. 38.

November 1, 1924, over 6,200 of its 50,000 employees were pursuing educational work offered by the company.[60] This included physics, salesmanship, business English, and a general course—in which were enrolled 500 of the most promising young men in the production departments of thirteen plants—covering the policies and methods of the company.[61] The Crompton and Knowles Loom Works, in the year 1923-24, had about 600 of its 2,500 workers enrolled in its evening courses on loom construction, mechanical drawing, blue-print reading, machine-tool operation, pattern making, molding, forging, welding, weaving, and the properties of iron and steel.[62]

Promotion in accordance with merit is of great importance, because the employee feels that he has more than a job—that he has the opportunity for a career, a chance to advance into jobs which he had dreamed of holding but which he could never see a way of reaching. And the workers who best appreciate the chance to win promotion by merit are likely to be the ablest and most ambitious in the force, precisely those who, if given no opportunity to advance, would be most active in organizing and leading trade unions. Unionism in the United States has always suffered because of the relative ease with which able wage earners could rise out of their class. Employers are now making advancement for superior workmen more attainable than ever before. In a generation or two, the effect upon the labor movement may be substantial.

Of the most recent developments in personnel practice, by far the most important is the endeavor of employers to make the jobs of their men more secure. Why have managers suddenly acquired such a deep and genuine interest in the stability of employment? The severe unemployment of 1921 is not a satisfactory explanation, because the grave depressions of 1893, 1908, and 1914 aroused no similar interest. Four principal circumstances appear to explain the present concern of business men with the regularity of employment. Possibly the most important has been the desire of managers to reduce labor turnover—a desire which was created, we have seen, largely by the war boom. It is apparent that whatever is done to make jobs attractive can have little effect if the workers regard their positions as only temporary. Nor is there much point in encouraging continuity of service, if, at frequent intervals, one-fifth to one-third of the force is laid off. A second reason for the interest of managers in stability of employment has been the urgent necessity of increasing the efficiency of labor. The extreme inefficiency of labor during the war and the great drop in prices during 1920 led managers to examine more carefully than ever before the causes of inefficiency. As a result, managers were profoundly impressed by the fact that many workers deliberately withhold production and use great ingenuity to conceal how little they are doing, because they fear that more output would mean less work. It was apparent to employers that this conscious restriction of output could be removed only by giving the men reasonable assurance of steady work. Finally, the interest of business men in security of employment was stimulated by their fear of radicalism and their desire for the good will of their men. Managers readily appreciated that nothing is more likely to make a workman radical than uncer-

[60] Swift and Company, *Year Book* (1925), p. 52.
[61] Ibid. (1923), p. 49.
[62] J. F. Tinsley, *New Phases of Industrial Management*, pp. 103-105.

tainty of employment, and nothing more likely to keep him conservative than the prospect of steady work. And as business men studied the problems of creating industrial good will, they perceived that most wage earners are not contented unless they have steady jobs and that all efforts to gain labor's good will must rest upon a foundation of regular employment.

The methods by which business enterprises have endeavored to stabilize employment are too numerous to describe here.[63] There is abundant evidence, however, that substantial results have been achieved. Thus, Procter and Gamble now guarantees its men 48 weeks of work in the calendar year. In consequence, labor turnover has dropped to the almost unheard-of rate of less than one per cent a month in a force of 6,500 men.[64] The Delaware and Hudson Railroad, by using a flexible working day and working week, has avoided laying off a single skilled worker since the plan was put into effect in 1923.[65] During the anthracite coal strike, the entire shop force was kept engaged by working five days a week, and by making repairs in advance of the need for them. The best evidence of the general progress in stabilizing employment is the decrease in the lay-off rate. The United States Bureau of Labor Statistics, collecting data for the period 1910-19 and for the year ending June 30, 1918, found an average lay-off rate of 13 per cent in a group of 261 plants employing the equivalent of 691,681 full-time workers.[66] For the period 1911-15, I found an average lay-off of 35 per cent among 78 plants employing 154,933 workers.[67] On the other hand, in 1926, the median lay-off rate among the enterprises reporting to the Metropolitan Life Insurance Company was 6[68] and, during 1927, 6.5 per cent.

The methods which have been discussed are the most important ways in which business men are endeavoring to make their men more efficient and more contented, but they are not the only ways. In concluding this description of personnel practices, it is desirable to indicate briefly a few of the many other methods by which enterprises are seeking to build up good will and efficiency. The Hammermill Paper Company provides garage facilities at a nominal figure, and sells gasoline to employees at one cent below the public filling-station price; the Spicer Manufacturing Corporation sells its men coal, gasoline, and oil;[69] L. Bamberger and Company employ a lawyer to advise employees, without charge, on legal matters;[70] and the Hammermill Paper Company provides free notary service and aid in filling income-tax returns. A number of enterprises maintain dental dispensaries, which give free examination, advice, and temporary treatment, and, in some instances, as in the case of Bausch and Lomb Optical Company, do permanent dental work at low rates.[71] Bausch and Lomb maintain an eye clinic, which gives examinations, and supplies frames and

[63] For an excellent description of them, see Professor H. Feldman's book, *The Regularization of Employment.*

[64] *Stabilizing Employment Plans, Law and Labor*, viii (May, 1926), 139.

[65] *Stabilizing Employment Plans, Law and Labor*, viii (May, 1926), p. 142.

[66] P. F. Brissenden and E. Frankel, *Labor Turnover in Industry*, pp. 80-81.

[67] S. H. Slichter, *The Turnover of Factory Labor*, pp. 86 and 92.

[68] United States Bureau of Labor Statistics, *Handbook of Labor Statistics* (1924-1926), p. 585.

[69] *Rules and Regulations* (April 21, 1924), p. 24.

[70] *Employees' Information Booklet*, pp. 10-11.

[71] *Instructions for Employees* (June, 1924), p. 7.

lenses far below cost;[72] L. Bamberger and Company have a chiropodist, who visits the store hospital two days a week and does work at a nominal charge.[73] The Standard Oil Company of California has arranged for employees to obtain loans for restricted purposes at five per cent interest, using their stock in the company as collateral.[74] The Employee's Handbook of the Public Service Company of Northern Illinois says:[75] "It is recognized that there are times when an employee may need temporay financial assistance, on which occasions the company stands ready to extend such assistance." Some personnel departments offer to advise employees in regard to personal problems. The Book of Information and Instruction for Employees issued by the Boston Rubber Shoe Company says:[76] "The Industrial Relations Department will gladly help any employee who has a personal matter on which he wishes counsel, such as sickness in the family, financial problems, the purchase of or renting of a home, and so forth. . . . You should feel free to go to the office (with your foreman's permission, if during working hours), with the assurance that your best interest will be served by so doing." The Employee's Manual of the Scoville Manufacturing Company[77] states that "it is the aim of the Industrial Service Department to render personal assistance to all employees in solving their personal problems. There are many instances when a situation can be faced more bravely and effectively if a friend is at hand to consult; the Employment Office undertakes to be such a friend." The Employee's Information Booklet of L. Bamberger of Newark[78] says: "If you need help or advice in finding a place to live, to board, to spend a vacation, or if you are worried about anything, consult with the Social Service Secretary, or see one of the Employment managers, or a member of the education department." Describing the personnel methods of the Commonwealth Steel Company, Mr. A. G. Morey says: "The men voluntarily bring many of their human problems to us, and a word of counsel, the use of our legal facilities, or other influences, have enabled us to be of service and advice to the men in many of their personal problems."[79] Among the cases recently handled by the employees' service division of the People's Gas Light and Coke Company of Chicago, were the following numbers of requests for several kinds of help: advice in investing money, 32; intercession for reduction of physicians' bills, 15; adjustment of difficulties with installment houses, 18; consultation on business affairs, 91; financial assistance in emergencies, 52; arrangement for hospital, surgical, or medical care, 190; advice in obtaining specialist for dental work, 22; advice in obtaining eye, nose, ear, or throat specialists, 43; assistance in drawing up wills, 33.[80]

IV

One of the best ways of appraising the significance of the new personnel methods is to ask in what degree they are responsible for the present

[72] Ibid., p. 7.
[73] *Employees' Information Booklet*, p. 9.
[74] Standard Oil Company (California), *Bulletin* (March, 1927), p. 5.
[75] Page 22.
[76] Pages 6-7.
[77] Edition of February 1, 1927, p. 25.
[78] Page 10.
[79] *The Commonwealther*, xiii (June, 1927), 4.
[80] *People's Gas Club News*, xvi (November 15, 1928), 7.

labor situation in the United States. The situation is characterized by four outstanding features; (1) a spectacular increase during the last seven years in the physical production per wage earner; (2) a substantial drop in union membership; (3) a large decrease in the number of strikes; (4) a low rate of labor turnover. The new labor policies have played an important part in producing these results, but it seems reasonably clear that a far more important part has been played by general economic conditions.

Between 1919 and 1925, the per capita production of workers engaged in manufacturing increased about 37 per cent. In other lines of industry the increase was almost as great. To some extent this great increase is attributable to the new labor policies. The practice of promoting in accordance with merit has undoubtedly stimulated many workers to produce more; and the interest which employers have aroused in saving and home ownership has probably increased the efficiency of many piece- and bonus-workers. Of special importance has been the greater security of employment, for which the new labor policies are partly responsible. The job has ceased to be merely a temporary position which the worker is bound to lose soon, and has become a valuable piece of property which he can probably keep for the rest of his life, *provided he meets the management's standards of efficiency*. The fact that he now has something worth keeping has produced a radical change in his willingness to do his best.[81] Finally, the creation of industrial good will has undoubtedly tended to make men more efficient. Its effect, however, has probably been primarily indirect rather than direct. Employees who are well disposed toward their superiors are not, because of that fact, necessarily more industrious or more painstaking. But good will does render workmen more responsive to demands made upon them by the management, and thus it enables alert and aggressive executives to obtain better results from their men.

The most important causes for the increased production per worker, however, have not been personnel policies. Undoubtedly the greatest cause of all has been the elimination of inefficiencies which grew up during the war and post-war boom, when speed was all important and when less than usual attention was paid to costs. A second important cause for the greater output per worker has been the movement of prices, especially the downward trend of non-agricultural wholesale prices in general and of interest rates in particular, and the tendency of wages to fall less than other prices and, during the last five years, not to fall at all. The great fall of prices in 1920 and 1921 created an imperative necessity that enterprises quickly and drastically reduce costs. This led managers to search as they had never searched before for ways of obtaining more output from fewer men. Falling prices have also hastened the normal tendency for production to be concentrated into the newest plants. These, as a rule, are precisely those which are best equipped and in which labor is most effective. The pronounced downward trend of long-time interest rates since 1921, the rise in wages between 1922 and 1924, and the stability of wages since 1923 have made it profitable for employers to replace methods of production which require less waiting and more labor with methods which require

[81] Stabilized employment means that enterprises are hiring fewer men for temporary jobs. The result is that a man who loses his job finds employment more difficult to obtain and unemployment becomes a more serious matter. Thus stabilization of employment tends to discourage resignations and to increase workers' fear of discharge or lay-off.

more waiting and less labor. Such changes, of course, increase physical output per laborer. Finally, production per worker has been increased by the abundance of labor. This in turn is a result of the concentration of output in plants where labor is most effective, of the spread of labor-saving methods of production, of the depression in agriculture (which has accelerated the movement of men from farm to city), and of the failure of wages to fall with the decrease of wholesale prices. Despite the restrictions on immigration, therefore, the supply of labor has been large in relation to the demand.[82] Naturally, only the best workers have been hired and there has developed a serious unemployment problem among the older and the less efficient men. And because wage earners have found jobs none too easy to obtain, they have hesitated to resign and have improved their efficiency in order to avoid discharge.[83]

The second outstanding feature of the labor situation is the drop in union membership. Since 1920, the membership of the American Federation of Labor has decreased about 30 per cent. This figure, however, is somewhat misleading because the building boom has enabled the building trades unions to grow. Between 1920 and 1923 the membership of 33 organizations which draw their adherents primarily from manufacturing dropped from 1,220,100 to 648,000, or nearly half. Between 1923 and 1926, despite the stability of the business situation, the membership of the same unions decreased nearly 18 per cent, from 648,000 to 532,000.

The precipitous fall in union membership between 1920 and 1923 was due principally to the withdrawals which normally accompany severe unemployment and to the break-up of unions after unsuccessful strikes. The failure of the strikes was, of course, due to the severe unemployment which prevailed throughout 1921 and most of 1922. About half of the drop in membership between 1923 and 1928 occurred in the International Ladies Garment Workers' Union, an organization which has been badly disrupted by the communists rather than by the employers. The remainder of the shrinkage after 1923 was caused primarily by the decrease of about 5 to 6 per cent in the number of workers engaged in manufacturing. Among the skilled craftsmen—who constitute the bulk of the union membership—the decrease was probably more than 5 or 6 per cent.

But have not the new personnel policies at least prevented the spread of unionism and thus are they not *indirectly* responsible for the fall in union membership? To this question the answer must be that the effectiveness of the new labor policies in checking the spread of unionism has not been tested, because in few cases has a determined effort been made to organize plants in which the new policies are found.[84] It is undeniable that during

[82] At certain times and in some places there have been serious labor shortages in the building trades. There was also a more or less general shortage for a few months late in 1922 and early in 1923.

[83] The evidence does not appear to bear out the oft-repeated assertion that the increase in output per worker since 1919 is primarily due to the use of more machinery or of more power per worker. I have analyzed the evidence briefly in my article: "The Secret of High Wages," *New Republic* (March 28, 1928), liv, 183-185. To some extent the efficiency of labor has probably been affected by installment buying, because the desire to keep up monthly payments on cars, houses, and radios and at the same time to maintain customary standards of living has undoubtedly stimulated piece- and bonus-workers to increase their output.

[84] The first real test of the new personnel practices is likely to come in the railroad shops. During the war, the railroad shop workers were strongly organized,

recent years the interest of wage earners in unionism has been weak, but this is most plausibly explained by the advance of about 11 per cent in the real earnings of factory workers between 1920 and 1926, and by the fact that, during most of the time since 1921, jobs (outside of the building trades) have been none too easy to obtain.

The third outstanding feature of the American labor situation is the drop in the number of industrial disputes from 3,630 in 1919 to 1,035 in 1926.[85] The number of employees involved fell from 4,160,000 to 330,000.[86] Undoubtedly the new personnel policies have tended to diminish strikes. But they are not responsible for this great decrease. Over four-fifths of the strikes in the United States are called by labor unions. The new methods of handling labor, however, have made greatest progress in non-union shops. Industrial disputes appear to be primarily products of price fluctuations. They are most numerous when changes in the cost of living or in wholesale prices cause workers or employers to seek changes in the customary wage rates. The remarkable fewness of disputes since 1922 is primarily attributable to two facts: the stability of the cost of living and the failure of the rather substantial drop in non-agricultural wholesale prices since 1923 to produce a movement to reduce wages. For the latter fact, however, as will be pointed out presently, the new labor policies are in some degree responsible. Important also in reducing the number of disputes have been the increase in the real earnings of factory workers, and the weakening of many unions by the depression of 1921, so that they have been unable to undertake aggressive organizing campaigns.[87]

---

but the unions were driven out of about half the shops in the bitter strike of 1922. Many roads which destroyed the unions have adopted the new personnel methods—"company" unions, group insurance, employee stock ownership, and security of employment. It is certain that the shop-craft unions will soon endeavor to reestablish themselves on the unorganized roads. Because the tradition of unionism still remains among these workers and because the men are largely skilled craftsmen, the efforts to reorganize the shops should furnish a real test of whether the new personnel policies make workers satisfied to remain unorganized. Thus far the effort to organize the employees of the Interborough Rapid Transit Company in New York City is the most notable attempt to spread unionism among the employees of a company which practices the new methods of handling men.

[85] *The Handbook of Labor Statistics* (*1924-1926*), p. 572. In 1917 there were 4,540 disputes, but the total number of employees involved was less than one-third the total of 1919.

[86] Ibid., p. 570. In the case of many of the smaller disputes, the number of employees involved was not reported. The figures given above include 2,665 disputes in 1919 and 783 disputes in 1926.

[87] The reduction in the number of strikes since the abnormal war period has been world-wide and has been quite as great in other countries as in the United States. The National Industrial Conference Board has estimated the number of workers involved in strikes and lockouts per 1,000 of population as follows:

	1920	1927
United States	40 (in 1919)	3
Germany	135	6
Great Britain	63 (in 1919)	2
Belgium	40	5
France	35	2
Netherlands	10	2
Canada	16 (in 1919)	2

Only in Australia has there been an increase. There the persons engaged in industrial disputes were 19 per 1,000 of population in 1919-20, and 25 in 1927.

The fourth outstanding feature of the labor situation is the low rate of labor turnover. Before the war, turnover rates in manufacturing averaged in good years not far from 100 per cent. In 1926, a fairly active year, the Metropolitan Life Insurance Company reports a median turnover rate of 47 per cent among several hundred factories.[88] In 1927, a less active year, the median rate was 41.4 per cent.

The protection of workers against arbitrary treatment, rewards for continuous service, and stability of employment have all, of course, tended to diminish turnover. Stabilization of employment has been doubly important. It has reduced turnover directly by decreasing the number of lay-offs, and indirectly by diminishing the necessity of hiring new men, among whom resignations and discharges are greatest.[89] But the outstanding causes for lower turnover rates have not been personnel policies. The most important single influence has probably been the condition of the labor market—the relative abundance of men and scarcity of jobs which have existed (outside the building trades) almost continuously since 1920. This is indicated by the fact that for several months early in 1923, when there was a shortage of men, resignations underwent a spectacular increase.[90] A second important influence has been the increasing efficiency of wage earners. Labor turnover is largely a function of hirings. It is greatest when forces are being expanded. The rising output per worker has made possible a gradual decrease in the number of men employed in manufacturing.[91] This has greatly diminished the number of hirings and consequently the turnover rate. A third reason for the small turnover has been the relative stability of wages since 1923. Resignations increase during periods of rising wages because men leave the plants which are slow in advancing wages to seek positions in plants which have increased their scales. This is well illustrated by the sudden jump in the resignation rate during the late winter and the early spring of 1923. In this time occurred nearly half of the entire increase in hourly earnings which marked the business recovery of 1922-1923.[92] During February, March, and April of 1923, the turnover rate (adjusted for seasonal variation) was higher than at any time between the middle of 1920 and the end of 1927.[93] Since the end of 1923, however, factory wages have been stable and labor turnover has been low.

V

But the fact that the new personnel policies have thus far produced only limited effects upon the labor situation in the United States should not lead us to underestimate their significance. In at least two respects they are likely to produce results of substantial importance.

In the first place, the new policies have materially strengthened the bargaining position of labor. The effect may not be sufficient to compel

[88] *The Handbook of Labor Statistics* (*1924-1926*), p. 585.

[89] The decrease in turnover tends to be cumulative, because as resignations and discharges decrease, hirings also decrease; consequently new jobs become more difficult to obtain and men become more reluctant to resign.

[90] See *Handbook of Labor Statistics* (*1924-1926*), p. 585.

[91] The number of factory wage earners decreased from 8,768,491 in 1923 to 8,351,257 in 1927. (*Statistical Abstract of the United States*, 1926, p. 745, and the *New York Times*, February 28, 1929, p. 12.)

[92] National Industrial Conference Board, *Wages in the United States, 1914-1926*, p. 27.

[93] *Handbook of Labor Statistics* (*1924-1926*), p. 586.

employers to increase wages more promptly in times of rising prices, but it is sufficient to retard or to prevent decreases in wages during times of slowly falling prices, such as the period 1923 to 1928. The new personnel policies have increased the bargaining power of labor because they have made the efficiency of labor depend more than ever before upon the willingness of men to do their best. As a result, enterprises find themselves compelled to retain labor's good will in order to avoid a loss in output. Consequently, when a fall in prices reduces the marginal worth of labor, it is not necessarily advantageous to reduce money wages—to do so might still further diminish the worth of labor by provoking a withholding of efficiency. The most economical (or the least unprofitable) course may be to incur some expense in order to increase the efficiency of labor. There is abundant evidence that the reluctance of managers to reduce wages in the face of declining prices since 1923 has been partly due to the fear that wage cuts would destroy the good will which has been built up at considerable trouble and expense.[94]

In the second place, although the new personnel policies are not responsible for the recent decrease in union membership, it is probable that they will at least retard the spread of unionism. Modern technology has tended to create class cleavage, by making the wage earner believe that he is destined always to remain a wage earner. Convinced that he has slight prospect of getting ahead as an individual, and that his welfare depends upon the welfare of his class, he becomes interested in organizing to improve the condition of his class. In the United States, with its rapidly expanding industries, the tendency of workmen to rely upon collective action rather than upon individual effort has been less pronounced than in Europe, but even here there has been a substantial growth of unionism, especially since 1897. Modern personnel methods are one of the most ambitious social experiments of the age, because they aim, among other things, to counteract the effect of modern technique upon the mind of the worker, to prevent him from becoming class conscious and from organizing trade unions. To the ablest, the most ambitious, and the most energetic workers, the very men who would resent most keenly the lack of an opportunity to rise and who would be most likely to become leaders of unions, modern personnel practice offers the chance of a career—promotion by merit through carefully graded steps and along carefully planned roads, and classes in which to prepare for more responsible positions. To the best men promotion thus becomes a more certain and often an easier way of gaining higher wages than is trade-union action. To the average and subaverage man, the wage earner who cannot expect to advance by unusual skill, knowledge, or exertion, and who is most likely to be interested in group action, modern personnel management offers security—steady work, protection against arbitrary discharge, a pension in old age, and, in some cases, insurance against sickness.[95] In addition, it

[94] Between 1923 and 1926, non-agricultural wholesale prices decreased over 9 per cent and, between 1926 and 1927, over 5 per cent. Hourly earnings of factory workers, according to the National Industrial Conference Board, remained practically stationary between 1923 and 1926. The slight movement was upward. Between 1926 and 1927, the hourly earnings of factory workers increased from 56.2 cents to 56.9 cents. (*Wages in the United States, 1914-1927*, p. 29.)

[95] The adequacy of the security is not here in question. Apparently it is sufficient in a period of stable prices to take the edge off the discontent of the wage earners, and that possibly is all that it is intended to do.

encourages him to form the habit of relying, not upon himself, but upon the employer, for help in the ordinary problems and even in some of the great crises of life. If the worker has a toothache, the company dentist will cure it; if he has a headache or a cold,[96] he can get treatment from the company doctor; if he or a member of his household needs an operation, the company doctor will help him find a competent surgeon; in some cases, the company optometrist will measure him for glasses, and the company chiropodist will treat his corns. If he has legal difficulties, he can obtain free advice from the company's lawyer; if his wife or children are sick, a nurse from the company will visit his home to render such assistance as she can; if he wishes to save money, the company will act as agent for a bank, deduct the money from his pay check, deposit it in the bank, and do the bookkeeping for him; if he needs to borrow money, the company will lend it to him at a low rate of interest; if he wishes to own his house, the company will build one for him and sell it to him on easy terms, or help him to borrow the money to build it himself.

The efforts of personnel management to check the growth of unionism suggest what is probably the most serious criticism of current labor policies. The criticism is essentially the same as that which John Stuart Mill made of paternalistic government. Mill said:

> A people among whom there is no habit of spontaneous action for a collective interest—who look habitually to their government to command or prompt them in all matters of joint concern—who expect to have everything done for them, except what can be made an affair of mere habit and routine—have their faculties only half developed; their education is defective in one of its most important branches. . . . There cannot be a combination of circumstances more dangerous to human welfare, than that in which intelligence and talent are maintained at a high standard within a governing corporation, but starved and discouraged outside the pale. . . . The only security against political slavery is the check maintained over governors, by the diffusion of intelligence, activity, and public spirit among the governed. . . . It is therefore of supreme importance that all classes of the community, down to the lowest, should have much to do for themselves; that as great a demand should be made upon their intelligence and virtue as it is in any respect equal to; that the government should not only leave as far as possible to their own faculties the conduct of whatever concerns themselves alone, but should suffer them, or rather encourage them, to manage as many as possible of their joint concerns by voluntary cooperation.[97]

Substitute "employers" for "government," and the words of Mill become peculiarly applicable to industry today. Clearly, modern personnel management does not encourage wage earners "to manage as many as possible of their joint concerns by voluntary coöperation." Plainly, it does seek to prevent the development of any "habit of spontaneous action for a collective interest."

The case against paternalism is probably weaker today than when Mill wrote. Only through some kind of paternalism, apparently, can the wage

[96] The Standard Oil Company of Louisiana even announces that it is prepared to administer cold vaccine to any employees who desire it.

[97] J. S. Mill, *Principles of Political Economy*, bk. V, chap. 11, section 6.

earner be protected against many of the hazards of modern life, or can he obtain the benefits of many scientific discoveries or the services of many professional experts. It is clear that employers, at little or no extra cost, can often give help which the worker could obtain for himself only at considerable trouble and expense. But is there not need among wage earners for more initiative and enterprise, for more mental independence, and for more disposition to rely upon coöperative self-help than modern personnel practice is disposed to encourage? Is it not, in general, desirable that men be encouraged to manage their own affairs rather than that they be deliberately and skillfully discouraged from making the attempt? And if much paternalism is inevitable, would it not be more satisfactory, from the standpoint of the community, that it be paternalism of the government rather than paternalism of employers?

45

Things Come to a Head: The 1930's

Collective Bargaining in 1934

EDWARD S. COWDRICK

Personnel administration in 1934 was monopolized largely by problems of collective bargaining. Other subjects, with the single exception of social legislation, were pushed temporarily into the background. The end of the year found collective bargaining problems even more involved and perplexing than they were when the famous Section 7 (a) was written into the National Industrial Recovery Act, although there were indications of early clarification of at least some of the doubtful points through expected court decisions in the Weirton case, the Houde case and the suits brought by the Goodrich and Firestone companies to block elections ordered by the National Labor Relations Board.

Section 7 (a), as everyone has been reminded many times in the past year and a half, reads as follows:

> Every code of fair competition, agreement, and license approved, prescribed, or issued under this title shall contain the following conditions: (1) That employees shall have the right to organize and bargain collectively through representatives of their own choosing, and shall be free from the interference, restraint, or coercion of employers of labor, or their agents, in the designation of such representatives or in self-organization or in other concerted activities for the purpose of collective bargaining or other mutual aid or protection; (2) that no employee and no one seeking employment shall be required as a condition of employment to join any company union or to refrain from joining,

Reprinted from *The Personnel Journal*, Vol. 13, No. 5, 1934-35, pp. 247-257.

Dr. Cowdrick was an active contributor to the personnel and labor research literature of the 1920's and 1930's.

organizing, or assisting a labor organization of his own choosing; and (3) that employers shall comply with the maximum hours of labor, minimum rates of pay, and other conditions of employment, approved or prescribed by the President.

It will be noted that in respect to labor the statute does these things:

1. It sanctions collective bargaining, without defining the term or setting forth the rights and obligations of the bargaining parties.
2. It imposes restraints upon employers, with no corresponding prohibitions directed at employees or labor unions.
3. It forbids forced membership in a "company union"—again no definition—without expressly including a similar restraint in respect to other labor organizations.

Whatever Section 7 (a) does or does not mean, it is certain that it was enacted at the demand of labor, and that at least in its early stages it was taken by the unions as a license for unrestrained organization. A drive for membership was started at once and has been prosecuted energetically throughout the intervening period.

This campaign for unionism was matched by a marked spread of employee representation. Representation plans were adopted in numerous companies after the passage of the Recovery Act; in others existing plans were extended, sometimes with alterations intended to bring them more fully into harmony with the law.

A Conflict of Philosophies

This parallel growth of unionism and employee representation brought into sharp conflict different schools of thought on the whole subject of collective bargaining. In the minds of unionists and their sympathizers, Section 7 (a) contemplated union recognition in the orthodox sense of the term, with contracts between employers and organizations of employees. Many employers, on the other hand, were convinced that contracts were not necessary; that employee representation fulfilled the requirements of the law as adequately as did unionism, and that collective bargaining meant simply the joint discussion of mutual problems. These employers contended that management was meeting its obligations under the law if it expressed, and carried out in good faith, willingness to meet with any representatives chosen by all or a portion of the working force and to talk over and try to settle any questions these representatives wished to bring up.

This fundamental conflict over the meaning of collective bargaining received further confusion rather than clarification from various official interpretations that were given in the earlier stages of NRA. Statements by General Hugh S. Johnson and by Donald R. Richberg at first appeared to support the contention of the open shop employers. This side of the controversy received further encouragement in President Roosevelt's settlement of a threatened automobile strike in March 1934, in connection with which he indicated a definite preference for proportional representation. In his statement at that time the President said: "If there be more than one group each bargaining committee shall have total membership pro rata to the number of men each member represents," and added: "It is my hope that this system may develop into a kind of works council in industry in which all groups of employees, whatever may be their choice of organization or form of representation, may participate in joint conferences with their employers." Later official pronouncements, however, cast doubt upon these early intentions and left the whole question in the utmost confusion.

In the meantime Senator Robert F. Wagner in the Congressional session of 1934 introduced his Labor Disputes Act in an effort to clear up controversial issues in the manner desired by the labor unions. This bill was defeated, but in the closing days of the session Congress enacted Resolution No. 44, under which the President appointed the National Labor Relations Board. About the same time Congress passed a revised Railway Labor Act in which were incorporated several of the features of the Wagner Bill.

Coöperation vs. Conflict

To those who had watched the gradual growth of confidence and understanding between employees and management during the years which marked the development of modern industrial relations, one of the most discouraging elements in the whole situation was the disposition of union leaders and their Congressional supporters to look upon precisely this coöperation and understanding as an evidence of something sinister and open to suspicion.

The original Wagner Bill in its list of "unfair labor practices," sought to interdict many established customs which had been looked upon as innocent or even praiseworthy. The author or authors of the bill apparently held the belief that the normal relationship between workers and management was one of conflict, and that the thing the Government had to do was to set down rules that would assure a fair fight. Scant recognition was given to the fact—so familiar to those experienced in industry that it has become a commonplace—that employers and employees normally spend little of their time fighting each other, and that their interests are more often common than antagonistic.

In this atmosphere of suspicion employee representation was under a severe handicap. Many of the older plans did not set up actual organizations of employees—the purpose had been to avoid building "company unions"—and were, in fact, voting franchises rather than associations. It was difficult even to discuss these plans in language intelligible to the Washington theorists. Employee representatives who appeared at the hearings on the Wagner bill often were perplexed by questions such as: "How many employees are there in your association?", or, "How often does the company union meet?"

Particularly was criticism levelled against any participation or coöperation of management in the collective bargaining activities of employees. Attacks were made upon the good faith of those representation plans—including some of the most successful of all—in which all matters were taken up in joint conferences without formal consideration by employees or their representatives in separate meetings.

In spite of these handicaps, supporters of employee representation, both workers and managers, made a sturdy defense and up to the end of 1934 they were holding their ground with fair success against those who were demanding that the Government "outlaw the company union."

While Congress, the Government and the National Recovery Administration were thus wrestling with the problems of collective bargaining, various labor boards and commissions had been busy with hearings and decisions on specific cases. In the absence of controlling court decisions the rulings of these boards form the most authoritative body of opinion as to the intent of Congress in passing Section 7 (a).

When the present National Labor Relations Board succeeded the old (Wagner) National Labor Board, it found itself at the top of a hierarchy of boards and commissions, some regional and some functioning for particular industries, some appointed directly by the Government and some set up under code authorities. Already there were many precedents, some of them conflicting, and a huge and uncodified mass of quasi-judicial opinion on all sorts of labor questions.

Four Leading Issues

The principal issues in controversy when the National Labor Relations Board took up its duties concerned the following aspects of labor relations:

1. Majority rule. Does the vote of a majority of the employees in a company or plant bind the minority, or is the employer under obligations to deal with all representatives or even with individual employees?
2. Definition of collective bargaining. Must the employer sign contracts with employee organizations or has he fulfilled his obligation merely by meeting representatives and discussing and trying to settle questions which they bring up?
3. The closed shop. Is it legal under Section 7 (a)?
4. Management's support of employee organizations. Does this cooperation invalidate the power of an employee association to function freely in collective bargaining?

Doubts regarding the majority rule and the essential characteristics of collective bargaining were resolved, so far as the National Labor Relations Board was concerned, in the decision on the Houde Engineering Corporation case. Under the direction of the old National Labor Board, Houde employees had voted at a special election to select an agency for collective bargaining. The majority vote favored a local union but there was a strong minority for an employees' association. The company, in accordance with the theory of collective bargaining held by many employers, had taken the result of this election to mean that it had both the privilege and the obligation to deal separately with the representatives of the two groups. It went ahead on this basis, meeting both sets of representatives and conferring on questions as they arose. The union, however, claimed that as representative of the majority it was entitled to be the sole collective bargaining agency for all employees.

This contention was upheld by the National Labor Relations Board in a decision in which it asserted that the company's policy of dealing with the two groups "resulted, whether intentionally or not, in defeating the objects of the statute." The board went on record with elaborate arguments, backed up by many legal citations, against the contention that the right of employees to "bargain collectively through representatives of their own choosing," meant that minorities were entitled to separate representation if they wanted it. This decision was at once recognized as contrary to many previous official pronouncements, including President Roosevelt's "proportional representation" statement in the settlement of the threatened automobile strike.

The majority rule doctrine of the Houde decision took on additional importance from the fact that it was coupled with an interpretation of collective bargaining which differed widely from that which had been advanced by many open shop employers. The board held that collective bargaining "is simply a means to an end. The end is an agreement," and ruled that the employer must "enter into negotiations with the union and endeavor in good faith to arrive at a collective agreement covering terms of employment of all employees within the class which was permitted to vote at the election."

It is significant that the two principles, majority rule and the obligation to try to reach binding contracts with representatives of employees, were embodied in the Wagner bill which failed of passage in the last Congress. Together they embodied what many lawyers maintain is a drastic addition to Section 7 (a). If the Houde decision is sustained by the courts in litigation now pending it will make a sweeping victory for orthodox unionism.

Naturally the full utilization of this victory is dependent upon securing the support of majorities of employee voters. In a respectable number of elections, most notably the one held at the plant of the Kohler Company, independent organizations have polled larger votes than were cast for the regular labor unions. The unions, however, prefer to take their chances under the majority rule rather than to become involved in anything resembling proportional representation. In taking this attitude, they rely partly upon the persuasive powers of union agents and union members, and partly upon the expectation that the results of an unfavorable election can be reversed in a later poll. Besides, the unions are traditionally opposed to dividing the field with actual or prospective rivals. The majority rule, while it does not, as some employers believe, necessarily involve the closed shop, unquestionably is a step in the direction of enforced conformity in all matters of collective bargaining.

What Unit for Bargaining?

In the Houde case the National Labor Relations Board did not pass upon the question of what employees should comprise a unit for collective bargaining; that is, whether all the employees of a plant were bound by the vote of a majority or whether certain departments or certain trades could demand separate representation. In several addresses after the Houde decision was rendered, in which he endeavored to reconcile that decision with previous statements that had been interpreted as upholding the rights of minorities to separate representation, Donald Richberg appeared to advance the view that the rule of the majority was binding only upon minorities that had participated in an election; that an independent group, if it wished to do so, could remain out of the general poll and choose its own representatives by vote of a majority of its own members. In a later decision, however, in the case of the Columbian Steel Tank Company, the National Labor Relations Board held that members of an employees' association were bound by a majority vote of all employees, even though the association had served notice in advance that it would not participate in the election.

The end of 1934 found the utmost confusion still prevailing over the combined issues of majority rule and the obligation of employers to make contracts with representatives of employees. Clarification by the courts, or further legislation by Congress, apparently will be necessary before workers or management know just what is the law on these vital questions.

As to the closed shop, few rulings have been handed down and the whole situation is nebulous. General Johnson in a Labor Day speech in 1933 said:

> If the employer should make a contract with a particular organization to employ only members of that organization, especially if that organization did not have 100 percent membership among his employees, that would in effect be a contract to interfere with his workers' freedom of choice of their representatives or with their right to bargain individually and would amount to employer coercion on these matters, which is contrary to the law.

The Government's attorney in the federal court case involving the Weirton Steel Company said: "The closd shop is impossible under 7 (a)."

The National Labor Relations Board, so far as this writer is aware, has not yet met the closed shop question squarely in a decision having general application and based upon the rights of employees under Section 7 (a). In one of its earlier decisions it held that a closed shop contract between a company and an employees' association was illegal, but stated that "the facts of this case do not require us to determine, in the light of Section 7 (a) of the National Industrial Recovery Act, the validity of a closed shop agreement with a bona fide labor union resulting in the discharge of employees not joining the union." In considering closed shop contracts with regular labor unions, the Board has sometimes approved and sometimes disapproved, depending upon the facts in each case. Probably the closest approach to a general approval of closed shop contracts is contained in the decision on the Bennett Shoe Company case (December 10), but even here the Board based its reasoning partly on the particular facts involved.

Controversy over Employers' Support

Employers' support of representation plans and of employees associations is another subject about which controversy has centered. Before the passage of the National Industrial Recovery Act it was generally taken for granted that the incidental expenses of operating a representation plan were to be borne by the company. Probably few, if any, employers would have objected to employees assuming some or all of this expense if they wanted to, but it simply didn't work out that way. Similarly, management assumed a greater or less degree of responsibility for preparing the terms of representation plans and for supervising their administration.

When questions arose as to the adequacy of employee representation to fulfill the collective bargaining requirements of Section 7 (a), these customary procedures immediately were attacked. Labor unionists and their supporters maintained that employee representatives in a works council could not serve as independent bargaining agents of the workers, so long as they met jointly with management representatives and received wage reimbursement for time occupied in their representative duties. It was further asserted that free choice of representatives by employees was impossible when elections were held on company time and supervised jointly by workers and officials. Here again employee representation suffered from a misunderstanding of its methods and purposes, and from the attempt to force it into too close an analogy with trade unionism. Critics found it convenient to ignore tangible evidence showing that in many companies employees for years had been selecting their representatives freely, and that the representatives had fulfilled their duties with complete independence.

On this issue the National Labor Relations Board has upheld most of the contentions of the union camp. In a number of decisions it has sharply criticized employers, not only for exerting undue influence to induce employees to favor local organizations in preference to trade unions, but also for furnishing moral encouragement and financial support to organizations of employees.

What Are Present Trends?

In the confusion of decisions and official statements, it is difficult to detect the real attitude of the Government toward collective bargaining or to trace tendencies with any degree of certainty. It is known that some highly placed officials believe the complete organization of industrial workers would be a good thing for the country.

So far as concerns the National Labor Relations Board, its decisions are clear and intelligible and prepared with the evident intention of building up a dependable body of precedent. The same thing cannot always be said for the statements of officials in the higher and lower governmental ranks. Moreover, the various regional and industrial labor boards have been turning out decisions in large numbers, sometimes with little regard to precedent or consistency. So far as this writer is able to learn, no compilation of these decisions of subordinate boards is anywhere in existence. The making of such a compilation and its analysis for the discovery of a developing governmental labor philosophy would be a fruitful project for research.

Even with the present incompleteness and sometimes inconsistency of authoritative rulings, some rather definite tendencies may be noted:

1. There has been an inclination toward acceptance of trade union doctrines as to collective bargaining. This inclination is manifested in the decisions of the National Labor Relations Board, some of which have been discussed in earlier sections of this article. In all fairness it should be added that the National Labor Relations Board and the various subordinate bodies were given the duty of enforcing a statutory provision, Section 7 (a), which was intended by Congress as a concession to organized labor. If, as sometimes has been charged, boards have gone beyond the intent of Congress and have written into their decisions ideas which cannot be justified by the statute, the remedy seems to lie with the courts.

2. Some of the subordinate boards, and recently the National Labor Relations Board, have shown a disposition to assume responsibility over matters, even of a minor nature, that were formerly considered to lie in the field of routine shop management. Questions of seniority rights, of discharge, layoff and rehiring, and of the assignment of individual workers to particular jobs have been subjects of complaint and adjudication. This tendency, should it become universal and be carried to extremes, might lead to something resembling governmental control of plant management.

3. In some industries labor boards have interfered in the internal affairs of representation plans or employees' associations, by taking control of the machinery for electing representatives. This tendency has not yet gone far enough to permit an appraisal of its ultimate results. It might assume much significance, especially if governmental boards should undertake to dictate the rules of both works councils and trade unions.

4. There has been some evidence of concern over coercion and intimidation by unions. In this connection it should be remembered that this type of coercion is not prohibited by anything in the National Industrial Recovery Act. Union sympathizers have justified this apparent discrimination by pointing out that if union agents resort to objectionable practices they can be punished under the criminal statutes or the police regulations of the states or localities in which the acts were committed. A suspicion that Section 7 (a) was somewhat one-sided in its application appears to have entered the mind of the President when in his statement regarding the settlement of the automobile strike he said: "The Government makes it clear that it favors no particular union or particular form of employee organization or representation. The Government's only duty is to secure absolute and uninfluenced freedom of choice without coercion, restraint or intimidation from any source."

This pronouncement, coming while hearings on the Wagner Industrial Disputes Bill were in progress before the Senate Committee on Education and Labor, was seized upon by critics of the bill and for a time it was understood that Senator Wagner himself was willing to have the measure amended so as to prohibit intimidation or coercion either by employers or by union agents. When a revised bill made its appearance, however, all that was left of this proposed reciprocal prohibition was the following rather humorous provision:

> It shall be an unfair labor practice:
> (1) For an employer to attempt, by interference or coercion, to impair the exercise by employees of the right to form or join labor organizations, to designate representatives of their own choosing, and to engage in concerted activities for the purpose of collective bargaining or other mutual aid or protection;
> (2) For employees to attempt, by interference or coercion, to impair the exercise by employers of the right to join or form employer organizations and to designate representatives of their own choosing for the purpose of collective bargaining.

It is perhaps significant that the National Labor Relations Board, acting in its mediatory capacity in the dispute between certain unions and the Great Atlantic and Pacific Tea Company, inserted in the stipulations of settlement the following sentence: "There must be no coercion or intimidation by any of the unions to compel any man to join a union."

Policies of Employers

We have dealt thus far mainly with what might be described as the external problems of collective bargaining—the clashes of interest between labor unions and their supporters on the one side and open shop employers on the other, and the pressure exerted to induce managers to adopt one or another type of labor administration. What, in the meantime, have been the developments within industrial organizations?

Here, again, there is little uniformity, although a few dominant tendencies may be traced. Naturally, employers have given more thought to labor policies in the last year and a half than in any equivalent period in the history of American industry. Any reckoning of the amount of time and energy spent upon these policies by officials of all grades—if such an account were obtainable—would be perfectly unbelievable to anyone not intimately acquainted with the internal processes of industry. Whatever doubt yet remained as to the importance of personnel administration in the managerial program has been brushed aside in the rapid march of recent events. It has become evident even to those who formerly doubted it that a defensible labor policy is essential to the successful management of any business organization, and that this policy needs to be understood and thoughtfully and intelligently carried out by everyone in the official ranks.

Thus we get back to an old principle of industrial relations—the importance of foremanship. Foreman training, with particular emphasis upon the handling of labor, has been given renewed attention during 1934. Employers have been reminded afresh—some of them through costly and humiliating experiences—that the best planned and best intentioned labor policy may be nullified by the unfairness or stupidity or ignorance of a single supervisor who does or says the wrong thing in a crisis. To avert blunders of this kind, many companies have taken extraordinary pains in making sure that the policies of management were thoroughly explained up and down the line and in instructing officials of all ranks in the attitudes they should take toward demands of employees.

But it is not sufficient that company labor policies should be supported by the bosses. They need the coöperation also of the workers. The guarantees written into the National Industrial Recovery Act practically put industrial relations programs at the mercy of the employees for whose benefit they are supposed to have been designed. No labor policy—and particularly no method of collective bargaining—is good enough to survive unless it can gain and hold the support of the workers. Here the companies which have built up long experience of fair dealing and mutual confidence are at a distinct advantage.

As to specific methods of collective bargaining, various policies have been followed. Some employers, voluntarily or of necessity, have accepted the full union program, recognized outside organizations, and signed contracts covering wages and working conditions. (In our pre-occupation with clashes of interest between unions and open shop employers, we should not forget that many companies have long been operating under union conditions with mutual satisfaction.) Other employers have adopted or strengthened representation plans or coöperated with their employees in doing so.

Gains for Representation

In the field of employee representation 1934 was distinctly a successful year in spite of persistent attacks. It is noteworthy in this connection that some of the representation plans which are now operating most successfully and which have enlisted the most loyal support of employees are among those adopted recently and, as it seemed, hastily. The success of some of these plans has surprised even the friends of employee representation, to say nothing of those critics who sneered at them as last-minute devices to escape unionism.

In some companies representation plans have been modified as to their terms or their methods of administration in efforts to bring them more completely into harmony with what were believed to be the requirements of the Recovery Act. Sometimes eligibility limits for serving as representative have been eliminated so as to permit employees, if they wished to do so, to vote for union agents or other outsiders. Sometimes citizenship or service requirements for voting have been removed. In numerous companies the management of elections has been made solely a responsibility of employees. In a few instances workers have been given the privilege to amend, without the consent of management, provisions which concerned election of representatives and other matters relating to self-organization.

As to whether or not these modifications in representation plans were necessary, there is room for difference of opinion. There are yet those who believe that a plan of the older type fully meets the requirements of Section 7 (a) so long as the employees themselves do not ask for some other method of collective bargaining. There is no doubt, however, that in many companies changes such as those described have been found expedient. In this connection it is worthy of note that some groups of employees, when alterations supposed to liberalize the collective bargaining machinery were suggested to them, either have refused to make them or have done so reluctantly and only to please the management.

Naturally almost all enlightened employers have taken added precautions to avoid even the appearance of influencing employees in their choice of representatives or of dominating the collective bargaining machinery.

All these developments have brought industrial relations departments sharply into the spotlight. The need for capable and intelligent personnel administration has been emphasized as never before. The increased responsibility of ranking executives and line officials has taken away no part of the burden carried by the professional personnel administrator. His duties have been increased, his responsibilities are heavier and the consequences of mistakes are more serious.

Frequently in recent months the statement has been made that nothing in Government or in industry is static; that all our institutions have moved away from the moorings of past years and that change will be a continuous program in the future. However accurate these statements may be—and certain allowances probably should be made for short-sightedness and lack of historical perspective—there is no doubt that many elements of our social and economic institutions are still in process of formation. Final results are obscure. There is little comfort for the man whose habits of thought are too rigid. Success in industrial administration depends as it never did before upon open-mindedness and the ability to make adaptations to changing circumstances.

46

Things Could Have Been Worse

The Destruction of the Labor Movement in Germany

ABRAM PLOTKIN

The factors that made it possible for the German fascists to take over the trade unions in Germany are many, but there are a few of first and immediate importance. To those who were on the ground between January 30 and the middle of May it was clear that the trade unions were incapable of withstanding prolonged resistance. What follows is an outline of the rapid developments that brought about their final destruction.

The Press

The first drive of the Nazis after police power was placed in their hands was against the trade-union press. It started on March 2, when the *Jungbuchdrucker* and the *Textilarbeiter* were suspended for two weeks. The *Deutscher Eisenbahner*, organ of the railroad workers, and the *Metalarbeiter* of the Metal Trades Federation, edited by Fritz Kummer, were suspended on March 10. All the other eleven publications of the Metal Trades Federation, the largest single federation in the Allgemeiner Deutscher Gewerkschaftsbund, were suppressed in rapid succession. The newspapers and magazines of Gesamptverband, an organization of 600,000 civil and municipal employees and in public-service utilities, were closed in short order.

Whole issues of the *Holzarbeiter Zeitung*, corresponding to the organ of the carpenters' union in the United States, and the *Gastwirtsgehilfen Zeitung*, issued by the Restaurant and Food Workers Union, were seized and destroyed. At the same time the leading organs of the central labor councils throughout Germany were either seized or *verboten.* As a result of this muzzling of the trade-union press by the Nazi police power, the workers were left without communication between themselves and their leaders. In a country like Germany, where the sources of information for trade-union members were almost wholly concentrated in their daily and weekly press, the shutting off of their news sources was like the cutting of an artery.

It may be asked why the workers did not fight back, as they did when their press was forbidden during the latter part of March, through the calling of a general strike until the *verboten's* were lifted? The answer is

Reprinted from the *American Federationist,* Vol. 40, No. 8, August, 1933, pp. 811-826.

Abram Plotkin was a general organizer for the International Ladies' Garment Workers' Union when this was written.

that it was impossible to call an effective strike against the Nazi press. In Vienna the S.D.P. unions controlled the printing rooms even of Nazi and monarchist groups. In Germany that control never was in the hands of the Social Democratic Party. A protest strike, therefore, would have brought no results, except perhaps to intensify the spirit of reactionism and add, no doubt, to the already growing lists of those who were in Nazi *Casernas* and concentration camps.

Physical Terrorism

Three lines of terrorism were followed by the Nazis. The first was to visit the headquarters of the different trade unions and demand that the Nazi flag be hung on the flagstaff of the building. The first squads were small, but if they met with a refusal, they would come back with several hundred more in squads of fifty, surround the building, search the premises for firearms, then make a bonfire of everything that displeased them. Pictures of Marx, Engels, Bebel, Leibknecht, Legien, Leipart, flags and banners that had been the treasures of the unions for many years and marked definite historical epochs for them, records of inestimatable value—all were thrown into the flames while the Nazis held a solemn festival around the fire.

In many cases they went further. In the Berlin Central Labor Council Building they wrecked the furniture in many of the rooms, opened the cash boxes and safes, and walked out with whatever they found. In Dresden, where the top floor of the Central Labor Council Building had been used as a hotel, the Nazis fitted up several rooms in sumptuous style, scattered condoms and whips about, and then invited the populace to come and see the orgiastic headquarters of the workers' leaders! The hotel in this case was turned into a Nazi *Caserna* and is now one of the Nazi military barracks.

There was hardly a trade union in Germany that, during the months of March and April, did not suffer from these visitations. Nazi striplings would walk in, with the police usually in the background, cock their revolvers, demand the keys, and proceed to search the premises. Invariably they would ask if there was any wine around, and would look surprised when there was none to be found. Refusal to meet their demands met either with a prompt beating or arrest. In one case witnessed by the writer, two girls in the Berlin Transport Union Headquarters, who could not explain the blurred writing on a mimeograph stencil, were arrested and kept in jail for several days. An appeal to the police was useless. Frequently the police were a party to the outrages that were committed. Moreover, the police themselves were intimidated and would do nothing against the Nazi troops. In some cases the unions resisted the raiders with force; in other cases the Reichsbanner men (the former military force of the S.D.P. and trade unions) fought alongside of the trade unionists against the Nazis. But it was a hopeless battle.

The Nazis were armed. The trade-unionists were without weapons of any kind, and the Reichsbanner troops had been ordered by the government to turn in their weapons, such as they had, to local authorities.

A second form of terrorism was used directly against trade-union leaders. Husemann of the Miners Union was among the first to feel the effects of this policy. Arrested, he was kept in a Nazi *Caserna* for ten days, and when released he was too ill to resume his activities. The chairman (also a member of the national executive committee) of the Transport Workers Council in Berlin was arrested by the Nazis, taken to one of the Nazi *Casernas* and forced to drink a quart of castor oil, and thrown out unconscious on the street for strangers to pick up and to take home. Not satisfied with their failure to properly intimidate him the first time, they rearrested him and gave him a fearful beating.

These persecutions, perhaps, were most virulent in such districts as Mecklenburg, Brunswock, Wurtemburg, the Palatinate, and in Bavaria. In these districts hundreds of organizers and secretaries of local unions had to leave for other parts of the country, or, as many of them did, take refuge in the forests. Even Leipart and Grassmann, two officials of the A.D.G.B., had to be taken to the hospital after their arrests. All of the trade-union leaders under arrest were first taken to the Nazi *Casernas* (the Nazis have been permitted to set up their own courts and maintain their own jails!); and once in there the men and women under arrest were treated with a brutality that has no parallel in any civilized country.

A special kind of terror was introduced in the factories. It consisted in ousting, by force, the social democratic members of the factory councils, either through dismissal or arrest. It should be remembered that every factory in Germany must, in conformity with the law, elect a factory council, whose work it is to enforce the national wage scales agreed upon between the employers and the union, the regulation of working conditions, discharges, lay-offs, etc. For many years the Nazis had entered the elections and placed their own tickets in the field in these factory council elections, but had never been successful. Now that Hitler was in power, they proceeded to oust these factory councils that had been elected. Thus in Bochum the transport workers elected eight men as their industrial representatives, of whom five were S.D.P. men. (The elections in this case were held prior to the taking of power by Hitler.) Immediately after the March 5 elections, the five S.D.P. men were arrested and jailed. The same thing occurred in the Siemen's Electrical Plant in Berlin (similar to the General Electric Company in the United States), and here some of the men were jailed and others dismissed. Among those dismissed was Erick Lubbe, a member of the Reichstag, chairman of all the Siemen factory shop councils in Germany and labor's representative on the board of directors of the Siemen's corporation.

After April 1 there was somewhat of a lull in these persecutions. Seldte, Minister of Labor, accommodatingly issued an order setting aside the factory elections that already had been held, and announced new elections some time in the future. On the day when the anti-Jewish boycott was at its height and the newspapers had no space for anything else, this decree was hidden in an obscure corner of the average newspaper.

The third method of direct physical force against the trade unions was to occupy or *besetzen* the trade-union buildings. The *besetzung* is different from the raids. The first lasted only a few hours. The Nazis would come in during the night, hang up their flag, break through the doors and search the building, and then disappear. The *besetzung* was the actual taking over of the buildings by the military forces of the Nazis. These preceded the final investment of the buildings on May 2, and were local actions, usually under the guidance of the local military post of the Nazis. Usually an incident would happen, as in Breslau, where a number of Nazis were hurt during a riot following a parade past the Gewerkshaftshaus, that would give the local arm of the Nazis an excuse, and a few hours later they would take over the buildings, bank accounts, books, etc., "in the interest of the Nazi state and to protect the workers' rights." The writer saw the *Besetzung* of the Gewerkshaftshäuser in Berlin, Dresden, Munich and in Bochum.

During the two months prior to May 2, there was hardly a city in Germany where the Gewerkshaftshaus was not occupied at one time or another. Every city in the state of Saxony suffered. It became a matter for congratulation if one visited a city where a *Besetzung* had not taken place. In one city, Frankfort on Main, the congratulations offered by the writer were premature. Three days after leaving a short notice in the press announced that a cache of firearms had been found on the grounds of the Gewerkshaftshaus and that it too was occupied. But through these occupations three important factors developed.

The first, as in Saxony, the military announced that Hitler had promised them work, and that they would not give up the houses until the work promised them would be forthcoming. The second was the impounding of the funds, not only of the trade unions but those of a number of the labor banks as well, and only enough funds were released as were needed for current expenses. The result was that many of the unions that had planned to get at least a part of their funds out of the country were thus checkmated.

But the most important results of these *Besetzungen* lay in a development not foreseen by the Nazis. They had expected that the masses would respond to this show of physical force and would welcome them with open arms. Nothing of the sort took place. If the masses were rapidly becoming demoralized, they were not, as far as the writer could see, taken in by the phrases and promises made to them by the Nazis.

Espionage

Still another factor made the lives of the trade-union leaders in Germany anything but a bed of roses. The censorship of the mails played no small part in contributing to the final breakdown. That letters were opened and read was the least problem for many organizations. The problem was how to have their mail reach them. In numerous instances information dealing with the *Besetzungen* could not be gotten through to Berlin except by courier from the Gewerkschaftshaus involved.

When the Gesamtverband was invaded on May 2 all of the employees were marshaled into the main hall of the building, and when the officers asked if there were any Nazis among them, the mail clerk, an old and trusted employee of the Gesamtverband, and the telephone operator stepped out of the ranks.

Later it developed that Reuter, private secretary of Polenske, president of the organization, was constantly in touch with the Nazis, as was Buchhalter, a member of the national executive committee! The subjects discussed and the decisions arrived at were known to the Nazis before the members of the organization, and in many cases members of the unions never knew what the decisions of the officers were because the communications got "lost" in the mails. In this case, even the communications of the president, confidential orders from the chief to his subordinates to all parts of Germany, were known to the Nazis before the ink on the signatures was dry.

The Week of May 1

The week before the first of May was a week of optimism. The skies seemed clear except for one small cloud—the first of May celebration announced by Hitler. The organizations had been asked to participate, but to both workers and leaders it seemed a travesty of the workers' holiday to celebrate it under fascist orders. Then came the government's ruling that the employers would have to pay the workers for the day. Then came the notice that those who refused to march and to take part in the celebration would be considered as being opposed to the government—no light offense in Germany at the present time. Those who refused to report and register with the Nazi shop committee would be subject to dismissal. When the leaders realized that to maintain official opposition would result in thousands of discharges, they yielded. The results were tragic.

In the morning the workers gathered in front of the factories, greeted the employers, and marched to the starting points where the parades were slated to begin. There were eleven such columns organized in the different parts of Berlin. Each line was presumed to parade one hundred thousand workers. In the three parades I witnessed it was doubtful whether more than half of those who were expected had come. Nevertheless more than a million people were assembled in the Templehof aviation field to take part in the demonstration. As the organizers anticipated, the excitement, the crowds, the fireworks, the adulation heaped on Hitler, had their effect. Even those who were embittered by the spectacle, one that had the air of a Roman holiday, were impressed.

Week of May 2

On the morning of May 2 I had an appointment with Martin Plettl, president of the Garment Workers Union. I phoned to make certain that he was in. The voice that answered was not the voice of the usual operator. I was asked my name, address and occupation. Only afterwards was Plettl's secretary permitted to come to the phone. I overheard instructions given her that she must speak only in German. Then came Miss Heinrich's hysterical voice. She could not speak to me . . . there was trouble . . . I would understand. Thinking it was another local *Besetzung*, I called the A.D.G.B. house but got no response. I then tried the Metal Workers Building. The phone bell rang but there was no answer. I then tried the Gesamtverband building and the same thing happened there. Fifteen minutes later I was in front of the headquarters of the A.D.G.B. It was surrounded by the Nazi military. The staff and records of A.D.G.B. were being loaded on police trucks. Ten minutes' rapid walking brought me to the new building of the Metal Trades Union on Jacobstrasse. The same sight there. I jumped into a taxi and drove to the Gesamtverband building on Michaelkirchplatz, at the intersection of Ingeluferstrasse, where the Gewerkschaftshaus is located. The street was roped off and the building surrounded on both sides by the military, while the complete length of Ingeluferstrasse was lined by Nazis. It was the end. Everyone of the heads of the thirty-one organizations in the A.D.G.B. had been arrested, and the important secretaries in the national office as well.

Plettl, with whom I had been intimate, Otto Schweizer of the Engineers and Technicians, Brandeis of the Metal Workers, Husemann of the Miners, Vomerhaus, organizer of the Brandenbourg district, Otto Engel, secretary of the Agricultural Workers Union, Franz Furtwangler, Walter Maschke, Frau Hanna, Kuno Broecker, Leipart and Grassmann, the two presidents of the A.D.G.B.—every one of the leaders arrested, not by the police but by the Nazi military troops. Fifty were arrested the first morning: the others were picked up in the succeeding days. This in Berlin alone—how many were arrested throughout Germany is not known and probably never will be known. For days those arrested were kept in the Nazi *Caserna.* Only later were they transferred to the city prisons.

In the afternoon the newspapers carried the first stories of the taking over of the trade unions and arrests and announcing its national character and direction. In every city and town in Germany where there was anything in the way of organized labor, promptly at 10 o'clock in the morning the Nazis marched in, arrested the leaders, ordered the office staffs to remain at their work, announced their "commissars" (the term was borrowed from the Russians by the Germans precisely as the Russians lifted it out of the French Revolution), and that henceforth there would be only one organization, free from the taint of Marxism, and that it will be the "future cornerstone of the Nazi State."

On the third every kiosk in Germany was plastered with posters announcing the "resurrection" of the trade unions. At the same time the newspapers carried the offer of the Christian Unions to join the Nazi organization, side by side with vague charges and innuendos against the incarcerated trade-union leaders. All of the newspapers joined in proclaiming a "new day" under the bountiful blessings of the Nazi control.

The following day brought the announcements of the appointments of Dr. Ley and Dr. Engels as the chief "commissars" to take the places of Leipart and Grassman; a mass meeting of the workers to be held in the Lustgarten on the fifth, where the new "commissars" would announce policy that will guide them in the handling of the workers and their problems; and that a national congress of the "new" union would be held on May 10 in Berlin.

The *Nachtausgabe* listed charges against the imprisoned leaders, charging financial corruption. The heavy stress is laid on the donations that the A.D.G.B. made to the S.D.P., the Reichsbanner and to the International Federation of Trade Unions!

Standing on Unter den Linden on Friday (5th), I watched thousands of workers as they marched in from their factories into the Lustgarten. Each factory's workers, as soon as the work was over, were met by contingents of Nazi troops. Squads in front and squads behind, and guards at the sides to make certain that no one slipped away; they passed in the thousands. Sickened, yet fascinated, I walked into the Lustgarten. I did not stay long. I stayed long enough to size up the crowd—there were perhaps between 60,000 and 70,000 workers present; there to hear the first principles of Nazi trade unionism as taught by their new "commissar," Dr. Ley. "I order you to stop thinking . . . I order you to keep silent and to obey orders. . . . And I order you not to question the things I demand of you. . . . We will know how to treat and exterminate the poison of Marxism out of our system. . . ." There was no applause and less enthusiasm. The German workers being told once more to conform and obey. Most of them seemed bewildered and it is doubtful whether they even know what has happened to their leaders; those who do know are keeping a discreet silence.

The Aftermath

Among the first orders of the Nazis to the workers was to demand a report from their cells on the number of arrests in the different communities in Germany! They were fearful of the consequences of the acts of their own followers. Then came an order forbidding workers from withdrawing from the unions—and that they must pay their dues and arrearages—or face the loss of their jobs. All of the organizations, the Catholic Unions, the A.D.G.B., etc., have been placed under one single control. They are rapidly being nationalized and their old spirit of class consciousness is rapidly being destroyed. What the Nazi aim is, no one as yet knows. They promised to formulate a program, but in the speech of Herr Hitler to the delegates attending the national congress on May 10, he said precisely nothing. Dr. Ley and Dr. Engels, aside from vague generalities, have been equally silent. The truth is that up to the present day they have no program except to destroy Marxism—and, for a while at least, will be more preoccupied with heresy-hunting than with programs. The following excerpt from one of the members of Gesamtverband, which reached the writer through underground channels, tells its own story. It is worth quoting:

> Our organization [he writes in behalf of his group] continues to exist. [The letter deals with conditions among governmental and public-utility employees.] The dwindling membership has ceased. The "Christians" have been annexed to the organization. All those employed in factories are obliged to join the organization under threat of dismissal. Yet, in spite of everything, thousands of our best functionaries [workers in the civil-service sense] are now in the streets without receiving their ordinary or unemployment relief. [In Germany the trades unions have built up their own unemployment insurance schemes.] In spite of having belonged to the organization dozens of years, comrades have forfeited all rights. Among our employees in the Reich [federal government] about fifty are either dismissed or in prison, while others have committed suicide.
>
> On Saturday we had a district leader conference at which commissars of the N.S.B.O. were also present. The session lasted eight hours; it was taken up with insults against our employees and functionaries. It was the worst meeting we ever endured. All our work was made nothing of, and words like "tramp" and "riff-raff" were comradely expressions. Matters will fall out so that the already reduced wages will be further cut in half, and employees who have received notice will be put out upon the streets. Passports will be taken away and the demand has been made that every employee who still belongs to the party [Catholic or Centrum] shall be denounced, so as to make it possible to dismiss him without delay.
>
> No more meetings take place. Only one man makes all decisions. We have only one hope—to get out of this misery as quickly as possible. We ask to be excused from writing, since we are all put under the strictest censorship. . . .

This letter is typical. It gives a hint of what may come, and requires no comment.

Did the German Trades Unions Have a Program?

When the writer arrived in Germany in November, his first impression was that the Communists had a program but no real power; that the trade unions had power but no program. He soon learned that the Communists' lack of strength was due to their failure to have a program of their own, and that the trade unions had only an outer appearance of power, and really had a program. The Communists wanted an organic unity with Russian bolshevism at a time when Russia dreaded such a possibility and would not have known what to do with it if it had come her way. The trade unionists and Social Democrats had opened the road to socialism in Germany through democratic means, but in the process they had greatly weakened themselves. When the crisis came both went down. Since it was upon these two groups that the workers, both in Germany and outside of Germany, depended, and had faith in, let us see what happened to them.

The Communist Party, in spite of its 6,000,000 votes, had no real strength. At the mass meetings of the C.P., where hundreds of thousands were present, one saw German workers in mass, but in the main they were the unemployed. If one will take the growth of the Communist vote in Germany and compare it with the growth of unemployment, he will find that the two parallel each other, yet in spite of the rapid growth of its vote the Communist Party in Germany was not gaining in membership. The Russian background to the movement, their many promises of revolution that did not materialize (the writer was told by Communists in Germany that the German Communists were ready but that the Russian Communists told them to wait), their splitting policy in the trade unions that won them very few adherents (but did incalculable harm to the trade unions), their occasional collaboration with the Nazis both politically and industrially, and their failure to take action when their Red Troops were dissolved, foreshadowed their end as a party of real opposition and revolution. One does not deny their courage or sincerity. They had both. But it must be insisted upon that they had no power and no program. and in the face of superior force, they went down, like all the other parties opposed to Hitler. The writer saw the counter-demonstrations ordered by the Communist Party as a protest to the Nazi meeting of January 22 arrogantly held in front of the Karl Liebknecht house, the Communist headquarters. Twelve thousand Nazi troops were addressed by Hitler; 16,000 police, with rifles and machine guns, guarded all the approaches, the roofs surrounded Bülow Platz, and rifles were trained on all the closed windows. It seemed that most of Berlin's population milled in the surrounding streets, trying to reach the Nazis who were deliberately provoking an outbreak. But the Communists had no arms, and aside from crowding and cheering and singing, no really serious disturbance occurred. It may be said that if real opposition had manifested itself on January 22, Hindenburg might have considered twice before appointing Hitler. But even the Communists had to think twice before sending their unarmed followers against the rifles and machine guns of the police. From that time on, a pessimism spread through the ranks of the Communists in Germany that marked their end, regardless of the turn of future events. And later, when Hitler was already in the saddle, and they were confronted with being outlawed, they threw overboard their past policy of noncollaboration with the Social Democrats, and were willing to vote with them in the Prussian Diet in order to elect an anti-Hitlerian cabinet. Such a policy, adopted three months earlier, would have made Hitler's arrival in power an impossibility.

But if the socialist trade-union leaders had a program, by the time Bruening came on the scene their power and influence on the nation had already been greatly undermined. On the conclusion of the war their program of necessity had to be two sided. They had to rescue the nation from the dangers of invasion. They had to rebuild the economic life of the nation in order that at some more propitious moment, socialism, which was their final goal, could be realized. The first presented almost insurmountable difficulties. The Communists wanted to introduce sovietism immediately, which would have involved civil war and intervention by the Allies had sovietism been successful; and this in a nation where hundreds of thousands were actually starving to death. And it must be kept in mind that under the Versailles Treaty all the property of the state was in jeopardy for reparations, as afterwards developed in the mortgaging of the German railways. Faced with these dangers, Carl Legien, president of the German trade union, steered away from these dangerous shoals and decided that to feed and to put the nation back to work was their first task, and at the same time to leave the doors open for the ultimate realization of their philosophic and economic doctrines. How far they were successful can be seen from both the internal and external changes that took place within Germany after the war, and the reconstruction of its external relations in the face of international hatred and opposition. The Weimar Constitution placed the German working class on a far higher plane than in any other country in Europe. Externally, the opposition to the revisal of the Versailles Treaty was slowly being destroyed.

To achieve these results, however, the socialists and trade unionists had to pay a terrific price. In the face of the injustices, inequalities and barbarous exactions of the Versailles Treaty, these leaders had to advise patience and caution. The signing of the Versailles pact (under such terribly humiliating conditions to Germany) afterward became one of the vehicles on which Hitler rode into power. The Ruhr invasion and the inflation that followed, the signing of the Dawes Plan and later the acceptance of the Young Plan, though seemingly concessions towards Germany, actually were body blows to German Social Democracy and to the trade unions affiliated with it. With every "revision" the German people only saw another humiliation, and listened with growing eagerness and attention to criticism directed at their leaders, until large sections of them were convinced that patience and caution would lead them nowhere. With this conviction came the growth of numerous parties of opposition, the emergence of the Catholic Centrum, the first manifestation of reaction when Hugenburg and his Junkers National Socialists became a power in the Reichstag with 107 members whom the acceptance of the Young Plan split, the growth of the Communist opposition and the rise of the Hitlerian National Socialists. And with the growth of these new parties, particularly the Communists and the Nazis, also came a growth of trade-union opposition. Thus the Communists first built their cells in the S.D.P. trade unions and tried to "capture" them. Failing in that policy, they tried to organize unions of their own. That they were not successful does not measure their effect. As a trade-union opposition they were able to circulate rumors and libels against their opponents, which too frequently were believed, and even if they led to no results for the Communists, they doubtlessly had an effect in creating a lack of faith and a demoralization in the ranks of the Social Democratic trade unions. The same tactics were used by the Nazi Party. They also established "cells" in the factories, and in some trades established their own factions as trade unions. And in some instances, in the late transport strike in Berlin, to be specific, called on the eve of the elections in November, 1932, the Communists and the Nazis combined in calling the strike—obviously a collaboration between these two enemies that could have had only one object—to smash the prestige of the Social Democratic leaders of the trade unions.

The persistent undermining of the trade unions could lead to but one result. By the time Bruening was appointed Chancellor, with dictatorial powers, the leaders knew that their strength had been sapped and that until the dangers of Communism and Nazism, particularly the latter, were disposed of, their program and their plans were in danger. It was then that the policy pursued by the S.D.P. and the trade unions, for the time being, underwent a radical change. With Hitlerism growing at a cyclonic rate (the causes of which are too many to enter upon in this discussion), the S.D.P. and its trade unions decided that it would be wiser to adopt the policy of tolerating the "lesser" evil, than to permit power to fall into Hitler's hands. That this policy was a temporary expedient is shown by subsequent developments. The discarding of this policy during the Von Papen régime undoubtedly opened the door to Hitler's entrance into power.

The policy of tolerating the "lesser" evil did not last for long. With Von Papen's appointment the left wing forces in the trade unions and in the S.D.P. were turned loose, and how thoroughly they wrecked that gentleman's aspirations was indicated in the election results. At the end of the count it was found that not a single party in the Reichstag was willing to work with him, and all that he could muster was less than 10 per cent of the membership of the Reichstag. But developments during the Von Papen chancellorship pointed in new directions. For one thing, Von Papen had thoroughly frightened the signatories to the Versailles Treaty and this resulted in practically eliminating reparations from the German budget. The second lay in Von Papen's attacks on the social and labor legislation in Germany. He gave the industrialists even more than they expected from him. Unemployment insurance was, to all intents and purposes, emasculated. Advance taxes, over which American publicists waxed delirious with praise, were used to subsidize employers who were willing to fight the trade unions, resulting in what almost amounted to a landslide of wage cuts and strikes, and the social as well as the labor legislation of Germany was threatened with extinction. The landlords and industrialists had, at last, found their man! But it was not to last long. When the election returns were in, the opposition to Von Papen was so strong that Hindenburg dared not reappoint him.

With Von Schleicher, Von Papen's successor, things took a different turn. Having learned from the experience of Von Papen, Schleicher decided to be more moderate. Von Papen's antilabor decrees were promptly annulled. Other decrees followed that stopped the epidemic of wage cuts. Trade-unionists became optimistic once more. Moreover, in the November elections, Hitler lost 2,000,000 votes and 30 seats in the Reichstag, and 30 more seats were deflected from him through an internal fight between himself and Gregor Strasse; while the industrialists, on Hitler's failure to at least hold his own in the November election, decided that Hitler's days were numbered and therefore cut off a large portion of their financial support. The writer saw two barracks in Berlin alone that had been closed for lack of funds. During the months of December and January the Nazi troops were sent begging on the streets of the cities of Germany to keep the organization alive and Hitler was compelled to admit being 5,000,000 marks in debt—a huge sum in Germany—the writer saw two barracks in Berlin alone that had been closed by the Hitlerians. It is therefore understandable, with these facts known, why, in spite of Schleicher's apparent liberalism, the left wing of the S.D.P. and the Trades Unions grew too optimistic. They were certain that Hitler was through, and wanted nothing to do with a man of the military caste who might have dictatorial aspirations of his own. Therefore, when Schleicher asked the socialist groups to continue the same policy of toleration that they had exercised during Bruening's time, they refused. It may be added that the older heads in the trade unions and in the S.D.P. were not entirely convinced that Hitler was through, and were willing to come to an understanding with Schleicher until the Hitlerian danger would be completely dissipated, but the left wing elements tied their hands and refused to go through with the programme. Unable to form a cabinet that would obtain parliamentary support, Schleicher handed in his resignation and left the door open for the Von Papen-Hitler-Hugenburg cabal that made it possible for Hitler to become Chancellor of Germany, take over the police powers of the state, and start his campaign of suppressing all opposition. Once Hitler was in, it was certain to all observers, that nothing short of war with a foreign power or a revolution at home, would ever succeed in dislodging him. And the German trades unions, after the years spent in rebuilding their national life, of fighting their way out of the injustices and exactions of the Versailles treaty, and of withstanding criticism and vilification from their enemies at home, were too weakened and demoralized to undertake a revolution. The wonder is that the crumbling of the weakened trade union machine did not take place sooner. On the contrary, it must have taken almost superhuman efforts on the part of German trade-union leaders to hold their organizations together as long as they did.

Only nit wits or those who are blind, therefore, will condemn the German trade-union leaders for being without a programme. Every step was carefully measured and every step carefully weighed. That their programme was, because of shortsightedness and over optimism, defeated, is true. But it should be borne in mind that if they erred in their plans, the criticism hurled at their heads ought not to come from the liberals. If their programme was smashed, and the trades unions along with it, it should be remembered that the error in their calculations resulted from the assumption of the left winger's policy and not from too much conservatism!

Moreover, it is hardly fair for the socialists, liberals, and trade unionists in the former allied countries, to, at this late date, criticize their German colleagues. Rather, it seems to the writer, it would be wise, and timely too, for these groups to stop and consider how much of the responsibility for the debacle in Germany should rest on their own shoulders. All of them knew the conditions in which German socialists and trade unionists found themselves after the forced armistice, and all of them knew that any party in Germany could not survive the Versailles treaty unless the injustices in this instrument were done away with; every one of them knew that Germany could not survive if the harshness and inequalities in that barbaric instrument of "peace" were applied in full force against the Germans. And in their failure to put sufficient pressure on their governments to at least mitigate the harshest features of the treaty they not only helped to bury the socialists and trade unions in Germany, but helped the reactionaries in Germany in their efforts to destroy all faith in internationalism.

One word more must be added. The writer was in Germany from November until May 8. He met, and was intimate with, many of the leaders of the German trade union movement,—during the darkest hours of the tragedy. They met both their fate, and the issues that confronted them, with genuine courage. It took courage to avoid pitfalls that might have led to the slaughter of tens of thousands of workers, and the victimization, perhaps, of hundreds of thousands more. It was doubly courageous to remain at their posts, as practically all of the national leaders did, until the guns of the Nazis ordered them into the lorry on their way to the military barracks. These leaders knew what was awaiting them. And they faced their arrests unflinchingly. When the real story is told to the German workers, when they realize that it was possible, through an irresponsible word or deed, to sacrifice them in mass on the altar of a gesture, and that the leaders refused and sacrificed themselves instead, then the German workers will honor their former leaders, and the world will join in the tribute.

The Future

What the future will bring to Germany no one really knows. Prognostications, especially on German affairs, are extremely dangerous. The Nazis have turned loose forces that they themselves do not understand. It may surprise many to learn that the most exciting things that have happened in Germany have come as an upsurge from below, and not from the government itself. The masses want work, and the most insistent ones are the very groups that Hitler and his adventurers have been most assiduous in organizing. It is not without reason that, at the numerous meetings the Nazi leaders are holding with the S.A. and S.S. troops, they must plead for more and more discipline. The anti-Jewish boycott (not yet ended though deprived of official sanction) was started by the S.A. troops in Munich, and it gained such momentum within a few hours that not one among the Nazi leaders dared to make an effort to head it off. There is ground for believing that the same forces operating from below forced the move against the trade unions on May 2. The general belief is that Seldte and Hitler would have liked more time, but the military leaders of the Nazi party, finding their troops getting more and more restless as the days passed, took this step to appease them.

If this is true, how much more additional pressure will come from below? And in what direction will the pressure from below drive the Hitlerian government? Will Hitler, for instance, use it to drive out of the cabinet the remaining members of the Hugenberg crowd, whose tariff exactions have already sent the cost of food to higher levels, a condition which has already resulted in sporadic rioting in the cities of the Ruhr? Or, finding that the unions, "the new corner stone of the Nazi state," are not contented with phrases about the indivisibility of capital and labor, and demand that wages, hours, social legislation, etc., be protected within the framework of the Weimar constitution, will he restrain the large industrialists of Germany who think that now is their grand opportunity? Or, will he go still further to the right, even against his own Nazi followers in the military branch of his party who carried out the investment of the trade unions on May 2?

All these questions will be answered, and in my opinion within a shorter period of time than the world believes. Germany is moving rapidly, much more rapidly than the intellects of Herr Hitler and his crowd of adventurers. The question in my mind, and in the mind of most of the former German trade-union leaders now is—what will come after Hitler? A monarchy? A military dictatorship directed by some yet unknown head of the Reichswehr? Or a repetition of the years of terror that existed in France during her upheaval? The last is not unlikely.

47

Some Repercussions of the Surge in Unionism During the Late 1930's

The Foreman and the Union

DON D. LESCOHIER

Let us start with the proposition that the adjustment of grievances and other problems arising in his department is an essential part of the duties of any foreman and that the establishment of collective bargaining in a plant does not change that fact. It may require some change in his methods, but it does not involve any change in his proper duties. Moreover, the foreman has the *right* to clear up the difficulties which arise in his department. No workman, either individually or as a member of a union, should ever be denied the opportunity to carry a grievance beyond his foreman, but the foreman should be the court of first resort.

Grievances always start in the individual department; they could not start elsewhere. Therefore, the foreman is the first representative of management and should be the first one contacted by an aggrieved workman or union shop committee, steward, or business agent. It should not be possible for a grievance under an agreement to go beyond the foreman for settlement until he has had an opportunity to consider it and to take action upon it.

This means that a foreman should have the power to make an adjustment with the union's representatives. Two points immediately arise: first, the scope of the foreman's powers and duties in a union shop in adjusting grievances and intradepartmental disputes; and, second, the competence of the foreman to deal with these problems. On the first point I suggest that the foreman (as well as his top management and the union) should

Reprinted from *Personnel*, August, 1938, Vol. 15, No. 1, pp. 18-25.

Dr. Lescohier was Professor of Economics at the University of Wisconsin when this paper was published.

consider the resolving of departmental difficulties due to grievances, misunderstandings, or failure of either party to carry out the spirit and purpose of the agreement as an essential part of the foreman's duties and rights. If any ordinary difficulty has to be taken up to his superiors or to top management for adjustment, either the foreman has failed in part of his job or his company has neglected to provide him with appropriate authority and training to carry out a duty which is rightfully his.

Short-Circuiting the Foreman

Why should a foreman have this power and duty? The answer is, because no one should come between him and his men. If he is to maintain an efficient, properly cooperating body of men in his department, the contacts of those men with the company must be continuously and almost completely through him. If the union can short-circuit him by going to top management, his prestige in and control over his department are seriously weakened. The same thing is true if top management short-circuits him by keeping all contacts with the union, including adjustments, in its own hands.

Top management, especially in industries newly organized, is very likely to do exactly this, partly because foremen are so often inexperienced in dealing with unions or lacking in definite training that would fit them to handle, in cooperation with the union, the problems which arise in their departments. It is also in part due to an excessive confidence on the part of top management in its own ability to handle industrial relations matters, and to an overestimation of its own and an underestimation of its foremen's knowledge and understanding of these problems. Sometimes, of course, top management is so baffled by the labor problems with which it is confronted that the head executives cannot believe that a subordinate might be able to solve such problems. Yet often that is so.

It is natural for the union to short-circuit the foremen (that is, to go directly to the seat of power without stopping to negotiate with subordinate executives), especially if the foremen lack the power to say "yes" or "no." Unions will be willing to negotiate adjustments with foremen only if such a procedure is the clearly stated and firmly enforced policy of the company and if the foremen have the power to get down to brass tacks with the union and to make settlements.

Top management tends to short-circuit the foremen because it is afraid that they will make mistakes. But it is better policy on the part of a company to accept with a shrug some mistakes made by the foremen, and to support the foremen's authority, than to force the foremen to obtain a managerial O.K. on every negotiation with the union that they carry through. After all, everyone makes mistakes; errors occur in every part of a business. Foremen now have to acquire experience in dealing with unions, and a certain number of mistakes are inevitable.

Perhaps the words of Frank Harrison, works manager of the International Harvester Company, should be remembered at this point: "We have found that a Harvester employee is still a Harvester employee, even if he does put on a button"; and negotiation with union men over grievances is, after all, negotiation with employees.

This brings us to the practical question: How can foremen be better trained for the competent handling of industrial relations problems which arise within their departments?

Three things are essential: first, the definition in black and white of the labor policies, practices, and procedures which shall obtain within the company; second, the definition in writing, for the foremen, of a set of principles to govern them in handling industrial relations situations; and third, specific training of the foremen for the handling of adjustments under the agreement in cooperation with the union.

A Definite Labor Policy

Formulation of a definite labor policy and a set of procedures is a task of top management. I am not referring to the agreement with the union. That constitutes the company's engagement with the union on certain specific matters, such as what wages and hours shall be, whether or not there shall be a closed shop, and other items of contract. But behind the agreement and broader than it are the company's own labor policies, covering many matters not mentioned in the agreement. For instance, such questions as vacations with pay, overtime, seniority, rules governing promotion, methods of labor selection and of wage payment, and the procedure to be followed by an employee with a grievance, *if they are not covered by the agreement*, ought to be covered by a definite "labor policy" clearly known to and accepted by both the company's executive organization and the employees. Other matters, whether not suited to coverage by a trade agreement or in fact not covered, such as policies to regularize employment, the selection of employees in layoffs, the handling of garnishments and assignments of wages, and the solicitation of funds for organizations outside the shop on company premises and time, should be covered by a printed booklet on company labor policies. The foremen and the workers will thus possess a clear definition of the company's policies on the many matters that may be involved in conflicts of opinion in the shop; and this labor policy will form a basis for definite action by the foremen on difficulties that arise. Indefiniteness should be eliminated on as many points of labor policy as possible by such written statements, *which should be discussed with the employees before adoption and publication.*

Guiding Principles for Foremen

Let us now consider the second point: the definition in writing, for the foremen, of a set of principles to govern them in handling specific issues. The following examples indicate what I mean:

- "The company wants its employees to feel satisfied at all times that their complaints and contentions receive full, free, and honest consideration and that the company wants them to be treated justly."
- "If a man *thinks* he has cause for complaint, this is just as real an issue as if he really has cause. Patience and forbearance are frequently necessary in helping employees to appraise a situation correctly. We want our foremen to aid their men to achieve a realistic understanding of shop matters, including personal difficulties."
- "It is the purpose of this company to provide the steadiest possible employment for its employees. Foremen are expected to give thought to the transfer of men to other jobs when work is slack in

their regular jobs. Furthermore, foremen, in the interest of stabilized employment, are instructed to consider all prospective discharges carefully, so that no arbitrary or unnecessary discharges occur."

These are simply suggestive of what I mean when I speak of written instructions covering principles of company policy. Such instructions are for the foremen, not for the body of employees. They must, of course, harmonize with the company's general labor policy and with the union agreement.

Supervisory Training in Union Negotiation

We come now to the third point: the training of foremen for intelligent and constructive dealing with representatives of the union on matters arising in their departments.

There is a large number of problems which cannot be covered adequately either by the agreement with the union or by the formal statement of the company's labor policies. I suggest the necessity of as careful training of foremen for fitness in handling these problems as they presumably have had in the mechanical knowledge required in their jobs.

It must always be borne in mind that the objective of training is to bring about a uniform and complete understanding of management's problems and policies in dealing with the unions, and in adjusting the day-to-day difficulties which arise, and to achieve uniformity of procedure in this regard—without putting a rubber stamp on the foremen's minds. It should be noted, further, that ideas as they pass down through an organization are bound to be diluted. It is necessary for foremen to grasp their company's labor relations policies very clearly if they are to observe them properly when dealing with problems in their departments or convey them correctly to the rank-and-file employees. For it must not be overlooked that the purpose of all supervisory training is the performance of the employee—in this case, the development both in the foreman and on the part of the union men with whom he deals of a desire for a fair, intelligent, and constructive handling of grievances, problems and interpretations under the union agreements.

In conclusion, I should like to list a set of general principles set forth by The B. F. Goodrich Company as basic to its labor relations policy:

- The careful thinking out, codification, and publication of the company's policies on all noncontroversial subjects.
- The discussion by top management, with the labor representatives, of all controversial questions and the incorporation of agreed policies and procedures into either the company's general labor policy or the agreement with the union.
- The systematic instruction of the supervisors in the policies arrived at, both on noncontroversial and on controversial subjects.
- The placing upon the supervisors of the responsibility for seeing that these policies are fully carried out in their departments and for adjusting any grievances or other difficulties which occur in day-to-day operations. The objective is always to enable the supervisors to settle a maximum number of problems without resort to superior executives.

- The periodical reconsideration and readjustment of the policies to conform to modifications in current economic conditions or changes within the structure and processes of the industry.
- Finally, the policy of permitting *no one* to come between the foreman and his subordinates insofar as day-to-day dealings are concerned—not even the personnel department or the union committeeman—except to facilitate conference and adjustment between the foreman and his men.

48

Some Odd Bedfellows

When Foremen Joined the C.I.O.

IRA B. CROSS, Jr.

"C.I.O. now demands right to sit on both sides of collective bargaining." Shortly before Christmas, in full-page advertisements and news releases from Coast to Coast, this headline gave credence to the belief, of quite a few readers, that in Detroit the C.I.O. was engaged in its first real step of taking over American industry. Previously, the automobile workers had made clear their demand that they be given a say in the setting of production standards, and with this newest statement made public, the Sovietization of manufacturing was apparently at hand.

C.I.O. Did Not Want Foremen

Customarily, there is always much more to a situation than meets the eye, and this incident provides no exception to the old axiom. In the first place, the Foremen and Supervisors Local Industrial Union No. 918, C.I.O., was not something new. It had been chartered on December 7, 1938. In fact, earlier in 1939 a sister local of this same organization out in La Crosse, Wisconsin, had conducted a strike, and the employees had refused to go through the picket line conducted by their foremen.

In the second place, it was with the greatest difficulty that the initial group of foremen convinced the C.I.O. that they should be granted a charter. At first, the C.I.O. did not want them in their organization, and now after the incident in Detroit which provided such unfavorable publicity, it is doubtful if any of the national officers are pleased that they did issue a charter to this thing which is neither flesh nor fowl.

Thirdly, the telegram which the foremen's union sent to the Chrysler Corporation, and which caused all the trouble, merely requested that the management meet with the duly elected bargaining committee of the foremen, in order to carry out the collective bargaining provisions of the

Reprinted from *The Personnel Journal*, Vol. 18, 1939-40, pp. 274-83.

Dr. Cross was at the Harvard Graduate School of Business Administration when this was written.

National Labor Relations Act. This message turned out to be a boomerang to the union, and a real bonanza to the Chrysler officials. It gave them gratuitously an unexpected bargaining point, which was most welcome to the company, after many days of seemingly stalemated negotiations.

To answer the questions in the minds of those who are interested in this unique problem of industrial relations, it will be well to determine: (1) Who were the persons behind this organization? and (2) What were the reasons for its formation?

Foremen Thought Employees Needed Union

Clarence Bolds, the president of this unorthodox union, is today a foreman employed by the Kelsey-Hayes Company in Detroit. He started there in September of 1929, and in the following April he was given the position he holds at the present time. He has an older brother, an officer in the International Typographical Union, from whom he obtained his first ideas on the subject of unionism. The Typographical Union, incidentally, for years has demanded that foremen employed in printing plants, under contract with the union, must carry cards in their organization.

When the A.F. of L. first undertook to unionize the automobile industry in the early thirties, Bolds, despite his foremanship, felt that the employees needed a union, and he lent his efforts to the formation of one of the first organized groups of Detroit auto workers. Later on, when the C.I.O. entered the picture, and the workers voted to hitch their wagon to John L. Lewis's star, foremen were excluded from membership in the union by legislative order. The C.I.O. wanted no part of the foremen, who always have been considered as being aligned with the management, and thus against the interests of the workers.

This left the foremen out on a limb. But when the organized workers began to exert concerted pressure on the automobile manufacturers, the foremen found themselves being moved still farther out on this same limb.

Changed Status of Modern Foreman

During all this trouble, two things happened which concern us here. Bolds, who had been interested in unionism from the start, retained personal contact with the men who were pushing the organizational drives. Although he was barred from any formal contact with the union, except as the union representatives in his plant might present grievances to him, he came to know various officers and representatives of the U.A.W., and frequently spent evenings talking with them. Secondly, the foremen began to find that the growth of organized labor was doing things which affected them, and their position was becoming hardly the job in the plant to be coveted.

The term "foreman" might as well be clarified here because it carries a different connation as between industries. The "foreman" in a typical automobile plant is not the boss over the employees in his department, in the same sense that one thinks of the foreman of a section gang on a railroad, or in a machine shop. At least he is no longer the boss under the union regime. Formerly, the foreman could hire and fire the men who worked under him. If he wanted to put his relatives to work, and he frequently did, such was his prerogative. If he didn't like the way a man spoke to him on Monday morning, after a hard week-end, he could tell him to "draw his time." This was customary practice throughout the industry before the unions came in. The foreman was the real boss, and in some cases he was a real tyrant.

When, however, committees of hard-boiled representatives of the organized workers began to confront top management with demands to be settled, with the alternative of having "your —— plant closed down," it became a matter of expediency to establish personnel departments. It was hoped that by centralizing the taking on and discharging of employees, grievances arising from indiscretion on the part of the foremen would be eliminated.

Furthermore, as competition between manufacturers became more keen, employers found it better to delegate the functions of production planning and scheduling, to special departments which were equipped to perform such work for the entire plant.

Workers Thumb Noses at Him

Thus, a foreman, now shorn of most of his authority and responsibility, found himself in the position where he might be handed an unexplained order from the production planning department, calling for increased output on his line. When he attempted to carry out this order the workers might thumb their noses at him, as they relied on their new-found protection of the union to protect them from "speed-up." If the foreman tried to drive the workers to meet the new schedule, the union would take a grievance up over his head to someone in the management, who possessed the authority to reduce the speed of the line, or "tell them the reason why." These men were no longer foremen; they became straw bosses, pushers, or gang bosses, whatever the name might be. As one man put it, "In each department there is one foreman—in the true sense of the word. Under him are other 'foremen' or gang leaders who do no actual productive work, but who as supervisors try to enforce the company's rules."

These "foremen" were smack in the middle, between the pressure of management to meet production schedules, and the pressure of workers to do just as little as they could get away with. These are the men who joined the C.I.O. Only a few isolated department heads were taken into the organization. The decision on membership for true foremen was left to the discretion of the individual plant divisions of the union.

Employees Cut His Pay

To add injury to insult, as one foreman explained it, "When I took the workers' pay checks around to them, I found that some of them were making more money than I was, and that generally I was getting only five or ten cents an hour more than most of them." In the past, when a company was confronted with a financial squeeze, wages were the first and easiest things to slash. When and how they were returned to the former level was pretty much left up to the employed.

A major objective of unions has been to set a contractual level of wages for a definite period, and relieve the employer of the temptation of reducing them during a pinch. In subsequent tight spots, employers would turn to this former "reserve" only to find that the wage scale of the workers was impregnable, for the life of the union contract. There was still a little flexibility in the organization, however, in the pay checks of foremen and the office force; so a "temporary reduction" of ten per cent or so would be levied on these individuals.

All in all, the foremen were becoming the "Forgotten Men" of industry. They no longer controlled the employment of the men who worked under them; even if they did recommend the discharge of an incompetent worker, the union usually could get him reinstated; they no longer had a say in the setting of production standards; they were the goats when the employer had to conserve his working capital; their hours of work were sometimes long and irregular; they had no assured job protection or seniority. In general, they were getting pretty well kicked around by both sides.

Right before their eyes, however, was being enacted a living example of what organized action could do. Many, not all, of the abuses about which the workers had complained for years had been corrected practically overnight through the magic of joining the C.I.O. Why couldn't they achieve the same ends by following in the footsteps of workers?

Foremen Have Difficulty Getting Union Charter

This was the thought that came to Bolds, and his fellow-foremen, late in 1938, as they mused over a ten to fifteen per cent salary cut, and a two-week stretch of work at half-pay. A small group of these men became inspired with the idea of organized strength, and applied for membership in the U.A.W.-C.I.O. The union would have nothing to do with them. They tried to get into the Architects and Engineers union, but with the same result. Finally, their efforts led them to Adolph Germer, then C.I.O. regional director for the state of Michigan, who was interested in their story, and promised to do something for them if he could.

John Brophy, director of the national C.I.O.'s organizational department, at first vigorously denied Germer's application for a charter for this group of foremen. Why should foremen, the agents of the employer—the perennial targets of abuse in almost every organizing campaign—be permitted to enter the ranks of organized labor? This looked like another ruse of the employers to undermine the union. Germer's sincerity and persistence finally bore fruit, however, and the C.I.O. officially recognized this group on the seventh of December, 1938. Listed as charter members are ten men—all foremen at the Kelsey-Hayes plant.

The primary obstacle of getting a charter overcome, the next job was to build the membership of the organization. Signing up the balance of the foremen at Kelsey-Hayes was easy. In two weeks and three days the membership in this company was practically 100 per cent. Almost immediately the men discovered that in the group action there lies strength. The company rescinded their wage cut, and dropped the idea of shifting the foremen from salaried positions to hourly rated jobs.

The U.A.W., however, was still not quite certain of the sincerity of purpose of this new organization. In order to prove that their intentions were the best, the representatives of the foremen's union took along the employees' grievance committee each time they went in to present complaints to the management. This practice continued for some time, and it was not until the Fall that the foremen's representatives met alone with the company officials to discuss the grievances.

Membership in other Detroit plants grew very slowly at first. Not that conditions were dissimilar in other auto factories—foremen simply are more conservative than production employees, and they weren't certain whether this new foremen's union was the answer to their problems. Working five to ten hours a day after they had clocked out of the plant, Bolds and his colleagues canvassed the homes of foremen of other companies, and addressed groups of them. Interest in the union grew as these other men listened to the persuasive description of the possibilities, and visualized what organized strength might do for them in their own plants.

Did Workers Force Foremen into Union?

During this organizing campaign, employers complained that their workers were forcing foremen to become members of the new union. In one company, subtle pressure was brought to bear on the foremen, when the employees refused to converse with them unless they were members of the C.I.O. Later, Chrysler publicly accused the U.A.W.-C.I.O., and the foremen's union of "working together." Although the head men of both groups staunchly maintain that there was no official sanction of assistance on the part of the U.A.W., there doubtlessly were many instances of covert and informal aid on the part of the local union men, in getting the foremen "interested" in this organization.

Foremen Get Signed Agreement

Finally, the foremen at the Universal Cooler Corporation were able to obtain a signed agreement, which stated that the company recognized the union "as the bargaining agency for its supervisory employees not eligible to become members of the U.A.W." In this contract, which was negotiated as a supplement to the U.A.W. agreement covering the productive employees, the corporation further agreed to a procedure for representation and grievance adjustment, seniority protection of a sort, a two weeks vacation with pay, and—this is the clause the men point to: "It is mutually agreed and understood that the Universal Cooler Corporation will not demand or request any act or action whatever of its supervisory employees which would tend to strain or break the existing harmonious and fraternal relationship between the United Foremen & Supervisors L.I.U., #918, U.C.D., and the I.U.U.A.W.A., Local #174, Universal Cooler Division." Paraphrased in the words of one of the foremen, this simply means "No longer are we to be forced to treat employees like heels."

This contract was dated on the 20th day of June, 1939. It wasn't long before word of this signed agreement, and of the gains achieved by the newly-organized foremen in other plants, began to get around the grapevine in Detroit. Before long, foremen throughout the city were inquiring as to how they might obtain membership in the union.

Building the Organization

The boys with the charter membership, however, went about building their organization on a very business-like basis. They refused to take in individual foremen. An entire plant had to come into the union as a division, before individual memberships would be accepted. That is, if enough foremen at, say, the Dodge Truck plant wished to sign membership cards, so that the executive board of the union felt that a separate division should be established for that plant, a subsidiary division would be formed. The job of further organization and administration of the affairs of this group would then be handled by representatives elected among the foremen in that plant. Eventually, eleven divisions, covering eleven plants in Detroit, were set up, and over 900 foremen were listed as regular dues paying members.

They rented an office where they might hold meetings and keep their records. This office, of course, had the title, "Foremen & Supervisors Local Industrial Union" painted on the front windows. The young lady, who worked in the office as secretary for the union, stated that frequently passers-by would stop, read the sign, and ask "Foremen and Supervisors? Why do they need a union?" Truly, it was a little difficult to understand.

Foremen Picket Plant

But in La Crosse, Wisconsin, the foremen at the plant of the Electric Auto Lite Company heard of this foremen's union in Detroit, but when they began discussing the possibilities of doing something similar for themselves, they were firmly told by management to forget about the idea. It seems that these men preferred a little more direct type of action to gain their ends. So, one day instead of going into the plant to work, they posted themselves at the company's gates, and informed the incoming workers that they, the foremen, members of Local Industrial Union #984 of the C.I.O., were on strike. This must have been quite a shock, and a distinct surprise, to most of the employees. Here were their bosses with a picket line of their own. Regardless of their first reaction, however, their decision was not to cross the picket line, so both straw bosses and workers joined in a "work holiday."

This group in La Crosse was unable to obtain official certification from the National Labor Relations Board, as a bona fide labor union. Their strike, and subsequent presentation of demands, however, rewarded them with an informal letter of agreement which contained, among other things of importance to the foremen, wage increases of substantial size.

Returning to Detroit in the middle of November we find the foremen's union, which still has attracted practically no public attention, just about to write the opening sentence in what may be the last chapter of their history as a labor organization. By this time, the Chrysler employees were getting set to break the endurance record previously set for strikes in the auto industry, by the General Motors' workers in 1937. Although a turkey-less Thanksgiving was in the offing, the picket lines were holding fast. During this time, foremen in the Dodge Truck plant had been doing various jobs around the plant, and they had been coming into the shop through the union picket line, although 48 of these foremen were supposed to be members of the foremen's union.

Management's grapevine had picked up the word that their foremen were joining the C.I.O., and the Chrysler people thought that it was time to find out how their foremen stood on this issue. Accordingly, one day, about the 16th of November, the management of the Dodge Truck plant quizzed foremen as to whether they were affiliated with this new union. It is understood that some of these foremen were pretty outspoken.

Foremen Are Laid Off

One of them is reputed to have said that his loyalty was a commercial product for sale, and that if the company wanted it, they could buy it—by improving the terms of his employment. Most of the men were not in the least afraid of the cross-examination, as a group of workers might have been, and readily admitted their affiliation with the C.I.O. According to the charges filed with the Labor Board, at the end of the working day, 47 of the 58 foremen in the plant were told that they were being laid off indefinitely, and were handed their pay checks. The foremen's union claims to have had 49 members in this plant. Forty-seven were laid off. Whether their union affiliation had anything to do with their being furloughed is a matter which will never be adequately proved. Nevertheless, the impression obtained by the foremen involved was unanimously to this effect.

Position Taken by Labor Board

Here at last was a chance to test the strength of the union. Previously, a few individual cases of discharges had been successfully contested. This case, however, involved almost the entire supervisory force of one unit in the Chrysler Company. On the 18th of November, a delegation from the foremen's union called at the Detroit office of the National Labor Relations Board. They told the Board representative that they wanted to file charges of an unfair labor practice against the Chrysler Company.

The Labor Board representative told these furloughed foremen, that it would first be necessary for the company to refuse to meet with them as a bargaining group, before proceeding with the filing of the charges. It was Saturday morning, and the company officials could not be contacted by telephone. Therefore, a telegram was sent to the company asking that the management meet with the foremen's committee for purposes of bargaining. Next day, the foremen's union made the front pages of newspapers throughout the country. In subsequent full-page advertisements, the Chrysler Company accused the C.I.O. of demanding the right to sit on both sides of collective bargaining. Little had the committee of foremen from the Dodge Truck plant realized the trouble that their telegram—a matter of formality in the procedure of the Labor Board—would cause. Nor did they anticipate what this would finally mean to their entire organization.

A Break for Chrysler

The U.A.W. union officials were taken by surprise when the Chrysler people waved this telegram in their faces, as bargaining on the strike issue was resumed on Monday. Although they knew of the foremen union's existence, they had no warning that the group might attempt to meet with the company at this most inopportune time. For a while the conference was in a turmoil, with the company men using this incident to get the upper hand. Finally, with the company's refusal to go further with negotiations, until the foremen's charge before the Board had been permanently withdrawn, the C.I.O. agreed to disband the foremen's organization, in the plants of the Chrysler Company, and cease all organizing activity in connection with their foremen during the life of the current contract.

The managements of other automobile companies in Detroit followed Chrysler's position, and the foremen found employers telling them "nothing doing," until the Labor Board handed down its decision on the cases which were pending. Faced with this impasse, the organization witnessed the substantiation of a prediction made by C.I.O. officials. When the founders of the union first sought their charter they were told: "Foremen cannot be organized because they aren't 'organization-conscious,' to the extent that workers are. When they are confronted with an obstacle they will drop out of the union rather than stick by it." A marked falling off in dues payments in each plant, after managements stood pat, and refused to meet with foremen's committees, bore out this original view.

Labor Board Unlikely to Recognize Foremen

The Labor Board has not yet handed down its decision on the four cases which involve the status of the foremen's union. It seems unlikely, however, that they will consider this group as a labor organization under the terms of the Act. "The term 'employer' includes any person acting in the interest of an employer, directly or indirectly." These are the words of the Act. To be sure, this constitutes somewhat of a borderline case, but despite the loss of their former authority as departmental bosses, it is difficult to see how, in the face of the Act's definition of terms, foremen can be classed as anything but agents of an employer.

The leaders of the foremen's union stoically regard their present predicament with this attitude: "We still have a fighting chance, but if the Board's decision goes against us we will be forced to liquidate our organization. Should this be our fate, we at least have the consolation of having served a worthwhile purpose, in bringing foremen out of the shadows into which they have been forced during the past few years. It was a tough battle while it lasted, but we have reminded management that they still have foremen on their staff, and if they want these foremen to be on their side, in the future, they had better take a little better care of them."

There has been some talk of these foremen setting up an independent organization, or affiliating with the A.F. of L. This seems a little unlikely, because for purposes of effective collective bargaining, the foremen's union really derived its strength from the C.I.O. through its close association with the rank and file of the United Automobile Workers union. As an independent group it could be little more than a fraternal organization.

Foremen Not Considered Union-minded

While the Detroit situation was still in the headlines, an official of the Steel Workers' Organizing Committee in Pittsburgh received a telephone call from one of the large steel companies. "We have just heard a rumor that our foremen are joining the C.I.O." "Well, why don't you do something about it?" barked the S.W.O.C. man. "If you'd treat your foremen half decently, they would have no reason for joining a union." After assuring the voice on the other end of the line that S.W.O.C. was kept busy enough with 550,000 steel workers, without bothering about a handful of foremen who aren't union-minded anyway, he hung up. Shortly thereafter, this company inaugurated a special series of conferences to find out what the foremen had on their minds, and the threat of their joining the C.I.O. dissolved into thin air.

At first sight, it would seem that the desire of foremen to become affiliated with labor unions constitutes a rather bad reflection on the management of their companies. The remark of one foreman sounded almost plaintive: "If we had only been treated by the employers as part of management, there would never have been a foremen's union." But up to now, management has been kept busy dealing with various employees' unions, and the plight of foremen has, in some companies, been overlooked. Now, however, management groups are concerning themselves more with discussions of this currently important topic.

The Foremen and Supervisors Local Industrial Union may shortly pass out of the picture, but it will have served a most worthwhile purpose if it has brought to the attention of employers throughout the country, the previously forgotten man—the foreman.

49

Some Thought Is Given to the Development of a Reasonably Stable Relationship

Union-Management Cooperation: A Psychological Analysis

IRVING KNICKERBOCKER and DOUGLAS McGREGOR

It has frequently been noted that union-management relations follow a fairly typical course of historical change. When a union is first organized in a plant, the relationship is likely to involve a high degree of suspicion and conflict. Usually this "fighting stage" gradually disappears and is followed by a relatively neutral stage characterized by a decrease of suspicion, a growth in mutual understanding, and in general a mildly friendly atmosphere. This is the stage of *successful collective bargaining.* Then, where circumstances have been favorable, a third stage in union-management relations emerges. This is a state in which suspicion and conflict have disappeared, and in which the atmosphere is one not alone of acceptance but of constructive joint efforts to solve mutual problems. The term *union-management cooperation* has been applied to this third stage of the historical process.

Union-Management Relations as a Process of Psychological Growth

This transition from stage to stage becomes more meaningful if it is viewed, not merely as a process of historical change, but as a process of psychological growth and development similar to that experienced by the individual as he passes from infancy through childhood and adolescence to maturity. The transition becomes even more meaningful if the emphasis is laid on the emotional aspects of the developmental process rather than on the intellectual aspects alone.

There are four important characteristics of psychological growth which apply equally to the individual and to union-management relations. In the

Reprinted from *Personnel,* November, 1942, Vol. 19, No. 3, pp. 520-39.

Both authors were faculty members of the Industrial Relations Section at the Massachusetts Institute of Technology when this was written.

first place, psychological growth is a slow and arduous process. It involves myriad small changes in thinking and behavior which normally occur imperceptibly day by day. While the rate of growth may vary somewhat, depending upon circumstances, sudden jumps occur rarely and then only as a consequence of rather severe crises. Thus some cooperative plans have emerged suddenly as a result of the very real threat of the complete bankruptcy of the company. This is not normal growth but an abnormal spurt brought about by a crisis.

In the second place, psychological growth is not an all-or-nothing process. Even the emotionally mature adult retains some childish habits. On the other hand, the child can in some ways be startlingly mature. The same thing is true of union-management relations. The growth process is uneven; maturity is achieved in one small way today and in another tomorrow. Many "childish" habits and ways of thinking are retained long after their usefulness has apparently disappeared.

The third characteristic of growth is that it may be arrested at any stage. Just as some individuals of 40 are still at an adolescent level of emotional development, so do some union-management relationships remain in the fighting stage for long periods of time. This characteristic of being arrested in the course of development is so common that real emotional maturity is rare among individuals. Likewise genuine cooperation between union and management is rare.

Finally, psychological growth—unlike physical growth—is a two-way process. Retrogression is not at all unusual. Occasionally, in a critical situation, mature habits and ways of thinking that have been acquired painfully and slowly will suddenly disappear, to be supplanted by childish ones that have been presumed to be long since dead. In an extreme sense this phenomenon may be observed when civilized people become barbarians under the stress of strong emotions (for example, in a lynching mob). The same phenomenon may be observed in a milder form when, in a cooperative meeting between union and management, someone inadvertently brings up a point which strikes at the heart of an emotional "blind spot" of one or more of the participants. Sometimes the results of the retrogression last not for minutes or hours but for months or even years.

In the end, the psychological growth of union-management relations is no more than the growth of the participating individuals. The situation in any given organization is exceedingly complex because of the varying extent to which one individual or another dominates the picture, and because a number of different individuals are participating in the relationship.

Management once dominated the relationship almost completely. During the past decade, the development of the union movement has changed the picture from one of *action* by management on the workers to one of *interaction* between them. Interaction is the means by which the relationship grows.

Difference Between Collective Bargaining and Cooperation

Collective bargaining and cooperation are terms referring to overlapping stages of development in union-management relations. Just as a relatively mature adolescent may be more like an adult than like the average adolescent, so may collective bargaining in a mature relationship resemble cooperation more than it resembles typical collective bargaining.

Collective bargaining is essentially a competitive process. It arose historically by carrying over to the relationship between union and management certain practices which were at one time habitual in the relationship between competing firms. The bargainer tries to outguess the other fellow, to hide his own motives, to play up the concessions which he grants his opponent, and to play down those which he receives. The process is reasonably well characterized by the metaphor of "playing one's cards close to the chest."

Union-Management Cooperation

Genuine cooperation, on the other hand, is a mutual effort on the part of individuals or groups to achieve jointly desired goals. It is not a bargaining process, even though it may develop from bargaining practices. Effective cooperation can occur only when the "cards are face up on the table." Regardless of appearances and "stage dressing," real collective bargaining is essentially characterized by conflict; cooperation, by mutual aid.

Both procedures have important roles in union-management relations. Collective bargaining does not disappear when cooperation emerges. There are some problems—notably wage negotiation—which are likely to remain matters for collective bargaining regardless of the degree of cooperation which exists between a union and management. There is nevertheless some shift as the developmental process takes place. Some of the things which were originally dealt with through collective bargaining come in time to be dealt with cooperatively. For example, a great many grievances come to be handled in time by cooperative means. As the union and management deal with each other, and as mutual trust and confidence begin to develop, there comes a gradual recognition that the real aim of a grievance procedure is the solution of common problems to the satisfaction of all concerned.

It is perfectly possible for union and management to cooperate on some things and to compete on others. What is not possible is for them to compete and to cooperate at once with respect to the same problem. Matters for collective bargaining (involving conflict) cannot at one and the same time be matters for cooperation (involving mutual aid).

What are the problems which lend themselves most readily to cooperative effort? One thinks first of the problems of productive efficiency; through cooperative effort it is possible to increase output and reduce waste, thus increasing the size of the pie. In addition, many companies have experimented with cooperative procedures for dealing with other problems. For example, although the establishment of the general level of wages is accomplished through collective bargaining, problems connected with the internal wage structure may be handled with considerable success on a cooperative basis. Job evaluation plans are rather widely administered today on a joint basis.[1] A few firms—like The Murray Corporation in Detroit—have had some success in the joint administration of wage incentive systems. Many problems connected with the formulation of a general labor policy such as would be printed in a booklet for new employees can be successfully handled cooperatively.[2] And there have even been

[1] H. B. Bergen, "Union Participation in Job Evaluation," *Personnel*, March 1942, pp. 261-268.

[2] D. D. Decker, "A Practical Supervisory Training Program," *Personnel*, November 1939, pp. 62-68.

instances where the union has cooperated with the company on problems connected with merchandising and selling.[3]

Basic Differences in Union and Management Organization

Certain basic differences between the management organization and the union organization materially affect the nature of the interaction that takes place, and thus influence the growth of union-management relations. The most important difference is in the way in which authority and responsibility are handled by the management organization and the union organization.

Industrial management is so organized that control is from the top down, with authority and responsibility delegated by the few to the many. Those at the top who have final authority are presumably the most capable and the most skilled of the whole management group. Control is exerted through the formulation of a policy which sets limits within which action may be taken, is usually fairly general and emphasizes long-range achievements, and is aimed at the promotion of a profitable enterprise.

Top management also exerts a fundamental control upon the rest of the organization through its methods of selecting and training subordinates. A certain degree of conformity with policy is required. A conscious control is exerted in this manner; however, men are selected as a result of unconscious influences which are even more important—a member of management chooses his subordinates not only to fill the logical requirements of his organization but also to satisfy certain demands of his own personality.

Finally, top management exerts control by issuing orders. These may be broad or specific, they may be called by a variety of names, but essentially they are orders which must be followed within certain limits of tolerance. Even the most liberal top management, using the consultative methods which are popular today, retains a veto power over the actions and decisions of its subordinates.

In union organizations, on the other hand, control is ultimately from the bottom upward, with authority and responsibility delegated by the many to the few. The many who control are usually less skilled and less capable than the leaders whom they control. The aims of the rank and file are likely to be relatively opportunistic and short-range, very specific rather than general in nature. Get this wage increase, settle that grievance to our satisfaction, prevent management from carrying out this course of action.

In the early stages of union-management relations, one of the chief aims of the union membership may be revenge.[4] This depends, of course, upon the past behavior of management. Where the desire for revenge exists, it is usually found that the provision of an opportunity for the open expression of accumulated dissatisfactions removes the necessity for other forms of revengeful behavior. When management has a sincere desire to eliminate past sources of frustration of its workers, there is little need to fear a long continuance of the revenge theme.

The union membership will also try to obtain specific improvements in

[3] Jules Hochman, *Industry Planning Through Collective Bargaining*, International Ladies' Garment Workers Union, New York, 1941.

[4] C. S. Golden, and H. J. Ruttenberg, *The Dynamics of Industrial Democracy*, Harper & Row, Publishers, Inc., New York, 1942, Chapter I, especially pp. 15, 16.

working conditions, and changes in procedural rules such as those of promotion and transfer. Finally, it will be the members' aim to obtain more money. The important needs for social recognition, security, and recognition of personal worth are difficult for the worker to put into words. The demand for money is tangible. It is therefore an excellent medium for the expression of these needs. Other aims of a different nature will emerge only after a slow educational process by which first the leaders and then the membership of the union have been brought to the point of thinking in long-range terms.

The authority of the union membership is exerted ultimately through its elected leaders. There is a vast difference between the elective process and the carefully controlled selective and training processes utilized by top management. In addition, at least during the early period of the union's existence, the union demands a greater conformity from its leaders than does management from its subordinates. Members of management sometimes display a kind of impatience which suggests that they expect to deal with the union in the same way that they would deal with the management of another firm. However, in the early stages of union-management relations, union leaders are specifically instructed delegates. They come to management with explicit instructions to obtain certain definite things. They are not carrying on negotiations within the framework of a policy, expressed or unexpressed.

As time passes and the union attains a greater stability and security, the control over its leaders is somewhat looser. They can begin to operate within the framework of a policy. Nevertheless, because a union local is basically a democratic organization, union leaders must constantly check the opinions of their constituents to see whether the decisions they are reaching in their negotiations with management are consistent with the aims of the membership. The rank and file always lag behind their leaders in understanding and in willingness to accept broad policies and long-range aims. A management that has been dealing with union leaders who have developed and broadened remarkably in perspective may be surprised to find them replaced at election time by a group of suspicious and antagonistic "fighters." The leaders have "sold out" to management—and they proceed to elect a new leadership that will "show management where to get off."

Influence of the Personalities of Management

It is obvious that the nature of the interaction between management and union will be influenced by the personalities of the participants. The growth will be exceedingly slow, and it may cease altogether at an early stage of development, unless the key members of management who regularly deal with the union have a genuine, secure confidence in themselves and in their ability to perform the functions of management.

The men who possess this self-confidence are quietly sure of themselves. They know that whatever happens they will be able to land on their feet. They are able to take criticism, even from their inferiors. They are tolerant—able to see and to face the limitations placed upon union leaders by the nature of the union organization. They can face critical problems in human relations objectively; their own inferiorities do not become involved. Consequently, they are able to take a long-range view of the union-management relationship.

The member of management who is lacking in self-confidence cannot treat union representatives as equals. He fears and suspects those with whom he deals, particularly if they are somewhat antagonistic and aggressive. As a result, he will be unwilling to take the necessary chances involved in the early stages of union-management cooperation. The first attempts at cooperation will be harried by hangovers from past competitive habits. Particularly when the past experience of both parties has been one involving a fair amount of conflict, they are likely to stub their toes frequently when they begin to attempt to cooperate. It requires real confidence to accept these slips and to go on without the feeling that there has been a dirty deal.

Influence of the Personalities of Union Leaders

The man who has rebelled violently against authority is rarely in management. He is, however, frequently found among those union leaders who are in power during the fighting stage of union-management relations. He is elected to his office because he possesses exactly the characteristics that the new and insecure union requires, and his first appearance across the table from management may cause a good deal of consternation. Such a man is likely to be resentful toward management and completely unwilling to bury the past in order to build a new relationship. Consequently, the growth of industrial relations is arrested so long as he is in power.

In the normal course of events, however, the union achieves some of its purposes, and with this achievement comes a measure of security. Men get tired of fighting (particularly when it is unnecessary), of fiery oratory, of being whipped into a frenzy at every union meeting. They are ready to elect to office intelligent leaders who are quietly confident and who possess skill in dealing with men. It is not until such men are elected to office by the union that the transition to later stages of union-management relations becomes possible.

The Quality of Foremanship

Interaction between management and union occurs chiefly (1) through meetings between middle or top management and union leaders; and (2) through the daily contact between foreman and union members. The union *leader* acquires an understanding of management's problems, learns the "why" and the "wherefore" of company policy, and forms his opinions of "the company" by means of his contact with the higher levels of management. The union *member* acquires his understanding and forms his opinions about "the company" (1) from what he is told by the leaders of his union; and (2) from his experience with his foreman. When there are discrepancies between (1) and (2), the union member accepts the evidence of experience.

It is obvious, therefore, that the foreman's methods of handling his men, his attitudes, and his personality are important factors influencing the growth of union-management relations. The poor foreman may prevent the execution of the most carefully laid plans for improving union-management relations. He may even provide the reason for the belief that better relations are impossible. Too often he does both, and management—unaware of the real circumstances—unjustly accuses the union of bad faith.

The good foreman, on the other hand, provides daily proof of management's real intentions. From his behavior the union members may obtain the substantiating evidence which their leaders need to sell them an enlightened, long-range program.

The growth of union-management relations, then, is vitally dependent upon the quality of men selected to be foremen, upon their training, and upon the degree to which they are made an integral part of management. Cooperation between management and union cannot occur until there is cooperation within the ranks of management.

Recognition of the Ability of the Average Worker

Management has a tendency to underestimate those abilities of workers that may be utilized for cooperative efforts. Aware of the long period of apprenticeship they themselves have served, many members are likely to feel it is absurd to assume that workers could be of material help in promoting more efficient production. This underevaluation of the worker's potential contribution is especially prevalent where management lacks real self-confidence.

The abilities of the worker which may be tapped for the cooperative effort differ from those of management. That is the main reason why they are valuable. Management typically has a generalized knowledge of engineering principles and of the production problems and processes in the plant. The worker, on the other hand, has a highly specific knowledge, drawn from his intimate daily contact with the process on which he is working and the machine he operates. As a result, he can often assist management materially in discovering ways of improving the process, of reducing waste, of increasing the efficiency of a machine. Out of his fresh perspective sometimes emerge suggestions and ideas which, although they may appear initially to be foolish, have real merit.[5]

Because the worker is likely to be overawed by management's knowledge and ability, he tends to keep his mouth shut for fear of criticism and ridicule. Management must have a genuine and evident respect for his ability before he will feel free to express himself. We are not suggesting that management must be prepared to put into practice every idea suggested by its workers if cooperation is to be effective. We are suggesting that the cooperation will be fruitless unless management has learned to deal with these suggestions in a way that does not injure the worker's rather shaky belief in his own ability along these lines. Also, management must be flexible enough intellectually to recognize potential merit in a fresh point of view, and to experiment with ideas that may seem revolutionary in the light of accepted engineering principles.

The existence of the ability denied the worker by management is often demonstrated when it is utilized to defeat management's purposes. It is the boast of many workers that they can "beat" any incentive system that management can devise, and the evidence tends to support this contention. The longer union-management relations remain in the fighting stage, the more strongly are union members motivated to utilize their abilities in order to outsmart management.

Willingness to Share the Gains from Cooperation

There are a number of possible gains from union-management cooperation which the worker will recognize as important to *him*. The motives

[5] Ibid., Chapters VIII, IX.

involved can be harnessed to the cooperative effort, however, only if there is a genuine willingness on management's part to share the resulting gains equitably.

The first of these gains is the economic one. There is plenty of evidence to suggest that the economic gains can be sizable, but there is not so much evidence of a willingness on management's part to share them equitably. Many suggestion schemes have been set up as a means of stimulating the worker's ideas for the promotion of greater productive efficiency. Even the more liberal of these plans, however, seldom grant the worker an equitable share in the results obtained. Too often they have a top award of $50 or $100, although the savings effected sometimes total thousands of dollars per year.

The traditional American philosophy has been individualistic. Consequently, it has been natural for management to seek ways of motivating individuals to be more productive, and to reward the individual for his efforts. During the past decade, however, there has been an increasing emphasis on collective goals. Social security, "share the work" plans, union organization, wage and hour legislation—all are *group* rather than individual phenomena. Actually, it is just as possible to harness motives to group effort as it is to individual effort. And union-management cooperation is a group effort. Although effective cooperation is unlikely if the contributions of the individual to the collective effort are ignored entirely, the economic gains can best be shared on a group basis.

But there is a growing realization today that the possibility of economic gain is only one of many reasons which keep the worker (as well as management) on the job. A second highly important motive is the desire for prestige and social recognition. Properly handled, this motive becomes a powerful asset to union-management cooperation, yet one of the major obstacles to successful cooperation has been the unwillingness of management to give the union proper credit for its contribution to the joint effort. The member of management who is not genuinely confident of himself feels that he loses face when his workers gain prestige for having contributed importantly to an increase in productive efficiency. Since the management of the productive processes is his concern and responsibility, any improvement which he has not instituted is essentially a criticism of his own skill. Naturally, then, he is unwilling to see others obtain praise.

The gains from union-management cooperation can be shared with the workers in another important way: in terms of job security. Certainly, if cooperation is effective, it will strengthen the position of the company competitively and to that extent make possible a greater stabilization of employment and greater guarantees of job security. With the experiences of the past decade still fresh in their minds, this is a matter of considerable importance to workers.

Some well-known instances of union-management cooperation in the steel industry and in the needle trades were begun as a last resort in companies that were about to go out of existence because of financial insecurity. It has been suggested by some critics that effective union-management cooperation can occur only under such extreme circumstances. It is more probable, however, that these cases represent a sudden maturing of union-management relations brought about by the necessity for surviving a real crisis.

Other potential gains from union-management cooperation are somewhat intangible. Chief among these is the interest in the "game" of running the company successfully. There is little doubt that this is a basic motive of management. When it is shared, some of the workers at least will begin to display the same loyalty to the company that is expected of management. This inevitably narrows the gap between management and union.

Union Security

When a union is fighting with management for its existence, union-management cooperation is impossible. Its leaders are motivated primarily to get more and more from management through collective bargaining so that they will remain in office and the workers will remain in the union. When the union has achieved some form of security (for example, a maintenance-of-membership clause, a union shop, or a closed shop), its leaders will no longer have to weigh every move in terms of what their constituents will have to say about it. They can weigh the problems which they discuss with management in terms of their real merit rather than in terms of their political significance for the union membership. They can count on time in which to educate their followers and in which to demonstrate the value of long-range rather than short-range goals.

Regardless of the merits of the case, there is little doubt that some form of union security is essential if union-management relations are to develop to full maturity. It may well be that a new formula for union security will be discovered which will be superior to any of those commonly used today. One which seems to have been almost entirely ignored is to share the gains of union-management cooperation between the groups that are cooperating—that is, management (or the owners) and the membership of the union. Thus there is a genuine motivation for joining the union, and the problems of coercion and freedom of contract are not involved. Union members may be unwilling to expend the effort required for union-management cooperation if the fruits are to be shared alike by members and nonmembers.

In general, union security is normally an issue only during the early stages of the growth of union-management relations. When these relations have reached the stage where cooperation is being seriously considered, the question of security is likely to be settled with very little argument.

Mutual Understanding

One factor which has not yet been mentioned specifically runs as a common thread through all those we have discussed. This factor is a genuine mutual understanding on the part of the participants in the union-management relationship. Only when this understanding is present is it possible for growth to occur.

Unless management understands the problems of the union leaders which arise as a result of the nature of a union organization, the behavior of the leaders will be viewed with suspicion and sometimes even contempt. Unless the union leaders can acquire a genuine understanding of the authoritative relationships of management and the consequences, they will remain suspicious and antagonistic. Unless management understands the worker's desires for security, social satisfactions, prestige, and the recognition of personal worth, union-management cooperation will appear to be a utopian idea entirely outside the realm of practicality.

On the other hand, unless the union can acquire a genuine understanding of management's desire for a productive enterprise, many of management's suggestions for improving efficiency and reducing waste will be viewed with suspicion. Unless the union members can acquire an understanding of the problems of their company, there is little point in cooperative effort to improve productive efficiency.

This mutual understanding is not a mere intellectual phenomenon. If someone says to you, "I want to explain how this machine works," and then proceeds to show you blueprints and demonstrate the operation of the machine in question, you will end (if he is competent) with an "understanding" of what he is talking about. But suppose someone says to you, "I want you to understand how I felt when I asked the boss for a raise the other day," and then goes on to describe his feelings as he approached the boss, his reaction when he discovered that the boss was in a bad temper because of a lost order, and his crushing disappointment when the request for a raise was indignantly refused. Whether or not you "understand" in this case depends not upon a mere knowledge of the facts but upon your ability to put yourself into the other fellow's shoes emotionally.

Union-management meetings are often carried on in an atmosphere of "being logical" or "sticking to the hard facts." When this atmosphere exists, a barrier is raised against the expression of feelings and emotions. The man who insists on logic and facts will almost certainly fail to get "out on the table" the nonlogical opinions and feelings which are important to real understanding. Cooperation under these circumstances is an impossibility.

50

Developments Since World War II

Collective Bargaining in the Postwar Period

ROBERT M. MACDONALD

In recent years, the collective bargaining system has been the subject of growing criticism for its failure to serve adequately the national interest. Although the criticisms vary widely in content and intensity and are often mixed with attacks on the quality of union leadership, they do reflect a fairly widespread concern that the effects of collective bargaining on the nation's economy are too disruptive to be tolerated much longer.

Reprinted from the *Industrial and Labor Relations Review*, Vol. 20, No. 4, July, 1967, pp. 553-577.

Dr. Macdonald is Professor of Business Economics at the Amos Tuck School of Business Administration, Dartmouth College.

The bill of particulars in this indictment is by now a familiar one and requires no detailed exposition here. In sum, the claim is made that collective bargaining, as currently practiced, has impeded the economy's growth, imparted an upward drift to the general price level, and periodically imperiled the nation's health and safety.

In the past, it is argued, these impediments and disturbances, though troublesome, were at least tolerable. More recently, however, as national and international problems confront the nation with sterner tasks—the need to eliminate poverty and injustice at home, to meet the challenge of foreign competition in domestic and world markets, and to fulfill economic and military obligations abroad—these impediments have become unduly burdensome. It is essential, therefore, that the parties to collective bargaining (principally the trade unions) adapt their methods and results to conform to the imperatives of a new and more demanding environment—either voluntarily through the exercise of self-restraint or involuntarily through the medium of public controls.

Since some of these issues are dealt with directly in other articles which focus on the wage-price guidelines and national emergency disputes, this essay does not attempt a full-scale evaluation of collective bargaining as such. Rather, it aims at providing the background and perspective necessary for understanding and judging the institutions and practices of the modern bargaining system. It reviews how bargaining patterns and practices have evolved in the postwar period, examines their current effectiveness, and comments on the prospects for change. The discussion is conducted with full awareness of the limitations and risks attending the analysis and projection of so diverse and dynamic a phenomenon as the bargaining system. Not only are generalizations about bargaining behavior often little more than statements of central tendency around which the range of variation is wide indeed, but the trends or patterns which are generalized are constantly subject to change as the participants search for new ways to accommodate to the needs of the changing environment. This latter condition makes especially hazardous the task of prediction, for what the future holds is limited only by the constraints of the environment and by the imagination and skills the participants bring to the bargaining process.

The discussion makes no claim to being exhaustive. On the contrary, it is limited to those changes which serve to illuminate the current status of collective bargaining practice and the probable direction of future developments. The first part of the article provides a general review of the evolution of bargaining institutions and practices in the postwar period. Subsequent sections examine within this framework the most significant patterns of change in the bargaining system—the development of the structure of bargaining units, the movement toward longer-term contracts, and the elaboration of private compensation systems.

Postwar Evolution of Collective Bargaining

Although the establishment of unionism on a broad scale dates from the 1930's and the revolutionary labor policies of the New Deal, the development of the modern collective bargaining system, especially in the mass-production industries, is in many ways an accomplishment of the post-World War II period. It is true, of course, that many bargaining relationships had their beginnings in the late 1930's as the new and burgeoning unions, encouraged by the Wagner Act, fought to extend their jurisdictions as rapidly as possible throughout their respective industries. Nevertheless, the prewar years were pre-eminently an organizing period for labor, and such relationships as were established were tentative and based on the most rudimentary forms of agreement. Consequently, when the war intruded and agencies were organized to settle labor disputes within the framework of the government's stabilization policies, these agencies were forced to impose their settlements on a private bargaining system which had only begun to develop its own institutions and practices.

Under any circumstances, the swift rise of unionism—from four million members in 1936 to thirteen million in 1945—was bound to create serious frictions in the economy. But the effect of wartime regulation, though offering in one sense a respite from the travail of accommodating a new and powerful force to the American scene, was probably to exacerbate the difficulties. If nothing else, the enforced industrial peace permitted tensions to accumulate and denied the parties an opportunity for a more gradual transition, thus concentrating their adjustment problems in the difficult months of the reconversion period.

Although it was evident at the war's end that serious labor troubles would accompany the removal of controls, it is doubtful that many were prepared for the massive wave of bitter strikes which poured across the nation in 1945-1946, affecting almost every major industry. In an effort to break the logjam, fact-finding boards were appointed in the major disputes to investigate the issues and recommend settlements. Eventually, under prodding from the President, agreements were reached and large-scale strife (with the notable exception of the coal industry) subsided; but not before a troubled public, alarmed by the power unions had demonstrated to disrupt the nation's economy, had become convinced of the need for firm controls. This need found expression, of course, in the Taft-Hartley Act, passed in 1947 for the specific purpose of protecting the individual and society against abuses of union power.

Union-Management Relationships Take Form

Granted that the Taft-Hartley Act may have encouraged unions and employers to intensify their search for ways of containing conflict (by posing the clear alternative of deeper government involvement in collective bargaining), it is nevertheless remarkable how swiftly the institutions and practices of the modern bargaining system were developed. Satisfactory accommodations, to be sure, were not reached overnight; antagonisms died hard, and there was widespread reluctance on each side to recognize, much less to accept, the legitimacy of the other side's interests and concerns. Too many companies, moreover, purchased peaceful relations at the expense of efficiency, granting concessions in the negotiation and administration of contracts which severely hampered the exercise of management initiative. An unknown but substantial proportion of these concessions were actually the legacy of wartime dealings, but the sources of concession were the same in the two periods.

Inexperienced management, operating in a comfortable economic environment where competitive pressures imposed at most a weak restraint on cost and confronted by powerful unions whose leadership was similarly inexperienced and often insecure in the face of factionalism and a militant rank and file, found it easier to practice appeasement than to accept the sterner task of organizational reform required by the advent of unionism. Appeasement naturally stimulated excessive demands, but even more, it encouraged resort to such coercive tactics as wildcat strikes and slowdowns as the means of challenging company decisions and securing additional gains. It made little difference in these situations that contracts often provided procedures for the peaceful handling of grievance disputes, including the right of appeal to arbitration. Where coercive pressures were rewarded, they were a swifter and surer method for accomplishing labor's ends.

Although it is tempting to attribute the loose work standards, costly incentive systems, restrictive seniority arrangements, excessive idle-time allowances, and other inefficiencies found to exist in the late forties and early fifties to the importunacies of aggressive unions, at least part of the blame clearly resided with management. Many employers were simply ignorant, shortsighted, or neglectful in their management of the labor-relations function; and through weak bargaining and lax administration, they permitted such practices to proliferate as long as their operations remained profitable.

Not all companies adopted the line of resistance in their initial adaptation to unionism. On the contrary, a significant number recognized from the outset the revolutionary consequences of collective bargaining for management and the need for radical changes in their methods of decision making and operation.[1] Companies in this group constituted, however, a distinct minority of American business, and they attracted only passing attention from others as long as the post-war inflation continued and profits were easily realized.[2]

Obviously, many of the relationships developed during the first post-war decade left much to be desired from the standpoint of efficiency. The fact remains, nevertheless, that the transformation of the bargaining system in this brief span of years was little short of phenomenal. It was a period, following on prewar and wartime beginnings, that witnessed the systematic development of the collective agreement into an elaborate network of rules for regulating all phases of the employment relationship. These detailed rules covered not only the traditional subjects of wage scales, working hours, job assignments, production standards, layoffs, and

[1] In these companies, organization structures were revamped to accommodate to the rising importance of the industrial relations function, long-range policies were formulated to guide actions in dealing with unions, and procedures were established to ensure that policies were adhered to at all levels of decision making. The importance attached to the administrative function was demonstrated in the upgrading and training of supervisory forces and in the adoption of firm disciplinary policies to be applied consistently in all matters of wrongdoing. It was characteristic of the management of such companies that they understood, even as they deplored, the political character of the union. And from this understanding flowed an awareness that freedom to manage was to be preserved not by appeals to unions to act responsibly but by adherence to policies designed to persuade union leaders and members alike that responsible behavior was simply a matter of self-interest.

[2] It is somewhat ironic, in the light of contemporary criticisms of collective bargaining, that the minority of companies adopting a firm approach were often maligned for their failure to effect a "constructive accommodation" with unionism. Apparently, expert opinion was lulled as much by the ease of profitmaking as were many of the practitioners.

the like, but also an increasingly complex array of supplementary wage programs which were radically altering the character of employee compensation systems. In addition, it was a period of experimentation with policies and procedures that would help contain conflict and stabilize relations. Some of the innovations adopted, notably the longer contract term, but also the use of joint committees to explore the more technical aspects of contract issues, were designed to facilitate negotiations. Others, such as the establishment of screening committees or the occasional agreement to promote educational programs in contract administration, were intended to foster the orderly and peaceful resolution of grievance problems. Thus, while abuses existed and responsible behavior was slow to emerge in many quarters, these shortcomings should blind us neither to the formidable tasks which confronted the parties during this period nor to their substantial accomplishments in fashioning workable relations.

The Post-Korean War Period

The end of the Korean War and the ensuing recession of 1953-1954 marked the finish of the comfortable economic environment in which collective bargaining had flourished for almost a decade. As competition returned in full force to domestic markets, many companies found themselves in serious financial difficulties and were compelled to embark on programs of stringent retrenchment and reform in order to meet the requirements of the new environment. Their problems, it should be noted, were not all attributable to poor labor standards; nevertheless, for a substantial number of companies, labor costs were badly out of line and improvement of labor practices was clearly a necessary condition for survival. The force of rising competitive pressures was readily apparent in the changed attitude of managements toward collective bargaining. Whereas in the past the majority of employers had been quite defensive and even passive in their approach to union relations, they now were compelled by market circumstances to adopt a more aggressive stance. Indeed, many of the strikes following the Korean War and continuing through the mid-1950's were less the result of employer resistance to new union demands than of employer attempts to recover prior concessions and to tighten up generally on administrative practices. Not all companies, needless to say, were equally successful in their quest for revised labor standards, but the results of settlements during the period leave little room for doubt that the overall quality of union-management relations (from an efficiency standpoint) was significantly upgraded in the mid-1950's.

If the immediate post-Korean years ushered in a harsher climate for collective bargaining, it was not until the late fifties and early sixties that the full impact of the change was felt. By this time, the American economy was in the doldrums, plagued by excessive and persistent unemployment, a sluggish growth rate, and a continuing deficit in the balance of international payments. Since the achievement of balance-of-payments equilibrium was premised on preservation of the exchange value of the dollar, a primary constraint on policy was the maintenance of price stability. What the economy also needed, however, was a vigorous expansion of aggregate demand in a setting which would encourage the exploitation of technological innovations so as to increase the efficiency of American industry and enhance its position vis-a-vis competitors in world markets. With the policy orientation so firmly settled on the need to contain price increases and foster technological change, it is not surprising that the environment proved uncongenial and even hostile to unions. Policy makers feared that the beneficial effects of expansionary measures would be dissipated by the tendency of collective bargaining to push up prices in advance of the realization of full-capacity output. In addition, there was widespread concern that union insistence on security programs and on the maintenance of outmoded work practices would deprive industry and the nation of the full advantages of technological improvements, thus inhibiting progress and compounding the danger of inflation.

Hardening Positions

It would be idle to contend that the public's concern with collective bargaining performance during this period was without justification. One can readily enumerate specific disputes—in steel, newspaper publishing, and the transportation industries—where bargaining behavior clearly deserved condemnation. A balanced judgment of the institution's performance, however, should presumably weigh accomplishments as well as shortcomings, and certainly it should proceed from a knowledge of the harsh realities of the times. The dominant social fact of the period was the failure of the economic system to meet the employment needs of the community. This fact alone was sufficient to strain the bargaining process. In the late fifties and early sixties, however, the scarcity of jobs coexisted with a rapid economic change—a dual condition which brought the efficiency requirements of employers and the security needs of workers directly into conflict.

The motivations of employers were straightforward enough: hard pressed by domestic and foreign competition and favored by economic circumstance and the climate of opinion alike, they simply found the times propitious for an all-out assault on labor costs. Hence, the so-called "hard-line" approach of management, which consisted simply of a concerted drive to seize the initiative in bargaining, roll back the size of wage settlements, and abolish or bypass allegedly restrictive work rules and practices. Unions inevitably were placed on the defensive. With unemployment already excessive and employers moving determinedly to curtail labor expenditures, union leaders had no alternative but to conduct a holding operation, attempting to shore up job opportunities against the corrosive influence of technological improvements, mergers, plant relocations, contracting out, and the like. Their concern for security was sharpened, moreover, by the failure of unemployment to decline with the resumption of economic growth.

For almost a decade union leaders and others had publicized the radical character of the new technology and its impact on particular company and industry work forces. However, the onset of persistent large-scale unemployment after 1958 encouraged a new view, namely that automation and related technological change raised productivity so rapidly that the economy could no longer provide employment opportunities for all who wished to work and/or altered the demand for labor so drastically as to render many workers of low skill and low educational attainment virtually unemployable. As a consequence, unions were compelled to direct their efforts in bargaining not only to the traditional task of providing cushions against the impact of change but also to the larger social problem of preserving and even creating employment opportunities—a function for which collective bargaining is particularly unsuited.[3]

In the light of these circumstances, it is small wonder that the parties to bargaining had difficulty composing their differences and that disputes in a number of industries—steel, meatpacking, longshoring, and transportation—were especially bitter and prolonged. The stakes were large and compulsions were based on considerations of survival. Nor is it surprising that the public's reaction was one of impatience and indignation, considering the ills which beset the nation and the tendency for government officials to label each new dispute a national crisis or calamity. Yet, even as the clashes were occurring and as editorials were proclaiming regularly the imminent demise of the bargaining system, the parties themselves were evolving programs and procedures which offered constructive solutions to the problems confronting them. In some relationships, it is true, antagonisms dominated and hampered the search for mutually beneficial arrangements. In general, however, there was remarkably little opposition to change per se, and in most instances where it did occur, such opposition proved temporary, awaiting the discovery of an equitable method of adjustment.

New Programs

Some of the programs developed in the period reveal a degree of ingenuity and inventiveness curiously at odds with the claim of critics that collective bargaining has lost its creative impulse. As examples of the diversity of approaches adopted, one need only consider the 1960 Mechanization and Modernization Agreement in the Pacific Coast longshore industry, the 1962 Long-Range Sharing Plan negotiated by the Kaiser Steel Company and the United Steelworkers, and the 1959 Automation Fund agreement entered into by Armour and Company and the Packinghouse Workers and Meat Cutters unions. These programs have in common the reconciliation of employer and worker interests in an environment of rapid change, but they chart widely different courses toward that objective. The original Pacific Coast longshore agreement, renewed with some revisions in 1966, consisted essentially of an exchange of work rules (embodying employee property rights) for an employee-financed trust fund (accumulated at the rate of $5 million annually) to be used for wage guarantees and early retirement and other benefits for fully-registered longshoremen. The Kaiser Long-Range Sharing Plan, on the other hand, combines a formula for sharing with employees any cost savings realized by the company, with provisions for protecting the employment and earnings of

[3] Union anxieties in the period were reinforced by the failure of union growth. The basis of this threat to the strength, if not the survival, of union organizations is well known. Rising incomes and technological change have produced, and continue to produce, shifts in the occupational composition of employment—from goods-producing to service-producing occupations and from blue-collar to white-collar jobs within the goods-producing sector. Since no reversal of these trends is in sight, the consequences for existing unions whose base traditionally is in the goods-producing, blue-collar sectors of the economy is obvious; they cannot expect to grow in membership with the work force and they may even suffer an absolute decline unless they can broaden their membership base to include white-collar and other groups that have so far resisted unionism's blandishments. Accordingly, the problem of worker security was compounded by the threat to institutional security manifested in the efforts of unions to prevent erosion of the bargaining unit.

workers displaced or downgraded by automation or improved production methods. The Armour Automation Fund, finally, is a fund financed by employer contributions to provide for the study of labor displacement and the development of programs to minimize the impact of change on the company's work force.

While the Kaiser, Armour, and West Coast longshore agreements are the most dramatic and most publicized examples of recent programs introduced explicitly to facilitate change, a wide variety of provisions have been adopted in a large and increasing number of agreements which seek in one way or another to accomplish the same objective. These measures include advance notice of change to the union; the use of natural or controlled attrition to effect reductions in the work force; arrangements for the retraining and relocation of employees displaced as a result of technological or economic change; and provisions for early retirement, severance pay, and supplemental unemployment benefits for discharged or laid-off workers. Taken together, provisions of this sort (which appear in different combinations in the majority of collective bargaining agreements) represent a sensible and equitable solution to a difficult industrial relations problem. Some of these devices are, of course, easily criticized, either on the ground that they reduce the potential cost savings of innovation or because they discriminate in favor of those workers who are already employed; but in a society that makes at best only minimal provision for income maintenance during periods of idleness, is often unwilling or unable to maintain employment opportunities, and has until recently neglected the need for the planned preservation and development of its manpower resources, these private devices have great social value and are probably a small price to pay for freedom to innovate.

Joint Study Committee

Recent innovations in collective bargaining have not been limited, however, to the development of substantive provisions for dealing with the problems of change. They also extend to bargaining procedures where mechanisms have been devised for the in-depth study of labor relations issues, away from the "crisis" atmosphere of the bargaining table. In some respects, these procedural innovations (to be found currently in steel, automobiles, longshoring, meat packing, glass, electrical equipment, and other industries) resemble the joint union-management committees established in the forties and fifties to consider issues—such as job evaluation or health insurance—which were simply too complicated to settle under normal negotiating conditions. What distinguishes the contemporary joint study committee, however, is its status as a more or less permanent supplement to the bargaining process, with responsibility for investigating problems referred to it during the life of the contract and even for recommending solutions to such problems where agreement can be reached. Although the typical joint committee is comprised of union and management representatives only, a few committees have broadened their membership to include neutral experts who may serve in a variety of capacities, ranging from mere advice on technical matters to full-fledged direction of the committee's activities.

The potential advantages of the continuous study committee are obvious. It provides opportunity for rational discussion and fact finding on complicated issues, invites a freer exchange of ideas and information between the parties, and encourages experimentation with novel approaches to both old and new labor relations problems. Furthermore, if competently staffed and conscientiously supported, it can lead to an overall improvement in the quality of union-management relations and to a form of continuous bargaining, wherein critical or urgent issues are studied and disposed of as they arise, rather than being left to accumulate as festering grievances which embitter relations and poison the atmosphere in which regular negotiations are conducted.

Currently, the majority of the committees which have been established confine their activities to defining problems and finding facts which will facilitate the work of the regular negotiating committees. In a few situations, however, they have been empowered to recommend, and even negotiate, settlements—with profound effects on the negotiating process as well as on the content of collective agreements. The Human Relations Committee set up in basic steel following the bargaining debacle in 1959 illustrates both the possibilities and the pitfalls of broadening the scope of the study committee's responsibilities. The HRC was authorized initially to plan studies and recommend solutions to such problems as wage incentives, job classifications, seniority, and medical care. Later, it was assigned additional issues in the areas of vacation scheduling, grievances, and contracting out. It is generally conceded that the improvement in steel negotiations in the early 1960's owes a great deal to the work of the committee.

In addition to its role in fashioning the details of settlements and inculcating a spirit of cooperation at the bargaining table, however, the HRC made possible the introduction of two innovations in the 1963 agreement which augured well for the future of collective bargaining in the industry. The first was the inclusion of "experimental" provisions on subcontracting and overtime assignments which were to be subject to continuing review by the committee; the second was an agreement providing that any recommendations made by the HRC during the term of the contract and approved by the parties would take effect immediately. Unfortunately, however, the very success of the HRC in introducing greater rationality into decision making and in substituting a more flexible and continuous form of bargaining for the frustrating rituals and rigidities of traditional negotiating procedures proved also to be its downfall. Thus, in the 1965 United Steelworkers' election, the leadership associated with the HRC lost to a rival slate of officers pledged to return decision-making authority to the duly constituted representatives of the members. An immediate casualty was the committee itself, so that what was probably the boldest and potentially most significant experiment toward continuous collective bargaining has for the moment been shelved.

It is doubtful, nevertheless, that steel can revert—or, for that matter, will be allowed to revert—to the old pattern of periodic crises which characterized negotiations in the forties and fifties. True, the present union leadership is currently more concerned with delivering on its pledges and consolidating its position than with its image before the public. But it is unlikely that either the public or the government will tolerate for long a return to the tiresome conflicts of the past or that an intelligent leadership can permanently overlook the substantial accomplishments of the HRC. The experience of the steel committee underlines, however, one major problem that must be resolved if study committees and continuous bargaining are to perform their potentially useful roles in the collective bargaining process—namely, the problem of integrating the mechanisms for continuous study, consultation, and negotiation with the traditional procedures for ensuring democratic participation in decision making. The defeated Steelworkers' administration was obviously deficient in this respect. If similar reversals are to be avoided in other situations, and particularly if the continuous study committee is to be allowed to develop its full potential as a mechanism for containing conflict and promoting cooperation, it is essential that the parties devise effective means, consistent with the need to preserve an atmosphere of free discussion, for keeping the rank and file informed on issues before the committee. This is assuredly a challenging assignment, but in view of the crisis of confidence which has overtaken union leadership in recent years, it is also an assignment whose successful accomplishment may do much to restore the respect of union members for the integrity and competence of their leaders, to say nothing of restoring the confidence of the public in the collective bargaining system.

Changes in the Structure of Bargaining

Accompanying these developments in bargaining attitudes, procedures, and agreements in the postwar period have been significant changes in the structure of the bargaining system. The dominant trend has been the growing consolidation of negotiating units and the increasing concentration of decision-making authority in the hands of national union officers. This tendency toward centralization is not of course unique to the postwar years, but has its origin in the natural drive of unions at all times to standardize labor conditions throughout the area of competition for labor's services. Nevertheless, the task of building effective bargaining structures must await at least the development of stable organizations that blanket most, if not all, of the important producers within particular product- and/or labor-market areas. This is a condition which was met in only a few sectors of the economy prior to World War II.

Statistical measures of the change in bargaining structure in the postwar period are not available. Nevertheless, the direction of the change is clearly identified in the centralization of decision-making power within union and employer organizations, the expanding size and scope of the bargaining unit, and the loss of independence or autonomy in subordinate units of the bargaining system.

In unions, the centralization of power reflects, in part, the natural urge of elected leaders to gather together the reins of control over the organization's major activities, thus minimizing the opportunities for ambitious rivals to challenge the incumbents. More importantly, however, it stems from the desire to increase bargaining effectiveness. If the union is to maximize its gains, if it is to develop a strategy for the attainment of long-run objectives, it must impose limits on the independence of component units. Unless it can develop a coordinated strategy and secure a common commitment to specific goals, it is constantly exposed to employer exploitation of its weakest members and hence to the destruction of hard-won standards and of possible gains for its membership as a whole. Even in the absence of bureaucratic tendencies, this need exerts a potent influence on the distribution of decision-making power and is no doubt the major factor responsible for the increasingly important role assigned to the national union in the bargaining process in the postwar years. It underlies the grant of authority to national officials to formulate bargaining demands, to coordinate negotiating strategy, and to pass on the acceptability of all contract settlements within the union's jurisdiction.

On the employers' side, the centralization of decision-making power has been largely a defensive response to the presence of unionism and the consolidation of union bargaining efforts. In the large, oligopolistic firm, whose operations are often highly decentralized and usually widely dispersed geographically, this response has taken the form primarily of centrally directed bargaining policies to which divisional and local plant managements are expected to conform. In the small, competitive firm, on the other hand, the tendency has been to join forces with other firms similarly situated, surrendering discretion in bargaining decisions to the collectivity of firms represented by the association. Regardless of the form it takes, however, the move to more centralized decision making is essentially an effort to combat the whipsaw tactics of the union or to secure otherwise a bargaining advantage.

Whether or not the centralization of power leads to multiemployer bargaining depends on the character of the industry, considerations of strategy, and the preferences of the parties. In small-firm, highly competitive industries, unions have invariably favored multiemployer negotiations as the only effective approach to the attainment and maintenance of high labor standards. In this, moreover, they have found the employers normally compliant, since bargaining on a market-wide basis lends stability to the industry's price structure, permits the pooling of bargaining strength, and provides each small employer with access to expert services in the negotiation and administration of the collective agreement. In the large-firm, oligopolistic industries, on the other hand, unions have pushed for company-wide (multiplant) bargaining, but the majority have abandoned their earlier interest in multifirm negotiations. This change of heart can be traced directly to the realization in the immediate postwar years that "pattern" bargaining on a single-company basis could accomplish superior results.

This procedure allows the union to negotiate first a favorable settlement with any one of a few key companies. The settlement then becomes the "pattern" for major competitors and the "target" for smaller firms in the industry or for firms in related industries. Deviations from the pattern can normally be expected as negotiations move outward from the "power-generating sectors" to smaller firms and to satellite industries. There are limits, however, to the union's willingness to retreat from the pattern, set by the need to preserve the integrity of industry standards and by the size and type of concessions required for a firm's survival.[4] The advantages to the union of pattern bargaining are obvious: The union is free to exert pressure on the employer most likely to yield a favorable settlement; it benefits from the reluctance of any one company to stand a strike while its competitors continue to operate; and it is able to vary the level of

[4] How much deviation in settlements actually occurs is difficult to measure. The "pattern" constitutes only part of the total bargain, covering mainly the adjustment in wages and major benefit programs. There is thus considerable scope for differentiation in non-pattern terms of the contract, and hence, in the cost of settlements, even in the absence of "pattern" deviations as such.

settlements in accordance with ability to pay without endangering the maintenance of standards in the industry.

Although pattern bargaining does not entail an expansion of the bargaining unit as such, it calls for a high degree of centralized control if the strategy is to be successfully implemented. That the unions have achieved this measure of control is evident from the changing response of employers. During the first postwar decade, most large corporations, intent on preserving their freedom of action or confident of their own bargaining strength or fearful that joint negotiations would encourage government intervention, strongly supported single-company bargaining. Since the mid-fifties, however, many of these same companies, aware of their vulnerability to whipsaw tactics, have had second thoughts on the matter and are now pursuing a more cooperative approach based on close consultation and exchange of information and, in some industries, on the development of a common set of proposals and a common strategy. There is no evidence as yet that the firms involved will ultimately seek joint negotiations. The example of the steel companies which have engaged in industry-wide bargaining since 1956, however, and the recent experiment in joint bargaining by five of the nation's major airlines would indicate that further extensions of the bargaining unit are possible.[5]

The Contemporary Structure

There are at present approximately 150,000 agreements in the United States, or roughly one agreement for every one hundred workers represented by labor unions. Since most of these agreements are negotiated with a single employer and cover only a small number of workers, the bargaining structure—judged by the size of the typical negotiating unit—is obviously highly decentralized. Indeed, this is one of the distinctive features of the American bargaining system, for negotiations elsewhere in the world are normally collective on the employers' side and the agreements commonly cover entire industries. The fact that the typical bargaining unit in the United States is small, however, should not be construed as evidence that decision-making power is equally dispersed. On the contrary, the practice of pattern bargaining and, in addition, the tendency for key settlements to radiate across industry lines result in a complicated network of relationships which significantly limits the discretionary power of any single unit. Furthermore, despite the small size of the typical bargaining unit, it is nevertheless true that workers are heavily concentrated in a relatively small number of large units. Thus, in 1961, the Bureau of Labor Statistics found that 8.3 million workers or about half the number under union contract, were covered by 1,733 major agreements, i.e., agreements embracing one thousand workers or more each. The nine largest agreements covered 1.9 million workers, or more than a tenth of total union coverage.[6]

[5] The outcome may depend in part, however, on the role the federal government assumes in the area of labor disputes. At present, the prospect of government intervention is probably a major deterrent to the formation of larger units. But if the growing tendency to intervene in any major dispute is not reversed, some companies may become resigned to the inevitability of government involvement in large-scale negotiations and more readily embrace the wider units that appear to offer them a bargaining advantage.

[6] "Major Union Contracts in the United States, 1961," *Monthly Labor Review*, Vol. 85, No. 10 (October 1962), pp. 1136-1144.

The pattern of these major contracts can be quickly summarized. Twenty-eight percent were single-plant agreements; 36 percent were multiplant, single-employer agreements; and the remaining 36 percent were multiemployer agreements. Although agreements of each type are to be found in the majority of industries, single-firm bargaining predominates in the manufacturing sector of the economy, whereas multifirm bargaining is the dominant form in the nonmanufacturing sector. With the exception of the railroad industry, where the centralized bargaining system is partly the result of extensive government regulation (and, one might add, the steel industry, where government intervention is more or less a habit), multiemployer agreements are largely confined to the small-firm, competitive industries—food, apparel, printing, furniture, and lumber in manufacturing; and mining, trucking, wholesale and retail trade, hotels and restaurants, services, and construction in nonmanufacturing. Clearly, the character of the industry, especially the size of firms and the degree of competition in product and labor markets, is the primary determinant of bargaining unit arrangements.

Current Developments in Bargaining Structure

Statistics on the size of bargaining units serve to describe the structure at a point of time and to measure the trends in structure over past intervals of time. Whether past trends are a relevant guide to the future, however, depends on the underlying determinants of change and our expectations with regard to their behavior. Considering the multiplicity of factors that affect the size of bargaining units and the distribution of decision-making authority among them, it would be hazardous to attempt to forecast in any detail how the bargaining structure will behave. Nevertheless, one can discern in recent experience a number of developments which will influence one aspect or another of bargaining structure in the next decade. These developments point to further growth in the scope and interdependence of bargaining units in some industries, but to a loosening of centralized control in others.

The principal factor encouraging consolidation is the continuing extension of the market. This is especially evident in the traditional "local-market" industries, where competitive areas are expanding rapidly under the impact of spreading urbanization, improvements in the technology of transportation systems, and the growth of larger companies with facilities located in a number of different communities. The effect of these forces is seen most dramatically in the trucking industry, where the Teamsters union has recently negotiated its first nationwide contract and now enjoys a convention mandate to further centralize its bargaining activities. But the same pressures are also at work in other industries (construction, retail food, baking, etc.), gradually expanding negotiating units and drawing the units in different areas into ever tighter relationships.

Operating in the same direction, but at another level, are the efforts of unions with representation rights in the same company to develop systems of joint or coordinated company-wide bargaining similar to the systems already established by the Meat Cutters and Packinghouse Workers in the meat-packing industry and the Auto Workers and Machinists in the aerospace industry. The aim of this drive, which has gained considerable momentum in recent years under the energetic sponsorship of the Industrial Union Department (AFL-CIO), is, of course, to enhance union bargaining power by eliminating employer opportunities for whipsawing. It is yet too early to predict the final outcome of these activities, since they naturally meet the firm opposition of employers. They do foretell a period of more effective interunion cooperation and may well result, in some situations, in multiunion bargaining units.

Less certain in effect, but nonetheless important, are the group of decentralizing pressures associated mainly with the so-called revolt of the local union memberships. This revolt, stemming from the dissatisfaction of subordinate groups with their role in the bargaining process, manifests itself in a variety of ways. It appears in the growing rebelliousness of the skilled trades in industrial unions, in the demands within company-wide bargaining systems for a stronger emphasis on the resolution of local problems, in the defections of subordinate groups from their parent organizations, in more vigorous election challenges to incumbent administrations, and in the reduced willingness of the rank and file to accept agreements negotiated by their representatives.

A careful analysis of the rise in intraunion conflict, which is gradually reshaping the power structure in a number of unions and bargaining units, would indicate that a multiplicity of factors are at work—many of them unique to individual situations. Much of the turbulence can be traced, however, to three general sources: the expanding scope of the bargaining unit itself, the character of the economic environment in recent years, and government policies that impinge on bargaining behavior.

Enlarging the scope of the bargaining unit enhances bargaining power, but it also magnifies the possibilities of intraorganizational conflict. Where the bargaining unit is narrow in scope—confined, say, to a single occupation in a single plant—the interests of members are likely to coincide and the job of developing internal agreement on objectives is relatively straightforward. As the scope of the unit expands, however, to embrace additional groups—different occupations or different plants—aspirations tend to diverge and even to conflict, and the difficulty of mediating these conflicts increasingly complicates the task of internal agreement. The larger bargaining unit is constantly under pressure, therefore, to satisfy each constituent group that there is more to be gained from the support of unit objectives than from reliance on the group's own bargaining power. When a strategic group is sufficiently dissatisfied with the unit's performance, there are but two alternatives: to redistribute power within the unit in favor of the group, or to accept the group's withdrawal. This is the basis of the skilled-trades problem in industrial unions. Here, the progressive disillusionment of the skilled craftsmen with industrial-union policies has forced such unions, under pain of mass defections, to adjust their bargaining procedures so as to strengthen the representation rights of skilled groups on negotiating committees and accord them a larger measure of bargaining autonomy.

The related problem of discontent among local union memberships is attributable in part to disagreement over the current distribution of decision-making power within bargaining systems, but in part also to recent changes in the economic environment. Except for the last two years or so, the period since 1958 has been marked by the coincidence of large-scale unemployment and rapid industrial change. Pressed by intensified competition, employers in these years were driven to exploit every means of improving efficiency, from plant shutdowns and the automation of production processes to a "hard-line" attack on work rules and practices which allegedly hampered management's flexibility in adjusting manpower. Understandably, these circumstances induced anxieties in the majority of workers about job security and fear for the preservation of local working conditions. With local issues dominant in the worker's mind, the company-wide bargaining systems developed in the roomier economic environment of the previous decade and geared primarily to the pursuit of monetary gains were simply found wanting. Hence, the difficulties experienced in the auto negotiations and others in recent years where local unions have refused to accept the signing of the company-wide agreement as a signal that local issues should be dropped or compromised.[7]

Lastly, it is clear that public policy has also contributed to the current unrest in unions. The encouragement given to craft-type units under the Taft-Hartley Act, especially since the mid-1950's, has increased the vulnerability of industrial unions to special group pressures. The Landrum-Griffin Act of 1959, by stimulating rank-and-file expression and by diluting leadership control, has had much the same effect. In addition, there is little doubt that the latter act has played a role in the increasing incidence of settlement rejections by local union memberships, though here it must surely share the credit with governmental pressures aimed at securing simultaneously adherence to the wage-price guidelines and peaceful contract settlements. Whatever else these policies may have accomplished, collectively they have encouraged fragmentation of the bargaining structure, increased the strains on the bargaining process, and complicated the job of peaceful settlement.

Whether the intensification of intraunion conflict is looked upon with favor or distaste depends on one's point of view. For those long troubled by the atrophy of the local union and the absence of effective dissent within unions, the tensions and adjustments are a welcome tonic that may yet reinvigorate the lifeblood of an ailing, if not aged, institution. For others, however, concerned more with the need to structure institutional relationships so as to minimize the incompatibility of collective bargaining with the national interest, the tendency toward fragmentation or decentralization is a disturbing, and even alarming, trend. The difference in viewpoint is, of course, an aspect of an old and troublesome dilemma—namely, how best to reconcile conflicting pressures on the leadership of unions (and of other private associations) to respond, on the one hand, to the aspirations of their particular constituencies and, on the other, to governmental determinations of the national interest. Each of us resolves this dilemma in his own way, the resolution turning on one's personal view of the proper functions of unions, one's weighing of the contributions of collective bargaining to society's well-being, and one's basic sympathy for the government's diagnosis of social needs and its ordering of national priorities. Whatever one's view of the ideal state, however, a realistic

[7] The recent election reversals also fit within this pattern, especially in the case of the United Steel workers. Although the issues in this campaign were complex, it is clear nevertheless that the repudiation of the McDonald administration turned in part on its inattention to local unions and local problems, its failure to respond to the special needs of different industry groups (in aluminum, non-ferrous metals, can making, etc.), and its tendency to allow the Human Relations Committee to usurp the prerogatives of the regular negotiating committee—in short, its commitment to an over-centralized structure of authority.

assessment of the possibilities for bargaining structure must accept at the outset the inevitability of closer government surveillance of the system's performance. If the vitality of the bargaining process is to be preserved, therefore, one cannot avoid the need to effect uneasy compromises between the right of dissent within unions and the need to establish bargaining relationships which facilitate the orderly settlement of disputes within a framework of shifting national interest constraints.

Whether the turbulence of recent years is likely to subside soon is a different and highly conjectural matter. On the positive side, changes in representation procedures, concern for more effective grievance handling, the adoption of forms of continuous bargaining, and the redistribution of decision-making power between national and local negotiations should help to reduce internal strains. At the same time, the restoration of full employment, the incorporation in recent agreements of a wide range of security or "adjustment" provisions, and society's acceptance of a growing responsibility for lightening the hardships of change should ease worker anxieties about the future. Whether these changes are sufficient to quiet the recent unrest, however, is a question that experience alone can answer.

Long-Term Agreements and Automatic Wage Adjustments

The adoption of the long-term agreement and its gradual spread throughout industry is another major development of the postwar period. Indeed, it has been called the most important single development in bargaining practice since the end of World War II. Long-term contracts were not an innovation of the postwar years, but what distinguished the type of agreement pioneered by General Motors and the United Auto Workers in 1948 was the inclusion of provisions making wage adjustments automatic at scheduled dates in the future. These automatic adjustments were of two kinds: a wage improvement factor designed to raise wages annually in line with economy-wide productivity advances and a cost-of-living escalator designed to maintain real wages (the worker's living standards) against movements in the price level of consumer goods. Interestingly enough, when the GM-UAW agreement was first announced, it evoked little enthusiasm and, indeed, a good deal of criticism in industry circles. Since 1950, however, its influence has become pervasive and its implications for wage policy are now a central concern of economists.

The GM formula, embraced first in 1948 and continued in all subsequent agreements with the UAW, was introduced shortly after the passage of the Taft-Hartley Act at a time when important segments of American management had adopted a hold-the-line policy on wages. The formula represented an attempt by the company to formulate a long-term wage policy, based on productivity and living-cost standards, which would reduce the conflict over wage-setting and hence the risk of government involvement in wage decisions. As Joseph Garbarino points out, the unique feature of the approach was the attempt "to develop a policy on the substance of bargaining, as distinct from a strategy for use in the bargaining process."[8]

The GM-UAW two-year agreement had not attracted any imitators by mid-1950 when a new five-year agreement, again incorporating the wage

[8] Joseph W. Garbarino, *Wage Policy and Long-Term Contracts* (Washington: The Brookings Institution, 1962), p. 3.

formula, was signed. In the fall of 1950, however, fear of inflation and wage controls occasioned by the Korean War encouraged a number of unions to demand cost-of-living escalator clauses in their agreements. As a result, by September 1952, over three million workers—or almost 20 percent of all workers under contract—were covered by escalator agreements. Automatic wage increases were less popular, covering only half as many workers, most of whom were under the jurisdiction of the UAW. With the post-Korean recession, interest in cost-of-living agreements subsided, and many were abandoned. The price rise following 1955, however, brought renewed interest in cost-of-living clauses, and by 1958 coverage extended to over four million workers in a variety of industries including automobile, farm equipment, aerospace, trucking, meatpacking, steel-aluminum, electrical equipment, and railroad.[9] The year 1955 also witnessed the beginning of an increase in agreements containing automatic wage increases. Apparently, the decision to adopt these agreements was partly opportunistic and partly a desire to experiment with long-term policies, signaling the parties' confidence in the government's ability to manage the economy and employer acceptance of the permanency of militant unions.[10] Thus, by the end of the 1950's, some five million workers annually were receiving wage increases scheduled in earlier-year negotiations.

The recession beginning in 1958 produced the usual pattern of abandonment of cost-of-living clauses. Inflation was no longer a threat, many of the employers who had adopted such clauses just prior to the price rise of 1955-1957 were opposed to their renewal, and most unions in any case were more interested in job security issues. As a result, coverage had fallen to only two million workers by early 1966. The elimination of escalator clauses did not affect, however, the increase in multiyear contracts with automatic wage increases. Thus, whereas only 5 percent of collective agreements provided for deferred or scheduled increases in 1954, the proportion had increased to 67 percent by the first half of 1966 and was still rising.[11]

More recently, since prices have resumed their upward trend, union interest has again turned to cost-of-living escalator clauses, and indeed this issue has been given prominence in recent disputes—as in the case of the Machinists' strike against the airlines in the summer of 1966 and the GE-IUE dispute in the fall of the same year. It promises, too, to figure prominently in the forthcoming railroad and steel negotiations. Many employers can be expected to resist these pressures or at least to try to modify the impact of escalator clauses by seeking limits on the allowable adjustment, longer adjustment intervals, and the elimination of adjustments to small price variations. In this they have the administration's support on the ground that escalator clauses intensify inflationary pressures. Similarly, employers have sought to modify the size of automatic

[9] *Monthly Labor Review*, Vol. 89, No. 9 (September 1966), p. iv.

[10] Garbarino, *op. cit.*, pp. 79-80.

[11] Bureau of National Affairs, Inc., *Facts for Bargaining*, Jan. 29, 1965 and July 14, 1966. The Bureau has also reported that the most common term for contracts is three years (47 percent), closely followed by two years (40 percent). Approximately a quarter of these agreements provide for reopening on wage and/or non-wage matters prior to the scheduled expiration date. BNA, *Basic Patterns in Union Contracts*, Sept. 9, 1965, p. 36:1.

wage increases (sometimes by extending the adjustment interval beyond one year), and they have sought to divert part of the increase to other benefits in an effort to hold down the size of the package. As yet, however, success has been limited, confined mainly to modifications of the cost-of-living clause.

Implications of the Long-Term Contract

From the economist's standpoint, the critical issues raised by the shift to long-term contracts are the implications for wage behavior. As might be expected, the economist's affinity for wage-setting mechanisms that ensure a ready response to changing market conditions makes him naturally skeptical of the practice of setting wages well into the future, even though, as a practical matter, he may recognize offsetting gains in the avoidance of annual tests of strength and in the increased predictability of costs. The concern for wage behavior goes beyond the flexibility issue, however, to the question of the inflationary potential of the long-term contract, i.e., to its effect on the secular movement of wages compared with that of the short-term contract negotiated annually.

The most intensive study of this aspect of wage policy concludes that long-term formula agreements of the GM-UAW type (especially where they coexist with agreements bargained annually) probably add to inflationary pressures, partly through their impact on wage behavior in recession periods, and partly through the effect of escalator clauses on the wage-price lag.[12] The argument concerning recessionary wage behavior derives essentially from the judgment that the long-term contract has been a major influence in making "the annual money wage increase virtually ubiquitous for the organized worker in the United States."[13] The wage-price-lag argument rests, on the other hand, on the notion that cost-of-living clauses "help to maintain or intensify an inflationary movement that starts elsewhere in the economy" by facilitating or speeding up the escalation process.[14] These arguments are persuasive, but they have not gone unchallenged. Other economists, for example, have concluded that unions with long-term contracts would probably have negotiated wages at least as high in annual bargaining,[15] or have argued that the only realistic alternative to cost-of-living escalator clauses is higher initial wage increases which *anticipate* the expected price rise, thereby *reversing* the adjustment lag and immediately generating inflationary pressures.[16] How one chooses between these views is a matter of personal judgment, for each rests on quite different assumptions about bargaining behavior and the nature of the inflationary process.[17]

[12] Garbarino, *op. cit.*, 163-173.

[13] *Ibid.*, p. 133.

[14] *Ibid.*, p. 64.

[15] Jack Stieber, "Evaluation of Long-Term Contracts," in Harold W. Davey et al., eds., *New Dimensions in Collective Bargaining* (New York: Harper and Brothers, 1959), p. 151

[16] See, for example, Alvin H. Hansen, "Inflation and the New Economics," *Challenge*, Vol. 15, No. 2 (November-December 1966), pp. 6, 41.

[17] Alvin Hansen places strong emphasis on the importance to stability of lagged adjustment to change, hence his preference for the cost-of-living escalator over the anticipatory wage increase. As he notes in his argument in favor of such clauses: "The lag is important. Stability in a market economy is largely a function of lagged adjustments. . . . It makes more sense to make the adjustment *after* the event than to force the issue before the event." *Ibid.*, p. 41.

There is, however, another difficulty in questions of this sort which further complicates the issue. Much of the investigation of the inflationary potential of long-term contracts runs in terms of money-wage effects to the virtual neglect of productivity effects which may also be important. It is universally conceded, for example, that management derives considerable advantage from long-term contracts—avoidance of the costs of annual negotiations, a more stable environment for forward planning, less idle time lost through strikes, etc. But if this is so, and even allowing that management pays some price to the union for these advantages, it surely follows that efficiency effects (as well as wage effects) are relevant data in assessing the inflationary impact of the long-term contract.[18] Similarly, even if one accepts that the multiyear contract has been instrumental in establishing the expectation of annual money-wage increases, so that wage rates do in fact rise more than they otherwise would in recessionary periods, it still does not follow that unit wage costs are affected to the same extent or even in the same direction. For as long as relative bargaining power is unchanged, adjustments that compensate for the incremental wage increase may well occur, and indeed are to be expected, in other employment terms.[19] Given these possibilities, which direct attention to the multidimensional character of collective bargaining and to the need to consider a wider set of effects, it is doubtful that a categorical case can be made for or against the inflationary potential of the multiyear formula contract.

As we look to the future, there is no reason to expect that the postwar trend toward non-reopenable, long-term contracts will soon be reversed. On the contrary, the complexity of the modern collective agreement and the highly technical, long-run character of many benefit programs make such contracts all the more desirable. The particular form of the contract may, of course, change from time to time. Experience demonstrates, for example, that the popularity of cost-of-living escalators is, with the exception of one or two unions such as the UAW, a function largely of price expectations. The automatic wage increase, on the other hand, is a more permanent feature of wage policy and will remain so as long as economic conditions and the balance of power in union-management relations are not drastically altered.

Government efforts to strengthen the wage-price guidelines could become a significant factor in determining private arrangements in this area. The administration has made an attempt in recent months to curb the use of escalator clauses as part of its anti-inflationary program, and stepped-up pressures would certainly reinforce employer efforts to avoid or modify such clauses. Whether the drive, even if successful, would have desirable results is another matter. Undoubtedly, a lengthening of the

[18] It could be argued that benefits accruing to the employer must be surrendered *in toto* to the union for the risks the latter runs in agreeing to such a contract. There is no reason, however, for supposing that the arrangement is not mutually beneficial; and indeed the parties' strong and growing preference for this type of contract would indicate that it is.

[19] The importance of looking beyond the wage bargain to the much broader range of terms and practices embraced in the collective agreement has been demonstrated time and again. The "hard-line" approach of management in the late 1950's, manifested in the drive to eliminate restrictive rules and other obstacles to efficiency, was reinforced no doubt by the recognition of serious constraints on the manipulation of wage rates.

wage-price adjustment lag or a ceiling on the size of wage adjustments or a reduction in the responsiveness of wages to minor or transitory price movements would have a beneficial effect from the standpoint of price stability. If pressed too aggressively, however, a campaign to undermine escalator clauses would surely force unions to demand anticipatory wage increases and even to threaten a return to annual bargaining—eventualities that are hardly likely to advance the cause either of price stability or of industrial harmony.

The Elaboration of Compensation Systems

Collective bargaining has been credited with many of the changes which have occurred in the wage patterns and practices of individual firms during the post-war period; the displacement of personal rate systems by more rational plant wage structures (based on job content analysis); the elimination or reduction of occupational rate differentials among plants in the same company; and to a lesser degree, the shift in some industries from incentive to daywork methods of wage payment. Important as such changes in wage systems have been, however, a more dramatic and more significant development of the last two decades has been the growth and proliferation of supplementary wage practices or, as they are often called, fringe benefits. Few of these practices, as such, are innovations of the postwar period; retirement plans, health insurance programs, paid leave, and even the provision of premium payments all have long traditions, especially for white-collar workers, that predate both the depression of the thirties and the advent of unionism. In addition, many of the specific programs received their initial stimulus in World War II from stabilization policies that were more permissive toward fringe improvements than wage increases. The postwar period is nevertheless distinctive in that it witnessed the rapid extension of such benefits to blue-collar work groups and the more or less continuous revision and elaboration of the programs in successive negotiations.

The spectacular growth of fringe benefits and their current importance in American industry are readily demonstrated. For several years now, the Chamber of Commerce of the United States has conducted surveys of fringe payments by a sample of American firms in the manufacturing and nonmanufacturing sectors of the economy. These surveys show that employer expenditures for fringe benefits in 1,181 companies amounted to 71.5 cents an hour in 1965, or 24.7 percent of payroll. They also show that for eighty-four companies reporting throughout the postwar period, fringe expenditures rose from 22.1 cents an hour in 1947 to 88.8 cents an hour in 1965, or from 16.1 percent to 28.1 percent of payroll.[20] The Chamber's estimates probably overstate the actual size of fringes for industry as a whole, since the sample is biased toward the larger, more prosperous firms. Nevertheless such additional information as is available

[20] Chamber of Commerce of the United States, *Fringe Benefits 1965*, Washington, 1966, pp. 9, 27. These figures exclude premium payments from the definition of fringe benefits but include such payments, along with expenditures for vacations and holidays, in the definition of payroll. When premium payments are treated as a fringe expenditure and the payroll base is redefined as "straight-time pay for time worked," the ratio of fringe payments to payroll in 1965 (for all firms in the survey) rises from 24.7 percent to 37.8 percent—or to almost two fifths of straight-time wages and salaries.

confirms that the current level of supplementary payments is 20 to 25 percent of labor compensation, and that this percentage has roughly doubled since the end of World War II.

Unionism as the Source of Fringe Benefits

Most students of industrial relations, while reluctant to assign much influence to unions in the wage and productivity areas, have no hesitation in attributing to unionism the major role in the development of fringe benefits. This conclusion, in our view, is worth examining more closely; first, because it hardly seems warranted, and second, and more importantly, because an examination of the issue brings to light certain conceptual difficulties in the measurement of union influence which, if ignored, are likely to distort evaluations of the institution's performance.

The view that unions should be credited as the primary agent in the spread of fringe benefits derives from the notion that these programs, because of their group nature, are not in the category of provisions likely to be introduced unilaterally by employers and from observance of the aggressiveness of unions in pressing fringe demands at the bargaining table. The reasoning here is surely misleading, however, for it is based on an oversimplified view of the problems of personnel management, a misconception of the nature of the bargaining process, and a failure to take account of the evolving requirements of an industrial system. Space limitations preclude a full discussion, but the considerations that underlie this criticism of the popular view can be briefly stated.

First, the idea that employers, absent union pressures, would have little or no reason to initiate fringe benefits is contrary both to fact and to the logic of efficient manpower management. Most of the types of benefit programs in existence today were originated by employers and usually for sound business reasons—to reduce the costs of turnover and absenteeism, to reward effort and improve efficiency, to take advantage of tax savings, and to aid in the recruitment of workers. The early plans, to be sure, were sometimes selective (or discriminatory) in their application, and benefit levels were invariably modest. But these characteristics reflected, respectively, the specific objectives the plans were designed to achieve and the employers' judgment that most workers preferred the bulk of their compensation in ready cash—a conviction that made a good deal of sense as long as incomes were close to the subsistence level.

Second, the union's drive for fringe benefits postdated the depression and passage of the Social Security Act in 1935. The depression brought abrupt changes in the social, political, and economic outlook of the nation, and especially a recognition of the worker's dependence on the vagaries of the labor market and his relative helplessness in coping unaided with the problems of unemployment, ill health, and old age. These were the forces which determined public attitudes and shaped the socioeconomic environment of the postwar period. In that environment, characterized by a growing awareness of workers' needs, sustained prosperity, and relatively tight labor markets, it is surely no more unreasonable to suppose that employers in their efforts to attract, retain, and motivate workers would have experimented with supplementary wage programs (already in existence for white-collar groups) than to assume, as many do implicitly, that they would have approached their personnel needs in a manner reminiscent of the early 1930's.

Third, the bargaining process, as it has developed, does not lend itself easily to employer initiatives. The good-faith bargaining requirement, for one thing, prevents the employer from introducing changes unilaterally. More importantly, however, the adversary nature of the relationship and the natural concern of union leaders that all gains appear as the sole achievement of the union dictate that most employers publicly adopt a firm stance even against proposals which serve their own interests and, under different circumstances, would readily be granted. Curiously enough, employer opposition to wage demands is seldom interpreted as evidence that in the absence of union pressures the course of wages would have been vastly different. Yet employer opposition to negotiated fringes is invariably accepted as a reliable indicator of what would have happened in a non-union market.

Finally, it is clear from even a cursory survey of social systems that the provision of protection against interruptions to income (through accidents, sickness, unemployment, and old age) emerges inevitably in the course of industrialization. Whatever the particular institutions of the labor market, it is everywhere the case that responsibility for the minimum welfare and security of the worker has fallen upon employers and/or government. It appears, therefore, that the real issues in this area relate less to the provision of basic protections as such than to the forms which programs take, the timing of their introduction, and the rate of their liberalization.

These considerations do not deny a role to unions in the development of protective measures against insecurity, but they do suggest that the influence of unionism is easily (and often) exaggerated. They also suggest that issues of this sort should be examined within a broader framework than has hitherto been used—a framework that acknowledges the needs of workers in an industrial society, accepts the realistic alternatives available in meeting these needs, and distinguishes the requirements of the system (the workers' needs) from the specific instrument created to fulfill these requirements (the union).

A similar but stronger conclusion about the effect of unionism on fringes is reached in the recent statistical study of the determinants of fringe expenditures by Robert Rice.[21] For years, proponents of the view that unions were the major influential factor in the development of fringes have claimed the support of government surveys which show that the incidence of benefit plans as well as the level of benefit expenditures are appreciably higher in the unionized sector of the economy. Rice's study, based on these same surveys, demonstrates, however, that variations in benefit expenditures are explained largely by variations in employee-earnings levels, and that the apparent causal relationship between expenditures and union status is a spurious one, reflecting mainly the fact that unionism's main strength is in the high-wage sectors of the economy. The assignment of a negligible role to unionism probably carries the argument too far, for an examination of fringe developments in specific industries makes it difficult to reject entirely the conclusion that unions were influential in the spread of such private programs as pensions and supplemental unemployment benefits (SUB), at least from the standpoint of

[21] Robert Rice, "Skill, Earnings, and the Growth of Wage Supplements," *Papers and Proceedings* of the American Economic Association, May 1966, pp. 583-593.

timing and the rate of benefit liberalization.[22] The absence of any clear statistical relationship between fringe expenditures and unionization casts doubt, however, on the validity of the claim that unionism has been the major causal factor in the growth of such expenditures.

Some Consequences of the Growth of Wage Supplements

The development of supplementary wage practices under collective bargaining has contributed materially to the well-being of the nation's wage earners. At least in the higher-paid occupations, workers and their families are now protected by an elaborate battery of private benefit programs which, in conjunction with the basic public programs, lighten considerably the burdens of ill health, unemployment, old age, and death. Indeed, in the income-maintenance area, these programs have already laid the groundwork for a shift to salary status for hourly-rated, blue collar employees and for a gradual transition to annual earnings guarantees for regular workers in a number of industries. Despite the beneficial consequences of these private plans, however, there are some weaknesses in the present mixed system of security programs that deserve attention in any objective appraisal.

The issue of the relative advantages of public versus private means of providing against insecurity, which turns on questions of social philosophy as well as on questions of economic efficiency, is beyond the scope of the present discussion. Whatever one's view on the appropriate mix of public and private provisions, however, it is clear that the present system of fringe-benefit financing raises some difficulties. One problem that needs only be alluded to briefly arises from the fact that many supplemental expenditures, e.g., those for insurance, holidays, and vacations, are employee-related rather than earnings-related. As a result, they do not enter into overtime calculations and thus tend to lower overtime costs relative to hiring costs. This progressive lowering of the effective premium rate has not discouraged workers from seeking overtime; consequently from the standpoint of establishing a premium rate that is just sufficient to attract the necessary supply of additional hours from a given work force, the newer rates are clearly closer to the optimum. Insofar as social policy (the Fair Labor Standards Act) is intended to discourage long hours and maximize employment opportunities at given levels of demand, however, the failure to relate contributions more directly to earnings has reduced the policy's effectiveness.

A more critical problem in the financing of fringe benefits arises, however, from the preferential tax treatment accorded employer contributions to private pension and welfare plans. As might be expected, the exemption of employer contributions from both the corporate income tax and the personal income tax has encouraged the funneling of increasing amounts of income into private, noncontributory programs. Even if one grants, however, that the encouragement of private supplementation of

[22] See Robert M. Macdonald, *Collective Bargaining in the Automobile Industry* (New Haven: Yale University Press, 1963), pp. 56-58. Actually, Rice found that unionization had had a significant effect on the *prevalence* of pension plans (Rice, *loc. cit.*, p. 588). His study did not investigate the effect of SUB separately, for the reason no doubt that plans of this nature have been confined to the auto, steel, rubber, and garment industries and have covered less than two million workers in recent years.

public programs is desirable social policy, the method employed is surely inequitable in that it offers lower effective purchase prices (through greater opportunities for tax avoidance) to higher-income groups who are in many ways least in need of protection. Preferential tax treatment of plan contributions, which amounts in effect to government subsidization of benefits for higher-paid employees, would appear less inequitable perhaps if the benefit levels under public programs were less meager. This is certainly not the case, however; and there is always the danger that the continued rapid expansion of programs at the private level, encouraged by federal tax policy, will divert attention and pressure from the need for substantial improvements in the public programs.[23]

Whether this danger materializes depends on the extent to which our recent stepped-up concern for the disadvantaged represents a basic shift in public attitudes toward the social security system. If Medicare and current proposals for liberalizing the OASDI program are harbingers of a new, more vigorous commitment to the security needs of the nation's citizens, then private plans will perforce accommodate, and private expenditures, relative to income, may actually decline. As long as tax policy and consumer preferences remain unchanged, however, total expenditures on security benefits (both public and private) can be expected to rise more rapidly than income, at least to the point where further deferrals offer no tax advantage.

Conclusion

This article has dicussed the major changes which have occurred in bargaining patterns and practices in the private sector of the economy in the postwar period. It has shown how developments in the bargaining system are a response both to the internal needs of the parties and to stimuli in the external environment. While an explication of these changes supplies a basis for predicting how the system may behave in the future, it does not provide grounds for assessing the overall effectiveness of bargaining institutions or the social and economic consequences of the bargaining process. Nevertheless, the discussion does have implications which are relevant to any contemporary assessment.

In recent years, rising public expectations, coupled with rapid and pervasive change in the society, have posed a challenge of adjustment for all contemporary institutions—social, economic, and political. It is perhaps understandable, therefore, that many observers of the labor scene have found collective bargaining wanting and excessively rigid in its response to the new environment. Judgments of this sort are based, of course, more on intuitive reasoning than on objective standards; nevertheless, the claim of inflexibility is surely not a valid criticism. Particular bargaining relationships, it is true, warrant censure on this score (measured against accomplishments elsewhere); but the record of the last two decades for the bargaining system as a whole is one of remarkable flexibility and adaptability to new and often trying circumstances. This record of vigorous

[23] The need for adequate retirement benefits at the public level is all the more critical when account is taken of recent private and governmental criticisms of existing private pension plans. As matters stand, it is estimated that private pension plans cover only 50 percent of employees and that the relative lack of vesting and portability rights and the tendency to fund past service liabilities over excessively long periods will deprive millions of these covered workers of any opportunity to draw benefits.

institutional adjustment reflects, on the one hand, the pragmatic attitudes and policies which have increasingly characterized the practice of bargaining in the postwar years and, on the other, the decentralized character of decision making which has fostered diversity in rule making and a willingness to experiment with novel approaches to old and new problems. A decentralized structure is not, of course, without disadvantages. It may, for example, make difficult, if not impossible, the task of securing compliance with national-interest objectives of the kind embodied in the wage-price guidelines (assuming compliance would serve the national welfare). It certainly has exacerbated conflict in industries, such as newspaper publishing, construction, and transportation, where unionism is at present too highly fractionalized. Granted these possible shortcomings, however, it is doubtful that any *feasible* alternative system devised to perform the same vital functions of assuring equity and fair treatment to workers in a democratic society would have matched the capacity for adaptive behavior exemplified in the present system.

The flexibility of the bargaining mechanism is revealed in the intricately varied and changing structure of relationships, in the continuous modification of bargaining procedures, and especially in the evolution of the detailed content of collective agreements. In the postwar period, collective bargaining has been instrumental in developing a wide array of income-maintenance and employment-adjustment measures which have added immeasurably to the security and well-being of wage earners and their families. Again, it is not difficult to find fault with some of these arrangements—to regret their limited or discriminatory coverage, to deplore their effects on mobility and costs, and to question on occasion their worth to the workers involved. In evaluating the measures adopted and in assessing responsibility, however, one does well to bear in mind the social and economic environment of the postwar years. Until very recently, Americans generally have been willing to tolerate prolonged periods of excessive unemployment, an inadequate system of income-maintenance programs, and an archaic set of manpower (or labor market) institutions. As a result, the burden of providing against insecurity of employment and income has fallen largely on individual workers or on the organizations they have created to protect their interests. In such a context, it is simply unreasonable (and largely irrelevant) to condemn collective bargaining because it is not the *ideal* instrument for solving social problems; for as long as society itself is remiss in providing conditions conducive to the acceptance of change, unions are bound to intervene and to seek in private negotiations measures that ease the burden on their constituents.

This does not mean, of course, that one should condone each and every bargaining practice; for the test is always whether or not the practice achieves a reasonable balance between the competing interests of workers and consumers. Economists are prone to judge the results of bargaining in terms of the competitive standard. This by itself, however, is too narrow a base for judging the utility of the bargaining system. Collective bargaining performs functions that are indispensable to the maintenance of a humane industrial society. It secures, above all, the worker's commitment to political democracy and a free enterprise economy. Consequently, evaluations of its worth and proposals for its reform, if they are to serve society's interests, must take account of the vital functions fulfilled by the bargaining system.

SECTION IV

Leaders in the Development of Personnel and Labor Relations: People and Organizations

This last section of the book is composed of a few selected articles describing interesting things people and organizations have done and philosophies they have espoused which have contributed to the development of personnel and labor relations. The papers included are not meant to be representative of any normative position or group but to describe early practices in the personnel and labor fields.

Although Business Week *suggests that John H. Patterson's behavior as owner and president of the National Cash Register Company was reputed to be like that of a mad ringmaster at a circus, his innovations in the personnel field are impressive. He was one of the earliest, if not the earliest, to invest heavily in training as an important personnel function, and interestingly, his training techniques, emphasizing visual aids, demonstrations, and role playing, would be considered modern in many current organizations. He developed a very successful suggestion system, as Worthington Holman's article describes. Patterson's own article shows him to be an early leader in recognizing that improved working conditions and employee satisfaction with the work environment were preconditions of effective performance. He understood the desirability of enhancing communication throughout the organization by developing written job descriptions and using organization charts. Perhaps most importantly, he inspired individual employees to exceptional levels of performance by emphasizing individual merit, egoistic and social needs of employees, and prompt reinforcement of good performance. He deserves far more recognition than he has received for his contribution to personnel management. Certainly his circus had few peers when compared on virtually any organizational success criterion.*

Samuel Gompers had some interesting thoughts, as reported by Samuel Crowther, when he attempted to visualize what he would do if he were in an employer's shoes. His emphasis on encouraging *his hypothetical employees to organize and join a union and his reliance on union-based employee committees to help foster profitability were undoubtedly a revelation to management readers in 1920. The relationship that developed between Sidney Hillman's clothing workers union and the management at Hart, Schaffner & Marx by 1938, which is portrayed by Morris Greenberg, does not seem too far removed from what Gompers seemed to be suggesting in his remarks.*

The automobile industry has developed into probably the best-known and largest industry in this country, and it seems appropriate to look at how things were done within it as another interesting indication of how personnel and labor practices have evolved over the years. Thus, we have included two articles describing employee relations in the Ford Motor Company by Drs. Li and Gannon. Li provides an interesting picture of what it was like from the employee's viewpoint to work at Ford, and Gannon uses a historical perspective to test his hypothesis that nonrational variables explain more organization behavior and performance than do rationally based decision models. After studying John Patterson, Samuel Gompers, Frederick Taylor, and Henry Ford, one cannot help but be at least partially convinced of the credibility of this hypothesis. Further, it is difficult to help but feel that although their motives were not completely pure and beautiful, no matter what they or other organizations did, it would not have withstood the devastation of the Depression. To some extent they may have been made scapegoats for events that were too much even for the federal government to handle effectively until World War II helped pull the economy out of its doldrums.

51

John H. Patterson: Pioneer in Personnel Programs and Policy Innovations

Famous Firsts: How Personnel Relations Was Born

BUSINESS WEEK

In 1903 the most intriguing tent show on the industrial scene was pitched at Sugar Camp, near Dayton, Ohio. The camp colony—more than 100 tents staked down in military formation—marked the National Cash Register Co.'s devotion to the wild-eyed notion that "salesmen are made, not born." Company founder John Henry Patterson was already well known for his radical ideas.

He had given his women employees backs to the chairs at their benches, and hot meals at noon. Workers were being sent off on occasional educational excursions and could take two baths a week on company time. Other health and recreational benefits plainly proved Patterson was simply spoiling the help.

The reformers of Teddy Roosevelt's time soon labeled such progressive programs "employee welfare" or "industrial betterment" activities. Patterson as early as 1897 had hired "Sister" Lena Harvey from a Dayton settlement house to join NCR as its welfare director. Elsewhere social secretaries, both male and female, began to create a new profession of industrial social service. Soon employees in every up-and-coming company found themselves enrolling in glee clubs, listening to lectures during luncheon, or attending, as at NCR, classes in scientific cookery.

War Baby. By 1911 when scientific management burst on the business world as the invention of Frederick W. Taylor and the industrial engineers who followed him [*Business Week*, Apr. 20, 1963, p. 94], personnel work in most of its human relations aspects was well established in everything but name. The name would wait till World War I had impressed the military jargon on management.

It was actually as early as 1894 that Patterson became the model for every factory owner-manager who would later discover the importance of employee training and morale. Most of the founding fathers of big U.S. businesses had their hands too full of production problems, or their heads too full of financial worries, to become innovators in the personnel field.

Patterson was forced into it, but his inventions in the then almost totally unexplored area of personnel management must be equally ascribed to his own freewheeling mind, egged on by a talent for flamboyant showmanship. This soon gave NCR the reputation for being something of a circus run by a mad ringmaster who had everyone on his staff jumping through hoops. However the show was characterized, it was all Patterson's. He held 55 per cent of the stock, his family the remainder.

Reprinted with permission from *Business Week*, June 26, 1965, pp. 92, 94.

Dedication. The "university under canvas" seemed to bolster this image. What wasn't so well understood was Patterson's sincere and serious dedication to education and to teaching methods that would still be called progressive decades later.

NCR's corporate school first opened in 1894, just 10 years after Patterson founded the company. In the meantime, he had invented the first sales manual, The NCR Primer, a standardized sales procedure that denied the traditional belief that a glib tongue and a winning personality were the secrets to success in business.

Patterson's men were instructed: "When you reach a town, go to the best hotel and secure the best room, if possible." But they were also told to memorize the 450-word sales presentation, and follow it to the letter. It was based on experience; it had been proved to give the best results. But this early application of the scientific method wasn't the end of it.

Lab Method. NCR's company school used the laboratory method of instruction. Model stores with real fixtures and dummy merchandise gave every student real-life practice in selling. Teaching was restricted to men who had had successful business experience themselves. What's more, the training included enough study of the problems of different lines of business to become a comparatively broad education in systematic business administration.

Patterson had graduated from Dartmouth College in 1867 and distrusted college educated men ever after. He also disliked engineers and accountants, but his "abolition" of NCR's cost accounting department in 10 minutes one day was only to demonstrate his impatience with reports that were both too long and too late to be useful. On that historic occasion, Patterson marched the entire accounting department to the boiler room and watched while the horrified bookkeepers one by one fed all their records to the furnaces.

Gimmicks. Above all else, Patterson liked to play the teacher, and his greatest joy was to use every attention-getting gimmick he could discover or devise. Charts, slides, films, and always the crayon and blackboard, would make the staff "see" whatever idea he wanted to put across. Business conferences and conventions took a new shape with this kind of showmanship. Role playing techniques, demonstrations, full-dress plays and pageants—all became tools in his training kit.

One of Patterson's biographers, Samuel Crowther, quotes him observing one day: "Business is only a form of teaching. You teach people to desire your product; that is selling. You teach workmen how to make the right product; that is manufacturing. You teach others to cooperate with you; that is organization."

His penchant for "teaching through the eye" led Patterson to chart his organization, giving his supervisors a clear picture of their position in the structure and their duties and responsibilities. NCR, like other expanding organizations, had had to departmentalize activities. But Patterson went further in writing job descriptions for all executives and supervisors—including himself as president.

Rejects. Much of his concern for management, long before scientific management had become fashionable, sprang from the discovery early in the company's history that $50,000 worth of cash registers sold abroad had been returned because of faulty workmanship. Patterson at once moved his desk to the shop floor and learned for himself that "poor work was the result of poor working conditions." In particular, cold lunches at the work bench were no help to efficiency and morale.

In 1896 he opened a dining hall that served his women employees two hot dishes and a hot drink every working day at a cost to each girl of 5c a week. In 1905, newly built Welfare Hall was seating 2,500 at a meal, but the cost to female employees had gone up to 25c a week. By 1918, NCR was serving more than one-half million meals yearly.

When Patterson built his next factory, he gave his employees America's first "daylight" plant with 80% of the walls of glass. Inside, the machinery was painted in light colors. Outside, landscapers prettied the place with flower beds and green lawns. By 1908 an army of 80 janitors was keeping 23 acres of floor space clean, sweeping the shellacked floors daily and scrubbing them once a week.

High Turnover. What such "betterment" work meant is difficult to estimate. The Welfare Dept. itself was dubbed the Farewell Dept. as Patterson hired and fired early personnel workers. But he always insisted that there was the best justification for his investment in education and employee relations: "It pays."

Apparently it did. When Patterson died in 1922, NCR employed about 10,000 and was claiming worldwide sales of $30-million yearly. Patterson had founded the company with an investment of $6,500 and a payroll of 13.

More than this, scores of NCR-trained executives were spreading the gospel of better management throughout U.S. industry: Thomas J. Watson of IBM, C. F. Kettering of Delco and General Motors, Alvan Macauley of Packard Motor Car, for example, all "graduated" from the Patterson campus to top positions in their own companies.

The corporation school movement that followed NCR's early demonstration of the idea led to the creation in 1913 of the National Assn. of Corporation Schools, an organization supported by General Electric, John Wanamaker, Burroughs Adding Machine, among other companies. And this, after several changes in name reflecting the broadening concern of management with personnel relations, in 1923 became the American Management Assn.

Today, the Patterson statue in Dayton memorializes him as "a pioneer in industrial organization and scientific management," among other virtues. Even in America, few local boys who make good end up in bronze striking a slightly Napoleonic pose astride their favorite horse—a hunk of heroic statuary in the city park. And monuments to the masters of scientific management are still rarer. Perhaps it helps if you were an Ohio farm boy named John Henry Patterson.

A 5,000 Brain-Power Organization

WORTHINGTON C. HOLMAN

There is a reason why the organization and business methods of the National Cash Register Company form one of the most interesting subjects for study and analysis to be found in the entire field of business.

Here is a company, organized twenty years ago with a force of two employees, a factory consisting of a single tiny room, two almost worthless patents, and a mere handful of capital, which has ever since maintained an almost complete monopoly of the rapidly growing cash register business of the world. There are dozens of typewriter companies, automobile companies, sewing machine and bicycle companies; but practically the entire output of cash registers used by the world's retail merchants comes from the factories of this one concern.

And it is a very large output. The stores of users of National registers, if placed side by side, touching each other, would extend in a continuous line from New York westward across the continent to Denver. The company's sales in the single month of May, 1904, approximated a million dollars. Its machines are sold in every civilized quarter of the globe, as far north as Alaska and as far south as Cape Town, South Africa. It may truly be said that its eight hundred salesmen have made the tinkle of the cash register bell heard around the world.

Why Two Hundred Competitors Failed

There has been scarcely a moment in its history when the National company has been free from competition—and most of the time its field has been crowded with competitors. In its twenty years of existence, approximately two hundred corporations, backed by millions of dollars in capital, have attempted to rival its product, and win the patronage of retail merchants—and there have been two hundred ignominious and costly failures. One competitor admitted on going out of business that he had lost nearly half a million dollars trying to perfect his product and build up its sale. Other competitors have lost like amounts.

The field was open to these competitors. There was no combination against them, no discriminating legislature, no system of railroad rebates or other collusion or alliance with outside forces. The National company had not a particle of influence or power, financial, political or of any other kind, outside its own walls. The market was open to competitors if they could win it. To ensure success it was necessary to achieve three results:

1. Make a product as good as that of the National company.
2. Make it at as low a cost.
3. Sell it with as much ability.

Reprinted from *System*, Vol. IV, No. 2, August, 1904, pp. 98-107.

Mr. Holman was a former employee of National Cash Register Company who later became associated with *System* as a writer.

A 5,000 Brain-Power Organization

These three things two hundred competitors failed to do. Most of them had plenty of money. Many had more capital than the National company. They could build factories, set up expensive machinery, hire any number of workmen, open a multitude of offices and put an army of agents in the field. They did all of these things. But they could not make the effort pay—they failed to win away the patronage of retail merchants. Nine storekeepers out of every ten who bought cash registers bought a National.

The success of the National Company in building registers that could not be matched, and in winning the absolute confidence and patronage of retail merchants has been due almost entirely to its remarkable organization. Brains, sheer original thinking, unusual methods, superior systems, have been responsible for every step of its progress. No competitor has ever been able to approach it in any of these points. Its competitors failed as the Russians so far have failed in their efforts against the Japanese—and for much the same reasons. They could not equal the foresight, the quickness and readiness, the individual enthusiasm and the discipline and perfect team work of their always successful rival.

How One Great Success Was Won by Organization

Patents played a comparatively small part in the National Company's success during the first half of its history, when its competitors were most numerous—although to-day its tremendous array of 900 patents and 379 styles of registers would prove an insurmountable obstacle to a competitor. But many competitors who came into the field eight or ten years ago had patents as good as those of the National company—some were better. They had not, however, manufacturing or selling systems in any way equal to those of their rival—their methods were awkward and bungling in comparison. To own a patent is only a single step toward a commercial success. In the factory and in the selling field there were a host of problems that perplexed them—problems that the older company had wrestled with and solved after many failures and much costly experimenting. If they were strong at two points—money and patents—the National company was strong at a hundred points. There were no gaps in the National circle. Its organization had gradually become rounded, complete, everywhere effective.

What is this organization? What have these manufacturing and selling systems, so successful in the past, developed into to-day? How does the National company do business at the present time? What are the causes of its ever-increasing success?

In this series of articles the answers to these questions will be given in due course as plainly, as specifically and as completely as possible.

How to Get the Full Earning Capacity of Employes

To understand the workings of a great organization we must look deeper than the surface. It is not enough merely to observe the detailed systems used—to catalogue or inventory the innumerable activities of the men in the organization. We must look behind and beneath these things and perceive their fundamental principles—the ideas on which they are based.

Every great organization is the concrete expression of a set of leading ideas. It is these which determine the character of the organization—just as a man's ideas determine his character and actions.

One of the main ideas underlying the NCR plan is that the company should get from every individual in its employ a full 100 per cent of his individual power and capacity.

The working out of this idea has had so much to do with the National company's success that it deserves to be described at some length. The present article—the first in the series on the company's methods, will confine itself to this single subject.

The tendency of most organizations, as they grow and ramify and perfect their machine-like workings, is to lessen the inspiration and efficiency of each individual member. As the number of employes increases, each man's individual importance grows less. He finds it harder to attract attention. He feels that he is effaced—buried in the great crowd of his fellows. He is apt to become automatic in his efforts—get into a rut, degenerate into a mere mechanical routine worker, with little interest in his work beyond the desire to hold his job. As a result, his employers get only a percentage of his full power and capacity.

You may teach a rowing crew the smoothest, most automatic machine-like stroke in the world; but unless the individual members of the crew have vitality, snap and dash, they will never break records.

It is the same with a business organization.

Employers know this. Every great business company believes in the theory of stimulating individual effort among its employes. But few corporations have been able to put the theory into any kind of satisfactory operation.

The minute a company manages to do so, its productive capacity increases by leaps and bounds, without any corresponding increase in expense.

At Dayton this theory has always been held as a kind of gospel. In shaping the National organization the aim has been to co-ordinate forces without weakening them—to bind individuals together into a smoothly working machine, and yet have the men who form the parts of that machine retain every last atom of their individual inspiration, power and efficiency.

The attempt has been successful. The typical National employe works like a horse. He is as full of steam as a locomotive boiler. Hundreds of National salesmen voluntarily work at certain seasons of the year twelve, fourteen, sixteen hours a day—from sunrise to midnight. There is a noticeable scorn of "whistle quitters" in the large office force at the factory. Men who watch the clock do so in defiance of the general spirit of their fellows. They are out of harmony with their surroundings, find their work and companions unpleasant, and soon leave. No man can long endure the silent condemnation of his fellows.

Night work at the office as a general rule is discouraged by the company. But the men are always ready for it, and expect no extra pay. They well know that they will get their reward in other practical ways. A year ago the general auditors' department, numbering over a hundred men, cheerfully worked three nights a week for a period of six weeks to meet an emergency that occurred during a rush of business. And a hundred other instances might be quoted to show the prevalence of this spirit in the organization.

The Secret of the "National Spirit"

A 5,000 Brain-Power Organization

The tonic that stimulates men to show a spirit like this is the tonic of opportunity. And opportunity is at every man's immediate elbow in the National organization.

Merit wins all the prizes there. Hard work, experience, knowledge of the business have their sure reward. Nothing else counts.

There are no relatives of the chief owners of the business in high places. There are no family friends or former social acquaintances of theirs or sons of social acquaintances scattered through the organization. There are no sons of important stockholders occupying positions worthy of better men.

The present general manager, who is also second vice-president, entered the business as an office boy. Sheer merit carried him through ten successive promotions to the head of the company before he reached the age of thirty. Under the National system of promotion he could not help arriving there; he was the ablest employe in the business. The company's methods automatically sift its employes and send the best men to the top as a sieve brings to notice the largest pebbles in a mass of sand.

Of the other twelve employes nearest the general manager in authority, nine began absolutely at the bottom, and one began only a third of the way up. Two—the general legal counsel and the chief patent attorney, came from high positions in other concerns. But their knowledge was of a kind that could not be acquired inside the organization. Two of the twelve leading employes began as office boys, three as clerks, two as stenographers, and two as workmen at the bench.

If this is true of the men at the extreme top, it is true also of the lesser leaders below them. The two hundred men who lead the National forces in various important capacities almost without exception have served at some time or other in the ranks, or very near them.

Quick Rewards as Incentives to the Workmen

Hard work then, faithfulness to duty, knowledge and ability grounded on experience have their invariable reward in the National organization. And that reward comes quickly. The company doubles its business, the size of its organization, and its need for men every few years. The sales doubled, for instance, between the years 1898 and 1902 in the face of all competition.

The unthinking reader may say that the company is fortunate in having a rapidity of growth that permits of a policy of much promotion from the ranks. This is looking at the case upside down. It was this policy of promotion from the ranks and other like points of policy that gave the company its rapid growth in the face of competition. Now that the impetus has been established, the policy works both ways to the company's advantage.

There is nothing like the power of an example. It is good for National employes to see all about them in desirable positions men who came up from low positions. No National rank and file man has to stretch his imagination very much to see in himself a future foreman, department head or district manager of salesmen. If there is a spark of ambition in him his surroundings are sure to fan it into a steadily burning flame. His thoughts are all on fitting himself for promotion. He grudges no time, no extraordinary effort that will enable him to move up a step.

It is men who work with this spirit who prove most profitable to employers.

How the Salesman Wins the Attention of His Superiors

How does the man in the ranks attract the attention of his superiors? This is easy if he has ability. If he is one of the company's salesmen, his daily sales are published in a daily paper which every member of the entire organization has an opportunity to see, and which most of them scan with intent eagerness. Everybody always knows the name of the agent who is leading in sales. Everyone can learn each day exactly what results each salesman is getting in his territory, each sales agent in his section, each district manager in his district. The photographs of leading agents are printed in the daily paper with their records. There are five thousand men who know the features of these leading salesmen as the American public knows the features of Roosevelt and Parker.

Contests are arranged between individual salesmen in a city, between groups of salesmen in a district—between different districts, and prizes and honorable mention are awarded for success. The spirit of pride runs so high that most men would rather have the honor of leading in these contests than pocket the money that goes with the honor.

Every good month's record brings the agent who makes it a personal letter of congratulation from the sales manager at the factory—sometimes from the general manager, and often from the president himself. At the end of certain periods, the names of leading agents are engraved on a bronze tablet on the outside of the administration building of the factory. The eagerness of National agents to win the honor of getting their names on this tablet will not be believed by casual readers.

When a National agent makes a trip to the plant of the company every department is open to him; every officer of the company he meets has a word of greeting for him. He finds that his face and his reputation are known all through the plant. If he is a leading agent, elevator boys stare at him with more awe than would be expected if he were a National league baseball pitcher. Clerks and office boys point him out to each other and quote his records.

There are thousands of National men, for instance, who can tell you off-hand that Mr. James, of Michigan, sold exactly 344 points in October 1902 (a point is $25.00 worth of business), and that Mr. Dennis of Maryland and Mr. Graham of New Jersey, beat that record in May, 1904, by selling 420 points and 346 points respectively.

The salesman is "the man who keeps the smoke coming out of the factory chimney." His visit to the factory gives the company a chance to honor his efforts. The general manager expects him always to call at his office for a few minutes. The president of the company is glad of a chance to shake his hand and show that he remembers his face, his name, and a good deal of his past history as an "NCR" man.

The salesman is human, and he goes back to his territory with a heart full of pride and loyalty to the company and its officers. He resumes his labors with a deep determination to better any previous work that he has done.

A warm spirit of pride and emulation in a force of salesmen is worth cold dollars and cents to the company.

Under a system such as this, no National agent can say that he lacks a chance to attract the attention of his superiors to his merits.

How the Factory Employe Is Stimulated to His Best Work

How does the able man in the factory rank and file attract attention? To answer this question I must digress for a moment.

The worst managed manufacturing plant in the world is a one-man, one-mind power plant, where the individual at the top does all the planning, originates all the ideas and starts all the improvements. When he is not devising changes for the better no one is. When he makes a mistake the entire plant goes wrong. He issues orders; those below him obey him blindly, not knowing the why or wherefore.

A better managed plant is one where the man at the top is supported by several other good men immediately below him, who also think and plan as he does. Such a plant is a two, four or six mind power plant.

The best managed plant of all is one where every employe in the concern, from general manager down to office boy, is alert to think and plan—where if there are a thousand employes the thought-engine of the plant is run by a thousand mind power.

In most factories the management conserves the horsepower that runs the engine, and lets the brain power go to waste.

Brains, thinking-power, ideas, are the best things a manufacturer can buy.

Often a successful business can be built upon a single idea.

It is the man with an idea who constantly changes the face of the world. It is not the man with a pair of large hands or a strong back.

It is the intelligent man that thinks who is most needed in a factory—not the automatic employe who does his work like a machine with his heart pumping all its blood to his hands and none to his brain.

How the Individual Is Made a Factor in His Company's Growth

A good many years ago the National company decided to make use of the brains of every man in its employ. The officers posted small boxes in the various departments, and asked every employe who could find fault with the materials, the tools, the machines, the methods of work, or anything else in his department—or in any other department—to enter a written complaint, and if possible, make a suggestion for improvement. The company promised that no foreman should read the complaints or suggestions, but that they should be referred directly to a committee of which the superintendent of the factory should act as chairman. Money prizes and promotions were promised as rewards.

Suggestions began to pour in by the hundred. A glaring searchlight of criticism was turned upon every least fault in the operation of the factory. No imperfection could exist long where hundreds of pairs of trained eyes were eagerly looking for it. No department dared turn out poor work when any man in the department to which that work was next passed on could secure a possible chance to win a prize by complaining of it.

In the next few years thousands of valuable suggestions were adopted. A new force had been added to the company's powers. With its several thousand-mind power plant the organization forged irresistibly ahead.

Mechanics studied the tools and machinery they were using. As a result of their suggestions certain departments in the factory gradually became filled with special labor-saving machinery and tools.

The office men were equally ambitious and thought out hundreds of short cuts to be used in their work.

Salesmen sent in criticisms of their registers they were selling. They suggested new devices to satisfy merchants' needs. They outlined what they thought would be the future needs of merchants. The invention departments were enlarged to a membership of sixty employes, who worked out these suggestions in practical form in addition to ideas of their own. Inventions and patents multiplied until the company to-day owns the astonishing total of 900 patents and makes over 379 different styles of registers.

The suggestion system did far more than supply the company with a constant stream of ideas. It had a deep effect on the morale of the organization. It has been and still continues to be a chief source of the remarkable keenness of interest and ambition which marks National employes.

This, then—the stimulation of individual effort—is the first of the several basic principles on which the NCR organization is founded.

Altruism and Sympathy as Factors in Works Administration

JOHN H. PATTERSON

The problems of to-day in factory management are not so much problems of machinery as of men; not so much those of organization as of personal relations. How best to develop the principles which are necessary for the solutions of these problems is the question with every thinking employer. There are few great companies in the world with organizations as complete or plants as well equipped as those of the great manufacturing establishments of the United States, and American manufacturers are anxious to retain their position of priority in the world. The one problem whose solution will assure permanence in the new commercial life of the nation is the adjustment of relations between employer and employee on a fair and humane basis. If American manufacturers and their workmen unite in enthusiastic development of one another's interests, they will retain their leadership.

The introduction of steam power into the manufacturing world drove the little blacksmith shop, shoe shop, the country dairy and weaver's loom, from the village into the city and opened many new problems. In

Reprinted with permission from *Engineering Magazine*, Vol. 20, January, 1901, pp. 577-602.

John H. Patterson was founder and president of the National Cash Register Company.

those early days, the small workman found it best to consider carefully the physical, moral, and mental welfare of his apprentice and his assistant. If it paid the small employer to do this, it will pay the great employer many-fold more to have the same thoughtfulness for the hundreds or thousands in his employ.

The difficulty will be to determine what is needed for this adjustment, and how to accomplish the arrangement even with the needs recognized. It would seem, however, that all will agree that among the essentials to economic production and a proper adjustment of relations are opportunity for thorough training of the workman, and his co-operation in saving and in perfect manufacture.

Some employers have sought to win this sympathy and assistance by large gifts to libraries, museums, and other public institutions open to working men. Others have aimed at it by a system of profit sharing, and still others, in increasing numbers, have sought it by introducing special features into their factories and by opening unusual opportunities to their people. This latter plan has as its foundation principles the ideas that an evidence of daily thoughtfulness will be surest to bring assistance and response; that a recognition of the laborer as a man with human aspirations, often with keen sensibilities and with love of home and comfort, will find a responsive chord within; and that poverty, lack of education, and narrow views are not necessarily evidence of a lower form of life.

It is with this in mind that a large number of employers are seeking to adapt their factories and methods to the needs of to-day. The personal experience of the writer and of others who are seeking by similar methods the same results, may not be out of place in this magazine. These are given as illustrations of what may be accomplished, and how it may be done, rather than as statements of relations to be closely followed. Thoughtful men to-day want not so much theories as facts. Hence, experience and actual work of the shop will be more acceptable than a discussion of what ought to be done.

It is difficult to understand why so much carelessness exists regarding the condition and ventilation of the average shop. The very first essential to the solution of the humane elements in the machine-shop problem is clean and well-ventilated buildings. It is often assumed that this is possible only for certain forms of light and clean manufacturing, but experience has proved that even in heavy machine shops, rolling mills, woolen mills, and paper mills, cleanliness and good ventilation are possible. The expense of accomplishing this is so small as compared with the increased output resulting from it, that one wonders that any company ever hesitates to accomplish these things. It does not require much force or a great expenditure of money to have clean floors and windows and to furnish fresh air. In addition to this, good drinking water, comfortable toilet rooms, and proper heating, will assure health and, therefore, better work. The National Cash Register Company's experience in this matter is constant proof of the value of bright and cheerful surroundings as well as of perfect cleanliness. Its buildings six years ago were completely remodeled and renovated, and from that time to this cleanliness, good ventilation and proper heating, have been emphasized with remarkable success. The Sherwin-Williams Co., of Cleveland, in its paint mill, and the Cleveland Hardware Co., in their rolling mill, have shown what can be done when proper inclination exists. In England are a number of very notable examples of the value of beautifying factory grounds and employees' cottages. The most prominent of these are the Lever Bros.' soap works at Port Sunlight, and the Cadbury cocoa works, at Bourneville.

Attention to personal comfort is another of the essentials in the recognition of the needs of employees. By this is meant thoughtfulness for comfort in work—proper arrangement for lunches and food—opportunities for rest, for baths, and for all those things which add strength and encourage contentment. When our company began its present system, it first provided stools with backs and foot rests for its employees. Then arrangements were made for the women of the factory to ride up and down on the elevators, if they chose, instead of climbing the stairways. Ten-minute recesses were given to the women in the morning and afternoon, affording them opportunity for relaxation. A large dining room was provided, in which a wholesome lunch is served each day at noon to two hundred and fifty or more of the young women employees of the company, the company furnishing the warm part of the lunch, and the young women supplying whatever additional they may desire. Baths were provided in all buildings, and employees were given twenty minutes each week on the company's time to take a bath. On one of the floors, a neat rest room was provided for the young women, for use in case of sickness or weariness. Cots are supplied in all the buildings for use in case of accident. Other companies have carried out many of these same ideas, some by fitting up rooms in their own factory buildings—as in the case of the T. B. Laycock Mfg. Co., of Indianapolis, and the Acme White Lead Co., of Detroit—while others have provided and equipped club houses, adjacent to the factory with the conveniences of lunches, baths, and reading rooms, open freely to all employees. The Gorham Manufacturing Company, the Joliet Steel Works, and the Eagle & Phoenix Company are illustrations of this idea in the treatment of employees.

It is not sufficient, however, to think simply of the physical wants. To accomplish one of the great aims of all such plans—that of securing intelligent operatives—it is necessary to afford the work people opportunities for mental training and mental growth. This idea when first advanced was combated in many cases, but employers generally are now agreed that skill and intelligence are essential to the highest accomplishment. Our first step in carrying out this idea was to give the fullest information to everyone regarding the company's work and business. This was accomplished by frequent meetings of a part or all of the employees, by conventions, by publications, and by announcements. A club consisting of the heads of departments and their assistants was formed, meeting frequently on the company's time in a large hall of the main building, provided for the purpose, with the object of discussing important topics relating to the general business and of receiving suggestions and complaints from the departments. Realizing that many of the employees needed instruction in simple mechanics, general meetings were held, where, by special entertainments, made interesting by the use of stereopticon pictures, instruction was given in the simplest elements of mathematics and mechanics. By these methods the company succeeded in proving to its employees that its motives were for their highest good and, step by step, their attitude changed from one of indifference and opposition to one of enthusiastic support. Other companies, like the John B. Stetson Company, of Philadelphia, have found these same ideas practical and have carried them out, adapting them to their own particular needs. The Cleveland Window Glass Company, the Acme White Lead & Color Works, and other companies have well-organized classes for instruction in special subjects.

One of the most thoughtful methods in the development of sympathy has been the system of prizes for suggestions, which has resulted in leading everyone to seek to assist and to give his best thought. This is accomplished usually by placing in the various departments an autographic register or a small box, upon which one may write his suggestion, or in which he may place the idea or complaint which he desires to present. Each man and woman is encouraged to think independently, and to watch for improvement in his own work and that of others. Series of prizes are offered, ranging usually from $10 to $50 each, covering a period varying in different companies from one month to six months. These prizes are usually open to all except heads of departments and assistants. As suggestions are received, they are carefully examined by one appointed for this purpose and when practicable, are put to good use and proper credit given. The occasion of the presentation in most of these factories is one of great interest and enthusiasm. In the practice of our own establishment it is always made an opportunity for bringing together the employees and their families. During the summer it becomes an out-of-doors gathering, at which thousands of employees and their families gather for pleasure and profit. This cultivates an *esprit de corps* which is felt throughout the entire factory. This company receives about 2,500 suggestions a year, a large portion of which may be put into actual practice. This same idea is becoming very popular among employers, the experience of the Eastman Kodak Company, Bausch & Lomb, and others proving in the highest degree satisfactory.

This encouragement to think for the interests of the company finds its expression very frequently on the part of employees in organization of clubs among the workers themselves. In this company, there are the Women's Century Club and the Men's Progress Club, meeting twice each month, with regular programs and carefully-wrought schemes of work. Relief-association organizations, for systematic assistance in case of sickness, are popular in many companies. Organizations for recreation or study are sure to be formed when a community feeling has been carefully developed among employees.

To assist in thus cultivating thoughtfulness, a factory library and reading room are valuable. It has been found that city libraries are always ready to co-operate in the development of this idea to the full extent of their ability. Stereopticon lectures, on all questions which will lead men to think, are very helpful and popular. It adds something to the intelligent work of the employee to know something of the country into which his product is to go. Therefore, practical talks on England, Germany, and other countries of the world, all assist in leading to thoughtful action in connection with the work. Quotations from good literature and suggestions on practical subjects, hanging in various places in the factory, all increase this thoughtfulness of the employee.

The duty of the employer in this problem is not completely fulfilled if he confines his efforts solely to his employees. Too often, the coming of a factory into a neighborhood is considered a misfortune, and has a depressing influence upon the value of residence property within its vicinity. This is not necessary and, with a little effort on the part of the factory people, it may be avoided. The factory may be made a center of life and influence for the entire neighborhood. A club house or settlement house immediately adjoining the factory premises, with qualified men or women in charge, will rapidly become a center of social, educational, and moral influence for the entire community. The "N.C.R. House" at Dayton is a little cottage in charge of a deaconess who gives her entire time to the needs of the community, and contains a library and reading room open to the neighborhood, a kindergarten for the children of employees and the neighborhood, and a room for the meetings of numerous clubs organized among the boys, girls, young people, and men and women of South Park. In addition to this, prizes are offered amounting to $300 a year, for the improvements in homes, yards, and surroundings. This includes planting in front yards, back yards, the cultivation of vines, window boxes, vacant lots, boys' vegetable gardens, and similar things which will add to the beauty and comfort of the neighborhood. So successful has this plan been in this case that the street facing the factory is regarded as one of the most beautiful working-men's streets in the world. The company in this case has set an example by beautifying its own grounds and surroundings in every way possible, seeking to accomplish the desired result by following the simple rules of good landscape gardening, and by the use of such shrubs only as the people themselves may cultivate if they desire. This idea is not wholly confined to this one company, though it has not been followed very extensively in the United States, outside of some of the older New England factory towns. The most prominent examples, perhaps, are in England, including those of the Lever Brothers' Company, of Port Sunlight, and Cadbury Brothers, at Bourneville. The Draper Company, at Hopedale, Mass., and the Cleveland Cliffs Iron Company, at Ishpeming, Mich., are further illustrations of this idea of neighborhood improvement and the use of prizes for good planting.

Mr. Law's Briar Cliff farms, in New York, are an illustration of what may be done toward helping workmen in their lives. His idea of kindness to men and animals is expressed in the mural declarations in the homes which he has erected on these farms for his unmarried employees:

Speak gently—it is better far
To rule by love than fear.

Going one step further in the recognition of this responsibility toward the neighborhood is the establishment of kindergartens, manual training schools, "pleasant Sunday afternoons," and other organizations under the encouragement of the company and its officers. This company has, for a number of years, supported a kindergarten open to the children of employees and of the neighborhood. It has a domestic-economy department, with cooking and sewing lessons for the girls of South Park and the young women of the factory. It has a boys' brigade and various boys' clubs for the lads, who are enthusiastic in their co-operation in all the plans that are made and who, with increasing care, assist in keeping the grounds of the neighborhood in a beautiful condition. A penny provident association offers opportunity for saving. A women's guild enlists the mothers for the best interests to their homes and their children. A choral society attracts the young people, while the "pleasant Sunday afternoon," or "Sunday school," as it is often called, furnishes an hour or an hour and a half of helpful interest each Sunday afternoon. This is intended not for teaching religious truth so much as for giving practical instruction in the true ideas of moral life. Two features of this plan will always give good results. One is the encouragement of the reading of the children by offering prizes to those who read and bring quotations from their reading each Sunday. The other is the use of the stereopticon for one-half hour at each gathering, with lessons in practical things that will be a help in the home life.

Such, in brief, is a suggestion for practical methods of influencing the assisting employees and the neighborhood, and thus solving the personal problem of modern manufacturing. The suggestions here made have not covered all that may be done, but are those which have been found practical helps in one or more factories of the United States. These efforts have been recognized as helpful not only by employees, but by the leaders of labor, religious, and social organizations. The kindly spirit which they indicate is reciprocated, both at home and abroad. The plan has been studied by prominent men and women and commended by students in many lands. The opinions of public men who have studied these efforts encourage their continuance as being the surest method of solving this problem. Carefully-compiled statistics show that they will help to reduce the cost of production, and the system indicates a growing improvement in the character of the working people and in the increasing advantages, both to the company and to its force. Because these things require little change from the usual methods, they are practicable under existing conditions, and because of their broad helpfulness, they must prove valuable to all classes of the community.

52

An Interview with Samuel Gompers

If I Were an Employer

SAMUEL CROWTHER

I asked Mr. Gompers what he would do if he were an employer—how he would manage the varied problems that confront the average open-minded employer—the man who wants to be fair. That is, I asked Mr. Gompers to step into the shoes of an employer. His answers are surprising—they differ totally from the usual conception of the union relation. I have studied industrial relations with considerable care and for a long time, but never before have seen unionist principles so clearly stated in the simple terms of everyday business affairs.

1. Would you have the relation between you, as an employer, and your employees personal or purely one of the bargain and sale through a collective agreement or would you endeavor to have both?

Reprinted from *System*, Vol. 37, April, 1920, pp. 722 ff.

Mr. Crowther was a prolific writer during the early part of this century concentrating on personalities of general interest to the public.

"I regard the human equation as the largest concern of business and I think that the only way to acquire the truly personal relation on a man-to-man basis is to arrange the basic hours and pay through a bargain with a responsible union body, for then there is no question of goodness on the part of the employer or of contentment on the part of the employee. The parties meet as buyers and sellers on a level plane and because each has something that the other wants there is no reason on earth that their bargain cannot be carried through with the same dignity, with the same mutual satisfaction, and with the same fairness of aim on the part of both sides that makes a present-day bargain between business men the beginning of a relationship.

"Nobody in these days would employ a salesman who would come back after having sold a customer and declare triumphantly, 'I did that fellow up all right. I got the best of him.' Any sales manager would discharge that salesman on the spot, for he would know that such a man would destroy and not build up trade. It is quite the same way in dealing with workers, and I am speaking not merely from a hypothetical position but as an actual employer.

"We have 100 people or so in the headquarters of the American Federation of Labor, all of whom are working under my general direction, and I do not think that it would be possible to have a more cordial relation than exists between us. They not only do everything I ask them to do, but they endeavor to anticipate my wishes in every respect and quite frequently do more than I want them to do.

"If I were an employer of general labor I should expect to bargain in the fairest possible spirit and I believe that I should receive fair service in return. Once we remove the union's suspicion of the employer and the employer's suspicion of the union, there is nothing in the world to prevent the most cordial relation—the sort of relation that we all like to have with everybody with whom we come in contact. The bargain would settle the questions of hours and wages; and with them out of the way, the road would be open for truly personal contact.

"When two merchants have concluded a bargain with which both are satisfied, one or the other usually says 'Let's have luncheon' or 'Let's have dinner' and they forget business and start to know each other. A similar condition exists in every place where wages and hours are arranged collectively and in a spirit of fairness. It is wholly contrary to the American union spirit to have an excessive formality in the relation between the worker and the man who employs him. Such formality obtains only when both sides are suspicious. Remove that suspicion and the formality vanishes. I have acted as mediator in no end of what appeared to be disputes between employer and employees, and not once has it happened that my decision has not been not only respected but deeply appreciated by both sides. And this has come about simply by removing suspicion. For instance, take the building trades of Boston. I acted there as mediator and I was an invited guest and speaker at their recent jubilee dinner at which the representatives of the employees and employers in this great industry participated to celebrate their renewed collective bargain. There were mutual respect and confidence.

"The interests of the employer and the employee are in no sense identical. Do not confuse that point. They have not an identity of interest, but they have a cooperation of interest—that same cooperation of interest which exists between a manufacturer and his best customer. No intelligent manufacturer will sell so much or at such a price that his customer must lose money. It is just as much his concern to see that his customer makes money as it is to see that he himself manufactures—for without the one there cannot be the other.

"Exactly this same kind of relation between the employer and the employees promotes good work and fair wages on the part of the employees and consequently a good output at a fair profit on the part of the employer. This manly relation is not possible with company unions or with any organization which ultimately depends upon the will of the employer, for then the necessary independence of spirit will not be present; deference is very apt to turn into servility.

"Many employers do not recognize the psychological change that comes about through union organization. The man who does not belong to an organization is very apt to say, 'What are you going to do with the boss? He has all the money. He has all the power. What is a fellow going to do?' I have heard the feeling of impotence expressed over and over again, and because the men feel that they are impotent, the employer, unless he is a very remarkable man, will feel much the same way and he may be gripped by the fetish of absolute, arbitrary power. He thinks that he is the whole show.

What Happens When Workers Organize

"The worker, on the other hand, when he organizes for the first time, usually acquires a swelling feeling of power. He begins to think that he and not the employer is in control—that is, he gets into exactly the same attitude of mind as is shown by the absolute employer. This is a well-recognized stage of union development and it is good for the men to get this feeling and for the employer to fear them just as the employees used to fear him, for out of the mutual fear arises in the course of time, and inevitably, the sensing by both that neither is running the show all alone—and that the only way for either to get on is through cooperation. That cooperation develops the very finest possible relation in which both sides are not only fair but independent and manly.

"Therefore, as an employer, if my men were not organized, I should insist upon their organization and I should put the matter of basic wages and hours out of the way through a collective agreement and should go on promoting the true idea that we are all associates in the same enterprise but approaching from somewhat different standpoints."

2. What relation would you officially have with the union—that is, would you consult with them on business affairs that touch labor, and would you place with them for their own confidential inspection a full record of your financial transactions? In other words, would you have anything in the nature of an advisory committee composed of the union officers and the company officers?

"I should, without doubt, consult frequently with the union heads and I should put before them my financial transactions, not, however, with the notion that whatever I have done is the best under the circumstances, but with the view of obtaining their cooperation to see if the one best way cannot be achieved. For instance, I should not ask the unions to lower their minimum standards of wages and living so that I might obtain contracts at a price lower than my competitors. It is truly unfortunate that so often an employer will enter into a contract, into a price-cutting excursion, in the hope of making the price out of his workers by lowering their wages instead of by increased operating efficiency.

"In order to obtain increased operating efficiency I should call in the union heads just as I should call in an industrial engineer, but even more frequently and on a more intimate basis. This would prevent dissatisfaction among my men by making wages always the last reduction instead of the first. I should know as an employer that high wages do not mean increased cost of production but, on the contrary, are the greatest possible incentive toward the invention of better machinery and tools in order that the worker's power may be extended to an almost indefinite degree. I should know that cheap men do not mean a cheap output. Wherever the human element is cheap you will find the methods and means of production in the most backward condition. I should pay high wages and I should endeavor by every possible means to eliminate the wastes from my plant, and to gain the maximum of efficiency without brutal driving.

"There is an impression that the unions are against machinery, are against the better ways of doing business, are against scientific management, and in favor of stringing out every job to the greatest possible extent. That, it is true, was the attitude of the old country. It is not the attitude of the American labor movement.

"The unions at one time opposed the introduction of machinery because both the workers and the employers saw labor-saving machines not as aids to production but as substitutes for men. I am in favor of every possible mechanical device that can substitute for human labor, but if the employer looks at the machine solely as an instrument to take employment from men he is bound to fail just as are the workers who oppose the machinery because it is going to cost them their jobs. That is the short-sighted view. The workers can break the machines, and they can destroy the blueprints, but the idea remains and if it is a good idea it will be put into force. Otherwise, we bar the economic progress of the world and encourage instead of prevent waste.

"But, looking at this question as an aid to production, it is the part of the employer to let the worker share in that profit by so expanding his business as to take care of the increased output. There should be no objection to this, for increased output means more, although not a higher percentage of profit, to the employer and it means more wages to the worker.

"A good illustration of the proper way to handle a situation of this kind was given by the printing trade. When the linotype came in, it was undoubtedly the idea of the printers to displace the hand compositors and to substitute girls. The unions met the situation fairly and so did the employers when the facts were presented to them. The employers realized that it would not be fair to throw out the men who had spent years in learning hand composition, that they were entitled to employment at decent wages, and that their skill would make the mechanical typesetters far more valuable than if the machines were regarded as substitutes and not as aids to better and more intelligent man-production. In consequence we have seen the whole printing trade expand perhaps a hundred times since the introduction of typesetting machines and similar devices, simply because these machines were regarded as additions to intelligence and not as substitutes for intelligence. A machine which is regarded as an addition to intelligence, as increasing the skill of the skilled man, benefits everybody. The machine which is regarded as a substitute benefits nobody—not even the man who thinks that by its purchase he is cheapening the cost of his production.

When the Community Benefits so Must the Workers

"No matter what machine may be invented, it will be the better for being operated intelligently, and therefore I take it that it is to the advantage of the entire community to bring on every possible kind of labor-saving machinery, to do everything we can to extend the power of the directing hand and to consider the machine as a tool which is more economical and efficient in the skilled rather than the unskilled hand.

"It is frequently said that there is no place for the unskilled man in the union organization and that, therefore, an employer in negotiating with unions is negotiating only with the more skilled and presumably the more intelligent labor and that this is essentially unjust to the unskilled man. It is my contention that every job is the better for bringing skill to it and that, although at one time it was correct to say that the unions found no place for the unskilled man, that is no longer true to-day. Not only have the more highly developed trade unions thrown open their doors to the helpers but also—and this is what so many people forget—many occupations formerly classed as unskilled have become skilled through organization. Hodcarriers were certainly passed as common labor, but now they are organized and in a way skilled. Surely the motorman of a trolley car is not to be classed as a skilled laborer if we recognize a certain distinction between skilled and unskilled more or less based upon the time required to acquire dexterity. A toolmaker is many years learning his trade while it is a stupid man who cannot learn to run an electric car within a week, although, of course, the refinements of the job take more than a week to master. But the motormen now regard themselves as skilled.

"I should not only endeavor to have all of my employees organized, but I should want to have them organized in such a way that I might, as an employer, consult with their representatives on constructive policies and not confine the consultation merely to differences. This constructive side has undoubtedly been neglected. It has been neglected because the suspicion between the employer and employees has commonly been so intense as to confine their activities to watching each other. Once they get together along the lines that I have outlined and check their suspicions, then there is room for that vast amount of constructive work which will so greatly improve industry in its every phase. Fighting produces battle leaders and it may well be that the conditions surrounding union organization have produced a number of leaders who have been compelled to be militant rather than constructive. This is undoubtedly a question of circumstance and not at all of fundamentals."

3. In what manner would you regulate the number of men to be employed, the tenure of employment, and would you call upon the union to aid in effecting such a program of production so as to avoid seasonal work, and insure 12 months output—that is, continuous employment? This would involve many large questions of procedure and would

include the consideration of working hours. How would you arrange the quantity and quality of the work done, the inspection of that work, and in general what the union is delivering under the collective bargain? Could you shift responsibility to the union for the delivery by the men of production rather than of mere presence?

"The answers to all of these various questions grow out of the adoption of a proper system of planning which will insure a full year's work. Seasonal work is the curse of American industry. It demoralizes both the employer and the employee. The employer gets in the habit of shutting down the moment that sufficient work is not afforded and the employee is continually harassed by a feeling of uncertainty and is easily led away into the delusion that by soldiering on his job he can prolong it. Here is a point in which the interests of the employer and the employee are not in conflict and where their best brains can well be pooled to take advice with production engineers for the planning of the work in such a way as to avoid slack seasons.

"It must be said to the credit of the Germans that in the greater number of their industries they did avoid seasonal work. It is to the discredit of our industry that in very few occupations is the employment at all constant. This is a very proper subject for the unions to cooperate upon with the employers' associations or with the individual employers—on the basis, however, that the last thing to be considered is shutting down the plant. With the growth of cost accounting, employers are beginning to realize that plant closing is a most expensive procedure, that manufacturing is not merely an adjunct to selling, and that the two have to coordinate and cooperate.

"It will develop that both profits and wages are too low because of the excessive waste of seasonal business. If capital and labor will only cooperate to war upon waste they will both find it far more profitable than warring upon each other. As an employer (and this is, of course, not so easy as it sounds, although I am convinced that it is not impossible) I should plan my production on a schedule, make my markets and prices accordingly, and then I should be in a position to bargain with my men on a 12 months' wage basis and abandon the chaotic and uneconomic notion of making all of my profits in six months and paying a wage based on similar principles. This would make a very great difference in the prices that I should charge, and to attain this end I should consult the union officers in order to gain that cooperative knowledge which is essential to good business, always taking as a fixed matter a minimum standard of living for those whom I employed.

"This minimum standard would necessarily follow as of course, for without it the intelligent endeavor that alone can result in the best business is impossible. I think that the fixing of standards of the amount of work and of quality of work, and inspecting to determine whether those standards are being lived up to, is peculiarly a matter for the workers in the plant, and I am in favor of committees elected by the employees as union men to take charge of these matters of detail in which a conflict of authority is so easy.

"I am in favor of putting more and not less responsibility upon the workers themselves and upon their union representatives. As an employer I should expect my employees to give me in return for their wages the fair value in work that we had agreed upon just as I should expect a customer to whom I sold on a fair basis to pay his bill and am confident that such responsibility would find ready response. If this fair return was not given then I should hold the union strictly responsible, and if the local officers should be derelict in respecting that responsibility then I should go to the highest authority of the American labor movement, for neither the employer nor the union can be permitted to go back morally upon a bargain duly and fairly made, but with the qualification, however, that since the bargain is a human one, circumstances that alter the conditions upon which the bargain was premised may so change as to make it inequitable. There are not many buyers and sellers who insist upon their pound of flesh no matter at what cost, and if we consider wage agreements as partaking of this nature then, both sides approaching fairly, there is no good excuse for trouble. If I considered that my labor agreements had become inequitable, I should want to have them equitably revised. Nobody can reasonably expect to succeed with a cutthroat policy."

4. How would you arrange wages? Would you have a wage committee or a shop committee and would you regard the union scale as a uniform dead level or as a minimum wage for that class of work, as, for instance, in the case of piece-work? Would you arrange with the union to guarantee the union scale, paying those who exceed that scale in proportion to their excess and firing those who do not come up to the scale? This would, in effect, be to regard the union day wage as merely a guaranteed minimum and then the wage itself would be based upon performance.

"The union wage is a minimum wage and it is arrived at as being in the nature of a safeguard against paying a man of a certain skill less than a certain amount for his day. But however erroneous may be some of the opinions on the subject, wages are paid out of the production and out of nothing else. Therefore, those who, in the name of unions, oppose the introduction of better methods of work are catering to ignorance and not to union principles.

"As an employer I should endeavor to distinguish between the union organization which is for the purpose of bettering society and those organizations which falsely call themselves unions and which exist for the avowed purpose of destroying society as we now know it and supplanting it with communism.

"I should pay my wages on performance and I should have a committee of the union with whom I could arrange the fair content of the day's work and thus guard against the danger of inhuman pace-setting.

"Pace-setting does not in the end result in higher production. When you consider the waste material and the steady deterioration of the human element through following too high a pace, you gain the true facts. If the union wage is to be regarded as a minimum it must be translated into a minimum amount of work, and that minimum amount of work is a matter on which the parties can fairly cooperate.

"Having fixed upon the minimum amount of work, we are to take into account that all men are not equal and there is no suspicion in the union doctrine that all men are equal in ability, and I should therefore arrange to pay my people in proportion to the amount of work they did above the standard—not at all in the way of a bonus, not as a gift, and not charitably, but with a mutual recognition of the fact that, if prices are calculated upon the man doing 10 articles a day, if he then does 20 articles a day the employer can well afford to pay the worker who produces 100% more, 100% more wages, because the overhead expense remains just the same. This is a principle recognized by most industrial engineers and it is perfectly fair to all parties.

"The chief objection from the worker's standpoint to doing more has been that while the employer gained largely from the excess, the employee gained little and often found that rates would be so reduced when he demonstrated his real ability that a new standard would be set under which a decent wage could be attained only by a killing day's work. I am decidedly in favor, wherever it is possible, of measuring the wage exactly by performance and of treating the union wage as a guaranteed minimum. If the standards were fixed by the men themselves or by the union officers, they would be fairly fixed, and those men who could not attain these mutually agreed-upon standards would very properly be discharged. Under such a mutual arrangement the length of the work day could be easily adjudicated on the facts, which is, after all, the only way that it can fairly be settled.

"As an employer I should be just as heartily in favor of the short work day as is, say, Henry Ford or any of our other progressive employers. Sustained effort is not possible beyond a certain length of time and if day in and day out the length of time is exceeded, the totality of production will suffer. Therefore, dismissing for the moment the human factor altogether and considering, as an employer, merely the amount of production I could attain, I should know that a regular amount of first-class production could not be reached unless I had an alert, active working force and that men who work more than eight hours a day, day in and day out, do not remain alert and active.

"We are so accustomed to the other kind of workers that sometimes we cannot recall the difference between the man in the fullness of his manhood and the one who, through long grinding, is only partially alive."

5. Would you evolve wage scales which carried with them bonuses, either individual or departmental, based upon the fact that after a certain production is exceeded, then the overhead charge becomes so much lower per unit of production that a considerable increase in wages may be made?

"This question I have already answered in the previous question. I should expect to share with my workers the increased benefit of large production, letting them know fully by arrangement with their committees just what it was we were sharing and why we were sharing it. The rates thus arranged would put a real premium on honest, active work and remove every possible difficulty in the way of higher and ever higher production. The idea of limiting production is a very pernicious one, but production will be limited until the two parties to higher production learn to cooperate."

6. Would you put the question of so-called scientific management up to the men and let them by their own committees with the assistance of production engineers evolve the best methods or would you accept the ideas as exemplified in the English unions that there is only one way of doing anything and that is the way it has been done?

"Only out of production can we all grow prosperous and every aid to production that does not involve human waste is a benefit to society. If the added production is gained at the cost of a human being then it does not help society, because even from a cold standpoint of economics it tends toward overproduction by destroying in the very making of the product those who would directly or indirectly buy that product. Whatever are the evils in the distribution of the products of work (and there are many of them), those evils are not going to be cured by producing less.

"That will not solve the problem of distribution. That will provide humanity with one bone instead of two to snarl about. As I said before, I am in favor of every possible device which will increase the productivity of human labor and increase its standards. This is best done with the assistance of science. There can be no objection to really scientific management—(not the so-called scientific management with its stop-watch methods and bonuses), that which is for the benefit of all of the parties to industry and not only of one. As an employer I should know that it would be shortsighted to expect to get steadily more from my workers and at the same time give them steadily less.

"The better industrial engineers who are interested in improving industry and not merely in coddling employers know this to be a fact and they regard an inequality in pay—that is, a pay which is less than the performance—as a waste of human resource, and pursue such wastes as belligerently as they pursue any other wastes.

"I think that scientific industrial instruction can best be given and possibly can be given only in cooperation with the workers and with committees of the workers so that none will have to work blindly. I am quite sure that the assurance that the improvement of methods will be for all will invite the most active cooperation on the part of the union officers.

"The old 'ca'canny' methods originated by the Scotch, the limitation of production, the idea that there is only a certain amount of work in this world to do and that it must be spread out thin, are dead and ought never to be revived, and will never be revived. As an employer I should discriminate between the union organized for work and the organization falsely called a 'union' which is organized to prevent work."

7. Would you put the matter of hiring and firing in the hands of a committee and an employment manager or would you fix the responsibility upon the union?

"This vexed question I should leave to an employment manager acting in consultation with the union, for in this way the fairest results may be secured. The turnover of labor is one of our most serious industrial problems and it has frequently come to my notice, this time speaking not as an employer but as president of the American Federation of Labor, that employment agencies have contributed to a very considerable degree to abnormal turnovers. In the past it has been not at all infrequent for foremen or superintendents to share in the fees paid to the employment agencies for jobs.

"It then became to the interest of these officials to have just as many men as possible hired or fired. I remember an incident of this kind with the late Senator Hanna. He owned blast furnaces near Buffalo and one day he telephoned from the cloakroom of the Senate that his men had gone on strike and would I come over and see him. I knew him very well and I had an inkling of what his trouble was, and so I went over to see him, especially since he was not at all a well man and could not very easily get around.

"I found him fuming—for if a blast furnace ever gets cold no power on earth can start it up again.

" 'What am I going to do, Sam?' he said. 'These fellows have walked right out. They are getting standard wages. What am I going to do? Can you get them back again?'

" 'I think I know what your trouble is,' I answered. 'These men have simply revolted. I happen to know that your superintendent gets a bonus from an employment agency on each man that is hired and he has developed a system of firing people and then reemploying them through the agency so that he and the agency can each get a little money. The men have revolted and don't you think it's about time they did?'

" 'Do you mean to tell me that's going on in my place?' he almost yelled. 'That's hell. I shall fire every one of them. But is there anything you can do?'

" 'There is nothing I can do officially,' I answered, 'because I have no power to command anything, but I shall see if I can get the men back and then we can adjust this employment matter.'

"I got in touch with the people on the long-distance telephone and they returned to work before the furnaces had cooled down. The senator soon discovered that what I had told him was a fact and it did not take him very long to get rid of the swindling foremen and superintendents. By the next time I talked with him matters had been adjusted and then he complained:

" 'But why didn't these fellows tell me about this condition? Why did they just walk out and leave me flat? It was so damned undiplomatic.'

" 'I suppose, Senator,' I answered, 'it is because we do not develop diplomats on 15 cents an hour!'

"Which is something that every employer might well bear in mind."

8. Would you endeavor to have any kind of committee or association among your employers who would discuss with you the ways and means for bettering the business and all who are associated with it without regard to what any other business is doing, and how would you avoid having these committees degenerate into merely legalistic bodies discussing and making rules as in England?

"I think it has been very well demonstrated by the English experience that the works committee as a whole is a failure and that far better results can be attained by union cooperative committees for specific objects. I do not believe in mixing the functions of industry. I do not believe in mixing the affairs of the counting-house and the workshop but I should delegate to committees elected by the men and solely responsible to the men, the settlement of many matters which arise which are peculiar to the shop and not to the industry as a whole.

"Where the industry as a whole is concerned it is to the advantage of both the employer and the employee that the minimum standards at least should be everywhere maintained, or the man who violates those standards will gain a temporary advantage over the man who preserves them and thus not only the worker but also the industry will eventually suffer. The matter of committees is not particularly complicated if we regard them not as a substitute for management but as an aid thereto and assign to each definite and not merely roving functions. They will not become merely legalistic quibbling bodies if they are operated in a spirit of fair play. There is not generally in America the same suspicion between the employer and the employed as in some other countries and I should not like to see that suspicion engendered so that the only dealings between the two are formal as between belligerent powers."

9. Would you further any community effort in the way of cooperative amusement, cooperative housing, savings or the like, where a distinct economy might be had by clubbing together?

"As an employer I should encourage my employees to form every possible kind of society which would add to their comfort, their education, their pleasure, or their well-being, provided always, however, that these societies could be organized by the people themselves and managed by them without interference from above. I am in favor of every such organization of employees and against every organization which is paternal in its scope or which is designed to hold the worker to his job by mixing up with that job something in addition to the job itself. For instance, savings schemes fostered by the employer and managed by him wherein the employee loses unless he remains a certain length of time have nothing to commend them and are an affront to manhood. Savings should be voluntary and managed from the outside. So likewise do I object to all of the enforced welfare work which treats the employee as an unintelligent animal needing the care of expert hostlers."

10. Presuming that you had evolved a system of harmonious working with the unions, what would you do in the case of a sympathetic strike?

"A sympathetic strike is absolutely against the principles of the American Federation of Labor. It has nothing to do with constructive union labor and is a weapon evolved by the anti-trade unionists to pave the way for the general strike with which they hope to destroy the present basis of society.

"Now, since you have, for the last two hours, placed me in the impossible position of an employer of labor, I ask to be released so that I may resume my lifelong position of speaking and acting as my preference dictates, that is in the name of labor."

53

Early Cooperative Relations at Hart, Schaffner & Marx with the Amalgamated Clothing Workers' Union

Working with Sidney Hillman's Union

MORRIS GREENBERG

Mr. J. E. Williams, arbitrator for the first seven years of the Hart, Schaffner & Marx agreement with the Amalgamated Clothing Workers' Union, in a long series of decisions, worked out and developed the philosophy; the best and most successful relationship can exist only where there is on the one hand a strong, aggressive, and efficient management, which has power and discipline to enforce its just needs, and on the other hand, a strong, well-knit, well-organized union.

A union deputy who speaks only falteringly for his people, who is not at all certain that he can carry out, or get the people to live up to, an arrangement which he makes in their name, is not of much use in any situation. It is in weak unions, badly organized unions, unions in so-called open shops or preferential shops, where they have to devote a great deal of thought and effort to maintaining their status that such deputies are encountered.

In such situations leadership is more concerned with small things, things which affect its own petty interests, than with larger, constructive matters.

Of course, it is asking a great deal of a management group which for years had a definite anti-union philosophy, to re-make that philosophy suddenly and completely because of the signing of a collective agreement. But unless they do and until they do, there will be trouble.

Design for Collective Bargaining

There is required at an early stage of the initiation of collective bargaining, as careful an analysis as possible of the basic problems of the particular industry, the setting up of machinery designed in the light of the facts of the situation to handle the matters that will come up from time to to time and the development of a proper spirit on the part of the members of management—the foremen, the superintendents, the timekeepers, the rate makers and so on—and of an understanding of the system so that they can administer it in a day-to-day manner in a way best calculated to get good results.

All of this is vague and general. I will try to give it a little more meaning by discussing some of these problems in a more detailed way to show they can be met, how a situation which is fraught with all sorts of possibilities for trouble can be so developed that these troubles are minimized and the best factors in the situation retained and strengthened.

Reprinted from *The Personnel Journal,* Vol. 17, 1938-39, pp. 200-211.

Morris Greenberg was employed at Hart, Schaffner & Marx when this was written.

Jointly Set Rates

Piece work is used for about 85 per cent of the work in our plant. I don't know of any wage payment plan that has been more roundly cursed by both sides, and with more reason, than piece work. All who have had experience in rate setting, and are familiar with the philosophies and theories of wage payment plans, know what an instrument for deviltry and damage an unlimited piece work system can be.

The old method of having rates set by management alone, everywhere gives rise to self-defense on the part of the workers, to loafing, soldiering and disregard of quality.

This does not happen any more in our plant. Piece rates are set jointly. All piece rates when set are carefully recorded. There is prepared a specification setting forth exactly quantity and quality of the work covered by the piece rate. In extreme cases, where a written description is not adequate, a sample of the work itself is put on file.

The right of discipline to maintain the specification, suspension of workers for failure to do work in accordance with the specification, in extreme cases the discharge of workers for failure to do the work as specified, rests in the hands of management.

Rigid Discipline Maintained

The impartial machinery has again and again confirmed actions of discipline taken on the part of the company to promote or enforce the maintenance of quality standards, and has gone farther. In cases where, through lax management, specifications have been allowed to lapse, the impartial machinery has seen to it that the firm is penalized. The firm need not come crying for sympathy to the impartial machinery for failure on its part to enforce its rights.

This will sound rather peculiar to those people who are skeptical about management's right of discipline under collective bargaining; that the machinery set up under collective bargaining has had to force management to exercise its rights. But that is the truth. And it has been, incidentally, a most welcome and efficient aid to management.

So we have accomplished two things. We have created in the minds of the workers of a feeling of confidence in the honesty and fairness of the rates. They must feel that way since they help make them. We have not only maintained but have done a great deal to strengthen the power of management to exact for these rates the quality levels to which it is entitled.

The third fear and bugaboo in respect to piece work on the part of workers, the fear of arbitrary changes in piece rates, is removed because the company channot change a piece rate. It can bring an action before the impartial machinery for the change of a piece rate, as can the workers, if experience demonstrates that an error has been made, but changes of that kind command confidence and respect.

Fat Juicy Rates

People frequently say to me, "Don't you often find that under that kind of rate making, the union takes advantage? The union enforces high rates here and there?" Yes, they do. We did find that, but that situation tended to correct itself in this way: A deputy is after all a representative, chosen by votes, and like most people so chosen, has to do what he can to maintain himself in favor with as large a group of his constituency as possible. If a deputy has been successful in putting over a cute trick and getting a nice, fat, juicy piece rate for a section, he is very quickly met by other sections saying to him, privately, "Look here, brother, I belong to this union, too. How about doing the same thing for me?"

In a situation where there is impartial machinery, an established rate structure, and specifications protecting the piece rates, that is a very difficult thing to do. The deputies in our situation, even if the rate making capacity of management had been more limited than it was, would soon have found themselves in a situation where it was to their own best interests to make piece rates that were fair and defensible.

It has tended to work out in that way, not because of any high-minded ideals on the part of the deputies—surely in the early days of our arrangement they were out to get what they could—but because the force of circumstances, the political necessities, the political repercussions of the things they did taught them that for their own interests it was better to have a sound, intelligently balanced rate structure. It removed pressures on them that they did not want to face.

The same thing is true and the same approach is possible with any rate system. I hold no special brief for piece work; but I think if I were organizing a new plant today and had free choice of a payment system, I would choose piece work, if the nature of the industry were such that rate making could be done intelligently.

Other Problems Aided

In setting up a decent wage payment system, one where there is tied into the making of the rates a definite specification of the work to be done for the rate, with the duty and responsibility of the company clearly established to maintain an exact performance of the quantity and quality of work for which the rate is set, you have gone a great part of the way to solving the quality problem.

To the extent that you place the mechanisms for adequate discipline in the hands of management, to enforce the quantitative and qualitative performance of the various specifications, you have solved the discipline problem.

All of these problems are interrelated. None of them stands alone. And that goes all the way through the entire field.

The maintenance of the proper quantitative level in production raised quite a lot of trouble in the beginning, and here again, as in the case of piece work, the end result was a forcing upon management by the impartial machinery, of a clear recognition of its duties and its obligation, of its part in the maintenance of a decent production level.

The problem of maintaining an even flow of work is frequently little understood and that is true in both union and non-union plants. In the non-union plants, with the same degree of understanding, less is done about it by management because less pressure is brought to bear on management to do things about it. Under a union arrangement, more pressure is brought to bear upon management to do things about it, with the result that in the long run, everything else being equal, management must be better and work flow more evenly. Management is forced in self-defense to be better under a system of collective bargaining.

Balancing Work Flow

It is obvious that in any system based on the division of labor, to maintain an even flow of work, the personnel in various sections or groups handling different parts of the work must be balanced. The plant, the equipment, must be available for the handling of the same quantity, and the same quantity of work must be fed to each section per unit of time.

It sounds simple and it seems almost silly to have to say it, but most violations of good management in the matter of maintaining flow of work are violations of just such simple and obvious common-sense rules.

If I have a section of tape sewers which has to turn out a thousand units a day and following them is a section of tape fellers which has to fell a thousand tapes a day and next to them is a section of tape pressers which has to press a thousand tapes a day, it is perfectly obvious that if the tape sewers don't sew a thousand a day, the fellers won't get a thousand to fell, they can't fell what they don't get, and so on down the line. If there are blocks in production and blocks in the earning capacity of the people in the sections that are affected, they give rise to serious irritations and complaints.

Under non-union operation, the standard attitude of management toward complaints of that kind by workers is, "It's none of your business. We're running this plant. If you don't like it, go work somewhere else." That is not management, that is an evasion of the problem of management, and a method under which bad management is perpetuated.

Positive Pressure of Union

Under a collective agreement, however, pressure is brought to bear when the tape fellers come and say, "Look here, you're forcing us to sit around and wait for no fault of our own; either give us work to do or pay us for waiting time." It forced good management down our throats. We had to be good managers in self-defense.

There has been another interesting development. Many people can see only the negative values in dealing with workers under collective bargaining schemes. They see collective bargaining machinery as a way to avoid trouble, a negative value, and they overlook the positive values. There are definite positive values and in my judgment, they often equal and in some cases outweigh the negative ones.

Here is one of these positive values: Under our system of operation, the girls in the tape felling section watch very carefully the people who come into the section preceding them. The plant starts to work at 8 o'clock, and if by 8:10 or 8:15 there are two or three people absent out of ten or fifteen, they don't wait very long before going to their shop chairman about it. The shop chairman gives the production supervisor a few minutes, a reasonable time, to get around to correcting that break. If within a reasonable time he has not done anything, the chairman calls the matter to the supervisor's attention. At first our management resented this interference with their ancient "right" but the company has learned to see the positive values in such a system. You can call it union interference if you like, but as the executive responsible for results, I call it coöperation. It is just as much coöperation if its motive is self-interest, as if its motive were something else. The result is the same.

Contributions to Management

It goes even farther because now a shop chairman not only announces that there are two tape sewers missing but he adds, "I'm sending over Susie and Mamie. In fact, they are over there now. Is that all right with you?"

The same thing happens in quality. Again, the motive is self-interest. If the tape sewer does a bad job of tape sewing and our quality supervisors do not catch it, the next section has a harder job to do the tape felling and stands a chance of being blamed for bad work which is not their fault. In self-defense they call the attention of the shop chairman to it, when, in the rush of work, something is overlooked.

In matters of production, in matters of quality, in matters of personnel management, we get a great amount of help from the representatives of the workers. Again and again, they will come to me and say, "Now, technically, in this situation you have the right to do so-and-so," or, "We have the right to do so-and-so, but don't you think it might be a better scheme if we were to do thus and thus instead, for these reasons."

Sometimes it is a better scheme, sometimes it is not, but the important point is that here is a type of constructive thinking, a positive contribution to management, that can come only through a decent, intelligent, and broadly administered collective bargaining arrangement.

Does Seniority Govern Layoffs?

No, seniority has nothing to do with it. Equal division of work is the rule.

We don't discharge except in individual cases for cause; and then they are discharged for cause, and seniority has nothing to do with it. If we have a certain number of cutters and have a very bad season, so that we have work for only one-third of the cutters, we have a choice of working that third full time for one or more weeks and then sending them home and calling the next third in full time for the next period, etc., or we can work the whole force one-third the number of hours. That is the principle we follow—equal division of work.

Do You Have the Check-off of Union Dues?

No, we do not. But what difference would it make if we did?

The union does not seem to need help in our case. We have what is technically a preferential shop but what is in fact a closed shop. A worker couldn't continue to work with us if he didn't pay his dues, not on account of what we would do; he could go on working there as far as we are concerned; but he would find it very uncomfortable.

Where there is a close-knit and well-organized union, speaking seriously, there isn't any problem of collection of dues and the question of who does collect them is a very incidental and unimportant one. Some people see red and froth at the mouth at the very mention of the principle of the check-off. Some of them sound as though the things the founding fathers fought for in our Revolution weren't half as important as the question as to whether the firm should, or should not check off the union dues. I think, personally, it doesn't make a bit of difference, but we do not collect dues.

Do You Have Trouble Introducing Labor-Saving Improvements?

In a general way, yes, but we have also been able to do quite a lot of that. There are limitations on us. For example, if a new machine came into the industry which would enable me to throw out 1,000 people, we couldn't go out today and just cavalierly throw them out. The union would sit down with us and work out the problem somehow. As a matter of fact, many such things have been done in the course of our arrangements with the union.

For one reason or another, there have been times when we have had surpluses of workers. We have paid dismissal wages, for instance, as a means of disposing of groups of workers from time to time. We have kept in touch and kept pace with the developments in the industry and with changes in our situation and have introduced improvements. It isn't easy; it requires negotiation in each case and working out the merits of the problem but the union officials have never taken the attitude finally of saying, "Despite your need and despite the situation, we won't let you do this." That is, they haven't persisted in saying that for very long. They have said it but they haven't persisted in this attitude.

How Do You Make Sure That You Will Have Enough Skilled Workers?
Does the Union Help? Does It Limit Apprentices?

There is no official policy on the subject but it tends to work itself out this way. We had a problem not long ago, a detail problem and yet one involving a few hundred people, where we were looking to make a quality change and at the same time we wanted to have a cost reduction. This is one of those impossible things like asking to have your pie and eat it too, but we were able to work that out.

The union worked it out for us, if we are strictly honest about it; and it involved, among other things, the taking in of about 200 new people, a type of worker that the union didn't have to supply. Had they been technical with me, they could have insisted on supplying 200 of such people as they did have, which wouldn't have been at all the kind we needed, all of them middle-aged or better. Instead of which they brought in from off the streets about 200 brand new people. Both they and we took care, in fact they insisted that we set an age limit and take no one over 22, just for the purpose of bringing in some fresh young blood at the time that we were reducing cost.

When we have experienced a shortage, the union has not interfered with me in training new people. For instance, sleeve sewing is one of the most highly skilled operations in making a coat. I would say it is probably the most highly skilled single operation there is in the making of clothing, and the best operators tend to be and become sleeve sewers. In the plant where there has been security of tenure since 1911, we have gradually begun in certain spots and at certain times to experience a shortage of sleeve sewers.

The union has seen this as their problem as well as ours. So we have taken younger workers from other parts of the shop who had the basis of experience and who we could most readily teach to do this other work instead of starting raw apprentices and teaching them. There has been no difficulty about that.

Gradually that works itself down to the end of the line, where we finally need a basting puller, and then we bring in somebody from the outside. There is no policy, but we haven't felt the pinch or the need of any people. If today we faced a sudden and sharp increase in volume, that would necessitate say a 50 per cent increase in productive capacity, it would be difficult but not impossible to secure the new people. The union would coöperate.

How Does Such a Union-Management Relationship Develop?

Up until the time of unionization in 1911, which came after a very bitter and bloody strike, there was nothing in the way of any relationship, any organized relationship, between the workers and the management. It was possible for Mr. Schaffner, for instance, who was a very high type of man, very cultivated and a truly educated gentleman in the real sense of the word, to say truthfully in 1911, in the course of the strike, at a public hearing as to the reasons and causes for the strike, that he did not know of the things that had been going on in his plant. It was not an evasion; it was not an alibi; he really didn't know.

The company operated at that time under a system where the superintendents were virtually independent contractors. It said to a superintendent, "Here is a factory, fully equipped. You manage it, and we will pay you a base wage, a salary of so much. We will meet all the payrolls, supply the work and the materials, etc. You get the help where and as you can and we will hold you to a cost of so much per unit. If your cost is better than that, you will get a bonus on such and such a scale." All the matters of hiring, firing, making of rates, changing of rates, were up to the superintendent. The firm neither knew nor cared. It was interested in one thing, that if it put in so many units to that factory per unit of time, it wanted so many units out, and it didn't want those units to cost more than a certain amount.

After the strike and the unionization, there then developed, very slowly, a system of relationships. Of course, the formal development was very rapid, because it was instituted almost on the completion of unionization. There was set up arbitration machinery that provided for committees of workers and committees of the firm and so on and so on. But this was more a formal creation than a real one. The real machinery, the real meeting of minds developed very slowly.

How Did You Develop the System of Joint Rate-Setting?

Our rate structure is a very peculiar thing. Our company is a little over fifty years of age and our rate structure is about as old. Before the union, the rates were made by guess. That is to say, the management by itself would set a piece rate at what it thought it ought to be. How they arrived at it I don't know and I don't think they did either.

When the company was unionized, the rate structure as it then existed was taken over bodily as a starting point. They didn't suddenly go to piece work from nothing. Then, there followed over the years a series of general wage changes, a general 20 per cent increase, a general 10 per cent reduction, such and such an increase, such and such a reduction.

Incident to some of the increases and some of the reductions, there were broad leveling-out processes. At one time, for instance, the union came along and said, "We want a wage increase. The cost of living has gone up." The arbitration machinery decided that in lieu of giving everyone a

20 per cent wage increase, they would give an increase of 10 per cent to all people earning from a certain amount up, and all people earning below that amount would get a 20 per cent increase. In other words, they tried to level out broadly, without any scientific approach to the question of the individual rate or the rate structure by groups.

The same thing was done again in wage reductions, where the less well paid groups were reduced somewhat less than the others. So the general rate structure is a thing that was inherited as a whole, had an arbitrary beginning and has since been subjected to general levelings and adjustments. We can't claim to have a scientifically set piece rate structure. The only thing that can be claimed for it is that, pragmatically and practically, it works.

In a general way, workers performing operations where about the same degree of skill is required tend to earn about the same amount. That isn't strictly true. There are some cases on both sides out of line, some sections that I could wish were earning more in relation to what others are earning, and some that are earning entirely too much considering the skill that is required.

So much for the general structure. Under the union arrangement there have, however, been many job rates made from time to time, as new operations are created or changes occur in old work. Those rates are made jointly. That is to say, a representative of the company and a representative of the union come in and study the operation and try to agree on a piece rate. Always or practically always they have a great many related rates to go by. There is very little that is really new in our industry. A new operation is probably just a variant of an old one, or it is a combination of parts of this one and parts of that one, for all of which there is existing information as to rates and earnings.

Where the two people cannot agree, they go to the trade board. The chairman of the board, who is really an arbitration board chairman, hears the dispute and writes a decision.

How Did Your Foremen Like the New Arrangement with the Union?

During the early years of the operation of our agreement the stumbling block lay right there. Our company kept on all its old foremen. These men suddenly had to take off their cloven hoofs and their tails and discard their pitchforks and put on the robes of angels—and they weren't too successful. It was a difficult change.

For the first few years Professor Earl Dean Howard administered the labor relations of our company. His job was largely that of educating and training the foremen. In a place as large as ours was then with as many ramifications employing as many people as it did that was possible only by his laying down rules. They were chiefly "Don'ts." A foreman may not do thus and so, unless he first gets permission from the labor department, or a foreman shouldn't say that and he shouldn't say this and if he did, he had to stand for the results. By that process of clubbing an education into their heads, they gradually learned.

I am afraid I will have to say they learned chiefly to do nothing. That is a bad way of putting it, but it is substantially correct. It took some time then before they began to re-assert themselves and began to see that the "don'ts" needn't be interpreted too literally, needn't be an injunction to cease doing anything. Slowly they began to learn from trade board cases, examples, and from all sorts of instruction the right way to do things.

It would have been cruel and ungrateful to have taken all these supervisors, foremen and superintendents and thrown them out and taken new ones, but I think the company probably would have done better to have weeded out where it couldn't educate. Instead of clubbing some of these men into a state of mind where I think they were next to useless, if they had transferred those they couldn't educate they would have saved a lot of trouble. Of course, that is easier said than done too.

These men were very skillful, able men. It took such a man to have been able to operate under the old system, because he wasn't just an employee, he wasn't just a foreman, he was virtually an independent contractor, who had to do everything for himself in a big plant, and that took a pretty able, aggressive man.

But in the first few years, there is no doubt about it that the labor department of our company took all the heart and much of the guts out of these men. They had to do it because these foremen just couldn't remember, just couldn't realize that there had been a basic change. They wanted to cut piece rates again; they wanted to fire workers again; they wanted to go on doing all the things that *they* knew were right. It was a tough job. That is one of the first and most difficult jobs that confronts any company newly entering into union relations, the conversion of the foremen.

What Happened to the Workers Who Did Not Want to Join the Union?

That was a problem that the union encountered. The union took over a thoroughly undisciplined mass of people, highly individualistic. The strike, as most strikes are, was organized and conducted and maintained by a minority, the most active, the most intelligent, the most aggressive group. That is what always happens. Many of the workers didn't understand where their interests lay and for a long time the foremen did their best to keep the groups divided and to keep them from joining the union.

When the contract was signed, all the membership didn't suddenly become union. All that happened was, the firm agreed to deal with this union for such of its employees as it represented, but nobody knew who it represented. The union didn't know and the firm didn't know. It took some time before all the workers came into the union; and that was a period of warfare and costly warfare.

It was a period of plotting and counter-plotting and put-up jobs on both sides and all sorts of monkey business, utterly silly, ridiculous, senseless and idiotic.

As we see it now this is the most short-sighted thing a management can do because during the whole time, the people who are unionized spend the bulk of their time getting the rest in, looking for complaints, looking for things they can get for their members that the others won't get, to show those that are not in the union that it would be to their interest to join. When that issue becomes settled there is a chance for the growth of a decent, sensible point of view, and coöperative relations.

This is the experience of every man in personnel management who has had to deal with a partially organized plant, whether he has tried to keep the groups apart or not.

54

Personnel Policies at Ford

A Summer in the Ford Works

CHEN-NAN LI

In the summer of 1925, I had the privilege of joining the Yale Industrial Research Group and of spending two months and three weeks in the Ford Motor Company. I worked in both the River Rouge Plant and the Highland Park Plant. I came in contact with not less than ten departments, the most important of which were the Motor Assembly, Grocery Store, Employment Office, Receiving, Battery, Compensation, Safety and Hygiene, and Sociological departments. My experience in the various departments and my observations of industrial relations at the Ford Plants were embodied in a rather detailed account entitled "A Summer in the Ford Motor Company." The manuscript is kept in the Yale University Library. Nothing regarding this first summer's work will be recounted here.

In the summer of 1926, I was again given the opportunity of working in the Ford Plants from June 23 to September 18, a total of two months and twenty-six days. The company very considerately put me in several departments in which I had not had time to work the previous year. I worked in the Glass Plant for over a month, the Garage for a week, the Motor Repair Department for three weeks, the Rolling Mill for a week, and the Power House for two weeks.

The fact that the Yale students were rapidly transferred from one department to another precluded, of course, the possibility of acquiring proficiency in any mechanical process that required much skill. But from the standpoint of studying industrial relations this was a distinct advantage. In the first place, it gave the student an opportunity to try a great variety of jobs. This enabled him to gain an insight into the nature of the conditions under which the workmen labored. The work in a modern factory varies all the way from jobs that require no skill at all to those that presuppose years of training; from those that involve only one or two simple operations to those that consist of a long series of fine movements; from those that require merely brute strength to those that demand engineering ability. To gain a comprehensive understanding of the working conditions, the student should experience as many types of work as possible. In the second place, it gave him an opportunity to come into personal contact with various types of working-men—skilled and unskilled, novice and expert, married and single, native and foreigner, conservative and radical. The Ford Motor Company is a gigantic organization. It is an organization that has some 100,000 men on its payroll, and that produces at normal times 7,000 cars every day. It combines a host of industries relative to automobile manufacture. It has its own coke ovens, blast furnaces, steel mill, rubber works. It manufactures paper, cement and artificial leather. It owns railroads and freight boats. It controls its own

Reprinted from *The Personnel Journal*, Vol. VII, 1928-29, pp. 18-32.

Dr. Li was at Yale University when this was published.

iron and timber supply. The student who worked in a number of departments could practically study a new industry each week. Furthermore, the company has thousands of up-to-date machines that perform a series of complicated movements at a single stroke. It is a novel and interesting experience for an academic student to operate, for example, a turbo-generator that makes 1,800 revolutions per minute, and to run a drill press that bores 48 holes in a single operation.

I was particularly fortunate to have spent two consecutive summers in the same firm. Such a huge organization must be studied from many points of view. After a second summer in the Ford Plants, the conclusions I had drawn in the previous year seemed to be rather hasty and sometimes not at all warranted. In this paper no detailed account will be given regarding the many jobs I had in the various departments during the summer of 1926. Suffice it to say here that in the Glass Plant I worked in the "Batch Room" (where the constituent elements of glass were weighed and mixed) at the furnaces, on a rolling machine, at the polishing wheels and on a great variety of miscellaneous jobs. In the Garage I learned to repair Fordson Tractors. In the Motor Repair Department of the Motor Assembly I learned to find out imperfections in the motor and to make proper changes and adjustments. In the Rolling Mill I worked at the finishing stands, where steel billets were rolled into finished products ready for shipment. In the Power House I worked at the boiler, the turbo-generator, the turbo-blower, the condenser and the air-compresser. At times I was engaged entirely in unskilled work, such as removing bricks and wiping machines. At times I was doing more or less skilled jobs, such as repairing motors and rebuilding the transmission of a tractor. At times I had to exert my whole strength. At times I could stand idly watching the machines work. Having worked in practically all the important non-production departments last year, I decided not to do any clerical work this year. This gave me more time to associate with the so-called "production men." In the following pages I shall endeavor to state my observations regarding the labor policy of the company and the life of a Ford workingman. The reader's indulgence is requested if, occasionally, facts treated in last year's report should be cited as evidences to support certain conclusions.

The Labor Policy of the Ford Motor Company

The labor policy of the company can be best discussed under the following headings:

1. *The Source of Supply.* The Ford Motor Company is cosmopolitan in its labor population. Nearly every nation on earth is represented on its pay roll. Besides native Americans, there are enormous numbers of Canadians and Europeans of every ethnological origin. South Americans and Western Asiatics also constitute a not altogether negligible minority among the Ford employees. To be sure, the Chinese and the Japanese are confined to students; but this is a fact for which the company cannot be held responsible. Although I should not say that racial prejudice has entirely disappeared in the Ford Plants, it is certainly not a part of the policy of the management. The Employment Office prefers a native to a foreigner, a northerner to a southerner, a Detroiter or a Michigan man to a citizen of any other city or state. This, however, is not a manifestation of racial prejudice. The company wants its men to be steady. The nearer to

Detroit the worker lives, the more likely it is that he will be a steady employee.

Another feature of the Ford labor supply is the employment of substandard men. In the factory one not infrequently meets the blind and the crippled. Though their number is negligible, their employment is something unique in the Ford Plants. The company has so many varieties of jobs at its disposal that suitable work can be easily found for any man not totally disabled. It must not be understood, however, that any handicapped man can find work in the Ford Plants. The substandard men are employed, not because they are substandard men, but because they have, in some way or other, been previously connected with the Ford Plants. In many cases they received the injury while in Ford employment.

Perhaps a few words should also be said here regarding the employment of women. Like the substandard men, the women are employed not because they are women. Most of the Ford women are wives or daughters of Ford men who have in some way been temporarily or permanently disabled. A woman whose husband is an active worker in the factory cannot obtain employment in the Ford Plants. I am told that Mr. Ford believes that a Ford employee gets enough wages to maintain a family in decent circumstances, and that his wife should take care of the home and not work in the factory for additional income. The Ford women receive the same wages as men. They are given work that allows them to sit down. In a factory where workmen have to be on their feet eight hours a day, the freedom to sit down must be reckoned as one of the greatest privileges that a person can hope to secure.

2. Provision for Labor Adjustment. One of the outstanding features of the Ford labor policy is that a foreman is deprived of the power to discharge a workingman. In case of disputes between an executive and a workman, or between one workman and another, the foreman can "lay a man off" for a period of ten days. Beyond that, the case must be referred to the Employment Office where a special officer takes charge of such matters. If, in the judgment of this officer, the foreman is wrong, the workman is usually retained, but is given work in some other department. Since the company has so many departments, such arrangements can very easily be made.

In the Ford Plants it is not at all hard to secure a transfer from one department to another, if the applicant has sufficient reasons to justify his request. Transfers are frequently given for medical reasons, or in recognition of some special aptitude or ability. The fact that the whole clerical force of the company is recruited from the rank and file of the manual workers, bears ample testimony to the readiness with which transfers are granted. Chronic drifters, however, are discouraged by every means. The company wants a man to stick to his job if there is no adequate reason for transferring him to some other department.

A man once hired is seldom discharged merely because of incompetency. He is given a chance to try many jobs. He is never obliged to quit unless every job should fail him. This is not likely to happen since so many jobs require little or no skill.

Another interesting fact in the matter of labor adjustment is the appointment of a negro to attend to the complaints of the colored people. A few years ago the feeling between the white and the colored workers in the Ford Factory was very acute. The negroes were often armed with dangerous weapons and were ready to resort to an "ordeal by combat" when the provocation seemed to them to be intolerable. Cases of bloodshed actually occurred. Numerous complaints were also heard from the colored workers that in the hands of white executives they were not given fair treatment in any case in which white men were involved. To remedy this situation, the company appointed a negro to work in the Employment Office whose special duty is to hear the complaints from the colored people and to bring about some satisfactory solution of their problems. While I should not say that the negroes are not at all discriminated against in the Ford Motor Company, they are, according to their own testimony, better off here than they would be in other manufacturing concerns.

3. Minimum Wages and Rate of Increase. With a few exceptions, every Ford employee gets $5 a day in the first and the second months and $6 a day in the third month. If a man should work for a couple of years, we can almost neglect the first two months and regard his minimum wage as $6 a day. The usual rate of increase is 40 cents at a time. The scale runs something like this: $6, $6.40, $6.80, $7.20, etc. After $7.20, increase is very difficult and for many jobs it is impossible. Most jobs are rated; but the workmen do not always get the amount specified. The increase of wages depends upon the nature of the job, the competency of the worker, and his relationship with the foremen. Though the foremen do not fix the wages, they make recommendations, and in that way they are very important factors to be considered. In the Ford Plants, however, foremen of different ranks know the workmen very well, so it is difficult for a single foreman to hold a man back on account of personal differences.

4. Vacations and "Lay-offs." The Ford Motor Company used to have one or two weeks' "lay-off" in the summer season. Various departments are shut down at that time and an inventory is taken of the capital stock invested in factory equipment. The company has never paid the men during vacations or on holidays. Even the foremen have to punch a time card and are paid on a daily wage and not on a monthly salary basis. Since the company has, however, in the past several years, given its employees very steady work throughout the year, two weeks' "lay-off" does not necessitate much financial loss to the workingmen.

In 1926 a great change took place in the Ford Plants. Nearly all departments were running only five days a week. The company has, through carefully experimenting on the five-day-week plan in several departments, found out that the amount of production is not in the least reduced under the new scheme. There were all sorts of rumors that wage adjustments would soon be made so that a workman would receive six days' wages for five days' work. Some men were betting with one another that wages would be increased when the next pay day came. The majority of the men, however, were skeptical.

5. Training and Education. For training and education, two organizations may be mentioned—the Henry Ford Trade School at Highland Park and the School Department at the Fordson Plant. The Trade School takes in boys at the age of twelve or thereabout. Instruction is divided into two sections; a week in the classroom, and two weeks in the shop. The boys are trained to be skilled mechanics. They are given a cash scholarship to meet their expenses. They work on production material and are expected to turn out articles which are actually used. Nothing is done merely for practice. Some academic work is provided, but it is given an intensely industrial tinge. Most of the graduates of the Trade School work in the Ford Plants as tool-makers, die-makers and machine repair men. The Trade School reaches only a fraction of the Ford employees; consequently, it is not an important factor in the matter of education for the workingmen. The School Department at the Fordson Plant caters more directly to the interests of the Ford employees. This department operates three schools—an electrical school, which offers training in electric wire and maintenance work; an apprentice school, which gives training in tool-making, die-making and machine repair work; and a service school which trains its students (the majority of them are from foreign countries) to be Ford service executives and repair men in this country and abroad. The service school has little to do with the regular workmen, since its students all expect to leave the factory on completion of their courses. The electric school and the apprentice school are distinct institutions for the regular Ford employees. These schools are open to all Ford men without any discrimination. Workmen can attend the classes in their leisure hours. No tuition is charged. Periodical examinations are held, and certificates are given to those who have satisfactorily completed their courses. Graduation from these schools is usually followed by a transfer to a better paid job or an increase of wages on the same job previously held. This powerful incentive has served to attract a fairly good number of ambitious workers. It must be borne in mind, however, that these schools only cater to the interests of those who aspire to be skilled workmen, such as electricians, tool-makers, die-makers and machine repairmen. Over 90 per cent of the Ford employees do not receive any classroom training at all. Division of labor has been carried on to such a point that an overwhelming majority of the jobs consist of a few very simple operations. In most cases a complete mastery of the movements does not take any more than from five to ten minutes. All the training that a man receives in connection with his job consists of one or two demonstrations by the foreman, or the workman who has been working on that job. After these demonstrations he is considered a fully qualified "production man." All that he has to do now is to automatize these few operations so that speed may be rapidly increased. For this group of men, it seems to me that some educational opportunities should be provided. Some academic work, particularly courses dealing with the use of the English language, should be offered. If they could learn to speak and write decent English and to read for pleasure, it would not only increase their social efficiency but open numerous ways of harmless enjoyment.

6. *Welfare Work.* The Ford Motor Company used to do very extensive welfare work for which a sociological department with a staff of over one hundred members was organized. When the company first raised its minimum wage to five dollars a day, it was understood that a part of it was the workman's share of the profit. This would be withdrawn from him if he was not living in decent conditions. The Sociological Department sent out a large number of advisers to visit the workmen's homes. They took pictures of the homes visited, and submitted reports on the conditions observed. It was on the basis of these reports that the company decided the qualification of a workman to receive his share of the profit. This work must have been very effective, since reports in the archives of that department give conclusive evidences of improved living conditions among

the Ford employees. When the other companies raised their wages, the five-dollar minimum of the Ford Factory was no longer as attractive as it used to be. The employees began to dislike the action of the company which now seemed to them to partake too much of the nature of paternalism. When opposition was apparent, the company deemed it wise to drop the whole scheme. The staff of the Sociological Department has been reduced, and the scope of its work limited again and again. Now its main duties are the investigation of the sick and destitute cases, the determination of the amount of aid needed, and the distribution of gratuity checks.

In connection with the welfare work, mention should be made of the commissary, which comprises four departments—a grocery store, a meat market, a drug store, and a shoe and dry goods store. The commissary caters only to the interests of the Ford employees. It sells from 10 to 15 per cent cheaper than other stores in Detroit. In the commissary at Highland Park the volume of business reaches at times $25,000 a day. In the summer of 1926 a similar store was opened at the Fordson Plant. It will probably outstrip the one at Highland Park in magnitude of business.

7. *Attitude Toward Unionism.* The automobile industry is regarded by union men as a stronghold of open shop policy. Like the other automobile manufacturing concerns, the Ford Motor Company does not recognize any labor or industrial unions. Bargaining, if there is any at all, is entirely on an individual basis. Shop committees and labor leaders are unknown. It is a current rumor that the Company has a very efficient secret service system with detectives scattered all over the factory to watch for any symptom of labor disturbances. Action is taken before any attempt on the part of the workmen to organize could come to fruition. This, I think, is much exaggerated. A secret service to watch for industrial troubles is hardly necessary, for the following reasons. In the first place, the foremen are always with the men, and everyone knows that the foremen have the interests of the company at heart. In the second place, during the eight working hours, men are supposed to be constantly at their jobs. Very little social contact between man and man is possible. Furthermore, it seems to me that the Ford workers are not at all disposed to unionize. Many of them are violent in their denunciation of labor organizations. If they have any disposition to unionize, they could get together without any difficulty when they are out of the factory. In the communities near the Ford Plants the inhabitants are predominantly Ford employees. There are all sorts of ways by which they could meet and discuss matters of common concern. Yet the workmen do not seem to be interested in fraternizing among themselves except on a very small scale. Such being the case, it is not at all necessary for the company to adopt an attitude of watchful jealousy toward unionism. Another thing that lends no small support to this statement is the fact that a Detroit paper entitled "The Daily Worker" which has many communistic ideas, and which, in its editorials, often advised the automobile workers to unionize, is allowed to be sold right at the gate of the Fordson Plant. The company has, to be sure, a factory service department which has so-called service men stationed at various places. Their chief duty is to look out for loafers and intruders, and particularly to prevent thieving.

8. *Personality in Industry.* Among the dehumanizing influences that have often been ascribed to the modern factory system, the most

important ones are speed, repetition, and lack of personal contact between labor and management. These are some of the inevitable consequences inherent in modern mass production and the extensive use of automatic machinery. Many authors have written on this subject and there is no need for elaboration here. In this paragraph I shall briefly discuss these features in connection with the Ford Plants.

a. Speed. No visitor to the Ford Plants ever fails to carry back the impression that the conveyor system speeds men to their utmost capacity. Each man is allowed only a limited time to complete his job and a limited space in which to execute his movements. Any delay on the part of one man makes it necessary for the whole gang to cease work. Repeated failures of this kind very soon eliminate the incompetent from the production line. Men are constantly in a state of nervousness and high tension. This, however, is only superficial observation. The speed of the conveyors has been so carefully regulated that, after a man has automatized his few simple operations, he can get his job done within the time allowed without undue haste and strain. If one is not unusually nervous or slow, he has no difficulty in working on the conveyor line. Then we must not forget that the conveyor system is only used in a few places in the Ford Plants. There are many departments where machines do the work, leaving little to be done by men. The workman has plenty of time to do his job, which sometimes consists in merely taking readings of certain measuring instruments. To a casual visitor the conveyor system is the most striking feature of the factory. He naturally falls into what we call in psychology the "fallacy of selection."

b. Repetition. Repetition is another indictment of the modern factory system. It is often asserted that monotony of work intensifies fatigue, creates disgust for work and produces mental abnormality. The Ford Motor Company is particularly known for its minute division of labor and the deadening monotony of its production process. The danger of repetition seems to me to be more imaginary than real. The human organism is remarkable for its adaptability to situations. After a man gets used to certain processes, change does not always appeal to him. In the Ford Factory there are abundant opportunities for men to exchange their jobs. But the men are not at all inclined to avail themselves of these opportunities. Most of them prefer to stick to their own jobs rather than to trade with others. Then we must remember that the workman spends only eight hours in his factory work. Allowing eight hours for sleep and one hour or so for going to and coming back from the factory, he still has seven hours for himself. He can find something different to do in his spare times to offset the monotonous effect of his factory work. Moreover, the minute division of labor is a necessary evil of the modern factory system. To say nothing of other factors, the increase of population and the rise of the standard of living alone would make it necessary to have mass production. Mass production is impossible without the extensive use of automatic machinery and the minute division of the production processes. Unless we are willing to return to the domestic and the handicraft stage of economy, it is highly improbable that we can avoid repetition in our industrial system.

c. Personal contact between labor and management. When the domestic system prevailed, the master workman and his apprentices and journeymen worked side by side in their limited concerns. Labor and management were hardly separable. The advent of the modern factory brought into existence a wide gap between the employer on the one hand and the employee on the other. The bigger the factory, the more detached the two parties become. This is true in all big modern factories, and the Ford Motor Company is no exception. The company, in order to secure maximum efficiency in such an immense organization, has to routinize and standardize many processes in handling men. To the management, a workman is a badge number and very little else. Fortunately, the relation between the foremen and the workingmen is a very intimate one. The Ford foremen are promoted from the rank and file of the workmen. They know all the jobs under their supervision through personal experience. So they are appreciative of and sympathetic with the workers in their departments. A new man might be somewhat irritated by the rough language the foremen use when speaking to the men. One of the Ford employees told me that he disliked factory work because there was to much "helling." By this he meant that the foremen constantly shouted "What the hell?" when anything went wrong. But when one gets accustomed to factory usage, he can easily notice that the foreman's attitude is, on the whole, a friendly one. He uses profane language as a matter of deeply ingrained habit. Many foremen fraternize with the men and, in this way, they help to bridge the gap between labor and management.

How the Average Ford Workman Lives

During my two summers in the Ford Plants I made it my rule to live exactly like a regular Ford workingman. I not only roomed and boarded with them, but participated in almost all their social and recreational activities. I visited many of their homes and cultivated some very intimate friendships with them. In this section I shall endeavor briefly to describe the life of a Ford workman.

1. Factory Life. A workman is, by regulation, supposed to spend eight hours every day in the factory. But as a matter of fact, he usually arrives from ten to thirty minutes before the work starts and leaves from five to fifteen minutes after the bell rings. Before he begins his work, he has to get his tools from the crib. After the work is over, he has to return the tools to the crib. He has to wash his hands and has to wait for his turn to punch his time card. All these things take time. Allowing from fifteen to twenty minutes for lunch and an hour or so for him to go to and come back from the factory on the street car or on a bus, it is safe to say that he spends in connection with his factory work from nine and a half to ten hours every day.

The time allowed for lunch varies with different departments. Fifteen minutes is the usual practice with departments where they run three shifts. Half an hour is also common, particularly with repair men. The Company does not provide lunch rooms but has arranged with a lunch factory to send wagon-loads of box-lunches to the Ford Plants at prescribed times. The company fixes the price and inspects the contents of the box-lunches. A box contains three sandwiches, a piece of pie, a piece of cake, and an apple, a banana or an orange. The whole box sells for fifteen cents. Milk and confectionery can also be bought from the wagon at very cheap prices. At the signal of a bell, all men rush to the nearest wagon. They form a long procession so that each man can take his turn. After lunches are secured, they seek for any convenient place to eat their meal. Many of them eat with unwashed hands. Fortunately the contents in a lunch-box are wrapped in wax paper so that there is no fear of contamination. Those who have homes in Detroit usually bring their lunches to the factory in tin boxes. The contents vary with different individuals. In general, they are better than the box-lunches sold at the wagons.

The shift changes once every two weeks, or, in certain departments, once every month. The day shift usually begins between 7 and 8 A.M. and ends between 3 and 4 P.M. The afternoon shift begins between 3 and 4 P.M. and ends between 11 and 12 P.M. The midnight shift begins between 11 and 12 P.M. and ends between 7 and 8 A.M. In departments where they run three shifts and change once every two weeks, a man works a fortnight on each shift in every 42 days. This, according to a concensus of opinion of the workmen, is rather upsetting to one's system. One is compelled to change his living habits once every two weeks. The midnight shift is particularly bad for one's health. Owing to family duties or noise in or around the house, one cannot sleep very well in the daytime. This means insufficient sleep and all its attending evils. What makes the change of shifts worse is that it necessitates almost a corresponding change for the members of the family, particularly for the worker's wife. She has to attend to his food and to see to it that he gets up in time and to control the children in such a way that noise in the house may be minimized. As things stand now, there seems to be no way to remedy this situation. Since the company has invested so much in capital stock and machinery it would be very poor business to run only one shift and let the plant be idle for sixteen hours every day. Then in certain departments, where there are furnaces, it is absolutely impossible to avoid three shifts. It is necessary there to maintain a constant temperature. Periodic cooling of the furnaces would entail inconceivable losses. Moreover, the increased expenses chargeable to overhead maintenance and fixed investment would raise tremendously the production cost of a Ford car, and, consequently, defeat the purpose of making a cheap car, which is the company's singular contribution to the public.

To return to the factory life of Ford employees, I must mention a few other facts of great importance. First of all, are the men terribly fatigued through hard work? To this question, I should say the man is fatigued, but not through hard work. This paradox needs some explanation. Practically all kinds of work that require much physical exertion are done by automatic machines. The company, we may say, has left nothing untried in the way of labor-saving devices. Overhead cranes are provided in nearly all buildings. Electric motors are installed wherever there is need for power to operate machines. Tools are so constructed that a minimum of application exerts the maximum of force. The position of the body and the movements of the hands have been, through years of experience, reduced to a definite form of procedure. Once the right procedure is acquired, all waste movements and unnecessary expenditure of energy are eliminated. Many men in the Ford Plants, however, get tired, not because they have too much, but because they have too little to do. The job of a machine tender, unlike that of an ordinary manual laborer, usually requires very little physical exertion. In many cases, he stands there watching the "Iron Man" work. He controls the switches, takes the readings of certain measuring instruments, and makes adjustment whenever anything goes wrong. Often it is his legs and not his hands that feel fatigued. The company requires everyone to stand up during the working hours. When the hands are not doing laborious work and the mind is not constantly occupied, it is quite natural that the feet begin to complain of the weight they are forced to carry. One of the workmen in a certain department said, when asked by the writer what he needed most urgently at the time, "Nothing but the freedom to sit down." This is certainly characteristic of the mind of most Ford workers in their working hours.

The description of factory life would be incomplete without inquiring into the attitude of the workman toward his job and toward the management. Jobs in the Ford Factory may be roughly divided into two classes—regular jobs and miscellaneous jobs. By regular jobs I mean those that require constant attendance. The miscellaneous jobs are those that occur here and there and from time to time, and are done by those laborers who have no definite jobs. For illustration, a punch press or a milling machine usually requires a constant tender, whereas a heap of dirt, or a pile of bricks to be removed, is only an occasional occurrence and does not require a special man to be on the job all the time. A regular job is usually expected to turn out a certain prescribed amount of product every day. The workman is responsible for what the schedule of production requires. He is naturally more or less conscientious toward his job. He works steadily, whether or not the foreman is present. The laborer who is doing a miscellaneous job is entirely different. He has little or no sense of responsibility. He tries to evade his work in every possible way. I worked at times with this class of workmen, and I had plenty of opportunities to observe how they contrived all sorts of ways to shirk work and to kill time. Once we were told to remove a heap of bricks with a wheelbarrow. An ordinary load consisted of about twelve bricks. One of the men had a wheelbarrow full of bricks. The heap seemed to have not less than sixteen. He told me to guess how many bricks there were. I said "Sixteen." He laughed and told me to count them. What should I find but eight bricks piled up in such a way that an empty space was left at the center, invisible from the outside. There were many other devices of this sort; but I need not stop to mention them here. I was constantly told by my comrades not to work fast. Whenever I happened to work faster than others, I immediately heard advice from all directions, such as "Take it easy," "Not piece work," etc. The miscellaneous jobs are not carefully supervised by the foremen. Whenever the foremen found the work slow, instead of hastening the workers they usually sent for more men. Such being the case, sometimes a ridiculously large number of men were engaged in a piece of work which could be done by half that number in less time.

The attitude of the Ford employees toward the company is, on the whole, very good. Here and there one may meet Bolsheviks and I.W.W.'s. But they are a negligible minority. The majority of the Ford workmen are fairly well satisfied with the existing state of affairs. They admire the ingenuity of Mr. Ford and the immensity of his organization. Some change in attitude, however, seems to have taken place this past year. Discontent is evident from the workmen's conversations. This is entirely due to the five-day-week scheme, which entails a serious loss in wages. Lots of men talk about quitting if the company will not take steps to adjust the wages.

I noticed in several places this sentence on the walls: "More money or we quit." This is certainly something that the management should take into immediate consideration.

2. Home Life. The Ford employees live under all sorts of conditions, from indecency to exquisite taste and refinement. The majority of them maintain a fairly high standard of living. An average Ford man may be described as follows: He is between thirty-five and forty years of age, a father of two or three children. His wife is somewhat, but not much, younger than he. She works hard at house-keeping and not infrequently gets a fairly good income through taking in roomers or boarders. He owns his house, or is paying for it on an instalment basis. If he does not own a house, he probably rents a whole flat. He has not only enough rooms for his household, but often one or two extra rooms to let. He has for furniture, carpets, davenports, comfortable chairs. He has a few pictures on the walls and a few books on his shelf. He probably has a piano or a Victrola. He has a telephone and sometimes even a radio. Of course his house is supplied with modern conveniences, such as water, gas and electricity. He owns a car, most probably a Ford. He and his family have three square meals every day. They rarely have delicacies; but their food is substantial and fairly well-balanced. When he puts on his street clothes, he is hardly distinguishable from an average American business man.

If he is not married, he is most likely between twenty-three and twenty-eight years of age. He has no home of his own. He is probably rooming in a private boarding house, sharing a double room with some other workman. The room costs each of them from $3 to $4 a week. He eats in a restaurant, spending from $1 to $1.30 a day on his board. He has some savings in a bank. He contemplates getting into some business or getting married or both.

3. Cultural Life. The average Ford employee, like the average American workingman, is almost destitute of any academic interest. He seldom has gone beyond the eighth grade. He has little or no interest in reading, except such things as concern his life immediately. He seldom goes to a library, attends a sermon, or listens to a lecture. His collection of books consists mainly of those antiquated grade-school textbooks he used to study while a pupil in the elementary school. He has no interest in art and no appreciation for music. So much for the negative side of this topic. To speak in positive terms, he reads newspapers every day without any interruption. He takes great interest in neighborhood gossip, in pool rooms and in drug stores. If he is a single man, he goes once or twice a week to concerts, burlesque, vaudeville, photoplays or public dances.

Meager as the cultural aspect of his life is, he appears to be a fairly intelligent and well-informed man. He has picked up, in the course of his life experience, a considerable amount of practical information. He is quite handy with mechanical things. He manipulates with some degree of dexterity electric appliances. He can do a fairly good job at painting, carpentering in and around his house. He knows a good deal about automobiles and can usually repair a car. He has some knowledge of business conditions, particularly in his own locality. He knows something about natural phenomena, such as weather changes, communicable diseases, common rules of personal and community health, etc. If we enlarge the term "cultural" to include all that is informational, the average Ford worker is by no means an ignorant individual, as one is apt to suppose him to be.

Although he knows nothing of the "ologies," he is efficient in and contented with his world of practical experiences. Unlike laborers in other countries, where social classes are well marked, he never thinks himself insignificant in the presence of well-educated men. His attitude toward college men seems to indicate that he must be secretly saying to himself: "You have education; I have something else. We are equals."

4. *Recreational Life.* In connection with home and cultural life, much has been mentioned which is more or less recreational in nature. To render this account complete, a few things will be added here. First of all, the majority of the Ford employees have cars. Many of them drive out in the late afternoons or go away for week-ends. Many of them go fishing and swimming on holidays. They play tennis, baseball, golf and billiards. Most of the younger men frequent parks, theaters, and dancing halls. A rather perverted form of recreation is visiting the so-called "sporting houses" of which, I am told, Detroit has an enormous number—greater than most of the big cities in the United States.

Summary

In the foregoing pages industrial relations at the Ford Plants have been treated from two angles—the labor policy of the company, and the life of an average Ford workman. The source of Ford labor supply is characterized by an almost complete absence of racial prejudice. The employment of substandard men and the equal treatment given to women have also been pointed out as unique features in the Ford Plants. Adequate provision for labor adjustment is evinced by depriving the foreman of his power to discharge a man, the readiness with which transfers are granted, and the appointment of a negro to hear the complaints of the colored men. Minimum wage is $6 a day and the rate of increase 40 cents at a time. "Lay-offs" are found to be rare, but vacation without pay is the practice at the Ford Plants. For training and education, two separate organizations are found—the Henry Ford Trade School at Highland Park and the School Department at the Fordson Plant. Training for highly skilled men is the sole objective of these institutions; consequently, the educational benefits reach only a very small fraction of the Ford employees. Welfare work centers on cases of sickness and destitution; and its administration is entrusted to the Sociological Department. Toward unionism, an attitude of indifference characterizes the Ford employees and an attitude of non-recognition represents the policy of the management. Of the human element in industry, three phases—speed, repetition and personal contact between capital and labor—have been discussed. Speed is found to be less than is usually reported by casual observers, the conveyor system being used in only a few departments. The effect of repetition is also found to be less deplorable than it is generally expected. Men get used to it through a process of "negative adaptation." Personal contact between the employer and the employee is almost nil, but the intimate relationship between foremen and workmen serves to bridge the gap between labor and management.

Four aspects of the life of an average Ford man have been briefly described. A workman spends more time in connection with his factory work than is generally believed. Opinions concur as to the upsetting effects of the frequent change of shifts. Due to the extensive use of automatic machines, men get tired not from physical exertion, but from psychological effects. The attitude of a man toward his work varies with the nature of the job. Though the relation between the company and its employees has, on the whole, been very good, the recent five-day-week scheme, without being accompanied by immediate wage adjustments, has introduced a serious cause for discontent. The majority of the Ford workers maintain a fairly high standard of living. At home, they are not entirely without modern comforts and conveniences. The average Ford worker lacks academic education; but the deficiency is, to some extent, made up by a considerable amount of practical experience. Various types of recreational activities are found popular among the Ford men. Some of them are perfectly wholesome; others need redirection.

Entrepreneurship and Labor Relations at the Ford Motor Company

MARTIN J. GANNON

Since World War II a significant number of organizational theorists have conceptualized the business firm as a rational decision-making structure.[1] The influence of such factors as the personal needs and values of the administrator are deemphasized in the rational decision-making model. However, an opposite viewpoint has been expressed by Philip Selznick, who believes that organizations are dynamic institutions infused with personal goals and values which complicate the "rational" decision-making process. Thus, Selznick emphasizes the concept that an organization or business firm must be studied as an historical institution rather than as a programmed and rational decision-making structure.[2]

A study of decisions made in a particular company may help to test Selznick's view concerning the actual operations of a firm. Such a study was completed by the author. The study focused on decisions in the area of labor relations and product development. Although a large number of firms might well serve as the source of information, the Ford Motor Company was selected primarily because more public information seemed to be available on this enterprise than of the majority of American companies.

Reprinted with permission from *The Marquette Business Review*, Summer, 1972.

Dr. Gannon is presently Associate Professor of Business Administration in the Behavioral Science Division of the Department of Buiness Administration, University of Maryland.

[1] See, for example, Herbert Simon, *Administrative Behavior* (New York: The Macmillan Company, 1947), 67-69.

[2] Philip Selznick, *Leadership in Administration* (White Plains: Row, Peterson, and Company, 1957), 31-32.

Rising Labor Problems: 1903-1913

The Ford Motor Company inauspiciously began major operations in 1903 at Strelow's plant, a reconverted wagon shop located on Mack Street in Detroit. Prior to this, Henry Ford had been a partner in some unsuccessful automotive endeavors: the Detroit Automobile Company and the premature Ford Motor Company. It was not until he associated himself with Alexander Malcomson and James Couzens that Henry Ford's operations began to function smoothly.

As many writers have pointed out, it was fortunate that Henry Ford was supported by the business acumen of James Couzens. During the years of their association Couzens, the Secretary-Treasurer, ran the business affairs of the company with unusual skill. Consequently Henry Ford was able to direct production, a job that was to his liking.

His relationship with his workers at this time was on a personal basis. Ford's background as a farmer and mechanic led him to identify with his workers. At this time employment in automobile plants was specialized with the result that skilled craftsmen filled most of the positions. Moreover, Henry Ford was able to maintain this personal relationship with his workers until approximately 1909, at which time the Ford Motor Company began to have on their payroll more than 1,000 individuals.[3]

Henry Ford was especially ambitious during these times. He wanted his struggling company to fulfill his own dream, one which other car manufacturers considered impractical: an inexpensive, all-purpose car which could be purchased by the average citizen. There was considerable opposition within the company management to this position, as only affluent individuals could purchase the highly-priced automobiles at the turn of the century and, as a logically incorrect consequence, companies generally felt that only expensive automobiles should be manufactured. Nevertheless, through his own persistence Henry Ford eventually achieved his desire of an all-purpose, inexpensive car when the Ford Motor Company decided to undertake production of the Model T.

In an important sense Henry Ford is the archetype of the Schumpeterian entrepreneur. Schumpeter defines an entrepreneur as an individual who combines a given set of resources so as to radically alter the consumption and production patterns of a society.[4] Until approximately 1930 Henry Ford performed activities which can be regarded as entrepreneurial.

During the first few years of its existence the Ford Motor Company manufactured several makes of automobiles. However, it was not until 1909 that actual production began on the Model T. In 1910 the Ford Motor Company moved to the Highland Park Plant. The work force had grown to 2,773. Routinization of the work became the pattern. During the year 1913 Clarence Avery and William Klann introduced the concept of a conveyor belt, which made possible the assembly line. By this time dissatisfaction among the workers had resulted in huge turnovers: There was over 380 per cent labor turnover in 1913 alone.[5] Undoubtedly mass

[3] Allen Nevins with Frank Ernest Hill, *FORD: The Times, The Man, The Company*, Vol. 1 (New York: Charles Scribner's Sons, 1954), 648.

[4] Joseph Schumpeter, *The Theory of Economic Development* (Cambridge: Harvard University Press, 1949), 66-74.

[5] Henry Ford with Samuel Crowther, *Today and Tomorrow* (New York: Doubleday, Page, and Company, 1926), 161.

production accelerated this trend, for no longer could most workers be accorded the status of skilled employees. Moreover, during the summer of 1913 grievances began to crystallize under the leadership of the International Workers of the World (IWW), a Communist-infiltrated union that appealed to immigrants, a large number of whom worked at Ford. Although small in number, this union served as a focal point for worker hostility. Finally, the country as a whole experienced a minor recession in 1913. For all of these reasons Henry Ford decided to combat the rising labor problems.

Benevolence: 1914-1920

The major event during the period 1914-1920 was the raising of wages from $2.34 to five dollars a day. On January 14, 1914, the announcement of the five-dollar day electrified the world. Overnight Henry Ford became known internationally as a defender of the worker.

As can be easily seen, there were undoubtedly business reasons for the implementation of the five-dollar day. An end to high labor turnover was an overriding consideration. Ford could acquire workers who were not recalcitrant but energetic in the fulfillment of their obligations.[6]

However, even though it is possible to impugn Henry Ford's motives in espousing the five-dollar day, nevertheless the host of other beneficial acts that he undertook during this period quickly dispelled most doubts as to his sincerity. In 1914 a Safety and Health Department was created. The year 1916 witnessed the opening of the Henry Ford Trade School. The popularity of this school was so great that in 1920 it had 15,000 applicants for 1,500 positions.[7] Acceptance in the school was largely based on need.

A startling policy initiated during this period was the hiring of partially incapacitated workers, ex-criminals, epileptics, negroes, and former inmates of mental hospitals. By way of contrast, no other large company had any policy comparable to this one. Moreover, it was not an ephemeral program, as even in 1934 approximately 20 per cent of the Ford workmen were in the physically disabled class.[8] Such farsightedness was and is highly unusual, as even today tradition militates against the hiring of less than "normal" workers.

The Ford Sociology Department was an important part of the foundation of Henry Ford's benevolence. This Department acted as investigator of Ford's workmen in order to determine their eligibility for the five-dollar wage. It had, however, more than this function. It gave advice to the Ford workmen as to how they should budget their money. While this Department was to an extent paternalistic, the situation of the workers necessitated such activity. For example, after receiving their first five-dollar-a-day

[6] Keith Sward espouses this viewpoint, and with some justification. As he shows, in 1916 approximately 30% of Ford workers were making less than $5 per day. The prospect of attaining the five-dollar day and of keeping it fanned worker interest. Henry Ford later admitted that the five-dollar day was one of the finest cost-cutting moves the company ever made. Keith Sward, *The Legend of Henry Ford* (New York: Rinehard, 1948), 57-58; Henry Ford with Samuel Crowther, *My Life and Work* (New York: Doubleday, Page, and Company, 1922), 147.

[7] Allen Nevins and Frank Ernest Hill, *FORD: Expansion and Challenge: 1915-1933*, Vol. II (New York: Charles Scribner's Sons, 1957), 341.

[8] Federal Trade Commission, *Report on Motor Vehicle Industry*, House Document No. 468 (Washington: U.S. Government Printing Office, 1939), 669.

pay checks, Ford workmen were besieged at the gates of the Highland Park Plant by all types of predatory salesmen.[9]

Under the auspices of the Sociology Department the Ford Motor Company conducted a language school for its foreign-born workers. Through this method Henry Ford helped in the acculturation of many individuals who otherwise would have found the American society impersonal and unapproachable.

Another aspect of this period was the profit-sharing system Henry Ford evolved for his workers. In 1919 the Ford Motor Company sold investment certificates to its workers in units of $100. Returns on such investment went as high as 14 per cent.

There were also minor indications of Henry Ford's benevolence which are noteworthy. For example, Ford opened grocery stores for his employees which, in 1919, were selling foodstuffs 25 per cent below market prices. This action contrasts sharply with the company stores still in existence in some coal towns in the United States. Another point of interest is that the *Dearborn Independent*, the newspaper owned by Henry Ford, supported the union in the steel strike of 1919.[10]

Labor, for its part, reciprocated Henry Ford's good will. In 1918 he decided to run for Senator from the State of Michigan. One of his ardent backers was the American Federation of Labor.[11]

In capsule form, it can be said that Henry Ford was benevolent toward his workers during this period. Prominent historians, in fact, are of the opinion that the only major labor reforms made during the early part of the twentieth century were those carried out by Henry Ford.[12] It is an unfortunate fact that Ford's policies were not imitated by other business enterprises.

Discipline of Labor: 1921-1929

In 1919 Henry Ford bought out the minority stockholders of the Ford Motor Company. This action made him the virtual autocrat of the Ford Motor Company. No one impeded his progress while, at the same time, the progress of the Ford Motor Company was blocked to such a degree that by 1922 the Ford dealers throughout the country unsuccessfully pleaded with him to make fundamental changes in car design.[13] His methods proved so rigid that many top executives left him, voluntarily or involuntarily, in 1921 and 1922. Among the members of the famous "Ford Alumni Association"[14] who terminated their stay at the Ford Motor Company at this time was William Knudsen, the brilliant engineer who sparked General Motors in its program of replacing the Ford Motor Company as the leader of the automotive industry.

Henry Ford and his company were, in short, losing ground. This state of affairs did not deter him from continuing his policy of manufacturing only

[9] Sward, *The Legend of Henry Ford*, 61.
[10] *Ibid.*, 145.
[11] *Ibid.*, 119.
[12] John R. Commons and Associates, *History of Labor in the United States—1896-1932* (New York: Macmillan, 1935), 79; and Walter Lippman, *Drift and Mastery* (Englewood Cliffs: Prentice-Hall, 1961), 57.
[13] Sward, *The Legend of Henry Ford*, 198.
[14] Samuel S. Marquis, *Henry Ford: An Interpretation* (Boston: Little, Brown and Company, 1923), 119.

the Model T. He listened to the advice of few if any of his subordinates. Indeed, he had much justification for this posture. Early in the history of the Ford Motor Company many of its executives vehemently objected to the manufacture of the Model T.[15] His introduction of the five-dollar day, which proved to be one of the best business propositions the company ever made, was first viewed as radical by many individuals, including John Lee, the first director of the Ford Sociology Department.[16] It is little wonder, then, that Henry Ford was reluctant to advocate new techniques of production, novel styles of cars, and the myriad innovations that would be necessary once the production of the Model T received secondary consideration. Moreover, sales continued on a high plane, even though there was a major business recession in 1921 and 1922. The *status quo* was sufficient at this time, at least for Henry Ford.

Henry Ford in 1920, then, was surrounding himself with sycophantic executives. At the same time, many of the farsighted projects initiated by Henry Ford during the years 1914-1920 had premature funerals. Dean Marquis, the dynamic head of the Ford Sociology Department, tendered his resignation in 1922 when he realized that the interests of the workers were not being supported. Henry Ford then closed down the Sociology Department. The plant foremen were again dictators of the workers; they could fire employees with no fear of reprisal. Even the press was stifled, as William Brownell, the editor of the *Ford News* who was partial to labor, resigned on December 31, 1920, and was replaced by a pro-management spokesman.

At this juncture it is appropriate to discuss the "published" views of Henry Ford concerning consumption and the rights of labor. While it is true that the majority of books published under Henry Ford's name were written by ghostwriters, nevertheless there is a consistency in viewpoint concerning consumption and the rights of labor which is remarkable. Further, this consistency was not only promulgated in written works but actualized in Henry Ford's relations with his employees. An understanding of Henry Ford's views will help in explaining the apparent paradox and seeming illogicality of Ford's treatment of workers.

Henry Ford had an advanced conception of consumption theory which, although expressed in simple language, was almost Keynesian. The more money that management paid the worker, the more industry's products would be consumed. Industry would benefit, consequently, through the payment of high wages.[17]

In his treatment of workers, however, Henry Ford was not so open-minded. While he paid laborers high wages when they did work, he felt little or no responsibility to them if they were laid off.[18] The industrialist's primary service is to the public and not to the workers. To make the workers secure while business is in decline is to harm industry and indirectly the worker. Moreover, workers could always find jobs once

[15] Roger Burlingame, *Henry Ford: A Great Life in Brief* (New York: Alfred A. Knopf, 1955), 60-61.

[16] Charles E. Sorenson with Samuel T. Williamson, *My Forty Years with Ford* (New York: W. W. Norton and Company, 1956), 139.

[17] Ford with Crowther, *My Life and Work*, 126; Ford with Crowther, *Today and Tomorrow* (New York: Doubleday, Page, and Company, 1926), 151; and Henry Ford, *Things I've Been Thinking About* (New York: Fleming H. Revell, 1936), 8-9.

[18] Sward, *The Legend of Henry Ford,* 226.

industry, after a relapse, began to advance again.[19] Such specious arguments were the basis of Ford's labor policy.

As indicated above, the workers had many grievances but few if any rights from 1921 until the establishment of the union at Ford Motor Company in 1941. After 1920 the workers were similar to low-grade soldiers in an army. Harsh discipline of workers became the standard practice.[20]

This regimentation of labor was accompanied by a lack of imaginative innovations. Henry Ford anticipated neither the used-car business nor the public's demand for "luxurious" models of cars. He still clung to his anachronistic dream of the all-purpose, inexpensive car. General Motors for the first time surpassed Ford Motor Company in sales in 1926 through the introduction of the more expensive but more luxurious models than the Model T, which was admittedly a durable car but, at the same time, a dreary one. Something had to be done, and Henry Ford acted in a grand but damaging manner. First, he made plans to build the River Rouge, a centralized plant which could produce cars with a minimum of effort. Over 100,000 men could work in this plant. All the functions necessary for the building of automobiles, from iron ore furnaces to the moving assembly line, were housed in this giant plant. Such integration, although detrimental in that flexibility was lacking to the extent that change-overs in styles became very difficult and expensive, did have the immediate impact of generating an efficient method of producing the Model A. Production of the Model A was then undertaken in 1927 at the River Rouge. While business was negligible in 1927 and 1928 due to these changes, the Ford Motor Company in 1929 bested General Motors in sales. It appeared as if Henry Ford would regain his position as the leader of the automotive industry, but this was not his destiny: The title was perennially worn by General Motors after 1929. The River Rouge Plant and the Model A were the final innovations of major import that were made by Henry Ford.

A few words concerning Henry Ford's policies toward labor that were implemented during this period (1921-1929) are appropriate. In 1926 he became the first large capitalist to initiate the five-day week. This action, however, was a gift of doubtful validity, for there was an immediate speed-up of work, added insecurity on the job, and a reduction of wages which averaged four dollars a week.[21] In 1929 Henry Ford announced the seven-dollar day. Immediately following this announcement, however, he cut back his labor force by 25,000. On top of this, Henry Ford started to increase his use of suppliers who were paid on a wage scale much lower than his own: In 1929 he had contracts with 2,200 outside suppliers; in 1930 the number rose to 3,500; and by 1931 it had reached 5,500.[22]

As had been emphasized, such actions were not in contradiction to Ford's philosophy of labor. Men have the right to high wages only when employed by the industrialist. Outside of this right Henry Ford believed that workers had prerogatives to little if anything else.

In this section the analysis of Henry Ford's relation with his workers has been pictured as negative in character from 1921 through 1929. However, it

[19] Ford with Crowther, *My Life and Work*, 47.
[20] Nevins and Hill, *FORD: Expansion and Challenge: 1915-1933*, 517-519.
[21] Sward, *The Legend of Henry Ford*, 175-176.
[22] *Ibid.*, 219-220.

is to be noted that many companies treated their workers just as badly or worse than did the Ford Motor Company. Also to be noted is the fact that, when Henry Ford did undertake revolutionary labor policies, he was not emulated but openly scorned by the majority of industrialists. Owing to the environment, it causes little astonishment that Henry Ford bullied his workers and had no respect for seniority rights.

Unfortunately the good will that Henry Ford had established from 1914 through 1920 and had maintained, with much difficulty, from 1921 through 1929 was to be eliminated during the nineteen thirties, at which time Henry Ford became actively hostile toward labor.

Intolerance of Labor: 1930-1945

The period of intolerance opened in 1930 with nothing more devastating than an edict banning the drinking of alcoholic beverages. The Ford Service Police, however, were soon in full operation. Under Harry Bennett this group was to serve as the oppressor of the workers. By 1938 the number of Ford Service Police was to stand at approximately 3,000 regulars.[23]

The old Henry Ford was gone; his entrepreneurial days were over. He was now acting as an anchor on the progress of the Company. It is true that in 1932 he did introduce the V8, but this was not a revolutionary model. As indicated above, General Motors continually bested the Ford Motor Company in sales after 1929; in 1933 Chrysler through the Plymouth moved into second place behind General Motors. While these events may have disconcerted Henry Ford, he made only feeble attempts to alter the situation.

The Great Depression was naturally a salient factor during this period. Layoffs were inevitable in every industry. But it is significant that, in Detroit, resentment was crystallized around Henry Ford. In March of 1932 the Ford Hunger March took place. Only a few hundred men were actually participants in it. Their demands were, in terms of present practices, quite conservative:[24]

> In behalf of the Ford worker as such, the hunger marchers demanded jobs, the right to organize, reduction of speed-up, abolition of labor spies, elimination of "graft" in the hiring process, two daily 15-minute rest periods on the Ford line, a six-hour day without reduction in pay, an unemployment bonus of $50 per man and free medical treatment for Ford men and their families.

Instead of meeting a sympathetic group of Ford executives, the hunger marchers were greeted by a barrage of bullets directed at them by the Dearborn policemen, who were naturally under the influence of the Ford Motor Company. Four individuals were killed and over a score were wounded. There was a public outcry concerning this event. Nevertheless, labor conditions at the Ford Motor Company became worse as the nineteen thirties progressed.

In 1933 the Ford Motor Company was again enmeshed in a labor dispute when one of its suppliers, the Briggs Company, stopped production. It is notable that this was the first major strike of the depression. Moreover, the

[23] *Ibid.*, 371.
[24] *Ibid.*, 233.

Briggs concern was, through a lease, working in Henry Ford's Highland Park Plant.

Many of the Briggs men had been working a 14-hour day for 10 cents an hour. They now demanded a nine-hour day, compensation for dead time, and a daily wage of $3.60 for women and $4 for men.[25] In other terms, they wanted treatment equivalent to that practiced at the River Rouge Plant. This, however, was not forthcoming. Partially through the support of Henry Ford the strike was crushed.

Trouble with labor constantly plagued the Ford Motor Company from 1930 through 1945. On February 26, 1934, there was a strike against speed-ups at the River Rouge Plant. It was quickly ground under foot. The Ford workmen either submitted to conditions then in existence or else they left.

Henry Ford, the former friend of the worker, was gradually becoming the symbol of resistance. Nevins and Hill cite three major reasons for union opposition to Henry Ford during the nineteen thirties.[26] First, the wage policy had collapsed. By 1940 Ford workers were actually being paid less than the employees of the other major groups in the automotive industry.[27] Second, the Ford Service Police terrorized the Ford workers. Beatings of workers were frequent. The Ford Motor Company, consequently, began to be primarily ruled out of fear for the job.[28] Third, the unions were aligned against Henry Ford because of his doctrinaire opposition to any form of labor organization. For these reasons, antagonism to Henry Ford expanded to incredible proportions.

1935 was an important year for labor in America, as the Wagner Act was passed at this time. It established the first national policy of collective bargaining. Under the protection of this act the United Automobile Workers (UAW) initiated a systematic campaign to organize union shops in the automotive industry. By the end of 1937 the entire automotive industry except for the Ford Motor Company had accepted unions. No violence of major import had been necessary to accomplish this unionization. But the Ford Motor Company proved different and difficult.

On May 26, 1937, the UAW began its program to unionize the Ford Motor Company. Under the direction of Walter Reuther and Ed Frankensteen the union organizers planned to distribute circulars to the Ford workmen on their way home from work. It was on the bridge over the Miller Road, which leads to Gate 4 of the River Rouge Plant, that the well-known Battle of the Overpass occurred. Ford Servicemen were awaiting the advent of the union organizers. When Reuther and Frankensteen arrived they were besieged by press photographers. As their pictures were being taken, Reuther and Frankensteen were ordered to leave the bridge by the Ford Servicemen. Although they started to comply, they were attacked by the Ford Servicemen. Reuther, Frankensteen, and several others ended up in the hospital. Approximately one-half hour later a second group of union organizers arrived. Although it had a large segment of women in its number, the group was also assaulted by the Ford Servicemen.

[25] *Ibid.*, 221.

[26] Allan Nevins and Frank Ernest Hill, *FORD: Decline and Rebirth, 1933-1962*, Vol. III (New York: Charles Schribner's Sons, 1963), 29.

[27] Sward, *The Legend of Henry Ford*, 347-348.

[28] *Ibid.*, 311.

Time was running out for the Ford Motor Company. However, Henry Ford's tactics of resistance were many and varied. By way of example, Bennett and Ford in 1938 manipulated Homer Martin, the first president of the UAW, into private negotiations. Through such a move they hoped to neutralize the UAW. When the executive members of the UAW became aware of these private talks, they impeached Homer Martin and elected R. J. Thomas as president.

Another tactic was the use of the familiar company union. Four company unions were organized at Ford in 1937 but they proved ineffectual.

A third tactic of significance was employed against workers in Ford plants which were located in St. Louis, Kansas City, Richmond and Long Beach in California. In 1937 Henry Ford appeared to have reversed his position by granting *de facto* recognition to the union at these plants. This stance brought the union out into the open. When the plants reopened for fall production, however, Bennett instituted lockouts and fired key union leaders.[29]

Despite these tactics Henry Ford was using borrowed time. By 1941 the UAW once again felt strong enough to organize the Ford Motor Company. All that was needed was a legitimate excuse for a strike. Such an incident occurred on April 2, 1941, when Harry Bennett discharged the eight Rouge employees who composed the grievance committee of the plant. The workers spontaneously began to walk off their jobs. Under the leadership of the UAW the workers surrounded the River Rouge Plant. They did not dare to stage a sitdown strike in the plant, as they realized that the Ford Servicemen would overpower them. However, the encirclement proved effective. On April 11 the Ford Motor Company capitulated.

The Ford Motor Company signed its first contract with the union on June 21, 1941. In an important sense 1941 was the critical year, as it was at this time that Henry Ford allowed the operation of the UAW in his plants. But the period of intolerance was destined to continue until 1945.

The span from 1941 through 1945 can be viewed from two levels: The intolerance by the Ford Motor Company of labor, and labor's intolerance of the Ford Motor Company. The first level is best illustrated in the case of Willow Run, a Ford plant located 35 miles outside of Detroit. This plant, which was to produce B24 bombers, was built in 1941. It had troubles from the beginning. The major problem was the housing of workers. Henry Ford did not want his workers living at Willow Run because it was a Republican district which enforced tax laws favorable to his interests. He believed that an influx of workers would be detrimental to him, since they would vote democratic and the tax laws would then be altered.[30] Through the efforts of the Federal Housing Administration this problem was eventually alleviated.

From 1941 through 1943, Local 50 of the UAW at the Willow Run Plant had untold difficulties. One man sat in judgment of the complaints of 35,00 workers. Turnover was the highest in the area. Things changed in November of 1943 when August Krech was appointed labor relations director. At this time Willow Run solved most of its labor problems and, under the plan mainly worked out by Charles Sorenson, initiated and sustained large-scale production of B24 bombers.

[29] *Ibid.*, 142 ff.
[30] *Ibid.*, 433.

The second level of the span of time from 1941 through 1945, labor's intolerance of the Ford Motor Company, was best exemplified in the number of work stoppages, which numbered 773 from the signing of the contract in 1941 until January 9, 1946.[31] The union regarded the company as an adversary; the workers activated work stoppages in violation of the contract.

In general, the span of time from 1941 through 1945 can be seen as a period of transition. The advent of Henry Ford II in 1945 was destined to even out the irregularities in the relationship between the company and the union.

Tolerance of Labor: 1945-19—

Henry Ford II was elected President of the Ford Motor Company in 1945. Although Henry Ford lived until 1947, his last few years were passed in relative calm away from the immediate operation of the company. It was at this time that the company was reorganized; Harry Bennett and the Ford Service Police were eliminated. An excellent example of this new outlook is provided by the history of labor relations at Ford Motor Company after 1945.

Immediately after taking office, Henry Ford II notified the union as to his plans concerning the contract negotiations scheduled to start in the near future. He wanted, he stated, two-way bargaining, that is, company security that the union would fulfill its part of the contract and union security that the company would perform in a comparable manner.[32] The Ford workmen were involved in countless unauthorized work stoppages. It was this aspect of the bargaining situation which was crucial.

This contract was negotiated with the usual amount of fanfare that is practiced in such relationships. Generally speaking, the contracts that the Ford Motor Company and the UAW have signed since this 1946 agreement are highlighted by their commonness rather than their uniqueness, since collective bargaining is industry-wide. The salient point is that, by 1946, the Ford Motor Company and the UAW established two-way bargaining acceptable to both of them. The old antagonisms lost most of their lustre as mutual confidence gained prominence.

The renewal of confidence in the company through concrete two-way bargaining was strengthened by other projects. John Bugas, director of industrial relations, instituted the use of attitudinal questionnaires in order to discover silent grievances of the workers. Henry Ford II, although he never completed his senior year at Yale, had been a sociology major and had been influenced by the ideas of human relations. The active implementation of such activities as questionnaire distribution, formation of plant sports teams, and the expansion of company recreational facilities promoted an identification of the workers with the Ford Motor Company. The results were promising. Labor turnover dropped from 3.8 per cent in 1946 to 2.2 per cent in 1947; the national average in manufacturing in 1947 was 2.8 per cent. Unauthorized work stoppages dropped from 94 in 1945 to 27 in 1946. Grievances were in decline at the same time: in 1946 there were 14,260 first-stage grievances, but only 11,207 in 1947.[33]

[31] Benjamin M. Selekman et al., *Problems in Labor Relations* (New York: McGraw-Hill, 1958), 362.

[32] "Two-way Bargaining Demand By Ford," *Business Week* (November 24, 1945), 93.

[33] Human Engineering Program Pays Off for Ford," *ibid.* (October 30, 1948), 89.

Formal recognition of the Ford Motor Company's excellent relationship with its workers was granted in 1948 when Henry Ford II received the Society for the Advancement of Management's Award for human relations in industry. In 1947 *Fortune* praised the company in the following manner:[34] "No question about it, Ford is now doing a labor-relations job second to none in the tense Detroit area. How much Henry II's earnest excursions into 'human engineering' have helped cannot be assayed, but certainly they haven't harmed."

This tolerance of labor has extended into the present. In 1952 the Ford Motor Company received the Award of Honor from the National Safety Council for its outstanding performance in preventing injuries to employees. Many of the farsighted projects which Henry Ford had espoused received renewed support, for example, the placement of physically handicapped workers, who numbered approximately 4,100 at the River Rouge Plant in 1953.[35]

Since this paper has directed much attention to the concept of entrepreneurship, it is only fair to say that Henry Ford II undertook innovating changes in the company that were reminiscent of his grandfather's early career. He surrounded himself with top corporate executives; he executed the change to new models of cars. Through such innovations Henry Ford II propelled the Ford Motor Company into second place in the automotive industry behind General Motors; Chrysler fell to third position. Although the company does not possess the selling power that it did in the early nineteen hundreds, nevertheless it has gained much ground under the innovating leadership of Henry Ford.

Discussion

The study of the decisions made in the Ford Motor Company in the area of product development and labor relations indicates support for Selznick's viewpoint that organizational decisions are permeated by personal values and that historical events have a strategic influence on performance. Certainly the decisions made at the Ford Motor Company over a period of fifty years reflected the personal values and needs of Henry Ford. For example, we can see that Henry Ford had high ego-strength and, correlatively, a high degree of self-confidence. In fact, his degree of self-confidence can be considered to be excessive, for he was convinced of the correctness of his decisions in spite of the obvious disconfirmation of the validity of his premises by actual sales figures. This high ego-strength and self-confidence probably resulted from his early success when he proved himself correct and his critics wrong regarding the production of the Model T. Such a high degree of self-confidence led to rigidity and resistance to change to the ultimate detriment of the company.

Henry Ford's labor relations policies also seemed to be the consequence of a distinct set of ideas. Apparently Henry Ford only recognized the right of workers to receive high wages when employed by the industrialist. If the workers were laid off, became sick, or were incapacitated, the industrialist had no obligation to provide for them. Such an outlook explains Henry Ford's antipathy to the unions who, according to Sumner Slichter,

[34] "Rebirth of Ford," *Fortune*, 35 (May, 1947), 86.

[35] Robert T. Ross, "Ford Plan for Employing the Handicapped," *Monthly Labor Review*, 53 (August, 1941), 1299.

have the following goals:[36]

> Collective bargaining, as carried on by labor unions with employers, has two principal aspects. In the first place, it is a method of price-making—making the price of labor. In the second place, it is a method of introducing the civil rights into industry, that is, of requiring that management be conducted by rule rather than by arbitrary decision. In this latter aspect, collective bargaining becomes a method of building up a system of "industrial jurisprudence."

In reference to price-making, Henry Ford was definitely ahead of his times, a fact evidenced by his introduction of the five-dollar day. Moreover, he supported workers through such far-sighted practices as the Ford Sociology Department and the hiring of partially incapacitated workers. Henry Ford, however, regarded such practices not as rights but privileges which could be and were withdrawn. In terms of the second aspect that is presented in the above statement—industrial jurisprudence—Henry Ford proved reactionary. Such a thing as industrial jurisprudence would destroy the rights of management whose safeguarding Henry Ford considered essential.

When Henry Ford II was elected President of the Ford Motor Company in the fall of 1945, he engineered many programs beneficial to labor. In a sense, the Ford Motor Company had come full circle from the days of the period of benevolence to those of the period of tolerance. This concept is given full expression in the following statement issued in 1955 prior to the agreement guaranteeing Ford employees the annual wage:[37]

> Years ago, when the elder Henry Ford instituted the $5-a-day wage, he was called everything from a madman to an anarchist by other American industrialists. We wouldn't be surprised to see Henry Ford II, who is fighting to take his company back to the top of the automotive heap, make as bold a move to win the favor of American workers as did his grandfather.

While it is difficult to make final generalizations, it seems that the application of Selznick's model would have benefited the Ford Motor Company. Neither Henry Ford nor his top executives such as Charles Sorenson explicitly outlined a systematic plan consistent with the needs, values, and history of the Ford Motor Company. If such a plan had been outlined, it is probable that the contradictory behavior and self-defeating activity of the Ford Motor Company would have been minimized both in the areas of labor relations and product development.

[36] Sumner Slichter, *Union Policies and Industrial Management* (Washington: The Brookings Institution, 1941), 1.

[37] "Changing World of Labor," *Christian Century*, 72 (February, 1955), 72.